FROM PORT T TO RAF GAN

From PORTT
to RAF GAN

An Illustrated History of the British Military Bases at
Addu Atoll in the Maldive Islands 1941-76

PETER DOLING

Woodfield

Second edition, published in 2004 by

WOODFIELD PUBLISHING
Bognor Regis, West Sussex PO21 5EL United Kingdom
www.woodfieldpublishing.com

© Peter Doling, 2003/2004

ISBN 1-873203-89-6

CONTENTS

ACKNOWLEDGEMENTS

This account of Britain's military use of Addu Atoll owes much to the interest shown by the many individuals who have helped me with my research over the years.

Inevitably, most of those who served at Port T and HMS Maraga are no longer with us and I very much regret that they have not lived to see a published account of their experiences during that most difficult period of their lives.

For their graphic accounts of life at Port T I am indebted to K Bell, K Bibby, A Brundrett, J Burgess, J Clark, L Cole, L Conlon, A Dobson, B Eddison, M Forte, R Gear-Evans, P Gerrard, R Godrich, P Harris, R Hawker, L Hobbs, E Ivermee, A Lawson, F Lewis, W Manners, H Mansell, J Marston, F Mathews, P McGuinness, K Peberdy, G Pitt, D Pyrke, H Russell, W Simpson, G Smith, F Smith, J Stamp, E Streatfield, J Thom, R Tuck, H Wilkinson and B Willis . In particular, my thanks go to two of the survivors from those early days; Kenneth Bell and Wilfrid Manners. Kenneth was in his early eighties when he found time, in between commuting to his job in Costa Rica, to meet me in London to discuss the problems he experienced when supervising the creation of Gan's wartime runway. Wilfred was also well past normal retiring age when he shared with me his wartime memories of Addu Atoll, loaned me his collection of photographs and gave me an introduction to Abdullah Afif Didi who, in corresponding with me from the Seychelles, increased my understanding of post-war life for the Adduans. My thanks also go to all those ex-mariners who sent me information about the ships which sailed the Indian Ocean and spent some time at Addu Atoll during the Second World War.

Understandably, more individuals have contributed to the history of RAF Gan than to that of Port T. For their help, so willingly given during my research into the post-war development and operation of the RAF's mid-ocean staging post, I thank them: without their contributions this would have been a meagre history.

In particular my thanks go to: Henry Probert for so frequently allowing me access to the Air Historical Branch archives; M Constable-Maxwell, E Cropper, W Edwards, P Ellis, R Fleming, B Gee, P Hill, W Kent, D Moffat, G Moss, R Mullineaux, H Rees, R Salmon, R Schofield, H Sheppard, B Spragg, I Thomas and A Whitlock, the eighteen former station commanders at RAF Gan who found time to answer my numerous questions, in many cases offering to provide photographs and memorabilia, to read my early drafts and correct my misunderstandings; B Bailey, G Bell, M Broome, G Brown, M Butler, D Chappell, M Graham, T Hayes, J Hoare, V Kendrick, E Lake, C Lawrie, L Moore, G Morris, J Parry, W Richards, D Robson, F Stillwell, D Taylor, J Upton and D Wishart, many of whom sent me photographs and papers and all of whom provided accounts of their time at Addu Atoll, adding to my knowledge of life on Gan during its days as an RAF base; Mrs T R Carpenter and Mrs D McGregor for sharing with me their memories of the time they spent at Addu Atoll as representatives of the Women's Royal Voluntary Service; Doctor Roger Wolstenholme for finding the time to write to me about the transfer of the medical facilities from the RAF; the staff at the RAF Personnel Management Agency for helping me to contact the former station commanders; the staff at the RAF Air Historical Branch, the Royal Air Force Museum, the Imperial War Museum, the Ministry of Defence Library and Photographic Library, the Commonwealth War Graves Commission and the Royal Air Force News for their help with my research.

Most of all, I owe a special vote of thanks to my long-suffering wife Patricia who, for far too long, has lived with my casual and seemingly never-ending search for information and with the ever-receding publication date for the Addu Atoll story.

VARIATIONS AND CONTRADICTIONS

The variations
English language accounts of the Maldive Islands and the Maldivians may be few and far between but they still manage to offer a confusing variety of translations from the Divehi. Thus the name of each of the islands which comprise Addu (or 'Addoo') Atoll (or 'Atol' or 'Atolu') differs according to the writer's choice of source.

In H C P Bell's monograph Gan is identified as 'Gamu' but I have not seen that name used by any other writer. 'Hithadhoo' is used on Admiralty charts and in some travel guides such as the Lonely Planet booklet 'Maldives' whilst Bell opts for 'Hitadu' rather than 'Hittadu' which was used in some of the military files and by some of the Adduans even though 'Hitaddu' seems to be the preferred version for both the military and the islanders.

Similar variations can almost certainly be found for most of the islands in the archipelago.

I have chosen to use the versions which were invariably used in the military records of the day and, in the case of Addu Atoll, are to be found on the seven-sheet mosaic of charts, in the series U885, prepared by the Mapping and Charting Establishment RE in 1970 from air photography dated March 1969 and incorporating names from the survey by N° 84 Survey Squadron Royal Engineers.

The contradictions
Any substantial account of events which have occurred in living memory will contain disputed details. Often, information obtained from official records will be contradicted by someone who was there and who remembers things differently. Far worse, for the researcher, is the discovery that official records often contain contradictory accounts of the same event.

The result is predictable. In this history, as in any other, there will be errors. My hope is that they will be of no real significance but, significant or not, I would welcome any substantiated contradictions; the Gan story will be all the better for being corrected.

COPYRIGHT

THE AUTHOR

Peter Doling, born in the North Hertfordshire village of Ickleford in 1934, attended Hitchin Boys' Grammar School from 1945 until 1950 when he became an apprentice with Geo W King Ltd, the Stevenage-based company of mechanical handling engineers. On completion of his apprenticeship and his Higher National Certificate studies he was employed by the company as a design draughtsman and by the local technical college as a part-time lecturer in engineering.

Under a deferred National Service obligation he joined the RAF in 1958 and served as an education officer for three years before returning to his previous employer to develop the company's supervisory and management training programmes.

Married, with two daughters, he continued to live in Ickleford until 1963 when he rejoined the RAF Education Branch. Promoted to the rank of Squadron Leader in 1968, he was posted to RAF Gan in 1971.

Eight years later, at the end of his tour as the senior education officer at RAF Brize Norton, he left the RAF to read Industrial Relations at The University of Bath.

Awarded an MSc in 1980, he was subsequently employed as a management studies lecturer at Havering College where he remained for seventeen years, employed for the last eleven as a senior lecturer specialising in strategic studies and operations management for post-graduate students.

I   The Maldive Islands

The islands

Down the centre of the Indian Ocean there lies an atoll chain in which are to be found some of the most beautiful and most dangerous groups of islands in the world. The Maldive Islands. Over one thousand of them, sitting on top of an underwater mountain range extending almost five hundred miles from north to south yet with a total land area of little more than a hundred square miles (Fig 1.1).

These countless spits of land, usually less than half a mile long and rarely rising more than five feet above sea level, are basically slabs of coral protected by the barrier reefs which prevent the Indian Ocean from washing away the entire island chain. Just over two hundred of the islands are inhabited and half as many again are given over to plantations, usually of coconut palms. The remainder are left to run wild (Fig 1.2).

Their beauty is that of the classical tropical island; palm trees over coral sands and turquoise green waters over exotic coral reefs hosting an astonishing variety of marine life. Sunsets in the Maldives are unforgettable and at night stars surround a moon bright enough to cast palm tree shadows on the white sands which edge the midnight-blue waters. But danger accompanies that beauty. On many islands insect-borne diseases are endemic. In the lagoons marine life ranges from predatory sharks to poisonous jelly-fish and any graze from the living coral is almost certain to result in an infected wound liable to become ulcerous. The currents around the atolls and the islands, strong enough and treacherous enough to sweep many of the islanders' boats out to sea each year, spell death for swimmers unwise enough to bathe in any but the calmest and most sheltered waters.

There are only two safe passages through the archipelago; one at the equator, the other at the 'One-and-a-Half-Degree Channel'. Elsewhere, the seabed is littered with the ancient wrecks of ships whose captains have incautiously attempted to traverse the Indian Ocean by sailing through the barrier created by the chain of islands and reefs.

The weather in the Maldives is typical of the tropics. Throughout the year the maximum daytime temperature in the region is remarkably constant at around eighty-six degrees Fahrenheit with the minimum, night time, temperature about eight degrees less. Humidity fluctuates considerably but is frequently over ninety per cent. Rain occurs on about one hundred and fifty days a year with the monsoons in the north often bringing over one hundred inches of rain a year to the affected islands, far more than the normal rainfall in the south although even there it is not that unusual for the annual figure to exceed one hundred inches.

Addu Atoll is well to the south of the monsoon belt but is nevertheless subjected to periods of heavy rain with a monthly total in excess of fifteen inches not at all uncommon during the wet season, which, whilst varying slightly from year to year, generally starts in October. The average annual rainfall at the atoll is around ninety inches but on occasions over one hundred inches have been recorded. The direction and speed of the surface winds at Addu Atoll vary with the seasons. In January and February the direction tends to be northerly or north-north-easterly, it then gradually backs to become predominantly westerly and west-south-westerly in April and May and southerly or south-easterly from June to August before reversing the cycle, returning to a northerly or north-north-easterly direction by January. Although the mean wind speed is less than fifteen knots there are wide variations over the months with a strong correlation between wind direction and mean speed. Gusts of over twenty-five knots occur on about one hundred days a year whilst gusts exceeding thirty-three knots are generally recorded on about thirty days. Over seventy-five per cent of those strongest gusts occur when the wind direction lies between two hundred and thirty and three hundred degrees.

Early Maldivian history

Given their unchanging lifestyle it is not surprising that until recently the Maldivians paid scant attention to their origins and their early history. Their aboriginal roots go back to India and Sri Lanka but for the best part of a thousand years the islanders have inherited mixed ancestry for they have been exposed to the racial influences of the Arabs for whom the Maldive

Islands provided a convenient staging post on the trade route to Malacca and China. It is thus quite likely that the Arabs were fairly well integrated into Maldivian society, particularly in the more northerly atolls where the present-day islanders display more traces of Arab and Indian ancestry than in the south where the racial characteristics are more akin to the Singhalese. Generally known as Maldivians, even though they call themselves the Divehi, meaning 'islanders', the people of the Maldives speak a language which, also called Divehi, provides further evidence of their early associations with the Arabs, Indians and Singhalese.

Little has been written of early Maldivian history and the oral accounts which have passed from generation to generation have been embroidered to such an extent that they have largely become mythical versions of long forgotten facts. Ancient inscribed copper plates or loamaafaanu refer to Koimala Kalo, said to be the first named King of the Maldives and the ancestor of the early sultans and sultanas. The inscriptions also provide glimpses of early laws and major events without giving anything like an historical account of Maldivian affairs.

The islanders have inherited no written descriptions of their earliest cultures; of the sun worshippers who left their symbolically carved stones scattered around the islands; of the people who built the island mounds nor of the Hindus and the Buddhists who followed them. According to Thor Heyerdahl they offer only vague references to the 'Redin', a mystical people to whom the islanders attribute the construction of the man-made mounds, or hawittas as they are called by the Maldivians, which are still to be found on some of the islands and which, even now, can be fifty feet or more in height and two hundred and fifty feet around the base. The Redin are not spoken of as Hindus or Buddhists although both religions existed in the Maldives before the middle of the twelfth century AD. It is likely that the Singhalese brought Buddhism to the Maldive Islands and it was probably the likelihood that the Singhalese would interfere or even come to dominate the affairs of the islands which caused the Maldivians, in 1153 AD, to abandon Buddhism, with its accompanying possibility of subservience to Serendip (now Sri Lanka), in favour of Islam which combined a degree of protection under the Islamic brotherhood with only a remote possibility of interference from the distant Arabs.

The Maldivians have subsequently remained faithful to Islam even when, in 1552 AD, King Hasan IX came under the influence of Portuguese missionaries and was converted to Christianity. His people regarded his conversion as traitorous and whilst Hasan was in Goa a rival, Muslim, sultan was proclaimed. In 1558 the Portuguese killed the rival sultan and replaced him by the Portuguese Governor/Sultan, Adiri Adiri. There followed fifteen years of oppression and bloodshed as the Portuguese tried to convert the islanders to Christianity. Eventually a Maldivian, Muhammed Takurufanu, and his two brothers spearheaded an attack on the Portuguese and killed Adiri Adiri. Takurufanu became the Sultan of the Maldives, the islanders remained Muslims and Christianity has been spurned ever since.

Early literature

The earliest accounts of the Maldivians and their culture were written by Arab, Roman and Chinese travellers but it was Ibn Batuta who, having served as an Islamic judge in the Maldive Islands for a year and a half in the middle of the fourteenth century AD, wrote the first lengthy description of life in the archipelago. It was over two and a half centuries before his account was bettered and, in spite of numerous references to the Maldive Islands by a variety of travellers it was more than one hundred and fifty years after Batuta served in the islands that they featured on the maps produced in Europe.

The earliest maps of the Indian Ocean originated from Ptolemy and from a succession of Arab geographers such as Al Idrisi but it is the Portuguese navigators who produced the best maps of the region with the 'Cantino' map of 1502 representing a significant advance in the recorded knowledge of the area. Early in the sixteenth century the cartographers were trying to reconcile the Ptolemaic tradition with the new knowledge and were often making the situation worse by taking liberties when using their own languages for place names and when allocating names to various territories. Thus there are early references, by Al Idrisi, to the islands called El-Roibahat *lying near Serendip* (Sri Lanka) *at seven days from El Komor* (Madagascar), *close together and countless in numbers*', a description which clearly fits the Maldive Islands. The name 'Roibahat' even suggests an origin for the name 'Addu' because Roibahat can appear in the old Portuguese as 'Rado' which easily corrupts to Addu.

Not until Diogo Ribeiro published his maps of the world, did a European-produced map first refer to the 'Archipelago de Maldives'.

In later years, as European traders sailed more frequently across the Indian Ocean, the details and the hazards of the archipelago received wider recognition. The coral reefs, the natives' hostility to strangers from the west, the endemic diseases and the Maldivian fever; all came to be feared. Little, however, was written about the islanders themselves and in Europe there was still no substantial published account of the island environment nor of the Maldivian culture until 1614 when Francois Pyrard of Laval described his experiences as a shipwrecked sailor taken prisoner by the Maldivians.

Pyrard had set out for the East Indies in 1601 on board the ship 'Corbin' which sailed from St Malo. The ship never reached her destination because the voyage, beset by a series of disasters, ended when she struck a Maldivian reef. Less than two decades after the Portuguese had imposed the bloodiest period of suppression in Maldivian history, Pyrard and his compatriots found themselves shipwrecked on an island where the inhabitants would care little for the difference between the Portuguese and any other fair-skinned strangers from the west. The men who survived the shipwreck thus became prisoners of the Maldivians and were treated so callously that all but nine suffered slow painful death from starvation and disease. Eight escaped on an improvised raft and were never heard of again. The ninth was Pyrard. He learnt his captors' language, was spared the ill-treatment meted out to his compatriots and eventually came to the attention of the Sultan who, anxious to know more about Europe and the Europeans, had Pyrard brought to the capital. Although still a prisoner, Pyrard enjoyed considerable freedom within the court and the capital, thereby receiving an insight into the Maldivian way of life. Frustratingly, he was unable to record his observations at that time. Eventually he found his way back to France but even then it was several years before he finally wrote an account of his adventures. Writing from memory he produced a description of life in the Maldives which was so accurate and so complete that few explanatory notes were needed when, almost three hundred years later, Gray and Bell produced the English translation of Pyrard's work.

Young and Christopher produced a brief account of their experiences and findings whilst on a marine survey in the 1830's but the first serious studies to be published were those of Harry Charles Purvis Bell who, whilst continuing to work with Albert Gray on the translation of Pyrard's text, wrote a whole series of articles between 1882 and 1893. Employed as an archaeologist by the Government of Ceylon, Bell's articles were initially the published findings of studies undertaken as part of his employment but in his post-retirement years his study of the Maldives and the Maldivians became a labour of love, his works respected and appreciated long after his death.

The people

The population of the Maldives has increased from just over seventy thousand at the end of the nineteenth century through eighty thousand just before the outbreak of the Second World War to almost a quarter of a million in the 1990s. The capital island of Malé, four hundred miles south-west of Sri Lanka, accommodated about eight thousand Maldivians in the late 1930s but is today occupied by some sixty-five thousand, all crammed into an area considerably less than one square mile.

The people, who tend to be short and slightly built, live on a diet of fish, coconuts, rice and locally grown tuber crops and fruit. They are dependent on imported food, especially rice which has become a staple element of their diet even though it is not grown in the Maldives. Their general life expectancy is little more than sixty although some islanders survive into their eighties or nineties (Fig 1.3).

Hard working of necessity and with a tendency to be pious Muslims, the islanders are inclined to be individually undemonstrative, not given to displaying much humour or any other emotion. Collectively, however, they can be highly demonstrative, bordering on the riotous to give vent to their feelings and to air their grievances. In their remote Moslem communities they tend to be distrustful, if not actually fearful, of strangers whilst their inclination to be hostile towards outsiders is a lasting legacy of their history. Only the most northerly and the most southerly communities have a reputation for hospitality towards strangers, the former as a result of Indian influence, the latter due in part to the legacy of the British at Addu Atoll and in part to the existence of an elite class whose forebears came south several generations ago.

Polygamy, permitted in Maldivian society, is not widely practised. The islanders do, however, have one of the highest divorce rates in the world, almost certainly because a man can divorce his wife merely by informing her that the marriage is over and then registering the divorce with the local official. The result is that on numerous islands many villagers will marry ten or more times, creating a complex pattern of local kinship in every community.

The crime rate in the Maldives is low and there are no prisons in the Western sense: those found guilty of a crime are either held under house arrest or committed to spend a given period in exile, banished without family to another island and forbidden to return.

On most of the islands the homes are little more than sparsely furnished huts which have been built by the householders using construction techniques which are primitive but effective. Raw timber from the ubiquitous palm trees is used for the frame. The walls and roofs are made from woven palm fronds; materials which are free, plentiful and easily worked even by youngsters, many of whom can split and weave a frond in under ten minutes (Figs 1.4 & 1.5). No windows or doors feature in these constructions: clear openings provide light, ventilation and easy access for the family, their chickens and the island's wildlife. In recent years corrugated iron roofs have become more common but, outside Malé, substantial coral stone houses remain beyond the means of most Maldivians even though building plots, allocated by the government, do not have to be purchased. Each home usually has one large room containing a 'swing bed' suspended by ropes hanging from the roof timbers and serving as a bed at night and a swing seat during the day. Observed by Francois Pyrard of Laval and described in his seventeenth century account of life in the Maldives, the swing bed is still in general use throughout the islands. A separate kitchen hut is commonly built to the rear of the main dwelling near a well which provides all the water for drinking and washing. On most islands there is no sanitation; the householders either use a designated area of the back garden or they use the beach. In view of their continual need for fresh water, it is surprising that rain water storage facilities, protected against colonisation by insects and larvae, have only recently been adopted, and that on very few of the islands.

Twentieth century history

The hereditary sultanate continued, with the occasional usurper, through the period of Dutch and French influence in the Maldives and beyond the signing of the protection agreement with Britain in 1887. Under that agreement the Maldivians retained their independent internal government but, in exchange for British protection against any foreign aggressor, forsook the right to conduct their own foreign affairs. It was an arrangement which led to a long-lasting amicable relationship between the two nations. The autocratic domestic rule of the Sultan continued virtually unchanged until 1932 when the first written Constitution of the Maldives was produced, to be followed by the election of a House of the People's Representatives and by the introduction of a constitutional sultanate. Hassan Nur-ud-din Iskander II became, in 1934, the first elected Sultan, serving until 1943.

Following Nur-ud-din's resignation in the middle of the Second World War, the country was ruled by a Council of Regency for two years and moved gradually from a constitutional monarchy to a republic. Amin Abdul Majeed Didi was designated as the second elected Sultan whilst he was in Egypt but he never assumed power and died in Colombo in 1952. In his absence, the country was effectively ruled by the Prime Minister, Muhammed Amin Didi, a forceful, innovative leader who is remembered with mixed emotions. In office and highly regarded in the early 1940s he was prominent during the discussions surrounding the 1948 agreement with the British government and when the First Republic of the Maldives was created on the 1st of January 1953 he became the elected President. He fell from grace, the First Republic lasted less than a year, and a constitutional sultanate was re-introduced with Ali Muhammed Farid Didi serving as the elected Sultan until 1968 when the Second Republic was declared. Ibrahim Nasir, the Prime Minister since 1957, became the President of the Second Republic and Farid Didi was banished to Colombo. Nasir remained as the President until 1978 when Maumoon Abdul Gayoom succeeded him. The 1948 agreement with the British government was revised in 1953 and further agreements were made in 1957, 1960, 1965 and 1976. The Republic of the Maldives is now a member of the Commonwealth and of the Assembly of the United Nations.

Twentieth century literature

For most of the twentieth century the English-language press largely ignored the Maldive Islands. Journal articles and occasional papers were published and although Hockly's work was published in 1935 it was Bell's monograph, published posthumously in 1940 (Fig 1.9), which was the major work on the archipelago. It was the tail-end of the century before Maloney published 'People of the Maldive Islands', a comprehensive study of life in the Maldives. More recently 'The Maldive Mystery', by Thor Heyerdahl, has provided some interesting glimpses of, and speculation about, early Maldivian history whilst the Lonely Planet guide 'Maldives' is a useful introductory text for modern-day travellers.

When Hockly's and Bell's accounts were written, Addu Atoll was special only in the sense that it was the southernmost atoll in the archipelago. Life there was as hard and as primitive as anywhere else in the Maldives. Visitors from other atolls were few because there had to be a good reason to make the long journey to the south of the equator: for the Maldivians, Addu Atoll lies on a route to nowhere. Few islanders left the atoll. The smaller fishing boats, or dhonis, which are still common throughout the Maldives (Figs 1.6 & 1.7) are not really designed for long sea journeys and only a few Adduans had been privileged to make the annual trading trips to Malé on board a buggaloe, a large trading vessel common in the archipelago at that time. Most of the Adduans had no concept of a different world beyond their horizon and few had ever seen a white man. That was to change dramatically with the onset of the Second World War when an alien military culture was to descend upon the atoll, changing forever the life style of the Adduans.

The twentieth century economy

In the 1940s and into the 1950s the Maldivian economy was in dire straits. Even when the traditional trade in coconut and fish was complemented with the creation of Maldives Shipping Ltd, the Maldives remained among the poorest nations in the world. The 1980s decline in the shipping industry was followed by a significant increase in tourism which had, by the turn of the century, overtaken commercial fishing as the major source of the nation's foreign exchange. On most of the islands, however, the main occupations have hardly changed over the centuries. For the men they are fishing and carpentry, especially boat building, which still entails the conversion of palm trees into planks and fittings by handsaw and adze (Fig 1.8). The cultivation of crops is not a full time occupation, is less highly regarded than fishing and is largely undertaken by women. Coir rope making, lacquer work, mat weaving and metal work all provide a limited amount of employment as does government office.

Away from the capital, bartering has always been a way of life. Money has little local significance in most of the island communities: it is primarily used for commodities which have to be obtained from Malé or Sri Lanka.

Life in the archipelago is certainly not life in a tropical paradise, even though visitors to the islands may receive such a first impression. Life is survival orientated in a culture which, on most of the islands, has changed but little for centuries.

Twentieth century health care

The rainfall in the Maldives provides an abundant supply of fresh water throughout the islands and helps to create lush vegetation, inland ponds or lakes and numerous swamps. In such environments insects thrive and until well into the twentieth century the major hazard ashore was disease, either carried by flying insects or lurking in the drinking water. When Commonwealth troops were stationed at Addu Atoll during the Second World War typhoid, elephantiasis, dengue fever, and malaria were all common and anyone foolish enough to drink the water from the village wells was almost certainly destined to become a host for a variety of intestinal parasites. By the late 1950s, when the Royal Air Force was establishing a base on Gan, disease was less prevalent among the villagers but typhoid, along with other less serious epidemics still occurred all too often at the atoll throughout the operational life of the RAF station. For twenty years the RAF's medical officers provided a local health care service unmatched anywhere else in the Maldives for at that time medical care was primitive throughout the archipelago. It has improved but little over the last twenty-five years with Malé, the capital, boasting the only noteworthy public hospital in the region.

There is now supposed to be a medical centre at each atoll but in practice many of the islanders still depend upon the services of a local hakim, a devotee of the ancient philosophy of natural remedies related to physiological humours, or the fandita man who heals through ritual and faith. Progression from the ancient to the modern is extremely slow, due partly to the nation's economic plight and partly to the entrenched cultures to be found among the isolated islanders.

Education

A decade after the end of the Second World War education consisted of little more than reading and writing closely linked to the Koran. Some of the primary schools in the archipelago were government-funded but many were financed through fees and voluntary contributions. They provided a very limited curriculum, merely building on the religious education undergone by virtually all children from the age of three or four. In the 1960s access to secondary education was limited to the children of those who either lived in Malé or could afford to send their offspring to the capital for an education which might subsequently be of little or no practical use on the home island. By the mid-1970s there were secondary education facilities on Hitaddu at Addu Atoll but they were under threat as a result of the British decision to abandon the Indian Ocean base. Even at the end of the twentieth century there were only two higher secondary schools, with courses up to English A level, in the archipelago; one in the capital and one on Hitaddu. Education at an overseas university has always been a rare privilege for a Maldivian and anyone so privileged can reasonably expect to achieve high office and membership of the elite group which controls the destiny of the nation.

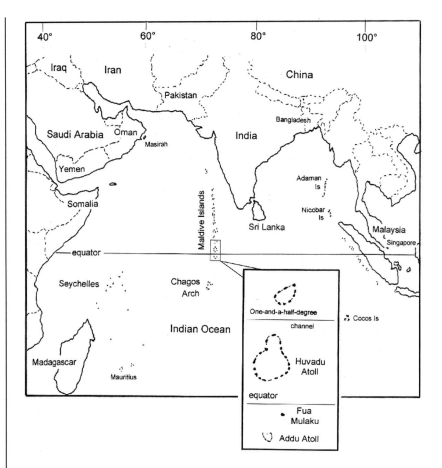

Fig. 1.1. Location of the Maldive Islands

Fig 1.3. Village elder with young companions.

Fig 1.2. Typical Maldivian island.

Fig 1.4. Traditional village home in the Maldive Islands

Fig 1.5. Young Maldivians with their palm fronds woven ready for use as roofing materials.

Figs 1.6 & 1.7. Maldivian dhonis, common throughout the islands.

Fig 1.8. Structural detail of a dhoni

THE MÁLDIVE ISLANDS.

1. ADDU ATOL.

Physical Features.

This beautiful little Atol, the most southerly of the Máldive archipelago, situated from 35 to 42 miles below the Equator and between 73· 1½ - 10 E. longitude, is perhaps the most perfect of the whole Group in its typical " atoll" form.

Shaped roughly like a half-moon, lying flat, concave-faced to North with horns projecting North-East and North-West, it stretches 10 miles East and West by 6½ miles North and South. The surrounding reefs have a contour of 20 miles; and appear both from the sea and the enclosed lagoon to be covered with continuous land, except for two narrow openings on the North and two wider to the South and South-East – the latter couple the only passages for ships. In reality, the coast line is broken up into islands, large and smaller, by gaps, more or less constricted and shallow, masked greatly by islets standing upon the outer reef.

Of the broader pair of passages, the more Southerly is that taken by Men-of-War and other vessels under steam, on rare occasions when such vessels visit this out-of-the-way Atol; the other two, suitable only for native sailing craft, occur in the middle of the Northern reef, one on either side of the centrally placed isle Kadu-hera ("Bushy Isle" of the Admiralty Chart).

Hitadu.

Hitadú is quite the most important and largest island in Addú Atol; being four miles in length by about three-quarters of a mile in breadth. Its population is more than double that of Midú and Huludú, the next in size combined.

In richness of vegetation, number of fruit-bearing trees large and small, wealth of fine grain, and root and garden produce, Hitadú rivals any of its fellows. A general air of prosperity and contentment seems to prevail. The men, strong and healthy looking physically, are engaging in manners, and display a quiet open demeanour refreshing to experience. Even the women appear in the streets freely unveiled, exhibiting less gaucheness and semi-timidity than noticed at that less sophisticated Island of the same Atol, Gan.

The streets and houses are well constructed, and kept up on clean and sanitary lines. One house at least – that of 'Ali Didi', a leading resident – in addition to being tiled and comfortably furnished, is set in a tidy garden of varied flowers.

Gan.

Gan (more correctly called Gamu) is the most Southerly Island on the Western reef. It is fairly populous having 558 inhabitants, who own six fishing boats large and small.

The vegetation, in places, is hardly less vigorous than seen elsewhere in the Atol. There are fine breadfruit trees; but, strangely, *Artocarpus integrifolia* grows neither here nor anywhere at the Máldives. A large expanse of low land is devoted to sweet potato cultivation. The Islanders houses are not built or arranged with that care and orderliness which mark Hitadú and Huludú dwelling sites; appearing to be more closely clustered and without any regular system.

The main road or street, well shaded and lined on either side by garden fences, leads from the landing place in the lagoon directly across the Island past a *"Maizánge"* (Council Room) to the *Hukuru Miskit*, or Chief Mosque of the seven found at Gan, which adjoins the seabeach on the West. This, a double-tiered structure, roofed and walled by cadjans, has a well-kept graveyard attached.

The small stony islet just inside the boulder zone of Gan, half way along the South-West shore, bears the same name (Addú) as the Atol.

Gan Ruins.

In the South-West portion of this Island and 200 or 300 yards from the beach, buried in heavy scrub jungle, interspersed freely with closely growing trees; among which *Hernandia peltala* (M. *kadu*) predominate, exist the sorry remains of what was once a Buddhist Monastery of no special pretentions.

This *Áráma* (to use the Sinhalese term) consisted, so far as ascertainable in the attendant circumstances, of but two ruined structures yet surviving, viz, (i) a Dágaba, now a miniature hillock of easy gradient, less than 30 feet in full height, but with no functional members remaining to mark its exterior form; and (ii) the base of an oblong *prákára* (encircling wall) , traceable above ground only on two of its sides, that formerly enclosed some buildings , the original position and dimensions of which must remain problematical owing to later-day reconstruction.

Inhabitants : Administration.

The inhabited Islands of Addú Atol number six in all. The census of 1921 reveals a total of 4,465 in the number of inhabitants; 2,340 males, 2,125 females occupying 782 houses. More than a third (1771) live at Hitadú; another third (1569) is divided between the twin Eastern Islands, Midú Huludú. The smallest population, little more than 200 heads, occupies Fédú.

Each Island is divided, for administration, into "Wards" (M *Avaru*) – two, three, four, six; and, for Hitadú, nine – served by *Khatib* and *Mudins*, with the Atol *Náibu*.

Fig 1.9. Extracts from Bell's monograph on the Maldives.

Section 1 – The Wartime Base

II   The Tentacles of War

During 1937 Japan, at war with China, was gradually isolating Hong Kong and was continuing to stage various incidents against the British and the Americans in the Far East. The British Chiefs-of-Staff, by then convinced that Germany was heading for war, knew that during the 1932 Shanghai crisis the Japanese had been ready to attack Singapore. Knowledge of the Japanese preparedness highlighted a potential dilemma: if Britain were to wage war against Germany, Japan might well take the opportunity to occupy the British colonies in the Far East either in support of the Third Reich or merely as a continuation of her expansionist policies. Whatever the reason, Britain would lose the strategic materials supplied by her Far Eastern colonies and might well find them utilised by an enemy nation. Moral obligations apart, the protection of those territories became an important strategic consideration and that led the Chiefs-of-Staff to regard Japan as a potential enemy second to Germany, relegating Italy to third place.

When German troops moved into Czechoslovakia, Britain's Committee of Imperial Defence had seriously to consider the depositions of British naval forces in the event of simultaneous war against Germany, Japan and Italy. Given inadequate naval resources to engage three naval powers it was agreed that the Home and Mediterranean fleets would take precedence; a Far Eastern Fleet would be formed and despatched as and when resources allowed. By the end of August 1939 the Admiralty had begun to withdraw units from the China Squadron, redeploying them in Home and European waters and in the Indian Ocean where they were likely to be needed for convoy protection duties. The defence of Britain's Far Eastern territories was essentially left to land forces operating with limited air and sea support. Britain's commitment to despatch a fleet to protect Australia and New Zealand from Japanese aggression was not abandoned but it was relegated to an intention which would be carried out only if events elsewhere so permitted.

Three days before Christmas 1939 it was decided that the Air Ministry should examine the possibility of laying down stocks of fuel on various Indian Ocean islands to enable the flying-boats from Trincomalee to move at short notice to the Seychelles, Mauritius or the Cape of Good Hope, thus enabling them to provide air cover complementary to the Admiralty's convoy protection programme. Within three months the first flying-boat mooring and refuelling facilities had been established at Malé Atoll in the Maldive Islands. This early development, a relatively minor aspect of the Indian Ocean war plans, established the potential military value of a base at Malé, confirmed the co-operative attitude of the Sultan and offered a ready-made solution when Italy's entry into the war put Allied shipping in the Indian Ocean under the threat of attacks by marauders operating out of the Italian Somaliland.

Britain, facing a fight for survival in Europe and unable, in 1940, to predict how quickly the Allied troops would overrun the Italian Somaliland in 1941, was simultaneously trying to maintain the defences of Hong Kong and the Malay peninsular whilst providing covert assistance to China and avoiding war with Japan. It was difficult enough to achieve all that even before the American, British and Dutch reactions to Japan's 'protective' occupation of French Indo-China in 1940 left the Japanese with insufficient oil to continue their campaign in China; then it became impossible. Impossible because it left the Japanese government facing a stark choice; abandon that campaign or capture the Dutch East Indies' oilfields, a move which would lead inevitably to war with Britain and America. Japan captured the oilfields.

From the East Coast of Africa to the Malayan peninsular Allied shipping was then under threat no matter where it sailed within the twenty eight million square miles of the Indian Ocean

Even before the Air Ministry had established an RAF refuelling depot at Malé, the Admiralty had been considering how best to counter the threat to Allied shipping in the Indian Ocean if, as was feared in 1939, Italy and Japan were to enter the war. It would obviously be difficult enough to protect Allied shipping even when safe port facilities were available but if the Indian Ocean ports were to be blockaded, some safe haven would be needed between South Africa and the Far East, well away from the mainlands of Africa and India, capable of being strongly defended and preferably located where there had been no pre-war activities from which an enemy could infer a wartime role. Such a location was most likely to be found among the Maldivian atolls. Certainly there was nothing new in the idea that Britain should establish a maritime base in the archipelago; such a proposal had already been published in the Ceylon Sessional Papers - in 1881 (Fig 2.1).

The islands had been frequently charted, probably because their military strategic value had been recognised by European powers since the early part of the nineteenth century. They were also so numerous that it would be difficult for an enemy to detect military activity on any one of them. For the Admiralty, the most southerly atolls had an added attraction; they were remote enough to ensure that any enemy attacking them would have to do so without land-based air cover and with severely stretched lines of support.

Of the various reports and charts from the early 1920s, when the Admiralty had surveyed much of the Maldivian archipelago, those produced by the 1923 survey team showed that Addu Atoll, the southernmost atoll in the Maldive Islands, met the Admiralty's criteria. All that was needed was an up-to-date assessment of the atoll's suitability.

Bearing in mind that the Air Ministry had already established a refuelling depot at Malé, the Admiralty staff did not expect to meet any objections to their suggestion that a naval base should be developed at Addu Atoll but they could not just send an expedition to survey the lands of an independent nation; before initiating a military reconnaissance of Addu Atoll they had to obtain permission from the Sultan. As expected, obtaining that was a mere formality; not only did His Highness Hasan Nur-ud-din Iskander II, give his permission, he even arranged for his nephew, Abdullah Alif Didi, to act as guide and interpreter for the survey team. No official reports of that survey appear to have survived but the personal recollections of Major W. Manners, a member of the team, are on record. He recalled:

'In the latter half of 1940 I was at Rawalpindi where I had been given command of, and was still in the process of forming, a new Lines of Communication Battalion. I received a message one day which was as mysterious as it was explicit, "...report to General Headquarters, Delhi, immediately and ensure that your baggage includes two manpack wireless sets, some old clothes, two pairs of plimsolls and some swimming trunks".

It was really rather worrying because I was a poor swimmer and the possibility that I might have to swim with a wireless pack on my back was

disturbing to say the least. My arrival at General Headquarters did nothing to allay my fears. No-one was able, or prepared, to explain what was going on. It was not until the following day that I was shown the naval charts of Addu Atoll and informed that I was to be a member of a reconnaissance party being sent to survey the atoll for possible development as a naval base. Security was obviously tight; no reference was ever made to Addu Atoll, the code name it had been given was 'Port T'.

The officers who made up the reconnaissance party came from the Royal Navy, the Fleet Air Arm, the Royal Engineers and the Royal Artillery and were under the command of Lieutenant Colonel Lukis. I was the communications specialist on the party and was accompanied by a Sergeant from the Royal Corps of Signals. We sailed from Ceylon aboard HMS Glasgow and our security was so tight that when we later returned to Ceylon my Sergeant didn't even know where he had been.

Our ship's boat landed us at a harbour on the island of Hitaddu where the party was met by Abdullah Afif Didi, a nephew of the Sultan. He spoke excellent English and acted as interpreter throughout our reconnaissance. I had a camera with me and photographed the arrival at Hitaddu. I also took some photographs of the local scene but unfortunately very few of them survived the war (Figs 2.2, 2.3, 2.4 & 2.5).

In addition to the village on Hitaddu there were villages on the islands of Gan and Midu. Near each village was a cultivated area but apart from that the islands were covered with palm trees, dense scrub and swamp. It was an unhealthy, insect-ridden environment.

Our party's health remained good, mainly because of the inoculations we had received before leaving Ceylon and because we lived on board ship, going ashore each day to continue our survey.

We concluded that the atoll could certainly be developed as a fleet anchorage and as a flying-boat base but we also observed that island clearance and swamp drainage, or infilling, presented an enormous task in an exceptionally unhealthy environment.'

DEFENCE

The importance of the Máldives in the event of maritime war in Indian seas in which England was involved, might be made considerable. Lying within two to three days' steam of Ceylon and the Coast of Hindústán - and therefore within easy reach of supplies - they could advantageously be selected as a rendevouz and temporary station, or as a point d'appui for war-vessels destined to harass the marine of the enemy in the East.

History affords at least one instance of the recognition by a European power of the utility of these Islands in time of war. Their admirable position did not fail to attract the watchful eye of the shrewd Dupleix, who occupied Málé (Sultan's Island) in 1754 with a detachment of French troops when engaged in the struggle against the English for supremacy of Southern India.

Fig 2.1: Extract from 'The Maldive Islands ... an account ... ' by H C P Bell.

Fig 2.3: Maldivian mosque, Hitaddu, 1940.

Fig 2.2: The first reconnaissance party landing, Hitaddu, Addu Atoll 1940 with Colonel Lukis standing at the stern of the dhoni.

Fig 2.4: Village school, Hitaddu, 1940.

Fig 2.5: Villagers launching a buggaloe off Hitaddu, 1941.

III   1941: The Creation of Port T

By 1941 the Air Ministry had developed flying-boat facilities at Malé atoll where emergency stores depots were under construction for the forces in the Far East. The Admiralty, by the middle of January, had declared its commitment to the development of a fleet anchorage at Addu Atoll and within a few weeks the Director of Plans, assessing the likelihood of having to despatch a fleet to the Far East, concluded that some fifty or sixty ships:

> '... may be despatched via the Cape to either Singapore or to an uninhabited base with no facilities whatsoever, situated approximately one thousand miles from Ceylon.'

The Stores Directorate, either unaware of the Lukis report or interpreting it pessimistically, started work on the supply plans for such a fleet on the assumption that the remote base 'Port T' would be uninhabited, would have no fresh water supply and that the fleet work undertaken at the base would be self-refits without shore facilities. Under those circumstances the supply problems would be severe but not insurmountable. Thousands of gallons of water would be required each week to run the tropical base and that alone would require a weekly delivery from Ceylon unless a local supply could be obtained either from the island or from distilling ships attached to the fleet. Securing a guaranteed local supply of several thousand gallons of fresh water each week would be the first priority if Port T were to be established as a fleet anchorage; without that the increasing threat from submarines in the Indian Ocean would make the delivery of water to such a remote location a hazardous operation and the more frequent the supply runs the greater the chance of alerting the enemy to the existence of the base.

Whilst the Admiralty's plans were taking shape, the shipping putting into Ceylon was increasing dramatically. By March the supply ships, the passenger ships on the Far Eastern route and the naval colliers and oilers passing through Colombo were totalling well over two hundred vessels a month and the need for improved air cover in the Indian Ocean was becoming ever more urgent. Of the various ways in which such cover could be provided, two options complemented the Admiralty's plans for the development of a fleet safe haven at Addu Atoll. The first was a proposal from the Commander-in-Chief, Far East, that a garrison should be established at the atoll and flying-boat facilities developed if practicable. The second was an Air Council plan for the establishment of a flying-boat group with headquarters at Colombo and squadrons in Ceylon, Mombasa and Durban, a plan which would require the development of operational facilities for the squadrons at various Indian Ocean islands, including Addu Atoll.

The Admiralty decided to support the fleet anchorage development with the establishment of a garrison on the islands but, pending a more detailed survey of the atoll, to defer the decision on the co-location of a flying-boat base. The fact that the British government did not have permission from the Sultan of the Maldives to build a military base on the atoll was virtually ignored and on the 23rd of August 1941 the Admiralty signalled the Commander-in-Chief, Mediterranean, the Commander-in-Chief, East Indies, and the Flag Officer Commanding, Royal Indian Navy, '... It has been decided to proceed with the defences at 'T' now. Request you will comply...' Within days a more detailed survey of the atoll was commissioned and Mobile Naval Base Defence Organisation troops in the Mediterranean area were being allocated to 'Force Piledriver' and 'Force Shortcut' ready for deployment to Addu Atoll.

Britain's request for permission to build the base was to be put to the Sultan by Colonel Brown RM but it was late September before the Governor of Ceylon wrote Brown's letter of introduction (Fig 3.1) and that was far too late for the Admiralty staff. They didn't bother to await the outcome of the diplomatic process, they took the permission for granted and before Colonel Brown was able to put the British request to the Sultan a detailed survey of the atoll had been completed, the Mobile Naval Base Defence Organisation troops had landed and work had started on the development of Port T.

The survey took place early in September, with HMS Mauritius spending from the 9th to the 13th at the atoll undergoing harbour trials in the lagoon and providing base accommodation for the survey teams. The accuracy of the Admiralty chart was confirmed, as was the suitability of the lagoon for submarine and torpedo test runs. The problems of constructing gun emplacements and link roads were analysed by the Royal Marines survey team while the underwater defence needs of Port T were assessed by the captain of the cable ship HMS Atreus who had travelled to Port T on board the Mauritius. His survey, hampered by the loss or inaccessibility of the charted bench marks and trigonometric stations, was focussed on the feasibility of installing controlled minefields, booms and indicator loops at the entrances to the lagoon. He estimated that the armoured submarine cable on board the Atreus was some forty thousand yards more than was required for the underwater defences at the atoll and he suggested that the surplus be used to run submarine communication links between Midu, Wilingili, Gan, Hitaddu and Bushey, leaving only the land lines and instruments to be provided from other sources. For some unstated reason the Admiralty would not give permission for the cable to be used at Addu Atoll; a decision which created significant and unnecessary problems in 1942 when inter-island submarine cables had to be laid.

On the 11th of September the Officer Commanding N° 222 Group, RAF Ceylon, flew to the atoll to complete the survey by investigating the lagoon's potential as a flying-boat base. Discovering that the main body of the lagoon was unsuitable for landing and take off due to the heavy swell, the numerous coral heads and the difficulty of laying moorings and flares he concluded that the eastern side of Hitaddu was the most suitable for flying-boat operations. His examination of the shore conditions confirmed that an RAF camp could easily be located on that shoreline, making aircraft servicing a relatively easy operation.

The Maldivians assisted throughout the survey but apart from the medicines, newspapers and cigarettes given to the atoll chief, they refused to accept any reward. Even the offers of rice, one of the islanders' staple foods, were consistently refused, providing a striking example of the control of the Sultan who had ordered that his subjects were not to accept gifts from any visiting ships without his permission. The fact that the Adduans were some three hundred miles from the capital, a seven-day journey on board a Maldivian boat, made no difference; they obeyed their Sultan.

In the Mediterranean the thousand marines and sailors destined for Port T were mustered under the command of Lieutenant Colonel W B F Lukis RM. Divided and designated 'Force Piledriver' and 'Force Shortcut' the troops embarked on HMS Glenroy and HMS Clan Forbes with Lukis, in overall command, on board the Glenroy. Force Shortcut, on board the Clan Forbes, was led by Lukis' second-in-command, Lieutenant Colonel L O Jones RM.

Unlike the Glenroy, the Clan Forbes had not been equipped as a troop carrier and conditions on board were appalling, even by wartime trooping standards. Jones, who had wanted to delay the ship's departure until improvements had been made, was supported by Lukis but both had been ignored: the Admiralty's insistence on the urgency of the operation over-rode everything. The two ships left the Mediterranean on the 20th of September and were given safe escort to Addu Atoll by the destroyer HMS Cornwall.

On board the Clan Forbes the troops soon discovered what they would have to put up with *en route* to Addu Atoll. It was bad enough that the 'light cruiser' galley had neither water heating apparatus nor baking facilities but there were other, far more serious, defects. There were four hundred and fifty-one servicemen in Force Shortcut. The ship carried no extra life-saving equipment except for a full consignment of lifejackets. There were no extra fire fighting appliances on board. The sanitation system consisted of ten latrines, without proper flushing systems, and no urinals. There were no drinking-water taps and no washing-water taps. Troops were crammed in to sleep where they could. The officers' accommodation consisted of six small wooden deck cabins, neither securely fixed to the deck nor waterproof. Each was just under seven feet square by six feet four inches high. Each contained four bunks. One of the survivors, former RN Leading Seaman John Stamp, recalled that the ship was over-run with rats, cockroaches and crabs. The bedding was alive. The troops came close to mutiny and it says much for Jones' leadership that he kept control of the situation for ten miserable days at sea. Much to the relief of everyone on board, the Clan Forbes anchored alongside the Glenroy and the Cornwall in the lagoon off Gan early on the 30th of September (Fig 3.2) and at eleven o'clock that morning the first Port T senior officers' conference was held on board the Cornwall. Four hours before Colonel Brown put to the Sultan the British request for permission to develop a military base at the atoll, Lieutenant Colonel Lukis RM had been officially designated 'defence commander, Port T' with Captain Mainwaring RN the 'senior naval officer, Port T'.

Colonel Brown was well received in Malé and from the report of his meeting with the Sultan (Fig 3.3) it is clear that the monarch avoided an embarrassing disagreement by readily acceding to the British request and offering to provide, at Maldivian state expense, all the help needed. There was, however, the implied proviso that no Ceylonese or Indian troops would be employed on Maldivian soil. It was a proviso which the British were to ignore.

Unaware of the conditions ashore, the twenty-two officers and four hundred and twenty-nine other ranks of Force Shortcut were understandably eager to disembark. John Stamp vividly recalled those first hours ashore, saying:

> 'Our top priority was to delouse ourselves, our clothes and our bedding. We erected canvas baths, filled them with sea water and disinfectant and soaked everything including ourselves. Only after delousing and drying out did we start to set up camp. There was little clear ground available outside the native villages but the troops quickly established a shore base, pitching our tents near the beach but well away from the local population. It took only a week for a transit camp site to be cleared on Gan and for smaller camp sites to be established on other islands.'

As the troops established themselves on Gan their problems began. The work was hard labour and it became even harder as sickness began to take its toll. Acclimatisation was difficult and was made worse by a particularly severe series of tropical storms which flooded many of the tents, turned several camp sites into swamps and left many of the troops with no alternative but to relocate most of their tents, salvaging what they could from the flood.

For most of the Adduans a strange new world, often quite frightening, was moving in on their islands. When the Matador lorries were brought ashore and driven up the beaches the villagers scattered. They had never seen such vehicles and they feared that their villages and their cultivated plots of land were about to be destroyed. Within days their fears began to come true as the troops started to tear down the palm trees. To the military, the trees were merely a hindrance but to the islanders they were an essential element in the local economy. Each tree provided a regular supply of nuts, coir and fronds for their plaited kadjan huts before ultimately providing timber. Each tree was privately owned and although each owner was due to be compensated for any losses he suffered, most believed that the compensa-tion would be inadequate. There was, however, nothing they could do about the destruction for it had the implicit approval of their Sultan and they remained subservient to him even when a significant part of their livelihood was being destroyed.

During October the Glenroy left the atoll, the Clan Forbes was sent to India for modification, the SS Corfu became the Port T base ship and the defence commander's headquarters was transferred from the Corfu to Gan on the 30th of the month. By then virtually all the troops in the Mobile Naval Base Defence Organisation were living under canvas (Figs 3.4, 3.5 & 3.6) and the villagers were becoming used to the strange events taking place on their islands. The Adduan men and the children were friendly rather than fearful but the women remained shy and withdrawn. For the men, life was a continual struggle for survival and, ever alert for any opportunity to make life easier, they quickly learned to take advantage of the military activity whenever possible, often without any understanding of the risks involved. They were, for example, recipients of an unexpected bonus for their families when the Royal Navy divers used underwater explosives to widen the Gan channel. Hundreds of stunned fish floated to the surface and were immediately seized by the villagers who were delighted to obtain their seafood without the effort of taking their boats out to sea. John Stamp recalled that as the blasting continued the villagers became so eager to beat each other to the spoils that 'many of them entered the water before the explosives were detonated and were none too friendly towards the troops for some weeks after experiencing the shock wave.'

The Mobile Naval Base Defence Organisations had been formed to undertake just the kind of development work envisaged for Addu Atoll. Conceived as exclusively Royal Marine organisations they actually included many 'hostilities only' Royal Navy personnel who had been kitted out in khaki at Eastney Barracks and temporarily assigned to mobile unit duties. They were ill-prepared for the tasks they faced and like the Royal Naval Reserve officers in the boat company, most of whom had been kitted out in khaki with puttees and pith helmets (Fig 3.7), they were even less prepared for the conditions they were to encounter during the construction of Port T. Except where the Maldivians had established their villages and cultivated areas, the islands were covered in scrub and riddled with swamps. Large land crabs, not usually aggressive but capable of inflicting nasty wounds on anyone unlucky enough to disturb them, added to the misery of the troops whose job it was to clear the scrub, drain or fill the swamps and convert the atoll into a defended anchorage. Rats were everywhere and the entire atoll appeared to consist of one vast breeding site for voracious, disease-carrying insects. Malaria and scrub typhus were hyper-endemic. Elephantiasis was common although those afflicted were seen only on Wilingili island where they were sent, often with their entire families, to live in an isolated colony. By the end of October sickness among the troops was increasing dramatically and, in anticipation of worse to come, the capacity of Gan's tented hospital was increased to ninety bed spaces.

Less hostile but nevertheless disconcerting on first acquaintance were the hundreds of small reptiles and the giant fruit bats which were to be found throughout the islands. The bats, bigger than any the troops had ever seen, would hang well hidden in any convenient tree or shrub during the daytime. On being disturbed they would take off with a considerable amount of noise and would often fly directly towards anyone who was nearby; veering only at the last moment to avoid what seemed to be an inevitable collision.

The beaches and the inviting water of the lagoon provided only slight relief for even there the troops faced a variety of dangers. The currents across the lagoon were strong enough to sweep any weak swimmer out into the Indian Ocean and even where no currents threatened, the marine life in the lagoon, as exotic as any in the Indian Ocean, was dangerous. Poisonous jelly fish, deadly stone fish, barracuda and sharks were common with the latter renowned throughout the atoll for attacking bathers in the shallows. Finally, the troops quickly learned that contact with the magnificent coral was likely to give them cuts or grazes which healed very slowly in the unhealthy climate, were a constant attraction for small parasites and invariably became ulcerated. In the words of former RN Signalman Philip McGuinness, *'I had eighty holes in my back. Quite a few lads had holes in their legs into which you could have put a pigeon's egg'.*

In that environment the troops laboured in protective clothing and lived in tents which quickly became mouldy and started to rot. For the first week ashore the servicemen worked for only six hours each day but it soon became obvious that they would never convert the atoll into a defended base by the deadline of the 1st of January 1942 unless they increased their working hours and after the 5th of October the working day was extended to twelve hours, starting at dawn and finishing at dusk, six days a week. Only on

Sundays was there a respite. The increase did at least leave the troops with little or no time to cause trouble or to dwell on their lot, a potential morale-sapping activity when work finished in the middle of the day. In any case, there were no leisure facilities to occupy them apart from board games and an occasional boxing match or film show on board one of the visiting supply ships. Prior to the 5th of October some of the men, bored by inactivity at the end of their six-hour working day, had even used their free time to earn 'pin-money' of no more than a pound a week as volunteer laundrymen on board HMS Corfu, washing the dirty linen from the tented hospital.

During those early days ashore several supply ships arrived from India and Ceylon, none more welcome than the SS Singu, a ten-year-old cleaned-out oil tanker which brought fresh water to the atoll. For the servicemen, drinking water was a precious, tightly rationed commodity because the so-called 'fresh' water in the islands' wells was highly contaminated and was actually the source of many of the local diseases. Until a local supply of safe and reliable drinking water became available the troops, banned from drinking from the villagers' supplies, consumed only that which was delivered twice daily by boat from the Singu to each of the thirteen islands on which the servicemen were based. Every month the Singu had to fetch a fresh supply of water from Colombo, necessitating the deployment to Port T of an alternative supply ship, usually the SS Appleleaf, and the employment of an escort ship, frequently HMS Scout, for a round trip of almost fifteen hundred miles in waters frequented by enemy marauders. Tight security was essential. Not only was Port T never referred to as Addu Atoll, individual island names were rarely used in written or radio communications; each of the thirteen islands was identified only by its allocated number (Fig 3.8).

The drinking water from Ceylon was far too precious to be used for anything else. Sea water was used for ablutions but it often caused skin complaints unless it was filtered through 'shower heads' consisting of suspended, suitably punctured five-gallon drums almost filled with sand which had to be frequently changed, an extremely tedious process. Whenever possible the troops took advantage of any tropical downpour to lather up and rinse off in the rain, frequently assembling on the beaches to do so. As former R N artificer Len Hobbs recalled:

'The tropical rainstorms often stopped as suddenly as they started, leaving the naked, lathered-up troops to finish their ablutions as best they could in the not-too-hospitable shallows of the lagoon. Such incidents

greatly amused the locals, some of whom were always within sight of this fascinating ritual.'

The Maldivians were understandably curious about the troops, their equipment and their lifestyle for the military had brought to the atoll an achievement-orientated culture, quite alien to the villagers who lived at subsistence level. The children were friendly enough and the servicemen, separated from their own families, invariably responded in like manner. The Adduan men tended to temper friendliness with caution whilst the women, who were rather shy even within their own communities, were generally happy to observe the troops from a distance. But far too many of the servicemen, equally curious about the villagers, had few inhibitions when satisfying their curiosity. Very few of them had ever encountered such a primitive community and they were understandably intrigued by the day-to-day life of the islanders whose territory they had invaded. They could, however, be quite insensitive to the feelings of the local population and had regularly to be reminded that, in accordance with Port T standing orders, anyone breaking bounds would be subject to disciplinary action (Fig 3.9).

The troops' lack of consideration for the islanders' privacy meant that the Maldivian interpreters spent much of their time trying to help the military and the Adduans to understand each other's culture and it was largely as a result of their efforts that problems affecting the villagers and the troops were invariably resolved amicably. The most serious and most obvious potential problem, molestation of the Adduan women by the troops, was tackled by a combination of orders and health warnings (Fig 3.10), a remarkably successful approach with very few servicemen having to be disciplined for failing to comply with the promulgated orders. The likelihood of disciplinary action or venereal disease undoubtedly deterred the majority of the troops and for those who were still inclined to ignore those risks there was a further very powerful deterrent, the rumoured retribution to be suffered by any offender unfortunate enough to be caught by the villagers. Undoubtedly exaggerated, the graphic accounts of mutilation were almost certainly enough to deter even the confirmed womanisers amongst the troops.

As the weeks went by, the military authorities and the Maldivian leaders were able to relax although both sides remained anxious to keep the servicemen and the villagers apart except for the essential co-operation among working groups. Boundary lines were established around the Adduan territories and the military establishments, the village areas were out of bounds to the troops and entry into the military areas was forbidden to all Maldivians except in the course of their duties. Even so, off-duty contact occurred because servicemen often received gifts of shells, fish or coconuts from the villagers and would frequently give soap, cigarettes and old cordage in return. Such exchanges never developed into an organised bartering or trading system although unofficial exchange rates developed with the price of a coconut increasing from one cigarette to ten in a matter of weeks. As this casual bartering became more frequent, individual trading between the troops and the villagers was made illegal for the simple reason that it was beginning to lead to off-duty contact between the two communities. Some fish and fruit was supplied for the garrison through an official trading system controlled by the atoll sheriff but the troops, living largely on tinned food, were quite prepared to risk minor disciplinary action for the sake of the fresh fruit which the villagers were willing to trade. For their part, many villagers would risk arrest by the sheriff for the sake of some soap or cigarettes. The result was that undercover bartering continued long after individual trading had been made illegal. Beer, a religious taboo for the Maldivians but an important dietary addition in the eyes of the troops, was infrequently traded although a few villagers acquired a taste for it and thought the pleasure worth the risk of being banished for a while to one of the small uninhabited islands, the normal punishment for any Maldivian found guilty of consuming alcohol.

The adverse living conditions and the growth of illicit trading inevitably led to some pilfering by the troops in order to improve their lot and to some by the villagers who had been unexpectedly shown an amazing variety of highly desirable commodities. Theft never became a serious problem because most of the Maldivians were very observant of their Sultan's orders and were well aware that in their close-knit communities very few actions went un-noticed; the near certainty of being caught was a strong deterrent. The islanders were also aware that the Port T orders gave any serviceman the right to apprehend villagers found 'loitering with intent' (Fig 3.11) and after a few of them had been arrested, handed over to the sheriff and punished, the number of thefts declined and remained low.

Whilst the troops of the Mobile Naval Base Defence Organisation were developing the garrison facilities the detailed reconnaissance report from HMS Mauritius was being studied by the Commander-in-Chief, East Indies, to assess the merits of incorporating a flying-boat base into the plans for a defended anchorage. As a result, the Air Ministry was informed by signal on the 15th of October 1941 *'Addu Atoll is suitable. Air Officer Commanding, Far East, will arrange for an advanced base for one flying-boat squadron to be constructed.'* The atoll's wartime role was growing.

November started with the men of Force Piledriver unloading one hundred and fifty tons of cargo from HMS Laomedan. The Force diarist, almost certainly unaware that he was recording two omens of the severe problems to come, noted on the first day of the month *'. . . the troops engaged on this stevedore work are beginning to show signs of tiredness . . .'* and, two days later, *'The first case of malaria has been diagnosed'*. By then, the monthly sick return was already showing that over a third of the servicemen were unfit for normal duties (Fig 3.12); the possibility that even more men were about to be incapacitated hardly bore thinking about.

They may have been in poor health but by early November the troops had made an impressive start on the major works programme. Roadways had been cleared, gun emplacements built, some coastal defence artillery installed and the first proof rounds fired on the 8th of November, just twenty-four hours before the Armistice Day service reminded everyone of the 'war to end all wars' (Figs 3.13, 3.14 & 3.15).

The Clan Forbes, modified in accordance with Jones' requests, returned from India on the 14th November, much to the relief of the men employed in the workshop unit. The ship's derricks, forty tons aft and eighty tons forward, could lift any landing craft out of the water for onboard repairs, a godsend in view of the number of landing craft propellers sheared on the lagoon's coral heads. For the remainder of the garrison, the ship's cargo was of far more significance than the derricks, for on board the Clan Forbes were 350 tons of stores along with two unexpected bonuses: the first mail to be received by the troops since leaving the Mediterranean and one thousand tons of fresh water in the ship's newly-converted tanks. As they began to unload the stores the troops were in good spirits but their mood changed when they discovered that much of the foodstuff, which had been transported in an un-refrigerated vessel, had decayed and had to be dumped overboard. That was a bitter blow for it came at a time when they also had to dump a consignment of inedible food from the Port T stores, where the storage conditions were little better than those on board ship. It was bad enough to be employed as stevedores but it was galling in the extreme to come to the end of the hard labour only to be told to dump most of the cargo in the lagoon. The troops were well aware that there had already been several outbreaks of gastro-enteritis in the camps and they could well understand the need to dump the decaying food but they were understandably angry that those responsible for the provisions had failed to store them properly. The loss of such a large quantity of food was a severe blow and the troops' resentment at having to dump it all in the lagoon was so strong and so obvious that after the Clan Forbes episode provisions were transported under far better conditions on board victualling ships, the storage arrangements ashore were improved and boards of survey were held every three or four days to write off any deteriorating provisions, ensuring that decayed foodstuff was dumped before it contaminated other stores. That helped to reduce the incidence of gastro-enteritis but the troops continued to fall victim to a host of other diseases.

Many of those were life-threatening but the first death among the men of the Mobile Naval Base Defence Organisation did not come from disease nor was it a serviceman who died. On the day the Clan Forbes returned from India, a civil engineer from Ceylon, Mr Gouray, became the first man ever to be killed in a motoring accident at Addu Atoll when he died after falling under the wheels of a lorry.

But with the tented hospital full to overflowing and the medical staff overwhelmed it would only be a matter of time before troops began dying from any number of tropical diseases and to relieve the pressure on the Port T medical staff and on the tented hospital H M Hospital Ship Vita was sent to the atoll. She arrived on the 20th of November and remained in the lagoon for four weeks, providing hospital facilities and treatment for more than a hundred servicemen. That was far more than the staff ashore could have coped with and after that successful visit the Vita was to become a familiar sight at the atoll, returning whenever an outbreak of any particularly virulent tropical disease reached epidemic proportions.

Although Force Piledriver was scheduled to remain at Port T until the defences had been fully installed, Force Shortcut was due to leave the atoll for employment on other Indian Ocean bases as soon as the camp sites had been established and the defence work at Port T was well under way. Thus it was that on the 26th of November 1941 the Clan Forbes, with Colonel Jones and most of the Shortcut troops on board, left the atoll. Most, but not all, because seventy-three members of the original Force Shortcut contingent were still hospitalised on board the Vita at that time and were taken onto the strength of Force Piledriver as soon as they were fit enough to return to duty.

Force Shortcut, with Jones in command, became a highly mobile force working on various islands in the Indian Ocean until the 20th of March 1942 when it was disbanded. Jones then spent some time on temporary duty in Ceylon before returning to Addu Atoll to replace Lukis as the defence commander.

By December, the men of the Mobile Naval Base Defence Organisation had achieved the most remarkable progress. They had cleared sites, filled in swamps, built roads, installed and tested coastal artillery and generally established a military tented garrison. The atoll had been converted into a defended base with the Gan Channel, the main entrance to the harbour, protected by a minefield controlled from a hut on the island of Wilingili. Submerged indicator loops spanned the channel so that if any metallic object passed over them its presence would be indicated on the screen which had been installed in the control hut where equipment was monitored twenty-four hours a day by sailors who could detonate the channel mines. The system had been installed and tested by mid-December and on the 17th the Admiralty was informed that 'Port T is now in operation as a defended port ... all shipping ... warned of underwater defences.'

The system may have been tested but the men who worked anywhere near the Gan Channel headland were understandably wary of it, particularly after a Port T order warned them of the possibility that the mines could be accidentally detonated by a passing vehicle (Fig 3.16).

The troops had created a defended port but they were in poor shape. Brought from Egypt and Crete, they were mostly debilitated even before they had started working in the island marshes and scrubland and as Christmas approached they were falling sick in ever-increasing numbers. They desperately needed the imminent stand-down which, when it came, would give them an opportunity to recuperate, to consume Christmas turkey, Christmas pudding and a fair quantity of alcohol in their inhospitable tropical environment (Fig 3.17).

Whilst the men at Port T were looking forward to their well-earned Christmas stand-down and the accompanying celebrations, the Admiralty's Director of Plans was setting out a paper which extended the atoll's role from that of a safe haven to '... *a main fleet base with maximum facilities for the maintenance of an entire fleet,*' a concept which carried dramatic implications for the labour force at Port T. That extended role could have heralded bad news for the men of Force Piledriver because they were in no condition to take on any extra commitments but, fortunately for most of them, Christmas was not just a rest period, it was virtually the end of their labours at Addu Atoll.

As implied in Colonel Brown's report on his audience with the Sultan, the Chiefs-of-Staff had always intended to send Indian troops to replace the units of the Mobile Naval Base Defence Organisation as soon as the initial stages of the construction work had been completed and on Boxing Day, much to the delight of the men at Port T, a warning order was promulgated informing them that an Indian relief force was due to arrive at the atoll on the 28th of December (Fig 3.18): their labours at Port T were coming to an end. By the 11th of January 1942 they would be over the horizon and, whatever their destination, they were all fairly sure that it was not likely to be as unpleasant as Addu Atoll.

Queen's House
Colombo (Ceylon)
26th September, 1941

Your Highness,

I have the honour to commend to Your Highness, Colonel C.T.
Brown, O.B.E., the Senior Royal Marine Officer on the East Indies
Station, who brings this letter and who desires to pay his
respects to Your Highness.

2.   The British Admiralty have in contemplation the undertaking
of certain defence measures in the Maldive Islands, the details
of which will be explained by Colonel Brown. A detachment of
Royal Marines is proceeding to the Maldives and I desire to
commend them to Your Highness' good offices.

3.   It is desired to start the necessary work as early as
possible in October. The Royal Marines will be responsible for
the work but there will, in the early stages, be a need for
labour for the building of piles, houses, etc., materials being
supplied, and it will also be necessary to find interpreters.

4.   I would be extremely grateful to Your Highness if you would
arrange that all possible assistance be given to Colonel Brown in
regard to the matters referred to in this letter.

5.   I trust that Your Highness is in the enjoyment of good health
and that you may long continue to rule over your dominions in
peace and prosperity.

I have the honour to be
Your Highness' obedient servant,

GOVERNOR

His Highness Hasan Nurruddin Iskander II
Sultan of the Maldive Islands

Fig 3.1: The letter of introduction which Colonel Brown presented to the Sultan.

Colombo
3rd October 1941

Sir,

I have the honour to place before you the following brief report on my visit to MALE on 30th September
1941.

I conveyed a letter from His Excellency the Governor and a present from yourself to HH the Sultan of the
Maldives and was received in audience by HH at 1500 hours. The outcome of this was that certain
members of the Maldivian Government, including the acting Prime Minister and Mr. Halmy Didi, who
had accompanied me from Colombo, sat in conference for about half an hour.

To these gentlemen I stated my case which was a request for native labour to assist in the erection of
certain structures required for the defensive preparation of Addu Atoll about to commence.

All material would be supplied by me and payment made for the labour employed.

Not only was my request favourably received but the Maldivian members stated HH would have pleasure
in supplying our needs at state expense. This was given official sanction later at a full meeting of the
council and a definite answer given to me at 21.00 hours.

In spite of my protests that it was not the intention of His Majesty's Government that the Maldivian
Government should be put to any expense whatever, that the stores and materials were on their way, if not
already at Addu, the Prime Minister insisted, after paying a glowing tribute to the Royal Navy, due to
whose protection he attributed over 100 years of peace, that this was a means of contributing to the war
effort.

I assured the Ministers that the defences were of a temporary nature only and would be dismantled soon
after the war. But one point was raised of which I took a more serious view and respectfully bring to your
notice. The acting Prime Minister stated that he sincerely hoped that no Singalese or Indian troops were
being employed. To this I truthfully replied that all my officers and men were white members of the
Royal Navy and Royal Marines. I was asked this question on two occasions and had he probed the matter
more deeply I should have had no option but to tell him the Royal Marines would eventually be relieved
by Indian troops.

It is obvious that the Maldivians have no desire for Indian or Singalese troops and their importation would
undoubtedly lead to trouble.

Although I am not directly concerned with the policy of reliefs for Royal Marines personnel, provided
they are relieved I consider it my duty to inform you of the facts and suggest that I might raise the
question at Headquarters SIMLA which I visit in the near future.

I have the honour to be,
Sir
Your obedient Servant,

COLONEL

The Commander-in-Chief
East Indies Station

Fig 3.3: Colonel Brown's report on his meeting with the Sultan.

WAR DIARY

In lieu of A.F. C.2118.

Unit....FORCE "PILEDRIVER".

Month and Year.....September 1941

Officer Commanding.:Lieut. Colonel W.B.F. Lukis,RM

Place	Date	Hour	Summary of Events and Information
At Sea	20th	1630	Weighed anchor. Ship's appointments:- O.C. Troops-Lieut. Colonel W.B.F. Lukis, Ship's Adjutant-Capt. J.I. Berry, Ship's S.Major-Q.M.S. G.W. Barnes, Ship's Q.M.S. Sgt. C.H. Bennett. Total strength:- 31 Officers and 583 O.Rs.
	22nd		T.A.B. Inoculation(50%) renewal injection for all ranks not inoculated since 31 Dec 40, commenced
	23rd		T.A.B. Inoculation ended.
	29th	1630	A.A. practice shoot.
	30th	0900	Port "T" sighted.
		1025	Anchored.
		1100	Conference in HMS "Cornwall" at which were present S.N.O. Port"T", Capt. Sir J. Paget Lieut. Col. W.B.F. Lukis, Major Salter, Lieut. Comdr. M.Fening, Lieut. Col. L.O. Jones Major Newling, Capt. J.I. Berry, and Capt. G.R. Borland. Lieut. Col. W.B.F. Lukis appointed Defence Commander Port "T". Capt. Mainwaring appointed S.N.O.
		1130	HMS Cornwall's whaler proceeds to entrance to no.5 island to recce depth of water at various tides and to buoy entrances.
		1230	R.M. party return from conference.
		1245	Conference of sub-Unit commanders.
		1400	Land recce party leaves "Glenroy", including Lieut. Col. W.B.F. Lukis, Lieut. Col. L.O. Jones, Major D. Johnston, Major Salter, Major J.F. Maxfield, Major N.A. Newling, Capt. J.I. Berry, Surg. Lieut. R.E.D. Wheeler, Lieut. C.M. Pond, Lieut. G.P. Cole and 5 O.Rs. Temporary shore signal point set up at no.5 island landing place.
		1430	Demolition party together with party from HMS"Cornwall" proceeds to no.5 landing place entrance to commence the deepening of the entrance by blasting.
		1730	Recce party returns.
		1830	Demolition party returns.
		2130	Boat and working party routine for the following day issued.

There was no change in command during the above period.

Fig 3.2: The official record of the arrival at Port T

Fig 3.4: Headquarters Camp and Hants Battery, Gan, 1941 (IWM Neg N° A28429)

Fig 3.6: 'Outpost of The Empire' Gan, 1941

Fig 3.5: Royal Marine camp, Hitaddu, 1941

Fig 3.7: Village walkabout, Gan, 1941

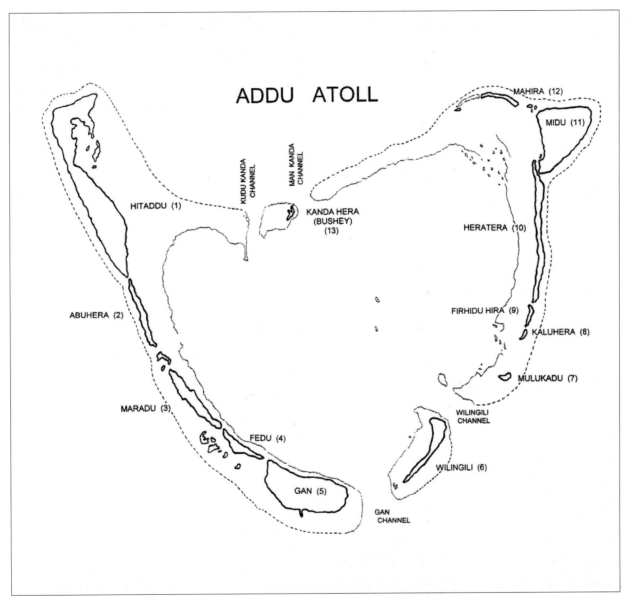

ADDU ATOLL

MAHIRA (12)

MIDU (11)

KUDU KANDA CHANNEL

MAN KANDA CHANNEL

HITADDU (1)

KANDA HERA (BUSHEY) (13)

HERATERA (10)

ABUHERA (2)

FIRHIDU HIRA (9)

KALUHERA (8)

MARADU (3)

MULUKADU (7)

FEDU (4)

WILINGILI CHANNEL

GAN (5)

WILINGILI (6)

GAN CHANNEL

Fig 3.8: The islands on which troops were based, Addu Atoll, 1941.

Bounds. Complaints have already been received from the natives in the village of Gan island that Europeans from ships have entered houses and taken photographs against the people's wishes. It is most essential that the extreme goodwill of the natives should be maintained. On no account are houses to be entered nor photographs of any people taken as they are most ignorant and frightened of being photographed. The native village is out of bounds, the route to the Southern beach via the native village is out of bounds. Disciplinary action will be taken against any officer or other ranks breaking bounds.

Fig 3.9: Extract from Mobile Naval Base Defence Organisation standing orders, October 1941, Order N° 33

Native women. The Sultan of the Maldives has made a gift of as much free native labour as shall be required. In return it has been promised that no native women will on any account be molested. All MNBDO personnel will avoid all cotact with native women. The percentage of venereal disease amongst the native population is believed to be very high.

Fig 3.10: Port T Order N° 2.14 dated 2 Oct 41

THEFTS BY NATIVES

Pilfering by natives has increased considerably during the past few weeks. In future, all natives not actually engaged in husbandry or working parties found loitering in the vicinity of tents on No. 5 Island will be apprehended and placed in custody and turned over to the Sheriff of Gan. All ranks may apprehend a native who they find loitering near the tents and will immediately take the native to an officer who may order the native to be placed in custody and inform the Interpreter of the action taken. The Sherrif from Mali has been informed of this course of action and has undertaken to assist in its execution.

Fig 3.11: Extract from Port T Order N° 56.228 dated 19 Dec 41

PORT 'T' FORCE STRENGTHS AND SICK RETURNS 1st./2nd. NOVEMBER 1941

Strengths at 1st. November 1941

	Officers	ORS
Force Piledriver	36	541
Force Shortcut	23	405
Totals	59	946

Sick report for 2nd. November 1941

Fresh sickness cases in 4weeks =	461
No. of individuals sick =	379
Sick admitted to wards =	111
Remaining in wards on 2 Nov.41. =	50
Average daily attendance for sick bay dressings etc. =	95

Fig 3.12: Port T sick report, 2nd November 1941

Fig 3.13: Roadway laid over swamp on Hitaddu. 1941

Fig 3.15: Coastal artillery on Hitaddu. (IWM Neg N° A28436)

Fig 3.14: Positioning the barrel of one of the coastal defence guns on Hitaddu. (IWM Neg N° A28434)

Controlled minefield cable. The resistance in the controlled minefield cable running alongside the road to Hants and HQ camp has been seriously affected by, it is alleged, lorries. Lorry drivers will take great care that their wheels do not touch the cable as further damage to a cable might result in the minefield exploding.

Fig 3.16: Extract from Port T orders.

CHRISTMAS FARE.

A consignment of turkeys, plum pudding, etc., has been received and will be issued by the Quartermaster in due course. The position of the beer stock has improved. All stocks will be allocated to Canteens on the basis of the ration strength on 23rd December of the Sub-units who use each canteen. For this purpose the Quartermaster's store, Boat Company on Island 5, Tented Hospital and Cumberland Camp will be included as one. Os. C Camps with Canteens will be informed of the distribution on 23rd December and should arrange for collection on the following day. A sum of rupees 600 has been received for the benefit of all troops for Christmas Day. It is proposed that in lieu of distributing beer free, to distribute this sum proportionally amongst the canteens on the same basis as above; except that the Boat Company personnel on H.M.S. "Ranchi" will be entitled to participate.

Fig 3.17: Extract from Port T orders

RELIEF OF M.N.B.D.O AT PORT "T"   This document if taken
                                    from Port "T" will be
          WARNING ORDER   treated as MOST SECRET
              by
  Lt. Col. W.B.F. Lukis, R.M.,
  Defence Commander, Port "T"   26 Dec. 41

1. INFORMATION
    (a) H.T. "THALMA" arrives at Port "T" on Dec.28th carrying the Indian
        Army relieving force comprised as follows:-
        Sub-Unit Name.   Strength   Ultimate destination.

        7th Heavy Bty & H.Q   294   Islands 5 & 6
        & attached sub-Units
        Garrison Coy.   178   Island 5
        8th Heavy Bty   86   Island 11
        9th Heavy Bty   86   Island 1.
    (b) s.s "CLAN FORBES" will arrive at Port "T" 7 Jan. 42 and will
        embark:-
        (i) Certain Stores from H.T. "THALMA", and possibly
        (ii) All M.N.B.D.O. heavy stores.
    (c) The M.N.B.D.O. will embark in H.T. "THALMA" with all personal
        baggage, small arms and E.Q. stores by 10th Jan. 42
    (d) H.M.S. "RANCHI" has consented to accommodate a part of the
        M.N.B.D.O. during the change-over.
    (e) There is no information as to the tonnage of the stores
        carried in H.T. "THALMA" for any island at Port "T" nor to be
        embarked in s.s. "CLAN FORBES".

2. SCHEME FOR THE RELIEF.
        The lack of information as to the tonnage of the stores in
    H.T. "THALMA" and as to the tactical stowage makes it impossible
    to plan any definite scheme for embarkation. The scheme as set out
    in the attached Provisional Outline Programme is based on the
    assumption that the stores are stowed to the best tactical advantage.
    It is hoped that it will be possible to accelerate the programme. If
    the 8th Heavy Bty. stores are stowed on top of the 9th Heavy Bty.
    stores the relief of Kent Bty. will be postponed until after the
    relief of Devon Bty, and the programme amended accordingly.

3. WORKING PARTIES
        Commencing 26 Dec. 41 all personnel will be required to form
    up into working parties irrespective of their normal work. M.L.C.
    loading and unloading will be carried out at every tide irrespective
    of the time of day or night. As a rule M.N.B.D.O. personnel will
    only be expected to load and unload M.N.B.D.O. stores.

4. CLEANLINESS OF CAMPS
        Indian Regiments are made to maintain a higher standard of
    cleanliness in the Camp than is usually achieved by white troops.
    All O.sC. Camps must ensure that the cleanliness of their camp on
    being relieved is of a higher standard than that usually achieved
    by Indian Regiments.

5. STORES
        The attached memorandum on handing over stores should be carried
    out in detail. All the Officers taking over will have a copy and will
    expect to find the stores set out for checking as it is suggested in
    the Memorandum.

Fig 3.18: The Port T warning order for the relief of the Mobile Naval Base Defence Organisation troops by an Indian Army force

IV   1942: Strengthening the Defences

During the first few weeks of 1942, most of the men in Force Piledriver departed, leaving the remaining construction work to be undertaken by a contingent of troops, all part of the Mobile Naval Base Defence Organisation, who arrived whilst the Indian relief force was settling in. Of the few servicemen who remained at the atoll some were fortunate enough to enjoy an all-too-brief fortnight's leave at Diyatalawa in the hill territory of Ceylon where a one-time prisoner-of-war camp, dating back to the Boer war, had been converted into a naval rest centre. Such leave, previously enjoyed only by the sick and by a few naval personnel, was a privilege; it never became commonplace in spite of numerous proposals that no-one ought to serve more than nine months at Addu Atoll without a break.

The Admiralty had, at the end of 1941, formally classified Port T as a 'defended port' which was all very well for the Admiralty but those who were there were under no illusions. The port was vulnerable. The installed defences were weak and were supported by deception. Some of the 'gun emplacements', which looked realistic enough from the air, actually consisted of felled tree trunks partially covered by palm fronds to create an impression of camouflaged artillery. There were no anti-aircraft guns on any of the islands even though the Chiefs-of-Staff had expressed their belief that any assault on the atoll was likely to include an air attack by up to two hundred carrier-based aircraft. Air cover for the base was minimal; rarely were the Allied forces' aircraft-carriers close enough to the atoll for it to be within combat range of their aircraft. It was left to the Catalinas of N° 209 RAF and N° 413 Royal Canadian Air Force squadrons to provide permanent air cover for the islands even though they were not based there; they plied the Indian Ocean, often for months between major inspections at Bangalore or Koggala. There were few RAF ground crew on Hitaddu; the Catalinas were largely maintained and repaired by the flight engineers, riggers and radio operators who made up the crews. On numerous occasions they were to be found working on aircraft which were afloat on a choppy lagoon and, adept though they were, it was inevitable that under those conditions they often could not work as quickly as they would have wished.

Even refuelling their flying-boats was a slow, tedious process with forty-gallon drums of fuel being manhandled from the island store into the Maldivians' dhonis and then rowed out to the aircraft where the fuel tanks had to be replenished by hand-pumping from a seemingly endless supply of drums.

The Catalinas were flown on regular patrols as part of the atoll's defence plan but, slow moving in the air and fully exposed when moored, they were themselves vulnerable. When not on patrol they sat alongside the Munro buoys just off the Hitaddu shoreline where divers, working from HMS Sovereign, had blasted away the coral heads to provide a clear take-off and landing area. Had the Japanese mounted a surprise attack during those early months of 1942 they would probably have found the Catalinas sitting in the lagoon like ducks in a shooting gallery.

To the senior officers at the Admiralty it was becoming increasingly obvious that, with the growing importance of the base, there was a need for an aerodrome at the atoll to enable Fleet Air Arm aircraft to operate permanently in the area, possibly alternating land-based and carrier-based tours. The Commander-in-Chief, East Indies, was in agreement and had, on the 3rd of January, informed the Admiralty that *The necessity to convert Addu Atoll from a lightly defended anchorage into a well defended base is fully appreciated ...* But he was only too well aware that if it were decided that an aerodrome should be constructed at the atoll the troops would be given unrealistic deadlines for the conversion of swamplands and jungle into a military complex complete with runways and all the attendant facilities: a situation which he sought to forestall by including in his communiqué a warning that '*...there are great physical difficulties...*'

The terms of reference for the 'Mauritius' survey had not referred to aerodrome construction at Port T and the survey report therefore only considered the atoll's suitability for flying-boat operations. Because of that yet another survey team was despatched to the atoll, led this time by Captain Huskisson RN whose brief was to investigate the possibility of building an aerodrome at the port. Huskisson and his team spent four days at Port T and concluded that an aerodrome could be constructed on Midu or on Gan.

Midu was identified as the preferred location although the difficult terrain on that island meant that three runways could be more easily constructed on Gan. Even before Huskisson's report could be properly considered, his verdict on the Midu site was confirmed by yet another reconnaissance party which had visited the atoll. Gan became the chosen site (Fig 4.1).

Somewhat unexpectedly, the Admiralty's investigations into the possible construction of an atoll aerodrome indirectly helped to solve another major problem: that of laying communications cables between the port and the other Indian Ocean bases. The Admiralty intended to add a diversion cable to the Seychelles-Colombo link, but the main British cable-laying company, Cable and Wireless Ltd., had no ship large enough to carry and lay the necessary quantity of cable. The only suitable ship was the John Mackay which, although British registered, was owned by the American Cable Company, a major international competitor of Cable and Wireless. The American company, almost certainly with government approval, refused to release the ship for use by a commercial competitor and was rewarded with the American Navy Department's open declaration of approval for the company's decision not to send the ship into the Indian Ocean war zone and risk losing it. In mid-January the Admiralty sent a signal to the British Embassy in Washington saying '...*Please help. Ship will not be at disposal of Cable and Wireless Ltd: only used for military communications, on Admiralty charter*'. Negotiations for the ship's release were at a stalemate when, on the 20th of January, Huskisson submitted his report. Then, on the 29th of January, the Admiralty learned that the Americans had informally asked whether the British intended to build an airstrip at Addu Atoll, implying that if such a development were proposed, the American government might help to persuade the American Cable Company to release its ship. That same day, the Admiralty informed the British Embassy in Washington that the '...*preliminary report on possible landing ground at Addu is favourable and it is intended to go ahead with construction*'. Within three weeks the American Cable Company had agreed to release the John Mackay later that year with a scheduled arrival at Port T by the end of August.

Whilst the negotiations for the release of the cable ship were being conducted, the Haitan, a 3,500-ton coal-burner, was *en route* to Addu Atoll where she was to be stationed for the next two years. Built in Danzig prior to the First World War, the ship had a chequered history. Before being hired by the Admiralty towards the end of 1941 she had served as a Chinese coaster as was evidenced by the anti-piracy railings which were still on her bridge and on her engine room approaches when she arrived at Port T. Prior to that she had spent some time as a passenger liner on the New York - Bermuda run, a far cry from her early service with the Russian Navy. She was commissioned as the Port T base ship on the 26th of January 1942 and her name was adopted for the shore station until the 27th of March when the Admiralty announced that the base was to be named HMS Highflyer. The change was short-lived. On the 4th of June the name Highflyer was abandoned and HMS Haitan was re-adopted. It made little difference; the base had been designated Port T and that *nom-de-guerre* remained in use until 1944.

Huskisson's report also triggered a rapid reaction from the Chiefs-of-Staff who were reviewing the functions of the atoll base and the threats which faced it. Within five days of receiving the report they had approved an atoll defence plan which included an air base requirement. Their intention was that the Fleet Air Arm would operate at least two fighter squadrons from the base. That clinched Port T's multi-service role and ensured that numerous reconnaissance parties and survey teams would descend upon the atoll because each service had its own special needs and priorities and each would conduct its own inspections. During the early months of 1942 the port probably became the most frequently surveyed base in the Middle East. Of the numerous reports made, only those from the 'Mauritius' survey and from the Huskisson reconnaissance appear to have survived; the recommendations made in other reports have to be inferred from the records of later meetings.

On the 25th of February Captain Briscoe RN arrived at Addu Atoll and took over as the naval officer in charge of Port T, inevitably becoming known to everyone as 'Noyk', the phonetic version of the abbreviation NOi/c. Within a week of his arrival the communications network at the port had been dramatically improved. Each shore station had been linked by telephone to the Haitan, which was anchored off the north shore of Gan, and the continuously-manned radio room on board the ship was providing a permanent link with the wireless station which, located at the north west extremity of Gan, was also continuously manned by naval telegraphists who alternated fourteen days duty on board ship with fourteen days shore duty under canvas.

Whilst Briscoe was initiating the improvements to the communications network a survey team, sent to the atoll from India and Ceylon, had started to investigate the nature and extent of the defences and other works needed to develop the port as a main fleet base complete with an aerodrome on Gan. By the 3rd of March they had completed their work, concluding that the entire atoll development plan would keep over a thousand men fully occupied for two or three years. The communications links around the atoll would require over seventy miles of cable, at least half of which would have to be laid on the coral shelves in the lagoon. Hutted accommodation would have to be built as well as defence installations, roads, bridges, piers and the three proposed runways.

The main recommendations in the report were accepted and brought prompt action. On the 10th of March, just seven days after the survey team left Port T, General Kandy ordered the immediate despatch to Addu Atoll of the first contingents of what was to become a garrison of over four thousand troops before the end of the year. Given that the three-runway aerodrome would cover almost a quarter of Gan island and that separation of the garrison forces from the indigenous population would have to be maintained, it was obvious that a military build up on that scale would deprive the troops of what little elbow room they did have. That potentially serious problem was ignored in the desire to develop the full military potential of Port T.

Kandy also set out the basic command structure for the atoll forces. A Royal Navy officer was to be in overall command with a Royal Marine officer as the fortress commander, a hierarchy amplified in a later directive from the Chief of the General Staff to the General Officer Commanding, Ceylon (Fig 4.2).

By the end of March it had become clear to those at Addu Atoll that, just as the Commander-in-Chief, East Indies, had anticipated, the Admiralty's site development schedule was unrealistic. With scant regard for either the site conditions or the physical state of the workforce, the Admiralty planned the creation of two aerodromes, one on Gan and one on Midu with the Gan aerodrome being required by May *'if possible'*. Every delay, and many were inevitable, increased the pressure of work and added to the frustrations and resentments experienced at some time or other by the military and the Maldivians alike. The villagers, usually friendly and cooperative, were at times resentful of the way in which their lives had, virtually overnight, been changed for the worse. The fishing, trading and cultivating on which their livelihoods depended were disrupted in part by their having to work for the military whenever required but mainly by the presence of an ever-increasing number of troops. The consolation for those employed by the military was that they received a regular, if limited, supply of provisions and perks in exchange for their labour. That was a highly desirable arrangement as far as the Adduans were concerned because the war had already created a shortage of food and other necessities throughout the archipelago. The other villagers, enjoying no such benefits, found that the local food shortages were being exacerbated by the illicit bartering with the hundreds of troops who were always ready to offer cigarettes in exchange for fresh fruit. In common with many of the older Adduans, those villagers with no access to the military provisions or perks resented the disruption and corruption. They were not even compensated by the provision of the one benefit they all sought: health care. The reason was simple. The military's medical services were far too stretched coping with sick troops to be extended to the Adduan population.

The islanders were both exhorted and consoled with the argument, put forward by their government, that they had to work for the defence of their own community and that that could best be achieved through the power of the Commonwealth forces who had come to protect them from the Japanese. It was an argument which did not stand up to close examination because it was obvious that if anything was likely to persuade the Japanese to attack such remote islands it would be the military build-up at the atoll. Without that activity the islanders stood a good chance of being ignored or, at worst, having their atoll occupied without a battle. It is debatable whether a more general call to endure personal hardship as a contribution to the overall defence of the Maldive Islands would have evoked a more willing response because the Adduans were notorious for their independent-minded attitude and, isolated from Malé, the capital, they might have reacted as unexpectedly as they were to do in 1959 when they made a unilateral declaration of independence. Almost certainly, the islanders co-operated in the exhausting and poorly rewarded work because refusal to do so, against the express command of the Sultan, would probably have been punished by banishment to an uninhabited island.

In spite of all the pressures, the day-to-day working relationships between the Maldivians and the troops remained remarkably good, largely due to the efforts of the interpreters who played such a significant role in helping with the integration of the British, Indian and Maldivian cultures.

If the islanders were experiencing some stresses, so too were the troops. The appalling working and living conditions were taking their physical toll and before long sickness had incapacitated half the garrison forces. Military funerals, always demoralising events, were fortunately few during the early days of Port T mainly because critically ill troops were sent to a military hospital in Ceylon whenever possible; the majority of the deaths thus occurred over five hundred miles away. There were some interments but generally those Christians who died at Port T were buried at sea, usually about a mile outside the barrier reef and occasionally, as John Stamp recalled, in the lagoon. With the arrival of the Indian Army personnel the number of troops at Addu Atoll increased dramatically and deaths and funeral ceremonies became more frequent with pyres for Hindus and island burials for Moslems and some Christians. But evacuation of the critically ill continued to be the normal practice with the result that fewer deaths were recorded at Port T than at any comparable military establishment.

Other factors, however, began to lower the servicemen's morale. Their diet, their limited leisure time and their sense of isolation; each was taking its toll.

Food, a focus of interest for troops the world over, was supplied by the Royal Navy and consisted mainly of tinned rations, with an occasional supply of fresh food including sheep and goats transported live from Ceylon for the Indian troops. The atoll did not bear enough fresh fruit to provide a proper diet for the villagers, let alone the troops. The local fishermen were not able to supply fresh fish for the troops because many of them were working for the military and the remainder were having to fish for longer hours in order to meet the normal demands of the villagers. Meanwhile, the quartermaster, making best use of a few inefficient oil-burning refrigerators and an occasional supply of ice from visiting ships, faced a permanent struggle to maintain adequate food stocks ashore in a climate which even caused rapid deterioration of tinned provisions. As one of the wartime survivors recalled '*I like corned beef, but not when you can pour it out of the tin*'. Whenever food supplies arrived at Port T they were distributed around the island for rapid consumption, a system which left the garrison highly dependent upon the safe passage of supply ships from Ceylon. Inevitably, the food storage conditions combined with other factors to create occasional outbreaks of food poisoning but the facilities were not improved until late in the year by which time over three thousand servicemen were based at the atoll. Those who were serving on board the Haitan were much more fortunate. Ex-Chinese coaster she may have been before she was brought into service with the Royal Navy but she still retained some facilities from her days as a passenger liner. Certainly there was far more food storage capacity than was needed for the crew. But none was made available for the shore-based troops. Briscoe, for whatever reason, did not permit them to use the Haitan in any way other than as a communications centre and an overflow sick-bay.

Leisure time during the early months of 1942 was negligible. The troops were kept fully occupied by their work and housekeeping which was conducted almost entirely during the daylight hours. A blackout, or to be more precise, a 'dim-out' had to be maintained throughout the hours of darkness for the simple reason that artificial lighting, visible across miles of ocean, was obviously out of keeping with an atoll supposedly inhabited only by Maldivians. Sunday, kept as a Christian day of rest, provided a very welcome break although for many it was the one day in the week when time, and energy, was available for the maintenance of personal equipment and the ever-present domestic chores which had not been completed during the previous six days. Active leisure pursuits were limited because the facilities were really no better during the early months of 1942 than they had been towards the end of 1941. Some volleyball courts had been marked out by the Indian units and a variety of impromptu ball-games would occur on most Sundays but the ground clearance programme was aimed at more serious utilisation than recreation and it was not until later in the year that several sports areas were laid out. No active recreational facilities were formally organised; participation tended to be spontaneous from among the few who had any spare time and energy. Time spent socialising instead of labouring was all that most of the men wanted and for many of the officers that meant an hour or two at 'The Signals Arms,' the soubriquet for Major Manners' tent which, by virtue of his being their bar officer, had automatically been adopted as their 'local'.

By the middle of the year a growing sense of isolation had begun to contribute to a general lowering of morale. The mail service from Britain, coming *via* India and Ceylon, was understandably sporadic and often long delayed. The troops were permitted to send only single-sheet censored airmail letters for micro filming in Colombo or Bombay before transmission to London where enlargements were made for delivery to the addressee, a system which meant that families in Britain did at least receive occasional reassurance that their loved ones, in some remote unidentified location, were still alive. As always, some were lucky, some were not. John Stamp recalled that none of his mail reached home for six or seven months and eventually his wife, fearing his death or capture had somehow gone unreported, asked the Red Cross to trace him, which they did. Radio reception for leisure or world news was virtually non-existent with only an occasional All-India programme being received. The British troops, like others in remote parts of the world, were thus largely ignorant of home and world events except for those which were described in the circulated official bulletins and in the occasional wad of newspapers which would arrive at the atoll. Invariably two or three months old, and often with a month's editions all stapled together, the newspapers were read avidly by the troops. Stamp also recalled that:

> 'At Port T even the Rotherham Advertiser would be read by everyone. In the absence of leisure listening on the radio, the lack of reading material was very frustrating. Books which did arrive at the atoll deteriorated quickly as a result of the humidity and the continual handling. Personnel living on board ship were somewhat better off in that respect for they had a small library.'

Morale among the Indian troops suffered for a different reason. They were within occasional rumour range of their homeland and as they heard of the Japanese attacks on India and Ceylon they worried about their families and longed to be with them. Their only consolation was that they were likely to return to India after a six-month tour of duty at Port T whereas the European troops, also serving at the atoll for six months, were unlikely subsequently to enjoy a home tour. Having become acclimatised they were more likely to be employed in the Middle East or the Far East for the remainder of the war.

Religious worship, so often a solace for troops throughout the world, remained, for the military, a personal matter. There was no padre at the base, no Christian church and no organised religious services. Most of the Indian troops were Moslems but they did not have their own mosques, nor did they use the mosques built by the Moslem islanders.

As if those factors were not enough to lower morale, there was a growing realisation among the troops that if the atoll were to become the main base for a retreating Far Eastern Fleet then it would also become a priority target for the Japanese. Port T could easily become the focus of a major battle from which there would be no overland escape. The troops who had come from Egypt and Crete began to wonder whether they had been brought out of the frying pan and put into the fire.

The officers had additional frustrations. Serving at Addu Atoll for an indefinite period they had the functional responsibilities for the development programme from start to finish. Unrealistic deadlines had been imposed upon them. They faced technical and environmental problems. Their workgroups had to be organised with particular regard to technical knowledge, skills and physical abilities, all of which varied enormously. The multi-cultural nature of the workforce demanded different leadership styles to develop and maintain effective working relationships. Few of the officers posted to the atoll had passed the basic Urdu examination and inevitably there were language difficulties within and between groups, especially in technical matters. As if those factors did not weigh heavily enough, the officers were finding it increasingly difficult to motivate men whose morale was beginning to decline along with their physical condition.

The officer in charge of the tented hospital probably had the most demanding and the most frustrating job of all because he stood little or no chance of solving the problems which confronted him. He found it difficult enough to provide medical treatment and hospital facilities for the troops but he was also responsible for all preventative measures intended to reduce the incidence of malaria and scrub typhus. The anti-malarial measures were almost non-existent, comprising little more than the provision of insect repellents, the strict enforcement of dress regulations and the use of mosquito nets. Very few men were permanently employed to tackle the source of the disease. The spraying programme was derisory. The troops were instructed to spray all the likely mosquito breeding sites throughout the atoll except for the wells which were being used by the villagers. This they were expected to achieve by using the two hundred hand-held spray guns, continually priming them from the buckets which, filled with a twenty-to-one kerosene-pyrethrum solution, they carried around the islands.

Scrub typhus posed a particularly difficult problem. The onset of the disease was dramatic with apparently healthy men collapsing without warning and subsequently suffering severe physical and mental effects. Because there was no real evidence to incriminate any particular species of insect as the typhus carrier, preventative measures had to be based on the assumptions that the culprit was a mite which frequented any area of dense vegetation. Spraying was therefore not a practical proposition which meant that the troops had to continue wearing full protective clothing whilst hacking their way through the undergrowth. That dramatically reduced their efficiency. Men obliged to labour whilst wearing protective clothing just could not complete a full day's work and the clearance programme quickly fell behind schedule. Worse still, the use of protective clothing delayed the work but failed to keep the troops in reasonably good health. For the first half of the year the hospital facilities, comprising an Indian general tented hospital, a naval tented hospital and the sick bay on board the Haitan, were overwhelmed. When, late in August, two very welcome additional tented hospitals arrived they were immediately put into service and almost immediately filled with patients. Hygiene control in and around the tents was a nightmare. Even after the nearby scrubland had been cleared, the tops of the palm trees played host to a variety of insects, reptiles and rats. Eventually one of the medical officers had all the tree tops removed, leaving the hospital tents surrounded by bare stumps. Even that idea backfired. Deprived of their tree top cover, large numbers of rats sought refuge in the hospital tents and were only driven out after a prolonged series of 'rat patrols' had been mounted.

Very different, but almost as frustrating, were the problems facing Major Manners, the Royal Corps of Signals Officer who had accompanied Lieutenant Colonel Lukis on the first reconnaissance of the atoll late in 1940. It was odd that he had been chosen to join the original naval reconnaissance party when both the Royal Navy and the Royal Marines had their own signals specialists but it was understandable that in 1942 he was then given command of a number of marines and instructed to install the communications network which would eventually comprise some forty miles of submarine cable in the lagoon and a further thirty miles of subterranean and overhead cable throughout the islands. The heart of the system was 'Atlas', the telephone exchange located in a Nissen hut near the fortress headquarters. His remit was to organise the installation of some ninety direct exchange lines to Atlas and provide several units with their own switchboards. Inevitably, he was under continual local pressure to complete the network but the various units at Port T so frequently presented him with changing requirements that he was eventually obliged to produce a complete communications plan which he took to Ceylon for agreement and for signature by the heads of all three services in order to counter the element of inter-service rivalry which was behind many of the changes. That settled, he had still to cope with the limited expertise of his workforce, most of whom had never worked with submarine cables and were totally unfamiliar with the necessary jointing techniques. Many hours were spent on demonstrations and on training: hours which could have been more usefully spent getting the job done if only a skilled workforce had been available. Laying the heavy submarine cables demanded both expertise, particularly in the jointing, and strength for there were no runners and sheaves to make the work easier. After each cable had been manhandled into the lighter and paid out into the lagoon, empty oil drums were used to float the end ashore where it was then hauled in by a team of the strongest men available.

Recovery and repair problems hampered Manners' progress. The submarine cables continually chafed against the coral and had frequently to be hauled up for repair. A Maldivian dhoni, dubbed HMS Mercury, was used for much of the cable laying until, heavily overloaded, it sank and broke up in the coral shallows in an area from which it was extremely difficult to recover the cable without damaging it. At one time, even the land-lines were not safe. Often the troops would lay several hundred yards of cable during the daytime only to return the following day to discover that it had been chopped up during the night. Calculated sabotage was suspected and overnight watches were mounted but it was several weeks before the culprit was caught. She was found to be a mentally unbalanced girl who was attacking the cables under the illusion that they were giant snakes. Once she had been identified the villagers took it upon themselves to prevent her from wreaking further damage, guaranteeing that, because she could not be made to understand the consequences of her actions, they would keep a close watch over her at all times.

In spite of all the difficulties which arose as a result of living and working in a multi-racial community isolated in a remote and generally hostile environment, there developed a strong sense of camaraderie amongst the troops. It was particularly strong amongst the shore-based officers largely because they saw the creation of a defended naval base and aerodrome as a collective responsibility and enjoyed excellent relationships with the shore-based fortress commander, Colonel Jones. Their group identity was strengthened because they felt no such collective empathy with the naval officer-in-charge, Commander Briscoe. He and his crew were widely regarded as the fortunate few because they lived on board the Haitan, which, in comparison with shore conditions, provided highly desirable accommodation. That was enough to create a 'them and us' feeling but it was fuelled by the fact that many of the Haitan's crew traded quite openly with the Adduans, a clear breach of regulations which provided them with a constant supply of fresh fruit and fish, much to the envy of the troops ashore. Briscoe and Jones, moreover, did not enjoy an amicable relationship. They were often at odds with each other for they frequently held diverse views on the priorities accorded to the different works to be undertaken. The situation was exacerbated by a command structure in which Jones, a Royal Marine Lieutenant-Colonel, was senior in rank to Briscoe, a Royal Navy Commander, but was his subordinate and could thus be over-ruled on decisions which he, with some justification, saw as his prerogative.

Even the sense of purpose amongst the shore-based officers and the camaraderie amongst the troops could not disguise the fact that by the end of March 1942 the troops were flagging as a result of the unremitting workload. They desperately needed something to boost their morale.

Ironically it was the Japanese activity in the Indian Ocean which provided it, for it brought the atoll workforce an unexpected reprieve from the constant demands for the early completion of the aerodrome. On the 4th and 5th of April a Japanese naval force sailed to the south of Ceylon, bringing increased submarine activity into the Indian Ocean and posing a threat to Allied shipping in the area. The Japanese then showed their local air superiority by launching a heavy air attack on Colombo on Easter Sunday, the 5th of April. At that time the Eastern Fleet was sailing, as it often did in eastern waters, as two separate groups comprising thirteen ships in Force A and sixteen ships in Force B. When the Japanese attacked Colombo the Commander-in-Chief, Eastern Fleet, was at Port T with Force A, six hundred miles away from the Japanese force and awaiting the arrival of Force B. HMS Cornwall and HMS Dorsetshire, steaming to rendezvous with their Force A sister ships, were sunk by the Japanese. The survivors from both ships were brought to Port T and, pending the arrival of a hospital ship, were treated in the sick bay of the Haitan and on one of the supply ships which was then at the atoll and which was hastily converted into a temporary hospital to cope with the emergency. As John Clark, then a nineteen-year-old RN telegraphist serving on board the Haitan, recalled; '... *Many of the rescued were so badly injured or had been so badly burned that deaths were inevitable. I don't know how many died but I do recall that quite a number were buried at sea beyond the atoll reef.*'

It was clear that the Admiralty's hopes that the Eastern Fleet, combined with the military pressure from America, would discourage any Japanese incursion into the Indian Ocean had proved false. Sommerville signalled an optimistic welcome to all his ships as they assembled at Addu Atoll (Fig 4.3) but he had to concede that Colombo had become too vulnerable a base for the fleet. The situation in the south of the Maldivian archipelago was no better. At Addu Atoll there were still no anti-aircraft defences and none was expected for at least two months. With the aerodrome construction delayed following the loss of one of the supply ships, the air defence of Port T had to be left to the flying-boats and any carrier-based aircraft which happened to be within range of the atoll. Port T could no longer be regarded as a safe haven. Sommerville accordingly split his fleet, sending Force B to Mombasa and withdrawing Force A towards the Seychelles from where the warships could continue to pose a threat to the Japanese fleet.

Within five days of the Japanese attack on Colombo the Commander-in-Chief, East Indies, had concluded that any attack on Port T could not be effectively resisted and that to continue with the build-up might well put more troops at risk and offer ready-made facilities to the enemy. He therefore proposed temporarily halting the entire atoll base development programme. The Admiralty agreed with his assessment and on the 20th of April called a temporary halt to the development of Port T, instructing Briscoe to concentrate on maintaining the existing defences and on improving the health of the troops, the environment and the recreational facilities. The plan to create a second airfield on Midu was abandoned in the knowledge that the original schedule had been so disrupted that if the development programme were to be reinstated all the available resources would have to be concentrated on the urgent creation of an operational airfield on Gan.

The consolidation work, which continued throughout May and June, brought little real improvement to the atoll's defences. The hours spent maintaining and repairing the Gan channel boom were to no avail because the boom, unable to withstand the strong swell, was eventually broken beyond repair and was temporarily abandoned pending the arrival of a boom trawler. That left the ships in the lagoon more vulnerable than ever to an attack by submarines which meant that the Hitaddu Catalinas had to be flown on dawn-to-dusk patrols.

There was no apparent benefit from the enormous effort expended on the destruction of the island's insect breeding sites even though the daily work of the clearance parties was supplemented by a collective effort devised by Colonel Jones who, aware that the coconut husks which lay waterlogged and decaying on every island provided thousands of breeding sites for mosquitoes, issued an order that every man would bring to his daily morning parade a coconut husk to add to the bonfires which the villagers maintained. In a matter of weeks the garrison territory was almost clear of such breeding sites and Colonel Jones was stuck, for the remainder of his time at Port T, with the nickname 'Coconut Joe'. The scheme had some psychological value but had a negligible effect on the insect population; the troops continued to fall victim to disease. Eight or nine months into 1942 it was still quite common for over five hundred men to be listed sick, preventing any fit personnel from being given leave in Ceylon.

The temporary cessation of the development programme did at least provide the troops with a reasonable amount of leisure time and gave them the opportunity to establish some formal recreational activities. Pitches were prepared for football, cricket and hockey with all three being played all the year round at Addu Atoll, supplementing the dhoni races, the film shows and the occasional boxing matches which were held on board ship.

The lull did not last. On the 24th of June the Admiralty and the Commander-in-Chief, East Indies, agreed to restart the development work at Port T even though the Flag Officer, Ceylon, was far from convinced that the enormous investment of resources on the atoll was either justified or wise. His correspondence with the Admiralty reiterated that the aerodrome project alone would require over one thousand men to manhandle ten thousand tons of sand and cement and, after unloading the cargo ships, to build some three hundred Nissen huts, thirty workshops and hangars, storage depots for fuel and weapons, the control tower, fire cover facilities and forty-seven distillation and refrigeration plants. Commenting on the uncertainty surrounding the deployment of any air squadrons to the atoll, he requested from the Admiralty an assurance that the development work would be of use in the foreseeable future, making the point that without such an assurance the effort could not be justified. No such assurance was given. In July, work was resumed.

By then the airfield construction programme was months behind the original schedule and there was no real hope of recovering the lost time even though the Royal Marine Engineers of 'Q' Company were already on board HMS Chitral and heading for Port T to lay the runways and to apply their expertise wherever else it was needed. Like all the Royal Marine Engineering units, Q company, which incorporated its own support services, could operate independently anywhere in the world, its seven hundred and twenty men providing expertise in every aspect of any engineering discipline from civil construction to vehicle maintenance. The company, under the command of Major K Bell RM, was ideally constituted for the work at Port T.

Bell was fortunate enough to be forewarned of the Gan environment and of the supply and construction difficulties awaiting his men at Addu Atoll. The construction of concrete runways on Gan would, it seemed, require thousands of tons of sand and cement to be imported from Ceylon and thousands of square yards of Sommerfield track to be brought from Britain or America. He was, however, aware that Dutch engineers in the East Indies had successfully laid coral-surfaced runways and his hurried research into the subject was later to be well rewarded when he was obliged to adopt the techniques for the Gan runways because of the dire shortage of the materials originally specified for the job.

HMS Chitral arrived at Port T in the middle of a tropical storm on the 19th of August during a major ground clearance operation on Gan, mounted as part of the aerodrome construction programme. The work necessitated the evacuation of all the villagers from the island and that caused considerable ill-feeling because they were having to leave their cultivated areas, huts, wells, mosques and burial grounds. Their community was split and they were accommodated on islands which offered worse conditions than Gan or where the best living and cultivation areas were already occupied and where additional residents were not particularly wanted. Their feelings for their own island were clearly shown by those who, evacuated to Hitaddu, set up their own small village community which they called 'New Gan'. They were not the only islanders to be moved to Hitaddu. Those whose homes were on Fedu found that they too had to be evacuated to make way for the military.

They too were relocated on Hitaddu and eventually 'New Gan' became 'Gan-Fedu'.

More than forty years later the upheaval was well remembered by Mr Abdullah Afif Didi, nephew of Sultan Iskander II and interpreter for the original reconnaissance party late in 1940. The evacuees and their belongings were gradually transferred to a special resettlement area at the southern end of Hitaddu. There the families had to resettle themselves as best they could for there were certainly no troops available to help. It was not just their homes which they had been forced to abandon, it was their cultivated land as well and that was a potentially serious problem because there was a general food shortage throughout the Maldive Islands and without their home-grown food the evacuated islanders were likely to face near-starvation. Incredibly, having forcibly evacuated the villagers, the British military ignored their plight until the poverty-stricken Maldivian government offered to pay the Royal Navy to provide food for them until the end of the war.

The evacuation was completed by the 31st of August 1942, just twelve days after the arrival of the Chitral. As the last of the villagers left, the troops realised that, either out of concern for the feelings and possible reaction of the villagers or out of lack of thought, the departing Maldivians had not been told to burn down their abandoned homes and fill in their wells before leaving Gan. The already overworked Indian troops were thus presented with the task of destroying the abandoned kadjan huts and filling in the village wells which provided countless insect breeding sites.

No-one welcomed the arrival of the Chitral and the men of Q Company more than Major Bond, the officer in charge of the Indian engineering troops and pioneer companies. For the three week period from the 20th of August to the 10th of September his list of main works to be carried out included the creation of as many yards of roadway as possible; the coral blasting for an underwater channel near Gan pier; the completion of the cookhouses and latrines; the siting of level pegs to complement a concrete survey; jungle clearance; clearance work for a second runway and the construction of a three-hundred-and-forty-foot jetty, a Navy Army and Air Force Institute store, two water tanks of ten thousand gallons each, a one-hundred-bed hospital, an operating theatre and dressing room, an ordnance workshop and a washing-water well. Frustrated through lack of basic materials, good equipment and fit men, Bond wrote in the war diary on the 1st of September 1942:

> 'The work is getting more than we can cope with ... with two hospitals to get ready, the installation of Fortress Headquarters and the miscellaneous jobs on hand ... The Auxiliary Pioneers are too weak to shift the twelve by twelve timber'.

The men of the Mobile Naval Base Defence Organisation lived on board the Clan Forbes whenever it was at Port T, were consequently in fairly good health and were still hard at work six days a week even though they had been at the atoll for some eight months. But, too few to do all that was on the unrealistic works schedule which Major Bond had been given, they also faced constructional problems which were compounded by the very limited range of materials available on the islands: coral, sand and coconut palms. Teak, needed in large quantities, was initially shipped from Ceylon but towards the end of 1942 the Royal Navy requisitioned that island's entire supply, leaving the Port T executives to obtain suitable timber from India or from as far afield as Canada.

Material shortages, worn-out equipment and weary men notwithstanding, the workrate was such that there was little time for the preparation of building plans as the war diarist, with obvious frustration, revealed on the 4th of September when he wrote that:

> 'The Superintending Civil Engineer never gives any drawings or designs but merely shows sketches in his notebook to some subaltern working on the job'.

By then the men of Q Company had started on the construction work which was to keep them at the atoll until the end of 1943. Old roadways were improved. New roads were laid where previously there had been trees and swamps. In the shark-infested waters off Gan the divers built a tubular steel jetty which extended three hundred and forty feet from the beach to the edge of the lagoon shelf.

The Q company troops had one advantage; they were well equipped in comparison with the garrison units which, like military units throughout the Indian Ocean, were continually in need of more and better equipment. That which had been provided for the garrison forces at Port T had often been obtained with difficulty from some other unit's holdings and all too often it had been released because it was in poor condition. Inevitably, plant and machinery frequently broke down. Some vessels sank, few causing more problems than the dredger which went down, or more inconvenience than the sixty-ton lighter which had been sent to Gan after being released from harbour duties in Colombo. Connected to the communications network at Fedu, the lighter carried about three miles of slack cable on board and when towed out to any visiting ships it could provide a direct ship-to-shore communications system. Within three weeks of its arrival it sprang a leak, sank and was neither recovered nor replaced, leaving visiting ships to communicate with the shore units by radio or visible signal. Then, within a month of that loss, one of the dredgers sank onto the coral shelf of the lagoon and for almost three weeks the recovery and repair work kept thirty-two men occupied, twenty-four of them employed to man the pumps for the divers.

But there was occasionally good news to counter the frustrations and the end of August saw one improvement which was welcomed by the quarter-master and appreciated by the troops. The Dutch ship Zuyder Kruis, a cable ship which had been converted into a refrigerated supply vessel, began to make regular deliveries of deep frozen food to the atoll which, accompanied by generous supplies of ice, provided frequent and very welcome relief from the normal tinned rations. Towards the end of October, the men of workshop company started to construct an ice plant and before Christmas a cool store was in use which certainly eased the quartermaster's problems even though the garrison remained dependent upon the food supplies which were scheduled to arrive from Colombo every three or four weeks, usually by the victualling and stores issuing ships SS Kutsang and SS Taiping.

The quality of the food had improved, but unfortunately the drinking water had become even more unpalatable. That brought to the atoll by the Singu or the Appleleaf was not unpleasant but the local supplies definitely were. The porous coral structure of the islands absorbed all the tropical rain which then formed a freshwater 'lens' some two or three feet below ground, effectively sitting on the more dense sea water. An analysis as long ago as 1879 had shown this water to be fit for consumption and the Royal Marine engineers had tapped into the lens with the eventual intention of pumping out enough water each day to satisfy all the garrison's needs. But the presence of several thousand troops on the islands had created special problems. The garbage and human waste created by the troops could not be dumped in the lagoon because it became trapped, eventually washing up on the beaches and creating yet another health hazard. There were insufficient resources to dispose of the waste out at sea and the use of latrine pits, waste dumps and smouldering incineration meant that the fresh water lens was likely to become heavily polluted. Until Q Company had built several incinerators on a large concrete slab, heavy chlorination had been practised to counter the threat of pollution and that had made the water even more unpalatable than it was in its natural state. Once the incinerators were in use and the chlorination reduced, there were fewer complaints from the troops, more of their drinking water was provided from the island's underground reservoir and far less had to be shipped from Ceylon.

Better food storage certainly reduced the incidence of dysentery and mild food poisoning but the attempts to create a healthier environment seemed to have little impact on the incidence of insect-borne diseases among the troops so that, in spite of Q Company's contribution, the construction work fell behind schedule to such an extent that the Chief of the General Staff, Ceylon Command, Brigadier General Angus; the Naval Chief of Staff, Captain Wedderburn RN; and the Superintending Engineer for the East Indies, Mister Wilson, visited the atoll on the 1st of October and spent three days with the fortress executives, discussing work priorities. Angus, unlike the fortress executives, was aware that whilst the men at Addu Atoll had been under severe pressure to develop the base, the Admiralty's policy on the function of Port T had been debated in Ceylon with the Flag Officer, Ceylon, writing, on the 1st of September, '... *confess I am still not clear of the use to which Gan is to be put*'. The discussions held at Port T early in October clarified the situation for Angus and, although the original concept of the atoll as a main fleet base was retained as an ultimate objective, the function of Addu Atoll had, within a fortnight of Angus's visit, been redefined as '...*an occasional fleet refuelling base with shore facilities for operating two disembarked Fleet Air Arm squadrons and facilities for fuelling flying-boats*' and the defence plan revised to reflect that change. The change of role also led to the cancellation of the Colombo-Seychelles cable loop project and when that happened the cable ship John Mackay, obtained with such difficulty and available only since September, was no longer needed. The ship duly returned to America after a mere one hundred and fifty-two miles of cable had been laid. The northern end of the abandoned cable was anchored to the sea bed and the southern end, at Addu Atoll, was bouyed on the off-chance that the project might be resurrected at some time.

During his visit, Angus, convinced that the project deadlines which had been set earlier were no longer valid, established a more realistic schedule for the construction of the aerodrome. The 1st of January 1943 became the new completion date for the main runway, with a serviceability state for occasional use, and the 15th of February became the scheduled date for the completion of a fully operational aerodrome. He also set out the works priorities for the fortress executives (Fig 4.4) and those, together with the less demanding schedule, went some way towards alleviating the pressure on the troops who were still fit enough to work. But it was the extraordinarily high levels of sickness at the atoll which really perturbed Angus (Fig 4.5) and immediately after his visit action was taken on the proposal, made in May by the Port T medical officers, that a thorough health survey of the islands should be conducted. By November, Surgeon Lieutenant R W Ross RM had been sent from Ceylon to conduct such an investigation. Ross, a bacteriology specialist who had relinquished a tropical research fellowship to volunteer for war service, was keen to undertake the study and appeared to be the ideal person for the job. Unfortunately he fell victim to scrub typhus shortly after his arrival at Port T and, as a result of the profound psychological disturbances which he suffered, he became aggressive to all and sundry, including Colonel Jones. At that stage it was not appreciated that Ross was suffering from Bush Typhus and Jones had no real alternative but to have him restrained and repatriated to Colombo. His bizarre behaviour and his derogatory report on health care at the atoll rendered him *persona non grata* even when he was well enough to return to work and that delayed the research project until a replacement scientist could be sent to Port T some three months later. The Ross affair caused a brief flurry of excitement in Ceylon but it was rapidly smoothed over by the senior officers responsible for the provision of medical services in that theatre (Figs 4.6 & 4.7).

Early November saw the first stages of the withdrawal from the atoll of the men of the Mobile Naval Base Defence Organisation. Their expertise, not then being fully utilised at Port T, was needed elsewhere, and their work was taken over either by Q Company or by the Indian troops. By the end of the month the aerodrome had become an exclusively naval project for use by Fleet Air Arm aircraft, N° 222 Group having confirmed to Air Headquar-

ters, India, that the RAF required nothing more than flying-boat facilities, for which moorings and operational services had already been provided at Hitaddu.

As a single-service development the project became much easier to manage although that did not necessarily mean that everything went smoothly for Majors Bell, Bond and Manners; there continued to be alterations to the plans, some stemming from inter-service bickering, others from honest opinions based on experience. The bickering gradually made the various Headquarters' staffs highly sensitive to accusations of interference and that occasionally led to a potentially serious reluctance to offer good advice, a reluctance exemplified by the silence over the location of the fighter control operations room. The room was originally located in the control tower and, sited near the runway, was in the most likely area of concentrated air attack. The staff at the Air Headquarters, India, on suggesting to N° 222 Group Headquarters' staff that it should be relocated, had been told not to interfere with what was a naval responsibility. Fortunately the correspondence was seen by a member of the naval staff who, appreciating the seriousness of the situation, hurriedly arranged a site visit, with the result that the operations room was re-sited four hundred yards to the west of the runway.

Throughout 1942 the troops lived under canvas even though simple kadjan huts, which could so easily have been built for them by the islanders, would have provided far more comfortable living accommodation in the atoll's hot and humid atmosphere. Those employed in the headquarters' offices, the engineering workshops or the hospital also worked under canvas throughout most of the day for those facilities were housed in tented accommodation (Figs 4.8 & 4.9), reflecting the works priorities which dictated that all the available men and materials had to be allocated to work which would improve the defence installations rather than the living and working accommodation.

By November the coastal defences set out in the October defence plan (Fig 4.10) were virtually complete and good progress had been made on the construction of slipways and jetties, on the bridges and causeways connecting Gan, Fedu and Maradu and on various general facilities (Figs 4.11, 4.12 & 4.13).

The possibility of a Japanese attack on the atoll was enough to persuade everyone at Port T that as the base neared completion there was an ever-increasing need to disguise the scale of the operation. There was no hiding the fact that the lagoon was providing a safe anchorage for the Haitan and if any of the Japanese spotter aircraft which were roaming the Indian Ocean were to discover the ship at anchor she would be open to attack. The same would be true if the Japanese were to discover the Catalinas moored off the Hitaddu coastline but if the full extent of the works at Port T were to be exposed the base was likely to be subjected to an all-out assault which it could not hope to survive. Camouflage and deception became the orders of the day, every day. Tented accommodation was mainly hidden among the palm trees; the jetties and causeways were constructed, as much as possible, to give the impression that they had been built by the Adduans for the convenience of their fishermen. The searchlights and observation towers on Gan and Wilingili were surrounded by palms and made to look like native-built structures (Figs 4.14, 4.15 & 4.16) whilst the exposed buildings such as the searchlight generator huts were kadjan structures which appeared to be nothing more than large huts used by the villagers (Fig 4.17).

There was, however one notable omission from the works under construction schedule; the one-hundred-and-eighty-foot early warning tower due to be erected on Gan. It had not been built for the simple reason that the Royal Navy had requisitioned all the teak in Ceylon and refused to export any of it, even for the defence installations at one of its own bases, Port T. A request had therefore been made for the tower to be fabricated in India, dismantled and shipped to Addu Atoll as a marked set of component parts. The request was being processed but no delivery date had been given.

As the troops set about clearing and levelling the aerodrome site they were confronted by a totally unexpected obstacle. Among the palm trees and the swampy terrain, and completely out of place on an atoll where the islands had little or no ground more than three or four feet above sea level, they encountered a hillock some twenty-five feet high with a base which was ninety yards in circumference. It was hardly surprising that no-one had remarked on its existence because it was completely overgrown and, overshadowed by the surrounding palm trees, had remained un-noticed by the military. The Adduans confirmed that they had been aware of its existence: they had not bothered to mention it because they had failed to appreciate that such a feature could not be left standing in the middle of a small three-runway aerodrome. It was not of their making and it had no religious or historical significance as far as they were concerned, hence their indifference towards it.

What the troops did not realise was that they had exposed the ruin of a Buddhist Dagaba which, built prior to the Maldivian conversion to Islam in the twelfth century, had attracted the attention of Bell's archaeological expedition in 1921 and was referred to in his monograph. To the men of Q Company it was no more than an inconvenience. They flattened it. With that out of the way they pressed on. By the 6th of December the site of Number 1 runway had been completely cleared and on the 7th the troops started to prepare the runway surface. It was hard labour, manhandling the enormous tonnage of coral obtained from the reef by blasting and drag-bucket dredging but the troops were in buoyant mood; they had been promised, in October, that over a thousand Indian troops would be arriving at Port T during December. The promise held, and by Christmas the number of servicemen at Addu Atoll had increased to over four thousand, more than at any other time during the war. The newcomers were fortunate. The worst was over.

The buoyant mood carried the old hands through to Christmas when they enjoyed their first significant respite for months with a forty-eight hour stand-down and reorganised watch-keeping shifts which gave everyone an opportunity to relax in the sunshine and think of the folks at home. The celebrations included as near a traditional Christmas dinner as the catering staff could create, a fair consumption of alcohol and a performance of 'Boogy-Woogy', the first of several variety shows to be staged by the men of the landing and maintenance unit of the Mobile Naval Base Defence Organisation who, unlike most of their compatriots in that organisation, remained at Port T well into 1943 displaying talents well beyond those required for their engineering duties.

In spite of all the frustrations and setbacks, the monthly progress reports clearly show that 1942 was a year of enormous achievement (Fig 4.18). By the end of December sickness was reducing quite dramatically, the construction programme was forging ahead, the men had more leisure time and the recreational facilities had been greatly improved.

SECRET (1)

PROVISION OF AIR BASES AT ADDU ATTOLL.

APPENDIX "A". - Sketch maps of GAN Island
& MIDU Island.

----

1.   NOTE.

The following data has been extracted from a report
by Captain Huskisson, R.N. who was detailed by the
Admiralty to conduct a reconnaissance of ADDU ATTOLL in
January, 1942.

2.   SUMMARY OF MAIN CONCLUSIONS.

(i) Of the numerous islands comprising the ATTOLL
only two - GAN and MIDU - are large enough for aerodrome
construction.

(ii) Flying boat facilities exist and are being
improved at the island of HITADDU at the WEST of the ATTOLL.

(iii) MIDU offers the better chances of a 3 runway
aerodrome (1200ˣ runways) and is recommended as the main
aerodrome, but owing to the swampy nature of the soil and
the dense coconut plantation, preparation will take a
considerable time.

(iv) In the NORTH EAST of GAN it would be possible
to construct 3 runways (1200ˣ, 1100ˣ and 1050ˣ) the
limiting factors in time being labour and material.

(v) Both aerodromes would therefore be suitable for
FLEET AIR ARM types.

(vi) Labour is extremely scarce and, in view of
other projects connected with the naval base and its defence,
it will be necessary to import labour from INDIA.

(vii) The majority of materials required for the
construction of concrete or tarmacadan runways, domestic
and technical accommodation would have to be brought by sea.

(viii) As alternatives to concrete or tarmacadan,
track runways are recommended. American steel plank or
Sommerfield track is suggested, and should be suitable for
F.A.A. aircraft.

(ix) The aerodromes at GAN and MIDU could be
developed to operate up to two F.A.A. squadrons each and
dispersion and camouflage of aircraft can be arranged without much difficulty, with prem the corr

(x) The plan for the defence of the Naval Base
envisages adequate provision of R.D.F., C.O.L. etc. and
warning should be reasonably good.

(xi) Meteorological services at ADDU ATTOLL are poor
and should be improved without delay.
    The principal winds encountered are :-

    S.E. Trade.   - July and August.
    N.W. Cross Monsoon.- December to March.

The duration of spells of high wind is short.

January is the dry season and most rainfall
occurs in July and August.

page .... 2.

(xii) Health conditions are poor and until they are
improved Indian troops should be relieved every 9 months
and British troops more frequently.

(xiii) Major maintenance of aircraft could be undertaken by H.M.S. "Unicorn" which is adaptable for this purpose.

Since Captain Huskisson made his
reconnaissance a further combined recce
party has visited Addu Attoll and has
just returned
    They confirm the above conclusions
but emphasise the difficulty of preparing
an aerodrome at MIDU. This would
take a considerable time and would
involve extensive clearing and levelling
operations

SABo.

Fig 4.1 (a). The summary of the main conclusions in the Huskisson report.

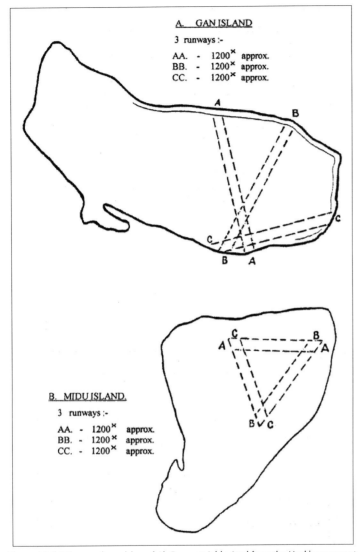

A. GAN ISLAND

3 runways :-

AA. - 1200^x approx.
BB. - 1200^x approx.
CC. - 1200^x approx.

B. MIDU ISLAND.

3 runways :-

AA. - 1200^x approx.
BB. - 1200^x approx.
CC. - 1200^x approx.

Figure 4.1 (b) Proposed provision of Air Bases at Addu Attol from the Huskisson report.

DIRECTIVE FROM CGS TO GOC CEYLON: 18 AUG 42

1. The higher control of the Ocean Bases of Addu Atoll ---- is by joint command under C-in-C Eastern Fleet (through FO Ceylon), C-in-C India and AOC India (through AOC Ceylon).

2. With effect from 15 Aug 42 C-in-C India will exercise his command through GOC Ceylon, but will remain responsible, in conjunction with C-in-C Eastern Fleet and AOC India, for higher policy. Air action will be co-ordinated by, and with, AOC No 222 Group, Royal Air Force.

3. With effect from 15 Aug 42 GOC Ceylon will therefore be responsible for:

    (a) Operational control
    (b) Training
    (c) Normal maintenance
    (d) Local administration of the military garrisons of Addu Atoll

4. GOC Ceylon will arrange with GHQ India for the necessary reliefs, despatch of labour, personnel, equipment and Engineer stores for any expansion of present defences and increases in existing garrisons.

5. Normal maintenance demands for stores will be met by HQ Ceylon Command. Any inability to carry out normal maintenance will be passed to HQ Ceylon Command for completion to GHQ India.

6. ----

7. Command

    (A) ADDU ATOLL

        (i) Base Commander

            A naval officer of appropriate rank.
            This is future policy.

        (ii) Defence Commander

            (a) junior to Base Commander
            (b) currently Lt Col L O Jones RM
            (c) the defence commander will co-ordinate all arrangements for the defence of Addu Atoll by the permanent garrison provided by Naval, Army and Air forces.
            (d) until a base commander is appointed he will in the event of attack, assume executive command of the whole garrison. He will NOT assume command of units of the Fleet or Air Force which may be using the base if they do not form part of the permanent garrison.

Figure 4.2. Directive from the Chief of the General Staff to the General Officer Commanding, Ceylon, clarifying the command structure for Port T, 1942.

```
TO                          FROM

   EASTERN FLEET                        C.IN C. E.F.

   I'm delighted to have you all in company.  Some of us
   are not as young as we used to be, but there's many a good
   tune played on old fiddles.

                              1704/3/42


              SHIPS IN COMPANY ADDU ATOL  -  APRIL 1942

   FORCE A                    FORCE B

   Warspite                   Resolution VA 3

   Indomitable (R.A.A.)       Royal Soveraign

   Formidable                 Ramillies

   Emerald                    Revenge

   Enterprise                 Heenskerk

   Napier (D.7)               Caledon

   Norman                     Dragon

   Nestor                     Griffin D 9

   Paladin                    Foxhound

   Panther                    Arrow

   Hotspur                    Scout

                              Nizam

                              Isaas Sweero


   Following parted Company a.m. Friday, 3rd April.  Hermes
   Fortune, Vampire, formerly Force B and Dorsetshire and
   Cornwalla of Force A.
```

Fig 4.3 Text of Admiral Sommerville's signal of welcome to the ships of the Eastern Fleet, Port T, 1942.

```
ADDU ATOLL: DEVELOPMENT WORKS PRIORITIES - October 1942

During his October visit to Addu Atoll, Brigadier General
Angus set out the following priorities for the fortress
executives:

Objectives:     Primary:    aerodrome

                Secondary:  rapid turn round of
                            supply ships


Priorities

First:      Accommodation for infantry battalion
            Anti malarial offensive
            Jungle clearing
            Stores building
            Site for third hospital section
            Perimeter road
            Fresh water storage

Second:     Aerodrome
            Cable station
            Move R.A.F. D.F. station
            Install 12 pdr guns
            Jetty for 400 ton ships

Third:      Slipway workshops for 72' motor boats
            Navigation beacons

Fourth:     1200' causeway Gan/Fedu
```

Fig 4.4 . Work schedule priorities at Port T, October 1942.

SICK RETURN 27 SEPT 42		
UNIT	No. Sick	% of Unit Strength
Q Coy RME	78	29
19 A W Coy	82	31
Sec 24 A W Coy	39	61
8th Sikh Pioneers	101	44
Aux Pioneers	227	60

Fig 4.5. Port T sick return for 27 Sep 1942.

Report from Surgn Lieut R.W. Ross, 1st Coast Regt, RM Galle, Ceylon

To Surgn Rear Adm RNA Hospital Colombo

Dated 18 Nov. 1942

Certain Medical Problems at Port T

There is a major health problem at Port T largely because of Malaria
and Bush Typhus, both of which are preventable.

Malaria

Nine months naval occupation has passed with no attempt at mosquito
control although malaria is hyper-endemic. A PO trained in mosquito
control and an LSBA have been resident for 3 months with no stores
and no control of labour. Mosquito survey results have not been
communicated to personnel. The carrier species has not been identified
and no adult mosquitoes have been dissected. The evacuated native
village is derelict and the huts swarm with mosquitoes; 300 wells are not
in use. All occupied huts should be sprayed, abandoned huts burned,
wells oiled and later filled in, swamps oiled, cleared and pumped out.

Bush Typhus

The vector has not been identified. The Hexapod lavol mite is probably
responsible. It is present in large numbers on dead coconut leaves and
a few on tree rats. It is a night biter living mainly in coconut palms,
not scrub. The camps are located among the palms although the island
centre is practically treeless.

Water

Water is imported 600 miles by tanker and stored near the landing jetty
in a tank covered with broken wire gauze. Indian labourers dip into it
for drink, sometimes bath themselves in it. Local water should be filtered
and chemically sterilised to release the tanker for other duties.

Need for action

Three weeks after the arrival of 250 men, 40 needed hospital treatment.
My own work was handicapped by my contracting Bush Typhus. Profound
psychological disturbances came with the disease and disturbed my
relationships with the executive officers. I am happy to offer my
services for the future research and duties needed on the island.

Fig 4.6 . Gist of the report on Port T medical problems, submitted by Surgeon Lt R W Ross RM.

Response from Brigadier W.R. Stewart DDMS, Ceylon Army Command
Dated 25 Nov. 1942

Malaria

The results of the survey conducted in June by the GHQ India
representative were given to the island personnel who thought them
unimportant.

The work on the wells poses a very large task. The swamps are more
extensive than thought and drainage poses another major problem.
Anti malarial discipline is being enforced and spraying undertaken.

Bush Typhus

Daytime clearing parties are bitten a lot. Parties now arriving
suffer less than earlier ones. Camp resiting is impracticable.
Mr. Carter, a government entomologist from Ceylon, will undertake
research on the vector.

Water

Local usage is recommended.

————— ooo —————

Letter From   Medical Officer in Charge, Royal Naval Aux
                 Hospital Colombo

        To   Medical Director General of the Navy, Admiralty,
                 London

        Dated   30 Nov. 1942

Col O'Dwyer ADH & P has recently visited Port T and was impressed
by the RN Tented Hospital run by Surgeon Lieut Zair RNVR with credit
to 2 medical officers running the hospital under most difficult
conditions. Anti-malarial work is being carried out by OC RN tented
hospital.

Surgeon Lieut Ross contracted Bush Typhus while serving at Addu Atoll
and, though he has made a complete recovery, it was thought inadvisable
that he should return. The reason for this is that in the early stages
he exhibited the symptoms of marked mental aberration associated with
the disease and, in consequence, not only fell foul of the Fortress
Commander but behaved in such a way to the natives as to make his
return undesirable.

It was not until after his reception in RN Auxiliary Hospital, Colombo,
accompanied by a report on his extra ordinary conduct, that the fact that
he was suffering from Bush Typhus was recognised.

Fig 4.7. Correspondence generated as a result of Ross's visit to Port T, 1942.

Fig 4.8 Headquarters' site general office, Gan, 1942.

Fig 4.9. Repair workshop, Gan, 1942. (IWM Neg Nº A28441)

DEFENCE PLAN FOR ADDU ATOLL.

APPENDIX A.—Proposed Defences.

APPENDIX B.—Plan of Addu Atoll Defence Area.

Function of the Base.

1.   The base at Addu Atoll is to be developed as an occasional fleet fuelling base.

Scale of Attack.

2.   Under existing circumstances, the scale of attack is likely to be limited to attacks by one or more armed merchant cruisers, submarines and midget submarines; such attacks may be preceded by reconnaissance by aircraft from armed merchant cruisers or submarines.

Air Raid Intelligence.

3.   T.R.U. station   1
    C.O.L. station (180-ft. tower)   1

Aerodrome Requirements.

4.   The aerodrome on Gan Island to be developed to enable two disembarked F.A.A. Squadrons to operate.
    Fuelling facilities only for up to six flying-boats.

Local Defences.

5.   The recommended scales of local naval, anti-aircraft and coast artillery defences are given in Appendix A, together with the provisions for early warning.

Land Defence.

6.   The responsibility of Commander-in-Chief, India.

Command.

7.   Officer Commanding Base to be appointed by Commander-in-Chief, Eastern Fleet, in consultation with Commander-in-Chief, India.

Fig 4.10 (a) The October 1942 defence plan for Addu Atoll.

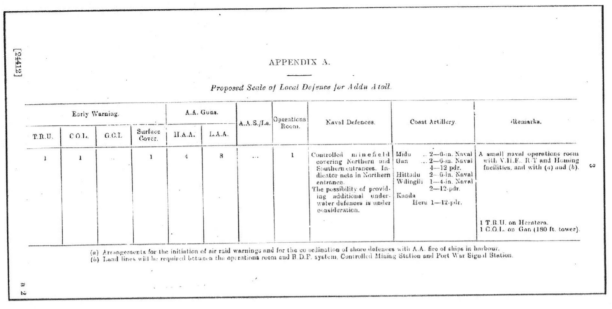

Fig 4.10 (b) Appendix from the October 1942 defence plan for Addu Atoll.

Fig 4.11. Bridge across one of the swamps on Midu, 1942.

Fig 4.12. Slipway and buildings at Maradu, 1942.

Fig 4.13. Minor pier, Gan, 1942. Source: L Conlon and A Lawson.

Fig 4.14. Observation tower location, Gan, 1942.

Fig 4.15. Observation tower construction, Gan, 1942. (IWM Neg Nº A28439)

Fig 4.16. Searchlight installation, Gan, 1942. (IWM Neg Nº A28440)

Fig 4.17. Searchlight generator huts, Gan, 1942.

ADDU ATOLL-MONTHLY WORKS PROGRESS REPORT - December 1942

The December diary contains:

a.   Routine reports of work under intense pressure to achieve ever faster work rate.

b.   50 men a day employed by medical authorities on anti-malarial work.

c.   250 yards of road that month.

d.   incinerators for 'night soil' to replace sea dumping. 1 done and working, 10 to build at 2 per week.

e.   piping from water boat to 10,000 gallon water tank laid. High level tank with gravity feed to distribution lorries.

f.   well being constructed for drinking water for whole island: water fit for consumption.

g.   brick making: 170,000 required for the wireless station at Hittadu, to be made on site.

h.   earthwork for No.1 strip 95% complete, No.2 strip just started.

Fig 4.18. Monthly works progress report, Addu Atoll, December 1942.

As the new year dawned the troops could view with satisfaction over one hundred thousand square yards of cleared land where previously there had been almost impenetrable jungle and swamps. Even more satisfying was the knowledge that much of the site clearance had been achieved with the most basic tools; manual labour had succeeded in conditions which had so frequently defeated the limited range of mechanical plant which had been sent to the atoll.

As soon as the ground had been cleared the engineers of Q company were expected to lay the north-west to south-east runway even though they had been informed that the Sommerfield track which, like all other suitable materials, was in great demand and short supply, could not be delivered because it had been earmarked for use elsewhere. Fortunately, Major Kenneth Bell RM, the officer commanding Q company, Royal Marine Engineers, had assumed, before embarking for Port T, that he might face just such a problem and had undertaken some very hurried research into the use of compacted coral surfaces for runways, a technique which had been tried with some success in the Dutch East Indies just before the war. Whether or not such a runway would be suitable for frequent use by twenty-ton military aircraft, a far more demanding application than had been reported on by the Dutch, remained to be seen. Given his limited resources and the urgency of the task, Bell could do no more than create the most solid runway possible.

He was sure that the compacted surface would need to be at least twelve inches deep to withstand continual use by the military and had calculated that even that minimum depth would require over ten thousand cubic yards of crushed material, an incredible amount to be blasted and scraped from the coral shelf for it would have to be compacted down from some two hundred thousand cubic yards of natural state coral. Admittedly, there was no shortage of explosives and the arrival of a drag-line excavator meant that his engineers would be able to provide a constant supply of loose coral. But getting it from the beach to the runway site would not be so easy because the three-quarter-mile route was along a road which the men of Q company had constructed for only occasional use by heavily laden vehicles.

Everyone was aware of the problems but there was no time to seek ideal solutions. The work had to be started. For a few days all went well. Then it rained. Within twenty-four hours a combination of moderate rainfall and frequent use reduced the route to a deeply rutted, suspension-damaging track. As if that were not bad enough, the collection and delivery system was grossly inefficient because there were no tip-up lorries available which meant that unloading at the runway site was a laborious manual process which threatened to delay the entire operation. The solution was simple, effective, and damaging for the lorries. Each driver was provided with a large rectangular plate which extended the full width of his vehicle's load bay and which had one end of a thirty-foot heavy-duty chain attached to its mid-point. Before the loose coral was loaded onto the lorry the driver would position the plate vertically at the front of the load bay, leaving the chain lying down the centre of the bay and hanging over the tailgate. The coral would then be loaded onto the lorry and the surplus length of chain thrown over the top. At the runway site the tailgate would be lowered, the end of the chain anchored to one of the heavy-duty rollers and the lorry driven away, leaving behind one full load of loose material ready for spreading and crushing.

The vehicles, continually drenched with salt water and bounced over rough terrain, had not been built to withstand such treatment. They needed repairing every few days and their life expectancy, estimated to extend to the end of the war, was reduced to a matter of weeks, generating acrimonious criticism of the Q company engineers from the supply services' staff in Ceylon and India. Bell rode all the criticism with a simple philosophy. He had few resources, a crucial job to do and a tight schedule. As far as he was concerned, a few worn-out lorries was a small price to pay for the completion of the runway on time. The first target date which he was working to was the 6th of February 1943. By that date the first runway was to be completed. It was. His men delivered the last few lorry-loads of material late in the afternoon of that day and, working by the light of vehicle headlamps, they finished rolling the coral surface at nine o'clock in the evening of the 6th.

It was on the 8th of February that Major Bell and his construction team first saw some real evidence of the value of their labours. That morning the fortress commander and his staff assembled to witness the first aircraft to land on Gan; at ten o'clock a Westland Walrus from HMS Gambia made a single approach run and a perfect landing (Fig 5.1). As it rolled to a stop there was a spontaneous outburst of cheering from everyone who had gathered to watch an event which, unknown to them, marked the birth of Gan's future as an international airport. The coral runway surface held firm. It was ready for the ultimate test of its durability: operational use.

The following day the convoy 'Pamphlet', *en route* from Aden to Freemantle, arrived at the atoll with several thousand Australian troops aboard, all headed for the war in the Far East. The troopships, all luxury liners requisitioned by the military, created a sight which impressed the servicemen and astounded the Maldivians. For the islanders in their dhonis the sight of the Queen Mary, the Aquitania, the Isle de France, the Nieue Amsterdam and the Queen of Bermuda with all their escort vessels provided an unforgettable glimpse into another world; never before had their remote atoll been visited by any of the great liners. The convoy anchored in the lagoon overnight but the Australian troops were confined to their ships, not because there was any possibility that some would desert but because they had left the Near East with a reputation for hard living and troublemaking which had made the authorities very cautious about letting them loose amongst the unsuspecting communities at Port T.

It was probably just as well that the Japanese fleet was occupied well away from the Maldives on the day that 'Pamphlet' was getting under way, for HMS Warspite, together with a dozen other ships including the Resolution and Revenge, was only a few hours away from the atoll, bringing the Commander-in-Chief, Eastern Fleet, to inspect the port. Confrontation at that time would undoubtedly have resulted in considerable losses on both sides, would probably have severely depleted the Allied stock of fighting and convoy ships and almost certainly have led to the destruction of Port T.

The Commander-in-Chief's visit confirmed his suspicions about the defences at Addu Atoll, causing him to express to the Admiralty his concern that the benefits of remoteness and the capacity to accept a large fleet were countered by the atoll's vulnerability and ease of observation from submarines. He argued that the atoll provided a nice hide out which should offer no more than the barest facilities necessary for the temporary accommodation of two squadrons. The Admiralty, generally in agreement with that assessment, actually had the whole subject of the Indian Ocean bases under review at that time and on the 20th of March instructed the Commander-in-Chief to abandon the boom defences at Port T and send the boom trawler Jan de Waele to the Levant, the first move in the reduction of the atoll base's function.

With the north-west to south-east runway operational, the Walrus aircraft from HMS Mauritius and Warspite made frequent landings to test the durability of the runway's coral surface and on the 18th of February a successful landing by a Royal Naval Air Service Catalina proved that the coral runway was satisfactory, at least during dry weather. The Air Ministry was duly informed that N° 1 runway was operational with limited support elements which included a mobile control, bowsers, some repair facilities and runway glim lamps for night-time use. There may well have been no occasion when an aircraft landed by the light of those lamps but any pilot who had tried to do so would have faced the daunting prospect of either locating a few pinpricks of light in the middle of the Indian Ocean or continuing to fly until his fuel ran out. The original plan to use the Gan airfield for Fleet Air Arm aircraft on shore-based detachment was apparently not implemented even though a Royal Naval Air Service station was established. The aircraft which did spend a significant amount of time at Port T were the Catalinas and the Royal Naval Air Service Sea Otter which, based on Gan and flown by an Australian, was employed on submarine detection flights whenever ships approached or left Port T, an almost daily occurrence.

Those early weeks of 1943 saw an impressive improvement in the health of the troops, brought about by a combination of widespread jungle clearance, land drainage, continuous attacks on the insect population and their breeding sites, the start of the dry season and the construction of hutted accommodation for many of the servicemen. By February the malaria cases were down to one hundred. Typhus cases, which had stood at one hundred and fifty in December, were down to nineteen and dysentery, reduced to only fifteen cases by February, was no longer regarded as a general problem. As the health of the troops improved, so too did their work-rate. By February the Maradu channel-blasting had been completed, fresh water was being continuously pumped at fifteen gallons a minute from the three-and-a-half-thousand gallon well which had been bored, buildings were being erected as rapidly as Nº 20 artisan works company could make the bricks and considerable progress had been made on the second runway.

The only task which had been abandoned was the construction of a causeway linking the islands of Gan and Fedu. The plan had been over-ambitious because the current in the Gan-Fedu gap was frequently far stronger than expected and the quantity of material needed for the causeway far greater than had been originally thought.

The obvious alternative, a road bridge, had been started towards the end of January and by the end of February, it too, was nearing completion. Similar progress had been made on the piers and the other inter-island bridges or causeways but the engineers were becoming frustrated. The rapid deterioration of the landing craft used to unload the supply ships and to transport loads between the islands was adding to the urgency of the work but it was impossible to complete any of the piers or bridges because the supply of planks from India had virtually ceased. Week by week the landing craft became more unreliable and week after week the construction workers waited in vain for the decking. Eventually the Headquarters' staff in India realised that there was an imminent crisis and made urgent arrangements to ship the necessary timber from Canada, some eight thousand miles away. It took a further six weeks before the planks arrived at Addu Atoll and just ten days for all the piers and inter-island bridges to be decked (Fig 5.2).

Even though the health of the troops had improved considerably by February the medical authorities were far from satisfied with the situation and on the 16th of the month Mister H F Carter, a government entomologist from Ceylon, arrived to continue the research started by Ross. By the 14th of March, when he left the atoll, he had studied the conditions on all the inhabited islands but his report (Fig 5.3) was inconclusive, primarily because he had been sent to the atoll during the dry season when mosquitoes were rarely seen. Given that kind of organisation by the staff in Ceylon who were supposedly trying to make amends for the earlier debacle, it became quite obvious to the garrison troops that they would have to continue to tackle the health problems as best they could without the benefit of clear direction from any expert in tropical diseases.

By March relatively few of the troops were unfit for duty and, with over four thousand servicemen and several hundred Maldivians to share the work, the days of hard labour were almost over. But for Lieutenant-Colonel M D Maclagan, the officer commanding engineering troops, who had taken over from Major Bond on the 14th of February, the frustrations remained. His March diaries refer to the routine demanding work, the increasing delays caused by equipment breakdowns and the seemingly inevitable supply problems which, by the 26th of the month, had left the atoll base with only enough petrol to last until the 2nd of April; just one week.

Nº 3 runway, started in March, took over five months to complete and even then the surface could not be consolidated because the roller was unserviceable. Nº 2 runway, started in April, was delayed both by equipment breakdowns and by the unusually high tides which prevented the collection of coral from the reef. To add to the problems, the dry season came to an abrupt end on the 7th of May and a tropical downpour the following day left an estimated three million gallons of water lying in the runway area, putting the aerodrome out of action for four days. The tropical storm did at least prove that the runway's compacted surface would not disintegrate in bad weather; it showed no signs of breaking up until the top three inches started to crack after a Liberator and eight Beauforts used it every day for a week. Even so, minor repair work kept it serviceable. Without doubt, Major Bell's coral-surfaced runway was a success.

With the increase in the number of servicemen at the atoll, it was obvious that something would have to be done to improve the leisure facilities for to leave some four thousand men trapped in a remote, overcrowded, all-male community on small inhospitable islands with few active leisure-time diversions was to invite trouble. Early in 1943 the fortress commander, only too well aware of the troops' needs, employed Maldivian labourers to prepare four sports pitches and within a few weeks football, hockey and cricket had all become fairly well organised with the results of the frequent inter-section and inter-service matches reported, together with snippets of local news, in the 'Haitan Sports Bulletin and District Reporter', a frequent, widely circulated and well-read duplicated sheet (Fig 5.4).

There were, however, very few leisure-time facilities for those who were not active sportsmen and, recognising that imbalance, Jones again seconded Maldivian labourers away from the main construction programme in March and employed them to build a cinema. Timber-framed with palm-frond walls housing bench seating for approximately six hundred, The Empire Cinema was opened on the 4th April 1943, providing for all the shore-based troops a facility which had previously been enjoyed only by those who were able to attend the occasional film shows on board the Haitan or on one of the visiting ships. The cinema, closed on Sundays, provided a weekly programme of six free film shows, generally comprising one English language film and five Indian films, a balance which fairly reflected the ethnic composition of the servicemen at Port T. Six weeks after the cinema opened the personnel of the landing and maintenance unit used it to stage 'Dreaming', another of their variety shows, again produced by Delafield and Bernacchi.

Improvements there were but the privilege of taking local leave was never extended to the shore-based troops. That was exclusively the privilege of the naval personnel who were serving on board the Haitan. As former RN telegraphist Harold Mansell recalled, they were occasionally given local leave but the concession was not extended to the Lascars, who made up the majority of the crew, nor to the Goanese who served as cooks and stewards; the only time they enjoyed the illusion of going anywhere was when the Haitan underwent steam trials around the lagoon after being at anchor for twelve months. Even though the shore-based servicemen would dearly have loved to spend a few days lazing on the beach they were never resentful towards the privileged few, they were actually very sympathetic towards those who served in the confines of the Haitan and they could well understand the need for them to spend some time ashore.

Throughout May, June and July and into August the weather remained stormy. Heavy rain alternated with high temperatures and strength-sapping humidity. Sickness increased. Morale sagged. There could not have been a better time for the Headquarters' staff in Ceylon to deliver the good news, announced early in June, that short rest-leave arrangements were to be introduced for the garrison troops. Those who had been at Port T for more than twelve months were told that they could look forward to an imminent short break in Ceylon. The relative newcomers were assured that their turn would come. The scheme started within days of the announcement and from late June onwards servicemen were leaving the atoll, initially in small groups of thirty or so, to spend fourteen days at Diyatalawa. For the remainder of the year a steadily increasing flow of personnel going to, or returning from, Ceylon supplemented the normal changeover of troops posted to or from Port T. For many of those who did not escape from the atoll during that excessively wet period there was one small consolation; they had moved out of their tents into hutted accommodation. Simple timber-framed structures with roofs and walls of woven palm fronds, the huts were more spacious than the tents, just as dry and had better ventilation. There was also the promise of better accommodation to come because additional, so-called permanent, prefabricated huts were due to be built for all the servicemen.

Even though they had been frequently drenched by the tropical storms, which had hit the atoll for almost three months, the troops had virtually completed the ground clearance programme by the end of July. The fighter control office was operational, navigation beacons had been erected on Maradu and Gan and the searchlight and anti-aircraft gun emplacements completed on Wilingili. The chain overseas low tower, however, posed quite a problem. Designed to stand one hundred and eighty feet high, the tower arrived as a loose collection of warped timbers, all badly drilled and with no identification markings or assembly plan. Given that winds in the region frequently gusted at over thirty-five knots, the troops had a potential disaster on their hands and it was hardly surprising that it was December before the tower was finally erected and handed over to the Royal Navy, subsequently to be manned by ratings from the Royal New Zealand Navy.

Although the atoll's defences had been greatly improved during the year the thirty-four servicemen who made up the permanent RAF contingent on Hitaddu had made no provision whatsoever for the defence of their territory, an odd situation which became the subject of correspondence between Headquarters N° 222 Group and Headquarters Ceylon Army Command (Fig 5.5). No physical barriers existed on the RAF site to hamper a hostile landing party and, incredibly, none of the RAF personnel had received firearms training. Colonel Jones was disinclined to allocate troops for the defence of the RAF unit and the Air Officer Commanding N° 222 Group saw the matter as a local responsibility for the land defence forces. The issue was left unresolved, with the RAF personnel maintaining the status quo. It is difficult to understand why they were so reluctant to establish their own defences and to undergo weapons training. Their camp had been sited where most of the ground clearance had been completed years earlier by the Hitadduans (Fig 5.6); they had no swampland or scrub to contend with and the Army had very quickly cleared what little undergrowth had to be removed. The hutted accommodation needed for drums of fuel and other stores had been built by the Army and the Maldivians; the jetty had been built by the men of the Mobile Naval Base Defence Organisation and the manhandling of the stores and the drums of fuel was undertaken mainly by Maldivian labour (Figs 5.7 & 5.8).

The RAF personnel were thus much better off than most of the troops at Port T and although they were apparently reluctant to work on the defences of their site or to undergo weapons training they did find time to improve the basic hutted accommodation which had been built for them. Most of the servicemen were content to apply their do-it-yourself skills to the creation of furniture with the ubiquitous palm trees providing ample wood from which to make bed frames and coir rope for the webbing. The officers chose to spend some of their time helping the Maldivians to construct an officers' mess ante-room. The kadjan-roofed, open-sided structure sitting on piles over the shallow waters of the lagoon must have been one of the most unusual ante-rooms in the world and was almost certainly the only one in which the furniture was made out of discarded crates (Figs 5.9 & 5.10). Living conditions on the RAF site were still very basic in 1943 even to the extent that much of the cooking was undertaken in a primitive outdoor kitchen (Fig 5.11) but at least the beach was pleasant and there was some clear space for those with enough energy to participate in the impromptu ball games which took place on most days (Fig 5.12). On balance, it seems that the RAF personnel had the best site on the islands, if for no other reason than the fact that elsewhere, space was at a premium; early in 1943 there were over four thousand servicemen living alongside the villagers, making the islands of Addu Atoll the most densely populated in the archipelago. They were also the only Maldivian islands with a traffic problem. So many military vehicles had been brought to the atoll that it became necessary to issue driving licences, to conduct driving tests and to employ motor cycle police on traffic control duties, an almost incomprehensible concept as far as the Adduans were concerned. The need was short-lived. Licences and traffic controls were introduced in mid-1943 but by the following year they were discontinued because troops were leaving the atoll to pursue the war further east.

As the garrison population increased the demand for fresh water grew to such an extent that three additional wells had to be bored, each much closer to the runway than was desirable. By October, in addition to the water taken by the Adduans from their village wells, ten thousand gallons of fresh water was being daily pumped out of the wells which the troops had bored on the larger islands in the atoll. That was enough for the four thousand service-men but there was little surplus and numerous bore holes were being sunk elsewhere to determine whether the atoll could yield additional supplies for the Allied shipping in the area. It is unlikely that enough fresh water could ever have been extracted to provide the naval ships with all that they required but the plan was abandoned anyway because the war zones were shifting and the fleet was operating further to the east. By then the local demand for fresh water was also reducing for, with the threat to India and Ceylon receding, several hundred troops were being transferred from Port T to the Far East: in October, over nineteen hundred servicemen left the atoll whilst just over fifteen hundred arrived, some returning from leave in Ceylon, others starting a new tour of duty.

That same month, the British Loyalty, a 1928 motor-tanker of almost seven thousand tons gross, arrived at Port T and dropped anchor in the lagoon which, unbeknown to anyone, was destined to be her final resting place. Requisitioned by the War Ministry in September 1939, and subsequently employed as an Admiralty fuel oil storage vessel, she was in poor condition. After being sunk by the Japanese submarine I-20 at Diego Suarez in May 1942 she had lain in the shallows for seven months, eventually being raised on or about the 20th of December. She finally left Diego Suarez early in October 1943 to take up station at Addu Atoll where she was to remain at anchor in the lagoon, serving as a storage hulk and refuelling station for Allied shipping in the Indian Ocean. For the next four or five months she invariably carried almost ten thousand tons of Admiralty fuel oil with the remaining capacity allocated to three hundred tons or more of coal, a few tons of petrol and a hundred tons or so of fresh water.

Although the rundown had begun in 1943 it would be well over two years before the last servicemen left the atoll and for them there were still some fairly hard times ahead. For the Adduans, an even more difficult period was looming, for there were severe food shortages throughout the Middle East in 1943 affecting servicemen and civilians alike with malnutrition so commonplace in the archipelago that it was becoming accepted as the norm. The troops at Port T were thus subjected to wartime rationing but they were not alone in that and they were certainly no worse off than their compatriots in Ceylon and India. The Adduans, with their local food supplies supplemented by the military to compensate them for the loss of their cultivated lands were actually better off than islanders elsewhere in the Maldives, most of whom could no longer afford to buy anything other than meagre quantities of food because the general shortages in India and Ceylon, coupled with the loss of the rice supplies from the Far East, had brought about a dramatic increase in the price of all imported foodstuff. Rice, not grown anywhere in the archipelago, was a staple food throughout the Maldive Islands and as the supply dwindled, many communities faced starvation. The military, becoming aware of the problem as a result of an RAF reconnaissance report and a series of Maldivian mail intercepts, mounted an investigation into the economic and political environment in the Maldives. The situation was found to be worse than anyone had imagined. There was a desperate food shortage throughout the archipelago with islanders starving as a result of the imbalance in the prices of imported cereals and exported fish. The only way to stave off a disaster was to provide emergency food supplies and to introduce a rationing system to provide the islanders with a diet comparable to that which was provided by food rationing in Ceylon. But rationing without import and export price controls would leave the poverty-stricken islanders unable to afford the basic rations to which they became entitled and it was obvious that the organisation of such a scheme throughout the islands was far beyond the capabilities of the Maldivian government which had neither the resources nor the expertise to cope with the situation. With hardly any debate, the Maldivian ministers handed over to the military authorities full responsibility for introducing and controlling the rationing and distribution of food throughout the Maldive Islands for the duration of the war. Control was exercised by the Headquarters' staffs in Ceylon with distribution by ships and flying-boats.

Port T was unlike any other atoll in the archipelago because the military had built on much of the land which had previously been cultivated by the Adduans with the result that local food supplies were, with the exception of fresh fish, barely adequate to support the islanders, let alone the troops. The Adduans were consequently even more dependent upon food imported from India and Ceylon than were islanders elsewhere in the Maldives and if the war had spilled deep into India in 1942 they would certainly have had to rely upon military provisions to avoid starvation.

Feeding the garrison troops under such circumstances would have also presented an enormous problem unlikely to be solved by the use of supply ships if war were waged in the subcontinent and across the Indian Ocean. Such a situation had seemed possible early in 1942 and, in an attempt to increase the locally-produced food supplies, several small-scale farming projects had been started to breed goats and chickens on the atoll. None had been successful because at that time there were other, more urgent, matters to attend to and animal husbandry had been undertaken in a very half-hearted fashion. But by mid-1943 the serious food shortages in the region led to the decision that the atoll should support sufficient livestock to provide significant supplies of meat, milk and eggs. Troops were allocated to farm duties and several hundred goats, chickens and rabbits were imported from Ceylon. The scheme was a complete failure. Many of the goats died *en route* to the atoll and those that survived were in such poor condition that they provided little or no milk whilst alive and very little meat when killed. The chickens quickly degenerated into a scrawny flock and, the final blow, the rabbits failed to breed. The plan was abandoned and the garrison forces continued to rely on imported food supplies.

The quartermaster at Port T was thus left with a severe problem. He had to develop and maintain a system of food rationing which sustained the troops and the Maldivians whilst ensuring that his food stocks were never exhausted before the arrival of the next victualling supply ship. That would have been an easy matter if the supplies had been sent to the atoll on a regular schedule, but they were not. The victualling ships arrived almost at random, generally unannounced and with varying stocks on board. The garrison's food stocks were frequently down to one week's supplies and on one occasion, at the end of October, only three days' provisions remained in the stores when the supply ship finally arrived. Although the Adduans had been only too well aware of the food shortages and equally aware of the improvement when control and distribution was handed over to the military, most of the troops were blissfully ignorant of the quartermaster's continual battle to balance the demand and the unpredictable supply. Like servicemen everywhere, they just continued to complain about the food.

By then, little was happening at the atoll to occupy their minds. The atoll's defence plan varied little from that of 1942 and it was most unlikely, after mid-1943, that Port T would need to be used either as a fleet hideaway or as a main servicing base. Also gone was the pressure of having to labour long hours in an attempt to meet the Admiralty's deadlines. Nevertheless, the base remained as an important link in the chain of military outposts between Africa and the Far East, providing refuelling and servicing facilities in sheltered waters. More importantly, from 1943 onwards it provided a communications link which was invaluable for shipping in the Indian

Ocean. For most of the operational life of Port T the base ship Haitan was the communications centre for all signals traffic with the outside world, maintaining a constant radio link with Colombo and transmitting messages for visiting ships which were thus able to maintain radio silence. The base ship, linked to all the atoll's shore stations by telephone, was backed up twenty-four hours a day by the port's shore-based unit located on Gan Point. Self contained, with its own transmitters, receivers and generator, the unit also provided accommodation for the shift-working signalmen. Each day Whitehall's British and Allied merchant shipping messages were received and retransmitted, on the commercial wavelength, from the Haitan. Many a seaman, rescued after his ship had been sunk, owed his life to the continuous listening watch for distress signals and to the rescue missions undertaken by the Royal Navy corvettes, generally HMS Balta or HMS Hoxa, which were frequent visitors to Port T from 1943 onwards.

As the port's communications role increased, Indian troops were deployed to Maradu to construct a concrete block building for use as an additional transmitter station but the project suffered a series of delays caused by the shortage of materials and the redeployment of labour and was eventually abandoned in favour of a timber built station on Gan, construction of which started late in October.

By Christmas 1943, when there was little likelihood of a serious attack on the atoll, employment at Port T had become, for many, a monotonous routine. The Christmas festivities provided a welcome break in their routines but it was obvious to the fortress commander and the naval officer-in-charge that the men were occupied but bored; morale was beginning to fall. Well aware of the speed with which morale can collapse when a sense of purpose is lost and knowing that competitive sport was one of the few activities which seemed to raise the men's spirits, the executives were enthusiastic supporters of the competitions against the visiting ships' crews who were invariably willing to field one or two sports teams, providing welcome diversions from the daily routines. The senior executives also seized upon any opportunity, no matter how brief or apparently trivial, to bolster the flagging spirits and thus it was that a few days after Christmas Sub-Lieutenant Alan Brundrett RNVR, then serving as a pilot with Nº 817 Squadron of the Fleet Air Arm, was ordered to 'beat-up' the atoll in his Barracuda aircraft off HMS Unicorn when the ship called into the port. He did not need to be told twice. For him it was an opportunity to enjoy the type of flying which, had it been practised on his own initiative, would have been a disciplinary offence. For ten minutes he gave a display of dives, turns and low runs, providing the garrison forces and the villagers with an exhibition of the Barracuda's performance and a reminder that the atoll base still had an important role to play, supporting the naval forces in the Indian Ocean.

At the end of December Commander Briscoe, who had served as the naval officer-in-charge at Port T since late February 1942 relinquished his command, handing over to Commander Coddrington-Ball RN. Briscoe became the first of only two officers to be awarded British Empire honours for wartime service at Addu Atoll, his OBE awarded in 1943 in recognition of his services during the major development period of the port with particular regard to the provision of facilities for the convoy 'Pamphlet'.

Within a fortnight Coddrington-Ball was to learn that Port T had served its purpose and was to be gradually run down.

Fig 5.1. The first aircraft to land on Gan.

Fig 5.2. Gan-Fedu bridge. (IWM Neg Nº A28432)

Report on investigations into Malaria, Filariasis and
Scrub Typhus at Addu Atoll with suggestions for control
by
Henry F Carter, Medical Entomologist, Ceylon

Malaria

The villagers living in Maradv, Hitaddu and Willingili were
examined for enlargement of the spleen, an indicator of endemic
malaria. Of the villagers examined, enlarged spleens were
found in over 53% of those aged under thirteen, 44% of those
aged thirteen to twenty and 22% of those aged over twenty.
There had been a recent outbreak of malaria. Every island
provides extensive breeding conditions for mosquitoes in the
swamps, village wells and water-holding coconut husks. The
mosquito species identified consisted of one Anopheline and
seven Culicines. Attempts to identify the malaria carrying
species were unsuccessful. Proof rests on detection of the
malaria parasites in the salivary glands of 'wild' females
of the carrier species and although Anophelines were suspected,
only two were seen in three weeks because the study was
undertaken during the dry season.

Filariasis/Elephantiasis

Most Elephantiasis victims are segregated onto Willingili,
generally accompanied by their families, resulting in a high
incidence of infected families. The Naval station at
Willingili is close to the native village. The Naval ratings
were checked and one 26 year old Goanese was found to have
microfilariae, the infective stage of the disease, present
in his blood.

Two of the eight identified species of mosquito were incriminated
as carriers of the disease.

Scrub Typhus

Rats, shrews and 'flying foxes' were examined, numerous mites
were found but the vector could not be positively identified.
Mites found on the rats were associated with Typhus endemic
in Texas but they do not live in the scrub like those mites
which cause scrub typhus in Malaya.

Fig 5.3 . A summary of Henry Carter's inconclusive report on malaria, elephantiasis and scrub typhus at Addu Atoll, March 1943.

The Haitan Sports Bulletin and District Reporter. 27 / 3 / 43

Soccer results during the past week.
R.M'S 4 R N 3.
Haitan 6 Ophir 1.
Haitan 1 Balta 3.
W.R.O's and C&P.O's 3. Haitan Rest 2.

Another Royal Marine versus Royal Navy match will take place at 17.45 on the R.M.E's pitch Gan on Sunday 28th (Today). So roll up in your hundreds and see the game of a life time. Don't forget to bring your rattles.

Hockey.
A. B. Burnell has taken on the work of organising a match in the near future. It is hoped that a game against the Indian Army on Gan will be arranged sometime this week. More names are still required, anyone who can wield a walking stick or swing a butchers cleaver should not hesitate to hand their names in.

Darts.
The Wardroom Officers team failed to beat the C&PO's darts team on their own "ground" …

Fig 5.4. Extract from 'The Haitan Sports Bulletin and District Reporter', Port T, 1943.
(Source: H Mansell)

Fig 5.5 (a). Correspondence relating to the defence of the RAF camp site on Hitaddu, 1943.

FROM:- Headquarters No.222 Group, R.A.F., Ceylon.

TO :- General Officer Commanding, Ceylon Army Command.
(Copy to Air Headquarters, India).
(Copy to Flag Officer, Ceylon).

DATE:- 8th April, 1943.

REF :- 222G/S/19/4/Air.

DEFENCE OF FLYING BOAT BASES AT ADDU ATOLL AND DIEGO GARCIA.

The Anti U-Boat Warfare Committee are contemplating the increased use of these Bases (as well as an additional Flying Boat Base at Male) for anti-submarine patrol and convoy escort. The additional accommodation that will be required is at present being investigated and you will be notified shortly.

2. While these Bases are being used only at infrequent intervals I am not unduly worried about the lack of defence. When, however, six Flying Boats are based at each Station and are carrying out regular anti-submarine patrols and convoy escorts I can well visualise that it would be to the great advantage of the enemy if they could deny the use of these Bases for our Flying Boats for a period and thereby obtain immunity for their submarines operating in that area.

3. Under the present scale of defence, a small but determined party landing from an enemy submarine could effectively destroy petrol stocks, W/T and D/F equipment and any Flying Boats that might be anchored there. It might well be a month or more before these facilities could be replaced and Flying Boats could again operate.

4. At Addu Atoll the R.A.F. camp is completely unguarded, not even being supplied with barbed wire.
At Diego Garcia two platoons of Indian Garrison Troops (medical category 'C') are stationed at the R.A.F. camp for defence purposes.

5. It is requested that you review these defence arrangements. It would seem to me that two platoons should be sufficient for the task provided that they are the right type of troops and equipped with a reasonable proportion of machine guns or light automatics, and that particular emphasis is laid to the safeguarding of petrol, W/T and the Flying Boats themselves.

6. Subject to the above, I only have two comments to make on the instructions you propose to issue to the Fortress Commander, Diego Garcia, forwarded to me under cover of your C.C.721/G/8 dated 3rd April, 1943:-

(i) I am not certain what is implied by para.3.
Although the R.A.F. contingent must obviously come under the Fortress Commander for defence purposes, and although the Fortress Commander will be in general administrative command of all troops, the R.A.F. detachment Commander must be at liberty to employ his personnel as he thinks fit, and will, of course, be in operational control of the Flying Boat Base.

(ii) I suggest para.7 be re-worded as follows:-
"The F.O. Ceylon and the A.O.C. are responsible for movement of the Station and Flying Boat Base respectively, in accordance with changing Naval and Air Force requirements."

Air Vice-Marshal,
Air Officer Commanding,
No. 222 Group, R.A.F.

No. 4401 G.
Fortress Headquarters,
ADDU ATOLL, 11th May, 1943.

Headquarters,
Ceylon Army Command.

Subject :- R.A.F. CAMP - ADDU ATOLL.

Reference your No. C.C. 19/G/14 dated 15 Apr 43.

I have received no request from O.C., R.A.F. Camp on HITADDU for the provision and erection of barbed wire.

2. According to O.C., R.A.F. Camp no provision has been made for the defence of the camp by them. There are 34 officers and men in the detachment, all of them technicians required to man the apparatus. None of them are trained in the use of arms. Five R.A.F. C.M.Ts are available.

3. Arrangements for the destruction of W/T instruments in the event enemy landing appear to be adequate.

4. In my opinion the camp site is extremely vulnerable and difficult to defend. The minimum tps required for successful defence would be one coy.

5. Up to the present time I have NOT allocated a Coy for this purpose as my commitments have been and continue to be very heavy and any further reduction in personnel would seriously retard the progress of construction.

6. To ensure adequate protection of the camp, without consequent delay in work, may one garrison Coy please be supplied.

7. If R.A.F. do NOT intend to provide personnel for the defence of the camp at any future date, may one extra Garrison Coy please be added to the units required as permanent Garrison on ADDU ATOLL vide para 14 of my MOST SECRET No. 2402 G dated 26 Apr 43.

(Sd) L.O. JONES.
COLONEL
FORTRESS COMMANDER.

Fig 5.5 (b)

COPY:

Subject :- Defence of HITADDU Island ADDU ATOLL.

C.C.6539/G/3.

A.O.C., CEYLON.

I attach a copy of a letter No. 4401 G. of 11 May 43, from the Fortress Commander, ADDU ATOLL.

At present the Fortress Commander ADDU ATOLL is not able to garrison HITADDU with a Company. This will mean that if the company is considered necessary, it will have to come from INDIA, this will take time and INDIA may not agree to the necessity of a company going to HITADDU.

The only real danger that I envisage against ADDU ATOLL is a raid from a submarine or lone raider, in which case I should have thought, that a few resolute armed men would be sufficient to deal with it.

As the defence of HITADDU Island is a matter affecting all three Services perhaps you would consider it advisable for this matter to be put before the next Commander's Meeting.

(SGD) H.E. WETHERALL
Lieut-General,
G.O.C., CEYLON ARMY COMMAND.

Fig 5.5 (c)

From : Headquarters, No. 222 Group, Royal Air Force.

To : Air Headquarters, India.
Copy to:- G.O.C., Ceylon.

Date : 21st May 1943.

Ref : 222G/S/19/4/AIR.

MOST SECRET

DEFENCE OF FLYING BOAT BASES AT ADDU ATOLL AND DIEGO GARCIA.

Further to my letter of even reference dated the 8th April 1943, addressed to the General Officer Commanding, Ceylon Army Command (Copy to Air Headquarters, India), I now attach copies of correspondence I have received from the Ceylon Army Command.

2.   I do not wish to press for additional defence measures at these bases for the following reasons :-

(i)   Diego Garcia already has two platoons of Indian Garrison Troops.

(ii)   Additional accommodation would have to be built at Hitaddu in Addu Atoll if it was decided to provide a small garrison.

)iii) Naval authorities consider it unlikely that a landing could be made at Hitaddu from the West.

(iv)   If considerable damage was done to the flying boat base, it should always be possible to operate Liberators from the runways on Gan Island, at any rate to cover the period until flying boats could again be operated.

3.   At the same time I must make it clear that no form of guard or picquet can be supplied from the very small numbers of R.A.F. personnel at Hitaddu. As land defence of these bases is the responsibility of the Commander-in-Chief, India, (as indicated in Defence Plan for Addu Atoll - D.I.O. (42) 120 (Final).), it is thought that G.H.Q. India should be aware of the position, as it may be desirable to review it again when these bases are being regularly used for Anti/Submarine and convoy escort work.

Air Vice-Marshal,
Air Officer Commanding,
No. 222 Group, R. A. F.

REGISTRY:
ATE 27 MAY 1943
AERIAL NO:

Fig 5.5 (d)

Fig 5.6 . Aerial view of the RAF camp site on Hitaddu, 1943. (IWM Neg Nº CF 619)

Fig 5.7 Maldivian labourers working at the RAF camp site on Hitaddu, 1943. (IWM Neg Nº CF 621)

Fig 5.8. The main fuel store at the RAF camp site on Hitaddu, 1943. (IWM Neg Nº CF 622)

Fig 5.9. The officers' mess ante-room, RAF camp site on Hitaddu, 1943. (IWM Neg Nº CF 624)

Fig 5.10. Off-duty officers in their ante-room, RAF camp site Hitaddu, 1943. (IWM Neg Nº CF 625)

Fig 5.11. Part of the 'field kitchen' at the RAF camp site on Hitaddu, 1943. (IWM Neg Nº CF 627)

Fig 5.12. Deck tennis at the RAF camp site on Hitaddu, 1943 (IWM Neg Nº CF 628)

VI   1944: The Rundown

As the Allied offensive built up in the Far East, Port T's significance declined and on the 8th of January 1944 the Flag Officer, Ceylon, held a meeting at Addu Atoll to discuss the reducing need for a military base in the Maldives. There was little to discuss. It was obvious that there was no longer any need to continue the airfield construction work: Addu Atoll had served its purpose but had become obsolescent. Equally obvious was the fact that most of the servicemen could be more usefully deployed to the Far East and, with their departure, the Indian general hospital could be reduced from a four-hundred-bed unit to a one-hundred-bed unit. Only the timing of the withdrawal gave rise to any serious debate and even that was rather short-lived. By the 25th of January the Admiralty and the Commander-in-Chief, Eastern Fleet, had agreed on a schedule and in mid-February, just one month after the completion of the road bridges linking Digi-Hera to Kafra-Hera and Midu to Heratera, the Chiefs-of-Staff approved the steady withdrawal of all coastal defence personnel and all army personnel not based on Gan, Fedu or Maradu.

Garrison company departed within a fortnight, to be followed, over the next four months, by the coastal defence personnel and Army personnel from all but the three islands in the south west of the atoll. The port's function was then redefined as '... *an occasional fleet fuelling base and a temporary base for flying-boats'*.

In anticipation of the Haitan's departure, plan 'R' was implemented, the construction of a multi-site shore-based naval communications station with wireless transmitters and towers housing the chain overseas low equipment, the transponder radar unit and the radio direction finding equipment. On the 1st of February the base was commissioned as a Royal Naval Air Service shore establishment and named HMS Maraga, the name being derived from the Maldivian Man-h-raga, the Divehi for a large black seabird. Typically, Maraga was commissioned but was incomplete. The wireless transmission towers, varying in height from eighty to one hundred and ten feet, were still under construction because the supply ships bringing the raw materials and components from India and Ceylon were running irregularly and were late with everything. The completion date for the ten towers was a vague *'as soon as possible'* which was just as well because the materials delivered during December 1943 had been enough to complete no more than four out of the ten. As the construction of the towers continued into the early weeks of 1944 no-one could have imagined that their equilibrium was about to be dramatically tested by a severe earthquake which, at approximately nine o'clock in the evening of the 29th of February shook every structure at Port T. Ron Godrich, at that time one of the ratings employed in the signals section on Gan, remembered that he and several other off-duty colleagues were in their bunks at the time. As he recalled:

> 'Our sleeping quarters were in a typical Maldivian kadjan hut; palm frond roof and plaited walls with openings for windows and a door. We slept in two-tier bunks which ran along the side walls of the hut and were joined by planks thus forming a continuous, but not particularly stable, structure along each wall. Restless sleepers could not avoid rocking the neighbouring bunks and it was rare for the night to pass without some of the disturbed sleepers forcibly expressing their opinions on the ancestry of the restless individual. When the earthquake struck, I and my colleagues immediately assumed that someone was rocking our bunks and we started to complain in no uncertain fashion. Then a few of us put our feet on the ground and discovered that it was moving. There was a shout of "earthquake" and we all rushed outside. The ground stopped moving but we all stood around expecting the earthquake to be followed by a tidal wave which would sweep across the island. We waited, not really knowing what to do for the best but luckily for us the tidal wave didn't materialise and we all went back to bed.'

Remarkably, only the permanent structures were damaged and those but slightly. The various Robinson-Crusoe-like towers remained intact; they were so flexible that they had merely swayed and vibrated during the earthquake as if in a tropical storm.

By the time the Haitan left Port T on the 4th of March the signalmen were already using the accommodation which had been built on Gan Point but the headquarters building, located near the jetty, was not commissioned until late September by which time much of Port T had been dismantled.

The transmitters, located near the runway, were housed in a building which included a workshop and living accommodation, the receivers being similarly housed in a separate building at the lagoon end of the airstrip near the Maldivian mosque and burial ground.

Although the war zone frontiers had shifted, the number of Allied ships operating in the Indian Ocean meant that rescue missions were still all too common. Many were undertaken by ships which responded to Mayday calls, rescued the survivors, and continued on their way. But the attack on the Khedive Ismail led to a far more complex chain of events. On the 12th of February the destroyer HMS Paladin was damaged when attempting to ram the Japanese submarine which had torpedoed the Khedive Ismail in the One-and-a-Half-Degree Channel. A salvage ship, the Salviking, went to the rescue of the survivors while the Paladin limped into the safe haven of Port T where repairs could be effected by the repair ship HMS Lucia. The rescue mission ended in disaster. The Salviking, with most of the Khedive Ismail's survivors on board, was within sight of Addu Atoll when she was torpedoed and sunk.

The Paladin, damaged but still seaworthy, set out once again on a rescue mission, with her crew only too well aware that a submarine, probably the one which had already got the better of the destroyer in the earlier encounter, was most likely lurking nearby and hoping to finish off the warship whilst her crew were picking up survivors. Much to the crew's relief, however, there was no sign of the submarine and the rescue went as smoothly as they could have wished. At Addu Atoll, Harold Mansell, a Royal Navy telegraphist who had picked up the Salviking's distress calls, watched as dozens of wounded were brought ashore, some walking, some on stretchers, nearly all with the slightly dazed, rather desperate appearance of men who had lived through the trauma of a successful torpedo attack. Those were bizarre circumstances in which to hold a reunion but that was what Mansell did when one of the survivors, looking at him in amazement, recognised him as a pre-war colleague from a Birmingham office.

The wounded were treated either on board the Paladin or in the tented hospital ashore until such time as one of the Ceylon-based merchantmen was available to transport them to a Colombo hospital. By the end of the month the survivors, the fit and the injured alike, had left the atoll as had the Paladin, adequately repaired for return to active service.

On many other occasions men were rescued by chance, as were seventeen seamen who were picked up on the 15th of April after their lifeboat was spotted by one of the supply ships which was headed for Port T. Adrift for forty-eight days with no protection from the blazing sun, almost totally exhausted and with their meagre food supplies long since consumed, they owed their survival to the rainwater they had been able to collect. Like many others who had been plucked out of the Indian Ocean they were brought ashore to be cared for in the tented hospital until they were strong enough to be sent to Ceylon. For several of them, the prognosis was not good but once they had left Port T they ceased to be the responsibility of the local medical officers and no records of their eventual fate were kept at the atoll.

Whilst the troops were preparing to leave the atoll, the villagers of Hitaddu were busy trying to sort out the local problems caused by their sheriff who had been appointed three years earlier by the Maldivian government. Matters apparently came to a head between him and the villagers on the 20th of February when he arrested several of them and accused them of illegal trading with the ships' crews in the harbour. The villagers were so incensed by his maltreatment of the alleged offenders that they destroyed much of his property and were only thwarted in their wish to give him a severe beating by the fact that his request to be taken into protective military custody was granted by the fortress commander. The islanders, wanting him to be returned to them for instant retribution, gathered in a crowd several hundred strong outside the entrance to the Hitaddu camp and there they waited for several hours before finally dispersing, deciding that the only way they would be likely to rid themselves of their sheriff was by submitting a formal complaint to Colonel Jones. That they did (Fig 6.1), creating a dilemma for Jones: it was one thing for the military authorities to become involved in a local dispute in order to protect the sheriff but it was quite another matter for them to act in a way which could be construed as interfering with Maldivian internal affairs contrary to the agreement between the British and Maldivian governments. Jones, who was due to leave within a few days, could do very little other than provide continuing protection for the sheriff whilst taking up the matter officially in order to avoid the necessity of providing almost permanent protection for the accused official. The Maldivian government was informed of the problem *via* its representative in Ceylon and immediately promised the Hitadduans that the matter would be thoroughly investigated, simultaneously issuing a warning of the consequences if the villagers were to take the law into their own hands. By then Jones had departed and the matter was left in the hands of his successor. Within three months Amin Didi, the Maldivian minister for home affairs, had arranged for the sheriff and his associate, the sheriff of Maradu, to be replaced by two representatives from Malé; Muhammed Didi being sent to Hitaddu and Husein Afeef Didi to Maradu. At the same time some of the village headmen and interpreters were replaced by Maldivians from the capital. The Adduans had got what they wanted, and more; their sheriff had gone, along with all his associates.

With the departure of the Haitan on the 4th of March only the British Loyalty remained permanently at anchor in the lagoon. Colonel Jones left on board the Haitan and Commander Coddrington-Ball took up permanent residence ashore combining, as the base commander, the roles of fortress commander and naval officer-in-charge. The rundown was well and truly under way and, in spite of the saga of the Khedive Ismail, the troops became rather complacent about the threat of enemy attack on the atoll. But at a quarter past two in the afternoon of the 9th of March any such complacency was shattered: the tanker British Loyalty was torpedoed whilst at anchor in the lagoon. The attack was made, not by the Japanese, but by a German submarine, the U183, which fired its torpedoes through the Gan Channel before making a getaway, remaining undetected even after intensive Catalina patrols of the area. One torpedo struck the tanker which then caught fire. The submarine captain, Fritz Schneewind, claimed that the British Loyalty had sunk but that was an optimistic addition to his list of kills. She did not sink but, with two of her tanks holed, she was badly damaged and by the following morning several thousand gallons of crude oil had spread over the surface of the lagoon and onto the beaches, polluting them for months. Damage limitation repairs were rapidly effected, her two damaged tanks were left open to the sea and the tanker, never intended to be a sea-going vessel again, remained at anchor in the lagoon, continuing to serve as a storage hulk and refuelling tanker, albeit with a significantly reduced capacity.

During April, Major Wilfrid Manners, the only other officer apart from Briscoe to be awarded British Empire honours for his wartime work at Port T, completed his job at the atoll and departed. He became a Member of the British Empire with his citation recognising the complexity of the task which he had so successfully undertaken.

The atoll's transponder radar unit and chain overseas low installations, constructed with so much difficulty, did not remain functional for long. There was no longer a significant need for an air raid intelligence service and on the 8th of May a signal from Whitehall declared the equipment redundant. Work started almost immediately on the removal of the Gan station and the Heratera station and tower. The one-hundred-and-eighty-foot tower on Gan which had caused so many construction problems was, with its turning gear, put onto a care-and-maintenance schedule.

During the first week of July almost three hundred servicemen left the atoll, leaving one thousand three hundred and forty-nine Indian troops at the base and reducing the British garrison to thirty-one officers and eighty-four other ranks. The troops were retained more to provide a labour force than a defence force and they found themselves dismantling or abandoning the installations on which they had so recently laboured in a vain attempt to meet the deadlines set from Whitehall. Four of the eight Bofors guns together with the coastal defence searchlights, which had only been reported in the war diary as '...ready for use' as recently as the 9th of March, had to be removed and shipped out. Nine of the gun emplacements on Gan and Wilingili, comprising one four-inch gun and eight twelve-pounders, were similarly declared redundant and the guns despatched to the Far East. Other sites which were closed in mid-1944 included the war watch centre on Midu and the six-inch batteries on Midu and on Hitaddu, where the guns were abandoned but not removed. On Gan the battery went onto a care and maintenance schedule.

Although construction work had given way to a dismantling programme approval was given, at the base commander's meeting in August, for the construction of '...a wall around the military cemetery', a feature which was to become a focus of interest for the Imperial War Graves Commission in later years.

Six months into 1944, with the rundown of the atoll base well under way, the Admiralty was seriously considering the post-war future of HMS Maraga. On the 14th of June the Surveyor of Lands, Ceylon, wrote to the Chief Surveyor of Lands, Bath, reiterating that the essential features of the wartime agreement between the British and Maldivian governments was that all stores and non-Maldivian personnel would be removed from Maldivian territory on conclusion of hostilities. Commenting that any wish to maintain a permanent post-war base on the atoll would raise a delicate political issue, the writer went on to suggest that:

> 'The problem is not one of financial implication but rather one of racial differences. The Sultan of the Maldives is not favourably disposed towards the spread of western civilisation amongst his people, and he is in fact averse to the intrusion of any foreigners, of whatever race, into the territory under his control. It is doubtful whether in the event of permanent occupation the Maldivian Government will be interested in rent, it is far more likely that the Sultan's goodwill to any such new arrangement will be obtained if he be accorded a salute of guns from time to time. In the circumstances if there is to be a new arrangement, it is suggested that the preliminary approaches should be made through Colonial Office channels'.

Given that the Maldivian government had wholeheartedly supported the Allied cause throughout the war and that the Adduans in particular had borne the destruction of their property with remarkably good grace, it was niggardly in the extreme for the Admiralty to consider the question of payment by the Maldivian government for any property left behind by the departing garrison or for the environmental benefits brought about by the development of Port T. But the possibility was referred to in that June letter, with the writer concluding, seemingly with some reluctance, that:

> 'Residual value will be more or less limited to the runways on Gan, the water supply installation, the causeways, slipway and wireless transmitter station buildings. In view of the Sultan's unfavourable attitude towards the emancipation of his people and development of his territory, it is considered there is no prospect of recovering anything under the heading of residual values, and in any case in the absence of money... settlement would have to be in the nature of a barter agreement.'

The Admiralty was not alone in considering the post-war future of the base. That was of even greater significance to the Adduans for whom a return to normality would mean the loss of the many advantages of sharing their atoll with the garrison forces. Although their cultivated land had been despoiled and their communities greatly disrupted by the military they had, by 1944, begun to benefit in several ways. They were living in a healthier environment as a result of the troops' ground clearance and pest control activities. Their normal diet, mainly of fish, rice and coconuts, had, since the 1943 investigation into food shortages in the Maldives, been supplemented with naval rations provided as part-payment for the work they did and that, together with frequent health-care advice and occasional treatment had undoubtedly improved the general health of the islanders. On a more mundane level their lives had been made easier because they were able to obtain sundry items through the NAAFI instead of waiting for one of their infrequent trading trips to Malé. Their NAAFI shopping, however, was of far less significance than access to the steady supply of materials which the military so readily discarded. The village communities utilised virtually everything which the Army scrapped, much of it the stuff of dreams for the poverty-stricken islanders. Cordage; corrugated iron; empty forty-gallon oil drums; non-ferrous metals; repairable tools; containers of any sort and the discarded tentage, which made excellent dhoni sails, were all sought after and occasionally fought over.

Standing firm between the affluent, profligate military and the poverty-stricken islanders were the sheriffs or headmen who attended the base commander's monthly conferences. They virtually controlled the allocation of surplus materials as well as making the initial decision as to which villagers, if any, should receive medical treatment. At every conference they negotiated the best deals they could, subsequently passing the benefits on to the villagers on a grace and favour basis. But they had no control over the rations received by the islanders as payment-in-kind for the work they did; the military authorities still allocated and distributed the food which they had continued to import for their Adduan workers ever since the 1943 crisis had led to the introduction of the payment-in-kind system. The islanders, unenthusiastic about the use of cash, were always keen to supplement their daily fare in any way they could, invariably responding to any offer of provisions as payment for their labour. It was an attitude which could not have been more clearly illustrated than by their response to an earlier military request for about six hundred pounds of fish each week for the troops. When payment was offered in cash the fishermen typically produced about twenty pounds of fish each week for sale to the military, keeping the remainder of the catch for their own consumption and for village bartering. As soon as provisions were offered in exchange for fish the supply exceeded the demand with the quartermaster being offered as much as a thousand pounds a week.

The headmen, partly at the behest of their government, but largely with the objective of increasing their own authority continually sought to control the distribution of payments-in-kind and by the end of October each of them was receiving a large daily allocation of provisions for redistribution among the Maldivian workers. That gave them one of the most effective controls they had ever had but it was not to the liking of many of the Adduans. The fishermen in particular were independently-minded enough to resent this latest development and they still tried to trade directly with the crews of visiting ships, regarding the returns as well worth the risk of being caught by the island authorities. That opinion changed after the September conference when the base commander reminded everyone that the regulations allowed British ships to fire on any of the villagers' boats which were persistently used for such trading. He also urged the headmen to stop their villagers' private trading by enforcing their own local law which gave the sheriff the authority to confiscate the boat, nets and fish of any Adduan found guilty of such a practice. The headmen needed no urging: they were probably even more anxious than the base commander to stop the illicit trading which was threatening their move towards a virtual monopoly over the supply of imported food. Within days they publicly announced that it was their intention to hand over to the sheriff any villager caught trading with visiting ships' crews. Almost immediately the practice ceased.

Having partially achieved their main objective the headmen were not averse to making whatever extra profit they could, particularly if that was at the Army's expense. Thus they would inflate the claims for payment-in-kind whenever they thought they could get away with it, which was quite often. Occasionally they would be incautious enough to submit a claim which was so obviously exaggerated that it was certain to be challenged, as had been the September indent for rations as payment for the hire of boats. Those indents were quite separate from the rations provided for the Adduan workers and were often slightly exaggerated but accepted after some debate. But submitting, as they did in September, a claim related to the hire of thirty-six boats and supporting it by documents authorising the hire of only four, exemplified the way in which the headmen would continually try to milk what they could out of the system.

There was, however, one man, Muhammed Didi, the sheriff of Hitaddu, who was largely aloof from the short-term practices of his compatriots for he had an eye to the future and something of an international vision. At the base commander's August conference he had obtained agreement for the military to start English language classes for the headmen. September 1944 may have seemed rather late in the day for such a useful development but Muhammed was not primarily interested in any immediate benefits, welcome though they would be. He was assuming that after the British withdrawal from Addu Atoll the Maldivian government would probably become far more involved in international matters than had been the case in the 1930s and from that premise it followed that those officials who could speak English would have an obvious advantage when career opportunities arose. As far as Muhammed was concerned, if any sheriffs were to be promoted he had every intention of being one of them; he joined the classes which started in November and continued until most of the garrison forces had departed.

Commander Coddrington-Ball departed early in October, leaving his successor, Commander Reid RN, with the prospect of an interesting month ahead. There were two significant visitors scheduled to arrive at Gan in mid-November; Admiral Louis Mountbatten, the supreme allied commander, South-East Asia, and Amin Didi, the Maldivian prime minister. Amin Didi's visit had been arranged to coincide with Mountbatten's so that the Prime Minister could meet the Supreme Allied Commander, introduce him to the local Maldivian officials and discuss the military situation in general and the future of Port T in particular. Judging by the complimentary entries in his private diaries, Mountbatten was most impressed by Amin Didi who, military matters apart, was genuinely concerned about the post-war future of the Adduans.

The Supreme Allied Commander arrived at Gan on the 16th on board an American B25 Mitchell bomber which had brought him from Ratmalawa. In his diary he referred to the Mitchell bomber as an aircraft which was fast but tricky to fly. That morning the Mitchell certainly lived up to its reputation for speed, landing at Gan at half past ten, with its Sunderland escort trailing some one hundred miles north of the equator, much to the amusement of the American aircrew. The latter part of Mountbatten's description of the B25 was to be borne out by events later in the day.

Mountbatten could hardly have come to Addu Atoll at a better time. The troops were still in low spirits after experiencing thirteen inches of rain in October, most of it during the last two weeks of the month. Their morale had also suffered a severe blow when, after overcoming all the trials and tribulations which had accompanied the construction of the base, they had been told to start demolishing it within a few months of its completion. But that was not all. They were understandably worried about their possible future deployment to the Far East where the fighting was continuing unabated. In one day Mountbatten gave their morale a tremendous boost. During his six hour visit he inspected the guard of honour, addressed a very large assembly, visited every unit at Port T, spoke to as many individuals as possible and showed a particular interest in the hospital and the work of the typhus research team. Quite apart from any political considerations, the Supreme Allied Commander's visit that month was an enormous success as far as the base commander was concerned.

As Edward Ivermee, who was serving as a Merchant Navy officer at Port T at that time, recalled:

> 'Mountbatten's common touch and his obvious honesty about the state of the war raised our spirits dramatically. For the first time, we felt that someone was really telling us the truth about what was going on. He made a tremendous effort to meet as many individuals as he could: he must have spoken to hundreds of men and there's no doubt that his visit gave us enormous encouragement.'

At twenty minutes to five that afternoon the Mitchell bomber, with Mountbatten on board, took off for Ceylon and was immediately in trouble. As the aircraft left the runway and began to climb, the rudder jammed hard-a-starboard, forcing the plane into a tight turn. The pilot, fighting to keep control as the aircraft dipped towards the sea, had only one opportunity to retrieve the situation and he took it. As the B25 veered towards an even tighter circle he managed to gain some control by asymmetrically increasing the engine power, finally putting the aircraft down crabwise as its uncontrolled circuit brought it over the end of the runway. With the Mitchell unserviceable, Mountbatten was obliged to wait for a replacement, ironically one of the Sunderlands which were patrolling the B25's intended flight path. He thus had an unexpected, and very welcome, opportunity to relax and to swim in the lagoon whilst the crew of the previously maligned flying-boat had an equally welcome opportunity to spread the story at the expense of the Americans.

During his visit the Maldivian Prime Minister took the opportunity to add his weight to the debate over the distribution of food supplied to the Adduan workers as payment-in-kind. For him it was an important matter, not because of any suggestion that the military authorities were failing to operate a fair system, but because he was sensitive to any criticism of his government's ability to organise the affairs of its own people through its atoll-based representatives. Such detail, however, was obviously not an issue for Mountbatten to deal with and it was left for Amin Didi and Colonel Johnson, who had accompanied Mountbatten to Gan, to discuss the matter with the base commander at his conference the following day.

The Prime Minister must have returned to Malé a very satisfied man for by the end of the discussions he had achieved more than he could reasonably have hoped for. He had been promised that the sheriffs would be given complete control over the food imported for the Adduan workers and the base commander had agreed to increase the ration allowances subject to the approval of the Headquarters' staff in Ceylon. Reid also proposed, without reference to Ceylon, to increase the payments-in-kind for November in celebration of Mountbatten's visit. That, as far as the sheriffs were concerned, meant that 1944 would end on a high note with each of them being allowed to distribute over a quarter of a ton of atta and almost one-and-a-quarter tons of rice during December. The base commander was just as happy as Amin Didi and the sheriffs. He had established an excellent relationship with the Maldivian Prime Minister merely by displaying some generosity whilst handing over a declining and, to him, a rather unimportant responsibility which the sheriffs would continually have sought to discuss until they had gained the total control which they were so anxious to achieve.

Mountbatten's visit may have been a great morale-booster but, rather surprisingly, one of the biggest factors affecting morale, the mail service, had hardly improved since the early days of Port T. Letters arrived about every three weeks, a delay which came to be regarded as unreasonable by the recipients after they witnessed the service provided for the three American servicemen who had been sent to Port T during 1944 to establish their own weather station. They were daily transmitting weather reports for the American forces in the Far East and for them, the delivery service to the atoll was superb regardless of whether it was military equipment or private mail which was being delivered. In the words of Edward Ivermee:

> 'They were incredibly well served by American aircraft. We always used to joke that they could get a special flight laid on if they needed some more Coke'.

By mid-December the military authorities had begun to consider in some detail the environment which they would be leaving behind for the Adduans. The Army no longer needed all the atoll land which it was occupying at the end of 1944 and as the garrison vacated some of its territory the local population was able to start replanting young trees on Gan to replace those uprooted by the servicemen. For the Adduans that was a highly significant activity heralding the inevitable return to a coconut-and-fish economy, albeit in a relatively scrub-free environment in which the swamps had been drained, roads provided and inter-island bridges constructed. Christmas 1944, the last at the atoll for all but a very few troops, brought the first and only visit of an Entertainments National Service Association (ENSA) party to Port T, a direct result, as far as the servicemen were concerned, of Mountbatten's visit the previous month. By then the troops at the atoll were in relaxed mood. The threat of attack had gone, the dismantling programme was proceeding without any great urgency and life was, compared with earlier times, fairly easy if not actually boring. Any diversion was welcome and the ENSA show was particularly so for it included one or two European females, a rare sight indeed for men who had been deprived of such company for years. The variety party's arrival and performance is remembered with some amusement by Ivermee who recalled that:

'The ENSA party, numbering no more than five, were brought to Hitaddu on board a Sunderland aircraft and had somehow managed to bring their own piano amongst their baggage. The visit provided a rare opportunity for the Army to score over the Royal Navy because the ENSA party was due to be met at the Hitaddu anchorage by a naval motor boat crewed by ordinary seamen who would take them to the Gan jetty where the senior naval officer at Port T would be waiting to welcome them ashore. Among the garrison's Army officers were several competent canoeists who had built their own canoes and who rowed out to meet the motor boat before it reached Gan. They persuaded the ladies in the ENSA party to board the canoes, subsequently to be rowed ashore some way from the Gan jetty and escorted to the Army officers' mess where they were generally made most welcome. The reception party at the jetty was left with little alternative but to extend its greetings and hospitality to the depleted all-male party, much to the amusement of the Army and the annoyance of the Royal Navy. The variety shows, given in the cinema, lived up to the old joke that ENSA

stood for 'Every Night Something Awful.' They were awful but were given a rapturous reception. The comedian was not funny but was wildly applauded just for making the effort of coming to such a God-forsaken part of the world. The entertainers had only to walk onto the stage to generate a deafening response from the troops. Such a reaction was not just restricted to the show times; the ladies were loudly cheered whenever they were seen around the islands during their brief visit to the atoll'.

It was without doubt the most popular entertainment ever given at Port T and it certainly helped to put the troops in better spirits for the last year of the war and their departure from the Maldive Islands.

Figure 6.1 Letter from the local population to the Fortress Commander.

Addu-Atoll 28th February 1944

From:-   The Local population of Addu-Atoll,

To: The Fortress Commander
          Fortress Headquarters   CONFIDENTIAL
          ADDU-ATOLL

Subject:- Detestation of the Civilian population to Sheriff,
and their complains against him.

Hon'd Sir

(Translation).
In view of the recent Civil disobedience here. It is necessitated both side to forward their grievances to you, therefore we are humbly going to submit our complains against the Sheriff, in the following paragraphs:-

He has been here nearly three years and within this period, we have seen him doing many illegal and tyrranous matters, on the interests of the people.

Why the provocation arose between the people and the Sheriff?

1.   On the 20th instant when the Sheriff was sailing on his round in the harbour, he found three country boats, belonging to Hittadu, were stopped there.   Then they all stopped at "Fedu" beach and he came on board the boats, questioned them saying you are coming from the Ships,   then they said, no, we did not go to the ships.   Immediately the Sheriff jumped on one of the boats and he hit the coxswain on his head four times with his strong hand; the man was injured seriously, and fell down in the boat unconscious. Then he turned to the crews and tied one of them, his hands back with thick coir rope, soaked in the sea and with sand. By tying his hands is such a wretched way, were cut deep. While they (his supporters) tying him, As he was getting much pain and irritation, he requested them, saying please have mercy, for the sake

of my Prophet. I wish if you would not hurt me so much, but they would not hear this and said this is Marshall Law time and not a time to remand your Prophet. Again he rushed to the rest of the Crews and hit them very strong blows with a Cocoa-Nut branch and Also kicked and pushed them over the ground as well as the second one. Out of them one small boy about 10 years old had too many blows here and there on his body and was injured a great deal. After finishing this grumble he ordered his supporters to take five of them back to Hittadu and kept them as prisoners in his cook-house with no medical assistance and properly fed. And he took the first and second man as mentioned above, in his own boat, to Midu, there too, he kept those too innocent fellows as in prison and advised the Local Sheriff there, not to behave with them well and to give them just a little food, no medical assistance, that is all. And when he was departing from Midu, it has been said by a reliable person that he said to the people there, I will crush everyone in the Atoll, in a similar way and I do not mean, I do not feel about their death, when I hit them. It is better to die some of them.

2.   In many public function he gives lectures disrespecting the Mohamedan Jurisprudence, which causes the people less believing of their relegeon. And under the present circumstances it is not necessary to refer for further explanations as it can be given in any juditial court of inquiry if it is wanted, with full details of witnesses.

3.   During his round from one to another Island, he used to have the fair sex unlawfully, in this respect he dose not have any hesitation in the Villages and the people hate him so much. According to the Muslim Laws such people must be punished very heavily but as he is the Sheriff, we were not able to object him on this matter and we kept patience too long.

4.   One day the Sheriff was caught red handed and the fact was made clear to the Local Magistrate by one of his supervisors and the former has summoned the woman and has punished her according to the Muslim Laws, consequently he wanted to revenge this disclosure of his suit by an inferior and the man was called in his office, after abusing him so much , hit him on the head very severely. His usual way of calling women into his own residence was, rides on the bicycle into the Villages at night and make them to follow him up to his house. In this way he has been found related to the boys as well. Such is his ill morals.

5.   Drinking of alcoholic liquor is absolutely prohibited in the Muslim Laws. It is sorry to say that the same thing was proved against him as we have found a half a bottle of "Whisky" in his own box.

6.   In answer to article No. 1 - of this statement. When we came to know of his cruel behaviour of the men on the 20th instant, sorrow and exhaustion compelled us to question the other members of his committee; Why were the arrested in the cook-house? The reply was we did not know anything about that. As he had arrested them without knowledge of the other members, the people assembled in the Village at about 2300hrs and proceeded to the cook-house to release them all. Suddenly we entered the Sheriff's compound and released the prisoners in

no time. During this adventure he was away from the Island and enormous damage was made to his clothing, stationary and house-hold we could not help, we had a big crowd, absolutely in the loss of patience. The people came back.

6-b.   On the following day at 1800hrs people were awaiting him at Hitaddu, jetty, and the boat was sighted approaching to Hitaddu, the boat was returned to the Jetty at 2100hrs, with only one man on board then he was asked by, where is the Sheriff? His reply was that he and the rest of the crews had landed somewhere on NEW GAN "Village" at Hitaddu. Suddenly the crowd made a big noise and the boat was sunk by them. thenceforward we marched up to NEW GAN "Village" to meet him and bring him back to Hitaddu, for investigation, but we could not able to find him then, so we returned to our respective "Villages".

6-c.   In the morning of 22nd, the people assembled again and when we were proceeding to New Gan "Village" on the way, they were reported by an Indian Officer, that the Sheriff is at R.A.F. Camp in his own quarter. So we had gone there and tried to get in touch with him but we were not allowed by the Guard to enter the camp area and held up us, as we were stopping there the O.C. R.A.F. had come to us and he informed us that it is impossible to hand the Sheriff over to you, but two of your men, be represented to him under my Guard and see him in my office.

6-d.   Accordingly we had sent two messegers from our side with full instructions to the Sheriff, that we are having such and such grave condition in the Village, resulting through his misdeeds and also that he is required in the Village for inquiry, which he promptly refused and said I have no longer resigned my authority upon your people and now I am under the British Govt. And I shall not go to Hitaddu any more. Again our messengers questioned him saying you are our Sheriff you ought to come with us, but he did not accept their words. So we came back to the Village with due patience and so are still

N.B.   we shall be much grateful and obliged if you will consider our present circumstances and try to settle this long disputed tyranny between us, on a right basic

        Trusting that you will give the matter your attention,
        we are at your service for further information, and remain

        Your most obedient servants,
        Civil population of Addu-Atoll,

        MALDIVES.

VII   1945/46: The Withdrawal

For HMS Maraga, 1945 was undoubtedly the year of the anti-climax. Given the ever-reducing threat to Allied shipping in the Indian Ocean there was no need to retain both an RAF presence and a Royal Naval Air Service station at Addu Atoll. The RAF, still operating flying-boat patrols from the Hitaddu base, had no further use for the Gan aerodrome and no wish to take over its administration. The atoll's distance from the 1945 battle zones meant that there was no likelihood that the base would host any disembarked Fleet Air Arm squadrons and the Royal Naval Air Service station was consequently closed down on the 20th of March. HMS Maraga was then re-designated as a refuelling facility and RAF observation centre.

The decision to withdraw all the garrison forces was confirmed on the 27th of April but, as in 1944, some of the garrison troops, whose military presence could only be justified for the first two or three months of 1945, were retained for their labour rather than their military skills; they were gradually withdrawn from the atoll during the year.

Quite apart from the three years of hard labour that had been expended in the creation and operation of Port T, the estimated financial investment amounted to one hundred and eighty thousand pounds of which one hundred thousand pounds had been spent on the development of the Royal Naval Air Service station, over sixty-five thousand pounds on the provision of a fleet base and more than fourteen thousand pounds on the installation of communications equipment, masts and towers (Fig 7.1).

To abandon such an investment seemed quite wrong, especially as the atoll offered an attractive fleet facility with an enormous natural harbour. The Admiralty briefly flirted with the idea of trying to retain the base for use in future emergencies but the idea was not taken up with the Maldivian government and the aerodrome, considered to be too remote and in too hostile an environment to be used by civil airlines, was, towards the end of 1945, handed back to the Maldivians who later re-established their village on Gan, cultivating some of the land and leaving the remainder to revert to scrubland.

Throughout 1945 the British Loyalty continued to supply fuel oil, fresh water, coal and petrol to the visiting ships and to HMS Maraga. But she was in a sorry state. Originally sent to the atoll because she was in generally poor condition, she had undergone minimal maintenance throughout her tour on station. Once established as a static storage hulk and refuelling tanker it was never intended that she would put to sea again but her fate had finally been sealed on the 9th of March 1944 when two of her tanks had been damaged in the torpedo attack and had subsequently been left open to the sea rather than repaired. The bulk of the ship's reduced capacity was generally taken up by fuel oil, the balance continuing to be allocated to one hundred tons or so of fresh water, a few tons of petrol and three hundred tons or more of coal, frequent deliveries of which were brought from India with over twenty-five tons a week being redistributed, mainly for galley use.

The fresh water was supplied from HMS Maraga, twenty or thirty tons at a time being brought to the British Loyalty by barge and stored in the forepeak or forward coffer dam. The British merchant seamen, two deck officers and two engineers, who served on board the tanker lived with the Indian crew in conditions which, whilst not very good, were certainly better than those ashore. But life on board the British Loyalty was quite monotonous. Conversation with the crews of visiting ships added a little interest but serving in a remote lagoon on board a small decrepit tanker which was sailing nowhere was bound to be a boring occupation. Even the trips ashore had little to offer except for the chance to swim in the shallows and relax on the beach away from the smell of the oil and the coal. The only exciting job, 'dressing' the buoys for the RAF, was actually one which would willingly have been abandoned because it was nerve-rackingly dangerous. When a Catalina or Sunderland arrived and had to be tied up to a buoy, one of the RAF aircrew had to lean out of the aircraft and, using a long boathook, had to haul in the wire loop which was attached to the buoy.

That was easy if the buoy was 'dressed' with the loop across its top surface but as the buoy moved in the lagoon swell the loops invariably slid down into the water making it virtually impossible to retrieve them by boathook from the aircraft. To overcome the problem a British Loyalty deck officer would take a small motor boat out to the buoy and hold it on station whilst an Indian crewman in the bows held the wire loop in the 'dressed' position. As the aircraft approached the buoy the motor boat would be held steady until the last possible moment before pulling rapidly away to escape a collision. That was a reasonable manoeuvre when the aircraft was a high-propeller Catalina but a frightening experience if the boat's motor misfired, as it often did, just as a Sunderland, with its low-slung propellers, bore down on it (Fig 7.2).

The atoll's channel defences, including a re-instated Gan Channel boom operated by the boom ship Teal, were still manned in 1945 because there was always the possibility that a lone submarine might be operating in the area. Land defences however had a much lower priority for the simple reason that an attack on the islands in 1945 was inconceivable. With the removal of that threat the pressure of the previous years had largely gone and there developed a far more relaxed, more tolerant atmosphere; incidents which would have brought retribution to the perpetrators during those earlier more stressful days were often tolerated during the last months of the military presence at Addu Atoll. One Merchant Navy officer who served on the British Loyalty throughout 1945 remembered many such incidents and his recollections provide an insight into the lighter side of life at HMS Maraga during the last year of the Second World War. As he recalled:

'A serious attack on the atoll may have been inconceivable but patrol vehicles, equipped with sirens to warn the troops of any such attack, were still maintained. Rarely was there a battle drill even though all of the troops, many of whom regularly carried arms, had individual battle stations. But a most effective test of the troops' reactions to the sirens was conducted in the early hours of one morning by two rather inebriated non-commissioned officers who commandeered one of the patrol vehicles and drove it, sirens blaring, around Gan.

Within minutes, the Indian troops were in position to repel an imagined enemy force. In the initial confusion some shots were fired, fortunately hitting no-one. Almost an hour went by before the Army officers were certain that the sirens had sounded a false alarm. They then had a problem because the Indians had been repeatedly warned about Japanese trickery and when a troop recall was sounded they would only leave their posts, mainly up the trees, when ordered to do so by officers or senior non-commissioned officers whom they recognised. Only when daylight came

was it possible to entice the troops back to normal duties by making personal contact with each of them.

The Army officers, who had always been aware that the troops needed something, apart from the common suffering, to identify them as a special group of men in special circumstances, openly displayed one sign of their own group identity: an unofficial shoulder flash. Permanently worn, even during official visits and inspections, the locally made shoulder flash consisted solely of a boomerang. It indicated the wearer's membership of the 'round the bend' club, offering silent comment on the effect which Addu Atoll could have on a person's mental state.

In some cases however it was difficult to know whether an officer's unusual behaviour was brought on by the environment or whether the local circumstances had merely provided an opportunity for him to practise his natural eccentricity. One such officer was the Major in charge of the engineering workshops. A pre-war film producer from Elstree studios, he had built a small car, akin to a buggy, which was his pride and joy. Fitted with one giant headlamp and an unsilenced stub exhaust the vehicle could be seen and heard over the length and breadth of the island. He became infamous for his joy-riding and his disconcerting habit of driving straight into the officers' mess rather like Toad of Toad Hall, scattering furniture as he came to an emergency stop. He never injured anyone for the simple reason that his imminent arrival was so obvious that no-one was ever caught in the danger zone.

As the war entered its final stages there was more time to relax. But increased leisure time brought problems. Without some sense of purpose there was a limit to the length of time anyone could spend on trivial activity without becoming bored. This was particularly so for the three Merchant Navy officers on board the British Loyalty and for them Saturday evenings developed into social evenings which provided a welcome break in their otherwise dull routine. A few Army officers were generally invited to dinner on board ship every other Saturday and on the intervening Saturdays the Merchant Navy officers invariably whiled away the evening wining and dining in the officers' mess ashore. The occasions became part of the social rituals which so easily built up at the atoll. Ashore, the evening's drinking and discussion gave everyone a chance to unwind, often in spectacular fashion, within the security of a group which was indulging in some rather bizarre behaviour within its own sanctum, witnessed only by the sometimes incredulous mess staff.

One common after-dinner practice was known as 'soak thy neighbour', a game which must have left the waiter totally bemused. The diners' choice of after-dinner liqueurs was generally limited to Cherry Brandy or Crème-de-Menthe, invariably referred to as 'red light' or 'sticky green'. Each was served in the most commonly used type of glass, a cut down beer bottle, its rim ground and polished as smoothly as any normal wine glass.

The officers would sit around in a large group, smoking, enjoying their after-dinner drinks and generally conversing. At some time during the evening one member of the group would ask a waiter to fetch a bucket of sea-water from the shallows off the nearby beach. The filled bucket would be ceremoniously placed on the floor in front of the requesting officer who, when he felt so inclined, would pour the water over any one of the others in his group. The unfortunate recipient, with his hair plastered to his head, his 'red light' or 'sticky green' topped up with sea water and his cigar bent and sodden, was expected to sit back in his saturated clothes and carry on his conversation as though nothing had happened; failure to do so would cost him a round of drinks. It was the victim's privilege to order the next bucket of sea-water and mete out similar treatment to some other member of the circle. So the process would continue until everyone was soaked but still sitting and conversing late into the night as though nothing untoward had occurred. Eventually the members of the group would retire, thanking each other for a pleasant evening and agreeing to meet again.

A less frequent, but not uncommon, Saturday evening event was 'burial at sea' which was reserved for any officer incautious enough to pass out under the influence of alcohol. A coffin was kept readily available into which the unfortunate inebriate would quickly be loaded. The coffin, with the 'body' aboard, would then be borne down to the beach to the accompaniment of the Dead March, hummed by all the 'mourners'. The lidless coffin would be launched out to sea, invariably overturning in a matter of seconds and dumping the drunken officer in the surf. He always came round at that stage. It was then his privilege to recover his own coffin and bring it back to the mess for further use in similar circumstances.'

By June, with victory already achieved in Europe, there was no need to continue the observation flights from HMS Maraga. The flying-boats were redeployed, the RAF personnel left the atoll, the base on Hitaddu was abandoned and that area was handed back to the villagers.

For the garrison force the sense of military purpose had virtually drained away. The atoll base, created through the labour of earlier years, was to be abandoned to revert to swamp and jungle. Life, however, was easier than at any other time of the war. The troops' workload was light and their health was good, which was just as well because the hospital had long since been replaced by a small hutted sick quarters leaving the men to rely upon visiting ships to provide any significant hospital treatment. Dental treatment was similarly provided by naval dental officers as had always been the case, for no dental officer had ever been based at the atoll. There was a sense of anti-climax but it was obviously offset by the conviction that the end of the war was in sight, a job had been well done and a return to normality was but a few months away. Contributing to that feeling of a job well done was the brief mid-year wave of publicity about the remarkable achievements of the troops who had created Port T. In June the BBC broadcast Major Manners' account of his cable laying experiences at Port T, subsequently publishing his comments in The Listener a few weeks before an Admiralty press release led to the publication of a variety of newspaper and journal articles paying tribute to the men who had built a military base where previously there had been jungle and swamp.

For the Maldivians the rundown of the port signalled an imminent return to a lifestyle devoid of most of the benefits brought through employment by, and trade with, the military. The Maldivian representatives who attended the base commander's meetings, understandably anxious to obtain whatever they could before the troops finally left the atoll, tended to make innumerable requests for commodities and perks; anything and everything, from tent canvas to hair cream, was desirable in their eyes. In other matters the Maldivians could only accept that some benefits, such as a more healthy environment, would remain but would probably not survive for very long because the islanders' return to a survival-orientated culture would leave them with little or no time for the maintenance of a healthy island environment.

On the 20th of September 1945 the Commander-in-Chief, East Indies, informed the Admiralty that there was no further naval requirement for a base at Addu Atoll and that action was being taken to close it down. On the 16th of October the Admiralty classified the base as non-operational even though personnel remained at the atoll well after that date to remove and despatch equipment and to reinstate many of the arable sites which were being returned to the Maldivians. By then the repatriation of personnel from the Far East was placing an enormous demand on the Allied shipping, little of which was routed through the equatorial channel to the north of Addu Atoll. The repatriation of servicemen from HMS Maraga was thus a gradual process until early December when HMS Jamaica was employed to evacuate the remaining Indian troops. After sailing from Colombo on the 7th of December, Jamaica dropped anchor in the lagoon at Addu Atoll in the afternoon of the 9th. With the last of the Indian troops on board, the ship set off for Ceylon shortly after sunrise on the 10th of December, the day on which HMS Maraga was officially placed onto a care and maintenance order.

That month also saw the departure, on board HMS Jamaica, of the merchant seamen who had manned the British Loyalty. Their ship, too broken down ever to be put back into sea-going service, and no longer employed as a refuelling station, had become a floating dump for the large quantity of materials and equipment which the military did not need, had no wish to transport to England and was reluctant to give to the Maldivians, largely through concern over the attitude of the Sultan towards the beneficiaries of such gifts. By mid-January all the unwanted military hardware, stores and worn-out lorries had been loaded onto the British Loyalty and on the 15th of January 1946 the twice-torpedoed tanker was scuttled in the lagoon just off Maradu where, on a calm day, she could, in the mid-1970s, still be seen from the surface onto which she occasionally leaked small quantities of oil.

For the few servicemen who remained at the atoll after the 10th of December, repatriation was on an opportunist basis which meant that the withdrawal continued until early in 1946 with the base being officially closed on the 21st of February and paid off on the 28th of that month. The departure of the last of the servicemen took place without any ceremony, merely the friendly farewells, the good wishes and the genuine expression of thanks to the Maldivians for all that they had tolerated and for their contribution to the Allied cause throughout the war. Given the scale of the world-wide post-war withdrawals it is hardly surprising that there appears to be no surviving records of the final departure nor any file reference to the last serviceman to leave the atoll. Whoever he was, when he left, the Adduans must have been convinced that their brief encounter with a Western lifestyle would never be repeated. They certainly could not have

imagined that in little more than a decade the British would again create a military base on Gan, that they, the Adduans, would stage a rebellion against the Maldivian government and that Abdullah Afif Didi would become the elected president of their breakaway republic, protected by the British military presence at the atoll.

For the islanders of Addu Atoll it was enough, at the beginning of 1946, just to concern themselves with the return to the coconut-and-fish economy of their survival-orientated culture.

ITEM	COST (£)
RNAS Station	
Runways, Taxiways, Roads	47820
Buildings	39150
Waterwells	5500
Minor Works	7530
Plan R	
W/T Transmitting COL, RDF,	
TRU, masts/towers	14350
Fleet Base	
Causeways, Roads	31450
Buildings	18950
Navigation beacons, jetty, etc	7930
Repairs, maintenance, minor works	7320
Total	180000

Figure 7.1: Works costs estimates for Port T, Addu Atoll.

Fig 7.2. Sunderland flying-boat and refuelling tender, Addu Atoll, 1943. (IWM Neg Nº CF 620)

Section 2 – The Post-War Period

VIII   Post-War Poverty and Politics

When the last of the Allied troops had left, the islanders were left to assess the effects of the occupation. Undoubtedly the best legacy from the war was an improved environment. Scrub land had been cleared, swamps drained, mosquito breeding sites destroyed and a road network created, complete with causeways linking many of the islands. On virtually every island there remained the buildings constructed by the troops, in the lagoon there were fewer coral heads to rip into the islanders' dhonis and on every major beach there was a landing jetty with that off the Hitaddu beach extending some four or five hundred yards across the coral shelf. (Fig 8.1) But the military withdrawal deprived the villagers of a source of income, a supply of materials and an emergency medical service. They had also lost the manpower which had brought about, and subsequently sustained, the environmental improvements. The islanders, once they reverted to a subsistence economy, would have little time to spend on the routine maintenance of their environment and without such maintenance the benefits would be short-lived. The scrub would soon reclaim untended ground and the number of insect breeding sites would rapidly increase.

Psychologically, the Adduans had experienced a culture shock. Living alongside the troops had made them only too well aware that life had more to offer than mere survival and they had, to some extent, developed a taste for easier living and for the pleasures, or vices, of the Western world. Their major problem in 1946 was that they had no local economy on which to build an improved lifestyle. Fishing and coconut growing re-emerged as their economic mainstays, providing food for the islanders and some products for export. Chickens were still to be found scratching around most dwellings and small quantities of fruit and vegetables were grown on the islands to add some variety to the local diet. But rice, a staple food for the Maldivians, still had to be obtained, like virtually every other commodity, from India or Ceylon *via* Malé.

The Adduans were too poor and their atoll too remote to attract merchant ships to their islands on speculative trading missions and they had nothing to gain by bartering with the equally poverty-stricken Maldivians who were eking out an existence on the islands to the north of Addu Atoll.

They were thus obliged to rely upon the Maldivian traders who sailed the archipelago in their buggaloes and vedis on a round trip of more than a thousand miles to the market places of Malé and Ceylon: a journey which was hazardous enough between Addu Atoll and Malé but even worse between the Maldivian capital and Ceylon with miles of open ocean to traverse in boats which were notoriously difficult to handle in bad weather.

The islanders did revert to their old subsistence-level lifestyle for the simple reason that they had no alternative; it was a case of adapt or starve, possibly even a case of adapt and starve anyway because there were storm clouds on the horizon, both literally and figuratively.

The climatic storms are a common feature of life on the atoll but they are rarely if ever devastating because the islands are well to the south of the monsoon belt. Gale force winds and torrential rain were common, but they generally lasted for no more than a few hours. Towards the end of July 1948, however, just when the islanders had successfully re-established their traditional lifestyle and were readjusting to their subsistence economy, the atoll was hit by the worst storm in living memory. For several days that month strong winds and heavy seas had prevented the fishermen from taking their dhonis outside the lagoon. On the morning of the 28th the winds became steadily stronger, driving sand off the beaches and bending all but the strongest palm trees. By mid-day the islanders were convinced that this was no ordinary storm and early in the afternoon, with the wind shrieking across the atoll, their worst fears were realised. The outer reef, their protection against the great rollers of the Indian Ocean, was over-run. A wall of water estimated at more than twice the height of a man tore across the reef and bore down on the islands.

No island escaped the onslaught. Gan, lying lower than the others and with fewer palm trees along its beaches, suffered the most. The wave tore across the island, uprooting trees as it went and hurling them against the villagers' fragile huts. As more and more debris was piled up the force of the water was gradually overcome so that by the time the wave had run the length of Gan it was no more than three feet high. The central depression on the island was turned into a saltwater lake with hundreds of stranded fish flapping helplessly in the muddy water. As the artificial lake began to drain away through a natural gully to the beach, the islanders, desperate to get what little benefit they could from the disaster, fell upon this unexpected supply of food. The variety of fish reflected the myriad life of the ocean with small colourful fish from the reef flapping alongside eels, tuna fish, barracuda and sharks.

The water flowing off the island carried with it large numbers of dead rats, together with the islanders' cats and chickens, all slowly drifting out to sea. What was left behind was devastation and a large enough number of dead animals to create a severe health hazard. The villagers of Gan were too pre-occupied to collect and burn the rotting corpses and in a matter of days every corpse had become a feasting and breeding ground for thousands of flies. The flies brought debilitating diarrhoea and sickness to the villages and with several hundred islanders incapacitated it became even more difficult for them to restore normality to the two village communities on Gan. No dwelling had escaped the devastation and no ground crops had survived. Salt water had contaminated the land and fouled all the wells except those on the northern edge of the island which had enjoyed some small measure of protection. It took months for the normal rainfall to mitigate the salt water pollution enough for the other wells to be used and for some of the crops to be re-established. The resourceful Adduans overcame their problems as they always did but it took them a year to return their island to something approaching normality and it was late in 1949 before the last traces of that devastating tidal wave had been removed. By then the only remaining indication of the disaster was the large number of young coconut palms growing where previously there had been mature trees.

Coping with the effects of the natural climate was difficult enough but coping with the effects of the post-war political climate in the Maldives was, for the Adduans, just as problematical. Prior to 1943 power in the Maldives had been vested in the Sultan under an hereditary system which, apart from a fifteen year interlude in the sixteenth century, had survived for over eight hundred years. The last of the hereditary Sultans, Muhammed Shams-ud-din III, was as dictatorial as his predecessors in spite of the supposed curbing of his powers by the 1932 constitution and by the partially elected legislative body, the Majlis. In 1934 he was forced to abdicate and with his departure the hereditary monarchy came to an end and an elective sultanate was introduced. Hasan Nur-ud-din Iskander II became the first elected Sultan and served until 1943 when he was forced to resign.

The Majlis nominated Al Amin Abdul Majeed Didi to succeed Hassan Nur-ud-din but he, in poor health and living much of the time in Egypt, was a reluctant recipient of the honour. Whilst not refusing the title of Sultan Designate he chose to defer his enthronement indefinitely, handing power to a Council of Regency which effectively meant handing power to Muhammed Amin Didi who presided over the Council. Britain formally recognised the Sultan Designate as the head of state but dealt with Amin Didi on all state matters. A highly intelligent and ambitious man, he was outstanding among Maldivians and for as long as Majeed Didi delayed his enthronement Amin Didi was not so much the power behind the throne as the power in front of it. In the early post-war period he was responsible for some of the most significant reforms ever introduced into Maldivian society, many of them beneficial but some disastrous for the effect they had on the national economy and on the lives of the islanders.

Amin Didi had the energy to match his ambitions and he was not content to limit himself to the post of Prime Minister. To increase his control he took on other commitments for the government and to increase his general popularity he widened his sporting and cultural activities. He became the self-appointed Minister for Foreign Affairs, Home Affairs, Finance, Education, Commerce, Public Safety and Justice. As if that were not enough, he added to his control over the nation's affairs by becoming the Commander-in-Chief of the Maldivian militia, a small but adequate force of some four hundred men who were responsible for internal security throughout the archipelago.

His reforms certainly brought about dramatic changes for women in the Maldives; they were freed from the veil, brought into public life, offered government grants to study in Colombo and encouraged to enter Maldivian politics. His other innovations brought electrical power to Malé, promoted improvements in the cultivation of coconuts and vegetables and established the government-owned Bodu stores to control the export of dried fish and break the Bohra merchants' near-monopoly on trade between Malé, Ceylon and India. That innovation, which also curbed the direct trade between the various islands and Ceylon to the disadvantage of the island traders, was tolerated because Amin Didi was so highly regarded. Even he, however, could not enforce his decree that all Maldivians should give up smoking.

His many non-political activities contributed to his popular image; he was the president of four local sports clubs, played for the national football team, was the president of a poetry society, wrote an English language guide book to the Maldives and two Divehi text books on Maldivian history.

His burning ambition was to bring the benefits of the twentieth century to the islands but his approach was economically so naive that it was doomed to failure. He initiated a construction programme to increase the number of public buildings in the islands and to provide more schools. He insisted on the creation of a football field in every sizeable village throughout the archipelago and, in a country where the only cars were in Malé, he instigated the creation of wide roads on all the occupied islands and a series of triumphal arches in the capital, declaring them to be in celebration of the imminent modernisation of the Maldives.

To accommodate those developments it was necessary to order the destruction of large numbers of coconut palms and breadfruit trees and to re-allocate cropland for use as football pitches, although at that time football, which was eventually to become a national sport, was a game for which the islanders had little enthusiasm. The destruction generated hostility from those islanders who relied upon their trees and small plots of land to feed their families and from those for whom such cultivation was a source of income. Fishing, the major industry in the Maldives and the major source of food for most islanders, suffered because most of the islanders who were forced to work on the roads and on the sports pitches were fishermen. Understandably, the islanders resented the intrusions into their normal working lives and the impact on their already low standard of living and yet they remained generally supportive of their Prime Minister.

Amin Didi then compounded the problems facing the Maldivians by borrowing heavily from Ceylon to finance his dreams. By the late 1940s the nation's economy was in such a poor state that virtually every islander was suffering. By the early 1950s the situation had become desperate. Ninety-eight per cent of the nation's export was fish for which Ceylon, the sole buyer, was able to name the price knowing that the Maldivians, with no modern trading vessels, would find it both difficult and expensive to open up other markets. For the Maldivian Council of Regency, Ceylon's domination of the market brought serious problems. During the war, when the import of food from India and Burma had become such a precarious business, Ceylon had sold the Maldivians as much rice, grain and sugar as it could spare and in the post-war years had loaned the Maldivian government the money it needed to invest in Amin Didi's vision of the future.

The balance of trade between the two nations had thus changed dramatically between the mid-1930s and the early 1950s. In 1934 Ceylon paid three million six hundred and forty thousand rupees for fish exported from the Maldives but received less than two thousand seven hundred rupees for the food which was exported from Ceylon to the Maldives. By 1945 the Maldivian government's annual imports of rice, sugar, grain and grain products from Ceylon were costing over one million three hundred thousand rupees and by 1951 the Maldivians' annual bill for food from Ceylon was two million rupees, paid out of the two million nine hundred thousand rupees received for the fish exported from the Maldives. The Council of Regency was thus faced with the task of paying for the nation's other imports, financing the loan from Ceylon and trying to fund a development programme for the Maldives out of approximately one million rupees. It was just not possible. Without some form of foreign aid it was inevitable that the Maldives would remain one of the poorest nations of the world, unable to revitalise its one significant industry, fishing, because it could not afford to import the materials to refurbish its fishing fleet.

Through the late 1940s, whilst the Maldivians were trying to solve their economic problems, British interest in their islands was focused on two matters: the care of the war graves at Addu Atoll and, unbeknown to the Maldivians, the possible construction of a British military airfield somewhere in the archipelago.

As far as the war graves were concerned the Maldivian government displayed the same generously friendly attitude towards Britain that had been so evident throughout the war. Just two months after Addu Atoll had been hit by the worst storm in living memory the Maldivian Government Representative in Ceylon, Ibrahim Ali Didi, informed the United Kingdom's High Commissioner in Colombo that the Maldivian government would meet all the costs of setting up and maintaining a war cemetery at the atoll rather than leave it to the Imperial War Graves Commission or to the British Army's Singapore-based Military Graves Registration and Inquiries Unit which normally did the initial work on the establishment of such cemeteries in the Far East and Asia.

It was really quite remarkable that the Adduans had not left the war graves on Gan to deteriorate along with the rest of their environment. But either out of respect for the dead or under orders from the Maldivian government they did apparently tend the graves, a fact which came to light in the early 1950s when the Imperial War Graves Commission was following up the Maldivian offer to provide individual headstones for the graves and to erect a memorial to those who had been cremated. Matters moved slowly in those days, especially when the Commission was corresponding, *via* the Commonwealth Relations Office, with a government which was in one of the more remote parts of the world and was pre-occupied with staving off economic disaster and starvation amongst its islanders. It would perhaps have been more efficient to have delegated to the Commission's Ceylon Agency, newly created in April 1948, the task of ensuring that the war graves in the Maldives were properly maintained. But, for whatever reason, the Commission chose to pursue the matter, *via* the Commonwealth Relations Office in London, with the Colombo-based High Commissioner for the United Kingdom who corresponded with the Maldivian government *via* the Maldivian Government Representative in Ceylon.

It was inevitable that such an extended chain of communications led to delays of many months and in 1952, without realising that political events in the Maldives and British military planning in London were overtaking their negotiations, the Imperial War Graves Commission was still corresponding with the Maldivian government, sending design details of the permanent headstones which the Commission would like to see erected over the graves and suggesting that the memorial to those cremated at Addu Atoll could appropriately be in the form of a set of panels ' *...to be fixed to the wall of the Gan cemetery ...*'

The British military planning which the Commission was unaware of but which was to negate all the plans for the war cemetery on Gan and lead to such dramatic events in the Maldives, began in the early post-war years when British troops were still deployed throughout the Far East. With India, Pakistan and Ceylon newly independent, the Air Council had to consider the vulnerability of the routes normally used by British military aircraft traversing the Indian Ocean. It was not thought likely that those three nations would curtail such flights through their territories in peacetime but the absence of any alternative air route across the Indian Ocean gave them a powerful bargaining position in any dealings with the British government.

If Britain were to become embroiled in further conflict in the Far East the reactions of those newly independent nations could not be predicted with any certainty and if the British military aircraft of the day were to be denied the use of the Indian sub-continent routes there was no alternative flight path between the east coast of Africa and the Far East. It was reasonable to assume that Ceylon would honour the mutual defence agreement of 1948 and provide staging facilities for all British aircraft in time of war but if India and Pakistan were not prepared to be just as co-operative, the short-range ferrying route for fighter aircraft would be lost and the medium range aircraft would only be able to use the Oman-Colombo-Singapore route by flying virtually unladen. The development of the Woomera test site in Australia and the outbreak of war in Korea proved the point; Britain needed to be able to dispatch military aircraft to the Far East without having to rely on the goodwill of foreign governments whose policies might differ from those of the British.

There were two other established air routes between Britain and the Far East, the Aleutian and the Central Pacific; the 'westabout' routes across the North American continent. Aircraft using the Aleutian route to Singapore covered approximately twelve thousand miles flying *via* Reykjavik, Goose Bay, Winnipeg, Vancouver, Anchorage, Adak, Sheymys, Hokkaido, Iwakuni and Manila. Those which used the Central Pacific route covered some fourteen thousand miles staging through the Azores, Bermuda, New Orleans, San Francisco, Hawaii, Wake, Guam and Manila. Using the westabout routes the RAF aircraft of the day would have taken some ten weeks to move a brigade group from Britain to Singapore, slightly longer than it would have taken to transport the troops by sea.

It seemed that the best way to satisfy Britain's strategic need would be to secure an independent air route across the Indian Ocean by building a series of staging posts on the islands which lay between the east coast of Africa and Indonesia. The Seychelles, the Chagos archipelago, the southernmost reaches of the Maldive Islands, and the Australian Cocos Islands were all conveniently situated as far as Britain was concerned and if airfield facilities were to be made available at each of those locations Britain and her allies would have the choice of trans-oceanic air routes. (Fig 8.2)

The Air Ministry staff selected the Seychelles, Diego Garcia and Addu Atoll as the most promising locations and, subject to the availability of a Far

East Air Force flying-boat, were ready by September 1951 to initiate a survey of all three locations.

Addu Atoll was not British territory and could not therefore be surveyed without permission from the Maldivian government. An Air Ministry approach to the Commonwealth Relations Office brought confirmation from the United Kingdom's High Commissioner in Ceylon that such a survey seemed to be covered by Section 5 of the 1948 agreement but also brought the suggestion that, if possible, it would be better for the Air Ministry to wait until after December when Amin Didi, the Maldivian prime minister, would be visiting Colombo and could be approached directly. Such an approach would avoid the confusion which was quite likely to arise if the request were to be made *via* the Maldivian Government Representative in Ceylon. The Air Ministry staff agreed that delay was preferable to confusion and on the 13th of December their patience was rewarded when the Commonwealth Relations Office was informed that the High Commissioner had spoken to Amin Didi who was happy for the survey to go ahead. The Prime Minister had added that he had recently been to Addu Atoll, could confirm that the old Port T and HMS Maraga buildings were still intact and, with great exaggeration, declared that the old runway was in excellent condition. The Air Ministry readily agreed to a later suggestion from Amin Didi that a Maldivian liaison officer should accompany the survey team to Addu Atoll and within a few weeks had made arrangements with the Headquarters' staff of the Far East Air Force for a Sunderland flying-boat to undertake the survey of the southern Indian Ocean islands from early September to mid-October 1952.

The survey, conducted under the codename 'Ship's Bunk' showed that in the Seychelles, on the island of Gan at Addu Atoll in the Maldives and on Diego Garcia in the Chagos archipelago it was feasible to build runways long enough to accommodate the next generation of long-range aircraft and if that were to be done trans-oceanic air routes could be established.

Relations with India, Pakistan and Ceylon were good enough for the Air Council not to regard the development of an independent air route as urgent, important though it was. Accordingly, the early Ship's Bunk report was supplemented with advice from the Foreign Office, the Colonial Office and the Commonwealth Relations Office before the Council met in 1953 to consider the situation. By that time the political situation in the Maldives had changed dramatically. Whilst the Imperial War Graves Commission

had been trying to discuss the war cemetery at Addu Attol with the Maldivian government and whilst the Ship's Bunk survey was being undertaken the system of government in the Maldives had been heading towards dramatic change.

There had, for several years, been little doubt that the Maldivians would eventually abandon their monarchy; the only uncertainty was the likely timing of the event.

In this instance fate took a hand when, on the 21st of February 1952, Al Amir Abdul Majeed Didi died. The Council of Regency continued to run the nation's affairs as it had done since 1943 but it faced the dilemma of how to replace the head of state. After almost nine years with a Sultan Designate who chose not to be enthroned there was a great lack of respect for the monarchy and growing support throughout the Maldives for the creation of a republic. Within the Council of Regency there was a general feeling that if the monarchy were to be abandoned, Amin Didi would be the best choice for election as the first President of the Republic of the Maldives. Certainly he was still generally popular because the islanders had not laid the troubles of the Maldives at his door. They blamed the absentee Sultan Designate for their troubles and credited Amin Didi with having brought the few post-war benefits which they had received. Only at government level and among the commercial executives had the undesirable effects of Amin Didi's activities lost him some supporters. Nevertheless, if a presidential system were to be created in the Maldives he remained the outstanding presidential candidate. He, however, openly expressed his opinion that although it was not a good idea to abandon the monarchy he had no wish to be their next Sultan.

It is almost certain that he could have restored the Maldivians' belief in the monarchy had he been willing to serve as an elected sultan but it is probable that he could foresee only a reduction of his power if he were to become the next Sultan of the Maldives. The real power for reform was in the hands of the government and the role of figurehead monarch would have meshed badly with Amin Didi's enthusiasm for initiating change: he had his finger in many pies and he was keen to retain the power he had. He would probably have preferred to see the continuation of the monarchy through the election of a sultan of his choice for he could then have continued to be the power in front of the throne. He was, however, open with his opinion that the Maldivians would probably accept nobody but him as head of state. Faced with Amin Didi's refusal to be considered as a candidate for election to the sultanate, the near certainty that no-one else would be acceptable to the people and the growing feeling in favour of abandoning the monarchy, the Council of Regency, acting under Article 80 of the Maldivian Constitution, organised a general referendum to determine whether or not the nation should become a republic.

While the views of the Maldivian people were being sought on the future of their monarchy, Amin Didi was seeking ways of easing the financial plight of his nation. In January 1952, through the Maldivian Government Representative in Ceylon, he had asked Britain for economic aid and on the 20th of March, just one month after the death of the Sultan Designate and three weeks before his nation's referendum on the future of the Maldivian monarchy Amin Didi arrived in Britain. He was seeking treatment in Harley Street for his diabetes but four days later he was in Downing Street, following up his earlier request for economic aid to rejuvenate the Maldivian fishing industry, to obtain some powered vessels and to arrange the provision of technical advice for the Maldivians on all matters from agriculture to the national economy. More precisely he was seeking, over a reasonably short but unspecified period, to repair or replace six hundred of his nation's fifteen hundred boats; to replace one hundred and fifty thousand yards of sail cloth; to obtain twenty tons of mild steel rod for making fishhooks and twenty-five tons of fish oil for treating the timber boats; to acquire two powered ships of two hundred and fifty tons each to ply mainly between Malé and Ceylon and a further two powered ships of fifty tons each to ply among the islands. In total he was asking for approximately one hundred thousand pounds, a reasonable enough sum if the Maldives had been a colony, for the Seychelles had received a quarter of a million pounds for a population which was less than half that of the Maldive Islands. But the possible provision of aid to an independent nation, albeit a British protectorate, created dilemmas for Britain.

The Maldivians could not sponsor themselves for assistance under the Colombo plan and if Britain had sponsored them it would have given the impression that the British government was trying to avoid its obligations towards the protectorate. Admittedly, Britain had cause to feel indebted towards the Maldivians. There was a lingering, but limited, sense of obligation towards them for their wartime support and for their spontaneous offer to create and maintain a military cemetery on Gan at a time when the Adduans had more than enough troubles to keep them occupied. Far more important was the fact that under the 1948 agreement the Maldivians had voluntarily given up their right to conduct their own foreign affairs, agreeing to allow Britain to negotiate on their behalf. For the British that was highly significant because it helped to keep the communists out of the Indian Ocean and that was worth paying for. Finally there were the Air Ministry's plans for a trans-oceanic air route. At Malé the Maldivians were already providing, virtually free of charge, all the facilities needed for the RAF flying-boats which were frequently to be seen in the lagoon and it would have been farcical, but not inconceivable, for Britain to be parsimonious on the matter of economic aid for the Maldivians and then to ask their government for virtually free use of one of their islands for the construction of an airfield to suit Britain's military strategy.

The upshot was a more detailed consideration of Amin Didi's request by a Cabinet Office working party on economic development in South and South-East Asia. From that working party came a proposal that a low key survey, without any prior commitment to provide help, should be undertaken by someone with expertise in the assistance of underdeveloped countries. Accordingly, Mr Milsum, a retired officer from the Colonial Services Agricultural Service, travelled to the Maldives on board the Ship's Bunk aircraft and conducted a brief investigation into the needs of the Maldivians. In his October report he recommended that Britain should supply the sailcloth, fishhooks and fish oil which had been asked for and should arrange for high quality timber to be imported from India because the effects of the Second World War embargo on imported timber were still being felt in the archipelago and without such imports the boat repairs and boat building would have to be undertaken using inferior timber from the islands or from Ceylon. His tentative conclusions on the provision of powered shipping led to a recommendation that a three-hundred-ton steamer and two ninety-ton motor launches would suffice for the trade runs and for inter-island communications. He also recommended the provision of foodstuffs rather than money and the provision of agricultural training to overcome the obsolete, inefficient methods which excluded the use of manure and which failed to check the effects of pests and disease.

Milsum's report was effectively the beginning of a five year saga in which the British government's behaviour reflected a desire to benefit from the strategically convenient location of the Maldives without any real desire to help improve the lives of the Maldivians, whose nation was one of the poorest in the world.

In the early 1950s Britain, still trying to recover from the effects of the war, was receiving economic aid requests from colonies around the world, many of which had suffered severely in the Allied cause. Under those circumstances it was understandable that the British government would be very reluctant to provide aid for an independent nation, albeit a protector-ate. Amin Didi was thus at a disadvantage: when asking for help he could do little more than appeal to the British government's sense of obligation towards the Maldivians and, unfortunately for him, that was rapidly waning. Early in 1952 he was in no position to negotiate or bargain because he had nothing to offer. Quite simply, Amin Didi was not likely to be offered very much until such time as British interests could be served by helping the Maldivians. That time was approaching because the Air Council was considering the development of Addu Atoll as a military base and if Gan were to be chosen as the favoured site for a mid-ocean staging post the Maldivians would undoubtedly benefit from the influx of capital which would accompany the arrival of the military. But Amin Didi, not party to the Air Council deliberations, remained unaware of the true reason for the pending survey of the southernmost islands in the Maldives. Unaware of Britain's dilemma, he was left with nothing more than the hope that the survey might eventually benefit his nation in some way.

Superficially, Amin Didi was, after his country's referendum on the 18th of April, in a better position than he had been in March when first submitting his request for aid. He had become the President Elect of an emergent republic, and that by a unanimous vote. He was also secure in that the change to a republic was overwhelmingly popular: ninety-nine per cent of the voters had declared themselves to be republicans who wanted the monarchy to be abandoned.

To give the Council of Regency time to agree on a new constitution, the sultanate was to end on the last day of 1952. The new status of the Maldives, and of Amin Didi, was to be established, with all due ceremony, on the 1st of January 1953. But for the President Elect there was a price to pay for such overwhelming support. He was, in an almost literal sense, expected to deliver the goods. If he couldn't do that before the end of 1952 he would certainly be expected to generate some signs of economic success early in the life of the new republic. The British ministers did not seem to appreciate the implications which accompanied Amin Didi's election; under the new constitution of the Republic of the Maldives a president was elected for a period of five years and although he could stand for re-election to extend his period in office he could also be deposed prematurely by the Majlis if he were deemed to be unfit for office through mental incapacity or misconduct. In effect he could be deposed for pursuing any course of action which was considered by the Majlis not to be beneficial for the nation or which rendered him unpopular with the electorate.

The Ship's Bunk survey report had, like Milsum's report, been studied by the Commonwealth Relations Office staff during November 1952. The implications of both had been carefully considered and a policy established that any negotiations over Britain's military use of Addu Atoll should not become entangled with negotiations over aid for the Maldives. Strict adherence to that policy of separation, together with military events in Korea deprived Amin Didi of the only bargaining point which he might have been able to use. What the British government failed to realise was that if the President Elect were not helped in his attempts to improve the quality of life for the Maldivians he was quite likely to be deposed and replaced by someone who would drive a very hard bargain over the use of Maldivian territory by the British military.

It was the declaration of a cease-fire in Korea which indirectly helped to bring about Amin Didi's downfall. By the first of January 1953 when the Republic of the Maldives was born and Amin Didi inaugurated as the President, he had failed to obtain an offer of help from the British government and was still unaware of the Air Council's interest in Addu Atoll. Unfortunately for him, the Korean ceasefire removed much of the urgency from the Council's deliberations, leaving the members to discuss the implications of the Ship's Bunk report almost at their leisure. It was thus well into 1953 before they first met to consider how best to secure a trans-oceanic air route from the Middle East to the Far East. By August they were no nearer a decision and they continued to display no great sense of urgency even after the 12th of the month when the communists in Ceylon showed that they could muster enough support to bring Colombo to a standstill and virtually immobilise the entire island. For a further eight months the council members continued to discuss the development options.

There was no perfect solution to their problem. Given staging post facilities on some of the Indian Ocean islands, the RAF's long-range aircraft would be able to fly, fully laden, from the east coast of Africa to Singapore or Australia without entering Indian or Ceylonese air space. Even if a new airfield at Addu Atoll were the only one to be built, it would still be possible to fly the Masirah - Addu Atoll - Cocos Islands route to the Far East with an eighty per cent load and the next generation of long-range aircraft would be able to fly that route fully laden. The medium-range aircraft were not so easily accommodated. If airfields were to be built in the Seychelles and the Maldives those aircraft would still only be able to carry their maximum loads to Singapore and Australia by staging through Ceylon and the Indian territory in the Nicobar Islands: only if flown unladen could they reach the Far East by staging through the Seychelles to the Cocos Islands *via* Addu Atoll or Diego Garcia (Fig 8.2). Because in-flight refuelling was unlikely to be developed to the extent required for medium-range aircraft to take on the long-haul work it had to be accepted that the island-hopping route across the Indian Ocean gave a rather limited, but nevertheless worthwhile, degree of independence.

Of the three suitable sites identified in the Ship's Bunk report that in the Seychelles, where the Air Council would certainly wish to create an airfield as the first stepping-stone between Africa and the Far East, was likely to be the most expensive to develop at an estimated cost of seven hundred thousand pounds. It was not so easy to decide whether the second airfield should be built at Addu Atoll or Diego Garcia. As far as costs were concerned there was nothing to choose between them: each could be developed for an estimated five hundred thousand pounds. There were two arguments to support the choice of Diego Garcia rather than Addu Atoll. To begin with, it was British territory and that weighed heavily in its favour for there was always the possibility that the relationship between the British and Maldivian governments, amicable enough in the early 1950s, could be soured as a result of the turbulence in Maldivian politics. It also offered the shortest route between the Seychelles and the Cocos Islands: a factor which was of less significance than Britain's territorial rights because, whilst the location was really no better than Gan for the trans-oceanic flights, its more southerly location was a disadvantage as far as fuel deliveries were concerned.

Whichever of the two sites were to be chosen the local population would have to be evacuated, for neither island was large enough to accommodate a military base alongside the indigenous communities. There was little doubt that the Diego Garcians would suffer far more from forced evacuation than would the islanders of Gan for they would have to leave their archipelago and settle elsewhere in the world; the Gan islanders could simply move onto a neighbouring island in their own atoll. That was not a consideration which influenced the members of the Air Council, it was seen as a political factor to be dealt with by the Commonwealth Relations Office. What was a consideration for the Council was the safety of the RAF's passengers who would be staging through the mid-ocean base. The council members were all too well aware that both Gan and Diego Garcia were in an area where tropical storms could close an airfield with very little warning and if only one of the sites were to be developed the nearest diversion airfield would be in Ceylon. There was a compelling argument for developing both sites so that each could serve as a diversion airfield for the other. As far as the Air Council was concerned the only argument against the idea of such a twin development was the cost. Consequently the council members submitted their views to the Chiefs-of-Staff Committee in April 1954, inviting the members to approve the construction of two airfields, one in the Seychelles and one at Addu Atoll. The committee was also invited to approve the construction of a third airfield at Diego Garcia, if it was considered to offer value for money. The Chiefs-of-Staff approved the first two and rejected the third.

By then, however, the political situation in the Maldives had changed even more dramatically than had been the case in 1952. The Republic had been born in style on the first of January 1953 with a durbar. Sir Cecil Myers, the United Kingdom's high commissioner in Ceylon who, in the afternoon, had signed an agreement to formalise the relationship engendered by the 1948 agreement, had represented Her Majesty the Queen at the ceremony. In his general report on the ceremony the High Commissioner commented very favourably on the organisation of the day and on the general orderliness of the people. He also contrasted the day's events with those of the similar ceremony in 1948 when no Maldivian women had been permitted to attend; they had been in purdah, viewing the ceremony from behind a specially erected wall. At the 1953 ceremony the effects of Amin Didi's efforts to bring Maldivian women into public life could clearly be seen. Very few of the female spectators wore veils and in the procession of the forty-seven members of the House of The People, eight were women.

For a while the President enjoyed the wholehearted support of the people but the honeymoon period was short-lived. Months of bad weather in the Maldives seriously reduced the fishing haul at a time when the President was palpably failing in his attempts to obtain aid. The already high cost of imported goods continued to rise, in part because of Amin Didi's earlier decision to abandon the official use of the Indian or Ceylon rupee in favour of the Maldivian rupee. Issued on par with the Ceylon rupee but backed only by Indian or Ceylon currency, it quickly ceased to have any value beyond the archipelago and was shunned by everyone who had any choice.

By mid-1953 the people were beginning to blame the new regime for all their problems and from then on the President's days were numbered.

That year, Amin Didi, a sick man whose diabetes and blood pressure were an ever-constant cause for concern, sought medical treatment in Madras during August. Whilst he was in India there were widespread calls from the business executives in Malé for his resignation, the opinion being openly expressed that his ability was declining along with his health. The calls were quickly taken up by the general public and that created a government crisis. The ministers reacted by suspending the constitution and appointing Ibrahim Ali Didi and his cousin, Ibrahim Mohammed Didi, to run the nation's affairs until such time as a general election could be held. When Amin Didi flew back to Malé in an RAF Sunderland there was a hostile crowd waiting for him and his ministers advised him not to go ashore on Malé island but to go instead to one of the smaller islands in the atoll. Reluctantly, he agreed and he was rowed to Dunidu where he was accommodated in a bungalow, was provided with servants and protected by guards. Whilst there he was persuaded, just eight months and three days after his inauguration, to resign his presidency. He remained on Dunidu after his resignation but he was not the kind of man to retire into obscurity and on the 31st of December 1953 he evaded his guards and returned to the capital island.

News of his arrival quickly spread, a crowd gathered within minutes and Amin Didi soon found himself being severely manhandled. He was rescued by government officials but there were injuries on both sides before he got clear. Several people were arrested, charged with causing an affray, tried, convicted and banished together with several of Amin Didi's supporters who were believed to have been attempting a coup with the intention of returning him to power. The former President's health deteriorated rapidly after the experience and on the 19th of January 1954 he died, not, as many newspapers reported, of injuries sustained in the affray but of natural causes. The real tragedy of Amin Didi was that he was a man of great ability and enormous energy but was so impatient to bring progress to the Maldives that he acted unwisely on far too many issues. With his resignation the British government lost a staunch friend who would certainly have supported Britain's use of Addu Atoll as a military base even though his country had been treated far from generously by the British.

The best that Britain could hope for was that Ibrahim Ali Didi would eventually be elected to fill the power vacuum created by the departure of Amin Didi. Ibrahim was an active sixty-five-year-old conservative and well respected elder statesman who had held himself aloof from the Amin Didi regime, had a record of very amicable dealings with Britain during the late 1940s when he had been the Maldivian Government Representative in Ceylon and was the one senior Maldivian politician who would be virtually certain to support the plans for the development of an RAF airfield at Addu Atoll. He was a man whose friendship could usefully have been cultivated but there is no evidence that the Commonwealth Relations Office staff made any special effort to do that.

Certainly there had been no lack of opportunity to strengthen the ties between the two countries. The failure to invite the Maldivian President to the imminent coronation of Her Majesty the Queen could have been reconsidered but was not, simply on the grounds that in 1937 the then Sultan of the Maldives had not been invited to the coronation and it was therefore not appropriate to invite a president whose status was deemed to be lower than that of a sultan. There had also been a fresh opportunity for Britain to offer aid to the Maldives when, in May 1953, Ibrahim Ali Didi made an impassioned plea to Britain, and to anyone else who would listen, for the immediate provision of a thousand tons of food grain to help avert a famine in the archipelago. Pakistan, itself a poor nation, responded with a gift of five hundred tons of rice and the Ceylon government, which had already loaned considerable sums of money to the Maldivians, offered a further loan of three hundred thousand rupees conditional upon it being used to purchase food from Ceylon. The British government, however, had ignored Ali Didi's plea for help.

Eventually help did come from Britain but it was not in response to the May appeal made by Ali Didi, nor even in response to the second, more urgent, plea which he made in September; it was a very belated reaction to Amin Didi's request of March 1952. Even though that request had been fully supported by the Milsum report it was late in 1953, some time after Amin Didi's resignation, before the British government agreed to provide the aid so sought after by the former President. For him, the promise of materials for the rejuvenation of the Maldivian fishing industry came too late. Ironically, one result of the delay was that the Maldivians gave Ali Didi the credit for this success, strengthening his position and making him even more pro-British than before.

The British offer was certainly not generous but it did guarantee that over a three year period virtually all the materials originally asked for by Amin Didi would be supplied: twenty thousand yards of sailcloth; one thousand pounds of cotton yarn; three thousand feet of quarter-inch diameter rod for making fishhooks; two thousand bamboo fishing rods; five tons of crude fish oil with which to treat the timber boats and four hundred pounds of lead. In total, the materials were sufficient to refurbish several hundred fishing boats and in the early months of 1954 when the first consignment began to arrive in Malé the Maldivians embarked upon a massive renovation programme for their fishing fleet.

By the time Britain had started to send the promised materials, the Maldivian system of government had undergone another upheaval. Ibrahim Ali Didi and his cousin had initially run the nation's affairs with the general support of the islanders but it had become increasingly obvious during the later months of 1953 that the Maldivians who had voted so overwhelming to abandon their monarchy had, after only eight months experience of a presidential republic, decided that they had had enough. They blamed Amin Didi and the newly created republican status of their nation for the continuing deterioration of the Maldivian economy and were openly voicing support for the return to a sultanate. A national referendum was held and the predictable result was that a large majority voted to abandon the presidential form of government and to reinstate an elected monarch as the Sultan of the Maldives.

The people chose Mohammed Farid Didi, son of the late Sultan Designate to be their next head of state and on the 7th of March 1954, less than two months after the death of their first President, the Maldivians enthroned Farid Didi. A general reshuffling of ministerial posts with Ibrahim Ali Didi becoming Prime Minister, by far the most significant appointment as far as the British government was concerned, followed the abandonment of the presidential system. Since the arrival of the materials for the rejuvenation of the fishing fleet had so fortuitously followed his international plea for help he had become even more highly regarded in Malé and, increasingly pro-British, he could be relied upon to support a request to build a military base at Addu Atoll although he was bound to be constrained more than Amin Didi would have been because the first President of the Maldives had been something of a law unto himself. If ever there was a good time for Britain to stop being parsimonious over aid to the Maldivians it was in 1954 when Ali Didi needed to build upon his recently acquired reputation and when Britain needed to establish an RAF staging post in the archipelago.

But the British ministers, still not committed to the provision of any powered shipping for the Maldivians even though they were generally sympathetic towards the idea, continued to prevaricate, arranging for Mr Cruickshank from the United Kingdom's High Commission in Ceylon to visit Malé in the latter half of 1954 to discuss the general situation in the archipelago and, in particular, the need for powered shipping. His report on the general situation merely confirmed all that had been said by Milsum and others. In essence the Maldivians needed practical help and considerable sound advice on everything from agriculture to national economics. His report on their need for powered shipping was straightforward enough but it was to be the starting point of a saga which lasted for several years and which was to show Britain, once again, as a country in which self-interest overrode a sense of obligation

The Maldivians had a solitary fifty-ton motor vessel and were thus almost entirely dependent upon sailing ships for their trade with Ceylon and India and for most of the inter-atoll trading in the archipelago. The two largest sailing ships were the government-owned 'Atthiyar Raham' and the 'Fathul Bari', both very much in need of repair. Britain's first proposal, made to the Maldivian Prime Minister in April 1954 *via* the High Commission in Colombo, was to repair the two ships and add an auxiliary power unit to the larger vessel, a proposal which the Prime Minister accepted very happily. In August, however, the two ships were inspected and found to be unsafe for use at sea during the monsoon period and that first proposal had therefore to be abandoned in favour of Cruickshank's second suggestion that a secondhand single-screw coaster should be purchased, probably at a cost of about fifteen thousand pounds. That alternative was acceptable to the

Maldivians provided the ship had a capacity of about thirty thousand cubic feet and was suitable for the type of work envisaged.

It was January 1955 before the British government, long on promises but short on action, began to search for a ship which would serve the Maldivians' purpose. By then Britain was virtually committed to the construction of a strategic base at Addu Atoll, only the approval of the Maldivian government and the financial details of the lease needed to be finalised. Given that Maldivian goodwill was central to the execution of Britain's military strategic planning it is remarkable that economic aid for the Maldivians should have been so reluctantly provided and that the provision of the promised ships should have developed into a three-year saga with Britain behaving in a way which would have tried the patience of any government in the world, let alone one which was trying to avert an imminent famine and was looking for help to a nation which it had generously helped in the recent past. By April, three vessels which had been short-listed on the basis of specification and price had been given a preliminary inspection. Each was found to be in poor condition and all were rejected. As the search for suitable ships continued it became apparent that fifteen thousand pounds was a gross underestimate of the market price for a fully powered vessel of around three hundred and fifty tons deadweight.

With the world demand for shipping steadily increasing, prices were rising even for elderly vessels in quite poor condition and it soon became obvious that at least thirty-five thousand pounds would be needed to buy the type of ship which the Maldivians required. By June the Commonwealth Relations Office accepted that there was no alternative but to argue the case for more money and, after many months, managed to obtain an extra twenty-five thousand pounds from the Treasury. That debate ran the affair into the beginning of 1956 with the search for a ship effectively in abeyance pending the Treasury decision. The arguments were protracted partly because of a suggestion, made at a meeting in Colombo on the 1st of September 1955, that the Maldivians lacked mercantile training and the technical skills needed to run a fully-powered ship and that when such a ship was eventually purchased it should be owned by Britain for three years during which time it should be managed by United Kingdom agents in Colombo for the benefit of, and at the expense of, the Maldivian government.

This rather arrogant suggestion, which attached strings to a previously unconditional offer, led the Treasury officials to ask for details of the costs, to the Maldivian government, of chartering a ship and of having a ship maintained and run by an appointed agent in Colombo. It was several months before they accepted that accurate comparative figures could not be obtained by the High Commissioner without details of the ship and its usage. It was January 1956 before that request was dropped and some eight weeks later before the Treasury was finally persuaded to allow the Commonwealth Relations Office to spend up to forty thousand pounds on a vessel. By then the fact that the original request had been for two ships, one for inter-atoll use and one for the Malé-Colombo run, had apparently been long-forgotten or ignored. The focus had shifted to the provision of one fully-powered vessel capable of making the Malé-Colombo run throughout the monsoon season, very much in accordance with Cruickshank's earlier recommendation to install an auxiliary power unit in one of the Maldivian sailing ships or, if that were not practical, to purchase one powered vessel to ply the Malé-Colombo route.

The worldwide search for a suitable ship continued and in April 1956 it appeared to have been successful. In Australia the MV Comara, a twenty-year-old ship some one hundred and seventy-five feet long with an operating speed of ten knots was up for sale and could be inspected, bought and sailed to Malé for a total cost of thirty-nine thousand seven hundred and fifty pounds. Although, at eight hundred and twenty tons deadweight, it was much heavier than the provisional specification agreed with the Maldivians it appeared to be such a good choice that the High Commissioner, following up the earlier proposals on the ownership and management of the vessel had, by the 7th of May, reached a tentative agreement with the Eagle Star Lines (Colombo) to manage the ship for three years at a cost of one thousand rupees a month plus five per cent brokerage on outward freight runs from the Maldives and one-and-a-half per cent or two per cent on inward freight runs. By mid-May the Ministry of Transport and Civil Aviation had confirmed that on a preliminary check the Comara appeared to be in good condition and was provisionally acceptable.

The Maldivian Government Representative in Colombo, on being informed of all this, consulted his Prime Minister by radio and discovered that he did not share the British enthusiasm for the Comara. He thanked Britain for the offer but declared that the ship was far too large and would be too expensive to run. He re-iterated that the Maldivians really needed two vessels, one with a capacity of one thousand five hundred to two thousand bags for inter-atoll work, the other with a capacity of five thousand to six thousand bags, and an approximate deadweight of three hundred and twenty-five to four hundred tons, for the Malé-Colombo route. In all probability it was Britain's attitude and not the size of the ship which had led to the Maldivian Prime Minister's rejection of the Comara. The casual assumption that the Maldivians would just accept the agency management scheme for the ship, provisionally arranged without any consultation, was insulting and although Ibrahim Ali Didi would never say so, it almost certainly brought about the rejection of this, the first suitable ship to be offered to the Maldivians since the promise had first been made two years earlier.

Whatever the reasons for the rejection of the Comara the result was a return by Britain to the earlier proposal to purchase an auxiliary schooner capable of sailing the Indian Ocean during the monsoon season. By July two ships which appeared to be suitable and which were for sale had been located. The High Commissioner informed Ali Didi of Britain's proposal to purchase an auxiliary schooner only to discover that the Maldivian Prime Minister was not over-enamoured of the idea. Consequently, the Commonwealth Relations Office was informed that Ali Didi was grateful for the help offered to the Maldivians and, although he appeared to have no objection in principle to the idea of an auxiliary schooner rather than a fully-powered ship, the all-important considerations were the condition and the capacity. His preference, however, was still for a fully-powered ship, to be owned by the Maldivian government and run by the Maldivian National Trading Corporation, an organisation which his government regarded as totally competent, with Maldivians holding four of the five directorships and an Indian with appropriate expertise holding the fifth.

Ali Didi discussed the British proposal with his cabinet ministers, subsequently passing on to the United Kingdom's High Commission in Colombo the result of their deliberations. The Cabinet's view was that for the Malé-Colombo run the Maldivians needed a fully-powered vessel with a capacity of thirty to thirty-two thousand cubic feet. They suggested that if it were not possible to buy such a vessel, one should be built, with the Maldivians contributing any costs in excess of the British offer of forty thousand pounds. If that were to become necessary the Maldivians could, during the

construction period, buy an auxiliary schooner to ply between Malé and Colombo. Then, with the newly-constructed ship commissioned, the auxiliary schooner could be relegated to inter-atoll work. Ali Didi accepted that, under that scheme, a captain and an engineer would initially be needed to train the Maldivians to operate the auxiliary schooner but that, he stated, could be easily arranged. He then added that, apart from the provision of suitable ships, he was keen to obtain radio sets for inter-atoll communication, preferably installing them before the trading ships began their operations.

The High Commissioner, rather surprised by this turn of events, sent a telegram to the Commonwealth Relations Office on the 24th of August 1956 giving details of the Maldivian government's proposals and adding:

> '...I made no comment on these rather ambitious plans. The Prime Minister's attitude throughout (has been) remarkably, even tiresomely, consistent. He has always said he wants two ships, one fully engined for Colombo/Malé, one smaller for inter-atoll work. Moreover, Maldivians are poor and no less greedy than other Asians and are reluctant to lose any part of the forty thousand pounds by accepting an inferior ship which does not fully meet their requirements.'

The response from London pointed out that it would take some twenty months and sixty-five thousand pounds to build a new ship whilst the cost of two auxiliary schooners, purchased and delivered to Malé, would be approaching forty thousand pounds, probably just leaving enough money to buy the radio transceivers which the Maldivians wanted. What puzzled the Commonwealth Relations Office staff was the apparent ability of the Maldivians to find the money to pay some twenty-five thousand pounds towards the cost of building a ship in addition to buying an auxiliary schooner. If they really could do that they could just as easily meet their needs from their own resources by buying two auxiliary-powered schooners.

The more likely explanation of course, was that the Maldivians had no real appreciation of the costs involved and actually had neither the cash nor the credit for such payments. It also seemed absurd to the Commonwealth Relations Office to provide a captain and engineer if the Maldivians claimed to be competent to operate the ships, subject, perhaps, to some diesel engine training. The matter was debated and argued over but the outcome was good for the Maldivians; the High Commissioner was given the authority to offer the Maldivian government two auxiliary powered schooners, one having a capacity of at least twenty-six thousand cubic feet, the other a smaller vessel with a capacity relevant to that of whichever larger vessel was purchased. The offer was to include the proviso that radio sets would be provided if, after the purchase and delivery of the two ships, there was enough money left out of the forty thousand pounds granted by the Treasury. The High Commissioner and the Maldivian Prime Minister exchanged letters confirming this arrangement so that there would be no misunderstanding and that left the way clear for Britain to make a firm offer for any suitable ship without risking a subsequent Maldivian rejection.

Ali Didi reiterated the need for a captain and an engineer for procedure familiarisation and for engine maintenance training, probably an arrangement which would be needed for about six months. The High Commissioner had by then become philosophical about the request, explaining in a telegram to London on the 31st of August that it was:

> '…tiresome to request this at this late stage but it is reasonable and ensures the ship will not break down through inexpert handling in the early stages. The Maldivians are increasingly keen to get help under the Technical Cooperation Scheme and this could be a harmless way of supplying it.'

By then it was the end of August 1956 and although Britain's plans to build a military base at Addu Atoll were well advanced, the provision of a ship for the Maldivians still seemed to be no more than a promise, at least until the 31st. Events moved rapidly that day. The High Commissioner informed London that an agreement had been reached with Ali Didi. The Commonwealth Relations Office immediately passed that information on to the Ministry of Transport and Civil Aviation, and was informed, that same afternoon, that there appeared to be four suitable ships available and that each would be checked as soon as possible.

Attention quickly focused on the Turriddu Scuderi which appeared to be the best ship although Ali Didi was concerned that the vessel, which promised eight knots, would only make an inadequate three or four in a monsoon. By mid-October the ship had not been surveyed and, whilst the Commonwealth Relations Ofice was becoming concerned about the delay, the owners took advantage of what they knew to be a sellers' market, procrastinated, increased the price and offered insufficient time to have the vessel's capacity measured. A provisional price of thirteen thousand pounds was offered and accepted in mid-November on condition that the buyer only conducted a superficial inspection. By then delivery of the ship from the Mediterranean to the Indian Ocean could not be made *via* the Suez Canal for at least several months and the Commonwealth Relations Office agreed that it would be best to let the deal rest until the canal clearance was well under way. That disappointed Ali Didi who felt that the deal would fall through. It did, but not, as he feared, because Britain was reneging on the agreement; it collapsed because of the attitude of the owners and the suspect condition of the ship. The Ministry of Transport and Civil Aviation had not, however, been idle during the protracted consideration of the Turridu Scuderi. Eight other ships had been located including two motor vessels, the Asoka and the Bhoja, which had been built for the Indian Navy as minesweepers for use in the Indian Ocean.

It did not take long for the Ministry of Transport and Civil Aviation to discover that all the auxiliary-engined schooners which were for sale at around twenty thousand pounds were in poor condition; one actually sank in a storm off Funchal before an inspection could be arranged. Once again the Commonwealth Relations Office was left with no real alternative but to approach the Treasury for a further increase in the grant.

Accordingly, C J Alport wrote to the Financial Secretary to the Treasury, Enoch Powell, with a proposal to purchase either two small ships to make up the required capacity or to obtain a fully powered ship of approximately thirty thousand cubic feet capacity to complement the Asoka or Bhoja which could be used for inter-atoll work. Before putting a price on his latest proposal Alport made the point that facilities for the new RAF base at Addu Atoll had been obtained on terms which were very favourable to Britain and that an important element in the discussions between the British and Maldivian governments had been the understanding that Britain would meet the Maldivians' shipping requirements quickly and reasonably generously. Conceding that Powell might feel that it would have been better to pay a more economic rate for the airfield than to confuse the issue with the general problem of economic assistance for the islanders, Alport could only confirm that that had not been done and it was therefore reasonable to compare the expenditure on shipping with the bargain-price lease obtained by Britain for the airfield facilities. Against that background Alport then asked for approval to spend an estimated eighty thousand pounds on ships for the Maldivians or, at most, a maximum of ninety-five thousand pounds.

So 1956 ended and 1957 began with the Maldivian government waiting for the ever-elusive ship while the British government was preparing to send the first group of servicemen to Addu Atoll to begin work on the RAF's Indian Ocean staging post.

There had never been any real doubt on the part of the British that the Maldivian government would allow them to build at Addu Atoll because there was a long history of Maldivian loyalty to the British Crown. But in the mid-1950s there were many factors which were likely to complicate what was, at first sight, a straightforward operation.

The Air Ministry's Works Directorate survey of Addu Atoll was not undertaken until late in 1955, by which time the trans-oceanic route had assumed greater significance because of political developments in the Far East and greater urgency because of the decision to use the RAF's Britannia fleet to transport troops between Britain and the Far East after 1958.

There were also the political developments in Asia and the Near East casting shadows over the Air Council's plans for Addu Atoll. The increasing mood of nationalism in Egypt could easily be picked up by the Maldivians either through Moslem fellowship or through the polemics at the University of Cairo where some of the most able Maldivians studied, often as a prelude to service in the Maldivian government. More significantly, the Indian government was arguing for a neutralist, non-aligned, policy for the whole of Southern Asia and was openly against the creation of new foreign bases in the Indian Ocean, particularly by the Western powers.

The advice received from the High Commissioner in Ceylon was no less worrying. His picture of the Republic of the Maldives was of a nation where there was no system of democratic opposition to the government; where the normal method of changing government was by revolution; where, for historical and geographical reasons, foreigners were treated with suspicion; where there was a continuing fear of loss of national independence; where the government would not wish to risk creating a permanent settlement of other Asians, especially of Hindus and Buddhists from India or Ceylon and where communications between the British and Maldivian governments were problematical, not least because there was no British Government Representative anywhere in the archipelago. It was true that the Maldivian Prime Minister would undoubtedly welcome the British plan to redevelop the old wartime base at Addu Atoll but there was some uncertainty about the new regime's attitude towards the plans, particularly in view of Britain's cavalier attitude towards the provision of aid.

There was, however, one major factor which was to Britain's advantage. The Maldivian nation was so poverty-stricken that its government was unlikely to block the development plans for Addu Atoll out of pique over the shabby treatment it had received from Britain since the end of the war. The development of a military base at the atoll would provide a much-needed boost to the Maldivian economy and it was therefore likely that, once the base had been established, future Maldivian governments would accept the British presence at Addu Atoll for as long as the economic benefits continued.

Fearful of the political complexities in the newly-created Sultanate, the British government attempted to secure tenure of Gan and obviate any political problems by asking the Maldivian government to consider selling the island of Gan to Britain rather than leasing it. That was asking too much. The idea met with widespread opposition within the Maldivian government and by the end of 1956 Britain was left with a simple choice: either accept leasehold tenure or abandon the development plans for Addu Atoll. Britain accepted the leasehold agreement and arrangements were made for work to start on the atoll sites on the islands of Gan and Hitaddu in 1957.

Whilst the Maldivians were intermittently trying to avoid mass starvation, abandoning and then recreating their sultanate and generally trying to regenerate their fishing fleet, and whilst the British government was mainly interesting itself in the military strategic value of the archipelago, the members of the Imperial War Graves Commission were continuing to ask questions about the war graves at Addu Atoll. In 1953 Amin Didi, the first President of the new Republic, had reaffirmed his government's 1949 offer to have all the work done on the Gan military cemetery, including the refurbishment and future maintenance of the necessary headstones and memorial panels, at his government's expense. By mid-1954 with Amin Didi dead and the sultanate recreated, Mr Zaki, the Maldivian government representative in Ceylon, had guaranteed that the new regime would honour Amin Didi's commitment. But the United Kingdom's High Commissioner in Ceylon was advising the Imperial War Graves Commission not to pursue the matter for a while, explaining that the new regime had troubles enough just struggling for survival. The establishment of a military cemetery on Gan thus became as protracted an affair as any other undertaking in which the Maldivians were involved. In September 1954 the High Commissioner sent to London two reports on the subject. The first, on the 24th of September, referred to a recent visit to the Maldives by one of the staff of the Trade Commissioner's Office in Ceylon who, on his return, reported that the Maldivian Prime Minister had assured him that the graves, all of which were on Gan, were properly looked after and that he, the Prime Minister, had promised to inspect them, to have them photographed and to send copies of the photographs to the High Commissioner. The second report, sent to London five days later, referred to yet another report, produced by the RAF, which quoted the Malé Postmaster General as saying that:

> 'Headstones have been erected: they are in the responsibility of the Maldivian Government vested in the Atol (sic) headman, the panels have been placed in the Gan cemetery to commemorate the dead who have no graves.'

Appreciative of the promise of a set of photographs and an apparent commitment to maintain the cemetery in good condition, the War Graves Commission was anxious to establish a pattern of inspections because experience had shown that the upkeep of war graves tended to be reduced after a few years. Accordingly, the Commission wrote to the Commonwealth Relations Office asking whether it would be possible for the High Commissioner in Colombo to make an occasional inspection of the cemetery, a suggestion which showed no real appreciation of the remoteness of Addu Atoll. The wartime airstrip on Gan had long since been taken over by scrub vegetation and by the 1950s Gan was accessible from Ceylon only by chartering a boat or by making a precarious twelve hundred mile round trip on board a relay of Maldivian boats which plied the islands but which did not make regular return trips from Ceylon to the southern atolls of the archipelago. On being advised by the Commonwealth Relations Office that the remoteness of the atoll left the High Commissioner with no alternative but to rely upon the goodwill of the Maldivian government, the War Graves Commission accepted the situation, agreeing that an annual enquiry of the High Commissioner would be more appropriate.

By April 1955 no photographs had been received and on the 21st of the month the High Commissioner informed the Commonwealth Relations Office that Ali Didi had not yet visited the cemetery but had reiterated the promises to provide care for the war graves and to send photographs of the cemetery and the commemorative panels. By December there was a message from the Maldivian Prime Minister saying 'I personally went and inspected the war graves. They were very well kept and looked after. I also gave further instructions for their upkeep.' The message was accompanied by a promise that photographs would be forwarded later. Finally, on the 2nd of May 1956, some four years after the War Graves Commission had first raised the matter, Mr Zaki, the Maldivian government representative in Colombo sent two sets of photographs to the United Kingdom's High Commissioner. One set showed the graves of Christian soldiers, the other showed those of the Muslim soldiers. The photographs were duly forwarded to the War Graves Commission, but were subsequently lost or accidentally destroyed.

The members of the Commission had, of course, been unaware of the British interest in establishing an independent air route across the Indian Ocean and of the Air Council's investigation into the possible development of Gan as a mid-ocean staging post. By the time that information reached them, the first RAF contingent had already established a base on the island and the men were beginning to clear the old wartime runway. the Commission's executive was left with no choice but to abandon their plans for improving Gan's military cemetery.

At the Commission's executive committee meeting on the 18th of July 1957 the issue was high on the agenda with the chairman explaining that the development of a military airfield on Gan meant that it would not be possible to erect satisfactory permanent headstones on the war graves. In the course of the subsequent discussion the committee members were reminded that in 1949 the Commission had accepted an offer from the Maldivian government to erect Commission-designed headstones on the graves of the twenty-six soldiers of the Indian Army known to have been buried at the atoll and a memorial to the forty-two who were known to have been cremated. Unfortunately, since the death of Amin Didi it had been almost impossible to obtain precise information about the provision of headstones and a memorial. The chairman explained that after the announcement that an RAF airfield was to be created on Gan the Commission had asked the Air Ministry for a report on the state of the war graves on the island and the effect of the construction programme.

The report had shown that there were four separate cemeteries on Gan and that it was impossible to establish whose remains were buried in which grave. Two of the cemeteries were in areas where new RAF buildings were to be erected and the remaining two were in the 'funnel' approach where structures above ground level were prohibited. The Air Ministry had therefore asked for the headstones, which bore no details of the interred servicemen, to be removed and had offered to provide land elsewhere on the island as a site for a memorial. In the report it was confirmed that there was no possibility that any of the graves would be disturbed by the construction work and it was suggested that the graves should remain undisturbed and that a monument should be erected as a memorial to the men of the Commonwealth armed forces who had died at the atoll and been buried or cremated there. The committee agreed that such a memorial should be erected. The Commission's chairman duly wrote to the Air Ministry and, late in 1957, an appropriate site for the monument was selected.

In January 1958 a letter from the War Graves Commission to the Commonwealth Relations Office set out the background to the affair, adding that the monument could not be erected until the airfield construction work was almost complete, probably in a year or two. The letter then continued:

'There remains the small but important point of the Imperial War Graves Commission's title to the little plot of land, no more than ten square yards, on which the monument will stand. They do not wish to own the site but merely to obtain some positive assurance that its use for the purpose of a memorial will be safeguarded in perpetuity. Can you please give us some general indication of the arrangement between the UK Government and the Maldivian Government for the lease of the island and advise us as to whom the Imperial War Graves Commission might approach to obtain the assurance I have mentioned?'

The reply from the Commonwealth Relations Office suggested that it would not be appropriate, at that time, to raise the question of use in perpetuity of the small plot of land. Incorrectly stating that Gan island had been leased from the Maldivian government for one hundred years, the writer added:

'You will no doubt consider this sufficient security for the time being. If you eventually wish to obtain a grant of the land in perpetuity it would be as well to leave any negotiations over for a year or two until the airfield is

formally established. We should then be asked to help with the negotiations through our High Commission in Colombo.'

There the matter rested until April 1960 when a letter from the War Graves Commission, by then re-named the Commonwealth War Graves Commission, raised the issue once more, saying:

'Although it would seem that security of tenure of the site of the memorial is established for the period of thirty years covered by the recent agreement with the Maldive Islands, the Commonwealth War Graves Commission is naturally anxious to obtain a grant to the land in perpetuity. I should be glad therefore to have your views on what steps should be taken to ensure that the tenure of the site of the memorial could be acquired by the Commission in perpetuity at the outset to cover any eventuality such as the closing down of the RAF base at Gan either before or after the conclusion of the period of thirty years.'

The timing of the proposal was unfortunate for it came during a period of acrimony and recriminations between the British and Maldivian governments as a result of the unilateral declaration of independence by the islanders at Addu Atoll. It was not therefore surprising that the reply suggested that the Maldivian government would regard with great suspicion any request for a gift of land, particularly of land at Addu Atoll. The advice from the Commonwealth Relations Office, to postpone any approach for at least eighteen months, was accepted by the Commonwealth War Graves Commission, the matter was dropped and actually appears never to have been pursued again. The memorial, which was erected on a small grassed area in front of the station headquarters at RAF Gan, is in the form of a rectangular stone pillar. On three of its faces there are marble panels bearing the names of those commemorated. On the fourth face a similar panel carries the following inscription in English, Hindi and Urdu:

1939 – 1945
THOSE COMMEMORATED HERE DIED IN THE
SERVICE OF THEIR COUNTRY

THE MORTAL REMAINS OF SOME WERE COMMITTED
TO FIRE AND OTHERS LIE BURIED ELSEWHERE ON
ADDU ATOLL

When the Commission's records were updated the original list of sixty-eight men was revised and the names of seventy men were inscribed on the memorial. Their ages are not given but the near-complete records held by the Commonwealth War Graves Commission show that they ranged from sixteen to fifty. Some may have been older; none was likely to be younger. Those honoured, and their ages where known, are:

Abdull Aziz, 28; Abu Sidding Abdul Huq; Alu Khan, 42; Anthony, 32; Appaduri, 24; Appu, 37; Bala Krishna Nair, 25; Banerjee, 28; Barkat Ali, 20; Baru, 36; Budiya Rahman, 27; Chandgi Ram, 40; Chhote, 36; Chiplunkar, 19; Dewa, 30; Dhana Singh, 24; Digambar, 28; Faqir Shah, 20; Gambhir Singh, 27; Ghulam Haidar, 16; Ghurahu, 25; Gopal, 22; Hajee Mea Baba; Har Chand, 28; Hasan Muhammad, 32; Inayat Ullah, 31; Jafar Ali, 28; Jagan, 29; Jahan Khan, 27; Joseph, 27; Kala Ram, 36; Kalu, 26; Khadim Ali, 46; Krishna Deokar, 36; Kumaran, 30; Lal Chand; Manickam, 26; Manikkam, 23; Mast Singh, 22; Mela Singh, 22; Muhammad Akbar, 21; Muhammad Alam, 50; Muhammad Aziz, 37; Muhammad Khan, 24; Muhammad Tufail, 40; Munuswami, 30; Nayadi Kutty, 21; Nur Muhammad, 30; Pillai, 23; Polu Ram, 32; Pyara Singh, 28; Rup Singh, 21; Rup Singh, 27; Sadhu Ram, 26; Sahib Din, 36; Sangappa Godemmi, 26; Sardar Khan, 21; Shah Ismail, 25; Shah Wali, 42; Shamsher Chand Katoch, 42; Sher Khan, 32; Sher Muhammad, 26; Tej Singh, 43; Teja Singh, 19; Thimappa, 21; Thurai, 24; Tunda, 28; Virappan; Yashwant Tukaram Chauhan, 22; Zaina Din, 50

The only names on the memorial are those of the Indian troops who died at the atoll. Those men who died there after being brought ashore from the Cornwall, the Dorsetshire and the Paladin under the circumstances described on pages 37 and 65 are not identified, nor are Lieutenant John Robb RM, an engineering officer who died there on the 28th of October 1942 and Sergeant Ernest Hinkins of Nº 2 Anti-Aircraft Regiment, Mobile Naval Base Defence Organisation 1, who died there on the 30th of November 1942.

There may well be others whose names are not recorded.

The memorial still stands where it was erected; respected and cared for by the Maldivians (Fig 8.3).

Fig 8.1. The Hitaddu jetty in the mid-1960s.

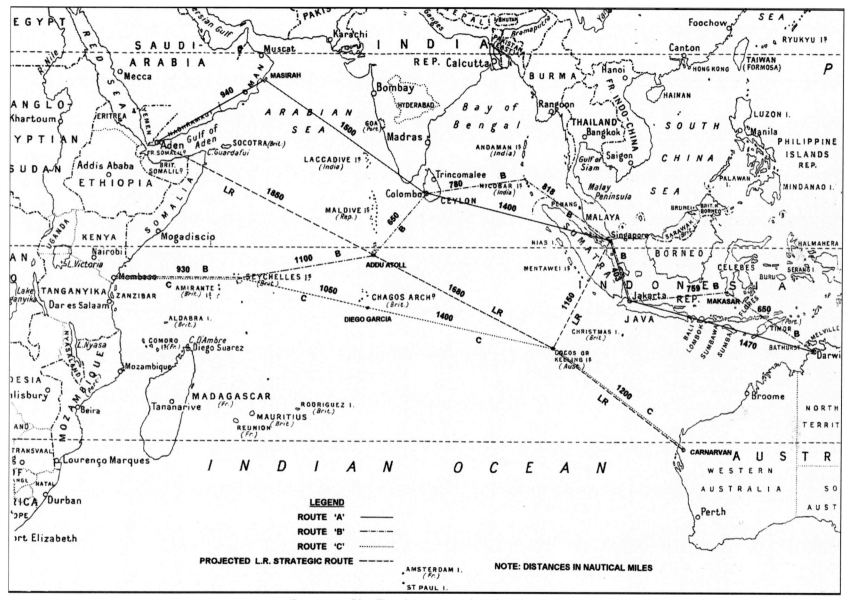

Figure 8.2. Possible military air routes across the Indian Ocean, 1960

Fig 8.3. The war memorial on Gan, 1971.

Section 3 – The Return of the Military

IX   The Ship's Flag Detachment

On the 16th January 1957 a small group of airmen, all members of the Airfield Construction Branch, assembled at RAF El Adem some twenty miles from the north coast of Libya. They formed the nucleus of what was to become a twelve-man unit which, under the command of Flight Lieutenant G.M. McNeil, was to be responsible for the first phase of the redevelopment of Gan as a military base. From El Adem the group travelled to Ceylon where they spent nine days assembling stores and equipment, recruiting the remaining members of the team, planning the mission and attending briefings on the sensitive political aspects of the redevelopment programme. On the 27th the twelve-man unit, by then officially known as the 'Ship's Flag detachment', sailed from Trincomalee on board HMS Modeste heading for Addu Atoll *via* Malé, the Maldivian capital. There, on the 30th of January, they were joined by the Maldivian Prime Minister, Ibrahim Ali Didi, who was to accompany them on the rest of their journey. The Modeste entered the Addu Atoll lagoon on the 31st of January and, after Ibrahim Ali Didi had spent some time ashore explaining to the Adduans what was to happen on the islands of Gan and Hitaddu, Flight Lieutenant McNeil and Flight Lieutenant Sellers, the unit's medical officer, waded ashore to locate a suitable campsite on Gan.

By a quarter past nine the following morning the twelve-man unit was ashore, surrounded by enough stores to last for six months. The ship's captain, worried because he was already sailing two days behind schedule, had the anchor raised before the disembarked servicemen had reached the shore and by a quarter to ten the Modeste had sailed out of the lagoon, leaving the men to their own devices. In effect, RAF Gan had been born even though the official postal address was 'Ship's Flag detachment, c/o RAF detachment China Bay'.

The first few hours ashore were hectic but by the end of the first day tents and marquees had been erected; a local supply of drinking water obtained; signals equipment set up; refrigerators installed and the first visitors from Ceylon greeted, hosted and despatched.

Of all those activities, the provision of drinking water had been the most fortuitous. The servicemen sunk their own tubewell early in the day only to discover that it yielded nothing more than a rather milky liquid which smelled strongly of hydrogen sulphide. That left them with the rather worrying possibility that, for at least the first few days, they might be forced to use the water from the village wells even though they had been given dire warnings about the health risks posed by those supplies. When they accidentally discovered one of the old Ship's Bunk wells they checked it without imagining that the water from it would be any better than their tubewell supply. Much to their surprise it yielded water which was drinkable even though it had a peculiar and rather unpleasant taste which just could not be eradicated even by the water purification plant which was installed later in the 1950s. Palatable only when consumed cold from the refrigerator, or when its natural taste was masked by some other flavouring, the water was at least plentiful and as more wells were sunk the local supply increased enough to ensure that none had to be shipped to Gan from Ceylon.

Signals contact, albeit rather poor, had been made with RAF Negombo but contact with the rest of the world could only be made by using Ceylon as a relay station; times and frequencies for transmissions were set from Ceylon, and classified transmissions were kept to a minimum because of the laborious cryptographic system. The arrangement had its advantages for the detachment commander who had dual, or possibly triple, reporting responsibilities. The Ship's Flag detachment was an element of the Far East Air Force, which had its Headquarters in Singapore, but Flight Lieutenant McNeil was responsible to Air Headquarters, Ceylon, for the administrative and functional affairs of his unit and directly to the Director General of Works at the Air Ministry for all construction work. Being only indirectly communicado as far as Singapore and London were concerned may have brought occasional frustrations but it had one obvious advantage: minimum communications meant minimum interference and that left him free to get on with the job as he saw fit.

The first-day visitors who flew in from Ceylon on board one of the RAF's Sunderlands were signals specialists whose interest was not in the day-to-day communications between Negombo and Gan, it was in the Hitaddu site because the intention was that Addu Atoll would become a communications staging post as well as an aircraft staging post and that would require a site bristling with masts and aerials. The plans for Gan already included one aerial farm but even if more could have been physically accommodated on the island they would not have been installed; the intended power of the transmissions was such that they needed to be sited some miles away from the runway to avoid electrical interference with the airfield communications equipment. Hitaddu, several miles across the lagoon, provided adequate separation which was the reason why Britain had leased part of that island along with Gan. The signals specialists arrived from Ceylon on that first day not because of the urgency of the Hitaddu project, which had a lower priority than the work on Gan, but because they were anxious to view the site and discuss the survey which was to be undertaken during the second half of February. They spent only a few hours at the atoll before flying back to Ceylon, apparently satisfied with what they had seen and discussed.

The first phase of the redevelopment programme was expected to last until the middle of March when another twenty men were due to arrive at Gan along with the airfield construction plant and the materials needed for the second phase of the project. During those first six weeks the dozen men in the advance party were expected, with the help of Maldivian labour, to create a base on Gan, to clear, as best they could, the old wartime runway which ran across the island and to remove any dangerous coral heads both from the Sunderland runway area in the lagoon and from the shore landing points. They were also expected to work on Hitaddu, completing a survey of the site and clearing as large an area as possible within the boundaries agreed with the Maldivian Prime Minister during the first few days ashore. Fortunately, the work on the Hitaddu site was not urgent and could, if necessary, be postponed until the arrival of the second group of airmen.

A preliminary reconnaissance soon revealed the extent of the work to be undertaken on Gan. Abandoned since the war, the runway had, like the rest of island, been taken over by scrub and trees. The wartime jetties had virtually disintegrated. The bridge connecting Gan to Fedu had lost its decking, leaving only a disconnected row of piers across the Gan-Fedu gap. In the lagoon the coral had been left to grow undisturbed for twelve years with the result that every navigation channel leading to the beaches was obstructed and, far more dangerously, large coral heads were lurking just below the surface in the area earmarked as a runway for the Sunderlands. Miraculously, no aircraft had fouled the uncharted growths but it was

obvious that coral clearance would have to be started without delay. Finally, there was the general health risk posed by the reappearance, over twelve years, of innumerable breeding sites for the diverse insect population of the island and for the colonies of rats which had thrived since the departure of the Commonwealth troops at the end of 1945.

Fortunately, much of the work required unskilled labour and there was no shortage of that, at least for the first week. Ibrahim Ali Didi was as keen a supporter of the redevelopment programme as his predecessor had been and he remained at Addu Atoll during those early days to ensure that the locally-based Maldivian government representative worked closely with McNeil, hiring and paying whatever Maldivian labour was required. With the Adduans initially employed on site clearance and on the erection of kadjan buildings the base camp improved rapidly and on the 6th of February the Maldivians even found time to make and erect a flagpole so that at half past two that afternoon, with all due ceremony, the detachment's first ensign was hoisted.

The arrangements for paying the Adduans to work for the RAF were simple, administratively convenient for the Air Ministry and financially attractive for the Maldivian government. McNeil, who held an RAF imprest account, was not involved in the payment of wages to the local labour force, his funds were intended solely for circulation within his unit because the Maldivians were not supposed to deal in Sterling. The Adduans were paid by their government's representative, each labourer receiving a measure of rice and two Maldivian rupees, less tax, for an eight-hour working day. On receipt of certified bills, the Air Ministry reimbursed the Maldivian government in Ceylon rupees using parity as the exchange rate even though the real value of the Ceylon rupee was at least double that and could often be traded on the black market at ten times the value of the Maldivian rupee. The Air Ministry thus avoided all direct dealings with the local labour force at a price considered worth paying whilst the Maldivian government made a handsome profit based upon the prevailing exchange rate.

For one week the Adduans worked well. Then, at the start of the second week, the village headmen put in the first Maldivian demand for a pay rise, asking for a minimum of three Maldivian rupees a day plus one-and-a-half measures of rice. Their argument was that with sixty or seventy men employed on site-work the fishing would suffer and the villagers' income would drop. That argument was immediately countered by reducing work on the jetty and the runway so that only half the labour force was needed, leaving those Maldivians who were no longer required by the RAF free to return to their fishing. That move deprived the Adduans of their bargaining point but the loss of half his labour force and the consequent delays to an already tight schedule obviously concerned Flight Lieutenant McNeil who, on the 9th of February, felt compelled to discuss the problem with the Maldivian Prime Minister.

The dilemma for Ibrahim Ali Didi was that he could not really be seen to support either side. He had the authority to order the Maldivians to accept the wage rates which had been set after consultation with their government but to have done that would probably have lost him the goodwill and political support of many Adduans who would have seen such an order as an unreasonable rejection of what they believed to be a legitimate demand. He could have sided with the Adduans but that would have caused him to lose face with the British government for he had promised all the labour that was needed at wages which he had negotiated and for him to have reneged on that agreement within two weeks of arriving at Addu Atoll would have severely damaged his credibility. Astute politician that he was, he offered no solution, although it is certain that the island headmen would have been made well aware of his displeasure. The upshot was that on the 12th of February he left for Malé on board an RAF Sunderland, leaving the labour dispute unresolved. As if to remind the airmen of the work still to be undertaken, the RAF's dinghy, with the Prime Minister on board, fouled a coral head whilst *en route* to the aircraft and Ibrahim Ali Didi had to be transferred to a shallow draft dhoni which took him out to the Sunderland, leaving the dinghy to limp back to shore for repairs.

It was typical of the Maldivians that the headmen did not allow the pay dispute to affect the personal relationships which they were gradually developing with the Ship's Flag officers. The medical officer, who had been prevailed upon to treat some of the Maldivians, was a welcome visitor to any village but all three officers received occasional invitations to lunch with some of the village headmen. Even on the 9th of February, when McNeil had dismissed half the labour force, all twelve members of the detachment were invited to a concert given by the Gan schoolboys.

Good progress was made in those early days in spite of having fewer Maldivian labourers than had been expected. By the middle of February the jetty had been completed; the channel lights buoyed; the runway clearance

work begun and the Hitaddu survey started. In the base camp, at the various worksites and in the only Maldivian village on Gan the medical officer was introducing a variety of measures to reduce the likelihood of having the twelve airmen succumb to insect-borne diseases, particularly malaria which was endemic on the islands. The servicemen, like their wartime counterparts, had been issued with small, handheld, knapsack sprayguns, primarily for use within their tents and their huts but after two weeks of pumping insecticide by hand they knew that the insects were winning the battle and that the airmen were likely to fall faster than the flies unless they could devise an effective and efficient method of spraying insecticide over the whole environment. Some ingenuity was called for and, after several days of trial and error, a 'swingfog' fumigator was developed which dripped a mixture of oil and insecticide into the exhaust of a portable petrol engine, creating a cloud of insecticide-laden smoke which carried into any nook and cranny. Wielded by Maldivians who soon became known as 'the swinging smokies' the fumigators were most effective in the kadjan huts and tents but were also useful among the shrubs in the working areas and undoubtedly helped to reduce the insect population quite dramatically within a few weeks. By then the villagers on Gan had begun to play their part in the battle against disease by following the medical officer's instructions and oiling their wells, each of which was a breeding site for mosquitoes and a potential source of infection.

The Headquarters' staff in Ceylon were aware of the Maldivians' pay demand but refused to increase the rates, assuming that the demand would be withdrawn when the Adduans realised that the airmen could get along without them. Permission was given, however, for the future employment of up to eighty Maldivians so that when the labourers accepted the rates of pay agreed between the British and Maldivian governments Flight Lieutenant McNeil would be able to deploy a large workforce to bring the works programme back on schedule. Sure enough, on the 20th of February, the headmen decided that they could not win the argument. They capitulated and the Maldivians who had been dismissed returned to work having gained nothing. Their return and the employment of extra labourers was welcomed just as much by the dhoni owners as by the detachment commander for they had a new-found business providing commuter transport. Any labourer who did not live on Gan had to pay a ferry fare to commute to and from work by dhoni even when unfavourable winds meant that the sail had to be lowered and the commuters were obliged to row themselves across the lagoon. When the passengers disembarked at Gan the dhoni was usually beached for the day because the owner had no crew for the return journey until the commuting labourers had finished their day's work. Providing the ferry service thus cost the dhoni owner a day's fishing and he was accordingly paid two men's wages for each such day: a far easier way of making money than taking his dhoni and his fishing nets out into the Indian Ocean for eight hours.

With the end of the dispute over wage rates, McNeil no longer had to worry about a labour shortage but he did have to schedule the site clearance work around the weather which could be unpredictable even during the dry season at the beginning of the year. When it did rain the Adduans tended to do little more than take shelter where they could whilst the servicemen generally spent some of their time trying to improve their living conditions. The weather-gods were kind that February which was just as well in view of the fact that the Maldivians were clearing the site by hand; even the deepest roots on the old wartime runway had to be removed manually to avoid excessive surface damage. During those early days in February there was far less rain than the servicemen had been led to expect. Although the occasional downpour forced everyone to run for cover there were none of the tropical storms which could so easily turn the island into one enormous quagmire. If anything, the labourers employed to clear the scrub from the old wartime runway would have preferred light rain to fall more frequently for every shower brought two benefits; whilst it was raining they were allowed to rest wherever they could find shelter and when the rain stopped they were able to remove even the most stubborn roots without the backbreaking effort required when working on hard-baked ground.

By the third week of the month remarkably good progress had been made with two thousand four hundred feet of the runway cleared of all but the deepest roots. The clearance work, however, had exposed a problem. The runway was only ninety feet wide. That had been adequate in wartime but it was ten feet narrower than the minimum required in 1957, and that inevitably led to even more work. Over the coming weeks labourers would have to be employed clearing more scrub, excavating, and then filling, a ten-foot wide trench across the entire width of the island.

After four weeks of backbreaking manual labour the scrub had been completely cleared across the centre of the island from the coast road along the north shore to that which bordered the southern beaches. By mid-March the ground was ready for the construction workers who were due to arrive on the 16th, the day the SS Maskeliya was expected to deliver the heavy plant and equipment which would be needed for the next phase of the re-commissioning programme.

In the lagoon, good use had been made of those coral heads which had been cleared from the navigation channels and the Sunderland runway area; they had been used in the construction of a jetty which had been built over several old wartime vehicle bodies that lay in the shallows. The construction technique had been simple. After being enclosed by sunken logs the old vehicles had been covered by the coral which, suitably compacted, provided a good foundation for the log decking which was added during the second week in March. That completed the structure and provided a jetty from which the RAF's marine craft could be loaded and unloaded without the danger of being holed by the coral heads which still pervaded the shallow waters off the beach. With the RAF dinghy repaired and the jetty completed, site clearance on Hitaddu could be continued without the tedium of a three-hour round trip by dhoni. It also meant that the RAF dinghy could be used to unload the Sunderlands, a welcome improvement over the use of dhonis which had never been designed to accommodate the heavy cumbersome pieces of equipment which they were often called upon to transport and which had, on several heart-stopping occasions, looked as if they would end up at the bottom of the lagoon.

On shore, the servicemen's campsite had been well established and included a collection of kadjan huts, simple timber-framed buildings with plaited palm fronds for the walls and roofs. Well ventilated, but surprisingly weatherproof, the huts provided, in Gan's hot and humid atmosphere, far more comfortable accommodation than the tents.

There was only one urgent task which could not be done in time by the Maldivians or by the airmen: the final clearance of dangerous coral heads from the Sunderland runway area. With N°s 205 and 209 Squadrons due to support the second phase of the construction programme by flying supply shuttles to Gan every Tuesday and Saturday it was obvious that the coral heads could only be cleared in time by blasting. A request to Air Headquarters in Ceylon brought a four-man team of Royal Engineers to Gan on the 2nd of March with general instructions to use their explosives experience wherever required. For them, the work was straightforward and they cleared the Sunderland runway area with ease even though the remarkable resilience of the coral meant that they were obliged to use much larger charges than they had anticipated. The engineers remained at the atoll until the 19th of March by which time they had cleared the lagoon runway, several navigation channels to the beaches and the coral shelf on the northern beach of Gan, thus providing a large access area for dhonis in what would eventually become a marine craft jetty and dhoni park. They did little however to clear the large coconut palms after discovering that, like the coral, palm trees were remarkably resilient and could be removed more quickly by bulldozer or axe than by the use of explosive rope.

Whilst the sappers had been clearing coral the Maldivians had been busy preparing for the arrival of the SS Maskeliya from England. The ship sailed into the lagoon at dawn on the 20th of March by which time a beach landing area had been cleared, the rafts which would be needed to bring the heavy plant ashore had been constructed and a petrol, oil and lubricants storage centre had been established half way between the north-west end of the runway and the camp site. In the lagoon, aircraft and marine craft moorings had already been laid by the crew of HMS Baron on the 15th of March, one day before the originally scheduled arrival of the Maskeliya and the same day that the Air Officer Commanding, Ceylon, had arrived at Gan to conduct an informal inspection of the work undertaken by the Ship's Flag detachment.

A few hours after the Maskeliya dropped anchor off Gan the additional twenty servicemen required for the second phase of the operation arrived by air. For them, the first two nights on the island were to be unnecessarily uncomfortable; they had to sleep where they could because their tentage had been stowed deep in the ship's hold.

No-one had imagined that unloading the Maskeliya would be an easy task. The Maldivians, short and slightly built, had neither the physical ability nor the experience to transfer heavy plant and equipment from the ship to the beach nor were they familiar with the use of the sheerlegs which would be needed to lift much of the cargo onto the jetty. As always, the weather had to be taken into account for although it was generally good in March, it was nevertheless likely to change with very little warning, whipping up the normal two-foot waves to a level which would make unloading impossible. Those problems, together with the added difficulty created by limited jetty facilities, an initial steep slope to the beach and a

lack of towing or winding equipment were identified by Squadron Leader Harding, an equipment officer serving with N° 41 Movements Unit, who, because of his beach experience, had been sent to Gan on the 9th of February to investigate and report upon the problems which were likely to be encountered when unloading the Maskeliya. Logically, he was subsequently detached to Gan to supervise the work which he had estimated to be a five-day task.

When the Maldivians realised what had to be unloaded they were visibly shaken. Admittedly, they were expected to transport very little of the cargo in their dhonis because the landing craft which was available to take the plant and equipment ashore could carry a thirty-ton load and with a sixteen-foot beam and a length of almost sixty feet it was large enough to take anything which they were unloading. But the heavy plant included an eight-ton and a ten-ton roller, two power graders, a bitumen distributor, a five-ton and two seven-ton tipper lorries, a tractor, a Land Rover and ten thousand gallons of bitumen in forty-gallon drums. The estimate of five days to unload the ship was far too optimistic. For three days the Maskeliya's crane operators and the RAF team, which now included nine marine-craft crew, needed all their expertise and ingenuity just to get the plant and vehicles ashore. Frustratingly, the caterpillar tractor was unserviceable which meant that it had to be towed ashore and left for repair when the intention had been to use it as the main workhorse, hauling the heavy plant and equipment up the beach.

Only the bitumen distributor had suffered any severe damage and as that would not be needed until mid-April there was ample time for it to be repaired. The rest of the unloading was not difficult, it was just so physically demanding that after two more days everyone was working at a noticeably slower pace. In particular, manhandling the drum stocks of bitumen, petrol, oils and lubricants was an exhausting, dirty job for which many of the Maldivians were physically unsuited. But eventually everything was ashore, the last load leaving the Maskeliya at six o'clock on the evening of the 28th of March, three days later than expected. At half past six, before that final load had even been hauled up the beach, the Maskeliya's captain, anxious to avoid any further delay, sailed his ship out of the lagoon and headed for Ceylon, taking with him the samples of the Gan water, sand and coral asked for by the Air Ministry staff who were waiting to conduct analyses of the materials which would be locally available for the main construction work on the island.

The servicemen's eight days of dawn-to-dusk hard labour had been briefly interrupted only for RAF Gan's first communion service, conducted on the 27th by the visiting Church of England padre from Negombo. It was hardly surprising, therefore, that on the 29th, the first day of a twenty-four hour stand-down, most of the servicemen slept through the day. But within twenty-four hours the temporary stevedores had recovered, were able to view with some satisfaction, and a certain amount of incredulity, the equipment and stores which they had brought ashore and were quite happy to spend time talking to the Far East Air Force press relations officer who had arrived forty-eight hours before the Maskeliya departed. Amongst the unloaded cargo even the NAAFI stores, dwarfed by the plant and the stacks of forty-gallon drums, were impressive and, whatever other shortages the thirty-two men might experience, they were unlikely to run out of alcohol or cigarettes: the administrative order for phase two shows that they had been allotted five thousand four hundred cans of beer, one hundred and sixty-eight bottles of whisky, one hundred and sixty-eight bottles of gin and one hundred and twenty thousand cigarettes.

As April began, morale was running high. The camp was much larger, the newcomers had been assimilated into the small community of servicemen and the unit was by then well equipped with transport, marine craft, fire fighting equipment and all the construction plant and materials needed to re-commission the old wartime runway. On top of that the state of health amongst the servicemen had remained good in spite of all the dire predictions which had been made when first they had arrived at Gan. The wartime records had obviously been studied and the lessons well learnt for the men had all been immunised against smallpox, typhus, cholera and the enteric fevers; they had been issued with mosquito nets and were subject to strict dress regulations intended to reduce the incidence of insect bites. No drinking water or kitchen water had been used without first being sterilised and tropical bleach powder had been added to all the other water used. Provided all those precautions continued to be observed there was every reason to believe that the twenty newly arrived servicemen would remain as healthy as those in the advance party.

For the Maldivians, Ramadan, the ninth month of the Muslim year, fell in April which meant that, faithfully observing the religious tenet of fasting throughout the daylight hours, they worked only in the mornings that month. In spite of that the re-commissioning work progressed rapidly. By the end of the month the old wartime runway area had been scraped clean down to the coral-surfaced landing strip which had been covered with compacted sand. The runway widening trench had been easily excavated, but filling it then posed something of a problem because hardcore was becoming an increasingly scarce commodity and the trench to be filled was ten feet wide for the entire length of the runway. Even though it was not deep, some fifty thousand cubic feet of hardcore was needed and there was no ready supply on the island. A wartime stockpile of two inch road-stones, discovered in the Maldivian village, quickly disappeared into the trench as did the hardcore obtained by demolishing a few old buildings. After that, some one hundred Maldivians had to be permanently employed shifting stones from the wartime roads and from the reefs until the trench was finally filled and ready for a surface layer to be added.

Elsewhere on the island the Maldivians could see increasing signs of the activity which would one day overflow into their village. The runway over-run and approach funnel were being cleared and the coast roads repaired. Insect breeding sites were being eradicated as any surface water, including the villagers' wells, was sprayed and oiled and as the undergrowth was stripped from the island. Much to the concern of the islanders it was not just the undergrowth which was being removed; many coconut trees were also being felled, rapidly reducing one of their sources of food and significantly affecting the income which they derived from the coir produced by the trees.

Their village, located towards the western end of the island, comprised some two hundred dwellings together with a school, a graveyard and several mosques to serve the five hundred or more Maldivians who lived on Gan. Aware that all their buildings would have to be razed to make way for the one-and-a-quarter-mile concrete runway which was to be laid down the centre of their island, the villagers clearly understood that they would have to be evacuated sometime during the year. Remarkably, in view of this threat to their community, the islanders' initial friendly acceptance of the servicemen never faltered, almost certainly because the Ship's Flag detachment had arrived in the company of the Maldivian Prime Minister whose presence at the atoll during those first two weeks of February had ensured that the Adduans were well aware of the importance of the redevelopment programme.

They had also been assured by their Prime Minister that eventually they would all benefit greatly from the British presence at the atoll and that those whose lives were initially disrupted would receive generous compensation for their losses and would be helped to resettle on other islands. Reinforcing that message, many of the older Maldivians had welcomed the arrival of the servicemen because they had worked with the British forces at the atoll during the war. They were aware of the benefits that were likely to accompany the return of the military and were only too willing to describe them to any of their younger neighbours who were prepared to listen. It was the vision of a better future for everyone which over-rode all the resentments and converted most of the objectors into willing helpers.

Few, if any, of the Ship's Flag personnel had ever encountered a survival-orientated culture such as that which prevailed at the atoll and they were understandably curious to learn more about the Adduan lifestyle; a curiosity which was partially satisfied by the hospitality enjoyed in February and during the two-day Easter stand-down in April when parties of up to half-a-dozen servicemen at a time were given guided tours of Maradu, Hitaddu, Midu and Fedu.

Within a fortnight the airmen were once again given some insight into life at the atoll when the Maldivians, celebrating the end of Ramadan with a two-day festival on the 1st and 2nd of May, invited all the servicemen to Hitaddu on the second day when the Adduans traditionally gathered on one island for their Eid festival sports day. Invited to compete in the dhoni race, the airmen soon discovered that they were no match for the smaller, slightly built, Maldivians and were beaten into fourth place in a six-boat race. They had, however, established what was to become a regular event during each of the English bank holidays which continued to be observed by the RAF even at Addu Atoll where, apart from those which were based upon a religious celebration, bank holidays had no significance. Gradually those extended weekend breaks developed into exhausting sports days which always included a dhoni race enjoyed equally by the servicemen, the Maldivian competitors and the boat owners who were paid for the use of the dhonis rowed by the servicemen and were generously compensated for any damage to their craft.

Invitations to visit the Adduan communities were not uncommon but day-to-day relationships were tightly controlled. Gan village was generally out of bounds for the servicemen and association with individual Maldivians was permitted only when it was a necessary aspect of a normal day's work. Trading with the Adduans was closely controlled and was limited to the purchase of local curios, which had to be paid for in Maldivian rupees obtained from the locally-based Maldivian Government Representative who was required to ensure that the islanders dealt only in Maldivian currency.

With Ramadan over, the Maldivians' reverted to their normal hours, starting their working day at seven-thirty, taking a mid-day break from half past eleven to half past one, and finishing work at half past five: a long enough working day which, for many Maldivians, was extended by at least three hours spent rowing to and from Gan.

By the middle of May some one hundred and forty islanders were employed on unskilled construction work but, with the first sand layer consolidated on the old wartime runway, the demand for such labour was declining. Coincidentally, the main fishing season started around mid-May and half the labour force abandoned the construction work to go fishing. That was a far greater loss of labour than McNeil could cope with but he was in no position to order the fishermen to return to work; they were largely free spirits who had their own priorities. He discussed the problem with the headmen and it was they who provided the solution by recruiting temporary workers from Hitaddu, providing all the unskilled labour which was needed.

With his labour problem solved and the airfield re-commissioning on schedule, McNeil was ready to greet Squadron Leader Schofield whose arrival, on the 5th of June, marked the official transition from 'Ship's Flag detachment' to 'Royal Air Force Gan'.

From then on Flight Lieutenant McNeil was free to concentrate on the re-commissioning of the wartime runway whilst the newly arrived station commander dealt with the day-to-day affairs which were to become increasingly complex as the construction programme gathered pace and the station commander's role became more politicised.

RAF Gan was a Far East Air Force station, which meant that Schofield reported directly to the Singapore-based Headquarters' staff on organisational, personnel and marine matters. For as long as the men of the Ship's Flag detachment remained at the atoll, McNeil continued to be functionally responsible to the Air Ministry's Works Directorate for the airfield construction whilst Schofield, until such time as a district works officer had been established at the atoll, dealt directly with the Singapore staff on works progress and problems. He had to report directly to Air Headquarters at

Negombo, the Ceylon base which was later renamed Katunayake, on all matters related to flights between Gan and Ceylon as well as on relevant aspects of meetings with the local headmen who were the representatives of the Maldivian government. The Ceylon-based staff were his political advisers but they had no direct contact with the Maldivian government in Malé; only the United Kingdom's High Commissioner in Colombo could deal with the Malé-based ministers and that only indirectly through the Maldivian Government Representative in Colombo. Schofield was thus expected to keep the High Commissioner informed, *via* the Air Adviser, on all Addu Atoll matters which might have political implications. The RAF Negombo staffs also featured in this complex network of relationships which had developed since February because they provided funds, rations, medical stores, mail, newspapers and some fuel.

Schofield thus found himself with as complicated an example of multiple reporting responsibilities as could be imagined and, given the remote location, the generally poor communications and the sensitive political environment, it was not easy to practise the selective reporting which would satisfy the diverse staffs, all of whom expected to be kept informed of events at Addu Atoll, whilst ensuring that Gan's small administrative centre was not buried under a mass of paperwork.

Section 4 – Politics and Power

When Squadron Leader Schofield arrived at Gan in June 1957 and RAF Gan was established as a Far East Air Force station, the Ship's Flag detachment had already made significant progress towards the re-commissioning of the old wartime runway and had created a base camp comprising a mixture of tents and kadjan huts including a rather basic structure which was used as the officers' mess, and a Robinson-Crusoe-style post office, later to be staffed by an Army Sergeant and a Lance Corporal. The fuel stocks had been moved into a rather small compound; an aerial site laid out; a temporary power house started and the camp cleaned up after being badly flooded by high seas driven ashore by strong winds. By the middle of June the bulk of the unskilled work had been completed and the Maldivian labour force had been reduced from one hundred and forty to one hundred, many of whom had been assimilated into semi-skilled jobs.

Schofield's arrival left Flight Lieutenant McNeil free to concentrate on the re-commissioning work which was just as well because he had encountered severe problems when laying the top surface on the old wartime runway and would have been hard pushed to find the time needed to deal with the remarkable variety of issues which was making ever-increasing demands upon the station commander's time. All had gone well with the runway preparation up to the 12th of July. On that day the first bitumen was sprayed, sanded and rolled but no matter how much it was watered the surface stuck to the rollers and tore. Fully exposed to the tropical sun, it was just not cooling down enough to be rolled.

After a frustrating period of trial and error, rolling was abandoned in the daytime and undertaken late in the evenings and into the night when the temperatures were generally in the low seventies Fahrenheit. Until late August, when the runway surface was finally rolled and ready for marking out, the airmen were able to work a normal dayshift only when the sun was obscured by heavy cloud and the rain brought the afternoon temperature down into the mid-seventies. For the best part of two weeks the noise created by the night-shift workers made it almost impossible for anyone to get a good night's sleep and that inevitably led to frayed nerves and short

tempers amongst the resident workforce with the result that seemingly trivial events would spark off reactions out of all proportion to the incidents. But on the 30th of August, the day when the re-commissioned runway was used for the first time since the end of the war, all that seemed to have been worthwhile. That day, twenty minutes before noon, a Bristol Freighter of Nº 41 Squadron, Royal New Zealand Air Force, arrived, stayed for two hours and then took off for Negombo. The newly-laid runway surface had survived its first real test.

With the work of the Ship's Flag detachment completed, the unit was disbanded and its members despatched to various parts of the world. In September Flight Lieutenant McNeil left Gan, his contribution to the reconstruction programme officially recognised with the award of the MBE.

Coincidentally, the 30th August 1957 was the date on which Richard Costain Ltd, the London-based civil engineering company, was awarded the main airfield construction contract. Given that the decision to build the airfield had been made over a year earlier that was unconscionably late in the day to award the contract for such a substantial project in such a remote location. Be that as it may, Costain's, with little appreciation of the site problems and the political manoeuvring which would bedevil the development, undertook to build a concrete runway down the centre of the island together with turning circles, hardstandings, taxiways, a road network, technical buildings and domestic accommodation, all by the end of January 1959.

By the beginning of September a community of European civilians was forming alongside the servicemen's tents and huts, extending the domestic site eastwards. Among the first to arrive were the NAAFI manager and the senior staff from the Air Ministry's Works Directorate. Within a few weeks they were joined by site engineers and plant operators employed by Richard Costain Ltd. Whilst most of the servicemen were living under canvas the European expatriates quickly had prefabricated buildings erected for themselves and kadjan accommodation for the Pakistani and Ceylonese workers who had been brought to Gan to work for Costain and the NAAFI. But Schofield's requests for better accommodation to be provided for the servicemen were rejected out of hand by the Air Ministry staff who refused to be drawn into debating the question of sub-standard accommodation. They merely reiterated their argument that the operational works were the first priority and that the airmen's lot would not be improved until all the higher priority work had been completed. All that Schofield could do at that stage was to allocate a few working hours to the general improvement of the communal amenities knowing that they would still be rather basic until a piped water supply had been provided throughout the domestic sites and, more importantly, a sewage plant had been constructed and commissioned.

As the number of expatriate workers grew the provision of such a plant was obviously becoming more urgent because the communal facilities were not only rudimentary, they created a potentially serious health hazard. The washbasins were fed only from the cold water tank, the showers were made out of perforated wooden boxes pump-fed directly from the wells and the sanitation system comprised bucket latrines with wooden seats and canvas surrounds. Maldivians were employed to empty the buckets into 'lavender lorries' which were then driven by airmen across the beach through the shallow waters south of Gan and out to the edge of the coral shelf. There the lorries' loads were dumped into the deep waters of the Indian Ocean, thus avoiding any contamination of the water supply which would certainly have occurred if latrine pits had been used anywhere on Gan. For the drivers who took the waste out to the edge of the coral shelf there was one major hazard: in choppy conditions it was not unknown for a vehicle to overturn on the uneven coral, simultaneously dumping the driver and the load in relatively shallow water, necessitating a rescue and clean-up operation for both the vehicle and the airman.

By November the influx of British and Asian workers had increased the non-Maldivian population of Gan to well over four hundred. The seventy RAF personnel found themselves living alongside some forty of Costain's employees and about thirty Air Ministry Works Department staff whilst in the south-western corner of the island the population of the Asian village had increased to nearly three hundred, comprising roughly equal numbers of Pakistanis and Ceylonese. The rapid increase in the resident population created more work with extra accommodation needed week after week and the support services, sanitation and general facilities having to be increased and improved. Much of that work could be undertaken by Maldivians but it meant that by the end of the year the number of Adduans employed on Gan had increased to three hundred, bringing the daytime population of the workforce on the island to over seven hundred.

That sudden increase in personnel was matched by the increased tonnage of freight brought to the atoll in November by the cargo ships which were to become such frequent visitors over the next few months. The Benledi and the Max Arlt brought a combined cargo of well over eight hundred and fifty tons comprising timber, vehicles, tentage and NAAFI stores whilst the Mastand arrived with a delivery of three hundred tons of equipment and materials for Costain. Tractors, excavators, lorries, cement, hutting, rice, kerosene, furniture and a general miscellany of essential equipment poured onto the island at a rate which left the stevedores little time to spare for anything other than unloading.

By the last day of the month almost two thousand tons of cargo, much of it extremely awkward to manhandle, had been brought ashore and that was not the end of it. The contract for the construction of the runway and other works to be undertaking by Costain Ltd called for forty thousand tons of cement, one hundred and twenty thousand cubic yards of crushed coral aggregate, seventy thousand cubic yards of crushed coral and natural sand, five hundred and thirty thousand cubic yards of natural coral hardfilling and sixty thousand tons of hutting, plant, machinery, fuel and miscellaneous building materials. Not surprisingly, the shipping schedules indicated that December and January would be even busier than November. With the confluence of the manpower, the machines and the materials the entire island was about to be converted into a building site.

For the Gan villagers, already taken aback by the speed with which the old wartime runway had been re-commissioned, the scale of the project was breathtaking. They could see that their island would soon be cleared of vegetation and they knew that their village huts, their mosque and their school building would be demolished. They readily believed that a one-and-a-quarter mile long concrete runway would be laid down the centre of the island and totally surrounded by the buildings and roads needed for a military airfield but what they could not believe was that such a runway would be laid and the airfield would be operational within eighteen months: their memories of the wartime construction programme and their vision of a concrete-covered island had given them the impression that they would spend years mixing concrete just for the runway, never mind the roads and the buildings.

Whether the airfield actually would be operational by the due date was debatable. Progress would inevitably be hampered by occasional bad weather or by the late delivery of materials and equipment, but serious delays were far more likely to arise from the need to discuss with Ismail, the locally based Maldivian Government Representative, the demolition of any structure or the destruction of any crops or trees, particularly the palm trees, every one of which had an owner who derived an income from the nuts and the coir. No matter how seemingly trivial the destruction might be, it was invariably a politically sensitive matter necessitating discussion and therein lay frustration for the two most senior civilian managers on the site; Costain's project manager and the Air Ministry's district works officer, who was responsible for overseeing Costain's work and co-ordinating the site work across the island to ensure that there were no significant delays.

December came and, with Gan beginning to resemble one huge building site, the major issue, the evacuation and resettlement of the Gan villagers, had still not been resolved. They had already decided that they did not wish to move to any other atoll in the Maldives, preferring to be re-housed on other islands at Addu Atoll as had been originally proposed early in 1957. The Air Ministry staff had already agreed that, pending the provision of imported prefabricated bungalows for the displaced villagers, Maldivians could be employed to build temporary kadjan housing for all the evacuees on sites chosen by the atoll committee. Some villagers, mainly those who had close relatives on the other islands, did leave Gan in November and settled alongside their relatives but there were too few of them for the bulldozers to begin the whole scale demolition which was required and those villagers who had remained on Gan, realising that they were in a strong bargaining position, had begun to hold out for additional compensation. Unfortunately, the project engineers, eager to clear the site, were occasionally wont to act upon a half-agreement with the result that during December a few village huts were demolished before prefabricated accommodation had been erected on another island for the evacuated families. It was an uncommon occurrence but one which was, before long, to be seized upon by Ibrahim Nasir, the Maldivian prime minister and used to justify his political manoeuvring.

The new year arrived, January and February came and went, site clearance and general construction continued and still the villagers remained on Gan.

By February 1958 a steady stream of merchant ships was arriving in the lagoon, frequently bringing three hundred tons or more of materials and equipment to be unloaded, usually with great difficulty, by Costain-employed labour often assisted by airmen who were temporarily working as stevedores. The Asian workers had limited expertise and lacked the equipment which would have enabled them to perform as efficiently as the ships' captains expected with the result that quite frequently there were differences of opinion between Costain's engineers and some disgruntled captain whose departure had been delayed and who was expecting his ship to be immediately unloaded even if that required the diversion of labour from some other works in progress. The result was a frequent conflict of priorities, invariably settled in favour of the merchant ships which had to be unloaded and turned around as soon as possible even if the supplies and equipment which they had brought were not immediately needed ashore and had to be unloaded and placed in some temporary holding area.

In spite of all the diversionary activity, steady progress was made on site clearance away from the village, on general construction work and on the maintenance of the fragile re-commissioned wartime runway which had shown ominous signs of wear and tear almost as soon as the Valetta shuttle service had been introduced. It had to be repaired and repaired until, on St Valentine's day 1958, when it was found to be undamaged after use by a fully-laden Beverley, it was declared serviceable and the airfield was officially designated as '...*operational during daylight hours*'. 'Operational' it may have been but that broad classification had to be qualified because the airfield facilities early in 1958 were still rudimentary: there was, for example, no air traffic control tower, just a small hut for the wireless operators who provided the crucial link with every Valetta flying from Trincomalee.

Within three weeks the runway surface was once again cracked and pitted and by mid-March, when the Air Ministry's Chief Engineer from the Far East Air Force Headquarters visited Gan, repair work had become an almost daily activity. On his recommendation, arrangements were made to remove the crushed coral surface and re-bed it to provide a much more substantial landing strip; an unwelcome time-consuming task which put the runway out of use for two weeks, necessitating the temporary reintroduction of the twice-weekly Sunderland flights from Ceylon. By the beginning of April the resurfacing was finished and the diverted labour was once more available to prepare the ground for the new runway. Unfortunately, on the

1st of January, the Maldivian government imposed an embargo on the demolition of the Gan villagers' buildings, and unless that were to be lifted the runway construction programme would, sooner or later, grind to a halt. The Adduans were certainly not going to break their Prime Minister's embargo by knocking down their own huts, nor were they prepared to give their permission for someone else to do it. All that the site engineers could get from them was an agreement to undertake any work other than the demolition of their village. That suited Nasir, for in his dealings with the British government he was trying to renegotiate the terms of the lease and if his embargo meant that the runway could not be laid he would be negotiating from a very strong position.

For Costain's site manager and the district works officer that was a worrying possibility until late April when they received the inexplicable, but very welcome, news that the Maldivian government had given permission for the contractors to clear a two-hundred-foot wide strip of ground through the village on the centreline of the new runway and to demolish the only two occupied huts which were located on the runway line. It was inconceivable that Nasir was not aware of this about-face and the only conclusion the site manager could draw was that the Prime Minister had not been informed of the precise location of the two buildings and had therefore failed to realise that if they remained standing the runway could not be laid. Far more puzzling was the concession to clear the strip of ground through the village for that effectively destroyed Nasir's bargaining position when dealing with the British government. Costain's engineers wasted no time on speculation, they immediately helped to relocate the two families and removed their huts.

The demolition of '... *the only two homes in the affected area*' is recorded in the station diary for April along with a reference to the government's permission to clear the central strip through the village but the subsequent works progress reports provide no further details of runway-line clearance until June when the diarist comments that the runway-line had been stripped of topsoil from the eastern end of the island to the intersection with the old wartime runway and a start made on clearing the trees to the west of that intersection. There are no notes to explain why the construction engineers had not immediately taken advantage of the April concession and cleared a central strip through the village, leaving any surrounding buildings to be razed later. It may be that, having demolished those two critically

located homes and having started the runway-line clearance from the east they just decided that they would continue to work from that direction and drive on through the village when they got there. If so, they took a risk because the Maldivian Prime Minister could quite easily have changed his mind and imposed an embargo on ground clearance and that, whilst not as easy to justify as the embargo on the demolition of buildings, would have been just as effective. Whatever their reasoning, the contractors did not immediately extend the runway-line ground clearance into the village.

With the increase in the number of Maldivians working on Gan came the risk that, sooner or later, any one of the illnesses which commonly afflicted villagers throughout the atoll would be brought onto the RAF base. Sure enough, in mid-May a significant number of servicemen developed diarrhoea and seven cases of dysentery were confirmed. It was a minor outbreak and the RAF's medical staff soon had it under control but the episode led to an immediate review of the building priorities and the addition of work which had previously, and quite remarkably in view of the unhealthy environment, been regarded as unnecessary. Additional ablutions and latrines were built; the kitchen which served the three dining rooms was rendered fly-proof and an annex was added to the station sick quarters to provide sick wards, a bathroom and stores. The Air Ministry, in addition to providing five thousand pounds for the extra work, modified the policy which decreed that the airmen would have to live under canvas until the operational works had been completed; the allocated funds included an allowance for a recreation room and sleeping quarters to be built for some of the sixteen non-commissioned officers and eighty airmen. All the work was straightforward and was given a priority classification with the station diary recording that everything had been completed during May with the exception of the servicemen's kadjan huts, three of which were finished with a fourth under construction.

When Wing Commander Kent took over from Wing Commander Schofield on the 5th of June he was immediately struck by the poor accommodation provided for the airmen so, in spite of the Air Ministry's policy on priorities and the use of the civilian workforce, he prevailed upon Costain's construction engineers to use some of their Maldivian labourers to build additional kadjan huts, each capable of accommodating about twenty airmen, which would serve until the prefabricated twelve-man barrack blocks, which arrived at Gan that month, could be erected and occupied.

The result was that, by August, the only airmen living in tents were the twenty-five RAF policemen who had decided to remain under canvas until the prefabricated accommodation became available.

With eighteen rain-soaked days, June was not the best of months for Wing Commander Kent to observe the builders' progress and yet, at the end of those first, rather unpleasant, four weeks he was able to see significant changes across the entire site. Apart from the removal of scrub and trees along much of the runway-line, the completed works included the concrete hardstanding at the eastern end of the island, the fourth of the airmen's kadjan huts and a NAAFI bulk store which had been built and brought into use.

Kinder weather in July meant that by the end of the month work was well under way on a range of buildings including the barrack blocks which had been delivered the previous month along with the prefabricated bungalow for the political adviser. But, as far as Costain's project manager was concerned, the most important development that month was the creation of a local quarry which would obviate the need to ship rock aggregate to the island. The company's engineers, after unsuccessfully searching the atoll for a dry-land source of rock which could be crushed to provide aggregate, had finally located a suitable supply in the coral shelf, some two feet beyond the low water mark between Gan's southern beach and the outer reef. The location was far from ideal but of the various underwater sites which the engineers had been forced to consider, that was the best. It covered a large area, was close to the beach, was in shallow water and could easily be sealed off. The sea could obviously not be kept out of the sealed-off area which meant that the quarrying was essentially an underwater operation carried out by drilling and blasting in between long periods of pumping undertaken to keep the water level as low as possible. The operation was a resounding success, supplying rock which, after being converted into aggregate, produced good quality concrete when combined with the hydrophobic cement which had to be used throughout the island.

Success was followed, as was so often the case, by setback with the need to divert labour to deal with an unexpected stretch of coastal erosion which had been brought about by the construction of the jetty. The problem had been noted in June but by mid-July it could no longer be ignored because the tidal flow, diverted by the jetty, had gouged out the beach to a depth of some thirty feet for about seventy yards to the west of the structure, creating a corresponding build-up of sand to the east. For almost a week labour had to be employed modifying the jetty to ensure that the wave action would restore the beach, more or less, to its previous state.

With its underwater quarry, modern construction plant, kadjan buildings and multi-cultural communities Gan was at that time looking more like a civil engineering site than an RAF station. That was not the only thing to surprise the senior officers who visited the base during those early weeks of Kent's period as the station commander. His lack of authority over the works programme, the seemingly disorganised Maldivian labour force employed on the site and the ability of Costain's engineers to manage the project successfully in spite of the local difficulties and constraints combined to present an image which few of them had expected. Then, when invited into the officers' mess, they would be somewhat taken aback to find themselves in a small kadjan summer house which, although boasting a refrigerator and a bar, provided little more than a meeting place in the shade. Few stayed overnight at that time but many of those who did would comment on the poor accommodation even though they had been enjoying the comparative luxury of a works department room whilst many resident servicemen were still living in tents.

Hosting such visitors was a time-consuming activity but it could pay dividends: exposing them to the vagaries of life at Addu Atoll was to every expatriate's advantage for word soon spread that Gan was not a good place to be and commiseration was often accompanied by a willingness to help.

August came and still there were no signs of the political trouble which was brewing. The construction work gathered pace that month with no major diversions of labour and only occasional delays when decisions were required from the atoll chief. By the end of August large quantities of coral rock were being quarried; the main power station had been connected to the RAF site; the first prefabricated barrack block erected; work started on the transmitter site on Hitaddu and the concrete foundation laid for the receiver building. It was also the month when the Royal Corps of Signals personnel arrived and started work both on Hitaddu and on Gan where they were to install a permanent telephone network. They soon discovered that although the aerial erection work on Hitaddu, where the site had already been cleared and surveyed, was straightforward enough severe problems had to be overcome on Gan where flooding and cable damage hampered the installation of the planned one-hundred line automatic telephone exchange and the corresponding network of cables. For the Air Formation Signal Installations Troop, Royal Signals, the most valuable piece of equipment was a high-powered water pump because the eleven-mile labyrinth of trenches required for the underground cables quickly filled with water which rose and fell with the tide, forcing the troops to lay the network in slimy conditions which inevitably reduced their efficiency. As if those frustrations were not enough, the twenty-eight members of the troop were also faced with the frequent accidental destruction, by Costain's employees, of the cablework which had been completed. The culprits were the plant operators who were using bulldozers to clear the site and would inadvertently, but all too frequently, sweep away the cables which had been positioned on or near the surface prior to final jointing, checking and laying. Many attempts were made to co-ordinate the site clearance work and the cable laying but none succeeded.

The result was that the planned telephone network was delayed for months, leaving only the very localised field-telephone systems to serve the RAF and works department areas. Far less frustrating for the troop was the work which they undertook to improve the very basic communication links which then existed between Gan and the outside world. At that time the signals caravan, actually an old wartime RAF van, provided radio-telegraphy links with the Far East Air Force Headquarters and with the United Kingdom's High Commission in Colombo. Even those links were not maintained for twenty-four hours a day because there were so few trained operators on Gan; each day the Singapore-based Headquarters' staff would be contacted around dusk and, unless there was a good reason for keeping the network open, the Gan watch was then stood down. There were no radio or telephone links between Gan and the other islands. On those occasions when it was necessary to contact a local headman on some matter, such as the inspection of possible resettlement sites for Gan villagers, messages would either be sent *via* one of the locally-employed Maldivians or, far more reliably, *via* one of the Valetta pilots who would be asked to detour over the island in question and drop a message. As the station commander recalled, '… *it always worked.*'

The signals troop remained at the atoll far longer than had been anticipated, working on the telephone network and on the meteorological and communications systems, both of which were relatively sophisticated for their day and both time-consuming to install, test and commission. It was the latter part of 1960 before the troop completed the last of its tasks and handed over all the systems and networks to a fourteen-man maintenance troop from N° 19 Signals Regiment, Singapore.

September 1958, with rain falling on sixteen of the thirty days, was another depressing month for the construction workers. They were obliged to cope, as best they could, with conditions which frequently left them wet and weary, either because they had been caught in the rain or because they had been working in humidity which, between the downpours, soared to levels which made the slightest physical effort enervating. It was hardly surprising that morale was low that month for any prolonged period of bad weather had that effect, not just because of the difficulties of working in-between the rainstorms and the frustrations brought about by the inevitable site flooding but also because the domestic accommodation and facilities were, for the most part, so basic that they hardly provided an escape from the capricious tropical weather. On top of that, virtually all of the few leisure facilities which did exist were outdoors and were thus essentially designed for dry-weather use. The only blessing was that, with the atoll well to the south of the monsoon belt, most of the storms which hit the islands were relatively short-lived even though they were rarely trivial. That month the construction workers found it hard to reconcile such a general description with the reality of life on Gan when, on the 9th, an already-sodden island was hit by eight inches of rain in just over ten hours, rendering the runway unserviceable, flooding most of the accommodation, throwing the construction work behind schedule and setting the pattern for the next three weeks. October, with rain on nineteen days of the month, was almost as bad as September even though the total rainfall for the thirty-one days was little more than six inches, an amount which was considered to be quite reasonable for that time of the year.

The delays continued to mount up and at the end of the month the concreting programme was still some six weeks behind schedule with other works not much closer to their planned status. On the 28th of the month the three hundredth Valetta flight to use the old wartime runway proved that the resurfacing had been successful although, as far as Costain's engineers were concerned, there had been an even more significant arrival almost three weeks earlier. On the 8th of the month, whilst a Valetta was *en route* to Gan, a near-gale-force wind blew up at ninety degrees to runway N° 33, the old wartime runway, creating hazardous landing conditions best avoided if at all possible. By then, work on runway N° 28, the island-long concrete runway, had progressed to the point at which four thousand feet of lean mix concreting had been completed and it was agreed that the inbound aircraft could land on that paved end of the runway by skimming low over Costain's concreting trains and their operators whilst they were still working. The landing and subsequent takeoff were uneventful but that aircraft, the first to use the island's concrete runway, heralded a new era even though it was to be another five months before the first Hastings arrived.

Early November brought no respite from the rain which continued to blight everyone's life. The construction programme fell further behind schedule, many everyday activities were suspended and the Remembrance Day parade was cancelled. As the month wore on the rain eased off, providing an opportunity for the contractors to make up some of the lost time but ironically, as the weather improved, shortages of materials and of some categories of skilled workers caused even more delays. For months, materials had poured onto Gan but time after time the site engineers had been left almost tearing their hair out as one ship after another delivered items which were not immediately needed yet failed to deliver anything like sufficient quantities of the materials for which the construction workers were waiting. Thus, in spite of receiving thousands of tons of supplies there was, by the end of September, no sheeting and virtually no remaining stocks of the most commonly used paints. There was, however, no shortage of cement because the SS Halvidar had delivered two thousand four hundred tons of that in July, providing an ample supply of the much-needed material but an unwelcome task for the labourers who had to unload, manhandle and store the forty-eight thousand one-hundredweight bags which made up that delivery and which were then supplemented by a further fifteen thousand such bags which were delivered during August. Unfortunately the concreting programme could not be brought back on schedule during the latter part of November for the simple reason that there was a shortage both of rock aggregate and skilled concreters. The shortage of aggregate was particularly frustrating for it could have been provided in abundance from the quarry were it not for the fact that the stock of explosive fuses had been exhausted. Within days the RAF delivered a consignment of those from Ceylon and quarrying resumed but the severe shortage of skilled concreters meant that even though those who were available worked virtually

unlimited overtime, the programme remained, at the end of November, six weeks behind schedule.

It was just as well for everyone's morale that there were successes to set against the problems and frustrations which came so thick and fast from early September until late in November: work had been started on a bulk-fuel installation; a coral crushing and batching plant had become operational; the first of the airmen's prefabricated barrack blocks had been completed and occupied and, on the 25th, the first prefabricated bungalow arrived for erection on Fedu. The intention was to have it erected and ready for occupation before the 10th of December and to invite all the Gan villagers to examine it before it was handed over to one of the families which had already been evacuated. The hope was that the villagers still living on Gan would be so impressed by what they were shown that they would all be keen to move, deserting the Gan village just as fast as new houses could be erected. With the village deserted, it would be difficult for the Maldivian government to justify a continuing embargo on further demolition and the contractors could expect to be given permission to raze it to the ground. The crucial factor at that time was thought to be the rate at which the prefabricated housing could be delivered and erected.

As the Christmas stand-down began, the construction programme was still behind schedule and the engineers were privately doubting their ability to complete the runway and the associated works on time even though the completion date had been extended to the 1st of May 1959 to allow for the changes which the Air Ministry staff had made to the contract and for the delays caused by the Maldivian government's political manoeuvring. The engineers' doubts came mainly as a result of the former because the changes had included a revised specification, requiring them to increase the length by seventeen per cent to provide the longest runway possible on the given line without extending it onto the coral shelf. The only good news for the contractors was that a dry-weather period was forecast for the first quarter of the new year and if that forecast proved to be correct there was a chance that their programme would be back on schedule by the end of March.

What nobody had forecast was the impact, at the end of December, of the visit by Ahmed Zaki, the Maldivian government representative in Ceylon. Although site clearance work was going on almost everywhere on Gan, there was still an embargo on the wholesale demolition of the Maldivian village and, even if the contractors cleared the runway-line strip strictly in accordance with the concession granted by the Maldivian government in April, the day was not far off when the continued existence of the village would bring the construction work to a halt. During the Maldivian minister's visit it became quite obvious to the station commander that Zaki had neither the inclination nor the authority to change the situation because the continued existence of the village still gave his government a strong bargaining point in its attempt to renegotiate the terms of the lease for the lands at Addu Atoll. He had been sent to the atoll to inform the Adduans that they were immediately to stop working on the construction programme, thereby supporting Nasir in his dispute with the British government. It was a message which the site engineers did not want to hear. But what they could not have imagined was that Nasir's ultimatum to the Adduans would actually help to bring the construction programme back on schedule.

XI   Towards the Rebellion

When the Ship's Flag detachment first landed at Gan, relations between the British and Maldivian governments were as good as they had ever been. The Maldivian Prime Minister, Ibrahim Ali Didi, a staunch supporter of the British plans to re-establish a military base at Addu Atoll, had faced no significant dissent from his ministers and his early visits to the atoll had ensured the co-operation of the Adduans.

The island base had been officially designated 'Royal Air Force Gan' with the arrival of Squadron Leader Schofield on the 5th of June 1957 and at that time there were few political concerns. The Maldivian Prime Minister had ensured that the atoll chief and the headmen would be cooperative, the minor labour disputes had all been settled and the airfield work was on schedule. By the 1st of September the old wartime runway had been re-commissioned, the men of the Ship's Flag detachment were ready to leave the atoll, the new airfield construction contract had been awarded to Richard Costain Limited and Schofield was awaiting the arrival of the company's project manager.

It was when Mr Ahmed Zaki, the government representative from Ceylon, and Mr Ibrahim Ali Didi, the Maldivian prime minister, visited the atoll in the third week of October that Schofield first realised that the redevelopment programme could easily be delayed as a result of political manoeuvring. The Maldivian Prime Minister was ostensibly there to discuss the arrangements which were being made for the evacuation of the Gan villagers, their resettlement onto other islands and the level of compensation which they should claim from the British. The evacuation schedule was of particular interest to Schofield because he knew that he would be under pressure from the Air Ministry's district works officer and Costain's project manager who wanted the villagers off the island so that their buildings could be razed and the land cleared for the new runway. It was also quite obvious that, in Ceylon, the Air Headquarters' staff and the United Kingdom's High Commissioner would have other expectations of him. They would want the evacuation to be organised with political sensitivity even if that delayed the construction programme for a few weeks. He seemed destined to become piggy-in-the-middle and he was understandably pleased to hear that Mr

East, the United Kingdom's representative from Colombo, would be flying to Gan in order to discuss the matter on site with Zaki and with the Maldivian Prime Minister. Schofield's hope was that between them they would agree on a schedule which the district works officer and Costain's project manager would have to accept.

That was not to be. Zaki and East privately discussed, but did not publicly disclose, suitable levels of compensation and Ibrahim Ali Didi was not prepared to set a timetable for the evacuation. To have done so would have provided his political opponents with ammunition and he did not intend to do that; he merely expressed an opinion that it would be better for the evacuation programme to be arranged by local agreement with the atoll committee through Mr Farouk Ismail, the atoll's resident government representative, who had arrived at the atoll in September, some three months after Schofield. With that, the two government representatives and the politician departed, leaving no-one at Gan any the wiser.

Before embarking for Addu Atoll in June, Schofield had been briefed, at the Commonwealth Relations Office, on the politically sensitive aspects of his new appointment and had been told that although there was no British political adviser at the atoll, nor indeed anywhere in the Maldives, there was a plan to establish one on Gan. But he had also been warned that the most likely appointee, a retired tea planter from Ceylon, could not be in post for several months. Thus, on the basis of one short briefing, the station commander was required to take on the role of British government liaison officer on all matters related to the redevelopment of the base. It was a politically sensitive role because he initially had to deal with the atoll chief on day-to-day affairs, with any visiting government representatives on wider issues and, later, with Ismail.

These diverse representatives, however, did not always have the same viewpoints and they tended to be wary of making any promises or decisions which might conflict with their government's current thinking. Schofield could seek advice from the United Kingdom's High Commission in Colombo on significant political issues but such requests had to be made through the Air Headquarters' staff in Negombo, and that tended to delay the process. The situation was far from satisfactory and, given the presence of Ibrahim Didi at the atoll, Mr East was quite obviously one of the more welcome visitors that October even though Schofield had not been party to the discussions he had had with the Prime Minister. There was nothing the station commander could do about that, he just had to get on with his job as best he could.

Because he was solely responsible for dealing with the political issues which bedevilled any decision affecting the Maldivians or their property he found himself, on far too many occasions, standing squarely between Farouk Ismail and the combined forces of the district works officer and Costain's project manager. Fortunately, he quickly established an easy working rapport with Ismail who, whilst living on Hitaddu, spent most of his time on Gan where, with the village headman, he worked in the most prominent building in the village; the old wartime communications centre on the north shore of the island. He was invariably available, spoke very good English and was very co-operative when faced with any straightforward requests such as those related to the provision of labour or the demolition of isolated buildings. More importantly, he had good connections throughout the Maldivian government, giving him a sound understanding of the ministers' views and a clear impression of what would be acceptable to them and to the Prime Minister. The result was that on most occasions the district officer's plans would be approved with very little discussion; only when faced with an unusual situation involving compensation or some politically sensitive matter, such as rates of pay or re-housing, did Ismail feel it necessary to refer a request to Malé. When that occurred, long delays would often arise because, until the RAF established a radio link between Addu Atoll and the Maldivian capital, Ismail could contact the appropriate government minister only by writing to him.

Responses to such referrals might not be received for several weeks, depending on the route chosen for the correspondence. Mail flown to Ceylon and then forwarded to Malé *via* the Maldivian Government Representative in Colombo might reach its destination in a few days whereas that sent in a dhoni would take a week to reach the Maldivian capital even if the winds were favourable for the whole journey, which they seldom were. It was a slow process getting a request to Malé but it was not difficult. Getting an answer was a different matter. If the reply were to be forwarded to the United Kingdom's High Commission *via* the Maldivian Government Representative in Colombo that would further add to the delay. There was also a political factor. By late 1957 the Maldivian Prime Minister was facing some ministerial opposition over the Gan agreement and when making decisions, particularly on the granting of concessions to the British, he had often to move slowly for fear of hardening that opposition. The result was that, even if the bureaucratic use of the proper channels were avoided, written requests associated with the redevelopment of Gan were likely to be deliberately delayed for purely internal political reasons.

This increasing disagreement within the Maldivian cabinet meant that Ismail was occasionally summoned to Malé either to explain what was happening at Addu Atoll or to be briefed on political developments in the capital. Flown to and from Ceylon by the RAF, he was always required to discuss Adduan affairs with the Maldivian Government Representative in Colombo before proceeding to Malé by boat. Invariably a summons to the capital meant that he would be away for up to two weeks, leaving Gan's station commander to negotiate with the village headman or the atoll chief whenever decisions had to be made which would affect the Maldivians. The headman and the atoll chief were not unfriendly but, understandably, neither of them had any intention of putting his head in a political noose by agreeing to proposals which were even slightly contentious. That left Schofield and the district officer frustratedly waiting whilst any but the most simple requests were passed from the village headman to the atoll chief or were held pending Ismail's return.

As far as the district officer was concerned, every delay was frustrating and, given his remit to co-ordinate the site work and minimise any delays, having to wait upon decisions from Ismail or Malé was particularly so. The result was that the station commander was frequently being urged to provide quick decisions when he just could not do so. There was an added complication. In the Air Ministry hierarchy the district officer was accorded the status of a Wing Commander and was thus senior in rank, but not in position, to the station commander. That didn't worry Schofield but it bothered the Air Headquarters' staff in Singapore and by the end of the year RAF Gan's establishment had been upgraded and Schofield promoted to the rank of Wing Commander with his tour of duty, as the officer commanding RAF Gan, extended from six months to twelve.

December came and, with Gan beginning to resemble one huge building site, the major issue, the evacuation and resettlement of the Gan villagers, had still not been resolved. The Maldivian government's suggestion, made early in October, was that the villagers should be moved to some other atoll in the archipelago. Another island called Gan, just north of the equator, had been recommended as a suitable location but the Adduans, who knew very little about that island, were obviously not prepared to accept their government's suggestion without first visiting what could become their future home.

Thus they decided that, sometime in October or November, a group of them would sail north, inspect the island and report back to their neighbours. Aware that the northerly Gan was two days sailing from Addu Atoll and anxious to have a decision as soon as possible, Schofield suggested to the Maldivians that the RAF's launch could take their reconnaissance party to the northerly Gan late in October as part of a navigation training exercise. Not surprisingly, it was a suggestion which immediately found favour with the islanders. When the launch arrived at the northerly island the reconnaissance party went ashore, discovering that the inhabitants of the only village on the island seemed friendly enough but that the island itself, smaller than the Adduan Gan and with a swampy interior behind the coastal belt of palm trees, was an unattractive place.

They quickly decided that they did not wish to settle there and on their return to Addu Atoll they painted a sufficiently unattractive picture of the island to persuade their fellow villagers that it would not be a good idea to move from their home atoll to the more northerly Gan. The Maldivian government did not force the issue of evacuation beyond Addu Atoll and, after considerable debate amongst the Adduans, it was agreed that the Gan villagers would be resettled onto other islands in their own atoll as had been originally proposed early in 1957. Anxious to hasten the process, the Air Ministry staff readily agreed to the Maldivian government's proposals that displaced villagers should be provided with housing built by the contractor's labour on sites chosen by the atoll committee, should be compensated for the loss of their crops on Gan and should be given a regular supply of rice until they had established fresh crops in their new locations. Each of those demands was easy to satisfy.

Reaching agreement on an appropriate level of financial compensation for the lost crops would probably take some time but, pending the delivery of prefabricated accommodation, temporary kadjan housing could be erected in a matter of days, and several tons of rice could be imported just as

quickly. It transpired that very few of the islanders were evacuated from Gan before Christmas even though the original plan, to resettle them elsewhere in the atoll, could have been started as early as September after the S S Max Arlt had brought some four hundred tons of rice to the atoll, enough to feed all the Gan villagers for three months after their evacuation. Some of the villagers who had relatives on the other islands did leave Gan in November because, like most of their neighbours, they were tired of living alongside an ever more intrusive building site and, given the opportunity to move into established communities on the neighbouring islands, they had gone. But there were too few of them for the bulldozers to begin the whole-scale demolition of the village and those Adduans who were still living on Gan had realised that they were in a strong bargaining position. Whenever an attempt was made to establish a final compensation package linked to an agreed evacuation date they would raise a whole series of problems related to their community, their school, their mosques, their graveyards, their trees or their crops and whilst each problem was being resolved the construction schedule, based upon the resettlement of the islanders before the end of November, was falling further and further behind.

Early in December whilst Ahmed Zaki and Ibrahim Ali Didi, the prime minister, were visiting Addu Atoll to check the evacuation and resettlement arrangements, they were hastily recalled to Malé. Flown to the capital on board an RAF Sunderland, they were accompanied by the station commander who was hoping for an opportunity to pay his respects to the Sultan and to discuss with the government ministers the general progress of the site clearance and the construction programme.

The visit started well. The Sunderland tied up in the Malé Atoll lagoon and Schofield, Zaki and Ibrahim Didi were met on the jetty by the Deputy Prime Minister and other cabinet ministers. Schofield, accommodated with the Sunderland's crew in a government guest house on Malé island, found that the Prime Minister, his deputy Ibrahim Nasir, the cabinet ministers and Zaki were hospitable, well disposed towards the RAF and apparently happy with the situation at Addu Atoll. Schofield, informed that he had been granted an audience with the Sultan the following day, was given a conducted tour of Malé and spent half an hour with Ibrahim Didi who talked about the plans to enlarge and deepen the Malé harbour, giving no hint of his imminent resignation even though he did say that, having done all that he set out to do when he first became Prime Minister, he hoped that he would soon hand over to a younger man. Schofield was escorted to the palace before eight o'clock the following morning and with minimal delay was able to pay his respects to the Sultan, finding him friendly but demonstrably intent on preserving his status by conversing only through Zaki who acted as an interpreter even though the Sultan was capable of conversing in English. The visit had been so successful as far as Schofield was concerned that he was taken aback to learn that, only hours after expressing his satisfaction with progress at Addu Atoll, the Prime Minister had been forced to resign over his mishandling of the redevelopment programme.

On Gan, Costain's construction engineers, eager to clear the site, occasionally acted upon a half-agreement with the result that during December a few village huts were demolished before accommodation had been provided on another island for the evacuated families. It was an uncommon occurrence but one which was, before long, to be seized upon by Ibrahim Ali Didi's successor, Ibrahim Nasir who, as the Air Ministry staff were to discover soon after Christmas, had very strong, and very different, views about the Gan construction programme.

It eventually became public knowledge that Ibrahim Didi had faced a variety of allegations, several of which were based mainly on complaints from the Adduans. Some, such as the claim that demolition was proceeding more rapidly than resettlement, were at best mere half-truths. In isolation, none would have been serious enough to bring about his downfall but in concert and in combination with other evidence they were enough to persuade his ministers that he had made a series of mistakes, the most serious being that more money had been spent on the Adduans than was likely to be received from the British government. The upshot was that he had been forced out of office. Farouk Ismail, who had effectively been Ibrahim Didi's representative at Addu Atoll, was not called upon to resign but he felt obliged to do so because of a difference of opinion with the majority of the cabinet ministers, particularly over the accession of Nasir. Zaki, the government representative in Ceylon, and son-in-law of the deposed Prime Minister, likewise chose to resign.

Ismail's resignation was not good news for Schofield because it ended a good working relationship and, given that Nasir was already voicing objections to the way in which the British were redeveloping Gan, it was quite likely that Ismail's successor at the atoll, holding an appointment within Nasir's patronage, would be obstructive rather than co-operative. It was also likely that Nasir would insist that every request from Schofield should be forwarded to Malé for a decision, a very simple technique for creating endless delays. There was every indication that a new, politically charged, era had dawned.

Schofield could do nothing to influence the Maldivians' political manoeuvring, he could only hope that Nasir would not set out to make life too difficult at Gan and that Ismail's deputy, Abdullah Afif Didi, would be just as amenable as Ismail had been. As it transpired, the events at Malé had made Afif Didi very cautious but he was certainly not obstructive and as far as Schofield was concerned it was much better to be dealing with Afif, the deputy atoll chief, than with Loutfi, the atoll chief, who was rather withdrawn in his dealings with the station commander and who, unlike Afif, was not able to converse in English. For the remainder of 1957 Ismail's absence and Nasir's accession made little or no difference to the local affairs at Gan. The construction work progressed slowly but surely towards the point at which the Maldivian village would have to be razed or the construction work halted. There were no clear indications of a looming impasse because there was no open discussion of the potential problem; whilst work was continuing no-one was inclined to raise issues which did not need to be tackled until the new year.

Every expatriate had been made aware, on arrival at Gan, that the more sensitive Maldivians could easily be offended by the behaviour of the newcomers, that seemingly trivial incidents could be blown up out of all proportion and that local events could escalate into political affairs. To be fair, the atoll officials were equally demanding of the islanders and were swift to punish those who digressed, particularly those convicted of crimes committed in the course of their employment on Gan. The difficulty was that those suspected of such crimes were likely to be interrogated by the RAF police and that in itself could evoke a reaction from the atoll chief.

It was therefore with some concern that Schofield learned of the theft, almost certainly by Maldivian employees, of cigarettes from the NAAFI. The theft, which occurred three days before Christmas, was significant not because of its scale but because it broke a pattern. There had, perhaps surprisingly, been very little pilfering by the Maldivians in spite of the frequent opportunities and the obvious attraction of so many of the commodities and the utilitarian items used by the expatriates. But on this occasion seventy tins of cigarettes, stolen when the thieves broke into the NAAFI shop, went far beyond petty pilfering. With Loutfi rather withdrawn, with Ismail's replacement, Abdullah Afif Didi, new in post and with a volatile political atmosphere, Schofield viewed the imminent investigation with some trepidation. Fortunately, the RAF police did not have to interrogate the two suspects for they were quickly apprehended in Hitaddu village which meant that the theft was regarded as a Maldivian community matter and was never brought into the political arena.

The speed with which the offenders were identified and arrested came as no surprise to the villagers for in the Maldivian communities it was virtually impossible to keep new acquisitions secret and the culprits had made little attempt to hide their ill-gotten gains. They were quickly tried, convicted and sentenced. Theft, a most serious offence in the Muslim world of the Maldivians, was compounded in this case by the fact that the stolen items belonged to foreigners who were virtually under the protection of the Sultan. Nevertheless, the sentences passed on the convicted men seemed remarkably harsh by Western standards; they were birched and banished from the atoll. Most of the expatriates were taken aback, for few of them had had any idea, before then, that under the Maldivian justice system banishment was the common alternative to prison whilst birching, although less common, was not that unusual. If, as seemed likely, the sentences were intended to deter any like-minded islanders from embarking on a similar escapade, they were certainly successful for serious theft by Maldivians never became a problem in spite of the number of Adduans who had both the inclination and the opportunity.

In Malé, Ibrahim Nasir was adopting a far-from-friendly attitude towards the British for he was convinced that his predecessor had had no right to lease land to the British government and from that premise he argued that the British had no right to be building a military base at the atoll. Within days of his accession he sought, and found, in the Gan evacuation programme, justification for impeding the construction work whilst avoiding direct political confrontation.

After the premature demolition of some of the villagers' homes during December the station commander had readily agreed that the deadline for the completion of the evacuation could be changed from the 31st of December to the 20th of January and the Maldivian ministers in Malé, aware of both the initial problem and the extended deadline, were reassured that such an incident would not occur again. Nasir, however, chose to exploit the situation and on the 1st of January 1958 the Adduans received their first indication of his intentions. Informed that their government would be sending a commission to the atoll to investigate the affair, they were told that, pending the arrival of that commission, they were to cease working on the demolition of the village and the evacuation of the villagers.

It was more of a warning shot than anything for at that time the construction schedule was not greatly affected by the embargo. Far more serious in the short term was the fact that, just before the commission arrived, trouble flared up between the Maldivians and the Ceylonese who had been brought to Gan to work for Richard Costain Ltd and the NAAFI. That should not have surprised anyone for many of the islanders had made no secret of the fact that they resented the influx of Asian workers and they wanted them repatriated. They had no great liking for the Pakistanis who had been brought to the atoll but they accepted them partly because they were fellow Moslems and partly because they knew that there were no Maldivians who could match their skills, experience and physical abilities. But, as far as the Adduans were concerned, the Ceylonese had no such saving graces and were consequently the prime target for the local troublemakers who, early in January, claimed that two of the Ceylonese had been having sexual intercourse with women from Gan village.

At the Maldivians' insistence an identity parade was held but the women could not, or would not, identify the alleged offenders. Later that day several Maldivians went to the Asian village to confront the Ceylonese. Tempers flared and that inevitably led to a fight which was broken up by one of Costain's British employees. Two of the Maldivians promptly ran back to their village and, claiming that a Gan villager had been killed, they rallied a group of volunteers to mount a punitive expedition against the Ceylonese. Alerted by a message from the Maldivian Government Representative, the RAF provost officer arrived at the Asian village just in time to stop a gang of young Maldivians from attacking the Ceylonese.

Meanwhile, the rumour had spread to other islands in spite of the Government Representative's prompt attempts to quash it. He did manage to stop a raiding party which was about to set out from Fedu but by then the islanders had become so incensed about the whole affair that, after holding a series of meetings, they informed him that no Maldivians would work for the Air Ministry or for Richard Costain until all the imported Asian labour had left the atoll. It was futile for them to issue such an ultimatum. The Asians had been brought to Gan because the Adduans, who were adept only in the use of hand-tools for carpentry and basic stonework, had neither the skills nor the physique to undertake the work which was to be done. Slightly built, they could not undertake heavy manual work nor could they sustain any reasonable manual effort for a full day, especially when that was preceded and succeeded by several hours rowing across the lagoon. The Maldivians' arguments that European workers could be brought in to replace the Pakistanis and Ceylonese were naive in the extreme; the Asians had been brought to the atoll because they were prepared to work for very low wages and to live in poor accommodation. European workers would have tolerated neither. Futile gesture or not, the Maldivians withdrew their labour, adding a further complication to the political manoeuvring which Nasir was about to start.

It was only a matter of hours after the Adduans had withdrawn their labour that an RAF Sunderland arrived at Gan, bringing Mr East from the United Kingdom's High Commission in Ceylon and a Maldivian Government Commission from Malé. Head of the nine-man Commission was Sheik Ibrahim Rashadi, a jovial apolitical Maldivian who had studied law at the University of Cairo and had been in government service for most of his working life. The interpreter who accompanied the Commission was Farouk Ismail, the former Government Representative at Addu Atoll who had felt obliged to resign from government service when Ibrahim Ali Didi had been forced out of office. Subsequently brought back into the government, he had been promoted into the Department of Justice and, with his experience of events at Addu Atoll during 1957, had been an obvious choice for membership of the Commission.

The United Kingdom's High Commissioner in Ceylon who, having received reports of the skirmish between the Maldivians and the Ceylonese, was concerned that there would be political repercussions affecting his office, had sent Mr East to Gan. Once East had been briefed on the fight, the subsequent withdrawal of labour and the general progress of the construction work, he returned to Ceylon to report to the High Commissioner, leaving the members of the Maldivian Commission to undertake their investigation. It transpired that they had no executive powers; they had been sent to the atoll to ensure that the evacuation of the Gan villagers and the accompanying demolition of their village had ceased. Not as well

publicised, but far more important as far as Nasir was concerned, was the fact that the members of the Commission had been instructed to study all the atoll officials' files and financial records as part of the investigation into the deposed Prime Minister's handling of the Gan affair; they had no remit, and apparently no inclination, to resolve the problems caused by the feud between the Maldivians and the Ceylonese.

On this occasion the United Kingdom's High Commissioner in Ceylon did not become embroiled in an argument with the Maldivian government because the members of the Commission considered the situation at Gan to be an internal problem to be resolved without reference to the British. The result was that after some discussion with the station commander and the Adduan employees the Commission persuaded the islanders to resume work on all the tasks which were essential for day-to-day living. Many of them accepted that as a fair compromise but the intransigent construction workers refused to return to work. They were still on strike when the Commission departed for Malé, leaving the British site engineers deeply suspicious that the members of the Commission, sensitive to their Prime Minister's views on the construction programme, had been more interested in prolonging the strike than in ending it.

Although the construction workers initially seemed determined to hold out against all demands for them to return to work their strike actually collapsed in less than a month, undermined by their employers and by the Gan villagers. As the Air Ministry's district works officer and Costain's project manager brought more Asians to Gan the Maldivians realised that the withdrawal of their labour from the construction site was of decreasing significance as far as the site engineers were concerned. The striking labourers were thus under some pressure to return to work before their employers decided that they no longer needed any of them. They were also under some pressure from the Gan villagers who, probably because they had become frightened of the Ceylonese, were asking to be evacuated as soon as possible. They certainly did not want the construction work delayed in any way and that gave the striking labourers an opportunity to resume work with minimal loss of face and, as if to oblige the villagers, the strike was called off.

As soon as they were back at work the Maldivians requested a pay rise. They did not state a figure, they merely claimed that for an eight-and-a-half hour day, two rupees seventy-five cents, the rate which had been agreed late in 1957, was inadequate. They were aware that rates of pay were not locally negotiable, that the demand would have to be referred to Malé by their government's representative at Addu Atoll and that they were likely to be employed on the 1957 rates of pay for several weeks before receiving a response from their government. They accepted all that and settled back into a normal working routine.

Towards the end of February another group of Maldivian ministers flew from Ceylon to Gan, sent there by Ibrahim Nasir as a reaction to the Adduans' pay claim. He did not believe that the Maldivians employed on Gan were poorly paid and, probably for his own political purposes, he chose to believe that their pay claim was merely a symptom of a much deeper problem which needed investigation. His ministers had a much simpler view of the situation. They believed that the Adduans were merely trying to extract as much as possible out of the obviously wealthy British. They were well aware that the wage rates for the Adduan employees at Gan had been set by the Maldivian government in consultation with the British government and were comparable with the wages paid for similar work in Malé. As far as the ministers were concerned the Adduans had no cause for complaint. But that was not the way the islanders saw it; they were convinced that they had a good case. They were paid in Maldivian rupees by their own government's representatives. The British government, however, reimbursed the Maldivian government in Ceylon rupees at parity with the Maldivian currency even though the unofficial market exchange rate made the Ceylon rupee worth anything from three to ten times as much as the Maldivian rupee.

Understandably, the Adduans felt that they should either be paid in Ceylon rupees at the official, parity, exchange rate or they should at least receive a large share of the profit created by their government's use of an artificial exchange rate in their dealings with the British. The Adduans did, after all, use a large proportion of their wages to purchase imported goods which were priced in Ceylon rupees and whenever they did that they were forced to accept an exchange rate which reduced the value of their wages by a multiple of anything up to ten. To add insult to injury, their government, apparently not content with the exchange rate profit, deducted income tax from the Maldivian currency payments which were made to the Adduans who were employed by the British.

Nasir's view of the pay claim as a symptom of a much more serious situation was later proved to be correct, but even he did not realise the seriousness of the underlying problem or the course of events which it would precipitate. In particular, he had failed to appreciate that the workmen were not the only Adduans who had become resentful towards their government.

As the bulldozers moved across Gan and part of Hitaddu the Adduan families saw their ground crops destroyed and their coconut palms felled. They wanted compensation but their government had promised nothing except assistance in resettling the Gan villagers whose homes were to be razed. Feelings were running high and within hours of landing at Gan the unfortunate government ministers were being harangued by a crowd of Adduans. When it became clear that the visitors had no executive authority to resolve the local problems which were the cause of such ill-feeling the villagers became so angry that the ministers, fearing that they were about to be manhandled, took refuge in the old wartime communications centre in Gan village. There they were besieged for over an hour with the islanders surrounding the building, banging on the doors and on the corrugated iron roof, chanting, shouting and loudly voicing their intention to kill any government representative who was foolish enough to step outside.

Eventually the ministers were rescued by the station commander who drove to the village in his Land Rover and brought them back to his office, safely negotiating a noisy, intimidating, but non-violent crowd of Adduans along the way. Having been rescued, the ministers had no inclination to meet the Adduans again. Considerably shaken, they left Gan on the first available aircraft heading for Ceylon. Their visit had certainly confirmed their Prime Minister's belief that there were deep resentments at Addu Atoll but how those could be eradicated without giving in to every demand posed a problem to which they had no immediate solution.

On the 6th of March the confrontations of January and February suddenly looked insignificant when Mr Heengama Wattalidiniya Symon, one of Costain's Ceylonese employees, was murdered; his skull smashed, apparently by a rock wielded with great force. The weapon was never found and, given the ease with which it could have been consigned to the depths of the lagoon, that surprised no-one.

An RAF criminal investigation officer was sent to Addu Atoll where he and his staff undertook extensive inquiries with the full cooperation of the atoll officials. But their investigation was fruitless. The murderer was never brought to justice and the case remained as the most serious unsolved crime throughout the operational life of the base. Suspicion obviously centred on the Maldivians because of their recent feud with the Ceylonese but nothing could be proved. The murder, the rarest of crimes in the Maldives and an event of enormous significance in the developing communities at Addu Atoll inevitably led to strongly worded exchanges at government level but not, surprisingly, involving the British government.

The United Kingdom's High Commissioner in Ceylon was involved only to the extent that the Ceylonese and Maldivian governments each requested an official report on the incident and on the subsequent investigation by the RAF. Once that had been provided the High Commissioner took no further part in the debate. But the affair led to bitter exchanges between the Ceylon government, which took the view that the crime must have been committed by a Maldivian, and the Maldivian government, which took the view that without sufficient evidence it was not possible to ascertain the nationality of the murderer. Fortunately the exchanges at ministerial level were not reflected within the affected communities at Addu Atoll.

There was no outbreak of violence, possibly because the Ceylonese accepted that the crime may not have been committed by a Maldivian and possibly because they were shocked by the enormity of the offence. Whatever the reason, Mr Symon's death persuaded Costain's directors that it was inadvisable to employ Ceylonese construction workers at the atoll whilst the feud with the Maldivians continued and within a few weeks they had paid them off, repatriated them to Ceylon and replaced them with Pakistanis. The only Ceylonese left at Gan were the few who were employed by the NAAFI and they were too few for the islanders to regard them as a threat.

Costain's move defused a potentially explosive situation because the Maldivians had never displayed any collective animosity towards the Pakistanis. If anything, they offered a guarded welcome to them as fellow Moslems but they had always openly displayed their intense dislike of non-Moslem Asians, particularly since the recent confrontations and they were quick to regard the repatriation of Costain's Ceylonese employees as their victory, claiming that their January demand for the repatriation of all imported Asian labour had been largely met. That did not mean that they were happy with the situation, it meant that they tolerated the influx of Pakistanis only because it was a preferable alternative to the continued employment of the Ceylonese and because they were not, at that time, in a position to prevent it.

Two months after the Maldivian ministers had beat a hasty retreat from Gan, the Adduans were still waiting for a reaction from Malé and the site engineers were waiting for permission to continue with the demolition of the Gan villagers' huts; permission which could come only from Nasir. The general assumption amongst the British site engineers was that the silence was a tactic intended to frustrate the Maldivian employees. Nasir, it was thought, would be quite happy if the Adduans, in their frustration, were to call another strike, thereby delaying the construction programme on Gan. The Maldivian Prime Minister would then try to turn the situation to his advantage by pressing the British government even harder for a new agreement on the redevelopment of the military base at the atoll. The strike would serve to reinforce his argument, already presented to the United Kingdom's High Commissioner in Ceylon, that his predecessor had exceeded his authority in signing the agreement and in organising a supply of cheap labour. The scene, they thought, was set for a confrontation. But it didn't materialise. Frustrated though they were, the Maldivians employed on Gan did not pursue their pay claim by calling another strike. Their experience earlier in the year had persuaded them that a withdrawal of labour would not wring any concessions from their employers and they were well aware that their own government would not be swayed by such action. The result was that the Adduans rather grudgingly agreed to undertake any work other than the demolition of the Gan village which was still the subject of an embargo from their Prime Minister.

That was the situation at the beginning of June when Wing Commander Kent arrived to take over from Wing Commander Schofield who had by then completed his tour of duty and could look back on his twelve months at the atoll with considerable satisfaction. He had seen the redevelopment programme gaining momentum week by week as the non-Maldivian population of the island grew from less than three dozen to over four hundred. With limited communications and with no political adviser anywhere in the archipelago he had picked his way through a political minefield largely resulting from the Maldivian government upheaval of December 1957. He was leaving behind a political scene which was superficially as calm as could be expected under the circumstances. He had established a good working relationship with the atoll chief and although the Adduans were resentful towards their own government they were generally co-operative. But he was also well aware that there were strong emotional undercurrents which made it almost inevitable that their resentment would, sooner or later, give rise to action.

Wing Commander Kent had, like his predecessor, been briefed on the political sensitivity of the redevelopment programme and had been made directly responsible to the Commander-in-Chief, the Far East Air Force, Air Marshal The Earl of Bandon. Nevertheless, he was expected to keep the United Kingdom's High Commissioner informed, *via* the Air Adviser in Colombo, on all events with political implications. From the outset he was made aware that seemingly trivial incidents at Addu Atoll were quite likely to be exaggerated by the Maldivians whose Prime Minister was always ready to submit a formal complaint to the High Commissioner in Ceylon. Kent was, in effect, left with little choice but to inform the High Commissioner of virtually any activity which touched upon the lives of the Maldivians. Unlike his predecessor, however, he was to have recourse to a locally-based political adviser who had been appointed by the Commonwealth Relations Office and was due to arrive in July. The adviser was a retired Army officer, Major Phillips, who, after leaving the Army, had spent some years as a tea planter before fully retiring to live in Ceylon. He had been appointed on the basis of his familiarity with the Maldives and his early availability but the latter seems to have been the more significant criterion for his experience in the archipelago consisted of little more than a brief stay in Malé. He spoke some Tamil and Singhalese but no Divehi and was thus unable to converse properly with any Maldivian who did not speak English. Nevertheless he was the appointed political adviser and, with no other responsibilities, was able to concentrate on the political aspects of the construction programme and on the political implications of the many day-to-day decisions which had to be made.

As a candidate for the job, Phillips was far from ideal but the Commonwealth Relations Office had found it extremely difficult to recruit anyone for the appointment and that had put him in a very strong bargaining position. He had virtually dictated the terms on which he would accept the offer. He was adamant that he would only go to Gan if his wife could accompany him and although that was contrary to the Air Ministry's policy he got his way. Rather than leave the post vacant, the Commonwealth Relations Office over-rode the Air Ministry. The outcome was that Phillips, who duly arrived in July, and his wife, who arrived a few weeks later, were provided with a bungalow which had been built for them at the eastern extremity of the island, overlooking the Gan gap. RAF Gan was an operational base for nineteen years and in all that time Phillips was the only man to be granted an accompanied tour of duty on the island, a clear indication of the concern which had been felt in Whitehall over the political ramifications of events in the Maldives at the time of his appointment.

In July, whilst the islanders' resentment was being fuelled by the politically-motivated embargo on demolition work and on any further evacuation of the villagers, the Maldivian government rejected their demand for higher rates of pay. That rejection increased the Maldivian employees' sense of injustice and their frustration even though they had half expected such a response. Frustration, however, turned first to disbelief and then to intense anger when they learnt that, with effect from the 31st of that month their taxes were to be dramatically increased. They had embarked on a pay claim but they were about to become considerably worse off. For the first time that any islander could remember, goods and commodities imported to the atoll were to be subjected to import duty based upon their cost (Fig 11.1). The list of items to be taxed contained 169 categories including some as broad as 'Maldive Products'.

The rates were punitive. 'Foodstuffs', with a ten per cent levy, were the least affected. Many items were subjected to one hundred per cent import duty whilst the broadly classified 'Maldive Products' were to attract a one hundred and fifty per cent tax. In view of the fact that everything except fish, coconut palm products and some fruit and vegetables had to be imported, the islanders, living at subsistence level, faced an immediate, and very serious, fall in their already marginal standard of living.

The amount of money likely to be raised by such taxation was of little significance compared with the exchange rate profits being made by the Maldivian government and it is difficult to believe that the objective was merely to raise money by taxing the islanders who had so obviously benefited financially from the redevelopment of Gan. A far more likely explanation was that the taxes were introduced to generate resentment rather than revenue and, by so doing, to create a belligerent labour force at Addu Atoll. The Sultan of the Maldives must have foreseen such an effect for he initially refused to approve the intended legislation, withholding his royal assent until his government, after further debate, passed the bill on a second reading. If his ministers had hoped that the Adduans' resentment would create labour problems on Gan they were to be disappointed. The islanders were close to rebellion but they contained their anger. In Britain, the staff at the Foreign and Commonwealth Relations Office had no idea of the tensions which were building up in the Adduan communities and which were destined to spill over into the international arena.

By the end of 1958 there was a general air of pessimism amongst the Adduans. They had borne, quite philosophically, the vagaries of the weather from early September to mid-November. For them, that was nothing out of the ordinary. The blow to their morale during that period had come not from the weather but from their own government which had informed them, towards the end of October, that in addition to the August increases in the rates of tax on imported goods they would be required to pay tax on all their sailing craft in the coming year.

The details were set out in the pamphlet, 'Notice to Owners of Sailing Craft', issued by the Maldivian Minister of Home Affairs (Fig 11.2). From that, they discovered that anyone who owned a boat would, after the 1st of January 1959, be required to register the vessel with the Minister of Home Affairs and would then have to pay an annual tax based upon the length of the craft. The smallest boats, up to twelve feet long, would attract a modest tax of no more than ten rupees a year but the annual tax on the large dhonis would amount to well over a thousand rupees. The intention was obviously to raise revenue by introducing a tax which, although applied to virtually every family in the archipelago, was heavily weighted against the traders and the entrepreneurs who had purchased large boats which were designed for open sea fishing but which, at Addu Atoll, were being used to provide the inter-island ferry services made necessary by the increasing need for Maldivian labour on Gan and the evacuation of the Gan villagers onto other islands. As far as the boat owners were concerned, the heavy taxation of the larger dhonis was designed to ensure that even more of their wages went to Malé.

For five months the Maldivians had suffered one blow after another. Their claim for a pay rise had been rejected out-of-hand; their government had introduced import duties which would fall more heavily on the Adduans than on any of the other southerly islanders. Their wages, irregularly paid since July, had not been paid at all since October and their supplies of rice from Malé had been significantly reduced. Now, they faced the imminent taxation of all sailing craft. Still they controlled their anger. But at the end of December, when Ahmed Zaki, the government representative in Ceylon, visited the atoll, their self-control finally snapped.

Ostensibly paying an official visit to view the construction works and talk to the islanders, Zaki was flown by the RAF from Ceylon to Gan where the station commander escorted him on a guided tour of the island. Although site clearance work was going on almost everywhere on Gan the embargo on further demolition of the Gan village was still delaying the runway construction programme in that area. The impasse was not just delaying the concreting operation, it was having a knock-on effect as cargo ships continued to arrive according to schedules which had been planned around the expected materials consumption rate. If the construction programme fell too far behind schedule or if the phased deliveries ran out of sequence the camp site was in danger of becoming one vast storage area because cargos had to be offloaded even though the few designated holding areas were certainly not large enough to accommodate all that was being delivered. Kent vividly recalled an occasion when a cargo of several thousand forty-gallon drums of aviation fuel had to be brought ashore before adequate storage facilities were available, leaving the island 'littered with drums full of fuel'.

During their tour of the island, it became quite obvious to the station commander that Zaki had neither the inclination nor the authority to change the situation; the continued existence of the village gave his government its strongest bargaining point in its attempt to renegotiate the terms of the lease for the lands at Addu Atoll. If anything, Zaki seemed upset by the friendly attitude of the islanders towards the British. The reason for that soon became clear. He had been sent to the atoll to inform the Adduans that they were immediately to stop working on the construction programme, thereby supporting Nasir in his dispute with the British government. As far as their Prime Minister was concerned, the Adduans would no longer be employed by the British and would therefore not be paid by their government agent after the end of December. If, ignoring Nasir's instructions, they continued to work on the construction programme, the wages which they were owed for November and December would be withheld and their government would cease to ship rice to the atoll.

Zaki was well aware that the islanders had received neither wages nor rice for about two months and he had, quite accurately, judged their mood as one of controlled hostility. He was also well aware that the message he had to deliver was, to say the least, unpalatable and he obviously had no wish to be around if the Adduans were to react violently to his government's ultimatum. Having decided that that was a distinct possibility, and having no wish to be the focus for their anger, he arranged for the document to be read out by Mister Loutfi, the atoll chief, at a public gathering on Hitaddu. Loutfi, a rather withdrawn individual, delegated many of his functions, particularly the rather unpleasant ones, to his deputy, Abdullah Afif Didi, who was thus inevitably delegated to inform the islanders of their government's latest instructions and ultimatum. Afif Didi was extremely adept at judging the moods of the Adduans and was invariably able to present his government's policies and proclamations in a way which promoted acceptance if not wholehearted support but on this occasion his talent for such persuasion was either not applied strongly enough or it was inadequate in the face of the Adduans' anger. They listened to him. Then, on that evening of the last day of the year, they finally allowed their feelings to boil over and, for the last few hours of 1958, they stoked up their resentment against their government and against the unfortunate Mr Zaki who had been cast in the role of unwelcome messenger.

Whilst Afif Didi relayed the instructions to the villagers, Zaki, having accurately judged the mood of the Adduans earlier in the day, remained on Gan. It was just as well that he did so for had he been anywhere on Hitaddu that evening he would undoubtedly have been attacked. His sense of self preservation saved him from that fate but at first light on the following day, the 1st of January 1959, some five or six hundred Hitadduans set sail for Gan. They were after Zaki's blood and they obviously thought that by arriving before five o'clock in the morning they would have no difficulty in catching him unawares. They were thwarted only because at four o'clock in the morning the New Year celebrations were still in full swing in Phillips' bungalow and the fleet of dhonis was seen heading for Gan.

The result was that at half past four the station commander was awoken by his room boy and Zaki who was seeking protection from the several hundred islanders who were on their way from Hitaddu. Wing Commander Kent was well aware that none of the buildings on Gan was capable of withstanding an assault by a determined mob but felt that, given the good relations between the RAF and the Adduans, they were unlikely to attack the station commander's accommodation which was, at that time, a room in one of the works department's huts. That therefore became Zaki's temporary refuge in the company of the political adviser and several RAF policemen who had been called upon to provide a security guard. It was obviously essential to get the minister beyond the reach of the Hitadduans as soon as possible but because no aircraft was scheduled to visit Gan that day he could not be flown to Ceylon until special flight arrangements had been made. Given that the islanders were determined to come ashore, there was no point in having an aircraft flown in from Ceylon until they had become tired of waiting and had gone home; if they thought that their quarry was about to escape by air they would simply assemble on the runway and prevent any aircraft from leaving.

With Zaki ensconced in the station commander's room, the islanders who had landed on Gan vented their anger on the Maldivian Government Liaison Officer's headquarters. They broke down the door, stole the cash from the safe and the documents from the cabinets. They then destroyed everything they could lay their hands on before setting to work on the fabric of the building, attacking it with such ferocity that they left it in need of major structural repairs. They chopped down the flagpole and tore down the Maldivian national flag which they later handed to the station commander as a souvenir, asking him to exchange it for an RAF ensign which could be hoisted to symbolise their change of allegiance.

With several hundred violent Adduans loose on Gan, Kent decided that Zaki's best option was to take refuge on board a supply ship, the SS Matheran, which, fortuitously, was anchored in the lagoon whilst the captain waited for an opportunity to discharge its cargo. Kent arranged for the minister to be escorted to the marine craft section, sending instructions for the crew to put him on board an RAF launch, get him onto the cargo ship, apologise to the captain and tell him that the station commander would come aboard to explain everything as soon as possible. By then Zaki was so fearful for his life that he just did as he was told, raising no questions and no objections. When the Adduans saw the launch making for the ship they guessed that their quarry was being spirited aboard and gave chase, narrowly failing to intercept the fleeing minister before giving up and rowing back to the shore.

Using the Morse communications link, the only means of contacting the Headquarters' staff in Singapore, the station commander described the situation he was facing, and was immediately given a promise that an aircraft would be sent from Ceylon to Gan to evacuate Zaki at first light the following day.

When Kent subsequently went aboard the Matheran, the captain could not have been more cooperative. He readily agreed to provide sanctuary for Zaki and even offered to weigh anchor immediately and sail for Ceylon to ensure the minister's safety and relieve the station commander of a very awkward political problem. It was an offer which had to be refused partly because of the costs which would have to be met but, more importantly, because the ship had not then been unloaded and would have had to return to Gan because the cargo was needed ashore. While Kent was discussing the seriousness of the situation with Zaki some forty or fifty dhonis, each filled to capacity with islanders, were headed out towards the Matheran, their crews and passengers all intent on boarding the merchant ship and dragging their minister back to Hitaddu for their version of instant justice.

Seeing the fleet of dhonis heading his way the Matheran's captain became concerned enough to follow the advice which he had previously discounted, rigging hoses and lines to repel boarders while Kent instructed the crew of the RAF launch to disperse the dhonis in any way they could. Authorised to harass the boats and prevent the islanders from attempting to board the ship, the RAF crew were also under implied orders to avoid damaging any dhonis or injuring any villagers, a necessary constraint if the Hitadduans were to be persuaded to go home without their anger being turned against the British. The crew of the launch successfully followed their orders, avoiding any collisions whilst weaving in and out among the boats, creating a wash which made the dhonis difficult to control and threatened to swamp those which came too close to the Matheran.

Unable to get at their minister, the Adduans began to head for home. Kent, in an attempt to defuse their anger, followed them in the RAF launch and spoke to the leaders, informing them that Zaki had authorised an issue of rice from the government store even though he had actually refused to agree to that when it had been suggested to him as a way of easing the tension. After they had calmed down the villagers collected their rice in orderly fashion and went home.

Zaki spent the night on board the Matheran. He certainly had no wish to venture ashore until an aircraft was available to take him back to Ceylon.

The following day, the 2nd of January, began quietly enough but the atmosphere was tense throughout the morning. The aircraft from Ceylon had been delayed and it was not until a quarter to four in the afternoon that it arrived, landing from a low straight approach to avoid giving too much warning to the islanders. They, however, were ready to set out for Gan as soon as there was some indication that their quarry was about to leave his sanctuary and when they spotted the approaching aircraft they manned their dhonis and set out for the Gan beach nearest the runway. The Maldivian emissary, in classical fugitive style, was smuggled ashore whilst his aircraft was turned round and refuelled as rapidly as possible. He was taken from the Matheran on board one of the RAF's landing craft which hit the beach as near as possible to the runway and disgorged a Land Rover in which Zaki was crouched low.

The vehicle was driven directly to the refuelled aircraft and within minutes, well before any of the Maldivians on Gan were aware of what had happened, their minister was aboard and the plane was airborne, headed for Ceylon. The pilot, at the request of the station commander, flew low over the oncoming dhonis so that the crews were left in no doubt that they were too late to prevent Zaki from leaving. Most of them were still a mile or more offshore and without exception they turned their boats and went home. The islanders had been out-manoeuvred but it was typical of them that they bore no ill-will towards the RAF. Those who were employed on Gan just settled back into a normal cooperative relationship content in the knowledge that they had seen off their unwelcome visitor.

The bombshell came twenty-four hours later, on the 3rd of January, when a group of Maldivians, led by Afif Didi, requested a meeting with the station commander. When Kent and his political adviser met them they announced that they had declared their independence from the Maldivian government and wished to come under British protection. They explained that the Adduans had long been discontented but that the latest taxes, combined with the order to stop working for the British, had finally pushed them into extreme action.

The islanders' declaration of independence created an awkward political situation. Kent explained to the deputation that their views and their request for British protection could not be acted upon locally but would be passed on to the British government. When news of the rebellion reached London, government ministers went rapidly from an initial state of incredulity to one of consternation. They realised that, under the terms of the agreement between the two nations, Britain could not recognise Afif Didi's *de facto* leadership of a so-called independent republic. The Adduans' unilateral declaration of independence was essentially an internal problem for the Maldivian government to resolve. To interfere in the affair would be to renege on every agreement made between the two nations since the days of Queen Victoria.

For the British ministers the embarrassing truth was that the rebellion had been brought about by the British presence at the atoll, that the rebels, well aware that their action was likely to provoke an armed response from their government, were openly assuming that they would be protected by the British military and that Britain could not allow the Maldivian militia to quash the rebellion.

It was obvious that any punitive expedition from Malé would be met by resistance from the islanders and it was equally obvious that the Maldivian militia, having won the battle, would take the Adduan ringleaders to the capital where they would be tried and banished, certainly for many years, possibly for life. Government officials selected for their ability to control difficult situations would then be brought in to run the affairs of the atoll and the Adduans would be made to suffer for their sins. They would also be left with the conviction that the British, to whom they had turned for protection, had betrayed their friendship by turning them over to the non-too-tender mercies of a vindictive government. The British could not afford to foster such hostility because some three hundred Adduans were employed on Gan and it was anticipated that that number would increase to over five hundred once the RAF station was fully operational. If resentment were to convert many of them into saboteurs it would be very difficult and very expensive to guarantee the security of Gan and of the Hitaddu site.

If the dilemma had been left to the politicians to sort out, the construction work would probably have been delayed for months but the station commander, Wing Commander Kent, banked on knowing what Air Marshal The Earl of Bandon, the air officer commanding-in-chief of the Far East Air Force, would want and he reached an agreement with Afif Didi that the Gan villagers would move and that the remaining structures in the village could all be demolished. He duly informed Costain's project manager, the Air Ministry's district works officer and the political adviser that he was immediately authorising the demolition of the village. The project manager was anxious to make an immediate start on the site clearance because the runway construction was already behind schedule,

the political adviser objected on the grounds that no such demolition should be started until political clearance had been obtained and the district officer expressed no firm opinions. Costain's project manager took Kent at his word and ploughed on.

The Earl of Bandon, responding to news of the Adduan's unilateral declaration of independence, arrived at Gan on the 6th of January and discussed the situation with all the executives responsible for the construction work. Being less constrained than the politicians, he then declared that, pending a political settlement between the British and Maldivian governments, Abdullah Afif Didi was to be recognised as the authoritative voice of the Adduans on all matters.

The islanders' unilateral declaration of independence also created problems for some of the officials at the atoll. The Adduans, individually inclined to be quiet and rather unassuming, tend collectively to be quite demonstrative on the subject of local and central government and the declaration of secession was quickly followed by demonstrations against local officials appointed by, or supportive of, the Maldivian government. The islanders gave them a simple choice: join our rebellion or leave the atoll. Some left. Others resigned their appointments and joined the rebels. The islanders agreed that, until such time as proper elections could be held, local affairs were to be run by a people's council made up of notable Adduans from the various islands. Abdullah Afif Didi was accorded the title of president of the council, a generally popular and certainly logical choice given his personal standing in the atoll. His education, his considerable experience of local and national government and his record of maintaining a good working relationship with the British, both during the Second World War and throughout the current redevelopment programme, clearly identified him as the outstanding Adduan of his time.

The scene was set for a saga which was to run for years, generating acrimony and mistrust between the British and Maldivian governments.

For the first time in history, import duties were levied on 31 st day of July 1958.

Duties are exacted in cash calculated on the cost price of imported goods as follows;-

1. Foodstuffs 10%
2. Dates 20%
3. Essences 30%
4. Children's requirements 15%
5. Honey 15%
6. Syrups (Lime Juice) 50%
7. Arecanuts 50%
8. Biscuits 40%
9. Butter 25%
10. Cakes 100%
11. Canned meat, fruits and vegetables 60%
12. China ware 30%
13. China ware (besides plates) 50%
14. Glass 25%
15. Feeding bottles 10%
16. Sucking bulbs 15%
17. Petrol 40%
18. Battery 50%
19. Electrical equipment 40%
20. Stoves 35%
21. Engine oil 20%
22. Sulphuric acid and poison 60%
23. Tiles, asbestos and iron corrugated or otherwise 20%
24. Cement 20%
25. Accessories required for bicycles and tricycles 20%
26. Luxurious accessories for bicycles 100%
27. Beedies, cigarettes and gudak 100%
28. Materials required for the manufacture of cigarettes, cigars etc. 40%
29. Live animals 40%
30. Makintosh 25%
31. Plastic materials 50%
32. Furniture (wooden ware) 30%
33. Cane 50%
34. Brass, copper and nickel 30%
35. Slippers 30%
36. Slipper manufacturing material 20%
37. Brushes 25%
38. Bath room equipments 50%
39. Playing cards 100%
40. Decorating articles 100%
41. Cinema film per 10' @ 1 cent
42. Corks 25%
43. Polishes 20%
44. Water bottles (rubber) 25%
45. Gold and silver 35%
46. Gold plated articles 100%
47. Caps 50%

55. Gram.Records 50%
56. Aluminium Ware 30%
57. Locks 20%
58. Joints 40%
59. Nails, Screws 20%
60. Cisterns, Tanks 20%
61. Curry-stuffs 15%
62. Tamarind 15%
63. Housing equipments 20%
64. Carpentery equipment 30%
65. Maldive products 150%
66. Coir products 150%
67. Coir ropes 150%
68. Watches etc. 40%
69. Iron and brass netting 40%
70. Iron, brass and lead pipes 30%
71. Vans and lories 40%
72. Motor cars and cycles 75%
73. Motor launches and dhonys 25%
74. Shaving equipment 30%
75. Soaps (talcum) 75%
76. Soaps (washing) 40%
77. Hukka and equipment 60%
78. Spectacles 20%
79. Sponge 25%
80. Cotton textile 30%
81. Textiles(general) 60%
82. Cotton yarn 15%
83. Thread 30%
84. Paper 20%
85. Printing materials 25%
86. Civet and musk 35%
87. Sago 25%
88. Files 30%
89. Scents and perfumes 60%
90. Thermos flask 30%
91. Shellac and lacquer 25%
92. Fire works 150%
93. Toys 150%
94. Fountain pen and stationary 20%
95. Pencils 20%
96. Drawing materials 25%
97. Colours (eatable) 60%
98. Fresh fruits and vegetables 15%
99. Ornaments- gold 100%
100. Musical instruments 50%
101. Salt 25%
102. Ornaments- ordinary 50%
103. Cutlery 30%
104. Wheat 25%
105. Cocoa 35%
106. Ovaltine 35%
107. Coats, trousers and ties 120%
108. Gunny bags- empty 30%
109. Engines 15%
110. Radios and accessories 40%

Fig 11.1. Translated details of the duties to be levied on goods imported by Maldivians. Source: Abdullah Afif Didi *via* V Kendrick.

Entirely New Tax imposed on **all sailing craft** with **effect** from the 1st day of January, 1959 :-

Registration of sailing craft :-

(1) Owners of sailing craft shall get their vessels registered at the Ministry of Home Affairs.

(2) A Certficate of Registration issued for each vessel registered shall bear a stamp of 1/- (rupee one) only.

(3) If a sailing craft is sold, exchanged or given away as a gift to another person, the same craft shall be registetred anew, in the manner stated above. Unregistered vessels will be fined, at the discretion of the Home Ministry.

The Tax or fee levied on all sailing crafts :-

The Maldivian measurement of length called a "Riyan" equals to 27 inches.

(1) A sum of Rs 2/- (rupees two) per riyan per year shall be levied on all sailing craft under 5 riyans in length.

(2) A sum of Rs 5/- (rupees five) per riyan per year shall be levied on all sailing craft having a length of 5 to 10 riyans.

(3) A sum of Rs 12/- (rupees twelve) per riyan per year shall be levied on all sailing craft having a length of 10 to 17 riyans.

(4) A sum of Rs 25/- (rupees twenty-five) per year shall be levied on all sailing craft having a length of 17 to 25 riyans.

(5) A sum of Rs 30/- (rupees thirty) per riyan per year shall be levied on all sailing craft having a length of 25 or more riyans.

———————————————

The above are extracts (translation) from the booklet entitled "Notice to Owners of Sailing Craft" issued from the Ministry of Home Affairs, Male, under the signature of Ibrahim Nasir, Minister of Home Affairs, on 15th October 1958.

Fig 11.2. Translated extracts from 'Notice to Owners of Sailing Craft'. Source: Abdullah Afif Didi *via* V Kendrick.

XII   Airfield Construction: January 1959 – January 1960

With Afif Didi recognised as the *de facto* head of the Adduans' so-called republic, the islanders could hardly have been more supportive. Anxious to escape from the ever-encroaching construction work and keen to be near the front of the queue for one of the new bungalows which were due to be erected on Fedu, many were almost queuing up to have their families relocated and their old homes demolished. Many of them moved to Fedu or Hitaddu to live with relatives or in temporary kadjan homes built by Costain-employed Maldivians organised by the atoll committee. All the evacuees were provided with a weekly ration of rice to compensate for the loss of their vegetable crops on Gan and were promised that they would be provided with prefabricated housing as soon as the units could be delivered and erected.

Under the new regime, Afif was totally cooperative and if he agreed that sites could be cleared, trees uprooted and buildings demolished that was good enough; the work went ahead.

For Costain's project manager there could not possibly have been a better start to the new year; no longer constrained by any of the Maldivian government's embargos, he was almost certain that the contract would be completed on time. He and his engineers, well aware that the Adduans' secession could be short-lived, decided that the best approach was to demolish the village as fast as the villagers could be resettled and to lay as much concrete as possible, thereby ensuring that when the Maldivian government re-established its authority at the atoll it would be faced with a *fait accompli*. Accordingly, a double shift system was introduced with site working starting at half past two in the morning and continuing until half past ten at night. As villagers moved out, buildings were demolished and the ground cleared. The bulldozer drivers ensured that there was not so much as a plant left where previously there had been palm trees, scrub and Maldivian buildings. Their efforts would have been noteworthy at any time but they were particularly so that January because the weather forecast for the month could not have been more inaccurate; twenty-hour working days coincided with an unpredicted and unexpected eighteen-day period of foul weather which brought gale force winds and almost sixteen inches of rain to the atoll. By the end of the month, site clearance was well ahead of schedule but, once again, foul weather had significantly delayed much of the building work.

Within days of the Adduans' secession the Maldivian government was embroiled in an argument with the British government and that was very much to the advantage of the construction engineers on Gan. With both governments pre-occupied with the rights and wrongs of the political situation, no politician was likely to become involved with the details of the airfield construction and that meant that the work on Gan and Hitaddu could continue uninterrupted.

The creation of the island-long runway was the obvious first priority but there was more than enough work to keep the increased workforce fully occupied, day after day. Throughout the first three months of the year additional labour poured onto the island as Costain's engineers worked to bring their programme back on schedule. By March there were over a thousand Pakistanis on Gan and their number was still growing towards the intended peak of approximately one thousand five hundred. This massive influx of workers at a time when labour rarely had to be diverted onto remedial work enabled the engineers to bring the entire project back on schedule within a matter of weeks even though workers had to be employed to build additional kadjan accommodation for the newly-arrived Pakistanis. By the middle of March the island had been split from end to end by the concrete runway and the daily progress on the associated concreting had been fast enough to be obvious to even the most casual observer with the turning circles, hardstanding and access tracks all completed. A variety of new structures had sprung up across the island, the most obvious being the four barrack blocks which were built and occupied before being completed, and the six aerial masts on what was to become Gan's aerial farm. The island was a hive of activity with Costain's engineers continuing to work with the unstated imperative to complete as much of the project as possible before the British politicians began to have second thoughts about the wisdom of recognising, and supporting, a rebel regime.

In spite of their desire to achieve as much as possible during those first hectic weeks of the year the engineers did not forget the evacuated Gan villagers whose departure had given them their clear run; some of Costain's labourers were employed on Fedu, laying concrete bases for the first consignment of prefabricated homes which was expected to arrive that month.

But whatever else happened in March, the event which raised everyone's spirit was the arrival of the first Far East Air Force Hastings on the 18th. Landing with a clear run down the length of the island, it signalled the beginning of Gan's days as a mid-ocean staging post capable of accommodating the next generation of the RAF's big jets. From then on the old wartime runway was redundant and the island-long runway was classified as operational. Costain's engineers had good cause to celebrate that day for with the inaugural flight they, and their project manager, became convinced that the airfield would be completed and in use, with all the essential signals and navigation aids, by the 1st of May.

In part, the rapid progress was due to the exceptionally good relations developed with the still-euphoric Adduans and to the rapport which had been established with Afif Didi and the people's council whose members were busy identifying and discussing the merits of additional sites for the further consignments of prefabricated homes. There were delays, but that was inevitable given the interdependency of so many of the tasks, the remoteness of the atoll and the vulnerability of the supply chain. But after the first three months of 1959 delays generally gave rise to opportunities for the redeployment of labour, as happened when the construction of the island's sewage plant had been temporarily halted due to the late delivery of the sewage ejectors. Occurring shortly after two shiploads of prefabricated accommodation had arrived from Singapore, it was an opportune time to redirect the sewage plant workers to Fedu where they could be employed laying concrete bases on the recently-cleared site for the resettlement village. At that stage in the construction programme redeployment was quite common but it rarely threatened to delay the project; it did little more than change the sequence of activities and, on occasions, it was beneficial in the longer term because it further improved relations with the Maldivians.

With nothing except the weather and the occasional shortage of materials to contend with, the construction workers made rapid progress and by the 1st of May the forecasts made by Costain's engineers were shown to be reasonably correct. The runway had been in use for six weeks, the loading tests had been satisfactory, its full length had been declared serviceable for any of the RAF's aircraft and the signals equipment and navigation aids had been installed. The only eyesore was the air traffic control centre which was sited in a kadjan hut overlooking the runway.

Two weeks into the month a Canberra, the first jet to stage through Gan, brought the jet age to the atoll, an event which left Costain's engineers elated and gave the Earl of Bandon a great deal of satisfaction because it provided clear evidence that his January decision to place his faith in Afif Didi and Costain's engineers had circumvented what could so easily have become a political impasse. On the 28th of the month, when he made another of his frequent visits to Gan, he made a point of publicly congratulating all those who had brought the project to fruition: as his letter to Costain's (Fig 12.1) shows, he had nothing but praise for the engineers who had completed the job on schedule.

Gan was operational with a full-length runway by mid-May but there was only a very limited supply of aviation fuel available at the base because the solitary bulk fuel installation tank, which had been completed and tested early in April, was still empty and would remain so for another month. It was mid-June before the arrival of the Shell tanker British Seafarer delivered two thousand five hundred tons of Avtur, creating, in the process, a very satisfied station commander and a very frustrated tanker captain. The waters were calm and the weather was good whilst the tanker was discharging its fuel which was just as well because the operation took twenty-seven hours, thereby exposing the inadequate capacity of the recently installed pipeline, a defect which would need to be remedied before the remaining bulk fuel tanks were commissioned.

Costain's main contract did not end with the completion of the runway and the associated hard surfacing, it continued until the end of August which meant that for some fourteen weeks those who had been laying the runway were redirected onto other works, and there was certainly no shortage of those. Top of the list of priorities was the modification of the fuel pipeline and the completion and testing of the four fifteen-hundred ton and two seven-hundred ton tanks in the bulk fuel installation: work which was finished by the end of May in spite of the fact that work schedules were disrupted on sixteen days by the ten inches of rain which fell that month. Evacuation and resettlement of the remaining Gan villagers was also high on the list of priorities and a group of Pakistanis was standing by ready to erect prefabricated bungalows on the Fedu site earmarked for the resettlement village which was to become known as Gan-Fedu. Typically, that work could not start immediately because there was a problem which exemplified the frustrating world of Addu Atoll; there seemed to be no easy way to transport the building panels from Gan to Fedu. The Adduans' dhonis were not capable of carrying such loads, the landing craft fouled the coral heads on the approach to the island and there just was not time to blast a channel through the coral growths and up to the beach. But, as was so often the case, a chance observation led to a solution. At low tide some Maldivians had been seen carefully wading from Fedu to Gan and from that it was reasonable to deduce that, at the right time of day, any lorry with good ground clearance could probably be driven across the Gan-Fedu gap. A trial soon established that, provided the vehicle kept to a very clearly defined route on the coral shelf, it could be driven between Gan and Fedu at any time during a critical one hour period spanning low tide, a period which provided ample time for a return journey.

By July, more Gan villagers were leaving their island to move into the newly erected huts on Fedu and by the end of the month, with twenty-two families having left Gan, the evacuation programme was ten days ahead of schedule. Unfortunately, Costain's engineers were certain that the work schedule which they had been given for the period up to the end of August was too optimistic and they stated, much to the displeasure of the staff at the Far East Air Force Headquarters, that completion dates could not all be met. After considerable disagreement and debate significant delays were avoided by juggling priorities and making compromises, mainly requiring temporary changes to the designated function of several buildings. Thus, by the end of the month, most of the airmen had been able to settle into newly built domestic accommodation but many found themselves working in a building which was not being used for its originally designated purpose.

The fire section, for example, continued to operate outdoors under a kadjan roof because the newly built fire engine shed was occupied by the accounts section which had been evicted from its former lodgings in the signals centre to allow N° 8 Radio Fitting Party to work on that building.

The air traffic control staff appeared to have been the most fortunate because the air traffic control centre had been moved out of a kadjan hut into the purpose-built tower, sharing it with the meteorological section which had been formed on the 2nd of June. The move was not, however, as attractive as it seemed because the air traffic control staff found themselves working in a tropical glasshouse without air conditioning; just one of the many temporary compromises made to sustain the momentum of the construction programme.

The working accommodation at the end of July was not all that had been hoped for but with all the major airfield works completed and with the improved domestic accommodation, it was obvious that life at RAF Gan would be far better in the coming months than it had ever been. As the servicemen's morale rose, so too did that of Costain's engineers for most of them would be going home at the beginning of September.

August saw the contractor's staff fully employed on general site work and on the continuing evacuation of families from Gan village. Evacuation was slower that month, mainly because the tides through the Gan-Fedu gap were much higher than normal, preventing the lorries from delivering the prefabricated housing panels to Fedu. Nevertheless, an additional seventeen families had left Gan by the end of the month and the forecast that the remaining villagers would all be able to move before the end of September proved to be accurate, with the last family leaving Gan on the 25th.

At the end of August Costain's two-year contract had been fulfilled at a cost of almost four million pounds and on the 3rd of September Brigadier Stewart, Costain's project manager, accompanied by most of the company's engineers, left Gan and returned to England. The few engineers who remained at the atoll were left to deal with any outstanding problems and to complete the handover to the works department officers who were to be responsible for all future development and maintenance work on the base. Virtually all the Maldivian labourers, whose contracts with Costain had been terminated at the end of August, became Air Ministry employees. Costain's Pakistani employees had all been engaged on fixed term contracts, none of which went beyond the end of September and as their contracts expired most of them were repatriated so that by early October only some three hundred and fifty Pakistanis remained on Gan, all of them recruited to work for the Air Ministry, some of them destined to remain on Gan for many years.

The transfer of responsibility from Costain to the works department engineers was a comprehensive process which was expected to take two or three months even if all went smoothly, which it rarely did.

The first serious problem came in October just as an epidemic of dysentery and food poisoning afflicted over a hundred personnel on Gan, many of them civilians employed by the Air Ministry. At the height of the epidemic, the station's water supply failed. For three days, whilst the engineers worked to effect the repairs, everyone was dependent upon the limited supply provided from bowsers.

It was ironic that the water supply should have failed in a month when almost ten inches of rain converted large areas of the camp into a quagmire criss-crossed with water-filled trenches and spattered with water-filled craters connected by flooded roads. In short, water was everywhere except in the pipes.

Dysentery and food poisoning among the labour force, urgent repairs and foul weather delayed the handover but by the beginning of December the Air Ministry-employed Pakistanis began to undertake the last of the demanding stevedore work, the removal of Costain's heavy plant. Left on the island when the main body of the contractor's engineers departed, the cranes, crushers, graders and rollers all had to be partially dismantled, lifted from the airfield into the landing craft and offloaded into the cargo ship which was riding at anchor in the lagoon, well offshore away from the coral reefs. It was slow, heavy work and the Pakistanis were more than happy when, on the 10th of the month, they saw the final load lifted onto the Clan McLennan and later watched as the ship sailed out of the lagoon carrying well over three hundred and fifty tons of the plant and equipment which they had virtually manhandled off the airfield and out to the anchorage. Further stevedore work was inevitable but with the removal of the heavy plant the labourers realised, with a sense of relief, that they were not likely to be faced again with the back-breaking task of manhandling such cumbersome loads.

Not until early in the new year was the handover completed to the satisfaction of the Air Ministry's district officer, leaving Costain's remaining staff free to depart and the district officer's staff to take over the responsibility for all future site works.

"MARVELLOUS PERFORMANCE" AT GAN

From :- Air Marshal THE EARL OF BANDON, K.B.E. C.B., C.V.O., D.S.O., R.A.F.

CINC/5

Headquarters,
Far East Air Force.
SINGAPORE, 17.

15th May, 1959

Dear Lindsay

I have sent a message to your chaps in Gan congratulating them on the very fine performance of completing the runway on schedule.

I would like also to thank you personally for all the efforts you have put in and for your extremely accurate forecast. Few people, except me, believed it!

Unfortunately I must agree that we will have to put off the ceremony on the 1st, June for the reasons you have given in your letter, but I shall look forward to seeing you there at a later date.

It really has been a marvellous performance and thank you very much.

Y. sincerely
Bandon

Mr. H.B. Lindsay,
Richard Costain, Ltd.,
III Westminster Bridge Road,
LONDON, S.E.I

On time again—and this time in the Maldives. Despite some factors, including a seventeen per cent increase in the runway length, which might have been expected to delay completion, the Gan runway was completed on schedule: a worthy achievement which brought to Mr. Lindsay the congratulatory letter, reproduced above, from the C.-in-C. Far East Air Force, the Earl of Bandon

Fig 12.1. The Commander-in-Chief's congratulatory letter to Costain's project manager, reproduced in the Company's house journal..

XIII   The United Suvadive Islands

The Earl of Bandon's recognition of Afif Didi as the *de facto* leader of the islanders brought immediate benefits for the Adduans and for the construction engineers for it meant that none of the Maldivian government's embargos remained; with nothing more than local agreement sites could be cleared, trees uprooted and buildings demolished. The biggest benefit came from the Gan villagers' readiness to leave their homes even though they knew that prefabricated housing was not available on the other islands. Still they went; many of them to move in with relatives or into kadjan huts built for them by Costain-employed Maldivians.

Those who chose to leave were all provided with a weekly ration of rice to compensate for the loss of their crops on Gan and were promised that they would be provided with prefabricated housing as soon as the units could be delivered and erected. As the exodus began the ground clearance programme gathered pace with homes being demolished as soon as they became vacant. The reasoning was simple. Even if a punitive expedition were to be immediately despatched from Malé, and that was most unlikely, it would take the militia at least two days to travel from the capital to Addu Atoll and if the demolition work on Gan were to be completed during the early days of the rebellion the Maldivian government would be faced with a *fait accompli* if, or when, it re-established its authority over the Adduans.

The euphoric Adduans, convinced that the British would protect them against any punitive expedition from Malé, did not remain isolated in their independence for more than a few days. News of the rebellion soon reached the populations of Fua Mulaku, the island which is generally referred to as an atoll, and Huvadu, the atoll which had been previously known as Suvadiva. The Mulakuans and the Huvaduans promptly declared that they wished to join the rebellion and when they too declared their independence Abdullah Afif Didi proudly announced that a new republic, The United Suvadive Islands, had been born. In their euphoria the Huvaduans and the Mulakuans ignored their vulnerability. It was a mistake for which they were to pay dearly.

Within days, no Maldivian national flags were to be seen flying over the islands of Addu Atoll; they had all been replaced by flags of the newly created republic. The design for the new flags combined simplicity and symbolism. Three horizontal bands; one red, one green and one blue, represented the three groups of islanders; the Adduans, the Huvaduans and the Mulakuans. A solitary star was displayed in each stripe, reinforcing the image of a triumvirate, and the crescent moon of the Moslem religion was positioned at the centre of the flag.

Afif Didi was not the only notable Adduan on the people's council but he was the obvious leader and it was clear that, for him, the early days of independence would be critical because the reality behind the local euphoria was that he and the other council members were expected to improve the lot of several thousand Adduans who had little food and virtually no money. They turned to the British and were immediately given the support of the Earl of Bandon. He arranged, as an emergency measure, for the rice element of the Adduans' wages to be provided by the RAF and for the cash element to be replaced by a chit system. Those arrangements immediately gave the people's council some credibility and when the islanders were told that the council would be responsible for distributing the rice and for supervising the exchange of wage chits for commodities obtained through the NAAFI the status of Afif Didi and his associates was enhanced even more. The Maldivians had not previously been allowed to buy goods from the NAAFI, partly because they were paid in Maldivian rupees which had no exchange value and partly because it was politically unacceptable for the Maldivian government's officials to concede that the Adduans could not obtain all that they wanted from the Malé-based traders who sailed to the atoll every few months. For the Adduans, being given access to the NAAFI order book was a dream fulfilled; it meant that they could work for the goods which had been unobtainable when the only currency they could offer was the Maldivian rupee.

Whilst the Adduans were settling quite smoothly into their new regime, the Maldivian government's political manoeuvring had started in Malé and Colombo. The United Kingdom's High Commissioner in Ceylon had been informed that the Maldivian Prime Minister was convinced that the British were conniving with Afif Didi and thus interfering in the internal affairs of the Maldives by supporting a revolution. It was an accusation which the High Commissioner found extremely difficult to rebut in view of the way in which the Adduan economy was being propped up by employment paid for in rice and NAAFI vouchers channelled through the peoples' council.

As far as Wing Commander Kent was concerned, sustaining good relations with Afif Didi and the people's council was highly desirable but for Afif Didi, maintaining a good working relationship with the station commander was crucial because the Adduans' declaration of independence had created problems which he, as the elected president of the nascent republic, was expected to deal with. The most obvious, and the most pressing, was the need to create funds to finance the government of the United Suvadive Islands. The equally obvious solution was to raise the necessary revenue through taxation; obvious but neither popular nor equitable and Afif Didi was far too astute to start his period of office with such a politically dangerous measure. A combination of modest taxation and the development of a trading company provided the answer. The newly formed government devised a seven per cent tax on all wages and benefits in kind for those employed by the British; collected leasehold payments from plantation owners who would normally have made such payments to the Maldivian government; imposed fines for those found guilty of offences under the largely unchanged criminal legislation and, most importantly for the financial health of the fledgling republic, formed the Adduan Trading Corporation. The corporation was a share company in which one thousand four hundred and twenty-six shareholders purchased a total of six thousand three hundred and forty-one shares priced at sixty-three shillings (£3·15) each to provide almost twenty thousand pounds of share capital. The company was given a virtual monopoly over Maldivian trading at the atoll with taxation of its profits providing a source of income for the newly formed government. A poll tax on every adult Maldivian in the atoll was also introduced but it was fairly short-lived because when Afif Didi saw that its unpopularity was likely to undermine his position he immediately rescinded it.

The republic soon faced its first major problem; near-starvation at Huvadu (Suvadiva) atoll. Ironically, this was the atoll which had been earmarked as a potential resettlement site for the Gan villagers and which had been visited, with the help of RAF Gan's marine craft, by an Air Ministry team the previous December to ascertain the suitability of the site

and the anchorage. The Huvaduans, like the Adduans, had received no supplies from Malé for several months but, unlike the Adduans, they had no other external sources of food and their own meagre crops were insufficient to supply the population's needs.

The United Kingdom's High Commissioner in Colombo had been made aware of the problem towards the end of 1958 and had offered, during negotiations over the Gan agreement, to help to alleviate the famine. The Maldivian officials, however, had shown little concern for the plight of the Huvaduans, denied that there was a famine and refused all his offers. At that time the British government would not take unilateral action to help the islanders because such direct interference in the internal affairs of the Maldives would not only have broken the long-standing agreement between the two nations, it would almost certainly have brought to an end the negotiations over the leasehold arrangements for the lands at Addu Atoll. But by the time the Huvaduans had joined the rebellion in the south and become part of the United Suvadive Islands the negotiations between the British and Maldivian governments had already broken down and when it became evident that the Maldivian ministers were either unwilling or unable to institute relief measures for the southern islanders the British government no longer felt constrained to stand idly by. A request for help was made by Afif Didi on behalf of the people's council and, either consequentially or coincidentally, the British government began to provide food for the Huvaduans from the stocks held at RAF Gan. It was a move which, quite predictably, infuriated the Maldivian Prime Minister.

At Addu atoll everything seemed quiet although the islanders, superficially elated with their new-found freedom, were actually living in a state of nervous tension. They were well aware that their government, whilst taking issue with the British over events at the atoll, would also be making plans to bring the rebels into line and to bring the ringleaders to trial. Rumours were rife. Reports of ships sailing south to bring the militia to Fua Mulaku, Huvadu and Addu Atoll were frequent and, until the 30th of March, were false. On that date the Adduans heard that the SS Elizabeth Boyes had sailed from Malé to Fua Mulaku, bringing militiamen who mounted two small-scale armed raids against the islanders. The Mulakuans, armed only with sticks and stones, eventually repelled the raiders by sheer weight of numbers but several of them received bullet wounds in the process. Four of the most seriously injured were desperately in need of medical treatment and were brought to Gan where the medical staff decided that although three of them could be treated locally one needed to be evacuated to Singapore for hospital treatment.

The move was vetoed by the Singapore-based Command staff as being politically too sensitive. The alternative, to send the patient to Ceylon, was more acceptable but when the medical staff there made it clear that they would not detain any patient who chose to leave their hospital, the political adviser on Gan immediately warned the station commander that Nasir would make political capital out of the affair if such an event were to occur. In the eyes of their government, the Mulakuans were rebels and if one of them were to be taken to Ceylon by the RAF and subsequently allowed to walk free the Maldivian Prime Minister would publicise, as widely as possible, the claim that the British were helping Maldivian criminals to escape from justice. The patient's needs however, outweighed the political considerations and, after considerable debate, he was flown to Ceylon. He received treatment, recovered, duly absconded and was not heard of again. Surprisingly, Nasir did not protest, presumably because he remained unaware of the incident.

As word spread through the islands of Addu Atoll, the injured Mulakuans' accounts of the fighting which they had survived became exaggerated, sending shivers of fear through the village communities. Conscious of the islanders' fears, Kent suggested that they could send an SOS signal to Gan by using a smoking bonfire in the daytime or by displaying a light at night. By nightfall on the 30th of March 1959 the Adduans had convinced themselves that at any moment the Maldivian militia would arrive at their atoll and force them into submission. That night the normally bright tropical moon was hidden behind heavy clouds, creating conditions which were perfect for a punitive force to land unnoticed. Sure enough, at eleven o'clock a light was flashed from Hitaddu where some villagers claimed to have seen a steam ship from Malé creeping quietly into the lagoon. The islanders, expecting to be attacked by a landing party at any minute, signalled for assistance from the RAF.

With no telephone network on Gan it took some time to alert all the servicemen but they were assembled as rapidly as possible, briefed on the situation and issued with the few available arms. The station commander set out across the lagoon in one of the RAF's marine craft while Wing Commander Thomas, the station commander designate, who had arrived at Gan earlier that week and was due to take over from Wing Commander Kent on the 2nd of April, was left in charge ashore. On arriving at Hitaddu Kent was told of the reports of a steam ship and of the islanders' fears of attack. One officer and twenty-four airmen were put ashore at Hitaddu to safeguard the RAF's property. The few Pakistanis who were on Hitaddu at that time were evacuated to Gan and the RAF's fleet, comprising one pinnace, one high speed launch and three landing craft, was then deployed to search in the dark for the Maldivian ship. Whilst the patrol was unsuccessfully trying to locate the intruder along the lagoon shoreline the villagers of Midu displayed their SOS light and the RAF's marine craft was duly headed across the lagoon to search the waters off their island. It was all to no avail. The search continued for some hours but as the sky lightened with the dawn the searchers realised that the whole affair was a false alarm triggered by the deep fears of the Adduans. There was no sign of any large ship even though the villagers' reports had been detailed enough to refer to '...a Maldivian crew and two motor launches on board'.

A night of apparently futile activity actually provided some valuable insights into people's attitudes and the servicemen's readiness to cope with a threat to the security of the base. The incident highlighted the fact that servicemen posted to Gan at that time had little more than the most basic training in the use of firearms and had not been required to undertake range proficiency training before embarking for Gan. Additionally, none had a clearly defined role in the event of an attack upon Gan or Hitaddu for the simple reason that, because nobody had believed that the atoll was likely to be attacked, there was no station defence plan. It was, however, heartening that they had reacted so promptly and had so cheerfully accepted the unexpected threat of armed conflict.

The affair thus led to the production of a defence plan for the leased territories and to the introduction of weapons training for all servicemen. It also enhanced the relationship between the military and the Adduans who had been greatly reassured by the reaction to their cry for help. They did not know, or did not want to believe, that the servicemen would only have engaged the militiamen in defence of British property and could not have gone to the rescue of any islanders outside the leased territories without creating an international incident.

If nothing else, the affair gave Wing Commander Thomas a vivid example of the unique responsibilities which he would inherit when he became Gan's next station commander.

That same month Major Phillips, the resident political adviser, also left, his contract completed. His departure was oddly timed, virtually coinciding with the change of command at Gan and depriving Thomas of any future opportunity to refer to the one man on the island who could discuss any situation in the light of Maldivian politics before and after the Adduan rebellion. For others at Gan, Phillips' departure was regretted for an entirely different reason; his hospitality had become legendary on the island, giving rise to the unofficial soubriquet for his bungalow: Vat 69. Phillips had been appointed on the basis that, if the post did not become redundant after a year or so, he would be replaced by someone from the Diplomatic Service and with the complex situation created by the Adduans' rebellion it was obvious that a successor would have to be appointed. Mr Humphrey Arthington-Davy was selected to take over from Phillips but he was not due to arrive at Addu Atoll until the 1st of May 1959 and thus met Phillips only briefly in London, learning something of the political manoeuvring in the Maldives without gaining any real appreciation of the Adduan environment. When, as scheduled, he did arrive at Gan on the due date it was too late for him to start asking questions about local *real politik*; the station commander had been in post for less than a month, Phillips had had no staff working for him, the file records were minimal and, with no telephone links to the outside world, the fastest means of communicating with the diplomatic staff in Colombo was *via* the military signals network, a system which was far too slow to use for a conversation. Arthington-Davy soon discovered that he had little choice but to work on his own initiative and to rely on his own judgement in a highly volatile political atmosphere.

Throughout his time at Gan he was to be involved in a seemingly endless round of devious political manoeuvring starting with the apparently innocuous change in the method of paying the Maldivians. On the 9th of April, three weeks before he had arrived, authority had been given for the Maldivian workers to be paid, *via* their people's council, in Sterling instead of in NAAFI vouchers. That helped to remove the embryonic black market which was developing between the Maldivians and the Pakistanis but it was ill-received by the Maldivian government ministers who objected to it on the rather dubious grounds that vouchers did little more than provide food in exchange for labour whereas payment in Sterling represented an unacceptably dramatic cultural and economic change for the Adduans. It was hardly a valid argument but it was adequate for Nasir's purpose which was to sustain a barrage of complaints against the British. Arthington–Davy was inevitably dragged into the disagreement, having to explain the situation to the High Commissioner in Ceylon who needed to rebut Nasir's claim that the British were planning to change the local culture at Addu Atoll into a Sterling-based cash economy.

That was not the only April development which the Maldivian ministers objected to. If anything, they were even more vociferous in their complaints about the assistance given to the Mulakuans who had fled from the fighting on their island, had reached Addu Atoll and had remained there rather than return to the violence and the near-famine on their home island. What incensed the Maldivian government was that the humanitarian aid provided by the RAF, and referred to by Mr Alport in his written parliamentary statement on the 19th of March, was extended, in April, to all the refugees at Addu Atoll regardless of whether they had fled to escape from violence or famine. To add insult to injury as far as Nasir was concerned, the Air Ministry had agreed to give Afif Didi a monthly allocation of twenty-two and a half pounds of rice, three and three-quarter pounds of sugar, forty-five coconuts and four pints of kerosene for each refugee, leaving the distribution of the rations to him, thus further strengthening his local reputation as a man who could persuade the British to provide for the islanders.

The Huvaduans who had reached Addu Atoll had, like most refugees, arrived in search of food but without money with which to purchase it or goods with which to barter. Their representative had explained that in spite of the supplies sent by the RAF early in the year there was still a famine at Huvadu because no food had been supplied from Malé for several months. That was one of the reasons why they had joined the rebellion and, whilst they were grateful for the hospitality and the monthly rations they were to receive from the RAF, they needed to obtain food for the islanders they had left behind. In short, they wanted to work for the British to earn the money needed to buy food and ship it back to their home islands. Once again, a proposal by Afif Didi was accepted by the British and by the islanders. Huvaduans would be employed on Gan and paid in cash on the understanding that their representative would take their earnings and purchase food for the Huvaduan communities. When they learned of this arrangement, the ministers in Malé were outraged. They regarded the Mulakuans and the Huvaduans as traitors for joining the rebellious Adduans and they made it clear to the United Kingdom's High Commissioner that in their eyes the British at Addu Atoll were not merely supporting the Adduan rebels, they were harbouring and supporting traitors from Fua Mulaku and from Huvadu. They blamed Arthington-Davy for either instigating or encouraging these local arrangements. He was, to the Maldivian government, virtually *persona non grata* within weeks of his arrival at Gan.

The Maldivian government's use of the press and the radio to condemn the rebels and castigate the British government for interfering in the internal affairs of the Maldives convinced Afif that some international publicity in support of the rebels' cause was needed. Ever an opportunist with a good sense of timing, he chose to write to The Times of London when the Maldivian government's media campaign was at its peak. His five hundred word letter setting out the reasons for secession, condemning the Maldivian government's record and asking for the United Suvadive Islands to be internationally recognised as an independent republic was published on the 29th March 1959 (Fig 13.1).

This was a further irritant as far as Nasir was concerned because it gave the impression that Afif and his conspirators were being given international press publicity with the active encouragement of the British.

Although Nasir and his ministers were at loggerheads with the British government the affair at Addu Atoll was a very minor event on the world stage and the letter, understandably, provoked only lukewarm international interest. That which was shown had little to do with the plight of the southern Maldivians, it had much more to do with the presence of the British military in the Indian Ocean and the opportunity for anti-Western governments to voice international criticism of Britain's continuing imperialistic adventures.

By mid-July the political scene at Addu Atoll was beset by reports that Huvadu and Fua Mulaku had been attacked by the Maldivian militiamen who had forced the islanders to surrender after a series of skirmishes in which the islanders' sticks and stones had been pitted against the militia's firearms. Inevitably, rumours were rife that the Adduans would be facing similar attacks within a few weeks. Afif could not quell the rumours; the best he could do was to assure the villagers that the British servicemen would physically protect them at Addu Atoll and the British government would

protect their interests when dealing with Nasir. Such assurances, given during a state of high tension may have been politically sound from Afif's point of view but they were potentially embarrassing for the station commander. He could certainly not expect to receive approval for any action which went beyond the protection of the leased territories, the non-Maldivian employees and British property. In short, the servicemen would no doubt mount whatever defence was required to sustain the operational capability of the base but would not go to the defence of the Maldivian village communities living on the various islands of Addu Atoll. If, however, he were to spell that out to the Adduans their faith in the British would vanish and with it would go their willingness to work and their leader's goodwill.

Coincidentally, July, the month in which the islanders heard rumours of attacks on Huvadu and Fua Mulaku, was also the month in which news reached Addu Atoll of a serious influenza epidemic in Malé. There were rumours of three thousand deaths at the capital and although that was obviously a gross exaggeration there were undoubtedly many people dying. The RAF's medical staff on Gan were put on standby to fly to Malé to provide the drugs, expertise and equipment which were not available in the capital and that brought the RAF doctors into the political arena as far as the Adduans were concerned.

The medical staff had often been accused by the Maldivian government of fostering anti-Malé feelings amongst the Adduans; now the villagers were letting it be known that they did not expect the RAF to go to the aid of the government which had consistently disregarded the health needs of the southern islanders. They made it clear that any such move would be seen as political and would jeopardise the good working relationships between the Adduans and the British although just what they meant by that was never spelled out. The influenza epidemic was confirmed by the Maldivian government but the offer of help from the RAF was refused, presumably because acceptance would have dented Nasir's pride, coming, as it would have done, so soon after his outbursts against the British. The fact that help would have come from Addu Atoll, the cause of the acrimony, rather than from Ceylon-based staff, made acceptance of the offer virtually impossible.

On the night of the 5th of August 1959 pandemonium broke out on Hitaddu. Villagers, roused from their beds, poured down to the beach where two large boats had been dragged ashore and sixty Huvaduans captured. The boats had crept unannounced into the lagoon in the middle of the night but had been seen by several Adduans who had alerted other villagers and organised a flotilla of dhonis to surround the uninvited visitors. There were thirty islanders on each of the boats and when challenged they did not resist arrest. They were searched, found to be unarmed, and taken away for questioning. The story which emerged confirmed earlier reports which had reached Addu and further fuelled the Adduans' fears. The two boats had come from Huvadu and the crews were able to give eye witness accounts of the attack on their islands. Several hundred militiamen from Malé had sailed south on board the Maldive Star with instructions to quell the rebellion in the southern islands. They had landed at Gadu on the 16th of July and at Tuandu the following day. The Huvaduans described the attacks as totally one-sided with the militiamen apparently firing at random. They estimated that eight villagers had been killed, a dozen wounded, many captured and flogged and about one hundred held on board the Maldive Star ready to be transported to Malé for trial. The militia force had been much greater than the small contingent which had attacked the Mulakuans earlier in the year and it was due to sail to Mulaku as soon as normality had been restored at Huvadu. After quelling any resistance at Mulaku the militiamen were expected to set out for Addu Atoll. The boats which had arrived off Hitaddu in the middle of the night were intended to be the first of a large contingent which would precede the arrival of the Maldive Star and two other boats, all with militia on board. The plan was apparently to infiltrate the islands of Addu Atoll with Huvaduans who were either supporters of the central government or who could be forced to follow orders for fear of future retribution if they refused. The intended infiltrators were under orders to spread worrying rumours and to create panic when the Maldive Star and its escorts sailed into the Adduan lagoon.

The recapture of Huvadu Atoll meant that the fleeing islanders who had arrived at Addu Atoll some weeks previously had become refugees and, as displaced persons at Addu, needed to be assimilated into the local communities until it was safe for them to return home, if it ever was. The Adduans, unsure what to do with the captured crews, eventually accepted that they had been forced to sail to Addu and although they were regarded with some suspicion they were allowed to settle at Addu Atoll as refugees alongside others who had already been accepted into the Adduan villages.

Afif immediately passed on to Gan's political adviser the news of the capture and the information which had been obtained from the prisoners. Military security on the leased territories was promptly increased and the Headquarters' staff of the Far East Air Force were informed of the potentially serious development. It soon became obvious that the Adduans expected to see the Maldive Star sailing into the lagoon at any moment and disgorging the militiamen who would force them into submission. They expressed their anxiety by staging a quiet, orderly demonstration on Gan, declaring their faith in the willingness of the British military to protect them and in their right to such protection as a reward for their loyalty and goodwill towards the British government.

The seriousness of the situation was obviously appreciated by the Command staff in Singapore because a series of defensive measures was immediately put into effect under the guise of an air mobility exercise, a ruse intended to reduce the interest shown by the British press correspondents who had become curious about the situation at Addu Atoll ever since Afif's letter had been published in The Times. On the 8th of August, just three days after the Huvaduan infiltrators had been captured, two Hastings aircraft and a Beverley flew from Singapore to Gan bringing one hundred men of the 1st Battalion, The Cheshire Regiment, complete with equipment and enough tentage for them to live under canvas on the airfield until they could be relieved by an RAF Regiment squadron. Two aircraft, a Dakota and a Twin Pioneer, were also despatched to take up reconnaissance duties at Gan alongside two Shackletons on detachment from Ballykelly. On the 15th of the month forty RAF Regiment personnel arrived on board XK 695, the first Comet to land at Gan; an event to be remembered by all those on board because the aircraft burst three tyres on landing. The remainder of the two RAF Regiment flights arrived the following day and the company of Cheshires left for Singapore.

The August development brought matters to a head between the British and Maldivian governments. The acrimony and the anger which had led to the abandonment of the inter-governmental talks earlier in the year had persuaded the British ministers that there was no point in discussing the latest turn of events; a hard-line approach would be far more appropriate. Accordingly, the Maldivian government was formally told that the British government regarded the operational state of RAF Gan, which included both the island of Gan and the transmitter site on Hitaddu, to be of paramount importance and if the Maldivian militia were to attack the Adduans, thereby disrupting the RAF's operations, British troops would defend the atoll. Force would be met by force.

Impotent in the face of such a threat, Nasir could only fume and resort to highly distorted and widely publicised versions of events in an attempt to bring international pressure to bear on Britain. It was a technique which was to continue for several years.

The situation was being taken with increasing seriousness by the British government. If the Adduans were to be attacked by the Maldivian militia any skirmishes which broke out ashore could easily be contained by the RAF Regiment squadron. The best defence, however, had to be one which would prevent the militiamen from landing and it was obvious that the RAF's locally based marine craft could not adequately take on such a role. What was needed was a naval presence significant enough to deter the Maldivian government from sending their militia to the atoll. The British Prime Minister decided that one Royal Navy ship would provide a more-than-adequate deterrent and the Admiralty was accordingly instructed to establish a rota of guard ships to be based at Addu Atoll to protect Britain's interests there. The Admiralty complied and the Caesar Class destroyer HMS Cavalier, the first of a series of guard ships to be stationed at the atoll, duly sailed from Cochin on the 6th of August and dropped anchor in the atoll lagoon off Gan's northern shore in the evening of the following day. From then on, one of the Royal Navy's ships was always on station in the lagoon with Carysfort, Crane, Cavalier, Caprice, Lagos, Loch Insh and St Bride's Bay rostered to undertake monthly spells of duty at the atoll.

Throughout September tension remained high in every Adduan village. The Shackleton, Dakota and Twin Pioneer aircraft continued to make daily reconnaissance flights, identifying nothing more sinister than a small boatload of Huvaduans who reached the atoll towards the end of the month. Bringing nothing more than a consignment of Maldivian government leaflets encouraging the Adduans to return to the normality of central control, they posed no threat, were arrested by the Adduans as soon as their boat entered the lagoon and were kept under house arrest until it was deemed safe to allow them to settle into one of the Adduan villages.

In spite of Britain's declaration that, if necessary, force would be met by force the Maldivian Government Representative in Ceylon was somehow given the impression that Afif Didi was ready to return to the fold because on the 9th of September he wrote to Afif saying:

> 'I have heard from the United Kingdom Office in Colombo that you are now ready to meet the representatives of the lawfully constituted government of The Maldives and as such I presume that you are ready to accept the authority of the Maldivian Government. If this be the case the Maldivian Government welcomes this news and would be glad to meet you in Malé.'

Afif's reply (Fig 13.2) made the Maldivian Government Representative realise that he could not have been more mistaken but, taking the opportunity to blame the British for the islanders' intransigence he wrote to Afif saying:

> 'I know no Maldivian in Addu Atoll is capable of drafting such a reply. Therefore, the reply itself is a further proof of the extent to which the United Kingdom authorities have been exercising their influence over the handful of people who are misled in Addu Atoll.'

It was hardly surprising that occasional parliamentary references to negotiations with the Maldivian government, the press releases on the RAF's Indian Ocean staging post, the Maldivian government's outbursts and Afif Didi's letter to The Times attracted the attention of British journalists. Most of them accepted that they would get nothing more than the press releases because Gan was not only Air Ministry controlled territory, it was so remote as to make it almost inaccessible without the help of the Maldivian government. There was, however, one enterprising journalist, Bertram Jones, who created a furore by flying to Ceylon and chartering a boat, the Sunfarer, to take him to Addu Atoll. His enterprise paid off. His one-man expedition gave the Daily Express an exclusive eye-witness report on events at the atoll and gave the British public its first insight into the bizarre political situation surrounding Britain's military presence in the Maldives.

The unannounced midnight arrival of the Sunfarer in the lagoon at Addu Atoll triggered off a great deal of activity ashore and on board HMS Crane, the RN guardship then at anchor in the lagoon. The sound of the Sunfarer's plunging anchor chain alerted several Adduans and they quickly spread the news of the new, as yet unidentified, arrival in the lagoon. As soon as the Crane's captain was sure that the newcomer posed no threat to the RAF base he took no further part in the affair, leaving the RAF's security officer to deal with the matter. Jones was invited ashore where he met the station commander and received a promise that a signal would be sent to London seeking permission for him to visit the RAF sites on Gan and Hitaddu. The journalist remained ashore for no more than twenty minutes but that was long enough for the Maldivians' bush telegraph to start relaying information to Hitaddu. By mid-afternoon a dhoni had been rowed out to the Sunfarer and Jones, still on board and awaiting a message from Wing Commander Thomas, was handed an envelope marked 'The United Suvadive Government's Service'. Inside was a note from Afif Didi saying:

> 'There is a rumour that you are a British Newspaper correspondent. I welcome you to the United Suvadive Islands and I shall be pleased if you will visit Hitaddu tomorrow to see for yourself how the people are enjoying liberty and freedom'.

Jones promptly accepted the welcome invitation and the next morning he was rowed ashore in one of the larger dhonis. The journey, which took some two and a half hours, gave him an immediate appreciation of the daily effort made by those islanders who commuted across the lagoon to work on Gan. Afif Didi, together with members of the people's council, spent several hours discussing with Jones the events which had led to the unilateral declaration of independence. They denied that Britain had played any part in the rebellion, explaining that the Maldivian government had never helped them to improve the conditions under which they lived, had left them to provide their own education service and, most importantly, had persistently refused to provide health care for the southern islanders. With the arrival of the British military, the islanders had begun to envisage a better life but had had their ambitions destroyed by their government's taxation proposals which were apparently designed to siphon most of the islanders' wages into the central government coffers. The proposals had been the last straw and had led to the creation of a new republic, The United Suvadive Islands.

Jones' perseverance paid off for he was allowed to visit Gan, to take photographs and to talk to the servicemen and civilians who were employed on the construction programme. His exclusive and somewhat fanciful report was published in the Daily Express on the 25th of November 1959, giving a very brief insight into the affairs at Addu Atoll and causing some amusement on Gan. Undoubtedly the report pleased Afif Didi who was keen to get as much publicity as he could, partly to espouse his cause internationally to the embarrassment of the Maldivian government and partly to work towards international recognition of the fledgling republic. The Daily Express articles caused a brief flurry of interest in Britain and led the Air Ministry staff to review their attitude towards press visitors to Gan.

It was difficult, having accepted the *fait accompli* presented by Jones, to deny other newspaper reporters the opportunity to visit the island and a full press visit to the base was subsequently arranged by the Air Ministry with the Far East Air Force Public Relations Officer from Singapore accompanying a group of reporters on a full tour of Gan. For Afif Didi, the opportunity was too good to miss; he wrote to every one of the reporters (Fig 13.3), briefly described the situation at Huvadu and Fua Mulaku, referred to the arrival of refugees at Addu Atoll and invited the group of journalists to visit the Adduan villages, an invitation which the Public Relations Officer declined on their behalf. For Afif, that was a disappointment but he was aware that he had at least used their visit to publicise, once again, the United Suvadive Islands. He was also astute enough to use the cyclostyled 'Times of Addu', a multi-page news sheet which had been produced on Gan every fortnight since the Adduans' unilateral declaration of independence, to ensure that the Adduan villagers were informed of his manoeuvring on their behalf (Fig 13.4).

Surprisingly, after excluding the press from Gan for so long, the Air Ministry suddenly adopted an almost unprecedented degree of openness about the RAF station, even giving permission for the Illustrated London News to publish two aerial photographs of Gan clearly showing the development of Britain's only strategic air base in the Indian Ocean. Bertram Jones had opened the door for other reporters. For how long it would remain open was another matter.

It was not until just after Christmas 1959, almost twelve months after the Adduans' declaration of independence, that news reached Gan that the Maldivian government had contacted Sir Arthur Morley, the United Kingdom's high commissioner in Ceylon, and suggested re-opening the talks about Gan. The Maldivian Prime Minister had suggested, and Sir Arthur had readily agreed, that Mr Ahmed Zaki could visit Colombo for preliminary discussions. Rather than have Zaki sail from Malé to Ceylon on board a Maldivian trading vessel Sir Arthur prevailed upon the Royal Navy to take him to Addu Atoll as a passenger on board HMS Mounts Bay.

That was three hundred miles out of his way but from there he could fly to Ceylon, courtesy of the RAF, and still arrive in Colombo far sooner than he could have done by travelling directly from Malé to Ceylon on board a Maldivian boat. Zaki viewed that schedule with some trepidation because on his last visit to the atoll, in December 1958, he had been fortunate to escape injury at the hands of the enraged islanders. With that in mind, cloak-and-dagger arrangements were made for his arrival at Gan and his almost immediate departure for Ceylon.

The carefully laid plans were, however, rendered pointless when the aircraft which was to take him to Ceylon became unserviceable, leaving an increasingly nervous Zaki waiting for the arrival of a replacement aircraft, quite unaware that his presence on board ship had been disclosed to the Adduans by one of the ship's Chinese stewards. Afif Didi, when informed of Zaki's arrival, expressed his complete faith in Britain's determination to safeguard the interests of the Adduans in any political dealings with the Maldivian government and instructed the islanders to take no action against the minister. The RAF's security staff were, like Zaki, unaware of the breach of security or of Afif's instructions; they continued their cloak-and-dagger operation for some fifteen hours until, at four o'clock in the morning, Ahmed Zaki was finally able to depart for Ceylon.

The minister's preliminary discussions with Sir Arthur Morley went so well that he was able to return to Malé with the draft for a new agreement between the British and Maldivian governments. Somewhat surprisingly, the Maldivian ministers were generally satisfied with the draft and indicated their willingness to recommend the text to their Sultan, subject to minor amendments which they wished to discuss. Within days, The Earl of Bandon met Sir Arthur Morley and Mr Alport on Gan to discuss the latest developments before boarding HMS Gambia on the 12th of February 1960 and heading for Malé. At their meeting with Nasir and his cabinet ministers they quickly negotiated acceptable modifications to the draft text. The result was a final agreement which was, perhaps appropriately, signed by the Sultan on St Valentine's day. In spite of the rapidity with which the agreement had been produced and the signing ceremony organised, the Earl of Bandon arranged for a ceremonial flypast of RAF aircraft to symbolise the apparent end of the political arguments and the acrimony generated by the construction of the RAF's staging post on Gan. Thus, within minutes of the signing of the new agreement, three Shackletons flew low over Malé, the sound of their Griffon engines causing the population to cease its day-to-day activities and wonder what had engendered such an unusual event.

For the rebels at Addu Atoll, however, the newly signed agreement boded ill, even though it appeared to provide them with some element of protection against the retribution which the Maldivian authorities would obviously wish to exact as soon as the opportunity arose. The main features of the agreement reiterated those of earlier agreements, confirming that the British government would refrain from intervening in Maldivian domestic affairs; that an airbase could be established and maintained at Addu Atoll for the protection of the Maldives and the Commonwealth; that the Maldivian government would give all possible rights and facilities needed for the operation of the airbase and would remain free to deal with other countries for education, economic, cultural and other non-political affairs.

The agreement gave Britain the use of Gan and part of Hitaddu for thirty years, spanning the period from 1956 to 1986. In exchange, the British government agreed to pay the Maldivian government one hundred thousand pounds immediately and to provide three-quarters of a million pounds over the next five years to aid the economic development of the Maldives, a vastly different financial arrangement from the two thousand pounds per annum specified in the original agreement. As for the dissolution of the so-called republic established by the Adduans, the Maldivian government agreed not to send any officials from Malé to reside at Addu Atoll until after a British representative had been established at Malé and both governments believed that Maldivian officials would not be molested on arrival at Addu Atoll. The letters subsequently exchanged between Nasir and Alport confirmed that Britain would attempt to bring about a reconciliation between the Adduans and their lawful government as soon as possible. There was no mention of the eventual fate of the rebels, nor, more importantly, of their leaders.

On the day when Sir Arthur Morley, Mr Alport and the Earl of Bandon set sail for Malé on board HMS Gambia, the Adduans had been informed by the atoll-based adviser on Maldivian affairs that Britain intended to sign a new agreement with the Maldivian government. When the islanders became aware of the contents of the agreement some began to waiver in their support for Afif Didi. More significantly, there were the first signs of a serious split in the leadership with three highly respected members of the peoples' council in favour of a settlement with the Maldivian government under the auspices of the British. Those three had all been educated abroad, had all previously been employed by the RAF in posts ranging from clerical officer to interpreter and were probably the only Adduans of a similar calibre to Afif. The loss of their support was a severe blow because Afif knew that without unanimity in the people's council, he stood little chance of sustaining the rebellion in the face of the latest agreement between the British and Maldivian governments. The villagers soon became aware of the split in the council and they also began to waver in their support for the rebellion, even though they believed that they would suffer dire consequences if central government authority were to return to their atoll.

The Adduans may not have been happy with the situation but the RAF Regiment airmen who were encamped on Gan's airfield certainly were. The threat of an armed incursion by the Maldivian militia ended when the agreement was signed and four days later, with the RAF Regiment no longer needed on the island, the airmen packed their tents and departed. On the 29th of February HMS Lagos, the Royal Navy's guard ship which had relieved Cavalier, sailed out of the lagoon, taking her delighted crew away from the boredom of static guard duty. Her departure, signalling the end of the stand-off, was a welcome sight for Wing Commander Thomas' successor, Wing Commander Constable-Maxwell who had arrived at the atoll twenty-four hours earlier and was understandably relieved to learn that the previously volatile situation had calmed down enough for Gan's defence forces to be withdrawn.

On the 2nd of April, in keeping with the rediscovered policy of friendly co-operation, the RAF's marine craft section sent a launch to Malé, taking Gan's senior works services engineer and a Far East Air Force staff officer to assess the suitability of Hululé island as a site for an airstrip and the neighbouring Dunidu, one of the smallest of the islands in Malé atoll, as a convenient location for a resident British representative. Dunidu was barely adequate and it was a lagoon boat ride away from the preferred location on the capital island of Malé but Dunidu it was and, as events unfolded, the island's distance from the capital, at first seen as undesirable, was subsequently to be a considerable advantage.

In spite of the general accord over the agreement, at least at government level, it was five months after the signing before Arthington-Davy, the Gan-based political adviser, was able to pay his first visit to Malé. Accompanied by a medical adviser, a Commonwealth Relations Office representative from London and by Gan's senior works services engineer, he was received by the Sultan, a clear indication of his change of status from *persona non grata* to accepted representative.

In subsequent discussions with Nasir virtually every aspect of the return to political normality at Addu Atoll was covered. The local implications of the agreement; the return to Addu of the central government's officials; the co-operation of the British; the provision of health care for the islanders; the construction of the proposed runway at Hululé and the provision of accommodation at Dunidu for a British government representative: all were considered. But no mention was made of the fate of the Adduan rebels. The Maldivian Prime Minister's deliberate avoidance of any discussion of their fate, indeed his refusal to be drawn into making any comment on that aspect of his plans, was duly reported to the United Kingdom's High Commissioner in Ceylon who was well aware that the Maldivian government had only recently quelled, with some loss of life, a further revolt at Huvadu, causing the Fua Mulakuans, also rebelling against their government, to surrender before being attacked. There was nothing the High Commissioner could do about Nasir's attitude apart from ensuring that Wing Commander Constable-Maxwell was fully aware of the potential threat to Afif and his co-conspirators.

True to his word Nasir arranged for accommodation to be built on Dunidu for a British representative, enabling Arthington-Davy to leave Gan for Malé early in October to become 'our man in the Maldives', his departure coinciding with that of Constable-Maxwell, whose ill health had led to his early repatriation, and the arrival of his successor, Wing Commander Cropper.

Within days of Arthington-Davy's arrival at Dunidu the airstrip at Hululé was in use with a Bristol Freighter of the Royal New Zealand Air Force making the first landing there on the 19th of October 1960. The runway, although unsuitable for aircraft any larger than a Valetta or a Bristol Freighter, enabled the RAF to establish an invaluable link with Ceylon and Gan for Arthington-Davy, supplementing the signals network which provided his only day-to-day contact with the outside world. Those aircraft types became quite frequent visitors to Hululé, providing *ad hoc* passenger flights and delivering bulky freight whilst the mail and any urgently needed medical supplies were invariably delivered by a Shackleton deployed from

Gan. Too large to use the Hululé runway, the Shackleton could only provide a delivery service to the British Representative by making low-level parachute drops.

Eight months after the signing of the new agreement, the Maldivian government appeared to be in no hurry to restore its authority at Addu Atoll, Nasir apparently being content to wait until Britain declared that the time was right for his officials to return to Hitaddu. Meanwhile, the Adduans, well aware that the game was up, could do nothing but wait apprehensively. Their fears were heightened in October when one of the RAF's marine craft returned to Gan from a navigation exercise around Fua Mulaku and reported the presence of several large vessels carrying Maldivians who were all dressed in military-style uniforms. The report convinced the Adduans that the so-called return to political normality would merely provide their government with its long-awaited opportunity to exact revenge on them. They believed that just over the horizon the militiamen were waiting. Knowing that resistance would be futile and that flight was impossible, they awaited their fate, praying ever more fervently as the tension built up.

Their prayers were to be answered.

The British government, committed by the 1960 agreement to '...*work for a reconciliation between the Adduans and the Maldivian Government*' was not working to an agreed schedule and was not prepared to recommend the return of central government officials to Addu Atoll whilst the Adduans continued to display open hostility towards such a development. Thus 1961 arrived without any sign of a return to political normality at the atoll. That, however, didn't mean that the Adduans' fears were dispelled and in January 1961 they surfaced with a scaremongering rumour that the Maldivian militiamen were planning to attack Hitaddu during the February observation of Ramadan. Although Afif Didi considered that to be unlikely, the opportunity was taken to rehearse the station's defence plan which required the servicemen to sustain the normal operational functions of the staging post whilst protecting the leased territories until the arrival, probably within forty-eight hours, of RAF Regiment personnel from Singapore or Britain.

The Adduans, still convinced that retribution would come their way as soon as the Maldivian government had the opportunity, were once again falsely reassured by the defence exercise, viewing it as a practical demonstration of the RAF's intention to defend them against their own government. The reality was that the station commander, like his predecessors, was under orders to take no action if the Maldivian militia were to attack the Adduans anywhere other than on Gan or on the transmitter site on Hitaddu. His brief from the Air Officer Commanding-in-Chief of the Far East Air Force was to defend that which was essential for the operation of the staging post, the communications centre and the search and rescue facility. That did not necessarily include the defence of the Maldivian labour force.

What it did include, by implication, was a commitment to prevent anyone from using the nearby islands as jumping-off points. It was left to him to decide just how he would do that with the few military personnel at his disposal; with a limited supply of weapons; no detailed defence plan and a political situation which was so sensitive that any local event was likely to attract international press coverage.

On Hitaddu, where the servicemen would have done no more than defend the transmitter site, there was a potential problem. The site was not likely to be encroached upon by any militiamen unless a large number of Hitadduans sought sanctuary there and that, of course, was quite likely. Just how the RAF contingent was expected to cope with a flood of sanctuary seekers was never clarified; the assumption being that the station commander would use his initiative to deal with the situation as it arose. The corollary was obvious; he would take the blame if matters got out of hand. As far as Gan was concerned, it was inconceivable that the Maldivian militia would attempt to land on the island even in pursuit of fleeing Adduans.

The real threat to that site was from the flood of refugees which could pour onto the island as soon as the militiamen sailed into the lagoon. There was no contingency plan for such a situation. The assumption, once again, was that the station commander would deal with the problem as it arose. At least he could reasonably assume that the airfield would remain operational even if the island became a temporary refuge for a thousand or more Adduans for, under the illusion that British troops would protect them against the militiamen, the last thing the islanders would wish to do would be to prevent the arrival of RAF reinforcements. They would therefore ensure that, whatever else happened, the airfield would not be obstructed. That would still leave the day-to-day problems caused by an influx of refugees and, even worse, with the politically explosive situation in which the Maldivian militia, possibly accompanied by one of their government ministers, were being thwarted in their attempts to restore central government authority at the atoll.

The British government would undoubtedly have been loud in its condemnation of any such Maldivian incursion but would not authorise any military action to protect the Adduans whilst the airfield and the transmitter site remained operational. Once the militiamen had established their authority throughout the atoll the refugees who had sought sanctuary with the British forces would almost certainly have to be returned to their own islands for they could not be physically accommodated in the leased territories even if the British government were prepared to consider such a politically embarrassing move.

The strain of living in permanent fear of an attack was affecting most of the islanders and by the end of Ramadan some on the island of Huladu were openly expressing the opinion that, with the latest agreement between the Maldivian and British governments almost a year old, it was time for the Adduans to return to their central government's fold. Thus, while Arthington-Davy, recently established on Dunidu as the British Representative in the Maldives, was trying to develop direct contact between the Adduans' leaders and the Maldivian government, an influential group of Huladuans was planning to disrupt the smooth working both of their people's council and of the RAF operations. They believed that such combined action would quickly pave the way for the arrival of central government officials. Their campaign began early in April when the eighty Huladuans who were employed by the RAF went on strike. It is true that not all of them were in favour of the action but feelings on Huladu were running high and the waverers were quickly persuaded to join the strike when the ringleaders threatened to smash any boats belonging to those who continued to go to work. The Huladuans made it clear to everyone that their dispute was not with the RAF but with Afif Didi's regime. They objected to their limited representation on the people's council; to unfair elections; to the way the council was running the atoll's affairs and, for good measure, to the choice and quality of goods at the Hitaddu trading post.

The strike certainly affected the day-to-day work on Gan and in an attempt to resolve the problem, an RAF representative, accompanied by an interpreter, sailed across the lagoon to Huladu. The islanders had seen him coming and by the time he arrived at their beach they had assembled a non-too-friendly crowd. He and his interpreter were allowed to land but as he tried to reason with the villagers they became openly hostile. Eventually their anger got the better of them. Gathering stones as they moved forward, they advanced menacingly towards the visitors who wisely beat a hasty retreat to their boat and pulled away from the beach in a shower of stones. It was left to Afif Didi to defuse the situation and he did so with typical political pragmatism. Only too well aware of the fragility of the Adduans' independence, he decided that unanimity was more important than the preservation of the recently established people's council. He did not resign the presidency but he did suspend the council on the 6th of April and declared that a ballot would be held to elect fifty-two representatives for a new term of office. The Huladuans were immediately deprived of their declared justification for going on strike, the election was held on the 17th of April and the newly-elected representatives held their first meeting the following day. Given greater representation on the council, the Huladuans had no excuse for remaining on strike and, outmanoeuvred, they returned to work. Afif had settled that affair and was firmly back in control but by then he must have been thinking that he was living on borrowed time with the illusion of an independent republic sustained only by his undoubted skill as a politician and his personal standing amongst the Adduans. The one certainty was that whilst he continued to have the support of the islanders, and whilst the British continued to condone his actions, he would fight on for what he believed to be right.

Whilst the British and Maldivian governments were still at odds with each other over the lack of progress towards the restoration of central government at Addu Atoll, the BBC was angling for permission to build a transmitter on one of the Maldivian islands to relay signals to India and the Far East, an idea that was politically sensitive because of the propaganda potential inherent in such a proposal. Both the Foreign Office and the Commonwealth Relations Office supported the idea but did not want the Maldivian government to know of the plan before the details had been finalised. Both expressed the hope that Gan's station commander could find some pretext to enable a BBC representative to visit all the main islands of the atoll in order to select a suitable site for a relay station.

To imagine that such a subterfuge would be taken at face value by the Adduans was to demonstrate a lack of understanding of their world. Afif Didi and his associates would immediately suspect that any request for a visitor to tour the various islands in the atoll was merely a cover for some political manoeuvring and with their recent disenchantment with the British politicians, they would suspect that whatever the true reason for the visit it would not be for their benefit.

For non-political reasons, the Air Ministry staff did not want such a visit to take place.

Siting a powerful BBC relay station near military communications equipment could create unacceptable electronic interference and they proposed that the visit should be postponed pending an investigation into the technical aspects of the plan. Of less significance, but nevertheless an aspect which would eventually be of some concern to the station commander if the relay station were to be built, was the implication that accommodation and services would have to be provided for the forty or more BBC staff who would be needed to operate it. They would undoubtedly expect accommodation at least on a par with that provided for the other British civilians on the base and that was likely to create two problems.

The first was the actual provision of buildings and services, a problem which would largely be resolved if the BBC staff were to be domiciled on an additional site yet to be chosen. The second was the potential for resentment which could be created among the servicemen if such a large contingent of civilians were to be given preferential treatment. If the relay station became a reality the best solution would be to house the BBC staff on another island in the atoll where they would largely be out of sight and out of mind.

The Air Ministry's concerns about the possible effects on the airfield's communications systems meant that the site investigation was postponed. But for the BBC, the Foreign Office and the Commonwealth Relations Office, the attractions of having a powerful transmitter beaming into Asia were so strong that the idea was never likely to be readily abandoned and it was, on later occasions, to cloud the political debate between the British and Maldivian governments.

It was not just the BBC that was attracted by the location of the new air base. There was increasing interest from the Americans for they, like the British, needed an Indian Ocean staging post. Both the Vice-Chief of the Air Staff and the staff of the Commonwealth Relations Office were reluctant to provide frequent-service facilities on Gan for the United States' Air Force partly because the increased use of the base on the scale envisaged by the Americans would lead to a considerable increase in the number of servicemen on the island and partly because such use would begin to undermine the authority of the RAF over affairs at the atoll. Fortunately,

from the British point of view, the leasehold conditions for the two sites at the atoll permitted only the occasional use of the facilities by American aircraft and that allowed the British government to turn down the American request without creating any ill-feeling.

There was little doubt that in a more favourable political climate the conditions of the lease could have been renegotiated but it was the reluctance to share the limited facilities which underlay the refusal, the leasehold conditions and the difficult political situation merely provided welcome justification for the decision. This reluctance was of some concern to the Foreign Office staff who saw it as a small but significant undermining of the 'special relationship' with the Americans and eventually that concern led the British government to offer the island of Diego Garcia, in the Chagos Archipelago, to the Americans for them to develop as a United States' Air Force base. It was an offer which led to the compulsory evacuation of the Ilois people, many of whom ended up living in poverty on Mauritius, their plight ignored by Britain until November 2000 when the islanders finally won a High Court ruling that they had been unlawfully removed from their land and were entitled to return to their islands and to be adequately compensated for their years of suffering.

The talks between the British and Maldivian governments gradually led towards what seemed to be a fair basis for an amicable settlement between the southern islanders and their central government. The Adduans, by 1961 the only rebel islanders who had not been forced into submission, continued to make demands in the name of the United Suvadive Islands. They were adamant that they would not accept any settlement which did not grant autonomous government to their republic with administration by freely elected councils; the unrestricted right to trade with other elected councils; the unrestricted right to trade with other countries; the freedom to travel abroad with passports issued by their own people's council and the return to Addu of those islanders who had been exiled by the Maldivian government.

Their demands were excessive and they knew it even though they would never admit it. Finally, they insisted that the agreement had to be ratified in Ceylon by the British government. For its part, the Maldivian government produced what seemed to be a fair basis for a settlement. The Majlis rejected the idea of a separate autonomous government as unconstitutional but went part way towards satisfying that demand by agreeing to delegate controls of local affairs to a locally elected committee under the chairmanship of an atoll chief appointed by central government, an arrangement that was introduced throughout the Maldives later in the year. They were not prepared to delegate the authority to issue passports but they did concede the right to obtain them locally rather than from Malé. They also conceded the right to trade freely with other countries; withdrew their objections to the employment of Adduans by the RAF; offered the Adduans an extra seat in the Majlis and, most significantly, offered a free pardon to everyone who had taken part in the rebellion.

Incredibly, the Adduans declared the government's proposals to be unacceptable. Expressing their determination to hold out until all their demands had been met, they continued to run their own affairs; to work for the RAF; to trade directly with Ceylon and to pay no central government taxes. Their reaction caused the Maldivian government considerable loss of face and left the Air Ministry with the dilemma of trying to satisfy conflicting political and operational responsibilities.

By June 1961 the British government was becoming frustrated by the intransigence of the Adduans and was seriously considering how best to put pressure on Afif Didi to reach an agreement with the Maldivian government. But news of events at Fua Mulaku and Huvadu put the attitudes of the Adduans into perspective and seriously undermined the British government's belief that the Maldivian authorities were willing to use due process of law in the return to normality rather than use force of arms to pay off old scores. The islanders of Addu Atoll had never been under any such illusions even though their central government was showing considerable restraint and tolerance towards them. They knew, and the British were about to learn, that tolerance and restraint did not normally characterise the Maldivian government's attitude towards the southern islanders.

Early in June eleven dhonis from Huvadu arrived at Hitaddu with over two hundred men, women and children on board, all trying to obtain food and clothing. They explained that they could offer nothing in exchange because their government had deprived them of virtually everything since their rebellion had been crushed in 1960. They camped in their boats just off the Hitaddu shoreline, clearly with no intention of returning to their own atoll and openly seeking to share with the Adduans the protection provided by the presence of the British forces.

Afif Didi, fearing that the two hundred Huvaduans could be the first of a flood of refugees, would not allow them ashore. For two or three days the refugees simply sat in their boats, making no attempt to land, gratefully accepting whatever food and water was offered to them by the Adduans and giving every indication that they were prepared to stay afloat indefinitely rather than return to Huvadu. The Adduans could have stopped supplying them with food and water but they were far too sympathetic towards the refugees to do that and, in any case, they were well aware that such deprivation could force the Huvaduans to attempt a landing on one of the inhabited islands and that would inevitably lead to confrontation which was the one thing which Afif Didi was anxious to avoid. Eventually, the Adduans were persuaded that the eleven dhonis were not the forerunners of a fleet and they permitted the refugees to settle on one of the atoll's unoccupied but habitable islands where they established their own small community. Afif was convinced that that was not the end of the matter. His view was that unless the Maldivian government abandoned the oppressive regimes imposed since crushing the rebellion in the neighbouring islands there would be further uprisings and more refugees sailing to Gan.

Part of Afif's prediction came true before the middle of June. At Huvadu no food had arrived from Malé since central government control had been forcibly re-established by the Maldivian militia. For the islanders at that atoll the last straw came with the refusal of their government officials to allow the near-starving villagers to obtain food by trading with the Adduans. The desperate islanders attacked the locally based government officials, capturing the wireless operator and his equipment before a message could be sent to Malé. Four of the officials managed to escape by boat, four were kept under house arrest and the remaining eleven were brought to Hitaddu with a request that they be sent back to Malé after receiving whatever medical treatment they needed. Afif was wary about becoming embroiled in this latest affair and refused to help the Huvaduans except by trading general foodstuffs for fish. He knew that a final settlement with the central government was too close for new life to be breathed into the rebellion and he would have nothing to do with the reconstituted United Suvadive Islands Council which the Huvaduans were establishing at their atoll. Ironically, the Huvaduans' arrival provided the final spur to persuade him to send a deputation to Malé in an attempt to reach a peaceful solution to the Adduan problem.

But other events were to overtake that plan.

The islanders of Fua Mulaku were, like the Huvaduans, facing starvation and they too took the law into their own hands, meting out their version of rough justice on the people they believed to be responsible for their plight. The upshot was that the number of deported government officials who ended up at Addu Atoll grew to twenty-eight, all obliged to live on Wilingili, the large, swampy, insect-ridden uninhabited island on the eastern side of the atoll. They suffered intense discomfort but that was seen by most of the islanders as a small price to pay for the sanctuary they had been given and for their isolation from the many Adduans who were in favour of demonstrating their hatred of the Maldivian government by physically attacking any official who was unfortunate enough to fall into their hands.

To some extent Afif was embarrassed by the presence of the deportees. Undoubtedly the conditions at Huvadu and Fua Mulaku were bad but it was also fairly obvious that the pardoned rebels of the earlier revolt were again active, largely out of jealousy over the new-found wealth of the Adduans. Afif did not want that sort of attention just as he was about to make peace with the Maldivian government, nor did he want the deported officials to remain at Addu Atoll where they provided a ready focus for troublemakers. Intent on getting the deportees back to Malé as soon as possible, Afif, on the 16th of June 1961, turned to Wing Commander Cropper for help, explaining that his immediate concern was to inform the Maldivian Prime Minister that the Huvaduan and Mulakuan officials, incommunicado for several days as far as the Prime Minister was concerned, were at Addu Atoll and safely under Afif's protection. Once that had been done and he had been given some credit for providing sanctuary, Afif hoped that the RAF would fly the deportees to Ceylon or Hulule.

By mid-June, mail drops to Arthington-Davy, resident on Dunidu Island in Malé Atoll, were quite frequent and letters from Afif to Nasir were duly included with the rest of the mail dropped on Dunidu on the 17th and 22nd of June. Within days, arrangements had been made for the RAF to fly the deportees directly to Hulule and by the end of June they had all been returned to Malé, little more than a week before Wing Commander Cropper was due to pay an official visit to the capital where arrangements had been made for him meet the Sultan. The visit went ahead as planned with Cropper, accompanied by the Arthington-Davy and Gan's station adjutant, meeting the Sultan on the 4th to '...exchange pleasantries and give

an assurance that the RAF would take no sides in the dispute with the southern atolls.' Six days later Arthington-Davy and the Maldivian Deputy Home Minister visited Gan and, before flying back to Ceylon with the station commander and the British Representative to discuss the situation with the United Kingdom's High Commissioner, the Minister talked to Afif about the return to normality.

At that time the reconciliation talks seemed to be at a critical stage; what was needed was for each side to compromise a little but not so much as to lose face. With the deported officials safely back in the capital and the Deputy Home Minister discussing the reconciliation, Afif judged that the time was right for him to send a delegation to Malé.

Carrying letters from their people's council, the chosen Adduans accompanied the Minister to Malé, convinced that they were making a significant contribution to the reconciliation process. Their journey was not totally wasted because it indicated a wish to achieve a settlement but it was fruitless for the simple reason that the Adduans' terms for a settlement seemed to be non-negotiable and it was unrealistic for them to expect the Maldivian government to cave in. At the same time, a second group of islanders set sail for the capital, deputed to deliver letters from their council to sympathisers in Malé, asking them to support the Adduans' proposals for a reconciliation. The letters, however, were never delivered because as soon as the deputation stepped ashore at the capital they were arrested and held in 'protective custody' for several days. When released, they were not inclined to spend any more time in Malé and they set sail for home as soon as they could.

It transpired that the timing of their journey could hardly have been more unfortunate.

They had arrived during an investigation into the discovery of antigovernment leaflets among the packaging materials in a crate sent to Malé from Addu Atoll, an offence later traced back to three Maldivians employed by the NAAFI on Gan. The deputation's failure to deliver the letters was disheartening but, in terms of contribution towards a reconciliation, it was of limited significance for it was unlikely that anyone in the Maldivian capital would have been prepared to express any sympathy or support for the Adduans during the government's investigation. The Maldivians responsible for sending the subversive literature to Malé lost their jobs but were fortunate to escape further punishment either from their people's council or from the members of the deputation who had been put to so much inconvenience.

As far as the staff of the Commonwealth Relations Office were concerned it was obvious that Nasir was increasingly anxious to regain control of Addu Atoll but would not believe that progress was being made towards normality whilst Afif continued to trade with the Huvaduans, with the Mulakuans and with a trading company called Moosajee's. Afif denied such trading but the pattern of events provided strong circumstantial evidence to the contrary. The recent revolts by the Huvaduans and the Mulakuans had been followed by the exchange of general foodstuffs from Addu for fish from the rebel islanders. Within weeks of that large scale bartering Moosajee's ship had brought fresh supplies to Addu Atoll and had exported the Adduans' surplus stock of dried fish. Nasir would never believe that such a chain of events was coincidental. His predictable interpretation of the situation must have been obvious to the people's council but the members gave no indication that they would cease such trading. In public, Afif and his supporters on the council remained confident that, whatever happened elsewhere, the Maldivian government would continue to be excluded from Addu Atoll until such time as the Adduans' demands had been met. As far as they were concerned, their trading was an irrelevant issue.

By July the members of the people's council had even clarified how far they were prepared to modify their demands, duly informing the Maldivian government, *via* a mail drop on Dunidu, of the concessions which the Adduans were prepared to make. These included the possible acceptance of the Maldivian national flag to fly alongside a special Adduan flag yet to be designed; a lump sum annual tribute to cover all government taxes and the lease money on the government plantations; the possible curtailment of trade with the Huvaduans; the issue of passports from Malé on the recommendation of the Adduan people's council and the education of Adduan children at schools in the capital or elsewhere. Added to the demands however was the requirement that Addu should be included in the United Kingdom's fisheries programme. For good measure, Afif Didi made it clear that he was not willing to change the name of the people's council to conform with practice elsewhere nor was he willing to send representatives to the Majlis.

Those proposals amounted to nothing more than an ultimatum of the kind already rejected by the Majlis as unconstitutional. Predictably they were again rejected. By then the Maldivian Minister for Home Affairs was losing patience with the Adduan rebels and on the 7th of July 1961 he wrote to Afif stating that:

> '...the pardon for your 1960 revolt has not been followed by obedience to the Maldivian Government. That pardon will be revoked in two months if you do not submit. There will be severe punishment for those who fail to obey'.

Three days later, in a confused approach so typical of the Maldivian government, that threat was seriously undermined by Ibrahim Nasir, the prime minister, who sent a message to the people's council to the effect that the government was anxious to forget past difficulties and that arrangements were in hand for allowing travelling abroad for everyone, including those who wished to travel for commercial purposes. It was obvious that the Maldivian ministers desperately wanted a return to normality at Addu Atoll but, given the presence of the British military on Gan and Hitaddu, just could not agree on how best to achieve that. It was also obvious that Afif and the other members of the people's council still represented the feelings of the overwhelming majority of the Adduans and it therefore seemed most unlikely that the Maldivian government would be able to re-establish its authority over the Adduans unless the British government, through the RAF, put more pressure on Afif Didi.

The opinions expressed by the Commonwealth Relations Office staff were clear cut. The 1960 agreement required the British government to work for a reconciliation between the Adduans and the Maldivian government. It was possible that Britain could actually be asked by the Maldivian Prime Minister to resolve the impasse by direct intervention, acting virtually as agents of the central government in Malé. That would not be difficult nor would it be particularly counter-productive because, with the major construction work completed, Britain was no longer so dependent upon Afif Didi and the Adduans.

Fortunately for Afif the Air Ministry staff viewed the matter differently. They were convinced that the RAF's interests would be best served by having the Adduans as co-operative neighbours, an impossibility if Britain were to take direct action in support of the Maldivian government's attempts to re-impose its authority over the islanders. Just as important was the Air Ministry's very strong sense of obligation towards Afif Didi and his supporters, obligation based upon an awareness that without their unilateral declaration of independence and their subsequent commitment to the construction programme the commissioning date for the RAF's staging post would almost certainly have been delayed whilst the politicians in Malé and in London conducted a long-distance argument over the rights and wrongs of the original agreement.

In August, Arthington-Davy, sympathetic to the Air Ministry's views, acted as a go-between for the Maldivian government and the Adduan people's council. On the 18th of August he brought to Hitaddu three senior Maldivians; the Minister for Home Affairs, the Attorney General and the Deputy Minister for External Affairs, all of whom wished to hold discussions with Afif and the other members of the council. The discussions were fruitless. The Adduans refused to modify their demands, claiming that the concessions which they had already made went as far as the islanders were prepared to go. The Maldivian ministers were just as adamant that they could not accede to the demands which the Adduans were describing as final. The talking ended and the ministers flew back to Malé empty-handed, making it clear to Arthington-Davy that they expected the British government to stop supporting Afif Didi and thus force him to accept the Maldivian government's terms.

The British government accepted, up to a point, responsibility for pushing Afif towards a settlement and chose to apply economic pressure on the Adduan community. In an attempt to undermine the Adduan Trading Corporation and hence the support for Afif and the people's council, instructions were issued prohibiting any Adduan from using any of the military communications facilities. That seriously hampered Afif in his dealings with Moosajee and clearly indicated that the British government was determined to push the Adduans into a settlement. The islanders however, gave no indications that they were ready to make further concessions.

The impasse continued.

In spite of their belief that they were gradually losing the support of the British government, the Adduans were determined not to give in. They clearly wanted a strong, like-minded man as their president and Afif had already shown himself to be just that, most recently during the August visit by the Maldivian ministers when he had arranged for the only member of the people's council who was openly in favour of negotiating with the Maldivian government to be held incommunicado for eight days.

When Wing Commander Cropper left Gan on the 3rd of October 1961 there had been no further progress towards a settlement and, politically, all was quiet. His successor, Wing Commander Ellis, had been briefed, before leaving for Gan, that negotiations between the two governments would almost certainly be resumed before long and that when they began, feelings amongst the Adduans were likely to run high and life at the atoll could become quite interesting.

If the British government had any doubts about the level of local support for Afif they were dispelled on Christmas Eve when a presidential election was held at the atoll. Four thousand two hundred and thirty-nine adults over the age of nineteen were allowed to vote and all did so. Four thousand two hundred and twenty-seven votes were cast for Afif. The remaining twelve votes were shared amongst the other five candidates.

Thus 1961 ended with Afif even more securely entrenched as president of the breakaway republic; the demands from the people's council rejected by the Majlis and the earlier pardons, theoretically at least, withdrawn as a result of the Adduans' failure to comply with the terms of the July letter from the Maldivian Minister for Home Affairs.

In January 1962 the Huvaduans and the Mulakuans paid the price for their mid-1961 uprising. The Maldivian militia were sent to the southern islands and within three days had taken control of Huvadu Atoll and the island of Fua Mulaku. Once again Addu Atoll became the destination for those who fled rather than be captured. They were not pursued, probably because the militiamen were initially pre-occupied and were subsequently deterred by the presence of a Royal Navy guard ship in the Addu lagoon. In a virtual re-run of the mid-1961 events the refugees, seeking British protection, camped in their boats just off the Gan shoreline. They were unable to land because the beaches were guarded, initially by locally-based servicemen and within twenty-four hours by RAF Regiment airmen, who were flown to Gan from the Far East. Within forty-eight hours the refugees had abandoned any thoughts of landing on Gan and found their way to the other islands on which their predecessors had settled some six months earlier. After four or five days it was obvious that no more refugees were likely to arrive, the RAF Regiment airmen returned to Singapore and the shoreline was kept under observation rather than under guard.

The refugees gave a graphic account of the fighting on the neighbouring islands, claiming that many villagers had been injured and several killed. It was obvious that their Prime Minister had become so incensed about the recurrent rebellions in the southern islands that he was prepared to send yet another punitive expedition from Malé and it was conceivable that he might have plans which went beyond the taming of the Huvaduans and the Mulakuans. In spite of the inter-governmental agreement he could be intending to move against the Adduans. If he were to do that it was crucial, as far as the British government was concerned, to adhere to the policy of using British troops only to protect the leased territories, not to defend the Adduans; it was one thing to deter the Maldivian government from mounting an attack but quite another to engage the government forces in armed combat.

Either way, international criticism of Britain's actions in the Indian Ocean was inevitable. But such criticism had counted for little in Whitehall in the past so it is hardly surprising that an attempt to break the deadlock by re-opening negotiations whilst maintaining a military deterrent was underpinned more by pragmatic reasons than by concerns for Britain's image abroad. If the Maldivian militia were allowed to attack the islanders while the British military stood by and watched, the Adduans' goodwill towards the RAF would vanish and without that the military base could only be operated at great expense.

There was another factor: the British government was hoping to lease more land at Addu Atoll and the Maldivian government would obviously never agree to such an arrangement whilst the British military presence at the atoll was effectively preventing it from regaining control over its own subjects.

The British plan was to extend the transmitter site on Hitaddu and to provide extra sites for the RAF on other islands in the atoll. Part of the Gan site could then be allocated to the Royal Navy for the construction of a naval tanker farm which would provide a strategic mid-ocean facility to replace the very limited refuelling service provided by the atoll-based tanker Wave Victor. In all, at least an additional seventy acres would be required, forty acres of which would be needed for the BBC's relay station which the Chiefs-of-Staff had, on the 16th of January 1962, approved as technically acceptable. If those plans were to go ahead, land would be needed on the other islands to provide overflow facilities for use during major exercises or emergencies and to accommodate the RAF elements which would be displaced from Gan once the naval tanker farm had been established.

The United Kingdom's High Commissioner in Colombo was thus instructed to open yet more negotiations with the Maldivian government with the clear intention of obtaining additional leasehold concessions at Addu Atoll. Although that would not be easy, he could at least point out that since Afif had been denied access to outside agencies for both private and commercial matters his problems were mounting up, his administration was having difficulty providing goods for the islanders and, as that situation worsened, it was likely that his support would wane. The December election results would have to be explained away as short-term support which would not be sustained in the face of a determined effort by the British and Maldivian governments.

From the British point of view the sanctions against Afif conveniently provided a sign of goodwill towards the Maldivian government whilst being accepted by Afif as understandable and therefore not a justification for developing any hostility towards the Royal Air Force. It was an ideal combination.

In February the High Commissioner submitted to Nasir a set of proposals intended to provide a satisfactory solution to the problems posed by the Adduans' recalcitrance. At the same time it was made clear to the Maldivian Prime Minister that in exchange for British help in restoring normality to the affairs of Addu Atoll there was to be no retribution exacted on the rebels. The proposals submitted to Nasir for consideration and discussion included the return to Addu of a Maldivian government-appointed atoll chief who would act as chairman of an atoll committee as envisaged in the previous year's legislation for local government throughout the Maldives.

Other suggestions included the election, supervised by the new atoll chief, of a new committee; the allocation of two seats on the Majlis for Adduan representatives; a maximum, at least for several years, of two non-Adduan administrative officers to assist the atoll chief and an embargo on the introduction of non-Adduan constabulary or militia into the atoll. The final, and most controversial, suggestions proposed a free pardon for Afif and all the Adduans in respect of the rebellion on the 1st of January 1959 and all subsequent events; an understanding from the Maldivian government that for several years no Adduan would in any circumstances be removed from the atoll for trial or punishment and an undertaking from the existing people's council that prior to its dissolution it would exert its influence both to secure respect for the authority of the Maldivian government and to ensure the personal safety of all government officials based at or visiting Addu Atoll.

If those proposals, which were highly protective of the rebels and represented considerable loss of face for the Maldivian government, were to be accepted as they stood there was little doubt that the British government would have to offer Nasir a face-saving deal of some sort. Economic aid or an increase in the annual leasehold charge, ostensibly to compensate for the revenue lost during the period of the rebellion, would be the most obvious way to appease the Maldivian government but Britain's dealings with the Maldivians had been exposed ever since Jones' story had been published in the Daily Express and any financial manipulation was bound to be scrutinised in Parliament. It was not therefore surprising that in March 1962 a steady stream of British ministers arrived at Gan, all seeking to explore the Adduan problem and apparently thinking that opinions reinforced by a brief visit to the atoll would contribute to any subsequent Parliamentary debates and somehow strengthen the British negotiating position at the meetings in Malé. Harold Watkinson, the minister of defence; Sir Arthur Morley, the United Kingdom's high commissioner in Ceylon and Sir Arthur Snelling, representing the Commonwealth Relations Office, were the most senior of the visitors and were probably the only ministers with a thorough understanding of the situation. Together they had to formulate the policies and the style for Sir Arthur to take into the negotiations; a difficult, politically sensitive remit.

The most obvious difficulty was the Maldivian government's perception, fuelled throughout the three-year affair by a variety of press reports in India and Ceylon, that Britain's proposals involved excessive loss of face for them. It was unfortunate that one such report appeared during the March discussions when The Times of India published an interview with a Maldivian, H B T Didi, who claimed to be the Crown Prince of the Maldives. In the report he described the Maldivian ministers as tyrannical puppets of their British masters, suggested that the Commonwealth Prime Ministers should discuss the question of granting independence to the Maldives and to the United Suvadive Islands and urged India and Ceylon to help the islanders to secure their independence. The Maldivian Prime Minister called upon Sir Arthur Morley to inform India that the Maldivian sultanate was elective, that no such dignitary as a 'Crown Prince' existed and that H B T Didi was actually a native commoner of Hitaddu island who had

been employed by the British Army in 1942, had later been arrested on a charge of theft and had escaped to Ceylon where he had lived ever since.

Such incidents were irritating rather than serious but they tended to offend the Maldivians' sensitivities and direct their attention away from the main issues. On this occasion, parts of the press report were, quite coincidentally, echoing some of the thoughts of Britain's Commonwealth Secretary who, unbeknown to the Maldivians, was questioning the wisdom of the British policy in this matter and was suggesting that it might be in Britain's best interests to work for the final secession of the southern Maldivian islands into a separate political state over which Her Majesty's government could maintain complete and undisturbed authority. Had Nasir been aware of such a suggestion he really would have had good cause to send the militiamen into the villages of Addu Atoll. As it was, the Maldivians, with no inkling of the discussion being held in the Commonwealth Relations Office in London, negotiated in good faith, initially with Sir Arthur Morley and subsequently with the Duke of Devonshire who, early in April, secured agreement on all the British proposals.

Both the Maldivian and British representatives were satisfied. What they did not foresee was the reaction of the Adduans.

When the Islanders heard the terms of this latest agreement they were incensed. They did not trust the Maldivian government, they feared the return of government officials to the atoll and they rejected the agreement out of hand. They planned to express their anger by holding a mass demonstration on Gan but when the station commander vetoed that for operational reasons they had to be content with a token demonstration on the RAF base and mass demonstrations in their villages. For a week they remonstrated and demonstrated, all to no avail. The British government, unswayed by the open hostility of the Adduans, went ahead with the plans to help restore central government authority at the atoll.

On the 15th of April 1962 the Duke of Devonshire, accompanied by a representative from the Commonwealth Relations Office together with the station commander and Afif Didi, drove out to the airfield to meet two Maldivian ministers who, with Arthington-Davy, had flown from Hulule on board an RAF Valletta, arriving at Gan at four o'clock that afternoon. News of their imminent arrival had spread through the local communities and as the aircraft landed some seventy dhonis containing an estimated thousand demonstrators reached Gan and disgorged about five hundred passengers onto the beach near the marine craft jetty.

Afif Didi, taken by surprise, certainly did not want the ministers' visit to be marred by violence; a demonstration formed no part of his plans. He immediately went down to the jetty and, using a loudhailer, asked the vociferous demonstrators who had landed near the jetty to leave the beach and get back into their dhonis. Many did so but many others remained in the shallows, refusing to climb back on board. Afif then went aboard an RAF marine craft and, still using a loudhailer, moved among the boats requesting them to disperse and return to their own islands.

They refused to do so.

The Maldivian ministers, visibly shaken by the hostility of the crowd, were well aware of the treatment meted out to other ministers in similar circumstances and obviously had no wish to have their names added to the list of government officials ousted by the Adduans. They, together with the British representatives, Afif Didi and two members of the people's council adjourned for tea in the bungalow which had previously been Arthington-Davy's residence. There they stayed, hoping that the demonstration would fizzle out once they were out of sight. That was a forlorn hope. Hundreds of islanders were rowing or sailing across the lagoon, their dhonis carrying as many men as could be crammed on board.

Within a few hours some two thousand Adduans had arrived just off the Gan shoreline. At least five hundred angry villagers landed near Gan's main jetty and some three hundred women and children marched from Hitaddu, wading the Gan-Fedu gap en masse. Thirteen RAF Regiment airmen of N° 15 Field Squadron had been flown from Singapore to Gan that morning but they could do nothing against hundreds of Maldivians without resorting to the use of firearms and that was never a realistic option. In the lagoon, the frigate HMS Loch Insh, on station as a guard ship, was similarly handicapped; there was no acceptable way of dispersing a swarm of dhonis in the shallow waters just off the beach.

The Maldivian ministers were becoming ever more nervous, fearing that the boatloads of islanders would land, overwhelm the RAF personnel by sheer weight of numbers and wreak their vengeance on those who had been unwise enough to travel to Gan as representatives of the Maldivian government. Afif had used all the persuasive powers he could muster before he left the jetty but it was over two hours before the remainder of those demonstrators who had come ashore were persuaded to return to their dhonis or to set off across the Gan-Fedu gap to return to Hitaddu. The dhoni crews, however, could not be persuaded to leave the shoreline. The RAF's marine craft were sent out to try to disperse the boats but as fast as some were moved along, others took their place.

At around six-thirty that evening Afif sailed back to Hitaddu, asking the demonstrators to follow him. They refused to do so and they spent the next hour and a half edging inshore. By eight o'clock they were so close to the beaches that many of them could have jumped out of the dhonis and waded ashore. It became obvious that unless some action was taken, or threatened, it was only a matter of time before some incensed islander leapt into the shallows to be followed by hundreds of others. The boat owners were therefore warned, through loudhailers, that even though the station commander regarded the Adduans as his friends and had no wish to harm them, fire hoses would be used to sink any dhoni that remained near the Gan shoreline. That was a very serious threat for the boat owners but still they ignored the warning until Ellis instructed the firemen to play their hoses into the water alongside the dhonis.

The effect was instantaneous. The dhoni owners' belligerence evaporated as soon as they saw a real threat to their craft. Without further ado they turned their boats round and set off across the lagoon. Even more remarkable was the fact that many of the departing Adduans were chanting '...*long live the Royal Air Force*'. They would have liked to have got their hands on the Maldivian ministers but they bore no grudge against the RAF for forcing them to abandon their vigil. The demonstrations, however, continued throughout that Sunday night in all the villages and on the Monday morning the islanders who worked on Gan came ashore as usual but then mounted a demonstration instead of going to work. At the same time scores of dhonis carrying Adduans who had no permits to land on Gan arrived offshore and recommenced the vigil that had been abandoned only eight hours previously. Once again there were over a thousand islanders wanting to get their hands on the government ministers from Malé and it was quite clear that for as long as the Maldivian officials remained on Gan, security patrols would have to be organised to guard the Gan coastline both day and night.

By mid-morning on the Monday the station commander was drafting a signal to the Far East Air Force Headquarters, warning of the likely need for more RAF Regiment airmen, together with fire and riot squads, to be sent to Gan. He was obliged to end the text with the statement 'As *signal being cleared further demonstration being mounted. Need more Regiment troops urgently*'. But within two hours he sent a cancellation of that request because it had become increasingly obvious that the Adduans were all intent on coming ashore and that it would only be possible to protect the Maldivian officials at the cost of disrupting normal military operations on Gan. Once again fire hoses were brought out and high-pressure water-jets were used to keep the boats at bay. (Figs 13.5, 13.6 & 13.7) It soon became obvious that the only way to restore law and order was to remove the focus of the islanders' hostility and it was therefore suggested to the government ministers that they should return to Malé as soon as possible. They readily agreed. By mid-afternoon they were airborne, heading for Hulule and grateful for having escaped unharmed.

The fifty RAF Regiment airmen who had been airborne when the Singapore-based staff received Ellis's second signal, arrived towards the end of the demonstration and remained on the base only until the station commander was certain that their presence was no longer needed.

The Adduans seemed to be satisfied with the results of their demonstrations for although they had been unable to get their hands on the ministers they had certainly made them run for home. The islanders had also clearly shown that they were not prepared to sit back and let the British help the Maldivian government to re-establish its authority at the atoll without the consent of the Adduans. If their demands, or concessions as they preferred to call them, were not met within the terms of the settlement they were determined to make life as difficult as possible for any Maldivian government official brave enough, or foolish enough, to visit Addu Atoll.

Following the April debacle the Duke of Devonshire accepted an invitation to attend a ministerial meeting at Malé. For him, it was an uncomfortable meeting. The furious ministers informed him in no uncertain terms of their displeasure at Britain's inept handling of the Adduan problem which, two years after the signing of the post-rebellion agreement, remained unresolved. He was also reminded that the rebellion was essentially an internal Maldivian affair which, but for the British presence at Addu Atoll, could have been settled in a matter of days by the Maldivian militia. The British presence had led to the rebellion and, for its own ends, the British government had supported and protected the rebels, thereby directly interfering with the internal affairs of the Maldive Islands, a blatant breach of one of the most fundamental clauses in every post-war agreement between the two governments.

The Duke was really unable to rebut what was essentially an unpalatable truth. He could only assure the Maldivians that it was Britain's firm intention to help re-establish central government control at Addu. He argued that the demonstrations which had just taken place showed how very difficult the situation was and how much extra preparation time was needed before matters could be returned to normal. It was unfortunate that, before asking for further land concessions he informed the Maldivians ministers that if their government chose to take independent action against the Adduans it would be regarded by the British government as a breach of the agreement and any offensive action by the Maldivian militia would be met by defensive force from the British servicemen at Addu. When he then went on to pursue Britain's need for more land at the atoll he immediately gave the Maldivians a bargaining point which they exploited by offering to lease the extra land required '...*within minutes of the restoration of central government authority at Addu Atoll*'.

With that statement effectively challenging the Duke to end the rebellion or forget the request for more leasehold territory, the meeting ended without any firm resolutions and with no plan of action.

The British government was thus left with three main options, each of which was accompanied by potential problems. The simplest option was to take no action to change the *status quo*. Once the Adduans were aware of that policy they could be relied upon to resist any Maldivian government attempt to return central authority to the atoll. Secure behind the British military presence, the islanders would provide a completely loyal workforce and would undoubtedly agree to provide more land for use by the British. Adopting such an action would, however, be a breach of the most recent agreement and would probably result in a Maldivian government complaint to the United Nations, leaving the British government to shrug off the international criticism which would ensue. Far worse would be the continual disruption on Gan and Hitaddu brought about by the Adduans' permanent fear of attack by the Maldivian militia and their resultant tendency to raise numerous false alarms to which the servicemen would be obliged to react. Living in such a permanent state of nervousness would inevitably affect the efficiency of the military operations at the atoll and that could become too high a price to pay for the benefits that might be achieved by adopting a policy which would fail to break the current deadlock. For the Adduans, opting to maintain the *status quo* would provide short term safety and the possibility of long term danger. If Britain were ever to abandon the base the Adduans would be at the mercy of their central government.

At the other end of the spectrum, the British government could add its weight to the Maldivian government and help to re-establish central government authority at the atoll by employing British servicemen in support of the Maldivian officials sent from Malé to govern the islanders. That would establish good relations between the British and Maldivian governments but would destroy the good relations between the Adduans and their British employers. It would undoubtedly provoke widespread strikes and would probably lead to acts of sabotage. Some nine hundred and forty Adduans were employed on the leased territories, just over five hundred and fifty of them by the works services department and without the co-operation of the Adduans it would be necessary to bring more Pakistanis to Gan to take over much of that work. It would also be necessary to employ more servicemen on the island, largely to provide greater day-to-day security. Finally, and perhaps most significantly, the Adduans' resentment could simmer for years, occasionally boiling over, as they sustained their hatred of central government authority.

If the British government were to choose to stand aside and let the Maldivian government re-establish its authority over the Adduans by force of arms the RAF's operations would almost certainly be severely disrupted by a flood of refugees seeking sanctuary on Gan. That would create an impossible situation for Gan's station commander. He would find it virtually impossible to remove several thousand Maldivians from Gan and would obviously be unable to keep the airfield operational if the Adduans chose to settle on the runway. Unless ordered to do otherwise he would have to resist any attempts by the Maldivian armed militia to pursue the Adduans onto the leased territories and if the British government were to approve such a pursuit there would be bloodshed on Gan. Even if the immediate problems associated with a stand-aside policy could be overcome, the relationship between the British and the Adduans would be irreparably damaged.

The third possibility was for Britain to renege on the agreement with the Maldivian government by formally recognising the breakaway republic and persuading other nations to do the same. The 'republic' would effectively consist only of Addu Atoll for Britain had no need, or interest in, the Huvaduans or the Mulakuans and would certainly not want a commitment to support those islanders or protect them from the Maldivian militiamen. The idea had its attractions and its supporters. It would give Britain a virtually free hand at the atoll for it would ensure the total co-operation of the Adduans and, more importantly, of the then president, Afif Didi. Such a move would definitely end the amicable relationship which had existed between Britain and the sultanate since the days of Queen Victoria and would probably become the subject of a debate in the United Nations with Britain almost certainly subjected to international criticism which could be shrugged off.

Any ending of the amicable relationship could be viewed pragmatically. The Maldivians needed influential and affluent friends. The British did not need the Maldivians, they just needed one of their atolls and that they already had. There was a risk that such a move would provoke the Maldivian government into inviting the Russians or the Chinese into the archipelago but the general opinion in Whitehall was that the risk was small partly because the Indian government, already indicating its desire to see the Indian Ocean as a neutral zone, had some influence with the Maldivians and would almost certainly persuade them not to offer any facilities to the Eastern powers.

But formal recognition of the United Suvadive Islands would not necessarily be beneficial for the Adduans. They would effectively be prisoners on the their own atoll for none would dare to venture to Malé or any other Maldivian island. Even worse, they would be at the mercy of the Maldivian government if Britain were once again to withdraw from their atoll.

There was little doubt that, from the British point of view, the best way to resolve the problem was to negotiate an agreement acceptable to Afif and the Adduans, preferably establishing Afif as the atoll chief with no non-Adduan government officials on the islands and with the payment of taxes to the central government at Malé. Such a solution could well be an impossible ideal because any settlement acceptable to Afif and the Adduans would almost certainly be unacceptable to the Maldivian government which had already conceded as much as could be reasonably expected of any government faced with a rebellion.

Years of negotiation was an unattractive option for the Maldivian ministers who were losing face as well as much-needed revenue for every day that the impasse continued. It was just as unattractive for the British because it promised continuing adverse international publicity and no possibility of leasing additional land at the atoll. There was little doubt that both the Maldivian government and the people's council could be persuaded to negotiate a mutually acceptable agreement if the British were to offer a large enough financial inducement but it had already been made clear in Whitehall that that approach would not be adopted: there would be no massive aid programme for the Maldives just to buy the agreement of the central government and the dissidents.

Afif Didi, for all his outward show of confidence in the British, must have been a very worried man. He had already accepted that the days of his fledgling republic were numbered. He could have been under no illusions about Nasir's desire to put him on trial for treason. He must have been equally certain that his conviction, a foregone conclusion, would most likely be followed by a life sentence of banishment to some uninhabited island in the archipelago, well away from Addu Atoll and incommunicado as far as his political associates were concerned. It is to the credit of the British government officials that none expressed a disagreement with the Earl of Bandon's outspoken assertion that there was a moral obligation towards Afif which over-rode all political considerations in the dealings with the Maldivian government. His thesis was simple: without Afif's help the RAF base could not have been built as rapidly and operated as smoothly as it had been and it was a matter of honour to ensure Afif's safety by granting him whatever protection or asylum was necessary.

The British government, apparently disinclined to take any positive action to break the deadlock, opted, virtually by default, to sustain the *status quo* for the remainder of the year.

The Adduans' nerves were tested during long periods of political silence and were almost unbearably frayed whenever reports of Maldivian government activity seemed to suggest an imminent confrontation with the Malé-based militiamen. They drew false comfort from the frequent arrival of short-stay military reinforcements on Gan for they failed to realise that on most occasions the servicemen were merely taking part in an air mobility exercise designed to test the RAF's ability to move troops around the world at short notice. Regardless of the reason for the influx of servicemen, the Adduans always breathed a collective sigh of relief when the troops arrived for they believed them to have been brought to Gan specifically to protect the islanders against the vagaries of their government, a misconception which was never dispelled by the British for it underpinned the goodwill from the islanders.

The Maldivian government, effectively impotent whilst the British remained at Addu Atoll, could only wage a war of nerves against the islanders and hope that publicity and propaganda would influence the British government to take more positive action to help restore central government authority to the atoll. The Maldivian ministers' frustrations could only be directly vented against one British official, Arthington-Davy on Dunidu. For him, life was made as awkward as possible. Domestic staff would fail to report for work and staff changes would occur without notice, creating a steady flow of inexperienced staff to disrupt the established routine. Basic supplies would fail to arrive on time or would be unobtainable. Maldivian workmen would arrive at Dunidu, start a construction project and abandon it before completion, leaving the British Representative and his staff to work on a site which frequently resembled an assault course in a builder's yard. Government ministers would be incommunicado for long periods or would fail to keep appointments, leaving Arthington-Davy cooling his heels in Malé for a few hours before returning to Dunidu.

Far more significantly there was, behind this irritating behaviour, the implied threat of violence.

The Maldivian ministers were always at pains to declare that they would never condone any violence against the British Representative or his staff but they were equally at pains to point out that crowd violence, which they could not control, could break out at any time and was indeed likely to do so for as long as the British government continued to support Afif Didi and the other Adduan rebels. If a spontaneous demonstration were to occur, the obvious target for the demonstrators would be the British contingent on Dunidu and it was unrealistic to expect the Maldivian government to prevent an angry mob from ransacking accommodation and injuring the occupants. It was, after all, little different from what had happened on Gan when Maldivian ministers had faced mob fury and the British military had been unable to cope without calling for armed reinforcements.

The implied threats had to be taken seriously by Arthington-Davy and by the British government, but, short of installing a high security perimeter fence and establishing an RAF Regiment contingent on Dunidu, there was little that could be physically done to forestall such an attack. Given that the adoption of defence measures to satisfy a siege mentality was diplomatically unacceptable, the best that the United Kingdom's High Commissioner could do was formally to remind the Maldivian Prime Minister that his government was responsible for the safety of the British on Dunidu. He did that, but, well aware that his reminder would carry little or no weight with Ibrahim Nasir, he also arranged for a Royal Navy ship to be on permanent standby within four hours sailing of Malé atoll and he warned Arthington-Davy to prepare a rapid evacuation plan for himself and his staff.

In the days of the monarchy in the archipelago it was customary for the Sultan to celebrate the beginning of each Maldivian new year by making a public speech. In June 1962 his speech focused on the troubles at Huvadu Atoll and at Fua Mulaku as having been inspired by the Adduans. Referring to the poor state of the Maldivian economy and the dire shortages of basic foodstuffs throughout the capital the Sultan laid much of the blame on the currency losses from Addu Atoll and declared that his government was active behind the scenes, a phrase which, to the Adduans, sounded ominous when linked to his separate statement on the increased recruitment into the Maldivian militia. It sounded even more ominous when the Commonwealth Relations Office disclosed that the British firm of Leonard Hunt and Co. had applied to the Board of Trade for a licence to export, to Malé, two hundred hand grenades, two hundred tear gas grenades and three Vickers machine guns complete with tripods and ten thousand rounds of ammunition.

Further checks showed that the Maldivian government had, over an eighteen month period, already ordered ten Stirling sub-machine guns with three thousand cartridges and five hundred pairs of handcuffs. Given that within the archipelago there was virtually no serious crime, that the occasional coup attempt was usually conducted only by a small group of dissidents and that the total strength of the Maldivian militia was no more than four hundred, the implication was that some punitive expedition was being planned. The most obvious target was Addu Atoll. This left the British government in a tricky position because refusal to grant an export licence for such an order placed by a legitimate and friendly government would attract considerable criticism in Parliament. Eventually it was assumed that whilst Britain continued to discuss the Adduan problem with the Maldivian government no direct action against the Adduans was likely and in the hope that negotiations in Malé would lead to an early and peaceful solution to the Adduan problem the provision of an export licence was delayed for many months under the general heading of 'muddle in Whitehall' .

In July 1962 Nasir wrote to Harold MacMillan, the British prime minister. After a preamble expressing concern over likely misunderstandings the text continued:

> 'I am certain you will not fail to do everything you possibly could to restore the firm foundation of the mutual goodwill which we had the privilege to enjoy in the past.'

Nasir then very clearly set out his understanding of the Duke of Devonshire's stance at the April meeting, saying:

> 'The summary of the Duke's reply could only be stated as follows which we note with utter frustration and disappointment:

A.   The British Government is still determined to try and settle the dispute peacefully.

B.   Should the Maldivian Government use force to settle the matter the British Government would use force to prevent such settlement.

C.   That he had legal advice from London that the exchange of letters between the High Commissioner and the Prime Minister is nothing in addition to the 1960 agreement, that the whole question still lies with the spirit of that agreement .

D.   That the British Government still feels certain obligations towards the revolt leader Afeef [sic] and that the reason for that is that he was instrumental in getting them the necessary labour for the construction of the base. When we listen to all these points being put to us by the Duke we were inclined that here was not a discussion but a dictation to us. We naturally felt shocked to listen to the minister making a categoric statement at point B, interpreted as a threat and a daring attempt, to interfere with the internal affairs of the Maldives.'

Accompanying the letter to Harold Macmillan was a lengthy report which provided a clear insight into the causes of Nasir's frustration and resentment. The document gave the Maldivian government's view of events, making the following claims:

- 'Construction of the RAF base at Addu Atoll had started in 1956 with no proper agreement between the two governments. Since 1957 the situation had deteriorated because the British Government had disregarded the wishes of the Maldivian Government and had unconstitutionally engaged a local labour force, paying the workers in Sterling and making goods available through the NAAFI.

- The natives [sic], simple fishermen, were prepared to do anything, even raise the Union Jack over their heads to keep in a rich state for life.

- Afeef took the opportunity to rouse the people in a revolt whilst his government was trying to agree on the construction of the air base.

- Afeef had attempted the same thing during the last war but because the British Government only needed a base at Addu Atoll until the end of the war it helped the Maldivian Government to apprehend all the rebels.

- Afeef has rekindled his old ambitions and because of the importance of the RAF airfield at Gan the British Government supported Afeef without any regard for the wishes of the Maldivian Government.

- The British support for Afeef led to a revolt at Addu Atoll which spread, with the Adduans' support, to Huvadu and Fua Mulaku.

- Never before in Maldivian history has there been a revolt of this nature among the normally peaceful contented people.

- Under Afeef's influence the natives tended to blame the Maldivian Government for hardships where none existed.

- Even if hardships had existed amongst the native populations that should only have been the concern of the United Nations, not of Britain which is only a friendly ally which has voluntarily agreed to defend the Maldives against external aggression and not to interfere in Maldivian internal affairs.

- When the 1960 agreement between the two governments was signed Addu Atoll was not under the control of the Maldivian Government and, in an exchange of letters, Her Majesty's Government promised to bring about a peaceful return to normality at the atoll as soon as possible. In two years nothing much has happened.

- The Maldivian Government has relied upon the agreement and never doubted Her Majesty's Government's sincerity until the Duke of Devonshire spoke of the British obligation to Afeef.

- Britain has no right to interfere in the internal affairs of the Maldives but has done so without any regard for the Maldivian Government the weakness of which, compared with Britain, is no excuse for such treatment.'

MacMillan replied in a typically bland diplomatic style, stating his interest in Nasir's views; his commitment to the maintenance of the long-standing friendship between the two nations; his regret at the misunderstanding which had arisen and his commitment to the restoration of central authority to Addu. He made no suggestions but promised that Britain would soon be ready with a firm set of proposals which he hoped would be acceptable to the Maldivian government after discussion with a British emissary whom he hoped to send to Malé by October.

MacMillan's suggestion of an October meeting gave Britain the chance to assess, through Arthington-Davy, the depth of the Maldivian plight referred to by the Sultan in his June speech. It also provided a period in which more pressure could be put upon Afif Didi and the Adduans. Accordingly, whilst Arthington-Davy was investigating, as best he could, the state of the Maldivian economy, the affairs of the United Suvadive Islands were being obstructed at Addu Atoll. Thus the captain of the SS Maskeliya, due to take Adduan goods to Ceylon, was persuaded that the cargo might be judged illicit, possibly leading to a dispute which would involve the ship's owners. Rather than take that risk he chose not to carry the goods.

With Moosajee already persuaded not to carry any more Adduan cargo Afif was left with a problem. Without access to outside shipping facilities his administration could not export the islanders' fish and import other foodstuffs. The loss of export facilities was not in itself crucial because the Maldivians were receiving total wages of about seven thousand pounds a month and, although some of that was spent in the NAAFI and some used for local dealings, about half of that seven thousand pounds was available for the purchase of goods from abroad. But to spend it on imports Afif had to transmit it to suppliers in advance because ships did not sail to the southern extremity of the archipelago for speculative trading with the Adduans. Finally, his request to transmit one thousand pounds a month from Addu Atoll *via* the RAF's accounts was refused and that effectively prevented his administration from importing any goods for the Adduans other than the very limited quantities which could be legitimately purchased through the NAAFI.

Even with the Adduan economy under siege Afif still had the overwhelming support of the islanders. But three highly respected Huladuans continued to argue that the Adduans should accept the agreement which the British and Maldivian governments had negotiated. Since early 1960 they had been arguing in favour of a settlement and their defection from the leading group of rebels had been initially seen as a severe setback for Afif Didi. They had, however, failed to attract enough lasting support to develop a significant opposition group; the nearest they had come to that was in April 1961 when the Huladuans had gone on strike but had been outmanoeuvred.

Afif, who brooked no opposition to his regime, saw those three defectors from his team as a threat and during the April demonstrations he made certain that they were kept securely under house arrest to ensure that they did not rally support, no matter how small, for the Maldivian ministers. Even after they had been released their position was precarious and in September they were once again in trouble following a visit to Gan by Arthington-Davy. It was almost inevitable that his visit would spark off rumours of another attempt to reinstate Maldivian officials to the atoll and on the 16th of September 1962 almost a thousand Maldivians, all believing the rumours to be true, crowded aboard a fleet of some one hundred dhonis and staged a demonstration near the Gan jetty. They were determined to show the strength of their feelings but they were not truly hostile and they dispersed after the station commander and Arthington-Davy addressed them and assuaged their fears. For Afif, the affair provided an opportunity to silence the three major dissidents together with six others whom he believed to be a threat to his authority. All nine were accused of trying to contact Arthington-Davy without the knowledge of the people's council and were placed, without trial, under house arrest for an indefinite period.

The Adduans' economy was in trouble but so too was the entire Maldivian economy. Arthington-Davy's investigations into that, undertaken in preparation for the British emissary's discussions with the Maldivian Prime Minister, revealed a situation which was near-critical. The nation was already known to be one of the poorest in the world with no foreign reserves and with a currency, the Maldivian rupee, which had no backing and was not accepted by anyone who had any other choice. By mid-1962 the collapsing value of the Maldivian rupee and dramatic food shortages in the archipelago had led to such an increase in bartering that cash sales were becoming the exception rather than the rule. The black market was rife in Malé. Heavy fines were being imposed on profiteers and hoarders and the licences of some Indian merchants had been revoked. There was an extensive building programme in Malé but, in common with other projects, the hospital which was to have been built out of aid funds from Britain had not been started. The government was so desperate for foreign exchange that it was even planning to lease some islands to foreign commercial organisations for copra growing.

Understandably, the Maldivian ministers were becoming increasingly anxious to start reaping some financial benefits from the development at Addu Atoll which had, prior to the rebellion, seemed to provide a golden opportunity for the Maldivians to drag themselves out of the poverty trap by building up some foreign currency reserves. But the hopes that Britain would be generous with its aid programme in appreciation of the very low cost of leasing the land at Addu Atoll had not been fulfilled and the saga of the supposed rejuvenation of the fishing fleet had done more harm than good to relations between the two nations. The profit the Maldivian government had expected to make by paying the Adduans in Maldivian rupees charged to the British government on parity with the Ceylon rupee had disappeared with the Adduans' declaration of independence and the British decision to pay the Adduans in Sterling. The final blow had been the loss of income from the taxation of the Adduans' new-found wealth; a significant sum for a poverty-stricken nation, as the affairs of the Adduan Trading Corporation indicate.

It seemed that Britain not only had the advantage of being effectively in control at Addu Atoll but was negotiating with a government which was desperately in need of a settlement in order to ease its crippling financial problems.

Snelling believed that in spite of all that, the Maldivian government was most unlikely to be pushed into cancelling the leasehold agreement with Britain in order to raise money by offering the atoll facilities to the Russians.

The practicalities of inviting a different foreign power into the Maldives and the long history of amicable relations with Britain did make it rather unlikely that they would end the protection agreement except as a last desperate measure born out of a feeling of impotence or loss of face. Financial necessity was a most unlikely reason for them to take such a drastic step.

Against that background the British ministers reconsidered the possibility of using economic aid to influence the Maldivian negotiators, developing a set of proposals which included an extension of the lease agreement to the year 2002 and the provision of an extra ninety acres of land at the atoll for British use, all in exchange for the reclassification of the existing fifty thousand pound loan as a gift with further long term economic aid valued at four hundred and fifty thousand pounds. Under the proposals the Maldivian government would also benefit by paying the Adduans in Maldivian rupees charged to the British government at the official exchange rate of thirteen to the pound and subsequently paid to the Adduans at the market value of the rupee which was only about one fifth of the official exchange rate. The proposals provided no new benefits for the Adduans. All they would get out of the settlement would be the security provided under the protective clauses and the concessions which they had previously rejected as inadequate.

Financially, the proposals were quite attractive for the Maldivian government but there were two flaws: the omission of a detailed plan to resolve the Adduan problem quickly and the insistence on a pardon for Afif and the other Adduans, a key non-negotiable clause in the British proposals. As Sir Arthur Snelling, the British emissary was to discover, those two flaws were to be the downfall of the British proposition for they carried a loss of face for the Maldivian ministers which was more important than the plan's financial attractions.

Sir Arthur went to Malé in the third week of October 1962 and remained there until near the end of November, negotiating with Nasir and the three government ministers who comprised the committee on the Adduan problem. His subsequent report clearly showed the difficulties he encountered. Mostly, it seems, they were of Britain's making. Nasir did all the talking for the Maldivians but only ever met Sir Arthur in the presence of the other three ministers. The atmosphere was initially quite promising with the Maldivians at least prepared to study the British proposals. Nasir,

however, was firm on the return of government officials from Malé to run the affairs at the atoll and would have nothing to do with the idea that Afif Didi should remain in any significant position of authority. The second meeting was postponed until the 4th of November pending further instructions from the British government subsequent to the events in Cuba which were far more demanding of attention than the events at Addu Atoll.

The twelve-day gap between meetings created some suspicions in Malé, with the local newspaper reports, always a good barometer of Maldivian ministerial feelings, progressing from initial puzzlement into open hostility. The British post-Cuba stance was firmer than before with the result that the second meeting was a setback for both sides when, in Sir Arthur's words, *'British firmness confronted Maldivian suspicion, hostility and intransigence'*. Time after time the British emissary sought further discussions and eventually he was accommodated at the third and final meeting on the 15th of November. At that meeting the atmosphere quickly deteriorated to such an extent that there was no point in continuing the debate. Sir Arthur, under orders to test Nasir's nerve by arranging to depart for Gan if a stalemate had been reached, did just that after the meeting, informing Nasir of his intention to go to Gan and await further instructions from Britain. The following day there were demonstrations in Malé against the British and rumour reached Sir Arthur that if they did not depart they would be kidnapped from Dunidu, manhandled into small boats, taken to Malé island and, if they survived that, sent to Colombo. The Maldivian government informed him that public opinion could not be controlled and that it was not safe for any British personnel to remain on Dunidu. Malé however, appeared to be even more dangerous and the only British workers based in the capital, six expatriates not associated with the British government or the military, left Malé and took refuge on Dunidu.

At that time the Royal Navy ship on patrol in the area was HMS Loch Fada and at Sir Arthur's request the frigate sailed into the Malé lagoon at dawn the following day, creating a great deal of fuss in the capital in spite of his explanation that the ship had arrived '...*to protect British lives and property in view of the expressed inability of the Maldivian Government to do so'*.

A complex relationship then developed between the British and the Maldivians. Sir Arthur's formal letters about Addu Atoll were being sent to Nasir *via* the Maldivian messengers; a steady flow of letters was coming from the Maldivian government to the six British workers who were sheltering on Dunidu, suggesting that they should go back to work in Malé even though their safety was not guaranteed; an amicable arrangement was made, at the request of the Maldivian government, for the sailors from HMS Loch Fada to blast a deeper and wider channel into the lagoon for the benefit of the Maldivian fishing boats whilst the local press reports, often bordering on the incoherent, became increasingly vituperative without ever hinting at the real reason for the presence of the British frigate.

On the 20th of November 1962 Sir Arthur wrote to the Maldivian Prime Minister describing the British efforts to restore normality to Addu Atoll, regretting the Maldivian intransigence and offering to take any messages to the Adduans. After waiting a week and sending a reminder Sir Arthur finally received a reply in Divehi which merely re-affirmed the Maldivian government's stance. He left for London *via* Gan on the last day of the month commenting, in his report on the failure of his mission, that '*His (Nasir's) bloody-minded attitude springs from suspiciousness of incredible depth - - - provoked by our determination to secure the safety of the Adduans.*'

Nasir had every right to be bloody-minded and suspicious of the British. With all the pent up frustrations which he set out in his correspondence with Harold MacMillan, with all his resentment over the April debacle at Addu Atoll and probably with memories of the protracted affair of the Addyyatal Rahman and the elusive nature of the British aid programme for the Maldives it would have been remarkable if he had been anything but angry, suspicious and intransigent. So incensed was he by the British attitude that he wrote to many of the senior ministers and prime ministers in the Commonwealth, to President Kennedy and to the Secretary General of the United Nations, all in an attempt to put pressure on the British and to make it clear that he was now in the mood to accept help from any foreign government prepared to offer it. To Harold MacMillan, Nasir wrote that Sir Arthur, although arriving at Malé with the apparent purpose of settling the Adduan problem, had actually been intent only on obtaining more land for Britain and a pardon for the Adduan rebels who had already been pardoned on three previous occasions at the request of the British. Such an obvious choice of priorities had made the Maldivian government deeply suspicious about Britain's motives and intentions and, ignoring the fact that his ministers had subsequently taken advantage of the warships' presence, he complained that the Loch Fada and the Caesar had arrived in the Malé lagoon without the permission of the Maldivian government.

Harold MacMillan, in response to Nasir's request to get the Addu affair settled and his complaint about the continuing presence of HMS Caesar, wrote to the Maldivian Prime Minister explaining the arrival of the warships and refuting Nasir's interpretation of Britain's priorities.

Whilst the airfield on Gan was operating efficiently enough to satisfy Britain's military strategic needs in the area, MacMillan was apparently quite prepared to take whatever criticism came from the United Nations or the Commonwealth Prime Ministers. Time was on his side. He obviously thought that if the affair dragged on long enough the Maldivian ministers, impotent against the British, would eventually accept any settlement out of desperation.

The failure of Snelling's mission left Arthington-Davy, together with a contingent of RAF personnel and the six expatriates who had fled from the capital, isolated on Dunidu and vulnerable to attack by any mob which might choose to sail the short distance from the capital island. A Royal Navy frigate was held on station within four hours sailing of Malé Atoll but that seemed to offer the Dunidu residents only limited reassurance. They requested that Sten guns, pistols and hand grenades be dropped onto the island in case the frigate should fail to arrive when called for. That request startled the Command staff, raising a vision of a last-stand encounter on Dunidu, and the request was dismissed out of hand on the grounds that armed men would simply invite greater hostility and would be hopelessly outnumbered against the Maldivian militiamen. The Singapore-based duty officer, urgently signalling the Air Ministry staff in London to warn them of possible military action led by the British Representative in Malé summed up the general feeling with his comment '*My faith shaken in judgement on the spot.*'

When Arthington-Davy was instructed to go to Addu Atoll and formally explain to the Adduans why Sir Arthur's mission had failed there was little doubt that Afif Didi had already heard of the failure but the formality had to be observed and the Air Ministry staff regarded this as a political matter best left to the civilian representative. Arthington-Davy's departure from Dunidu defused the potentially serious situation because the Maldivian government never concerned itself with the junior staff who worked for him; they were consequently left unmolested and unhindered in their day-to-day activities.

Thus Arthington-Davy's visit to Gan, arranged to satisfy protocol, was almost certainly more valuable for its side effects than for its original intent; it defused the situation at Dunidu and it maintained the non-political status of the RAF in the eyes of the Adduans.

1963 started with the Maldivian government once more expressing its frustration in no uncertain terms. Nasir had again written to MacMillan expressing the view that after almost five years without any central government control over the affairs at Addu Atoll it was fairly obvious that Britain was unable to find a solution which would be acceptable to the Maldivian government, the Adduans and the British. He had repeated his earlier comments that the British presence had actually led to the rebellion and was now preventing him from solving the problem, as he could so easily do with the national militia. Finally, he played what was probably the only trump card he had left. He declared that it was time for the protection agreement with the United Kingdom to be brought to an end.

That posed a serious possibility for Britain and by 1963 it was no longer as unlikely as it seemed.

The Maldivian economy was getting little benefit from the lease of the atoll, the government was losing face and Nasir might just be frustrated enough to make such a move. The implication was that, if the protection agreement were terminated, Britain might end up losing its newly built strategic base and seeing it handed over to some other foreign power, possibly to Russia. To reinforce the seriousness of the situation the Maldivian Attorney-General used the Malé radio broadcasting service to address the nation at about the time that Nasir's letter was expected to reach the British Prime Minister. Quotations from the broadcast were sent to the Commonwealth Relations Office by the British Representative in the Maldives. They made strange reading. The Attorney-general, a powerful orator when the occasion demanded, worked hard to arouse anti-British feeling among the Maldivians with comments such as:

> 'I'm sure you, my noble countrymen, are fully aware of the vicious and treacherous nature of British Imperialism. You are witnesses to the speed with which it has transformed those innocent hearts of our brothers and sisters into scheming and violent ones' and 'Our lives are a small price to pay for the salvation of our country. Our enemy is in the last phase of his world domination. Let us ... rid ourselves of this vicious enemy of our freedom. Let us each to his task and do or die.'

The letter and the speech were backed up by a similarly strange and vitriolic series of articles in the Maldivian newspapers where, under headings such as 'British Invasion of the Maldives', the Maldivians were once again able to read the old allegations that the RAF had instigated the rebellion at Addu Atoll.

In Britain, the situation was considered to be potentially serious enough for the Joint Intelligence Committee to commission a report on the possible use of the Maldives by the Soviets. The report turned out to be only partially reassuring. Pointing out that there seemed to be no great advantage for the Russians to move in to Addu Atoll and no signs that they wished to do so the authors commented that India and Ceylon, both against politicising the Indian Ocean, were friendly towards Britain and would almost certainly try to dissuade the Maldivians from inviting the Russians into the region.

The Russians' occasional presence in the archipelago was largely discounted on the grounds that although they had made several cultural visits to the islands there was no evidence that the relationship with the Maldivians went beyond the cultural and in a clear indication of that the Maldivian government had refused a Russian request for their survey vessel, Vityaz, which had been near Malé in February 1960, to survey the archipelago. The fact that Soviet merchantmen, each presumably on a 'listening watch', were often in the Indian Ocean just over the horizon from Gan was equally dismissed as the normal behaviour of the major powers in international waters. There remained, however, one serious possibility; the Russians might wish to lease Addu Atoll simply to deny Britain the use of a strategically significant mid-ocean staging post.

That possibility bothered Sir Arthur Snelling and, anxious to try, yet again, to break the impasse he initiated an investigation into the Adduan economy and the stability of the local political system. Accordingly, Mr Peter Moon, who was employed at the British High Commission in Colombo, was tasked with the investigation and required to produce a report which would support his recommendations on how best to restore central government authority without creating local unrest. He was sent to Gan in January and took up residence in what had once been Arthington-Davy's bungalow.

Snelling probably saw the commissioning of yet another report as a constructive move but the Maldivian ministers must have seen it as just another example of Britain's prevarication and excessive concern for the wishes of the Adduan rebels.

Moon had been employed in the High Commission in Colombo since 1960. There was little doubt that he would bring an open-minded approach to his investigation and would produce a report which might be contentious but which would undoubtedly offer a variety of recommendations based on good evidence. That he did.

His report disclosed that, both commercially and politically, all was not as well as Afif made out.

The local administrators and the Adduan Trading Corporation were essentially re-distributors of Sterling, paying out fourteen or fifteen thousand pounds a year and, in the case of the administrators, providing services for the general benefit of the community.

Initially, the Corporation, with its headquarters on Hitaddu and a trading post on every inhabited island in the atoll, had been a significant source of income for the atoll's administration. Cash sales were combined with a system of barter using credit notes redeemable only against goods supplied to the Corporation from Moosajee's, an Indian trading company with a long history of trade with the islanders and a well-established credit arrangement for dealings with any businesses, including the recently formed Adduan Trading Corporation. The spread of shareholders meant that over one thousand four hundred islanders had a vested interest in the success of the Corporation and would quickly report any illegitimate trading which might undermine the company's monopoly position.

There were twenty-six people working full-time for the Corporation together with numerous part-timers who were employed as and when required to move goods around the islands. Control was ostensibly in the hands of a close colleague of Afif, whilst most of the administration and book-keeping was done by a Tamil clerk who believed himself to be on secondment from Moosajee's even though Moosajee himself had stated that the man was no longer one of his employees. Detailed records were kept but they were not in any conventional form. In 1962 the Corporation's turnover on NAAFI-supplied goods alone had amounted to some fifty-nine thousand pounds, providing enough profit to pay the Corporation's overheads and contribute to the revenue needed for the basic public services provided under the atoll's new regime.

But there were problems. A dividend had only once been paid, no accounts had ever been submitted to the shareholders, trade with Moosajee was grinding to a halt and the Corporation's debts to the Indian company were growing.

During the fifteen months prior to Moon's report the value of the Corporation's issued credit notes was some twenty-four thousand pounds but the measures taken by the RAF to curtail the Maldivians' trading with outside agencies were dramatically affecting the company's solvency. Almost twenty-five thousand pounds worth of Adduan produce held by the Corporation was awaiting export but was deteriorating to such an extent that its value was probably down to eighteen thousand pounds. The islanders had recently been unable to barter their produce because the goods supplied by Moosajee were virtually exhausted and until Moosajee had been informed that produce was available for export from the atoll he would not be sending further supplies to the islanders. By February 1963 the Corporation was in deep financial trouble.

Apart from the deteriorating produce, the assets included some goods of indeterminate value in Colombo and approximately seven thousand five hundred pounds in cash, some five and a half thousand of which was held by the NAAFI as a deposit on ordered goods. The Corporation admitted debts of just over twenty thousand pounds to Moosajee and a liability for just over one thousand pounds worth of circulating credit notes. The credit notes, together with the total debts for the company and for the atoll's administration were the subject of a dispute, with Moosajee claiming that Afif Didi, as head of administration, owed his company some forty thousand pounds, quite apart from the Corporation's debt. Afif strongly denied that so much was owed, claiming that the debt was no more than twelve thousand pounds.

Regardless of the actual amounts which were or were not owed, the figures being bandied about were staggering for an economy in which the most senior Maldivians employed as overseers in the works services department were paid less than five pounds a week, with unskilled labourers receiving no more than half that.

It was obvious to Moon, but not, apparently, to the Adduans, that the whole economy of the so-called republic was about to collapse unless the islanders could re-open their overseas trade.

The republic and the Corporation provided employment for one hundred and ten people, but their salaries were far from generous. The most junior employees, the office clerks, were each paid five pounds a month whilst Afif Didi, the president, received only thirty pounds a month. The list of atoll employees included twenty-seven policemen, the village headmen, the magistrates and the teachers. All were paid out of taxation which raised just under seven thousand pounds in 1962. The Corporation, however, cost approximately eight thousand pounds to run that year when the Gan-Fedu and Midu branches had been opened and when the senior director was being paid more than his president. The most obvious options for improvements were all politically unpalatable and none had been implemented by March 1963. A levy on shareholders who had only once received a dividend or seen an increase in the company's profit margins would have been extremely unpopular and could have threatened Afif's hold on the presidency. Any suggestion that running costs should be reduced would have implied a reduction in everyone's wages or in the number of employees; less threatening politically but obviously unpopular. Afif had no wish to face up to the problem. He merely continued to press for the removal of the ban on his use of the RAF communications network which was effectively a ban on the Maldivians' overseas trade.

There were not, early in 1963, any widespread worries among the islanders about their economy. As far as they were concerned Gan continued to be a source of wealth with employment as high as one Gan worker per household in Gan-Fedu village, reducing through one per three households in Huludu to one per seven households in the rather remote Midu which was several hours rowing time from Gan. Understandably the seven or eight hundred Maldivians on the British payroll, all of whom were well able to support their families, were not unduly worried about the Corporation's problems.

There were other workers who were similarly unconcerned, the craftsmen whose work had been increasingly in demand ever since the British had started to employ local labour. Many Adduans were investing in coral stone houses, paying about two hundred pounds for the basic structure to be built and subsequently employing carpenters and other craftsmen whose expertise was needed to complete the work.

It was the fishermen who were suffering more than most through the lack of trade because they could only sell their catch locally and with most families able to do their own fishing, the supply of fish far exceeded the demand. The coconut growers were also faring badly for they were selling few coconut products and were still having to employ people to care for the trees. Nevertheless the lessees of the coconut plantations were still the wealthiest men in the atoll because they had accumulated enough capital over the years to weather the temporary lack of trade.

With the help of an interpreter it was easy enough for Moon to talk to the atoll's executive committee and to many of Afif's supporters for they were still very much in the majority. He was even given free access to the three dissidents who remained under house arrest for having voiced their opposition to the *de facto* government led by Afif and declared themselves in favour of a reconciliation with the Maldivian government. None of them was suffering and only one needed an interpreter. They told Moon that they saw the restoration of central government authority as inevitable and wished to negotiate a peace deal with the promise of a free pardon.

Afif Didi wanted nothing to do with that idea and had kept them under house arrest because they were too important and too influential to be left roaming around.

Far more difficult for Moon was the task of trying to assess the general level of support among the islanders for the reconciliation favoured by the three dissidents. In theory he was free to talk to anyone but in practice the villagers were frightened to voice any comments against Afif or his government, particularly if they had to speak through an interpreter. They were all aware that several Adduans who had tried to contact visiting government officials had been arrested, accused of some other offence and either banished to Huvadu or put under house arrest, a fate which continued to await anyone who was unwise enough to make public comments in favour of a reconciliation with the central government.

Afif's control relied upon the Adduans' belief that the British government would protect them. His philosophy was simple; any sign of dissent among the islanders had to be quashed before it undermined that belief and gave the British the impression that his support had declined to the point at which Maldivian officials from Malé should be brought to the atoll. Everyone was watched, everything was reported. The slightest suspicion that a villager was no longer totally loyal to Afif was enough to cost him his job on Gan, frequently on some trumped-up charge of misbehaviour.

One Adduan in particular, Mohammed Saeed, was caught in the political crossfire and was to pay dearly in the future both for supporting the RAF operations at the atoll and for working for a reconciliation with the Maldivian government. He refused to visit the political adviser's bungalow for fear of subsequent arrest but he did contact Moon. He explained that previous contact with the British Representative had put him under suspicion and he was fearful for his future. Only because Moon had been given a job involving day-to-day contact with the labour force, thus reducing the obvious exposure of individual informants, had Mohammed Saeed made his approach. That had been true of many such contacts but few had been as frightened as he. Moon, unable to do anything to alleviate Mohammed's fears, could hardly have foreseen the treatment which was to be meted out to Saeed over the next few years.

One outcome of Moon's discussions with Afif was the release, early in March, of the three dissidents who had been so long under house arrest without trial. Afif had told Moon that he was in favour of their release but it was a council matter; a fine point in view of the fact that the council did what Afif wanted. However, the councillors met on the 9th of March and agreed to the release, simultaneously ordering the release of all other prisoners regardless of their offences, thus saving the council's collective face over the release of political prisoners only.

By mid-March Moon had completed his investigation and produced his report, concluding that, in spite of the imminent economic collapse of the fledging republic, Afif's administration was widely supported. There were several reasons for that. Afif was an even-tempered, flexible individual with a sufficiently ruthless streak to hold on to his presidency for as long as he had British support against the Maldivian government. His personal standing was very high. The Adduans were more prosperous than at any time in their history. Finally, there was a widespread belief that the British government would continue to exclude the Maldivian government from Addu Atoll and would eventually recognise the breakaway republic. Even those Adduans who doubted that tended to support Afif because they did not believe that the British could protect them if central government rule returned to their atoll.

Moon made several recommendations, starting with the removal of the United Suvadive Islands' flags which still flew throughout the islands even though Afif had agreed to their removal when the 1960 agreement had been signed. He suggested that the Adduans should be instructed, by the widespread distribution of Divehi language leaflets, to remove their flags, arguing that such an instruction would be symbolically very significant.

Referring to the hostility faced by a significant group of islanders who were in favour of a settlement with the Maldivian government, Moon recommended that they, together with those Adduans who generally co-operated with the RAF when any Maldivian government representatives visited the atoll, should be employed on Gan. They could thus be more easily protected against the vagaries of the people's council, and such protection could best be effected by ending Afif's role as unpaid civil labour liaison officer and replacing him with a Maldivian employee known to be neutral.

Moon's report exposed the existence of two police forces on Gan: the RAF's military police and a covert police force operating as an undercover extension of the official republican police. Describing that situation as undesirable, Moon proposed that Maldivian policemen should be employed by the RAF and amalgamated with the military police. He also suggested that the RAF should distance itself from the republic. That would be relatively easy to do, starting with the direct payment of all Maldivian employees, thereby ending the arrangement under which the Adduan administration distributed cash and rice, still issued as payment-in-kind, to the Maldivians employed on the leased territories. If that move were to be followed by a refusal to supply the atoll administration with a wage sheet on which to base the seven per cent income tax which had to be paid by the wage-earning islanders the message would be clear; the RAF was preparing for the return of central government authority to the atoll. Increasing economic pressure could then be applied to lower the Adduans' standard of living, reducing the attractiveness of their so-called republic.

Moon's final recommendation was highly contentious. Afif Didi should be removed from the atoll.

His reasoning was that Afif's education, personality and political acumen were not matched by any other Adduan and if he were to be removed there would be no-one capable of taking over the presidency and sustaining the crumbling republic. Given the ever-increasing problems facing the atoll's administrators, Moon was convinced that Afif could be bought out with a generous offer of asylum. He believed that the Adduans' reaction under such circumstances would depend upon the manner of Afif's removal. If that were discreet, the shock of his disappearance would probably lead to no more that a stunned, half-hearted reaction. If, however, the Adduans were given warning of his departure they might mount a series of demonstrations. He suggested that any such disruption would be short-lived and would quickly be replaced by apathy which would provide a good opportunity for the re-introduction of Maldivian officials to the atoll. He was convinced that the islanders would be unlikely to cause too much trouble because they knew that the British could allow the Maldivian government to re-establish its authority over the Adduans merely by standing aside whilst Nasir sent in the militiamen. Moon believed that the islanders, bereft of Afif Didi's leadership, would generally accept the return to normality and would almost certainly be co-operative if they were to be convinced that the British would protect them from the retributive intentions of Nasir and his ministers by ensuring that all the terms of the agreement were scrupulously observed..

As if telepathically aware that events at Addu Atoll were moving towards normality, the Maldivian Prime Minister abandoned, temporarily at least, his animosity, surprising Arthington-Davy enough for him to signal the Commonwealth Relations office in March saying '...*entirely amicable meeting with PM. Nasir happy, relations returning to normal. No indication why.*'

Nothing, however remained constant for long when dealing with the Maldivian government and in April the Chief of the Defence Staff had to signal the Commander-in-Chief, Middle East, to warn of a possible threat to the British Representative at Malé. The rapid evacuation frigates, one on station just over the horizon from the Maldivian capital and one at Addu Atoll, were under orders for a naval exercise and their withdrawal would have left the Dunidu contingent vulnerable just when anti-British feelings were beginning to run high again in Malé. If the Maldivians were to blockade the airstrip at Hulule, as they had previously done by covering it with a hundred or more felled coconut palms, the unarmed Dunidu residents would be isolated and unable to resist any attack.

Remarkably, the Chief of the Defence Staff proposed to protect them by dropping a parachute platoon onto Dunidu as soon as the airstrip had been put out of action, a perfectly feasible military plan which was so politically naive that he would never have been allowed to implement it.

Fortunately he had no reason to seek government approval for such a move because the Maldivians needed to keep the airstrip open during the summer for the convenience of some Ceylonese schoolteachers and some Maldivian school children. It was typical of the Maldivian ministers that they ceased railing against the British just long enough to ask for help, formally requesting that an occasional RAF shuttle service be provided between Ceylon and Hulule throughout the summer to provide transport for the Maldivian children, who were to go to school in Ceylon, and for the Ceylonese teachers, who were coming to work in Malé. The British government, as obliging as usual on all trivial matters, agreed to provide such a service, scheduling the RAF flights as a series of round trips from Ceylon to Hulule to Gan and back to Ceylon, thus simultaneously providing a regular service connecting the High Commissioner in Ceylon, the British Representative on Dunidu and the political adviser on Gan.

The only problem was that the RAF would not classify the ill-maintained, poorly-equipped runway on Hulule as suitable for passenger flights, it was strictly an 'essential operations only' airfield. But the Maldivians, not really that concerned about safety, had neither the money nor the inclination to repair the airstrip and the executives of Air Ceylon, the airline which most frequently used the airfield, had no intention of spending money on it. If the RAF were to use it for military supply flights but not for passengers the Maldivians would undoubtedly see that as obstructive behaviour rather than safety consciousness and the Commonwealth Relations Office, anxious to build goodwill whenever possible, suggested that the British government could bear the cost as an element of *quid pro quo* for the use of Gan. That sounded reasonable enough but it was not agreed, it merely sparked off a lengthy debate with the Treasury.

In June the Queen's official birthday had provided an occasion for the Maldivian ministers to demonstrate their unanimity by boycotting the British Representative's party and for the Maldivian press to attack Britain with one article declaring '...*our blood boils to see our rights and legal claims being crushed and fragrantly* (sic) *superimposed by the use of prestige and influence of Britain*'. The fact that the Maldivians were hoping that the British would repair the Hulule airstrip as a goodwill gesture was of no consequence, the public diatribe continued unabated.

That same month Britain's desire to bring about a settlement between the Adduans and their legitimate government was given fresh impetus when the Royal Navy, already interested in establishing a naval tanker farm on Gan, proposed a survey of the atoll to assess its suitability for use by nuclear-powered submarines. Such use, which was almost certain to be resisted by India and Ceylon once they became aware of it, was, according to the Admiralty, covered by Annex 1 to Article 1 of the 1960 agreement and could therefore be undertaken without informing the Maldivian government. Although the survey was not made at that time because of the sensitive political situation, the idea of using the atoll as a base for nuclear powered submarines was not abandoned, it was merely shelved until such time as the Admiralty felt that the political climate was more favourable.

While the debate about Hulule airfield was going on, Moon's report was being considered by the British government and a draft plan of action, incorporating most of his recommendations, was being formed. The plan seemed simple enough. First of all, Afif Didi and his supporters would be offered asylum. When they had left the atoll the way would be clear for officials to be brought in from Malé. Once they were in post and the new administration was seen to be honouring the terms of the agreement, the British government would resume the aid programme to the Maldives, financing the construction of a hospital in Malé, the provision of maritime equipment and the improvements both to the harbour and to the oil storage facilities.

Moon's job ended once his report had been studied and accepted and he duly returned to England. It was left to Mr D C Rounthwaite, the newly appointed political adviser at Addu Atoll, to deal with the local reaction to the implementation of the report. He arrived at Gan on the 12th of July just as Snelling was managing to break the deadlock over the runway repairs on Hulule by suggesting that the work should be started as soon as possible because Duncan Sandys, the secretary of state for commonwealth affairs, would be flying to Kuala Lumpur for the Malaysian celebrations at the end of August and was planning to stop overnight at Malé to talk to Nasir.

Although the British government had no wish to spend money on the Hulule airstrip, Duncan Sandys' itinerary provided an opportunity to justify the expenditure on the basis of a 'minister-on-board' flight. The Singapore-based Command staff, notified of the decision to effect the necessary repairs, were unimpressed by the justification. Their alternative proposals, to improve the fire fighting facilities on Hulule and to provide temporary medical services for the airfield by seconding a doctor to the island, were rejected. But they made their point about unnecessary expenditure by acknowledging the ineffectiveness of the runway drainage system and

suggesting that Sandys' flight schedules should be arranged so as to ensure that his aircraft's arrival was timed to avoid landing on a wet runway, a tongue-in-cheek proposal which was studiously ignored. The repairs were completed in August. That same month the Maldivian press once again berated the British for their behaviour in the southernmost reaches of the archipelago, claiming that convicted criminals were being offered sanctuary at Addu Atoll. The Adduans had never been under any illusions about the difficulty of sustaining an illegitimate independent republic in the south of the archipelago. Their only trade routes to the north ran past the Maldivian capital and that made it inevitable that sooner or later one of their vessels would be captured by the Maldivian government. Sure enough, in mid-August, an Adduan fishing boat which had set sail for Ceylon was blown off course, was seized and taken to Malé. The fishermen were tried and convicted, their boat was confiscated and they were banished to 'criminals island'. They managed to escape and reach the Indian territory of Minicoy from where they were repatriated to Addu Atoll, providing an opportunity for the Maldivian press to accuse the British of harbouring convicted criminals at Addu Atoll under the protection of the RAF.

Rounthwaite had been at Gan for little more than a month when the captured Adduan fishermen were put on trial in Malé. It was not a good time to try to persuade the islanders that, as far as their dreams of independence were concerned, the game was over. But he did what he could, threatening ever-increasing economic pressure and openly declaring that the British government would remove Afif Didi if he opposed the reconciliation. One month later he was no further forward. The tide of events was, however, flowing against Afif and his supporters with the British High Commissioner in Ceylon, Sir Michael Walker, visiting Gan at the beginning of September to meet Hugh Fraser, the secretary of state for air, and Duncan Sandys, the secretary of state for commonwealth affairs.

On the 8th of the month Duncan Sandys went to Malé where he and Ibrahim Nasir signed an agreement which committed the British government to help restore Maldivian central government authority to Addu Atoll by the end of 1963. The agreement effectively drove the final nail into the coffin of the Adduans' unilaterally declared state of independence. In return, Britain was granted permission to extend the Hitaddu site by up to fifty acres to accommodate, under terms of tenure essentially the same as those for the existing site, a BBC relay station to be operated either by the

British government or by the British Broadcasting Corporation. For Nasir, there was an additional benefit: Sandys' undertaking that British aid to the Maldives would be resumed as soon as the political problems had been resolved.

On the 12th of September 1963 a telegram was sent from the Commonwealth Relations Office in London to the British High Commissioner in Colombo informing him that 'Agreement signed, aid scheme resurrected, hospital work to resume at once.' The signing was hardly likely to be news to the High Commissioner because an official communiqué setting out the terms of the agreement had already been released in Malé three days earlier. But the telegram served its main purpose, it authorised the resumption of work on the long-delayed hospital project. Even before the communiqué had been released in Malé Duncan Sandys had returned to Gan in order to make a statement to the atoll headmen.

His message was unequivocal: the time had come to restore political normality to the atoll.

The islanders were told that that would be done as soon as possible and certainly no later than the end of the year. Sandys confirmed that the agreement included the granting of a full pardon in respects of all past acts in connection with the rebellion so that no-one who cooperated with the Maldivian government in future needed to fear retribution for past behaviour. There were no exceptions to the pardon and he publicly stated that he had every confidence that it would be fully implemented. To round off his statement Sandys assured his audience of the firm friendship of the British government towards the people of Addu Atoll whom he hoped would continue to live happily in peace and prosperity. The irony of such a closing remark was not lost on his audience who realised that, for the first time, the British were working to a deadline for return to political normality and that by the end of the year the Adduans would once again be under the control of men they hated and feared. The idea of living happily in such circumstances was inconceivable. As for living prosperously, central government taxation had been one of the major causes of their revolt. They fully believed that, once back in control, their government would seek to recoup the losses suffered during the islanders' flirtation with independence and would embark on a punitive taxation programme for Adduans implemented under the pretext of a redistribution of wealth to ensure that the Maldivian nation shared the financial benefits of the British presence at Addu Atoll.

The headmen expressed their hatred of the Maldivian government in no uncertain terms and left Duncan Sandys well aware that the Adduans would forever believe that the British government had finally sold them out for the sake of fifty acres of land for the British Broadcasting Corporation.

The reaction to Sandys' statement clearly showed the depth of feeling among the Adduans and, bearing in mind the previous demonstrations which the islanders had mounted, one flight of the N° 1 Field Squadron, RAF Regiment, was deployed to Gan from RAF Butterworth, the airmen advertising their presence by daily practising their anti-riot techniques in full view of the Maldivians who came to work on the island.

Rounthwaite was left with the task of following up Sandys' statement to the headmen and persuading the islanders that the best thing for them to do was to work for an amicable return to political normality. It was a thankless task. He tried to visit each village in order to read out Duncan Sandys' statement, to be as persuasive as he could and to distribute copies of the statement. But he couldn't travel as rapidly as the rumours. The Adduans' intelligence grapevine had prepared them for some official announcement and by the time Rounthwaite reached Fedu, the first island on his itinerary, the villagers had already heard the rumour that they had been sold out for the sake of a BBC relay station.

When they heard the full text of the statement they, like the atoll headmen addressed by Duncan Sandys, realised that for the first time the British were working to an imminent deadline. Taken aback, they reacted angrily. Almost without exception the villagers who had assembled to hear the news tore up their leaflets in disgust, declaring that they would rather die than accept the agreement. They harangued Rounthwaite to such an extent that he eventually abandoned his attempt to persuade them of the wisdom of his advice and moved on to Hitaddu. There he found that the news from Fedu had preceded him, the villagers were waiting for him and there was no possibility that he could immediately persuade them to work towards a return to political normality which would end their period of illusory independence.

So it was wherever he went.

The villagers were angry, the council members would not believe the promise of a free pardon for everyone and the women, probably fearful of the retribution which might fall upon their menfolk, were strident in their opposition to the implementation of the new agreement. Afif, with his dream of independence finally shattered, was in no mood to help Rounthwaite and, although some of those who made up the anti-Afif faction said privately that they would co-operate, none was prepared to say so in public.

It was two days before Rounthwaite reached the village of Maradu-Fedu and received the first sign of a breakthrough. It came only after he spent hours at Maradu trying to win over the villagers by working through their village councils. At Maradu village he was eventually told that he was no longer welcome as a political representative although he would be welcomed as an individual on a personal basis. At Maradu-Fedu however the villagers did not reject the agreement out of hand. They were not keen on it but they were prepared to discuss it, albeit guardedly.

The Maldivian press, with a recent history of seizing on any opportunity to publish rather hysterical anti-British articles, had even managed to capitalise on a recent RAF search and rescue operation for some Huvaduan fisherman, thought to be adrift in the Indian Ocean, by reporting that the Huvaduans had escaped from Addu Atoll and that the RAF was searching for them. But the pending resolution of the Adduan problem was sufficiently welcome for the press to publish a '...forgive and forget' philosophy, at least for the time being. It would have been very different had it become generally known that plans were afoot to grant asylum to Afif Didi and his family. Sandys had readily accepted that Britain had a strong moral obligation to Afif and would grant him asylum if he so requested but had never mentioned that when dealing with Nasir for to do so would have destroyed the negotiations. Subsequently explaining the situation to the Maldivian Prime Minister would not be easy but could be done by arguing that Afif was undermining the reconciliation and had therefore been granted asylum, possibly in the Seychelles, to ease the return to political normality at the atoll.

That politically expedient argument would not have been too gross an exaggeration because Afif's influence and standing were still extremely high. But the breakthrough which started at Maradu-Fedu was beginning to spread and the idea that a return to political normality was inevitable was taking hold. Afif tried to counter that by using his influence with the village councils and by issuing instructions that no Adduan boat was to take the political adviser ashore, a restriction first encountered by Rounthwaite on the 15th of September when he was met some one and a half miles offshore from Midu and told not to land.

Nevertheless he went ashore by RAF dinghy but then had to spend some considerable time persuading the Midu and Huladu headmen to call a meeting of their two councils. When the councillors eventually met they unanimously rejected Rounthwaite's arguments for amicable reconciliation even though he had spent an hour and a half trying to persuade them that such an approach would be best in the long run. Rather surprisingly, in view of the fact that Huladu had long had a hard-core of Malé supporters, they were less friendly to him on a personal basis than were the councils on other islands, a clear indication that Afif had influenced them to close ranks against the common threat.

The following day the political adviser, hoping to have sown the seeds of change, called a halt to the one-sided discussions which were in danger of becoming counter-productive. Time was needed for the seeds to germinate even if there was a danger that Afif would use Rounthwaite's temporary withdrawal to boost the Adduans' resolve to stand fast and find out just how far the British were prepared to go to support Nasir.

One week into the selling of the agreement Rounthwaite could claim some success. There had been no demonstrations against the proposals, the Adduans were still well disposed towards the RAF and it seemed that most of them believed that the British government was serious in its intent to resolve the Adduan problem before the end of the year. Finally, three influential islanders had admitted in private that they would co-operate in the implementation of the agreement.

On the debit side nearly all of the Adduans viewed their government's promises with disbelief. Almost without exception they believed that they had been sold out for fifty acres of land. An emotional 'Die before submitting' rallying cry was developing which could easily become the prelude to large-scale disruptive demonstrations. Rather worryingly for Rounthwaite, the people's council had instructed Afif not to go to Gan, where he was employed as the labour relations officer, in case the British tried to remove him from the atoll. That instruction was disconcerting because it meant either that the councillors genuinely mistrusted the British and were determined to safeguard Afif to serve as the leader of a continuing rebellion or that they suspected that Afif's resolve was wavering and that, given the opportunity, he would seek asylum with the British and leave his associates to face the infuriated Maldivian officials in the not-too-distant future.

Unfortunately, Rounthwaite had no immediate way of knowing which was the case.

With the political adviser *persona non grata* on all the islands it was difficult to counter any propaganda emanating from the village councils and it was therefore decided that it would be best left to all the expatriates at the atoll to explain the British stand to the Adduan employees. Admittedly, that was not a very effective technique but it was the best that could be done in the circumstances. It was also decided that HMS Loch Lomond, which had been at anchor in the lagoon since the 6th of September, should leave; in the eyes of the Adduans it was a symbol of British protection against the forces from Malé and the removal of that symbol would be highly significant. Thus, on the 25th of September 1963 the Loch Lomond departed and the Adduans, unaware that the ship would simply be over the horizon on exercises at sea, were convinced that they had been deprived of their naval protection.

In Malé the Maldivian press had a new target: Afif Didi. With the obvious intention of trying to swing public opinion against Afif, and thus gain popular support for whatever retribution should befall him in the future, the Maldivian newspapers began to provide so-called details of atrocities committed by Afif against the Adduans. It was already becoming obvious that when political normality returned to Addu Atoll, he would be in great danger regardless of the terms of the agreement so recently signed.

Any lingering doubts about Afif's determination to resist the return of central government authority to Addu Atoll were dispelled as information reached Gan about his activities. He was playing on the fears of the Adduans by making all manner of dire predictions about what would happen when the Maldivian officials were back in control at the atoll. The villagers, with clear memories of earlier food shortages and with recent knowledge of near starvation at Huvadu, were particularly worried by the suggestion that once political normality returned to the atoll the Royal Air Force would no longer provide them with food as part-payment for their labour, nor would the islanders be permitted to purchase foodstuffs from the NAAFI. They were beginning to rally around Afif and, already embarked on a campaign of non-cooperation, were quite ready to threaten violence to anyone who voiced support for the Maldivian government.

On the 20th of the month, at a mass meeting on Hitaddu, the islanders discussed strategies for attacking the Maldivian officials when they eventually arrived at the atoll.

Afif, told to put a stop to the intimidatory tactics, failed to do so. On the 21st of September his appointment as labour relations officer was terminated, partly because of his failure to co-operate and partly to undermine the credibility of his predictions which were assumed by the islanders to be based on inside knowledge obtained by virtue of his appointment. The headmen were all informed of Afif's dismissal and of the intention to seek a replacement.

The dilemma for the British government arose from the fact that Afif had become an embarrassment but was morally entitled to British protection. If he were to be abducted by the British for his own protection he could sue and Britain would face international censure. Neither would be disastrous but both were best avoided if possible. The only tactic which could be easily adopted was to make Afif's position untenable and to grant asylum if he were to ask for it. That he would surely do sooner or later, especially if such an option were to be favourably mentioned by the political adviser. With that in mind, the pressure on Afif was increased by the announcement that at the end of the month the RAF would take over the distribution of rice to all Adduan employees thus pushing Afif to the sidelines and making it more difficult for him to collect some of the taxes on which his administration depended.

Although Afif's appointment as the labour relations officer had been terminated easily enough it was no easy matter to find a replacement because any Maldivian accepting the job was, in effect, publicly declaring that his support for the implementation of the new agreement was so strong that he was willing to take over the liaison job from which his president had just been sacked. One Adduan who was prepared to accept the job knowing that he would face considerable hostility from the other islanders was Mohammed Saeed, a capable and intelligent Adduan who already had an entrepreneurial interest in the operation of the Maldivian hotel on Gan. He was duly appointed. What no-one could have foreseen was that not only would he have to cope with the local hostility but he would, in the not-too-distant future, also have to cope with considerable antagonism from the Maldivian government whose cause he had espoused when he was appointed as Afif's successor on Gan.

It did not take long for the local resentment against Saeed to manifest itself. On the 22nd of the month feelings were running high among the islanders and a signal was sent to RAF Butterworth to alert the Officer Commanding N° 1 Field Squadron, RAF Regiment, to the likelihood that a further contingent of Regiment airmen would be needed at Addu Atoll. The following day there was a minor demonstration on the shore near the main jetty on Gan and although that was easily quelled, the Singapore-based Command staff were asked to provide further assistance.

On the 24th a fleet of dhonis started to arrive at Gan bringing some three hundred agitators from Hitaddu, all demanding that Saeed be handed over. They had apparently been aroused by rumours of the covert arrival of Maldivian officials and the raising of the Maldivian flag on Gan. The agitators had, however, chosen a bad day because three Hastings had arrived at Gan a few hours earlier, bringing the second and third flights of Regiment airmen from Butterworth where they had been on standby since the 22nd. Their arrival brought the RAF Regiment detachment on Gan up to squadron strength and they were ready to deal with any demonstration which the Maldivians might mount. Their presence was not only enough to persuade the agitators to abandon their plans and to sail back to Hitaddu, it marked the turning point in the Adduans' resistance to the return of political normality. Their belief that the RAF forces were there to protect them in their independence had been dramatically undermined in a few days and was finally shattered by that display of strength in support of the new labour relations officer.

At half past four in the afternoon of the 24th of September Afif Didi, finally accepting the inevitable, rang Rounthwaite, confirmed that his village would accept the terms of the new agreement and requested a meeting. He and three delegates arrived at Gan at half past five and confirmed the capitulation. That night his house was surrounded by hostile and abusive villagers protesting that he had misled them. They did no damage and eventually dispersed, some determined to fight on and some seemingly resigned to defeat. Within twenty-four hours those villagers who were in favour of conceding had begun to win over those who still wished to hold out against their central government. Afif Didi told the members of the people's council to submit their capitulation in writing and he duly presented their statement to the political adviser on Gan at ten o'clock on the morning of the 25th while the flags of the United Suvadive Islands were being lowered and the Maldivian national flags were being hoisted throughout the atoll.

The station commander and the political adviser had a private discussion with Afif and gave him until noon that day to decide what he wanted to do.

In spite of the Maldivian government's promise of a full pardon the British were genuinely concerned for Afif's safety. They had long been persuaded, but would never publicly admit, that at best he was likely to lose his liberty for many years. At worst he would lose his life. But this was the man who had certainly earned all the protection which the British government could provide. He had unstintingly served the Allied cause during the Second World War and had suffered banishment in the early post-war years because the Maldivian government had not forgiven him for fostering thoughts of independence among the Adduans when the wartime naval base had been created at the atoll. More significantly, it was he more than anyone who, throughout the construction of the airfield in the late 1950s and early 1960s had ensured that the work schedule was maintained even when the Maldivian government was being obstructionist. On the 26th of September, he wrote to the political adviser saying:

> 'I accept the Maldivian Government authority to be restored in Addu Atoll and I hereby undertake that I shall respect and remain loyal to the Maldivian Government and their officials and also obey fully their orders and commands. I humbly request to the British Government to be kind enough to extend to me and my family the full protection of the British Government for our own personal safety.'

There was never any doubt that he would be offered asylum, even though it was not to be on the basis of that request. When Rounthwaite signalled Arthington-Davy for confirmation that Afif's request was adequately worded he was asked to explain to Afif that his letter was considered inadequate for the British to use as justification for the help which it knew would be loudly condemned by the Maldivians as political interference in the internal affairs of the Maldives. Afif, anxious to be granted asylum to avoid the reprisals of his government and of some disenchanted Adduans, was perfectly happy to write whatever was appropriate and, adopting the wording recommended, resubmitted his request saying:

> 'I accept the authority of the Maldivian Government and have no wish to obstruct in any way the re-establishment of that authority in Addu Atoll

but in view of the position I've held in recent years my presence in the Maldives might be embarrassing to the Maldivian authorities and to myself. In the circumstances I think it would be in the best interests of everyone if I were to go elsewhere and I shall accordingly be grateful for any help you can give me and my family to go to the Seychelles'.

He was immediately told that arrangements would be made for him and his family to be resettled wherever they wished.

At four o'clock on the afternoon of the 27th of September 1963 HMS Loch Lomond arrived under orders to carry Afif and his family to the Seychelles. At nine o'clock on the morning of the 30th of September, in recognition of the friendly relationship which had developed between them during a politically turbulent year, Wing Commander Hill was on the Hitaddu jetty to bid farewell to Afif and his family. Their departure was a quiet affair with no reaction from the Adduans for they had finally accepted that their brief period of independence was over and had, on the 26th of September, requested the immediate return to their atoll of the Maldivian government's representatives, with all six headmen promising a friendly welcome for the officials and seeking permission to go to Malé to capitulate and to swear allegiance to their government. The British government arranged for Afif and his family to live in the Seychelles and rewarded his services to the Crown with a pension. The collapse of his dreams of independence and prosperity for the Adduans and his voluntary exile for the sake of his family and his own future came as a devastating blow to Afif, made worse by the fact that his frail elderly mother was unable to leave home with the rest of the family and died just three days after Afif was obliged to bid her farewell.

So ended the local involvement of the man who was arguably the most outstanding Maldivian ever to have held office at Addu Atoll. As he sailed for the Seychelles he could look back on a life which had brought success, deep frustration and notoriety before ending in personal tragedy. Born in 1916, he was still a young man when, during the inter-war years, he first became a prominent member of the Adduan community, his university education combining with a family background which had given him considerable commercial and political acumen and had ensured him a place among the Maldivian elite. Ever-ambitious for his fellow Adduans, and for himself, he spent most of his years trying to persuade his fellow

islanders that life, if organised in concert with other nations, need not be a day-to-day struggle for survival.

During the Second World War he had become convinced that the Maldivian government would take all the benefits from the development of Port T but would have no interest in enhancing the lives of the Adduans either during the lifetime of the naval base or in the post-war era. He had believed that the way forward for the Adduans was to build upon the Port T facilities once the war was over and that vision led him to his early unsuccessful attempt to persuade the islanders to declare their independence. It was an attempt which gave him his first experience of Maldivian government retribution when he was briefly banished to a penal island.

There appear to be no file records detailing this early rebellion but it seems certain that Afif made a fundamental mistake; he misjudged the political mood of the time. His attempt to lead a rebellion came at a time when the British government needed the facilities which were available in Malé as well as in Addu Atoll. The Allied cause and the post-war world order was uppermost in the minds of the British politicians and not one of them would have sacrificed the Maldivian government's support for the sake of an unknown rebel. Not surprisingly, the British co-operated with the Maldivian government to quash the rebellion and thereby helped to bring Afif to trial.

When re-admitted to Maldivian society he returned to Addu with his vision of independence intact but discreetly hidden. For years this intelligent well-educated man must have been deeply frustrated by his awareness that life could be so dramatically improved for the Adduans if it were not for their government's seeming indifference. Then, in 1957, the reappearance of the British military had brought to the surface his vision of prosperity for the islanders. The employment of Adduan labour to help with the construction of a new military base could undoubtedly have provided the foundations for a future trading economy as the Adduans became wealthier and that must have seemed, to Afif, like the answer to a prayer. He became totally committed to the construction programme and had been completely loyal to the Maldivian government throughout the time that Ibrahim Ali Didi was the Prime Minister. He had remained loyal during the early months of Ibrahim Nasir's period in office even though the Adduans had been ordered to cease working on the construction programme after the 1st of January 1958. It had taken twelve months of government prevarication to persuade Afif, with his unrealistic vision of independent prosperity for the islanders, to lead them in a unilateral declaration of independence. That move, borne of frustration and anger had been doomed from the start because Britain, a mere leaseholder at the atoll had never been in a position to safeguard for ever the future of the rebel islanders even if the political will had existed.

Afif had had his day and his only consolation was that it had lasted much longer and ended far less violently for the Adduans than for the Mulakuans and the Huvaduans. The demise of the so-called republic was inevitable. The timing may have been in doubt but the end was predictable; an incensed and suspicious Maldivian government would eventually be back in control at Addu Atoll with many Adduans suffering for having taken part in the rebellion and with Afif ending his days either on a penal island or living with his family in exile.

Afif's departure and the capitulation of the islanders marked the end of the United Suvadive Islands and the beginning of a new chapter in the saga of the British military at Addu Atoll.

Figure 13.1 Abdullah Afif Didi's letter to The Times.

The Secretariat,
Hitadu,
United Suvadive Islands.
TO THE EDITOR OF THE TIMES

Sir,

We have noted with interest statements in the Press and radio concerning the present political situation in the Maldives and in particular reports of the various utterances of the Malé Government representatives in Ceylon and London. To present our side of the picture is the aim of this letter.

Some of our reasons for the secession from Malé – the old capital of the Maldives – are as follows: the indifference of their administration to the elementary needs of the people of these islands – food, clothing, medicine, education, social welfare, etc. for many years we have been reduced to serfs and bled by extortionate taxes and levies. At the commencement of this year further taxes were imposed and the people who had nothing left to give revolted.

Bear in mind that we have not a single doctor for 18,000 undernourished people, nor any medical supplies whatsoever. We have no schools , no means of communication, no public utilities. All this is certainly the fault of Malé. Epidem-ics of Asian flu, malaria, enteric, typhoid, diarrhoea, conjunctivitis, etc, sweep our islands periodically during the year, and in 1958 we had a serious outbreak of dysentery causing deaths. We appealed to Malé for help. They refused and very piously told us to go on reading the Quran! The RAF doctors came to our aid, supplied medicine and visited the sick day and night. Can you wonder that we hate Malé?

Our main export from these islands was dried Maldive fish which we sent to Malé for sale in Ceylon. Payment was made to Malé in Ceylon rupees but we were forced by Malé to accept Maldivian rupees in return. One Maldivian rupee is worth only half a Ceylon rupee and we had then to buy what food we could afford from Malé at Ceylon prices.

The presence of the British in Addu Atoll had absolutely nothing to do with the will of the people to break from Malé. Attempts have been made before and as recently as 18 months ago men were imprisoned for trying to make an improvement. The RAF at Gan Island had no knowledge of our intention to make an uprising on the first day of 1959 – it was calculated action by the people to show Malé that we are determined never again to submit to the despotic rule of a government of one family.

We wish to make it clear that we have set up a government unanimously elected by the will of the people. We are a state of 18,000 people willing and able to support ourselves in spite of Malé. We are now the United Suvadive Islands. Our immediate policy is betterment of our people, friendliness to all nations and in particular to the British who have sincerely helped and wisely guided the Maldives whenever we desired to do so in the past.

We are in favour of the staging post and radio station at Gan and Hitadu Islands respectively, which must bring economic development and prosperity to our islands. We earnestly appeal to your great and generous country and people for help and understanding. We have been inhabiting theses islands from time immemorial, possessing thereby inalienable rights over them, the ownership thereof certainly cannot be claimed by the Malé Government. We, therefore appeal to the British Government to kindly grant us facilities to open negotiations at once with a view to conclude a Treaty of friendship and cooperation between Her Majesty's Government and the United Suvadive Islands.

We hope the British Government and people will appreciate the justice of our cause and recognize the United Suvadive Islands at once.

Yours truly,

ABDULLAH AFIF DIDI,
President, The United Suvadive Islands

THE GOVERNMENT OF THE UNITED SUVADIVE ISLANDS.

SECRETARIAT:
HITTADU ADDU-ATOLL,
UNITED SUVADIVE ISLANDS.

28th September 1959.

To,

MALE REPRESENTATIVE IN CEYLON.

I am in receipt of your message forwarded through the United Kingdom High Commission in Ceylon. Your message has been considered by the People's Council and the Executive Council and I am authorised to make the following reply:-

Having suffered the callous, brutal and ruthless exploitation by the Male Government, the People of Addu, unprompted by any outside authority, spontaneously threw off the tyrant's yoke and declared their independence on January 1st this year. The more particular causes for this were :-

(1) The extortionate taxes which reduced the Islanders to penury and from which they received no benefit in the form of educational, medical or indeed any other facilities.

(2) The with-holding by the Male Government of the wages of all those who were working under their directions with the Royal Air Force on Gan and Hittadu.

(3) The refusal of the Male authorities to issue any foodgrains to the Islanders, in spite of their responsibility to supply the subsistence rations to Islanders displaced from Gan, and to make part payment of wages in rice to those working on Gan and Hittadu, and

(4) The orders of Male Government that no one should in future work for the United Kingdom Authorities on the construction of the Staging Post, which would have deprived the Islanders of a source of livelihood.

Reduced to misery, starvation and penury by the actions of a remote and grasping Government, indifferent to their sufferings and distress, the People of Addu, despairing of receiving justice from the tyrannical family regime in Male, and determined to lead their own lives in peace and happiness, declared their independence. Later the People of Fua-Mulak Island and Huvadu Atoll, of their own free will and accord, joined the people of Addu and the United Suvadive Islands was established, by the unanimous will of the people.

There can be no Government except with the consent of the Governed. The present Government in Male was not elected by the people of Huvadu, Fua-Mulak or Addu, nor do any representatives from these places sit in the Majlis

2

The Maldivian Government in Male can therefore make no claim to represent in any way, or to exercise any authority over the people of the United Suvadive Islands.

(إِنَّ اللّٰهَ يَأْمُرُكُمْ أَنْ تُؤَدُّوا الْأَمَانَاتِ إِلَى أَهْلِهَا وَإِذَا حَكَمْتُمْ بَيْنَ النَّاسِ)
(أَنْ تَحْكُمُوا بِالْعَدْلِ إِنَّ اللّٰهَ نِعِمَّا يَعِظُكُمْ بِهِ إِنَّ اللّٰهَ كَانَ سَمِيعًا بَصِيرًا)

The Maldivian Government in Male, disregarding the Sacred Teachings of the Holy Prophet, on Whom be Blessings and Peace, brutally attacked the peaceful and unarmed people of Fua-Mulak in March and Huvadu in July. Many innocent persons were shot and others flogged and dragged away from their homes and families in chains, and their fate is not known. Private property was looted and women raped.

These actions, abhorrent to all decent people, have increased the determination of all the people of the United Suvadive Islands to resist, and if necessary lay down their lives to prevent the return of an authority under which they have suffered injustice and neglect for so long.

Never the less the People of the United Suvadive Islands, desiring only to lead their own lives peacefully and free from outside interference, and in peace and harmony with their neighbours, and brothers, the Maldivian People of the Atolls north of the 1½ (One and half degree) channel welcomed the offer of good offices made by Her Majesty's Government in the United Kingdom in their statement of August 7th.

It is a matter of sincere regret to us that the Maldivian Government in Male rejected this offer. It is our hope that the Maldivian Government in Male will reconsider their decision, and will accept the offer of good offices by Her Majesty's Government to reach a peaceful settlement with the People of the United Suvadive Islands.

(وَإِنْ طَائِفَتَانِ مِنَ الْمُؤْمِنِينَ اقْتَتَلُوا فَأَصْلِحُوا بَيْنَهُمَا فَإِنْ بَغَتْ)
(إِحْدَاهُمَا عَلَى الْأُخْرَى فَقَاتِلُوا الَّتِي تَبْغِي حَتَّى تَفِيءَ إِلَى أَمْرِ اللّٰهِ)
(فَإِنْ فَاءَتْ فَأَصْلِحُوا بَيْنَهُمَا بِالْعَدْلِ وَأَقْسِطُوا إِنَّ اللّٰهَ يُحِبُّ الْمُقْسِطِينَ)

A.Afif Didi., (President)
UNITED SUVADIVE ISLANDS.

Fig 13.2. Afif Didi's reply to the Maldivian Government Representative in Ceylon. Source: Afif Didi *via* V Kendrick.

SECRETARIAT:
Hittadu Addu-Atoll,
United Suvadive Islands.

7th Jimadil A'khir 1379.
8th December,   1959.

Gentlemen of the world press,

        Welcome to Addu-Atoll. The people of the U.S.I.
are very happy that you have come from distant places to see
for yourselves how we are living our lives free from the tyranny
of the Male Government under which we have suffered for Centuries.

        On 22nd Jimadil A'khir 1378, which corresponds to January
1st 1959. The people of Addu-Atoll declared their Independence.
Within two months the people of the Fua-Mulaku Island and Huvadu
Atoll also threw off Male's yoke, and together we formed the United
Suvadive Islands. A democratic Government was set up by the free
votes of the people but so far our newly formed Independent country
has not been recognised by the countries of the world. This has
caused many difficulties for us and we hope that as a result of
your visit, the world will learn all about our struggle and recognise us as an Independent country.

        For 4 months we enjoyed our freedom in happiness and
then the Male Government made a brutal attack with their armed
forces on the totally unarmed and peaceful people of Huvadu Atoll.
Many people were shot and many were deported to Malo after being
flogged and we do not know what has happened to them. Unable to
face an armed attack as they are separated from us by 25 miles of
open sea, the people of Fua-Mulaku Island were forced to surrender
to Male and their leaders also have been flogged and deported.
The population of both Huvadu and Fua-Mulaku have since then been
deliberately starved by the Male Government, and about 100 refugees
have come down here seeking our help.

        For our parts the people of Addu-Atoll, although unarmed,
are determined to maintain their freedom by every means.

        In September the Maldivian Government in Male called me
to Male. Copies of their message, our reply and their rejection
of our offer to seek a peaceful settlement are attached to this
statement. Not having any intention of permitting our people to
live in peace, free from their tyranny, the Male Government has
blamed the British for interfering in our affairs.

        We welcome the presence of the British in Addu, as we
welcomed them during the last war. Our people have lived under
British protection for the last 70 years, and we hope that this
protection will be continued in the future. We have not taken part
in any discussions about the lease for the R.A.F. Base at Gan. The
British Government has negotiated with the Male Government who have
no authority to speak us. Any negotiations must be held with our
representatives as Gan is part of our territory and it is only the
people of the U.S.I. who can make agreements concerning them.

        The construction of the airfield at Gan has brought
great prosperity to our people. For the first time in our history

employment is available, we get regular food supplies, we receive
medical aid when necessary, and a new way of life is open to us.
Can you wonder that we are determined to keep our Independence
from a Government who have deliberately kept us ignorant, backward,
poor and frequently half starved for centuries? We only wish to
live our lives in peace and happiness.

        You are most welcome to see any of our Islands and ask
anyone any questions you wish. We hope that as a result of your
visit, the peoples of the world will know more about us and will
sympathise with our struggles.

        We hope that you will enjoy your short visit and take
away many pleasant memories of our Islands.

                              A.Afif Didi,
                    President of the United Suvadive Isles.

Fig 13.3. Afif Didi's letter to the visiting reporters. Source: Afif Didi *via* V Kendrick.

Fig 13.4. The Times of Addu: Source: Afif Didi.

Fig 13.5. The arrival of the demonstrators, Gan, April 1962.

Fig 13.6. The crowd beginning to wade ashore, Gan, April 1962.

Fig 13.7. Playing the hoses to disperse the demonstrators, Gan, April 1962.

Fig 13.8. The dhoni lines in quieter times.

XIV   The Turbulent Return to the Fold

Although the departure of Abdullah Afif Didi and the islanders' capitulation marked the end of the rebellion it was never likely to mark the end of the acrimony which had so soured relations between the British and Maldivian governments. The British ministers were well aware that Nasir would be incensed by their decision to grant asylum to Afif, they just could not predict how he would react. They could only hope that Afif's departure from the archipelago would mark the beginning of a new era.

For Britain, the Adduan capitulation brought immediate benefits. There was no longer a need to station a Royal Navy guard ship at Addu Atoll nor to maintain one within a few hours sailing time of Dunidu; the frequent deployment of RAF Regiment troops and general reinforcements to Gan became unnecessary and the British press lost interest in the story which had at one time or another provided copy for most of the national newspapers.

Predictably, Afif's departure did not bring an immediate end to the political malaise. The Adduans, deprived of Afif's leadership, caved in and, following the example set by their village headmen, declared that they were all ready to reaffirm their allegiance to the central government by travelling to Malé and signing the loyalty book. They arranged to send representatives to the capital and they wrote letters of submission which could hardly have been couched in more submissive terms stating, as they did, *'To the Honourable Prime Minister of the Maldives, with many salaams to Your Excellency we humbly submit...'*. Every clause of their government's suggested settlement agreement was covered in the letters of submission and every clause was accepted.

Nasir, however, was still openly committed to ending the protectorate status of the Maldives even though he had declared his willingness to retain the Gan agreement and the general defence agreement with Britain in spite of his deep, and justifiable, suspicion whenever he was dealing with British ministers.

As Afif was preparing to leave Addu Atoll, Arthington-Davy was active both on Dunidu and on Gan. In his signal from Malé to Colombo on the 29th of September 1963 he says *'Saw Nasir this a.m. He surly, suspicious,* *annoyed that Adduans had not sent delegation in own boats, annoyed that he unable to name delegates, enraged on hearing of Afif's asylum, said he would not cooperate with HMG on anything. Accused Sandys of trickery, deceit, bad faith....'* It was obviously an early morning meeting because the station diary records that he visited Gan that day, just a week after his return to Dunidu following a three-day visit to Addu Atoll.

With Afif heading for the Seychelles and Arthington-Davy back on Dunidu, Nasir continued to rage against the duplicity of Duncan Sandys whom he accused of supporting Afif the rebel rather than the Maldivian government. Within days the press in Malé picked up Nasir's mood, abandoned the 'forgive and forget' approach and embarked on yet another vitriolic campaign against Britain. Claiming that Adduans were being shot to cover up British sins the newspapers carried such comments as '. . . *dead men tell no tales, we know the trick'.*

To back up his anger and his recriminations the Prime Minister had Arthington-Davy's Maldivian staff and boat crew arrested on a trumped-up charge and then generally made life as difficult as possible for the British contingent on Dunidu. He also refused to take over the administration of Addu Atoll, apparently in the hope that the ensuing muddle would disrupt the RAF's operations, causing the British considerable inconvenience and reminding them of his displeasure. He then decreed that the Adduan delegation would, although pardoned in accordance with the agreement, be required to remain at the capital until he was prepared to see them and that, he said, would not be until affairs were back to normal at Addu Atoll.

Nasir's widely publicised rift with the British government soon had repercussions on Hulule, where British vehicles and equipment were sabotaged, and at Addu Atoll, where the islanders would hear any threatening radio messages broadcast from Malé. Although there was little doubt that much of Nasir's reaction was a face-saving exercise which would eventually be followed by the return of the government officials to Addu, it was undoubtedly a period of considerable concern for the safety of the British personnel on Dunidu and of the Adduans who had set out for the capital in good faith to swear allegiance to their government. In an attempt to resolve the problems, Sandys sent a personal message to Nasir. It went unanswered. That was hardly surprising given that Nasir had already written to Sandys setting out the reasons why he was intending to establish fully independent sovereign status for the Maldives through amendments to the 1960 agreement. In that correspondence he had promised to safeguard Britain's interests in the archipelago but had also expressed his intention to '... *let Addu wait until the 1960 agreement has been revised.*'

Had the Maldivian Prime Minister known the true state of affairs at Addu Atoll he would probably have been a much happier man because on the day that the British Representative informed him that Afif had been granted asylum, the British High Commissioner in Colombo had been informed by Rounthwaite that a state of administrative and financial chaos existed throughout the Adduan community. Mohammed Saeed and Ahmed Didi were working hard to restore some order to a state of affairs which would have already led to widespread local unrest had it not been for the recently introduced arrangement whereby the rice rations for the Maldivian labour force were distributed by the RAF. Mohammed and Ahmed were discovering what Moon had already commented upon: the administration's accounts were in no recognisable conventional form, the Trading Corporation's shareholders had only ever received one dividend and no annual accounts had ever been submitted for their approval. Even more revealing was the fact that the bank was nothing more than a large box which was said to contain some one hundred thousand Maldivian rupees. The casualness of the whole affair was staggering and, given that the Adduan Trading Corporation was at the heart of the islanders' economy, such laxity all but destroyed the reputation of the former officials.

Against such a background it was fortunate for Afif Didi that all the luggage which he and his family had taken to the Seychelles had been meticulously searched before their departure. It was an action which, whilst apparently not very sensitive, was actually to his advantage because once he had departed it would have been all too easy for any anti-Afif faction to have made wild accusations about his absconding with the wealth of the republic in his baggage. At least the thorough search effectively ruled out that particular accusation.

Whilst the Adduans were trying to sort out their local troubles and worrying about Nasir's failure to send any government officials to their atoll, their Prime Minister, refusing to talk to Arthington-Davy, was leaving all Adduan affairs to be dealt with by his ministers. Through them, Nasir was demanding that Afif be brought back to the Maldives and, with twenty other nominated Adduans, should sail to Malé and swear allegiance to the government. The Prime Minister was also adamant that Afif would not subsequently be allowed to return to Addu Atoll for at least six months, during which time he would be free to settle anywhere in the Maldives.

From London, the Commonwealth Relations Office staff, having formulated seemingly innocent counters to Nasir's claims of British duplicity, recommended an approach which would be seen by the Maldivians as being more in sorrow than in anger. Afif had, after all, been pardoned and was a free man whose request for asylum had been granted.

As far as the Adduans were concerned, it should be seen as reasonable that it was their village headmen who should go to Malé to capitulate and to swear allegiance to the central government because they, unlike the villagers nominated by Nasir, were elected representatives of the village communities. As for transport, it was obviously unnecessarily laborious for the headmen to sail three hundred miles in a buggaloe when they could so easily be flown directly from Gan to the Hulule airfield. The pretence of innocent failure to imagine that Nasir might want the troublemakers to make an arduous boat journey, might want their boats in Malé where a pretext could be found to confiscate them and, most of all, might want to get his hands on the defeated rebel leaders, fooled no-one. It was a typically transparent diplomatic subterfuge.

Neither the Maldivian nor the British governments had given the Adduans any explanation for the non-appearance of the Maldivian officials whom they were expecting and the islanders, becoming increasingly suspicious and quite fearful of their own government's intentions, could not understand why there had been no response to their letters of submission which Arthington-Davy had delivered to Malé. They were obviously unaware that although the staff at the Commonwealth Relations Office were doing their best to improve relations between the Adduans and their government there seemed to be no easy way to break the deadlock created by Nasir's obduracy and until that could be achieved there was really no alternative but to sit back and wait, worrying though that might be.

With Afif's departure, Rounthwaite tried to adopt the role of trusted adviser to the islanders but he was, to a certain extent, hamstrung by the politics of the situation. He continually emphasised that Nasir was angry with the British government, not with the Adduans and yet he was honest enough to suggest that it was not a good idea for any Adduans to sail to Malé. He spent time in every village explaining the situation and yet he knew that to the villagers it was obvious that he was concealing the true state of affairs. He tried to persuade them to work closely with their local administration and yet he knew that there was a risk for those who allied themselves too closely with the one-time Afif faction. It was apparent to the islanders that there was an impasse between the two governments.

Rounthwaite felt obliged to inform the British Representative in Malé that, due to the administrative shambles at the atoll, the Adduans were not likely to be co-operative or even manageable for much longer. He forecast that they would be out of control within a fortnight. That turned out to be an unduly pessimistic assessment even though there seemed little doubt that their local government organisation was heading for a complete breakdown.

By mid-October 1963 the islanders had learned the names of the twenty Adduans whom Nasir wanted to report to Malé and that information fuelled their fears. The political adviser initially proposed that he should release full details of all Nasir's demands but then, displaying his frustration with Britain's attempts to resolve the affair through friendly negotiation, he signalled the Commonwealth Relations Office with the suggestion that Nasir was bluffing and that Britain should call his bluff by declaring that Afif would not be brought back to the Maldives and that Britain would not negotiate payment of the islanders in Maldivian rupees until central government officials had taken over the local administration at Addu Atoll. Furthermore, he suggested, Nasir should be told that Britain would not even consider a revision of the basic agreement until normality had been restored to the atoll's administration for at least twelve months.

His proposals were unacceptable, presumably because they were considered to be counter-productive in the hostile atmosphere which prevailed. The staff at the Commonwealth Relations Office were even reluctant to publicise the British side of the story and expose Nasir's intransigence although the Maldivian press continued to publish anti-British articles whilst avoiding any mention of the letters of submission from the Adduans. Some of those newspapers reached Hitaddu where the Adduans were quick to realise that the strong anti-British comments were a reflection of their government's views. Increasingly concerned by the prospect of control from Malé they openly demanded that Afif should be brought back to the

Maldives on the grounds that his asylum should not be allowed to endanger the future of eight thousand islanders. When their demand was rejected out-of-hand by the political adviser they became uncooperative both towards Rounthwaite and their own atoll committee, almost precipitating a return to the chaotic state of affairs which had developed during the days of the republic.

So the affair dragged on until the end of November when Don Raha, a wealthy influential anti-Afif Adduan, decided, with nineteen other islanders, to set sail for Malé with the intention of trying to hasten the reconciliation process and the return to normality. The journey was planned against the advice of Rounthwaite, the atoll committee and the headman of Maradu-Fedu, providing yet another opportunity for dissent among the Adduans. Several influential supporters of Don Raha, mainly traders, became openly antagonistic towards the atoll committee which was in danger of losing the last vestiges of its authority. Only after a great deal of discussion were the committee members persuaded to quieten down and allow matters to run their course.

November 1963 had not been a good month for the British contingents at Malé atoll. On Dunidu all the recently-replaced Maldivian staff had resigned, including the boat crew who had taken their boat with them. That left Arthington-Davy, three RAF signals specialists and an RAF Regiment officer marooned on the island until the Far East Air Force Command staff arranged for additional servicemen to take over the work abandoned by the Maldivians. The resignations, intended to make life difficult for the British Representative actually worked, within a few days, to his advantage because the Maldivians were replaced by RAF personnel together with a Royal Navy Petty Officer and the ratings needed to crew the naval cutter which replaced the Maldivian harbour boat.

On the nearby island of Hulule, the site of the only Maldivian airstrip, an RAF Warrant Officer and two airmen, all members of the Airfield Construction Branch had, until mid-November, been supervising the local workforce which was repairing and extending the runway. That work, long delayed by the political manoeuvring of the British and Maldivian governments had been restarted early in November but had been abandoned in the middle of the month, brought to a halt by widespread sabotage and theft. The sabotage seemed to be pointless. Vehicles and equipment had been badly damaged and over a hundred gallons of petrol poured away.

The thefts were easier to understand; utilitarian items were always likely to be stolen by the Maldivians and the theft of medical equipment could be explained either as theft for resale or as theft for some secondary purpose. Regardless of the motives, the overall result had been to delay the re-commissioning of the only civilian airfield in the archipelago. The lack of concern shown by the Maldivian Prime Minister created the obvious impression that the sabotage was officially condoned if not actually encouraged, an impression reinforced by the fact that only after Arthington-Davy had made several vigorous protests to Nasir did the Maldivians belatedly agree to mount guard over the remaining stores and equipment.

What may have persuaded Nasir to provide guards for the Hulule site was not so much the British Representative's protestations as an invitation, from Duncan Sandys, to visit London to discuss the revision of the 1960 agreement. Whilst life was being made difficult for the British contingents on Dunidu and Hulule Sandys' letter, despatched on the 5th of November, was travelling its circuitous route to Malé, reaching the Maldivian Prime Minister, *via* Arthington-Davy, on the 24th. The invitation to visit London, extended after a preliminary suggestion that, as a matter of urgency, Nasir should send his government's officials to Addu Atoll, obviously pleased the Prime Minister for he replied with unusual promptness. After thanking Sandys for his willingness to consider his proposals for the revision of the 1960 agreement he expressed a preference for the talks to be held in Malé rather than in London, adding that he still deplored Afif's departure for the Seychelles and reiterated that he had no intention of despatching any officials to Addu Atoll until the Afif affair had been resolved. But the impasse appeared to have been broken. Nasir was again prepared to talk to British representatives, he had become a little more co-operative over the Hulule affair and within a fortnight he seemed to confirm the change in his attitude by welcoming Don Raha's deputation.

Matters then developed, as was so often the case in dealings with the Maldivians, in contradictory ways. Abdullah Jamal and another Adduan had also set out for Malé in November and had returned to Addu Atoll on the 14th of December after travelling to Fua Mulaku on board the Maldivian hospital ship The Golden Ray which was touring the Maldives and which had brought several government officials to Fua Mulaku. Jamal and his associates reported that the large Adduan delegation headed by Don Raha had been well received in Malé. They also brought back a letter from the Minister for Home Affairs acknowledging the submission of a great many of the islanders and informing them that an Adduan business centre had been established in the capital as part of the normalisation process. That augured well for the future as did the accompanying decree from the Sultan requiring the Adduans to elect a new committee for the atoll.

Meanwhile, officials from on board the Golden Ray had re-established government order at Fua Mulaku, arrested five pro-Afif ringleaders of the local revolt, sent them back to Malé as prisoners and broadcast a denunciation of six Adduans who were deemed not to have helped the government either by their service on the atoll committee or by generally working closely with the Royal Air Force. The activities of those newly-arrived officials immediately undermined whatever good had been achieved by the letter from the Minister of Home Affairs. On learning of the events on Fua Mulaku, the Adduans immediately voiced their consternation and in a series of noisy but generally peaceful demonstrations loudly declared that their central government could never be trusted.

As Christmas approached, the Maldivian ministers seemed suddenly to realise that the Hulule airstrip would be needed during the last ten days or so of December for a series of shuttle flights between Malé and Ceylon. It was customary, at that time of the year, for the Maldivian children who attended school in Ceylon and for the Ceylonese teachers temporarily employed in the Maldives to return home for a Christmas holiday, and ignoring the incongruity of their requests, the ministers turned to the British Representative for help, asking him to expedite the Hulule repairwork and to ask the RAF to provide a series of passenger flights for the teachers and the schoolchildren. Arthington–Davy, in accordance with the newly-emerging spirit of co-operation, discovered that the Hulule runway would be back in service by the time the school holidays started and obtained permission for the RAF to provide the few passenger flights required. That, theoretically, put Nasir under an obligation to him but in practice it probably achieved nothing except to give Arthington-Davy the satisfaction of knowing that Nasir could be reminded of this co-operation when next the mood changed, as it surely would.

In the mid-December atmosphere of fear and uncertainty at Addu Atoll, Rounthwaite was keen to have a new atoll committee elected before the 31st of the month, the deadline for a return to normality according to the September agreement between the British and Maldivian governments. He got his wish, with an election on the 20th and a new committee in office by the 22nd. One member of the six-man committee was Abdullah Jamal from Maradu who had carried out the orders from Malé to hold the election and who, on being elected, informed the other five elected members that as soon as the committee had been established, the first order they would receive from their central government would be for the Adduans to go on strike in order to disrupt the RAF's operations at the atoll. Given all that they had done to assist in the construction and operation of the base, Jamal's elected colleagues were aghast at the idea that a return to normality was to be accompanied by a general strike. But they felt powerless if the order came from Malé. They contacted Rounthwaite and, in Jamal's absence, spoke freely of problems on the horizon, forewarning the political adviser but not offering any way out of the situation.

The return to near normality at the atoll meant that by Christmas 1963 the islanders were subjected, through their newly-elected atoll committee, to the central government controls over trading and to the taxation which had finally pushed them into their 1959 declaration of independence. Virtually all of the controls reflected their Islamic culture; Maldivians were not allowed to possess pigs or pig products, dogs, alcohol, obscene cards or pictures, contraceptives or any images for worship. Only the Maldivian government was allowed to possess firearms, gunpowder, opium or the narcotic ganga. It was theoretically possible for an ordinary Maldivian citizen to obtain a government permit for the possession of poisons, acid, copper sulphate, dangerous animals and insulting or objectionable literature but in practice the applicant had to provide such a compelling argument for possessing any of those items that they were, in effect, all banned.

The Adduans could accept all those controls without too much concern even though, with such ready access to Western society's commodities, they were probably more tempted to enjoy certain forbidden pleasures than were islanders elsewhere in the archipelago. But the tax regulations were hated by all. As far as the Adduans were concerned, their central government had devised the regulations in order to squeeze as much revenue as possible out of the southernmost islanders who had, since the arrival of the British, achieved the reputation of being the wealthiest Maldivians outside Malé.

It was easy to see why they believed that the regulations had been designed with them in mind. Necessities which had to be imported were taxed at fifteen per cent, which was seen as an acceptable level even though it was effectively a tax on rice, their staple food. Curry powder, dates, candles and kerosene all attracted a fifteen per cent import tax. Glue, used in considerable amounts by the boat builders, was taxed at forty per cent whilst the tax on 'non-essential' food, such as the eggs and loaves of bread available through the NAAFI at Addu Atoll but unlikely to be imported anywhere else in the archipelago, were liable to a one hundred per cent tax. Luxuries, also readily available to the Adduans but rarely imported elsewhere in the Maldives, attracted punitive tax rates. Chocolates were taxed at one hundred and fifty per cent whilst utilitarian items, such as pillows, were subjected to import duty of three hundred per cent. The final sting in the regulations was the imposition of a two hundred per cent tax on all manufactured goods covered by an additional, comprehensive, list of taxable items.

For those Adduans employed on Gan there was always the possibility of avoiding such taxes by purchasing goods from the expatriates. Such trading was illegal but it did happen, albeit on a small scale. It was the NAAFI shop which offered the Maldivians the most obvious, and illegal, method of obtaining tax-free goods because the shop staff were not tax collectors for the Maldivian government and they left the Adduan buyers to declare their purchases to their own tax collectors.

That system worked reasonably well when applied to the purchase of durable goods because it was virtually impossible for any Adduan to buy such goods without his neighbours and his fellow workers knowing about it. To get the items home he had to provide proof of ownership by showing the goods and the appropriate receipts to the security staff employed to prevent the illegal removal of any items from Gan. That was done quite openly in the queue for the homeward-bound dhonis and there was no way of knowing how many of the queuing Maldivian commuters might tell the local tax collectors what they had seen. The villagers were also well aware that even if there were no informers in the queue, news of any significant purchase would soon spread through their village grapevine. It was just not worth trying to avoid the payment of import tax on such purchases because the risk of arrest and conviction was far too high.

But for consumables, especially food, it was essential for the NAAFI to limit the sales to the Adduans to avoid undermining both the Maldivian tax system and the registered Adduan traders. Thus no Maldivian was allowed to purchase more than twenty cigarettes a day from the NAAFI shop or more than one loaf of bread, or its equivalent in cakes or biscuits, and a small quantity of immediately edible food.

There was nothing the islanders could do about the tax regime but, once again, their resentments were building up.

As soon as the atoll committee had held its first meeting, five of the members set sail for Fua Mulaku and the Golden Ray to confirm the results of the election and the final submission of the Adduans. Delayed by bad weather, they did not reach the hospital ship until the 30th of December on which date it set sail for Malé. At Addu Atoll the islanders, unaware of the delays affecting their delegation and by no means convinced that the election of a new committee meant that all would be well, monitored the radio transmissions from the Golden Ray in an attempt to gather news of their delegates' reception. When they intercepted a message to Malé asking for five hundred wrist chains they jumped to the worst conclusion possible. That description could have referred to an unusually large quantity of medical stores but the Adduans could think of only one interpretation: handcuffs.

The year ended with the Maldivians participating in the customary dhoni race at Christmas before organising a few guided tours of their villages. They were as near certain as they could be that their government officials would celebrate the new year by ordering the withdrawal of all Maldivian labour from Gan and they were obviously anxious to demonstrate that, even though there were political clouds on their horizon, their local goodwill remained.

Day-by-day the atoll officials had to live with the open hostility of the villagers who were convinced that the return of central government control would be followed by a return to hard times and as 1964 began, the islanders, resentful because of the punitive levels of imminent taxation and fearful for their safety in the coming months, waited nervously for the arrival of the officials from Malé. The British government, however, was generally relieved that the saga seemed to be drawing to a close with the Maldivian government at least nominally in charge of affairs at the atoll. That much was quite obvious from Duncan Sandys' letter to Nasir effectively pointing out that should he fail to seize the opportunity to restore his government's authority at the atoll the Adduan problem would be his to solve, not Britain's.

Like the Adduans, the RAF communications staff were monitoring the radio transmissions from the Golden Ray and on the 2nd of January one of the last transmissions to be monitored gave a disconcerting, but hardly unexpected, picture of events on Hulule. During a conversation between two Maldivian ministers the news of further sabotage on the island the previous day was greeted with considerable pleasure and an openly expressed hope that such acts would continue during 1964. The conversation provided unwelcome confirmation of the Dunidu contingent's rather precarious position.

The sabotage on Dunidu and Rounthwaite's report of the likely withdrawal of all Adduan labour from Gan was taken seriously by the Chiefs-of-Staff who, early in January, were producing contingency plans for the reinforcement of Gan and for the evacuation of British residents from Malé Atoll. They saw no significant problems in providing military personnel to take over the work normally done by the Adduans on Gan but it was obvious that the creation of rapid evacuation facilities for the British residents on Dunidu would be politically much more sensitive. Life was not pleasant for the British contingent but events in Malé were not serious enough to justify an overt Royal Navy presence in the area even if such a politically provocative arrangement were to be approved by the British government. The upshot was a typically English compromise. The Chiefs-of-Staff assumed, in spite of evidence to the contrary, that a gradual increase in hostile activity against the British residents was far more likely than any sudden action. They then produced an evacuation plan based upon an Admiralty instruction which ensured that there would always be a British warship within four days sailing of the Maldivian capital. That was not particularly reassuring for the British residents but it satisfied the main criterion which was to avoid the political confrontation which would have been inevitable if the Royal Navy's presence had smacked of gunboat diplomacy.

As the month wore on an interesting political situation was brewing for Wing Commander Moss who had arrived at Gan on the 16th of January to take over from Wing Commander Hill whose tour of duty as Gan's station commander was completed at the end of that month. Like his predecessors, Moss had been given a briefing at the Commonwealth Relations Office in London before flying to Addu Atoll. On being told at that briefing that there was a highly regarded resident political adviser, Rounthwaite, on Gan he optimistically thought that he would be able to concentrate on operational matters, leaving all political matters to his adviser. But he soon discovered that, on Gan, operations and politics could not be separated and that the officer commanding RAF Gan had to be as much a politician as a station commander.

Officially-condoned sabotage was easily provoked at Malé atoll but not at Addu Atoll where the villagers were still well disposed towards the RAF. There were, however, some islanders who were feeling particularly resentful towards the British government for having precipitated the demise of their breakaway republic and at the beginning of 1964 a large number of broadsheets was being circulated throughout the atoll, fuelling a wave of anti-British propaganda.

The distribution of the sheets was apparently being orchestrated to coincide with the return, on the 13th of the month, of the five-man delegation which had been to Malé and which was expected to be carrying a set of government directives to be implemented at Addu atoll. If the broadsheets were to be believed, the unwelcome directives would be seen by the villagers as the result of Britain's failure to protect the Adduans' independence.

On their return the Adduan delegates publicised the orders which had been drafted by their central government for implementation in January, well in advance of the arrival of any central government officials. It transpired that much of the document was uncontentious, confirming the results of the December election, recognising the membership of the atoll committee and appointing Moosa Ali Didi, Afif Didi's brother-in-law, as the temporary atoll chief. That appointment, seen as a goodwill gesture from Malé, was probably made in the hope that Afif's downfall had provided a salutary lesson which would be well remembered by everyone, especially his brother-in-law who would be expected to regard the appointment as an opportunity to prove that he was a reformed character, fully committed to the central government.

But many of the government's other instructions were badly received for they seemed to have been drafted with the intention of disrupting the operation of the RAF base by imposing restrictions on the islanders' co-operative working practices. The villagers, by then facing up to the reality that they had lost control of their own affairs, had little alternative but to comply. But they remained deeply resentful, especially of the way in which their standard of living was being reduced by the unavoidable levels of taxation and by the increasing controls over their trading with the NAAFI.

It soon became obvious that the Maldivian government's tactic of alternating periods of reasonable amicability with periods of hostility was to be duplicated at Addu Atoll as soon as the Adduan delegation returned from Malé with clear instructions to the atoll chief on the style he was to adopt in his dealings with the RAF. The first indication of that occurred in January when a number of large-scale thefts of building materials and equipment led to a widespread investigation by the military police. The atoll chief, by then very anxious to remain in favour with Nasir, and already making daily accusations about the RAF's treatment of the Adduan workforce, issued instructions that the Maldivian labourers were to report every incident, no matter how trivial, to their headmen, adding that anyone known to have disregarded his instructions would lose his job. The effect was predictable. The number of complaints grew and the RAF authorities were obliged to investigate each one, no matter how trivial it might seem.

The Adduans' anti-government feelings were so great at the beginning of 1964 that two of the most senior members of the atoll executive approached the political adviser with a proposal to withdraw the submission of allegiance to the Sultan and again declare independence under British protection. The Commonwealth Relations Office staff, informed of the proposal *via* the British High Commissioner in Ceylon, rejected the suggestion out of hand, leaving the Maldivians with no alternative but to work under their central government's regime. Nevertheless, the proposal, coming from such influential Adduans, rang political warning bells in London. It was obvious that the slightest wavering by the British government was likely to be seized upon by the islanders as an excuse for resurrecting the breakaway republic of the United Suvadive Islands and if that were to happen it would almost certainly spell the end of the fragile relationship between the Maldivian and British governments.

For one group of villagers the newspapers which their delegates had brought back from Malé were far more worrying than the latest set of government orders. It was no great surprise to discover that every issue contained the sort of vitriolic anti-British articles which were invariably published whenever the government wished to arouse the fervour of the capital's population but it was a shock to see, prominently displayed against that rabble-rousing background, the names of those Adduans who had been blacklisted by their government for conspiring with the British. One of the islanders, Mohammed Saeed, was completely taken aback when he discovered that his name was on the list. He, after Afif Didi's departure, had toured the atoll with the political adviser and helped to persuade the Adduans to accept the authority of their central government. Often he had been subjected to threats from the more militant villagers who resented the role he had taken on and he was still in fear of reprisals. He just could not understand why he should have been blacklisted. He was probably so politically naive that he had failed to realise that, as far as Nasir was concerned, his crime had been to contribute to the relatively smooth organisation of the atoll's labour force for the benefit of the British at a time when the Prime Minister had been hoping that the islanders' administration would collapse in chaos.

Saeed was well aware that any citizen blacklisted as a result of political activity would normally obtain redemption by signing the book which was kept in Malé and although that was often a formality even he, politically naive though he was, was well aware that secession was not a run-of-the-mill misdemeanour and it was painfully obvious that once he left Addu Atoll he would be exposed to government retribution. The mere thought of visiting the Maldivian capital alarmed him. He sought the opinions of the political adviser and the newly-arrived station commander who, after some prompting from the Commonwealth Relations Office staff, suggested to Saeed that he should go to Malé, sign the book and get the matter over and done with. Thus reassured, Saeed decided that he would join a group of forty Adduans who planned to set sail early in February, all heading for Malé and all intending to reaffirm their loyalty to the Sultan. Moosa Ali Didi, recently confirmed as the temporary atoll chief, further boosted Saeed's confidence by nominating him as his representative and asking him to discuss with the central government officials a variety of day-to-day matters affecting the Adduans.

Having to make such a lengthy hazardous journey was penance enough for most of the islanders but the authorities in Malé obviously considered it to be insufficient for Saeed and two of his companions. As soon as they landed the three of them were arrested, ostensibly on currency charges, and held on one of Malé Atoll's small islands, known locally as prisoners' island, pending trial. Saeed was given no opportunity to present himself as his atoll chief's representative and no opportunity to enter into discussions with any

government official. For him, his arrest was the beginning of a saga in which he called desperately but unsuccessfully for help from the RAF and the British government.

Saeed, like any Maldivian who was thought to have supported the British at Addu Atoll, was in many respects a victim of the anti-British atmosphere in Malé which had led to the demonstrations in the capital and the renewed sabotage on Hulule which, during the first week of 1964, had left the airstrip so badly damaged that it could be used only for essential military flights. That sabotage, together with the continuing anti-British campaign in the Maldivian press, had provoked Duncan Sandys into writing to Nasir on the 11th of January expressing his concern and requesting that the Maldivian government should put an end to the practices which could obviously not be occurring without government approval. He pointed out that the cessation of sabotage and of the anti-British campaign by the press would create a friendly atmosphere for the conduct of negotiations on the revision of the 1960 agreement. He might just as well not have bothered because the British Representative was refused permission to deliver the letter in person and discuss the contents with Nasir; he was obliged to leave it with one of the government's minor officials. By the end of the month no reply had been received and it had to be assumed that Nasir had no intention of responding to Sandy's requests.

By the end of January 1964 the anti-British campaign at Addu Atoll, developed as a result of the government orders brought back from Malé by the Adduan delegation, had begun to quieten down. That was more a consequence of the departure, for Malé, of most of the atoll's pro-government faction than of the efforts of Rounthwaite, for he had been banned by the atoll chief from addressing any public meetings in villages throughout the atoll. Nevertheless, the political atmosphere remained chilly. The pro-government Adduans, together with two members of the atoll committee, had been summoned to the capital, ostensibly to discuss the future of the Adduan Trading Corporation. Most of their fellow islanders, long since persuaded that their government would use any pretext to lure groups of Adduans to Malé, believed that no such discussion would be held, they believed that this seemingly innocuous summons was nothing more than a ruse and they were quite certain that retribution awaited any Adduans who were called to the capital, even if they were known to be government supporters.

By mid-February several boatloads of Adduans had returned from the capital, all bringing news of the anti-British atmosphere which existed there. There was an unabated press campaign against the British actions at Addu Atoll and the general hostility towards the Adduans for the trouble they had brought upon their government. When, at the end of the month, one returning group of islanders brought news of the arrest of Mohammed Saeed and his two companions on currency charges the Adduans were badly shaken. Such offences had been committed by virtually every islander at the atoll and the Adduans suddenly realised that, at the very least, they could all be convicted of tax evasion during their period of independence. They also realised that their government was quite likely to use such a ploy out of vindictiveness if the islanders were seen to be supporting the British when their Prime Minister was covertly supporting anti-British activities.

That realisation led to a general deterioration in relationships between the RAF and the Adduans and led to the resignation of Ahmed Didi, the political adviser's interpreter, who, prior to his visit to Malé, had played a very significant part in fostering good relations with the atoll committee and the villagers. Like most Adduans, he had decided that it would be politically expedient to distance himself from the British until he could be certain that what he was doing was acceptable to his government. By the end of the month the atoll officials had become so cautious in their dealings with the British that the United Kingdom's Deputy High Commissioner in Ceylon, briefly visiting Gan to discuss the political situation, was refused an audience with the atoll chief and was obliged to return to Colombo without having had any useful discussions with the senior Adduans who were running local affairs.

Moss, having arrived at the atoll during a period of quite devious political manoeuvring by the Maldivian Prime Minister, took an early opportunity to fly to Hulule and meet Arthington-Davy. The visit, which helped to establish a personal relationship between the British Representative and Gan's station commander, was invaluable. It gave Moss a better understanding into Nasir's political manoeuvring and an eye-opening insight into conditions in the capital, on Hulule and on Dunidu. On Hulule he was shocked to discover that the runway which had been repaired prior to Duncan Sandys' visit in 1963, and which was still being used for regular civilian flights to and from Ceylon, was in no better condition than a Second World War emergency airstrip. The central area was deeply grooved through continual use and, as a subsequent inspection confirmed, the compacted sand had been washed out from underneath the surface, allowing grass to grow through the numerous cracks. There was nothing that Moss could do about that except to ensure that the dangerous state of the runway was brought to the attention of the Singapore-based Command staff and the RAF pilots who flew supplies and mail to the Dunidu contingent.

March saw an increase in Nasir's authority over the Adduans when the first significant consignment of food arrived from Malé and was distributed in accordance with precise instructions issued by the central government. Increased control was accompanied by a rise in anti-British activity when, in the middle of the month, the Hitadduans were ordered by their government not to report for work on Gan for three days. No explanation was given. As far as Nasir was concerned the Hitadduans were not entitled to an explanation, they were simply required to obey orders. By far the largest proportion of the local labour force came from Hitaddu which meant that the stoppage considerably complicated the RAF operations on Gan, exactly as Nasir had intended.

The incident provided a clear example of the way in which the Maldivian government intended to work towards the restoration of its authority at Addu Atoll, the return of Afif Didi and, eventually, the total independence of the Maldive Islands.

There was really very little that the political adviser on Gan could do about the situation. The atoll chief was acting under orders; significant numbers of Adduans were sailing to the capital and returning with all kinds of threats ringing in their ears and the ministers in Malé were making the islanders ever more fearful about the future by threatening to drive the British out of the archipelago. Accordingly, Rounthwaite decided that his best move would be to visit the Commonwealth Relations Office in London to discuss the situation at the atoll and his role in the light of his decreasing influence with the Adduans. Aware that his departure would leave the recently-arrived station commander with no political adviser other than Arthington-Davy on Dunidu, Rounthwaite spent several hours briefing and advising Moss on the complexities of Maldivian politics before leaving for England on the 30th of March. Within days Moss received an intelligence report which warned that the Maldivians were intending to sabotage the runway on Hulule. Informed of this, Arthington-Davy, remaining characteristically relaxed, declared that the airstrip was far too important to the

Maldivians for them to put it out of action. Within twenty-four hours he was proved wrong. His flash signal to Gan was terse: *'Airstrip sabotaged, runway closed.'*

The sabotage left the British Representative and his staff isolated on Dunidu. It also left Wing Commander Moss with the task of organising the dropping of supplies, mail and diplomatic papers onto Hulule. Fortunately he had experience of that type of operation in Malaya, was able to inform the Command staff of the requirements and to give Arthington-Davy advice on how best to prepare a drop zone. The situation, however, caused considerable concern at the Air Ministry and Moss was summoned to London by the Vice-Chief of the Air Staff. Within hours he was on board a flight to RAF Lyneham and working through the papers which gave him an essential understanding of the political situation in the Maldives. At Lyneham he was cleared by customs without leaving the airfield, was transferred to a waiting Pembroke and flown to RAF Northolt. From there he was taken by car to Whitehall and, still without sleep since he left Gan, was ushered into a meeting of the Joint Chiefs-of-Staff. They were dressed, as was usual, in civilian clothes, and did not introduce themselves. That left Moss not knowing who was who but not unduly bothered.

Invited by the Vice-Chief of the Air Staff to offer a solution to the Maldivian problem, the recently-appointed station commander suggested that the political situation could best be brought back to normal through the negotiation of a new treaty with a totally independent Maldivian nation. That implied the renegotiation of terms for the lease of lands at Addu Atoll, which Moss saw as a reasonable concession for the British government to make in view of Britain's military needs and the Maldivians' economic plight. Given that the Vice-Chief of the Air Staff and the Commander-in-Chief of the Far East Air Force did not often see eye-to-eye with the staff of the Commonwealth Relations Office, Moss may very well have struck a chord when voicing his opinion; either way he was asked to stay behind and work through the night with the team responsible for producing military plans to cope with the increasing instability in the Far East.

After finishing his business with the planning team and catching up on his lost sleep, Moss visited the Commonwealth Relations Office to discuss the situation at Addu Atoll and Rounthwaite's reducing role. The discussion led to the conclusion that the political adviser's mission had been completed and Rounthwaite was accordingly instructed to return only briefly to the atoll to tidy up his affairs before his permanent departure on the 13th of April. Coincidentally, the Maldivian government had requested his removal from the atoll and, although that request was ignored, Rounthwaite's departure no doubt gave Nasir the satisfaction of thinking that he had provoked an immediate British response.

The visit to the Commonwealth Relations Office also gave Moss an opportunity to comment on the circumstances of Mohammed Saeed's arrest. He explained that Saeed didn't deserve to be treated so badly for he had successfully trod a difficult and very narrow path, displaying a remarkable degree of loyalty to both sides in the dispute. He also made the point that Saeed's case was a far bigger matter than the fate of one man because every Adduan knew that the British had pledged his safety and he had been arrested. If Saeed were to be left to his fate the Adduans would never again believe any British promises of protection against prosecution or persecution by their government. The point was made but there was little that the staff at the Commonwealth Relations Office could do without jeopardising Saeed's future even more.

Moss was not to be left in London for long. The Commander-in-Chief of the Far East Air Force had been made aware that, whilst the political adviser had been visiting the Commonwealth Relations Office, the Dunidu contingent had been isolated and Gan had been left under the command of a Squadron Leader because Wing Commander Moss had been summoned to Whitehall by the Vice-Chief of the Air Staff. Unhappy with that situation, the Commander-in-Chief arranged for Wing Commander Thain, a Singapore-based Transport Operations staff officer, to be detached to Gan to stand in for Moss who was not at all surprised when he received a curt signal from the Commander-in-Chief ordering him to return to Gan on the first available aircraft. Within hours Moss was airborne.

With Arthington-Davy isolated and Rounthwaite at the end of his tour it was obviously desirable to create as short a reporting chain as possible between Gan and Whitehall and Moss had, as a result of the Whitehall meeting, been instructed to report directly to the Vice-Chief of the Air Staff on all political matters even though he was to remain responsible to the Commander-in–Chief of the Far East Air Force for all operational matters. Having one of his station commanders bypassing the normal chain of command and reporting directly to the Vice-Chief of the Air Staff did not please the Commander-in-Chief. He protested but his protest was rejected;

for the remainder of his tour Moss was directly responsible to the Vice-Chief of the Air Staff on political matters and was required to do no more than keep the other interested parties informed of any significant developments. That list of interested parties went far beyond the military network and after Rounthwaite had left Gan, Moss also inherited the political distribution list and had to ensure that the United Kingdom's High Commissioner in Ceylon, the staff at the Commonwealth Relations Office and Arthington-Davy on Dunidu were all kept fully informed of the political manoeuvring at Addu Atoll.

April 1964 started badly for the Dunidu residents. On the 4th of the month Arthington-Davy met the Maldivian Prime Minister and presented him with a letter from Duncan Sandys' who, incensed by the isolation of the British Representative and his staff, had written to Nasir demanding that he put an end to the anti-British activities in Malé. Predictably, the British Representative was given a frosty reception and received no reply to the letter which had been written as a necessary diplomatic protest but which had probably done little more than persuade Nasir that the Maldivian tactics were finally causing the British to take notice of what could happen in the archipelago if they continued to ignore the Maldivians' grievances. Subsequently the anti-British campaign in Malé increased.

Any work which was for the benefit of the British contingent on Dunidu was stopped and Hulule once again became the focus for the Maldivians' anger. They had already sabotaged the airstrip at the end of March by dragging a hundred or more felled trees onto the runway, intending to do no more than obstruct it but actually managing to damage the already-weakened surface to such an extent that, even if the tree trunks were to be removed, no aircraft could safely use the airstrip. Early in April, to reinforce the message that the Royal Air Force was not wanted in the archipelago, the Maldivians attacked every building used by the British on the airfield, systematically looted the stores and sabotaged any piece of British-owned equipment which they could not steal.

The damage to the runway created a problem for Arthington-Davy's staff because it meant that supplies for the Dunidu residents had to be dropped onto Hulule. The Dunidu contingent had a pinnace to get them from their base to Hulule but they did not dare to leave it unattended. Neither could they afford to leave the dropped supplies unguarded for fear that they, like the other stores, would be commandeered by the Maldivians. Enough manpower had therefore to be provided to guard the pinnace, protect the piles of supplies, transport the goods to the beach, load the pinnace and run a shuttle service between Dunidu and Hulule.

Throughout such an operation the servicemen who manned the pinnace and protected the supplies on Hulule were vulnerable to attack as were the staff who remained on Dunidu during the operation. Given the volatile nature of the Maldivians who had sabotaged the airfield it was risky to send unarmed men to collect the supplies and on the 10th of April, in response to a request from the British Representative, weapons were dropped to the Dunidu-based servicemen who were ready and waiting on Hulule. On every subsequent trip the arms were overtly worn and the Maldivians, unsure of the way in which the servicemen would react if attacked, kept their distance. The weapons were never fired except on the practice range on Dunidu but they served their primary purpose, they kept the Maldivians at a distance.

As the situation at Malé deteriorated, a Royal Navy guard ship was diverted towards the Maldivian capital and held on station below the horizon outside Maldivian territorial waters. It provided the Dunidu residents with an evacuation facility which could be made available within hours but gave the Maldivians no opportunity to complain about gunboat diplomacy.

On the 14th of April a large number of Maldivians arrived on Dunidu ostensibly to fell trees. What they actually did was to fell a few trees wherever such activity interfered with the work of Arthington-Davy and his staff. The felled trees and debris were then left where they could cause the most inconvenience. When not chopping down coconut palms the Maldivians made as great a nuisance of themselves as possible, harassing the Dunidu residents without physically assaulting any of them. Coincidentally a further letter from Duncan Sandy's was delivered to Malé the following day, withdrawing the British request for additional land for a BBC relay station and also informing Nasir that a revised version of the 1960 agreement was being prepared. Nasir did not reply to the letter but after a few days there was a noticeable reduction in the harassment on Dunidu.

The Maldivian press, however, continued to publish belligerent articles about the British presence in the Maldives and ended the month by announcing that the amnesty granted to Afif Didi had been withdrawn, a claim neither confirmed nor denied by Nasir.

The events at Malé were mirrored at Addu Atoll where Moss had returned only to discover that the political situation was becoming more complicated day by day. At an amicable meeting with the atoll chief and two members of the atoll committee the friendly discussions were focussed on domestic issues avoiding, as much as possible, the political considerations. There was, however, no doubt about the chief's commitment to non-cooperation and Moss could never be sure what problems were about to surface.

The station commander's sudden recall to Gan became more understandable as he learned that the deteriorating political relationship between the British and Maldivian governments was coinciding with a looming crisis in Indonesia and the consequent plan for the RAF's V-force reinforcements to stage through the base during the coming weeks. He also learnt that the Air Officer Commanding the Far East Air Force had become so concerned about the possibility of any reinforcement operation being disrupted by the actions of the Maldivians that he had introduced a standing order requiring a Far East Air Force Group Captain from Singapore to take over command of RAF Gan should Moss be recalled to London or on any other occasion if the Maldivian labour force got out of hand.

As the Indonesian crisis grew and the V-force began staging through Gan the island became more and more congested. Aircraft were parked in every available space and airmen were accommodated in every available hut and in tents on the airfield. Then, at the height of the activity, fighting broke out amongst the Maldivians. The first warning sign came when a Maldivian employee asked for a secret meeting with the station commander. Employed in the works services department the man had no political status but had strong leadership potential, was pro-British, antagonistic towards the Maldivian government and not very supportive of the atoll chief. Moss refused to get involved in clandestine meetings, particularly with a potential insurgent, but the request sounded a warning and put him on his guard. He did not have long to wait. At around nine o'clock the following morning he received a message from Hitaddu: *'Fighting has broken out among the villagers'*. As he was reading the message the Maldivian employees, alerted by their own grapevine, started a mass evacuation from Gan, pouring towards the quayside and either clambering on board the parked dhonis or waiting for the boats which were on their way from Hitaddu to complete the evacuation.

Signals flashed from Gan to London, Singapore and Ceylon. The message was brief: *'Native labour left'*.

Moss was well aware that he could implement operation Econium to bring reinforcements to Gan but he was already faced with an overcrowded island and had no wish to make the situation worse by bringing in even more resident servicemen before it became essential. He therefore asked everyone to cope without the Econium personnel until the pressure became too great. He needn't have bothered. The Senior Air Staff Officer for the Far East Air Force held a teleprinter conference with Moss and then announced that he was implementing Econium. Within twenty-four hours the reinforcements arrived and, for good measure, the tradesmen and general duties airmen were accompanied by a flight of RAF Regiment personnel.

The Regiment airmen were welcomed because on previous occasions they had proved to be the ideal deterrent; Maldivians who had been tempted to come to Gan and disrupt the RAF's operations had thought better of it when they had learned that they would be met by armed servicemen. The airmen, well aware of the efficiency of the island grapevine, made certain that their presence on Gan became common knowledge throughout the atoll. They started each day by staging an armed parade in full view of those islanders who, in spite of the fighting in their villages, were to be found queueing outside the RAF medical centre each day. The airmen then moved onto the football pitch where they spent the remainder of the morning undergoing anti-riot training. The ploy was simple and effective for at no time did the village combatants threaten to bring their fighting onto either of the RAF's leased territories.

The information filtering out of Hitaddu confirmed what Moss had surmised. The pro-government and anti-government factions had finally resorted to violence to settle their arguments and there, significant among the leaders of the anti-government faction, was the Maldivian who had been so anxious to meet secretly with Moss whose stance on that had been vindicated far sooner than he had expected.

Events then unfolded in a manner which was all too familiar in the Maldives, be it at Malé or Addu Atoll. Within hours, injured villagers began to arrive at the station's medical centre, asking for treatment. They saw nothing incongruous about leaving the RAF in the lurch, entering a running fight in one of the villages and then asking the RAF's medical officers to treat their wounds and patch them up so that they could return to the fray. The medical officers, who had no axe to grind, treated the injured without debating the rights or wrongs of the situation. But what they were doing was always likely to be interpreted from a political standpoint because every Maldivian was on one side or the other and most were looking for evidence of biased treatment from the RAF. The situation was made even more sensitive when, on the first day of the fighting, the atoll chief asked Moss for help to crush the anti-government rebels. The station commander was well aware that the British government would studiously avoid any involvement in the fracas but nevertheless he passed on the request to Whitehall. The reply was immediate and predictable: ' *You are to maintain a position of neutrality* '.

That was easier said than done with injured Maldivians coming to Gan for treatment and others coming to purchase essential supplies from the NAAFI-run Maldivian trading post, as they were quite entitled to do. After five days of local fighting Moss again signalled Whitehall saying: '*Must have guidance - there is limit to this neutrality lark .*' He was wasting his time. The only guidance he received was the reiteration of the instruction to remain neutral. His only satisfaction was the knowledge that his exasperation with the politicians had registered in Whitehall.

The next day a deputation of five Maldivians came to see Moss. The group was led by Moosa Ali Didi, the atoll chief, and included at least one island headman. Moosa, whose head was wrapped in a heavily blood-stained bandage giving testimony to his having been caught up in at least one of the skirmishes which were still taking place across the atoll, presented himself as a representative of the Maldivian government and formally requested assistance from the RAF to put an end to the fighting.

When told that the conflict was an internal affair for the Maldivians to resolve without British involvement he pointed out that a leading member of the anti-government faction was publicly claiming that he was supported by the RAF, a claim which many villagers would continue to believe unless the station commander openly declared support for the atoll chief. Moss offered Moosa a compromise. An RAF pinnace and crew could be put at the chief's disposal to tour the atoll. The service crew would do no more than provide transport. Moosa could say what he liked to the islanders at each port of call but the station commander had no intention of being involved in any way. The offer was accepted and the following day Moosa toured the islands. Moss had no idea what was said to the villagers but the chief's use of the pinnace obviously helped to persuade the islanders that he had the support of the RAF. They deserted the anti-government group and the fighting ceased within hours of Moosa's tour. Moosa's main adversary was arrested and was assumed to have been tried, convicted and banished to some remote island for he was not seen again on Gan.

It was frustrating and irritating for Moss that as soon as the local affairs were back to normal the atoll chief once again became difficult to deal with. The reasonably amicable relationship which had existed prior to the recent troubles had always been fragile but had survived as long as domestic issues were discussed in isolation from any political aspects. Even then, however, there was no doubt about the atoll chief's general tendency towards non - cooperation to conform to his government's line. It was not therefore a great surprise when, on the 26th of April, Moosa withdrew all Maldivian labour for the day without notice, supposedly to carry out communal work throughout the atoll. The atoll committee workers had by then become almost schizophrenic, finding fault with anything and everything. Often the members of the committee would complain quite forcibly, half-apologise for having to do so and then ask for some favour from the RAF. It was virtually a case of '*Sorry, but we are acting under orders. Can you let us have some more diesel?*'

Whilst trouble was flaring up at Addu Atoll, Arthington-Davy, on Dunidu, had become even more isolated. Whenever he visited the capital he was followed by large numbers of hostile Maldivians shouting abuse at him and swearing to rid the Maldives of the British Imperialists. Eventually the Maldivian government warned him and his staff to remain on Dunidu for fear that the hostile crowds in Malé might turn from oral abuse to physical violence. He and his staff were then refused access to Hulule where, on the 2nd of May, the Maldivians had started to repair some of the damage which they had inflicted upon the airstrip. The exclusion was officially justified as being necessary for the safety of the British contingent who, if they were to visit Hulule, would be confronted by angry Maldivians, resentful that the British at Addu Atoll had pushed them into sabotaging their own airfield and then having to undertake time-consuming and expensive repair work.

The order to remain on Dunidu was a blow for the British contingent because, with Hulule providing the only suitable drop zone, their exclusion from the island prevented them from receiving anything by air. Irritatingly, they were also prevented from collecting drinking water from Hulule, the source of the most palatable water in Malé Atoll. Arthington-Davy, left with nothing more than a teleprinter link with the outside world, thus became totally dependent upon the Maldivians for the delivery of supplies and mail. His isolation lead to a scenario worthy of Gilbert and Sullivan when, on the 11th of May 1964, he received from the Commonwealth Relations Office a draft revision of the 1960 agreement together with a request that he should deliver it to the Maldivian Prime Minister. Denied access to the capital he eventually had to entrust the document to one of the Maldivians in charge of a coconut-picking party on Dunidu and hope that it would be passed on to Nasir for his consideration.

In London, the Chiefs-of-Staff had become seriously concerned that the volatile nature of Maldivian politics and the unpredictability of the Adduans was likely to threaten the security of the Indian Ocean staging post for the foreseeable future. With 'Econium' already implemented as a result of the recent fracas at the atoll and with RAF Regiment airmen temporarily ensuring the security of operations at the base there was little else they could do about the immediate situation apart from raising the military profile of the atoll by dispatching an Army regiment to Gan and stationing a Royal Navy guard ship in the lagoon. Whilst the former was considered to be unnecessary and undesirable in view of the overcrowding already created on Gan, the latter was seen as a simple option with no implications for the RAF's accommodation or facilities at the atoll and it was implemented with little or no debate. HMS Loch Lomond, the first of a succession of guard ships, duly arrived at the atoll early in May. Once again RAF Gan was 'under Royal Navy protection' for the foreseeable future.

By 1964 the military facilities at Addu Atoll had become strategically so important and the behaviour of the Maldivian government so unpredictable that the Chiefs-of-Staff, at a meeting on the 7th of April, seriously discussed the merits of severing Addu Atoll from Maldivian jurisdiction. The idea had been raised in committee on the 3rd of April and the Air Force Department had been instructed to discuss with the Commonwealth Relations Office how best to operate from a seceded atoll given a hostile Maldivian government and either a hostile or a co-operative Adduan population. Such a military evaluation was predictable but discussing the option with the Commonwealth Relations Office was remarkable in view of the way in which the British government had broken Afif Didi's hold over the Adduans

and had publicly declared an intention to help the Maldivian government to re-establish its authority at the atoll.

The joint perception was that if the British government were to renege on the most recent agreement with the Maldivian government it was unlikely that the Adduans would be hostile towards the British. If they were to be given long-term assurances of protection there was little doubt that they would once again secede from their government and would continue to work enthusiastically for the British military.

There remained, however, the possibility that as a result of recent experience they would not trust the British to protect them in the long term and would consequently become hostile neighbours.

Atoll reinforcement and defence plans were therefore drawn up showing the number of servicemen required to operate the base under such circumstances. The picture which emerged was worrying. To sustain the RAF operations and the construction work it would be necessary to employ servicemen or Asian civilians to replace some 800 Adduan workers. The plan assumed that the BBC's request for land would be abandoned and various reinforcement measures implemented to increase the number of servicemen and aircraft at the atoll to counter any attacks by Maldivian militia or infiltration by hostile Adduans. The Achilles heel of the military's operations at the atoll was the Hitaddu site which, on an island with a local population of some four thousand, was manned by only twenty-five servicemen.

The only clear access to the site was *via* the 400-yard pier which projected across the shallow waters of the coral shelf into the lagoon. Under siege, the site could not be defended without force of arms. Gan was far easier to defend but to protect the two sites against infiltration and sabotage several hundred Army personnel would have to be based at the atoll and a Royal Navy presence maintained in the lagoon. The soldiers would have to live under canvas on the airfield, an arrangement which would be acceptable only if troops were to be seconded to the atoll on a series of short-stay detachments. Even then the facilities on Gan would be stretched near to breaking point with almost two thousand young men crammed onto an island where the total area of less than eight hundred acres was mostly taken up by the airfield and its associated buildings.

For the Chiefs-of-Staff the exercise provided confirmation that, whatever short-term measures were adopted, the atoll base could only be efficiently operated in the long term with Maldivian co-operation, at least from the Adduans and preferably from the Maldivian government. Nevertheless, they believed that it was possible, albeit undesirable, to operate the base defensively, approved the idea of secession as a last resort and adopted it as a contingency plan. With that behind them, they could view the political developments in 1964 with a slightly more relaxed attitude, hoping that co-operation would come out of the inter-governmental manoeuvring but prepared, if necessary, to operate the mid-ocean base in a hostile environment.

In May, quite unexpectedly, some encouraging signs emerged to indicate that, regardless of what was happening in the Maldivian capital, the political climate was improving at Addu Atoll. That month, when Moosa Ali Didi was visiting Malé, the Maldivian government appointed a temporary atoll chief, Weliduge Moosa Didi, and he, much to the surprise of the British, started his period of office in a friendly, co-operative manner. After amicably and helpfully discussing service matters with Moss during their first meeting he agreed that the islanders should continue to take part in the dhoni race during the Whitsun festival and he then extended a surprise invitation for the servicemen and civilians on the Gan and Hitaddu sites to take part in organised visits to some of the atoll villages. It was an unexpected and highly significant gesture of friendship from such a senior government representative.

Later that month there were also small but encouraging signs from Malé. The Deputy Minister for Home Affairs had obviously received the draft revision of the 1960 agreement *via* the coconut-picking party for he had responded by sending an alternative text to the British Representative on the 20th of May. He had also eased the restrictions on the Dunidu contingent, allowing them to resume their visits to Hulule. They were thus once again able to collect their own drinking water and the supplies dropped either by the Valettas of 52 Squadron or by the 205 Squadron Shackletons. By mid-June the political tension in Malé had eased to such an extent that on the 16th of the month Arthington-Davy was invited to meet Nasir to clarify certain aspects of the Maldivians' proposed text for the revised agreement, hopefully in preparation for detailed negotiations to be started in Colombo. Following that amicable and constructive meeting the British Representative suggested to the Commonwealth Relations Office that it was an opportune moment for the British contingent to leave Dunidu, thereby removing the obvious focus for any local resentments which might build up and sour the improving political atmosphere. The suggestion was accepted and on the 18th of June 1964, with the permission of the Maldivian Prime Minister, HMS Loch Lomond steamed into the Malé lagoon and evacuated Arthington-Davy and the service detachment. From Malé they were brought to Gan and from there the British Representative flew to London for talks at the Commonwealth Relations Office.

Arthington-Davy's assessment had been correct. With the removal of the local focus for resentment at Malé the demonstrations and sabotage had became pointless and they ceased even though the Maldivian press remained hostile.

At Addu Atoll the station commander had quickly realised that Weliduge Moosa Didi was quite genuinely a kindly, fifty-year-old who was a professional atoll chief rather than someone who had come to office by virtue of commercial success, personal wealth or political nepotism.

In May and June the relationship could not have been more amicable and in those early weeks it grew strong enough to be unaffected when, at the end of June, Weliduge received instructions from Malé to be less co-operative. Fortunately he had by then established his own ideas of an appropriate degree of co-operation and he largely chose to ignore his new instructions except for those which referred to visits. He was instructed to ensure that the only Adduans who visited Gan were those who were either employed by the British or were needing medical treatment. He was also ordered to stop the organised tours which he had arranged for the servicemen and the civilian expatriates and was informed that, in future, visits to the atoll villages could only be made with the express permission of the Minister for Home Affairs in Malé. The restrictions, which really amounted to no more than precise implementation of the 1960 agreement and of some of the clauses in the new draft agreement, obviously reflected the Maldivian government's view that the political atmosphere at Addu Atoll was becoming too friendly. They did not, however, bring about a noticeable deterioration in local relationships.

June saw the arrival of a team of investigators from the Ministry of Public Buildings and Works and from the Far East Air Force Headquarters with a remit to study two politically sensitive subjects: the pay and conditions of the Maldivians employed at Addu Atoll and the possible Maldivianisation of jobs undertaken at that time by Pakistanis. The Maldivianisation study was simple enough because a significant number of Pakistanis were employed in jobs which Maldivians could be trained to do within a year or two. All that was needed was the commitment of time, effort and resources to a training programme. The principle of Maldivianisation was therefore accepted by the Command staff with little debate and the implementation was left to the local initiative of the RAF and Gan's district works officer. That seemed reasonable enough but it was to become a contentious issue over the years with the Maldivians continually expecting faster and more extensive Maldivianisation than could be achieved with the limited training resources made available.

The investigation into the pay and conditions of the Maldivians was not as straightforward even though it was certain to lead to recommendations for improvements in both. It would be the extent of those improvements which would trigger off a debate and that was bound to involve the Maldivian government as well as the British Treasury. As far as conditions of service were concerned the Maldivians had few entitlements to paid holidays, agreed periods of notice or compensation for injuries. The team quickly decided that all Maldivian employees should be accorded the entitlements enjoyed by the Pakistanis, namely six working days paid absence per annum, eleven paid public holidays per annum, seven days notice of normal discharge and, subject to set criteria, payment of workmen's compensation for industrial injuries or illness. Even those basic entitlements could not be agreed locally because they introduced a charge on public funds and could therefore only be implemented with the approval of the Treasury. The team's recommendations had therefore to be submitted to London for consideration.

The Maldivians' rates of pay presented a more complex subject. Maldivian employees typically worked a six-day, forty-eight-hour week starting work at six-thirty each morning, finishing at three-thirty each afternoon and taking a one hour meal break around mid-day. Some were required to start earlier or finish later, some chose to work seven days a week and a few were required to work overnight. Their working arrangements accommodated their religious practices, leaving them free to take individual prayer breaks each day and to worship in the mosque each Friday. During Ramadan they worked only until mid-day. They were paid hourly wages with pay rate variations based upon a variety of criteria across four trade groups. Their cash wages were supplemented with just over one pound of rice per day for

each employee. In mid-1964 the wages paid for a eight-hour day, including the cash value of the rice, ranged from 5/4d (27p) for roomboys through 6/10d (34p) for labourers and 7/4d (37p) for laundrymen up to 9/10d (49p) for head labourers, timekeepers, clerks and interpreters.

Dovetailing in with the wages were the fees paid to the owners of the dhonis in which most of the Maldivians travelled to and from work. If the wage rates were revised then the travel costs would also have to be adjusted. Finally, there were the Malé factors to consider; the Adduans' wage rates had initially been agreed with the Maldivian government on the basis of a fair comparison with wages in Malé and in order to avoid yet another inter-governmental disagreement any proposed pay rises would have to be subjected to a similar comparison. Complicating any such comparison was the fact that the Adduans had one advantage over the Maldivian workers in Malé; they were paid in Sterling which was far more valuable for trading with Ceylon than was recognised by the official exchange rate. They were thus able to purchase the imported essentials and still have money to spend on the goods available from the Maldivian trading post on Gan or from the seven Maldivian shops which were located in their villages and which generally offered a range of goods at prices lower than those in the Gan trading post.

The investigators from Singapore were well aware of the advantages which the Adduans gained by being paid in Sterling but they were also aware that such payment would be discontinued as soon as the Maldivian government regained complete control over the affairs of the atoll. The reason was simple. The government could make a handsome profit by paying the Adduans in Maldivian rupees and then obtaining repayment from the British government at an artificial exchange rate which varied almost at Nasir's whim.

Finally, there remained the vexed question of taxation. Since declaring their independence the Adduans had paid no taxes to central government and when normal taxation returned they would suffer a significant drop in the purchasing power of their wages.

By the end of June the investigating team had done all that it could at Gan and it returned to Singapore from where the team members could complete their report and submit it, with their recommendations, to the Ministry of Defence. Their recommendations were founded on their belief that Britain should establish a permanent Maldivian labour force with twentieth century conditions of service as soon as possible. Although the Adduans were aware that details of the team's recommendations would not be released for several months their expectations had been raised. With whetted appetites they began to look forward to significant improvements in their pay and conditions.

Their general mood of optimism and friendly co-operation lasted until the 8th of July. On that date Moosa Ali Didi returned from Malé, his appointment as atoll chief confirmed. Within hours of his arrival at Hitaddu he had destroyed the optimistic mood of the islanders and had begun to undermine their relationships with their British employers. It was not that he had any personal axe to grind, he was simply acting under instructions from Malé where it had been made quite clear that his new appointment was conditional upon his implementing whatever orders he was given. The villagers soon learnt that his orders included the introduction of the taxes which had been announced in 1958 but had never been applied at the atoll. The 1964 list of items to be taxed was even more detailed than that produced in 1958. Houses, boats and palm trees were all listed, together with foodstuffs and every other necessity of life which was likely to be traded in their coconut-and-fish economy and every luxury which an islander might purchase.

The rates of tax ranged from fifteen per cent for essential foodstuffs to three hundred per cent for luxury goods such as pillows. It was immediately obvious to the Adduans that outside Malé, the capital, they were almost certainly the only islanders in the archipelago who could afford the so-called luxuries which were to be so highly taxed. More than that, they almost certainly had the highest proportion of house owners and boat owners anywhere in the Maldives, including Malé, for they had tended to use their wages from their British employers to improve their housing and to buy boats as a precaution against loss of employment on Gan and the subsequent need to revert to fishing as a means of earning a living. It was small comfort for the villagers to learn that they would not be required to pay retrospectively; they were still facing a reduction in their subsistence-level standard of living when they had genuinely been looking forward to some significant improvement. They were convinced that the new system of taxation had been very carefully constructed to penalise the Adduans, who were fortunate enough to be employed by the British, more than any other group of Maldivians.

As if the imminent re-appearance of central government taxation was not bad enough, Moosa had also been given orders to pursue a policy of non-cooperation with the British, a policy intended to hamper the continuing development programme but which would inevitably create problems for the Adduans in the process. As far as the British were concerned, the only good news was that the Maldivians had not been ordered to withdraw their labour. That was probably because Nasir could remember only too well the reactions of the Adduans when Zaki had told them to stop working for the British.

Moosa, however, had a variety of tactics to make life awkward for the employers and he used them all. Problems would occur where previously there had been none. He became uncooperative over the provision of labour and he continually demanded changes such as the cessation of dhoni line searches, the closure of the labour relations office and the provision of double pay for workers employed on Fridays and public holidays.

Complaints would be made over seemingly trivial matters and would be formally raised with requests for full investigations. To ensure that his tactics had maximum impact Moosa banned all direct contact between the atoll committee and the RAF's Maldivian Affairs officer, informing him that, until further notice, his only contact with the committee was to be in writing through the atoll office. He even banned the RAF medical and hygiene teams from visiting any territory outside the military sites although he was well aware that such a restriction, whilst having no immediate impact on the operation of the base, was very much to the disadvantage of the Adduans.

He was doing no more than applying to those teams the restriction which applied to all expatriates at the atoll but the effect was to deprive many villagers, particularly the elderly and the infirm who were too ill to be brought across the lagoon to Gan, of the medical treatment available through the RAF. Every Adduan was well aware that the advice and supervision provided by the teams had been largely responsible for the considerable improvement in the general health of the villagers and had significantly reduced the incidence of malaria at the atoll. Now, in one move, Moosa had undermined the preventative measures and deprived the villagers of the on-site services of the medical officers. The villagers, already irritated at having to work to orders which seemed to be causing more problems for them than for the British, bitterly resented this latest sign of Moosa's hard-line approach.

By the end of July their resentment had grown into open hostility and Moosa was becoming increasingly nervous as their antagonism threatened to turn into violence. Information leaked from his meetings made it clear that he was under orders from Malé to pursue hard-line anti-RAF policies in the hope that the British would eventually decide that the continued use of Gan as a mid-ocean staging post was becoming more trouble than it was worth. If they could be persuaded to develop one of the alternative island sites in the Indian Ocean Nasir would have achieved his objectives. The British would be ousted from Addu Atoll and the islanders who had cost his government so much in lost revenue and loss of face would be forced back into a subsistence culture after experiencing a tantalisingly short period of relatively good living. They would also be left unprotected and that would suit Nasir who made no secret of his wish to bring the Adduan rebels to justice. The potential loss of revenue for his government was seen as a price worth paying, partly because he still doubted whether his government would ever receive the agreed payments and partly because he believed that financial aid could be obtained without the need to lease the lands at Addu Atoll.

There was really very little chance that Nasir's plan would have been successful but, ironically, it was the atoll chief who began to undermine it when he realised that his uncooperative stance had resulted in the loss of his own perquisites from the RAF. At the end of July Moss was assured by Moosa that he was personally very pro-British but was acting under orders from his government. The atoll chief did, however, indicate that he hoped that it would be possible to adopt a more amenable approach in the near future and he hoped that in the meantime he would still be permitted to purchase diesel oil and various other items from the RAF, preferably in confidence to avoid any embarrassing comments from the members of the atoll committee. As far as the station commander was concerned Moosa's request was perfectly reasonable. The items could all be legitimately sold to the atoll chief and if he were to feel slightly embarrassed by the transactions that was his affair. Certainly it was better to have him beholden to the British rather than to have him resentful towards them and if he wished his dealings to remain confidential his anxieties might generate more co-operation than any ephemeral gratitude.

In a matter of days Moosa's obligation to the RAF was tested because trouble which erupted on Hitaddu seemed likely to lead to a considerable worsening of the political atmosphere between London and Malé. Most of the Hitadduan labour force openly resented the attitude of the atoll chief and on the 4th of August 1964 two events brought matters to a head. Several Adduans who had been involved in a fracas on board their dhonis near the Wave Victor had been reported to Moosa. They were subsequently tried, convicted and punished on the 5th of August, the same day that the atoll chief met a deputation of shareholders in the then defunct Adduan Trading Corporation. The shareholders had already lost the Corporation's entire stock because as soon as Afif Didi had left the atoll the Maldivian government had ordered the closure of the islanders' shops, confiscated goods to the value of some four thousand pounds, sold them and kept the money.

At the meeting on the 5th the chief informed the shareholders that their government also had no intention of returning their share capital and that if they were in difficult financial circumstances they should demand a pay rise from the RAF. The meeting broke up in pandemonium. Moosa immediately had sixteen members of the deputation arrested and within the hour there was a rapidly spreading rumour that they had been bound and beaten. That was enough for the villagers. Acting on a rumour, they seized the chief and put him under house arrest. The atoll committee really had no alternative but to support Moosa and in an attempt to put pressure on the villagers the committee members declared that no Maldivians were to work for the British until the atoll chief had been released and matters were back to normal. That move backfired because the villagers, facing the loss of their wages as well as their share capital, turned against the committee members. The leaders of the demonstration sent an assurance to the RAF's Maldivian Affairs officer that this latest uprising had nothing to do with any move towards independence, it was solely related to the non-return of the share capital. For the station commander, recent experience suggested otherwise. He was certain that any villagers' demonstration was likely to get out of hand and overflow onto Gan if allowed to do so and as soon as the Maldivian labour had been withdrawn he had implemented part of the Econium reinforcement plan and that enabled a significant number of airmen to be released for security duties. The RAF police had been issued with anti-riot equipment and smoke grenades, shoreline patrols had been set up and the station's defence flight put on permanent standby.

From the RAF's point of view the timing of this latest withdrawal of labour could not have been much worse. Because of the Indonesian crisis heavy demands were being made on the personnel and the services on Gan as the Canberras and V bombers staged through the base along with the reinforcements which were being sent from England to the Far East. Because the Regiment airmen based in Singapore had already been deployed elsewhere an RAF Regiment flight had to be sent to Gan from RAF Lyneham. The flight arrived on the 7th and within hours guards had been posted around the marine craft unit, where several dhonis had made a night-time approach before being scared off by searchlights, on board the Wave Victor and around the Hitaddu site where the staff were armed only with pickaxe staves and dustbin lids. Within twenty-four hours of the Regiment airmen's arrival the number of shoreline patrols had been increased, night-time patrols introduced, and the leased territories were reasonably secure.

At the Ministry of Defence and the Commonwealth Relations Office the staff were becoming disillusioned by the Adduans' continual plotting and counter-plotting. They were anxious to keep news of this latest problem out of the press even though the British government's reaction to the events showed an unyielding commitment to the return of central government control to the atoll. It had been decided that if Moosa Ali Didi were to be ousted by the Adduans, the British government would have no dealings with anyone chosen by the islanders as their atoll chief. Furthermore, the British would employ no Maldivian who supported such an insurrection. The message was clear but it did not have any immediate effect because the atoll committee, temporarily under the popular leadership of Ahmed Salih Ali Didi, had already withdrawn all Maldivian labour in an attempt to secure Moosa's release.

It was four days before the atoll chief actually managed to escape from house arrest and by then the atoll committee had declared that the RAF was to blame for instigating the revolt. That became the first test of Moosa's sense of obligation towards Moss. He could either agree with the committee, which would inevitably lead to a further souring of the relations between the British and Maldivian governments, or he could disabuse the committee of that opinion and allow the affair to be settled as a local internal matter. After some correspondence with the station commander and a meeting on Gan on the 11th of August the atoll chief agreed that the committee was mistaken.

The members then agreed that the Maldivian employees from all the islands except Hitaddu should return to work the following day. That they did, thereby allowing the RAF's emergency measures to be scaled down. It took Moosa another week to bring the situation on Hitaddu under control if not actually back to normal. The villagers, however, were polarised with the majority in support of the leader of the anti-Moosa faction but a significant minority in support of the atoll chief.

Moosa then had ninety of his rival's most vociferous supporters arrested and that swung the situation in his favour, at least as far as control was concerned. On the 18th, all but seventy-eight of the Hitadduan workers returned to Gan. Those seventy-eight absentees were among the ninety villagers arrested a week earlier, many of whom were claiming to have been paid by the RAF to stage a revolt. The station commander, however, had already reminded Moosa that it would be more appropriate to thank the British rather than accuse them, for if they had shown any support for his rivals the atoll chief would almost certainly have been deposed. Moosa readily appreciated that fact but he faced a dilemma. If he were to thank the British he would be out of favour with Nasir. Alternatively he could save face and please his Prime Minister if he chose to offer the RAF as a scapegoat and unjustifiably accused the British of fomenting trouble at the atoll once again. To his credit, he passed the obligation test by assuring Moss that when he sent a report of the affair to Malé he would exonerate the RAF from all blame. Apparently he kept his promise for neither the Maldivian government nor the Maldivian press accused the British of inciting yet another Adduan rebellion.

Moosa banned the Maldivians from talking to the British about the troubles on Hitaddu, warning them that anyone who was found to have broken the ban would automatically lose his job. That was an effective move for although the assumption on Gan was that the rebels would be sent to Malé for trial, it was many weeks before news finally filtered back from the capital that all of the accused had been tried, found guilty and sentenced to five years banishment.

September brought no respite in the interminable Maldivian game of blowing hot and blowing cold. The atoll chief, seemingly regretting his earlier objectivity, or possibly under some pressure from Malé to recant, wrote to the station commander and accused the British of being behind the Adduan's recent revolt. The claim was immediately rebutted but the incident gave some indication of the pressures on Moosa to make life awkward for the RAF.

There was a generally fractious mood among the islanders during the early days of the month and there seemed to be a strong likelihood of yet another withdrawal of labour, the mood and the threat both stemming from the growing feeling among the Adduans that their wages and allowances, essentially the same in 1964 as they had been in 1958, should be increased at least to compensate for the imminent taxation. Once again the station's defence flight was put onto alert, an RAF Regiment flight was flown in from Singapore and the Econium reinforcement plan was put on standby.

On the 7th of the month several Maldivians refused to show their passes on landing at Gan and on the 8th even more joined in and that led to some hustling and jostling. Tempers became frayed and the following day the Maldivians staged an early morning demonstration at the dhoni lines. In the resulting fracas several RAF policemen, some British and some Pakistani, were slightly injured. By nine o'clock that morning all Maldivian labour had been withdrawn from Gan and the islanders were on their way home, leaving Moss to call for Econium reinforcements to be flown in, together with a second RAF Regiment flight which was on standby at Lyneham.

Later that day several members of the atoll committee came to Gan, declared that it was all a misunderstanding and promised that the workforce would be back as usual in the morning. The delegation then suggested that all requests for Maldivian labour and all complaints about Maldivian employees should go through the atoll chief who should be permitted to have a representative present whenever an RAF policeman was interviewing any Maldivian employee. Moss agreed to implement all the suggestions, giving Moosa the same degree of control over the Maldivian labour force as that which Afif Didi had enjoyed in 1959.

The delegation had promised that the workers would return to work and sure enough, on the 10th of September, all the Maldivian employees, except for the fifteen ringleaders who had been sacked by the RAF, reported for work as if nothing had happened. Undoubtedly the rapid arrival of some of the Econium reinforcements had helped to persuade the islanders that they might be wise to return to work before their jobs were taken over by the military. Similarly, the arrival of the RAF Regiment airmen almost certainly persuaded them that it would be unwise to start any trouble.

The Maldivian government was keen to make some capital out of this minor event, coming, as it did, so soon after the revolt against Moosa Ali Didi. The leading players in that fracas had been banished for five years but Nasir, unwilling to concede that his government's policies and Moosa's style had brought about the short-lived insurrection, was looking for a scapegoat. He thought he had found one in the RAF's Maldivian Affairs officer on Gan and he demanded his removal from the atoll on the grounds that he was a political agitator. The British government studiously ignored the demand, leaving Nasir more disgruntled than ever.

While the Maldivian and British governments continued to discuss the revisions to the 1960 agreement another problem reared its head at the atoll. Malaria and other insect-borne diseases were on the increase amongst the villagers, a predictable consequence of the atoll chief's insistence that no medical or hygiene teams would be permitted to visit the villages or any land not leased to the RAF. On Gan and on the Hitaddu site there were virtually no problems because of the considerable measures taken to destroy the breeding grounds and to kill the insect population by using the now familiar squad of 'swinging smokies'. Knowing what could be achieved through cooperation, and keen to make the islanders aware that the hygiene squads' exclusion from the villages had not been initiated by the RAF, the senior medical officer had displayed the chief's letter in the station medical centre. A furious Moosa, accusing him of being a political agitator trying to undermine the chief's status, refused to lift the ban. In an attempt to resolve the impasse the station commander wrote to the atoll chief on several occasions but his letters were either ignored or were answered with a negative.

The ban meant that several of the Maldivian labourers employed in the hygiene section were no longer needed and on the 6th of October twelve were made redundant. Moosa immediately demanded their reinstatement and when that was not done he withdrew the remaining Maldivian labourers from the hygiene section. The station's medical officer replaced them with Pakistanis and was again accused by the atoll chief of being a political agitator keen to foment trouble and personally responsible for the earlier laxity of the spraying programme on the islands.

Those accusations were followed by a request for higher pay and better conditions for the Maldivians still employed in the medical section, a request which was passed on to the Far East Air Force staff and the Ministry of Defence for consideration and to the United Kingdom's High Commissioner in Colombo as part of a general report on health care at the atoll. Subsequently the High Commissioner's representative approached the Maldivian government with a request for permission to resume spraying throughout the atoll and for inter-governmental talks to be started with a view to improving the pay and conditions of the Adduans. No reply was received on either matter. Later that month a Maldivian broadsheet was released in Ceylon giving the Maldivian version of the recent events at Addu Atoll. It consisted of the usual accusation of beatings and wounding of Maldivians by the British, serving only to emphasise the impossibility of trying to deal with the Maldivian regime.

By October the Singapore-based Command staff were discovering that any plans to improve the pay of the Adduans were likely to be delayed by the Maldivian government which quite clearly did not want the Adduans to become too wealthy. Meanwhile Moosa was threatening to ban overtime working or withdraw all the Maldivian labour unless improvements were forthcoming. He would not however, contact Malé to seek approval of his demands nor would he put those demands in writing because he wanted to deny his role in the matter if his government were to disapprove. He contented himself with making demands and declaring that his government would approve of his actions.

The Command staff held a very pragmatic view; a permanent Maldivian labour force should be established with good pay and conditions. That would establish the RAF as a good employer who paid on merit, not under duress or as a reaction to labour problems. If good pay and conditions whetted the Adduans' appetites for Westernisation their relations with their central government could well be damaged even more but it was up to the British government to tell Nasir that he couldn't have it both ways. Either he accepted the implications of the RAF's role as a good employer or he risked facing another separatist movement.

If the Adduans continued to press for better pay and conditions and to take industrial action in pursuit of their claims there were very few options open to the RAF. The current continual use of military reinforcements was both disruptive and expensive and if Moosa were to order frequent short duration stoppages the Econium personnel would end up being shuttled between Singapore and Gan, spending more time embarking, flying and disembarking than actually working on the base.

Such disruption could be avoided if more Pakistanis were brought to work and live on Gan and although such recruitment would show the Maldivians that they were not indispensable it was an expensive option and was contrary to the British policy of Maldivianisation. It would be less expensive to recruit Moslem workers from Malaya but they were not particularly good employees away from home and those who were married would only travel abroad with their families.

Arthington-Davy was made fully aware of these issues and of the fact that it was impossible to isolate the questions of pay, working conditions and industrial relations at Addu Atoll from the negotiations over the new agreement between the British and Maldivian governments. That left the British Representative, if he managed to gain access to the Maldivian Prime Minister, with the unenviable task of trying to persuade Nasir of the merits of the Adduans' claims. That, it seemed, was unlikely to happen in the remaining few months of 1964.

At the beginning of October, the atoll chief was refusing to visit Gan and was as obstructive as ever, insisting that all contact with him had to be in writing through the atoll committee. Information leaked from his meetings indicated either that he was committed to his government's anti-British policies or that he was presenting a false image in the knowledge that what he said would certainly be passed on to the RAF's labour relations officer and probably on to the government ministers in Malé. He continually declared that he wanted nothing from the RAF and that he would rid the atoll of the British. Fate decreed otherwise because on the 15th of the month he had an unpleasant surprise when the Maldivian government announced that the Hulule airstrip was to be repaired by a communal effort which would require the provision of labour from each of the forty-three inhabited atolls in the archipelago.

The runway had been divided into forty-three sections and each atoll had been allocated one section to repair. Work was to start by mid-November. For the Adduans this meant the provision of some seventy or eighty islanders at a time when bad weather was making any boat journey hazardous, never mind the three-hundred-mile trip to Malé. Moosa was on the horns of a dilemma. He dare not refuse to provide any workmen but if he were to do the obvious thing and ask the RAF for help he would stand accused of being too friendly with the British. After some agonising he chose to explain his dilemma to the station commander. Moss was always genuinely pleased to help the islanders and on this occasion there was an obvious opportunity to do that and to leave the atoll chief once more under a sense of obligation even though the station commander was certainly not persuaded that that would influence Moosa's behaviour to any great extent. As soon as the chief had explained the problem, Moss initiated a marine craft unit navigation exercise which would require a launch to be taken on two return trips to Hulule island in Kalamadule Atoll. For good measure he also approved the loan of tents and equipment for the labourers who were to travel in the launch. Moosa was on tenterhooks. He had committed himself for the benefit of the Adduans but was expecting retribution when his Prime Minister heard what he had done. Fortune favoured him at the expense of the islanders in the north. Just as he had resigned himself to being summoned to Malé, typhoid broke out in the more northerly islands of the archipelago. The plan to assemble workers from forty-three atolls was abandoned and the order to provide labour was replaced by an order to send money to the government so that local labour could be hired to repair the runway.

Although that opportunity to leave the chief with a sense of obligation to the RAF was lost, the chance arose, in November, of providing a far more personal service for the briefly friendly and co-operative Moosa. By that time there was a miscellaneous collection of ex-Costain tipper trucks, dumpers, concrete mixers, lorries and construction equipment, all no longer needed on Gan but not valuable enough to transport back to England. Moosa bought the entire collection at a bargain price but then had to transport it to Hitaddu. Once again he asked for help and once again Moss was happy to oblige. The surplus equipment was shipped across the lagoon on board one of the RAF's landing craft and, for good measure, Moosa was offered an increase in the quota of fuel which he was allowed to purchase each month; without that he would be unable to operate the additional plant and vehicles which he had acquired.

By then the chief had obviously decided that the time was right for him to ask yet another favour of Moss for no sooner had the ex-Costain equipment arrived on Hitaddu than he asked whether the RAF marine craft fitters could replace a defective bearing in his launch. Once again help was willingly given.

Rather surprisingly, a *quid pro quo* came within a matter of weeks when a Russian research vessel, the Vityaz, visited the atoll as part of an Interna-tional Geophysical Expedition. The Russian captain requested permission for his crew to go ashore onto Hitaddu which presented a rather unwelcome prospect for Moss because, although the atoll chief was not generally inclined to allow foreign ships' crews to visit any of the inhabited islands, there was always the possibility that he might allow the Russians ashore solely to embarrass the British and, once ashore, the Russian crew would have been perfectly entitled to wander along the public footpath which traversed the Hitaddu communications site. But at the time of the Vityaz visit Moosa was indebted to Moss even more than usual and, knowing that the station commander did not want a group of Russians walking through the military communications site, he refused permission for them to land on any of the inhabited islands. The crew had therefore to content themselves with a shore visit only onto the beaches of Wilingili. Moosa accepted an invitation to go aboard the Vityaz but the Russian captain's invitation of on-board hospitality for the station commander and his officers was politely declined.

Throughout the latter part of 1964 there was thus a strange political climate with publicly ostentatious ill-will from the atoll chief cloaking a much more amenable attitude which was only ever displayed in private. Above all else, Moosa was fearful of reprisals if any of his Adduan enemies reported adversely on him to Malé. Undoubtedly he was walking a political tightrope because he made it clear to the station commander that, no matter what his personal feelings were, he could not be seen to be friendly whilst his government was at loggerheads with the British. He privately admitted that many of his political actions were not merely unpopular with the Adduans, they were patently detrimental to their well-being, the most obvious example being the rapid increase in the number of islanders, now up to about seventy a month, who were contracting malaria since the RAF's medical and hygiene teams had been banned from the Adduan villages.

Quite apart from the increased incidence of malaria, that exclusion order had led to an increase in the number of villagers coming to Gan for general medical treatment and although it could not account for the truly dramatic increase in demand which had occurred since 1963 it certainly contributed to the burden falling upon a medical service which had never been intended to provide health care for the islanders. In part, the medical staff were compounding the problem by their commitment to treat anyone in need and in part the problem was being created by the Ministry of

Defence with the unofficial acceptance that refusal to provide treatment for the Adduans would have given the Maldivian government another argument to use in its continuing disagreement with the British. Whatever the reasons for the increase, a rise in consultations from nine hundred in 1963 to over fourteen thousand in 1964 coupled with a rise in outpatient treatments from twelve hundred to almost twenty two thousand over the same period clearly indicated that some controls would have to be introduced regardless of the political capital which the Maldivian government might make out of such a move.

Politically, 1964 ended the way it began, in a state of turbulence. The islanders, confused and fearful that matters would get worse once their government was back in control at Addu Atoll, had convinced themselves that their conditions of employment would worsen, their trading would be curtailed and their incomes would be more highly taxed. At international level the Maldivians were still arguing with the British, making veiled threats, fuming at their own impotence when confronting British intransigence, resorting to hysterical outbursts in their national press and rounding off the year on the 20th of December by requesting the removal of Arthington-Davy whom they no longer recognised as the British Representative in the Maldives. The timing of that request was odd because there were, at the end of 1964, some indications that the British and Maldivian governments were close to an agreement which would finally resolve the Adduan problem. Discussions between them, however, were few and far between during the early part of 1965, almost certainly due to the onset of Ramadan, the observance of which invariably brought a politically and socially quiet period to the archipelago.

The final agreement was close because the British had chosen to ignore the Maldivian government's blatant breach of that section of the 1960 agreement which had included guarantees that no Adduan would be punished for having taken part in the rebellion. In January 1965 eighty of those Adduans who had been called to Malé had been arrested, convicted on charges of staging or supporting the rebellion and exiled for periods ranging from one to fifteen years. The Maldivian government was unrepentant in the face of criticism and the British government, faced with the certainty that to pursue the issue would be to bring about yet another collapse of the inter-governmental talks, chose to ignore the Maldivians' display of bad faith. The convicted islanders were left to their fate. The atoll

chief, however, returned from Malé in good spirits because, with his appointment confirmed, he would not have to stand for re-election in August and could therefore weather any temporary disaffection on the part of the Adduans. His feeling of security was reflected in his dealings with Moss whom he later contacted about the possibility of obtaining a new electrical generator to supply power for the Hitaddu network.

He may have felt reasonable secure but it was very noticeable to the station commander that, for the first time, the Adduans took no minutes at that meeting.

By March 1965 the intermittent discussions between the two governments had resolved all but a few relatively trivial differences. Some, but by no means all, of the final stumbling blocks were more related to loss of face than to significant political issues. The British could not, for example, immediately agree to the withdrawal of Arthington-Davy from the Maldives but were quite prepared to arrange for his transfer at a time when such a move did not appear to be a response to a Maldivian demand. The BBC's request for land at the atoll, a request which had so irritated the Maldivian Prime Minister when it was raised by the Duke of Devonshire, had not been favoured by the Commonwealth Secretary since the previous April's meeting with the Chiefs-of-Staff and he therefore chose not to pursue it, allowing the negotiators to concentrate on more important issues.

There were, however, two very significant issues still to be resolved: the control of illegal trading by the Adduans and the use of Maldivian currency at Addu Atoll.

The demand for the elimination, by the RAF, of illegal trading between the Adduans and any visiting ships was one which the British certainly could not accept, either immediately or in the future. Acceptance would have put the RAF in the position of policing a thoroughly unpopular Maldivian law and, apart from the practical difficulties of enforcing the law, would have led the Adduans to resent the way in which the British were controlling an aspect of Adduan life which was not legitimately any concern of theirs.

The proposal to replace Sterling by Maldivian rupees for the payment of all wages to the Adduans employed by the British, was not in the same category as the elimination of illegal trading but it was an issue which could seriously affect the supply of Adduan labour. The wage levels had been agreed and paid in Sterling since the islanders' unilateral declaration of independence. If the Maldivian government were to take over the payment system a government agent would pay the Adduans in Maldivian rupees at the official market exchange rate and the Maldivian Government would be reimbursed by the British at a rate which would profit the Maldivian exchequer. The Adduans' wages would be dramatically devalued, they would probably blame the British for agreeing to the arrangement and many of them could well decide that it was not worth being employed for little more than twenty per cent of the previously agreed wages. Not surprisingly, it was an issue which was to become the subject of considerable disagreement over the next few months.

From the 12th to the 16th of March Moss attended a series of meetings in Colombo at which the British High Commissioner sought agreement with the Maldivians on the wage levels for the Adduans and the currency to be used. In the background was the understanding that the wage rates were likely to be increased as a result of the study undertaken in June 1964. It soon became obvious that the Maldivian government would not really pursue the idea that the Adduans should be paid in rupees, largely because there was an alternative approach which would be almost as rewarding for the government, more flexible, administratively simpler and devoid of the risks associated with the exchange rate. The Maldivian plan was to establish both a differential system of taxation, which would be loaded against the Adduans, and a trading control system which would transfer money from the Adduan economy into the Maldivian exchequer.

The islanders were already aware of the taxes that they would have to pay when they were once again under the control of their central government because the atoll chief had visited Malé in February and had returned with the latest proposals for income tax, purchase tax and annual licence fees or ownership tax. The government claimed that the taxes and licence fees were the same throughout the archipelago but, even if that were true, it was not really the point. The taxation system seemed to have been designed so that the Adduans would be affected more than any other group of islanders. Income tax would be of greater significance at Addu Atoll than anywhere else, with the possible exception of Malé, for the simple reason that hundreds of Adduans were receiving weekly wages in cash. Elsewhere in the archipelago wages were not that significant because most islanders eked out a living in a fish-and-coconut economy where bartering, a form of trading which was so difficult to tax, was far more common than cash trading. Income tax was also to be levied on benefits-in-kind, which were almost unique to Addu Atoll and were thus of little or no significance elsewhere in the Maldives.

The phrase 'benefits in kind' obviously embraced the weekly rice issues which formed part of each Adduan employee's pay but it also imposed taxation on the estimated value of the scrap furniture, old oil drums and general bric-a-brac which the Maldivians were allowed to scavenge from the Gan scrap heap every Tuesday before the heap was shipped out to be dumped at sea beyond the atoll's outer reef. As far as purchase tax and annual licence fees or ownership tax were concerned the effect at Addu Atoll would be greater than anywhere else in the Maldives for the simple reason that the Adduans had access to, and had acquired a liking for, items which had been selected for punitive taxation levels.

Purchase tax was as high as three hundred per cent on some items whilst the monthly ownership tax on a luxury such as a radio was set at one pound two shillings and sixpence (112 ½ pence) which represented twenty hours gross pay for a Maldivian labourer employed on Gan. For anyone eking out a living by fishing and small-scale crop cultivation such taxation levels would put all luxuries out of reach whilst even those employed by the British would find it impossible to maintain the quite modest lifestyles to which they had become accustomed. The Adduans were incensed but impotent. They needed no reminding that in January eighty of those called to Malé had been arrested and, convicted of staging or supporting a rebellion, had been exiled for periods of from one to fifteen years. The islanders at Addu Atoll were understandably submissive.

At the meetings in Colombo the Maldivian representatives insisted on checking every detail of the pay and conditions of the Adduan work force. Rates of pay; benefits in kind; hours; holidays and dhoni hire rates, each was examined in fine detail and, by the 16th of March, after a great deal of hard bargaining, the British High Commissioner was convinced that the two sides were close to an agreement. Even though their government's taxation programme would make a mockery of any pay rise the Adduans might receive as a result of the 1963 survey, the Maldivian officials were adamant that the programme would not be changed. It was akin to blackmailing the Ministry of Defence. Either the Adduans would have to receive a very large pay rise, which would actually make it cheaper for the Ministry of Defence to recruit more Pakistanis to work and live on Gan, or they would just have to put up with a considerable reduction in their already low standard of living, which would almost certainly make them resentful and would affect the working relationships at the atoll.

The Maldivian negotiators were fairly sure, given that the Chiefs-of-Staff were reluctant to increase the resident population on Gan and were fairly anxious to maintain amicable relations with the Adduan population, that the Maldivians would receive a large compensatory pay award. The impression they gave was that their ministers were now quite prepared to see the Adduans enjoying greater prosperity than before and becoming increasingly better off than Maldivians elsewhere in the archipelago provided that the central government received a major portion of any such new-found wealth.

By the end of March 1965 the serious negotiations had been completed and the British High Commissioner had embarked on a series of discussions with the Maldivian representatives in order to clarify the details of an agreement under which the Maldivian government retained its intended taxation programme and Britain was not held to be responsible for policing the Adduans' illegal trading with visiting merchant ships. As if to reinforce the complexity of that particular issue and to demonstrate why the British would have nothing to do with the problem, the SS Everglory, a merchant ship frequently contracted to deliver supplies to the NAAFI, re-appeared at Addu Atoll early in April to the undoubted delight of the Adduans, the amusement of the British and the frustration of the Maldivian officials.

By then, Wing Commander Moss, whose original tour of duty had been extended five times to cover a politically turbulent period, was in the throes of handing over command to his successor, Wing Commander Scannell. Among the many abiding memories of his sixteen turbulent months at the atoll was one which gave him enormous satisfaction because it illustrated that in spite of all the political manoeuvring he had managed to establish as genuine a relationship with Moosa Ali Didi, the atoll chief, as he could have wished. On the 11th of April, his penultimate day on Gan, two Maldivians brought him a farewell present from the chief: a live turtle. It was a generous gesture which left him in a quandary. He could not bring himself to have it killed for the dinner table even though fresh turtle on the menu was something of a delicacy. Nor could he insult Moosa Ali Didi by returning his gift. His solution was to have the turtle returned to the sea and to write a very appreciative letter to the chief explaining, with regret, that he would not be permitted to take the turtle back to England. With his letter Moss sent Moosa a pen asking him to accept it as a token of a friendship which could continue for as long as they could write to each other.

Moss, like every other Gannite, would never forgot his experiences at Addu Atoll but it was the circumstances surrounding Mohammed Saeed's arrest which were uppermost in his mind day after day long after returning to England. Many months after handing over to Scannell and leaving the atoll Moss wrote to the Maldivian Affairs officer on Gan asking for news of Saeed and was delighted to hear by return of post that as his letter arrived at Gan so too did Saeed, released from Malé and allowed to return home.

Neither he, nor anyone else, could have imagined what the future held for the unfortunate Saeed.

Wing Commander Scannell was fortunate enough to arrive at Gan just as the political arguments between the Maldivian and British governments had ended, at least for the time being. In Colombo, discussions continued in an atmosphere of friendly co-operation and by June details of the new agreement had been hammered out with plans for the usual exchange of complimentary letters. In July the Sultan of the Maldives, His Highness Mohammed Farid Didi I, accompanied by the Honourable Ibrahim Nasir, the Maldivian prime minister, arrived unexpectedly in Colombo, apparently for medical treatment. The British High Commissioner, whilst respecting the reason for their unexpected visit, took the opportunity to make arrangements for the new agreement to be signed and, with little ceremony, he and the Maldivian Prime Minister signed the documents on the 26th of July in the High Commissioner's residence. They also agreed to meet again in Malé on the 28th of the month for a more formal signing ceremony. The already well-established details of Maldivian independence together with the protection agreement with Britain were all incorporated in the document and complemented by details of leasehold arrangements for the lands at Addu Atoll.

Britain emerged from the ceremony with very favourable terms. Her Majesty's Government was granted the use of Gan and part of Hitaddu free of charge until the 15th of December 1986 provided all the conditions of the agreement were met. There was nothing in the agreement about the use of the Maldivian rupee as the official currency for the payment of Adduan employees although there were two conditions related to wages and trading. As far as wages were concerned the agreement required that, by the 28th of July 1966 all Maldivians employed on the military sites would be paid only in cash; the use of rice issues as payment-in-kind was to be discontinued no later than that date. There was no mention of the illegal trading which the Maldivian government was so anxious to eradicate but there was a clause which prohibited any Maldivian from trading directly with the NAAFI, a practice which had grown dramatically since 1960 but which was to be replaced by the establishment of Maldivian government - nominated traders who would act as intermediaries between the NAAFI and the Adduans. That was a desirable arrangement as far as NAAFI staff were concerned because it meant that the Maldivian government would be able to collect its dues *via* the nominated traders.

Sir Michael Walker, based in Ceylon, became the first British Ambassador to the Maldives and it was agreed that until Maldivian passports became internationally accepted, he would issue British passports to those Maldivian citizens whose applications had been approved by their government. The agreement did not require any British political representation to be established in the Maldives, thus leaving the way clear for Britain to recall or transfer Arthington-Davy without appearing to accede to a Maldivian demand.

In effect, Britain had been given strategic facilities at Addu Atoll in exchange for the already-agreed eight hundred and fifty thousand pounds in economic aid, one hundred and fifty thousand pounds of which was due to be paid in 1965. It was a remarkable about-face by a government which had so loudly declared its intention of ridding the archipelago of the British whom they had accused of inciting a revolution in the southern atolls. Given that background it was remarkable that Nasir had settled for no more than the aid package agreed in 1960 and the anticipated tax revenue from the Adduans when he could almost certainly have demanded, and got, far more than that.

Amongst the Adduans there was a general feeling of relief that the two governments had reached what seemed to be a final agreement. They did not know exactly what had been agreed but their view was that the agreement signalled the end of the inter-governmental acrimony which had pervaded for over five years and that, they were convinced, would allow them to go about their daily business without fear of attack. They were not under the illusion that life would be easy in the coming year just because the political climate was more settled at national level; they knew only too well that local politics were still simmering and were always likely to come to the boil. They were also well aware that with the return of their central government's authority at the atoll they would be closely watched; already they had been ordered to build accommodation on each of their inhabited islands for five members of the government militia from Malé and to provide accommodation on Hitaddu for a Government Representative. It was quite obvious to all of them that, in essence, they were to be supervised by their government's military police and their behaviour reported to Malé by a locally based official.

In July the atoll chief announced that atoll committee elections would be held in August. His announcement coincided with the return to the atoll of Mohammed Saeed who had finally been released from Malé after his arrest some sixteen months earlier. A firm believer in justice and in the rights of the individual as espoused in the Maldivian constitution, Saeed had paid dearly for helping to persuade the Adduans to accept the authority of their central government. Released after being detained for fifteen months he returned to Addu Atoll just in time to stand as a Hitaddu candidate in the atoll committee elections, timing that was to lead to a slightly embarrassing situation for the station commander.

When Saeed had been arrested, Rounthwaite and Moss had both been taken aback but, realising that to take issue with the Maldivian government over Saeed's treatment would merely have prejudiced his case even further, they could do little more than recognise his work for Rounthwaite by promising that he would receive back pay for the period of his absence. Although no-one had envisaged his being away for so long, both Scannell and the RAF's Maldivian Affairs officer felt that it was right to continue to honour that promise in view of the manner in which he had been persuaded to present himself to the authorities in Malé.

But Saeed's candidature in the forthcoming local election identified him as a political rival of the atoll chief and the Command staff in Singapore considered that it would be unwise to issue his back pay before the local elections had been held in case that were to be interpreted as providing support for his political campaign. For the same reason he was not immediately offered a job in place of that which had ended when the political adviser had left. That was typical of the way in which even slightly sensitive issues were dealt with by the Command staff who had learned that in Maldivian affairs nothing was trivial and anything could be turned into a political issue. Wing Commander Scannell ensured that they were well aware of Saeed's previous work for the RAF but it was to no avail; the message to the station commander was:

'...the issue of his back pay will be dealt with after the August elections and the question of his re-employment must await the approval of the Maldivian Government'.

Saeed was indignant about such cavalier treatment from his previous employer particularly in view of his work record but, like most Maldivians, there was nothing he could do about it except complain. That got him nowhere because he was complaining to a Maldivian Affairs officer who agreed with him but was unable to re-employ him or to issue his back pay.

Relations with Moosa had been quite good since his February return from Malé and as the August elections approached they became even better. Confirmed in office by his government, he did not have to stand for re-election but was still apparently anxious to be seen working for the good of the Adduans. In late July and early August he had several friendly meetings with the station commander at which it became obvious that, probably acting under orders from Malé, he was no longer pursuing the idea of removing all non-Maldivian Asians from the atoll even though that had been such a high priority for him in May. He had shifted his focus and wished to discuss the future loss of the rice issue and a compensatory pay rise.

Even though it was of interest to those Adduans who were employed on the military sites it was hardly an urgent matter because it had already been agreed that some seven thousand pounds of rice would still be issued as payment-in-kind each week until the middle of July 1966. Subsequently, employees who would previously have qualified for a rice issue would be entitled to a free meal each day so the debate was about a sum of money to represent the difference between the value of the rice issue and the value of the free meals. Tied in with this was a request that the NAAFI should be allowed to sell more rice to the Adduans once the free issues ceased because, with most of the trading buggaloes laid up, the islanders would have difficulty obtaining supplies from elsewhere. But all this was a year hence. It was not a serious debate; it was a preliminary warning of discussions to come and it served Moosa's purpose which was to ensure that the Adduans knew that he had the issues on his agenda.

The local election campaigns ran amid vague accusations of the mismanagement and embezzlement of the Adduan Trading Corporation funds and of blackmail and threats against those who dared to voice such opinions. Voting took place throughout the atoll on the 15th of August. Rather surprisingly, in view of the hostility shown to him by most Adduans when he had helped Rounthwaite to extol the virtues of a return to central government authority in 1963, Mohammed Saeed was elected to represent Hitaddu on the atoll committee. He promptly declared that he would rather work for the RAF on Gan than serve on the committee. As he had expected, that provoked Moosa into reporting the matter to Malé with a request that Saeed be permitted to work for the RAF.

The request was approved with remarkable speed, a delighted Saeed promptly resigned from the atoll committee and by mid-September he had taken up employment on Gan as an RAF interpreter, a job which he planned to hold at least until 1966 when he hoped to go to India on a university scholarship. The atoll chief, pleased to see Saeed moving to the sidelines of the political arena, was just as satisfied. The only sour note to an arrangement which was otherwise to everyone's satisfaction was that Saeed had been awarded only one hundred pounds back pay for the sixteen months he had been away from Addu Atoll. Quite apart from the fact that he had lost a considerable income from the operation of the Maldivian hotel, that sum was totally unrepresentative of the wages he had lost, was to become the focus of ill-feeling from Saeed and was to lead to acrimonious debate between the RAF staff on Gan and the Command staff in Singapore.

As soon as the latest agreement had been signed and relations with Britain were virtually back to normal, the Maldivian government set about trying to establish its position in the world by asking Britain to sponsor its application for membership of the United Nations Organisation and by seeking world-wide recognition of its independent status. The Chinese, ever eager to seize an opportunity to extend their sphere of influence, were among the first to recognise the Maldivian nation and to enquire about the establishment of a mission in Malé. As early as August, the Ceylon Daily News published a report which, under the heading 'Peking jumps to it in the Maldives' reported that 'Chou-En-Lai wishes the Maldives success in their efforts to oppose imperialism and colonialism...'

The Maldivians, mindful of the likely long-term benefits of maintaining good relations with Britain and of the short-term plans to ask the British to help with the reconstruction of the Hulule runway, accepted the British perception of the Chinese as being unwelcome political troublemakers. Given that the presence of the friendly British had already brought a rebellion to the archipelago it is likely that the Maldivians were not averse to the Chinese *per se*, they just did not want to offer a toehold in Malé to any other nation. The upshot was that the Maldivian government welcomed its recognition by China but declared that an established Chinese presence in the capital was not desirable.

With the Maldivian and British governments apparently on friendly terms once again and with the local political differences at Addu Atoll apparently resolved, Wing Commander Scannell could reasonably have been looking forward to a period of operational stability during which Econium would not be implemented, the Adduans would not mount any demonstrations and the RAF Regiment reinforcements would not be called upon. Any such hopes were shattered in September when Pakistan and India squared up to each other and brought political and religious differences into the Pakistani community on Gan. The affair, described on page 267 was short-lived and by mid-October the only noticeable reminders of the problem were a few vacancies in the Pakistani workforce and a slight change of attitude on the part of some Pakistanis towards those compatriots who had agitated for repatriation. After that experience Scannell was more aware than ever of the operational impact on Gan of events across the globe.

At least he could reflect that, at local level, Maldivian affairs seemed to be running as smoothly as could be expected. Relationships were generally amicable and there were even small gestures of friendship from the atoll chief which would have been unheard of twelve months earlier. Thus the station commander and five others, swimming off Wilingili, became the first servicemen allowed to set foot outside the leased territories that year when they were invited ashore by the chief and when the Air Officer Commanding, the Far East Air Force, on an informal visit to Gan in June 1965, was invited by the atoll chief to tour Hitaddu village Scannel was pleasantly surprised and rather intrigued because such an invitation, rarely extended to visiting officers, was normally reserved for those occasions when the chief was hoping to obtain some *quid pro quo* in the form of help from the RAF. On this occasion, however, it seemed to be no more than a genuine gesture of friendship.

The apparent desire to improve the relationship between the Maldivians and the Gan communities was sustained for months with occasional social contacts, particularly with the Adduans' fellow Moslems, the Pakistanis.

Nevertheless the improved relations had not helped to resolve one important problem for the Adduans: there was still no organised approach to the creation of a healthy environment for the villagers. Reducing the incidence of diseases which all too frequently ran to epidemic proportions was really a public hygiene and medical problem but it had taken on a political dimension with the result that logical arguments from the RAF medical officers were of little avail. The Maldivian government would only allow the RAF medical teams to visit the Adduan villages in exceptional circumstances and there was certainly no possibility that they would be allowed free access to organise the activities of a hygiene team even if the team were made up of Maldivians. Nor would the medical officers be given permission to establish clinics outside the leased territories. The best that could be done was to provide treatment on Gan for the ever-increasing number of Maldivians, many of them from as far away as Fua Mulaku or Huvadu, who were finding their way to the medical centre. For the medical staff, spending so much of their time treating Maldivians whose ill-health was a direct consequence of the environment in which they lived, it was frustrating in the extreme to be prevented, for purely political reasons, from tackling the causes of so much of the misery.

The atoll chief's disagreement with the RAF's senior medical officer in October 1964 and the subsequent employment of Pakistanis to man the hygiene section had created a situation from which the chief could only extricate himself with some loss of face and he was unlikely to do that just to alleviate the health problems of his villagers. A partial solution had been developed in January when the atoll committee finally ceased insisting upon the re-employment of Maldivians in the hygiene section and actually wrote to the senior medical officer asking for spraying equipment to be given to them for use in the villages. They would not, however, let any non-Maldivians into the atoll settlements either to undertake the spraying or to supervise the work. The result was inevitable, only the timing of the next epidemic was in doubt.

It was in May when the inevitable occurred; malaria and infective hepatitis struck down so many villagers on Hitaddu that it seemed to be only a matter of time before some islanders died.

With several hundred Maldivians coming to Gan each day the epidemic was quite likely to spread across the atoll like wildfire and a worried atoll chief felt obliged to ask for help. He contacted the senior medical officer and, when trying to explain why the epidemic had occurred, had to admit that, incredibly, the villagers were refusing to use the spraying equipment which had been provided by the RAF because they claimed that they were not being adequately paid for the amount of work entailed. The senior medical officer, aware that the epidemic could severely disrupt the operation of the RAF base, immediately offered to employ the villagers on hygiene duties at a fair rate of pay. Nothing, however, could be arranged that easily in the political climate of the time and the atoll chief did not dare to accept the offer without first receiving official approval from Malé.

When the Maldivian Minister of Health learnt that the proposal would involve the presence of European supervisors in the Adduan villages he vetoed the plan, leaving the islanders to hope that the epidemic would burn itself out before the death toll became too great, and the RAF's senior medical officer to hope that it could be prevented from spreading onto the military sites.

Their hopes were partially realised and then dealt a savage blow. Deaths amongst the villagers, where the very elderly were particularly at risk, were fewer than had been anticipated and frequent health checks of the Maldivians employed on the military sites helped to prevent the diseases from spreading into the expatriate community. Then, in October, typhoid broke out among the Adduans. The outbreak was confirmed by the RAF's medical staff on the 18th of the month and a signal sent to the Command staff in Singapore informing them of four confirmed cases of typhoid among the Maldivians on Hitaddu and a further three suspected cases.

Although all the Europeans, Pakistanis and Ceylonese had been inoculated against all the diseases which they were likely to encounter at the atoll, the openness of the RAF's Hitaddu transmitter site, which was bisected by a public right of way for the villagers, was a cause of some concern, as was the number of Hitadduans employed both on that site and on Gan. The atoll chief was in favour of inoculating all the Adduans but, quite apart from the cost of such an operation, the medical officers could foresee problems both with the timescale, for approximately nine months was required for a person to receive the series of three injections, and with the diagnosis of typhoid cases which were masked by the initial fever reaction to the inoculations.

Moosa, well aware that his failure to ensure the implementation of an adequate spraying programme had helped to bring about the present situation, was in a dilemma. Very reluctant to ask his government for permission to allow the RAF medical staff to supervise such a programme in the villages he explained that he would prefer his government to be approached through the British High Commissioner, presenting the problem as one of concern to the British.

When that suggestion was turned down, he was left with little alternative but to inform his minister of the situation. His radio link with the capital meant that his request was dealt with immediately and Moosa, on learning that the Maldivian Minister of Health had given permission for an RAF medical team to visit any of the villages to treat the sick and to supervise the spraying programme, seemed more relieved to hear that he would not be called to Malé to account for his failures than he was to hear that his request had been granted. The chief's relief on escaping criticism from Malé combined with the team's work in the villages helped to foster good relations through November with the medical team being welcomed wherever they went and the station commander, accompanied by the Maldivian Affairs officer being given an escorted tour of Maradu and Fedu, yet another unheard of gesture of friendship from Moosa.

It took just one month for relations to become soured, this time as a result of a cost-cutting decision by the district works officer. In December he dismissed fifty Ministry-employed Maldivians and the chief retaliated by refusing to supply labour to unload a ship on the 23rd of the month, the day before Ramadan started. The district officer simply drummed up enough casual labour to get the job done with the result that the chief visited Gan on Christmas Eve and, after some discussion, agreed to co-operate. It seemed, however, as though the recent period of goodwill had come to an end, at least until the chief needed help of one sort or another.

Whilst the major cause for concern at Addu Atoll had been the outbreak of typhoid so soon after the other epidemics, the Command staff in Singapore had been addressing the question of repairs to the airfield on Hulule. The Vice-Chief of the Air Staff had already agreed to provide advice and help, which would generate good publicity, but was not prepared to provide funds out of the defence vote. It was not so much that the Hulule project was excessively expensive, it was simply that it was a foreign aid matter, not a defence matter and experience had long since shown that foreign aid matters, especially those involving the Maldivian government, tended to become sagas with escalating costs.

The Far East Air Force Command staff had informed the Ministry of Defence in September that radar and lights were not needed, that the bitumen and cement would cost no more than twenty thousand pounds but that shipping costs for delivery to that remote part of the world would amount to an additional nine thousand pounds.

The British High Commissioner, however, had received the Maldivians' multi-page request for materials and equipment for Hulule, a request which went far beyond the supply of bitumen and cement. It included radar equipment and runway lights and ranged from Land Rovers to hacksaws; everything that could possibly be needed to re-establish and operate the airport had been listed.

The Defence Adviser in Colombo was not prepared to offer anything more than expertise and the loan of construction plant so the Maldivians' request was passed to the Commonwealth Relations Office in London, subsequently becoming the focus of lengthy discussions *via* the British High Commissioner in Colombo. The upshot was that Britain provided expertise, the loan of some construction plant and money for the purchase of bitumen and cement. The Maldivians were left to provide the necessary shipping, the equipment and the labour force, an arrangement which left them disgruntled but not really surprised.

The project started early in January 1966 and suffered a series of setbacks, the worst occurring later that month when the City of Victoria, a Panamanian-flagged vessel owned by the Maldivians, was shipwrecked on a reef near Hulule. Fully laden with bitumen, the ship was abandoned by the crew. Only the tenacity of the Maldivians saved the cargo which they loaded into their dhonis before the shipwrecked vessel disintegrated.

In spite of the setbacks the Maldivians completed the project virtually on schedule, re-opening the airfield on the 27th of March.

1966 began quietly enough at Addu Atoll. If the works department dispute still rankled with the atoll chief he gave no signs of it. Throughout January he was as friendly and co-operative as when the RAF medical teams had been dealing with the outbreak of typhoid. Then, in the first week of February, he asked for help to retrieve a marooned launch, a request which seem innocuous enough but which was to lead to unforeseen problems.

Moosa was one of only six Adduans who owned a motor launch. His, named Scout, had originally been purchased by the Adduan Trading Corporation for four thousand four hundred pounds and was in good condition because it had frequently been repaired in the RAF's marine craft unit. The atoll chief had never had any qualms about asking for such work to be done, even when he had been making life difficult for the station commander and, out of goodwill, his requests had never been refused.

The other five launches were not as reliable as Scout and one was apparently marooned at Huvadu, having broken down on the way back from Malé. Rather than send his own launch, the most reliable of the six, to retrieve the one which had broken down, Moosa asked the station commander if an RAF launch could be sent out on a rescue and repair mission. Scannell readily agreed to that and the RAF boat crew set out, accompanied by Mohammed Saeed who had volunteered to act as the interpreter.

The RAF launch entered the lagoon at Huvadu Atoll, angering the local chief who had not given the RAF crew permission to sail into his waters. Discovering an interpreter on board, the chief's anger focussed on the luckless Saeed who was to pay dearly for his offer to accompany the crew. By the time Moosa's launch had been repaired and the rescuers and rescued had returned to Gan, the Huvaduan atoll chief had informed Malé of the invasion of his territory. As a result Moosa was reprimanded by his government and instructed to ask the British for nothing. Fearful of being seen not to give his wholehearted support for this instruction he banned the Adduans from participating in any activities not directly related to their employment, even ending the Morse Code training as well as the social activities such as football matches against any RAF teams.

The Maldivian government also instructed any Maldivian who had accompanied the RAF to Huvadu to report to Malé and that worried Saeed who had already had one close encounter with the Maldivian legal system. His experience of previous intervention on his behalf, by Rounthwaite, made him too frightened to accept an offer for the RAF to intercede, particularly at a time when Nasir was away and his deputy seemed to be encouraging the growth of anti-British feeling in Malé.

Saeed duly went to the capital in mid-February 1966 where he discovered that his fears were fully justified. As punishment for assisting the RAF and encouraging the crew to take their launch into the lagoon at Huvadu

Atoll he was held in Malé for almost twelve weeks and then kept for a further six weeks in the detention centre on Guido, a small penal island at Horsborough Atoll. His case provided a clear illustration, if any were needed, of the way in which any Maldivian who, in the eyes of his government, became too closely associated with the British was made to suffer. For Saeed this latest run-in with the authorities in Malé was merely a brief chapter in what was to become a saga for he was, over the years, to be treated by his government in a way which was obviously intended to be an example to other Adduans of the fate which would befall them if they stepped even slightly out of line. That made life precarious for some of the islanders who genuinely wanted to help the British but were frightened that they would be reported by someone wishing to ingratiate himself with the authorities or just acting out of personal animosity.

The treatment meted out to Saeed combined with the rebuke from Malé certainly affected Moosa's behaviour. Obviously anxious to give his central government no chance to discredit him, he became obstructive on every aspect of the Adduans' involvement with the British creating, in the process, some inconveniences for the RAF and hardship for many Adduans. The blanket permission for Gan's medical officers and hygienists to go into the island settlements was replaced by a system whereby the weekly programme of visits had to be submitted to the British High Commissioner in Colombo for approval by the Maldivian Government Representative. Inevitably, such a system meant that approval was not given in time and the scheduled visits were cancelled, leaving the villagers suffering, the doctors irritated and the atoll chief feeling secure in his relationship with his own government.

In those early months of 1966 when the Maldivian government was reacting over-sensitively to the incursion into Huvadu Atoll, the British government was considering the implications of allowing the French Air Force to use Addu Atoll as a regular staging post. Like Britain, the French needed to fly military aircraft to the Far East to support their nuclear test programme and the Maldivian government had already given blanket clearance for one year for unarmed French military aircraft to over-fly or stage through the Maldives even though Article 1 (2) of the Partial Test Ban Treaty implied that Britain should deny the French the use of Gan's facilities for flights even indirectly related to their nuclear test programme. The British government was well aware, however, that the French had already taken a tough line with the United States of America by threatening to refuse the American military the right to over-fly French territory if the American government would not allow Mirage II jets and KC 135 tankers to over-fly America .

The concern was that, if denied access to the facilities on Gan, the French would apply the same tough line against Britain as they had against America and with over five hundred operational flights and one hundred non-operational flights over France every month, the RAF would have found re-routing both inconvenient and expensive. The Defence and Overseas Policy Committee studied the implications of the French request and opted for a purely pragmatic approach, advising the Secretary of State for Defence that Britain could cope with any hassle from the Maldivians far more easily than from the French and that it would be best not to be too fussy about the use of Gan. Thus the French were given access to the airfield at Gan and were asked for nothing more than assurances that their military aircraft which used the facilities were not carrying materials related to the atomic test programme. The French were presumably quite happy to provide whatever assurances were required in the knowledge that the British would not enquire too closely into the matter for fear of exposing a subterfuge. The Maldivians must have suspected that the conditions of the lease for Gan were being broken but they chose not to confront the British over the issue, probably because proof would have been so hard to obtain and with the 1965 settlement so close to the final stages of implementation they did not wish to continue with their usual practice of making wild and unsubstantiated accusations. The result was that for the next ten years French military aircraft staged through Gan whenever they wished without ever becoming the focus of any political exploitation by the Maldivians. The Adduans were not bothered about the use of the staging post by French aircraft carrying nuclear weapons, they only involved themselves in matters which affected their daily living and that was certainly not so in this case.

The political manoeuvring which did concern the Maldivians early in 1966 was that which came as a result of the re-appearance of typhoid at the atoll. The first cases were diagnosed late in February but the atoll chief dared not invite the medical officers into the villages to treat or vaccinate any of the islanders even though there was every chance that without medical intervention the Adduans would be struck by an epidemic. Early in March the Maldivian government, anxious to show that it was not leaving the matter to be dealt with by the RAF medical teams, sent their hospital ship, the Golden Ray, to the atoll on an investigative visit.

The medical staff on board were accompanied by Hassan Didi, the Maldivian deputy minister for home affairs who was friendly enough but was under orders not to allow any non-Maldivian personnel to go beyond the boundaries of the leased territories. Whilst reserving judgement on the vaccination of every Adduan who worked on the military sites, he readily gave his permission for Gan's medical officers to vaccinate all the food-handling Maldivians employed by the British. He, and the doctors from the Golden Ray, accepted an invitation to dine in the officers' mess on the evening of their arrival, much to the concern of the atoll chief who accompanied them and who spent the evening on tenterhooks worrying that in the general course of conversation some remark might be made which would land him in trouble with his government.

The investigation into the Adduans' health problems was a sizeable task and whenever the Maldivians undertook any large-scale operation there were problems. True to form they ran into difficulties during their visit in March when their ship's engineer reported that the Golden Ray's generators had become unserviceable and he was unable to repair them with the spares and equipment at his disposal. Also true to form, the Maldivian minister promptly turned to the RAF for help which, as always, was willingly given.

With the ship's generators repaired and the Adduans' health problems assessed, Hassan Didi and his medical team set sail for Malé, promising that the Golden Ray would return in a few weeks, bringing medical staff and anti-typhoid vaccine. The promise was kept. In May the ship returned with two World Health Organisation doctors on board who supervised the medical staff throughout the vaccination of over seven thousand nine hundred Adduans during the week that the ship spent in the lagoon. As before, Hassan Didi accompanied the medical team and again ensured that the RAF medical staff were not involved in the vaccination programme.

On the 12th of April 1966 Wing Commander Scannell, having completed his one-year tour of duty, handed over command of RAF Gan to Wing Commander Rees who, arriving in between the visits by the Golden Ray, was given an early introduction to Maldivian politics to complement the briefing he had been given in London prior to his departure for Addu Atoll. As his senior medical officer pointed out, it was all very well for the Maldivian government to mount a vaccination programme with the help of the World Health Organisation but it would have been so much more effective to have permitted the RAF staff to supervise the work of the hygiene committees which had been set up in every village but which were patently not doing a proper job.

One month after the first visit by the Golden Ray five new typhoid cases were confirmed and there was no way of knowing whether there were other unreported cases amongst the villagers. One thousand four-ounce tins of sterilising powder were available for the hygiene committees who were reported as having sterilised no more than twenty wells out of an estimated one thousand five hundred drinking-water wells at the atoll. The committees did not respond when asked how much chlorine they needed, seemingly because the members were frightened of the political implications of having any involvement with the RAF; they had seen what had happened to Mohammed Saeed.

Saeed actually returned to the atoll on the 23rd of June, having spent some eighteen weeks in Malé and on Guido, on charges which were apparently not upheld. He came back to his twenty-pounds-a-month job grateful for the help he had received from the British High Commissioner in Colombo and keen to resume his work as an interpreter. He was also anxious to settle the question of back pay, both for this latest absence and for his previous, sixteen-month period. That, inevitably, had to be referred to the Command staff in Singapore.

Saeed, however, didn't have time to settle down, let alone wait for a decision from Singapore on his back pay. On the 12th of July, just two weeks before the atoll chief was due to attend the Independence Day celebrations in the capital, Saeed was again ordered to report to Malé. Once again he needed the support of his employers but, on being made aware of the situation, the British High Commissioner, whilst agreeing that Saeed seemed to be suffering some rather harsh treatment, made the point that he was a Maldivian national and that Britain had no real justification for becoming involved with the Maldivian government in this affair. The High Commissioner did promise, however, that he would mention to Sattar, the Maldivian minister, that Saeed's frequent removal was an inconvenience to the RAF, a rather odd approach to take in view of the fact that Sattar would certainly have been pleased to know that the RAF was being inconvenienced, a fact which did not auger well for Saeed's future.

Abdullah Jameel, the Malé-based son of the Maldivian Chief Justice, was appointed temporary atoll chief at Addu Atoll to cover Moosa's absence but his arrival didn't change the local politics of health care to any appreciable extent. At first he refused to accept any sterilising powder in spite of the approval given by the Maldivian government and the instructions for use given by the World Health Organisation doctors. The situation had become so impossible that on the 20th of the month the station commander signalled the British Representative in Colombo and the Far East Air Force Command staff saying:

> *'I am in tears of frustration. We have asked, nay begged, both the atoll chief and the newly arrived acting atoll chief to accept the chlorine powder for water sterilisation. Our most recent letter stated that we had been informed by the Malé Government that they had instructed the atoll office to accept the powder. There has still been no reaction. Ahmed Salih, the English speaking Hitaddu village headman and atoll committee treasurer who is in charge of well chlorination was speaking to Hughes this week. Hughes actually saw Dr Tawil's written instructions given during the visit in May. These described how to calculate the quantity of powder needed, clearly stating that it was desirable to treat wells on every island at least fortnightly when powder was available.*
>
> *It was emphasised that we had all the supplies needed and we have been trying for weeks to get the Adduans to accept. Salih said he no longer has any water sterilisation powder even for wells of known typhoid houses but that he could not take powder without the authority of the atoll chief who would need permission from Malé. I begin to think that it may be easier to treat rather than prevent typhoid since the only means of delivery seems to be aerial bombardment.'*

The signal seems to have started a chain reaction from Colombo to Hitaddu *via* Malé for eventually, on the 25th of July, Jameel allowed the atoll committee to accept five hundred tins of powder. Word soon came back to Gan that the World Health Organisation instructions were not being followed but without permission to supervise the work there was little the senior medical officer could do short of blackmailing the Adduans by threatening to withdraw all medical services from the non-entitled islanders until he was satisfied with the water sterilisation programme and that was not something he was prepared to consider. All that could be done once the powder had been delivered was to wait and hope that the villagers would eventually see the sense in following instructions which were intended to protect their health.

In the week that Jameel arrived at Addu Atoll, the Maldivian government had licensed the traders referred to in the 1965 agreement, thereby introducing the generally unpopular changes in the trading arrangements for the Maldivians. From that day all official trade with the Adduans had to be channelled through traders who were under government control and who could lose their licences unless they correctly implemented all the regulations on trading and on the taxation of goods. Their nominations, on the 15th of July, came the day after the Maldivian employees on Gan and Hitaddu received the last issue of rice in lieu of wages, again in accordance with the 1965 agreement. That left the traders in control of the supply of a staple food as well as general commodities. The villagers were angry. They believed that the traders would be used as agents of their government to squeeze every penny that they could out of the islanders.

The Adduans had only a few days grace before the eight nominated traders set up their organisation on the 4th of August and they made the most of it. For the last two weeks of July they bought all that they could in order to avoid the pending taxes. They bought as much rice as they could store without it deteriorating, as much fuel as they had cans for and as many general items as they could afford.

The station commander was well aware that the new arrangements would have a dramatic effect on the Adduans' lives because a considerable percentage of their pay would be taken in taxes levied through the traders but there was no quick solution which could be offered. Wage rates for the Adduans were roughly in line with those paid by Brown and Company, the only significant foreign employer in Malé, and were linked to the Pakistani wages paid at Addu Atoll. If the British Treasury were to agree to a substantial pay rise for the Adduans, and that was unlikely, the islanders could then find themselves priced out of work by becoming more expensive than the Pakistanis. All these considerations were explored at the Far East Air Force conference attended by Rees and his Maldivian Affairs officer from the 5th to the 8th of August but no decisions were reached: the message to the Adduans was '...*be patient, we are working on it'*. That was hardly a reassuring comment in view of the fact that the situation had been discussed in considerable detail during the negotiations which led to the signing of the 1965 agreement, but it seemed to be the standard response whenever any suggestion was made that incurred expenditure for the benefit of the Maldivians.

The staff at the British Treasury dragged their heels whenever possible, even to the extent of avoiding the payment of legitimate debts for as long as possible, and preferably for ever. Whereas the Adduans had come to expect that sort of attitude from their own government they had not expected it from the British. Now they felt hard done by on three counts.

They had never received any payment from the funds of the defunct Adduan Trading Corporation and the shareholders, assuming that their government had confiscated the Corporation's funds without formally stating so, had given up hope of ever receiving any money.

They felt let down by the British who had never paid them compensation for the trees which had been destroyed during the construction period even though the Air Ministry had agreed to pay fourteen thousand pounds to the Adduans and six thousand pounds to the Maldivian government. Frequent signals from the station commander to the Air Ministry on that issue had brought no action and the islanders had eventually decided that they had been robbed of what was legitimately theirs. In total they were some thirty thousand pounds out of pocket in an economy where three pounds a week constituted a reasonable wage.

Now they faced the third financial blow: increased taxation and no signs of a pay rise.

The islanders, remarkably patient with the RAF but still angry with their government, took any opportunity they could to reduce their tax burden and, as if in answer to their prayers, the SS Everglory sailed through the Gan gap and dropped anchor in the lagoon on the 6th of September. Owned by the Tek Hwa shipping company in Singapore the Everglory was an occasional visitor to Addu Atoll, delivering supplies to the NAAFI and bringing heavy equipment or materials for the RAF.

The atoll chief and the station commander were both well aware that the Maldivian government only permitted foreign shipping into the lagoon at Addu Atoll on the clear understanding that direct trade between the ships' crews and the Maldivians was illegal. The law was clear enough but to the Adduans the Everglory was one giant floating warehouse filled with goods which they wished to buy and which the ship's Chinese crew was only too willing to sell. The station commander was in an invidious position. If he deployed the marine craft unit's boats in an attempt to prevent the islanders'

dhonis from approaching the Everglory he would sour relations with the Maldivian workforce. If he did not try to prevent the illegal trading he would be providing the Maldivian government with yet more ammunition to use against the British. The impossibility of trying to prevent the Adduans from trading with the Everglory's crew was neatly summed up in the signal which he sent to the Singapore-based Command staff on the 7th of September saying:

> 'Everglory entered lagoon approximately midnight September sixth boarded by Adduans whilst making way. The Officer Commanding Marine Section boarded as soon as he could force a passage through local fleet and presented letter to master from me asking him not to trade. Master agreed to put up notice forbidding trade but said it would be impossible to enforce. By this time bicycles, bales of material and cases of all types of goods found in Eastern bazaars were pouring over the sides into local boats. Queues formed outside most cabins. Impossible to estimate amount of Sterling changing hands but many locally employed Adduans are known to have sums of approximately one hundred and fifty to two hundred pounds on them leaving Gan yesterday.
>
> Would suggest something in the region of ten to fifteen thousand pounds will change hands as, apart from NAAFI, this is the main outlet. Atoll chief has asked Malé for instructions but he has had no reply so is doing nothing for fear of reprisals from Malé. He has ignored all our requests and have just sent him another request over the radio asking him to stop dhonis approaching ship. I do not expect any action, locals very much resent our interference on their red letter day and in our own interests of good relations I have made it quite clear that it is Malé that wishes to stop this trade.
>
> Will no doubt get usual untruthful report from Malé and it is painfully obvious that they only wish to make relations between Adduans and RAF as difficult as possible. Between midnight and seven a.m. about two hundred Adduans including some nominated traders boarded Everglory and at present ship is surrounded by dhonis. Do not feel I can take any further action to stop trading except to watch and observe the festival of Everglory colourful and picturesque and bringing happiness to all Adduans'.

During the ship's first night in the lagoon an RAF patrol observed large quantities of goods being transferred from the ship into dhonis owned by prominent Adduan citizens. The patrol observed and reported but took no action.

The merchantman left the atoll on the 9th of September and the affair was allowed to die down with remarkably little comment from Malé. The reason for that became clear later in the month when it transpired that some of the goods obtained from the ship by prominent Adduans were consigned to Malé, leaving no doubt that the Maldivian officials, despite their public posturing over illegal trade and their attempts to blame the RAF for such breaches of the law, were condoning such behaviour and, in some cases, were personally benefiting from it.

At least Moosa had been spared the embarrassment of coping with the Everglory episode for he had been in Malé, returning to Hitaddu on the 22nd of September to take over from Jameel. The Adduans were not at all happy at his return because his renewed over-cautious and generally obstructive attitude did not allow them to foster the kind of relationship which they preferred to have with the British. They were, however, very careful to avoid falling foul of him because they had taken note of the fact that whereas their chief had returned from the capital, Saeed had not.

It was almost certain that the chief's rediscovered obstructiveness resulted from his experiences in Malé which, given Saeed's complaints about him, could not have been as pleasant as he would have wished. Certainly he appeared anxious not to be involved with the RAF in any way which could be misconstrued by his government and one predictable result of that approach was that the health care of the Adduans became increasingly based upon treatment rather than prevention.

The Command staff in Singapore, recognising the additional, albeit unofficial, demands being made on the medical staff had already agreed, in June, to take onto the RAF establishment the Adduans employed to treat other Maldivians in the Gan medical centre. But as the demands on his staff continued to grow, the senior medical officer formally requested an increase in his budget for the treatment of Maldivians from five thousand pounds per annum to ten thousand, a request which would not be answered for months.

Whilst waiting for a response he sought information from about fifty Maldivian employees in an attempt to discover how many of the Adduans' wells were being chlorinated. According to them only about five per cent were being treated and even those were not being treated daily. The result of such inactivity was that most of the five hundred tins of powder which had been handed over in July were reportedly still in the atoll office in October. It was obvious that unless the chlorination programme was supervised on site by RAF staff, the Maldivians would never bother about it, they would just wait for the next epidemic and then ask for help.

There were many periods, and the last quarter of 1966 was one such, when the behaviour of the local Maldivian officials was quite incomprehensible to a European. They would suddenly embark on a pattern of non-cooperation for no obvious reason and although it could generally be assumed that some radio message from Malé had brought about such a change that was not always so. On many occasions local behaviour which was unhelpful and, in some cases, actually harmful to the Adduans was also contrary to the expectations of the Maldivian government.

Whether or not the atoll chief had been offended by the medical officers' continuing attempts to initiate a well-chlorination programme throughout the atoll was not clear but October saw the start of several more months of obstructive behaviour by the atoll officials. They scrupulously applied every policy which benefited the Adduans but would have nothing to do with any activity which indicated a measure of Maldivian goodwill towards the British. Thus paid employment, medical treatment and trading continued as normal as did the frequent requests for help in various ways, rarely followed by any thanks for the assistance rendered.

This uncooperative attitude did not generally extend beyond the atoll officials; the vast majority of the Adduans remained friendly and helpful. The Maldivian government, well aware of the situation, added legitimacy to the atoll chief's behaviour, even to the extent of telling him not to arrange a local demonstration of the Maldivian 'fish dance' for the entertainment of the Air Commander when he visited Gan in November, an event which was of little or no significance, but a snub which was important to the Maldivian ministers.

Some of the ill-feeling on the part of the officials may well have stemmed from the fact that an RAF check on the prices of goods sold to the Adduans by the nominated traders, who were mainly supplied from the NAAFI, disclosed that in three months prices had generally increased by fifteen to thirty per cent, in several cases had more than doubled and in some instances had increased to almost three and a half times the August price. Some of the increases were undoubtedly due to the imposition of taxes set by central government but taxation could not be blamed for many of the price rises. Nor could they be explained away as business expenses, for the traders had negligible overheads and purchased their commodities on very favourable terms from the NAAFI.

All of these points were explained to the Maldivian employees who had complained that they were finding it increasingly difficult to afford the commodities supplied by the traders and were beginning to ask when their pay would be increased. Moosa, aware of the check into the profits being made by the traders and the disclosure of information to the Maldivian employees, responded by complaining to his government about the behaviour of the RAF police when investigating recent thefts from Gan. His complaints of the detention and interrogation of Adduan employees and of by-passing the atoll chief when dealing with Maldivians had a hollow ring to them in view of his refusal to speak to or correspond with the RAF's Maldivian Affairs officer but they had the effect he desired. His govern-ment's representative in Ceylon complained to the British High Commissioner in Colombo who then sought an explanation from Gan's station commander.

The police investigations which the atoll chief had been referring to related to the theft of four tons of cement, seventy-two gallons of paint and several hundred packs of cigarettes, a significant crime on an island where the Maldivians found it fairly easy to remove the spoils of petty pilfering but where considerable ingenuity was needed to abscond with any sizeable haul. The investigation had been partially successful, with two hundred packs of cigarettes having been already recovered when the atoll chief made his complaint to Malé. Subsequently the investigation, which continued to be successful, had to be conducted with an awareness that it had become politically sensitive and that it was being undertaken at a time when the relationship between the atoll chief and the station executives had been soured.

By December 1966 Moosa was not responding to any of the RAF's attempts to contact him. He had become so anxious not to upset his government in any way that he even radioed Malé before giving approval for twelve Hitaddu children to attend a Christmas party on the communications site on Hitaddu where their parents were employed.

Towards the end of 1966 the Maldivian traders, sensitive to any possibil-ity of criticism from Malé and unhappy about the way in which their prices were being monitored, decided to purchase all their rice from Rangoon instead of buying it from the NAAFI. The Rangoon rice was cheaper but delivery was unpredictable and just before Christmas the supplies failed to arrive. By then the NAAFI stocks had been reduced to reflect the reduced demand and when the traders were once again obliged to obtain their supplies from Gan they found that they could not obtain all that they wanted. Within a matter of days the rice stocks at the atoll were critically low.

Rice was a staple food for the Adduans and large regular supplies were needed for a population which had almost doubled since 1958 and which, at the end of 1966 was approaching ten thousand. The NAAFI had never failed to provide whatever quantities were needed and when the Maldivian traders failed to guarantee a regular supply, feelings against them began to run high. Fortunately for them Ramadan had started on the 13th of December and most of the islanders, when fasting through the daylight hours, tended to be rather lethargic which meant that the rice consumption that month was lower than usual. As the rice stocks dwindled, those factors saved the traders from being assaulted and, luckily for them, the Rangoon supplies arrived before the NAAFI stores were empty. The traders had learnt a lesson and the station commander was simply relieved that the RAF had not had to contend, on top of everything else, with rice riots by the labour force and the inevitable request for the RAF to fly supplies in from Ceylon or India.

Throughout 1966 the British had continued to dangle in front of their Adduan employees the same old carrot, improved pay and conditions for all their Maldivian workers, which had been used for the last two and a half years. Just before Christmas yet another team from Singapore arrived at Addu Atoll to investigate, once again, the conditions of service for the islanders. The intention was not to introduce changes in the near future but to produce a report with recommendations for consideration at the Ministry of Defence, simultaneously demonstrating to the Maldivians that the matter had not been forgotten. It was difficult for the Adduans to believe that the British were seriously considering any increase in the wage rates which had been set in 1958 and which ranged from just below ninepence (approxi-mately 3 ½ p) an hour to one shilling and sevenpence (approximately 8p) an hour for a few of the more senior employees. The lack of any pay rises during their period of so-called independence had not been of any great concern to the Adduans for those were years of very low taxation and cheap trading. But those advantages had gone and the islanders were beginning to complain that the British were forever investigating the matter but showing no serious intention of changing anything.

So the year drew to a close with the RAF executives being cold-shouldered by the Adduan officials and with the islanders feeling let down but very cautious in what they said or did. They knew that Mohammed Saeed was still detained in Malé and they knew that anyone who stepped too far out of line was quite likely to join him. What they were almost certainly unaware of was that Saeed believed his situation to be so precarious that he had written to Sir Stanley Tomlinson in October to ask for help in his struggle for justice, a request which the High Commissioner had turned down after discussing it with Rees who agreed that any offer of help for Saeed would be seen by the Maldivians as interference in their internal affairs and would thus almost certainly prejudice Saeed's case.

During the first week of 1967 the atoll chief asked for help for a bugga-loe said to be in difficulties as it approached the atoll. An RAF launch was sent to rescue the boat and its crew, only to discover that the buggaloe, a vessel incapable of tacking because of its design, merely needed a tow against an adverse wind. This incident, coming only a few days after the theft of three hundred and sixty feet of terylene rope from the Hitaddu site finally provoked the station commander into writing a letter of protest to the chief. He received no acknowledgement.

The same wall of silence met the NAAFI manager when he invited the chief and the nominated traders to a meeting to discuss trading arrange-ments and the provision of a dependable supply of rice for the Adduans.

There seemed to be no way in which anyone could initiate a dialogue with Moosa. Even the medical officers, whose services were so valued by the Maldivians, could not evoke any response from him even though they were still anxious to discuss the chlorination programme which continued to be a bone of contention. Gan-Fedu, where an unsupervised group of hygiene labourers employed by the RAF was spraying the wells and their environ-ment, seemed to be the only village in which the wells were being properly treated. Elsewhere, chlorination was unsatisfactory.

The general impression was that the atoll committee, wary of establish-ing too close a relationship with the British, was just not bothering to organise the work and the villagers wouldn't dare to do anything without the committee's backing.

In January influenza hit the Adduans. Although it was unlikely that this particular outbreak was of the strain so feared in the days of Francois Pyrard of Laval, any such outbreak amongst the Maldivians was potentially devastating, as evidenced by various accounts of epidemics and mass deaths over the centuries. The RAF medical officers, anxious not to risk the possibility of multiple deaths, supplied vaccines to villagers whom they had trained to give injections. Banned, by the atoll chief, from visiting the villagers themselves, the doctors just had to hope that as the epidemic spread across the atoll the vaccines were being administered. Within days rumours were reaching the senior medical officer that villagers were being charged for the injections but it was just not possible for him to determine the truth. His questions went unanswered and his accusations provoked no response from the atoll chief or any of the atoll officials. Whatever the politics of the situation, the epidemic passed, its effects probably mitigated by the vaccine but with no thanks due to Moosa who would not even acknowledge the role of the RAF's medical services in the affair.

There was a slight thaw in the political atmosphere after mid–January, just enough for the Maldivian officials to progress from stony silence to frigid civilities. It seemed to have been brought about by the December combination of a children's Christmas party on Gan, and inter-island dhoni race and the chief's awareness that improved pay scales and job descriptions for Maldivian employees had been submitted to the Far East Air Force Headquarters by the station commander.

The two-and-a-half-hour party was for the children of all the Maldivians employed on Gan and, attended by some one hundred and fifty youngsters, was an event which could hardly be ignored by the Adduan officials. That was also true of the inter-island dhoni race three days later when the islanders, servicemen and Ministry of Defence civilians all competed in the customary three-mile race.

After that the political thaw set in. February brought the British High Commissioner from Colombo to Gan with Air Marshal Rochford-Hughes, the air commander of the Far East Air Force. They expressed a wish to pay a courtesy visit to the atoll chief as part of their itinerary and, much to the station commander's surprise, such a visit was approved by the Maldivian government.

Accordingly they, accompanied by the station commander, the senior medical officer and the senior administrative officer, landed at Hitaddu in the afternoon of the 26th of February and were met by the Hitaddu headman, Ahmed Salih Ali Didi, who accompanied them to the atoll office where they met Moosa and the interpreter. It was the first time that the station commander had met the chief since May 1966. Moosa was a highly intelligent man, shrewd, with a strong personality and a better knowledge of English than he was prepared to admit. Firmly in control of the atoll, he was nevertheless under the Malé thumb and, whilst admitting that he wished to co-operate with the British, was at pains to point out that he was always constrained by his government's policies of the day. It was difficult, given the recent course of events, for the station commander to take seriously the chief's reference to the need to maintain goodwill but the opportunity was too good to miss and it was suggested that the chief should meet Rees every month. Effectively cornered, Moosa asked the High Commissioner to take up the idea with the Maldivian government, saying that once approval had been obtained from Malé he would be happy with such an arrangement.

The upshot was that, by March, meetings were back in favour and the atoll chief was pursuing a variety of benefits including revised rates of pay for Maldivian employees and the Maldivianisation of more jobs on the leased territories. That didn't mean that he felt free to act according to his own instinct. He even initially refused to accept a Far East Air Force plaque, saying that he would need permission from Malé before he could accept the gift which had been sent to him by Rochford-Hughes in appreciation of the hospitality extended to him the previous month. Relations continued to improve as the month progressed. The chief, pleased to be informed that the Singapore-based Command staff had sent their final proposals on Maldivian pay and trade groups to London, was happy to discuss any matters relating to the Adduan work force and was co-operative in helping to control the increasing number of Maldivians seeking medical treatment on Gan. In return Rees was only too happy to provide technicians to repair the chiefs' faulty Mercury radio telephone set and to arrange for a works inspection of the wiring in the atoll office on Hitaddu.

The radio provided the chief with a direct link to the Maldivian officials in Malé and he was so anxious for it to be repaired quickly that he was quite willing to allow the RAF technicians to effect the repair *in situ*. That repair was simple but the inspection of the atoll office revealed that the building needed rewiring and the works department staff accordingly gave Moosa a rewiring diagram, recommended a Maldivian wireman capable of doing the job and offered to inspect the work once it had been completed. They were simple enough favours but they led to the best relationship with the chief for a year. The station commander was even invited to tour the village, to have tea with Moosa and to accept a Maldivian polished wood cup which the chief offered him when accepting the Far East Air Force plaque, thus ensuring an official exchange rather than the one-sided acceptance of a gift.

At least there were, early in 1967, no matters of significance for the British and Maldivian governments to discuss with each other; at international level all was quiet. In part this was due to the continuing sensitivity of the station commander who worked on the simple basis of informing the atoll chief and the High Commissioner in Colombo and, through him, the Maldivian government, of any pending activity at Addu Atoll which could possibly give rise to a complaint.

Such events were becoming less frequent but one which was potentially sensitive was the firing of meteorological rockets from Gan. The meteorological staff on Gan were planning a series of Skua rocket launches as part of their research into atmospheric conditions in the region and although the programme was not planned to take place until 1968 the Maldivian Government Representative in Colombo was informed of the plan early in 1967 and was invited to send a representative to view the launch. He was also advised that prior to the launch it would be necessary for the RAF to search the rocket-case landing area to ensure that no-one was in the danger zone. It was patently the kind of activity which, although innocuous, would have created a diplomatic incident if the British had embarked upon the search and launch programme without first informing the Maldivian government. The plan provoked no adverse comments from the Maldivians and no representative attended the launching.

The welcome thaw in the chiefs' attitude was not, unfortunately, mirrored by the government ministers in Malé which meant that, as far as the chief was concerned, friendliness and caution had to go hand-in-hand if he wished to remain in office. He was so cautious that in April, when invited to a farewell meeting with Wing Commander Rees, whose tour of duty ended on the 21st, he sought permission from his government minister who, predictably, demonstrated his control over the chief by not responding to his request until after Rees had departed, thus ensuring that Moosa was unable to meet Rees and Wing Commander Fleming, Gan's new station commander, for a joint discussion.

It was several weeks before the chief, accompanied by the Hitaddu headman and an interpreter, met Fleming. In spite of the earlier rebuff he was overtly friendly and assured Gan's newly-appointed station commander that he would continue to work closely with the RAF. He was as good as his word, although his interpretation of working closely was rather one-sided, allowing him to accept, and acknowledge, favours which would previously either have been refused or would have been accepted without thanks. A few weeks later, when one of Gan's marine craft rescued two dhonis and their crews from the Gan gap where they were in danger of being swept out to sea, Moosa demonstrated his changed attitude by writing a letter of thanks to the station commander even though he was well aware that it was politically dangerous for him to acknowledge in writing any such obligation.

He could not, however, throw caution to the winds in his relationship with Fleming for he was well aware that his behaviour would be regularly reported to Malé and that he would be called to account if he were to be seen to be too friendly towards the British.

The result was that when accepting help he would often respond in mixed fashion, locally expressing his appreciation whilst formally notifying his government of some unsatisfactory aspect of his relationship with the RAF. That was disconcerting for the station commander who, whilst pleased to accept the gestures of appreciation and the easing of some of the restrictions which so beset the working arrangements for the Maldivians, was well aware that the chief's criticisms were likely to generate official complaints from the Maldivian Prime Minister to the British High Commissioner in Colombo. Such complaints were rarely taken seriously but the High Commissioner was always obliged to ask Gan's station commander for an explanation which meant that Fleming and his staff had to become adept at rebutting the various fictions emanating from Moosa, an art which they had to develop even though they had better things to do with their time.

The mid-year provision of new radio aerials for the atoll chief provided a typical example of the way in which Moosa would react whenever he thought that some local malcontent might accuse him of being over-friendly or over-cooperative with the RAF. He had been offered new, more effective, aerials for the atoll's radio link with Malé. Such a gift was actually in the interests of the RAF because improved communications between the chief and the ministers in the capital might lead to quicker decisions on matters affecting the operation of the base. The chief accepted the new aerials without any hesitation and, in an unheard of gesture of appreciation he even offered Fleming a plot of land on which to build a house, an offer which the station commander could not possibly accept. The chief, however, had a public image to preserve and when, a mere two or three weeks later, the aerials had not been erected he complained to his government about the slow progress and asked for the matter to be taken up with the British High Commissioner.

Then, still playing the two-faced game, he suggested to Fleming that when the RAF technicians, who had delivered and sited the aerials, returned to complete the installation they should be accompanied by the senior medical officer with whom he would like to discuss the general state of health among the villagers. The medical officers could hardly credit such a dramatic reversal of attitude in six months but were quick to take up the invitation. By August they had been invited to tour all the villages to check for evidence of what the chief described as an '...*unusual and widespread disease*' causing fever, vomiting and diarrhoea.

The chief's invitation was, however, modified by the officials in Malé who refused permission for anyone other than the senior medical officer to tour the villages, relenting only when he refused to undertake such a tour on his own. The ministers' prevarication led to a four-week delay which meant that the tour was conveniently made during a staff visit by the Principal Medical Officer for the Far East Air Force who accompanied the team on their visits to Maradu, Midu, Huladu and Fedu. Tests were carried out on several hundred villagers without disclosing any evidence of a mysterious disease, leaving a suspicion that the chief had exaggerated a minor health problem among the villagers in order to obtain his government's permission for the medical team to tour the atoll, an arrangement which had previously been politically unacceptable but for which a precedent had now been created.

The station commander's monthly meetings with the chief continued to be generally constructive with Moosa essentially, and quite correctly, interested in exploiting every situation in a way which kept him in favour with his government whilst providing benefits either for himself or for the Adduans. Thus in June, when an establishment review identified some over-manning amongst the Maldivian workers, it was entirely predictable that he would threaten to withdraw the entire Maldivian work force if any Adduans were to be made redundant.

The Ministry of Defence staff, however, had already decided to allow natural wastage to reduce the number of employees to the correct level and when the chief was informed of this he expressed his appreciation. He then found a simple way of slowing down the normal wastage rate, thereby protecting some of the Maldivian employees at the Ministry's expense. He merely reminded the Maldivian interpreters that if they helped the RAF against the interests of any Maldivian, they would be transported to Malé to face criminal charges. That reminder severely hampered any RAF police investigation into charges against Maldivians, thus reducing the likelihood of any Adduan being dismissed for gross misconduct, a charge which was common enough to create more labour turnover than that from voluntary resignations. The result was that it took almost four months for natural wastage to reduce the number of Maldivian employees to the establishment level, a process which had been expected to take no more than six weeks.

Only two events disturbed the political scene during 1967, one a continuing local saga, the other an unexpected event which was of minor international significance and which came close to creating a very embarrassing situation for the British government.

The latter event involved the French ketch Vadura which sailed into the lagoon and requested permission to stay long enough for the crew to repair some damage sustained during bad weather at sea. After leaving Addu Atoll the ketch headed north but, in distress, sailed into the lagoon at Huvadu Atoll. The crew was initially given a friendly reception and half of them went ashore. Once out of sight of the ketch they were overpowered by the islanders who then boarded the vessel and attacked the remainder of the crew. Although the only fatality was the ship's dog, several of the crew were injured and the ketch suffered some damage, particularly to the wireless room where the equipment was smashed. News of the event quickly reached Gan via the Maldivians who were in radio contact with the Huvaduans.

The Commander-in-Chief of the Far East Air Force, who was visiting Gan when the Vadura ran into trouble, favoured sending one of the RAF's marine craft, complete with an armed rescue party, to the aid of the French crew. The political repercussions of such a move, at a time when the Maldivian government was still silently fuming over what it saw as Britain's arrogance over the last decade, would at best have been embarrassing and at worst have led to moves by the Maldivians to terminate the lease of land at Addu Atoll on the grounds that armed interference in the internal affairs of the Maldives constituted a gross breach of the agreement.

It was not easy for the station commander, who was expected to be sensitive to the political nuances of everything which the RAF did, to tell his own Commander-in-Chief that the idea of an armed rescue mission was just about the worst idea he could have come up with. Tact prevailed however and it was left to the French government to raise with the Maldivians the question of compensation for the results of the unexpected reversion to behaviour more in keeping with the time of Francois Pyrard of Laval than the nineteen sixties.

The Huvaduans, it seems, were not provoked in any way except by the mere presence of the vessel in distress. It can only be assumed that their relatively recent experiences with the Maldivian militia had left them resentful and spoiling for a fight which they could win. The crew of the ketch had probably just been unfortunate enough to provide the islanders with an opportunity to vent their feelings on foreigners who were in the wrong place at the wrong time.

The other event, the continuing local saga, revolved around Mohammed Saeed, the Maldivian employed by the RAF as an interpreter, who had been so unceremoniously shuttled back and forth between Addu Atoll, Malé and various detention islands at the whim of the Maldivian government. In July he was told that the Ministry of Defence staff had agreed to award him two hundred pounds back pay, some nine months salary. That was little more than half the salary he had lost during his detention. It was certainly not generous, given the circumstances of his initial departure for Malé and the original promise that he would continue to be paid his normal salary whilst he was away. But the Ministry staff were not prepared to offer any more and Saeed accepted that final offer with good grace.

He also received the unwelcome news that he was once again to report to Malé.

On his arrival in the capital he was arrested on charges which were not disclosed to the RAF and taken to Wilingili island before being confined at Makunudu Faroe in Tiladummati Atoll until late August when he was released and allowed to return to Addu Atoll. There appeared to be no logic in his frequent removal from Addu Atoll and, given the fairly calm political state, it was difficult to accept that the Maldivian intention was merely to disrupt the work at the base. The suspicion that Saeed's frequent recalls were initiated by the atoll chief, who wanted his own nominee in the interpreter's post, hardened when, after no more than a few weeks back at Addu Atoll, Saeed was again summoned to Malé and charged with anti-government activities, the details of which were, once again, not disclosed to the RAF either officially or covertly. Judged guilty, Saeed was sentenced to five years banishment on Fadiffolu Atoll. With Saeed banished the atoll chief was able to ensure that only those Maldivians acceptable to him would apply for the job. As a result, Saeed's successor had to be regarded as a communicant to the chief on all matters and although that made life awkward at times it also provided an opportunity to feed selected information to the chief in the hope that it would influence his subsequent behaviour and benefit the RAF.

Saeed's banishment, the villagers' health problems and the use of the Maldivian section building on Gan, the so-called Maldivian hotel, became linked through local politics during 1967. The building had, during the Second World War, been the Royal Navy's headquarters for HMS Maraga but had come to be owned by Saeed who derived an income from the operation of the restaurant and accommodation facilities. It had been closed immediately after the typhoid outbreak of 1965 and subsequently condemned by the district works officer, as being in need of rewiring, and by the senior medical officer, as a health hazard. The Maldivians working on Gan were thus left with no restaurant facilities and, more importantly, no occasional overnight accommodation.

Saeed would only repair the building if he could subsequently run it as a hotel but had he embarked on such a private commercial enterprise on Gan he would undoubtedly have found himself in even more trouble with the Maldivian authorities. Rather than risk further harassment from Malé he effectively relinquished his ownership of the building and left the way clear for the RAF to bring it back into service. In May the decrepit kadjan roof was replaced by corrugated metal, the building was rewired, the first floor accommodation refurbished and the ground floor restaurant equipped to the satisfaction of the senior medical officer.

Because of the sensitive political climate no individual Maldivian was prepared to run the hotel and it was therefore left to the atoll committee to operate it under a franchise arrangement made with the RAF in mid-year.

Within a matter of weeks after the re-opening, the building had to be requisitioned to provide isolation ward facilities for victims of yet another outbreak of typhoid among the Maldivians from Hitaddu. The by-now-familiar procedures, based upon the World Health Organisation guidelines were implemented and the outbreak was successfully contained. Nevertheless, in September, when Fleming completed his tour of duty and handed over to the new station commander, Wing Commander Mullineaux, there was still a strong possibility of a typhoid epidemic among the islanders. It was hardly an auspicious time for Mullineaux to assume command but the typhoid control measures very quickly proved to be so successful that the outbreak was restricted to a total of only five confirmed cases with two deaths, one being that of a two-year-old Maldivian girl who had died in the Maldivian hotel. Once again a typhoid epidemic on Gan had been averted and by December, when no further cases had been confirmed, the typhoid outbreak was deemed to be over and the Maldivian hotel had reverted to its normal function.

When Mullineaux took over from Fleming the atoll chief, in recognition of the fact that the RAF's medical staff had very efficiently controlled the typhoid outbreak, was even more co-operative than he had been throughout the year. That, however, changed in a matter of weeks and he demonstrated his readiness to make life un-necessarily awkward for the station commander by referring to the Maldivian government matters which could very easily have been dealt with locally.

His first opportunity arose when, early in October, three airmen wandered outside the leased site on Hitaddu into an uninhabited part of the island, a clear breach of the leasehold agreement and, for the airmen, a disciplinary offence.

They were seen by some Hitadduans who reported the matter to the Maldivian Government Representative on the island. He, with the approval of the atoll chief, reported the infringement to Malé. From Malé, the offence was reported to the Maldivian Government Representative in Ceylon who was instructed to pursue the matter with the British authorities. He complained to the British High Commissioner who referred the complaint to the Far East Air Force Command staff in Singapore and to Gan's station commander. Mullineaux had then to investigate the complaint and send a report to the Command staff and the British High Commissioner. His report flowed back through the chain of relationships until it reached the atoll chief and the Government Representative on Hitaddu. By then the airmen had long since been reprimanded and a great deal of time had been wasted. But on Hitaddu, Maldivian honour had been satisfied.

Throughout 1967 the traders, like traders elsewhere in the archipelago, were unhappy with the scale of the excise duties levied on all imports and with the extent of their government's control over trading with other nations. In particular they resented the controls imposed on their dealings with India, Ceylon and Burma, the suppliers of nearly all the staple goods. They were convinced that Nasir had initiated all the controls with the eventual aim of replacing the private traders by a network of government agents operating throughout the Maldives, creating a government monopoly in external trade. By the latter part of 1967 there were thirty officially designated Maldivian traders at the atoll and the goods sold to them by the NAAFI had been subject to import duties levied by their government ever since the system had first been established as a way of controlling the islanders' illegitimate, untaxed trading.

The Maldivian government, so frequently seen to be indifferent to the complaints of its citizens, may have been swayed by the reaction, through-out the archipelago, to the imposition of the recently increased excise duties but if that was so, no word of it leaked out. What did happen, much to the surprise of the British and the delight of the Adduans, was the removal, late in 1967, of all excise duties normally payable by the traders. On the 3rd of November the Maldivian Government Representative in Ceylon wrote to the British High Commissioner in Colombo saying:

> 'The authorities in Malé have requested me to inform you that with effect from the first of November 1967 customs duty payable by the author-ised traders of Addu Atoll will be waived.'

There was no explanation and the islanders did not seek one. On one of the few occasions on which their government had done them a favour they were certainly not going to enquire why. For the RAF there was no direct benefit but there was the indirect advantage that with a reduction in the local cost of living the Maldivians might be prepared to settle for a modest pay rise in the near future.

With their government's welcome bonus to look forward to, the majority of the Adduans may well have started the new year in a better frame of mind but there were rather worrying rumours of imminent political change in Malé. Initially fuelled by the atoll chief's increasing remoteness, the rumours were strengthened by the Maldivian government's failure to answer an early request from Gan's Maldivian Affairs officer for the British High Commissioner and the Air Commander of the Far East Air Force to meet the atoll chief during their brief visit to the base. If the rumours from Malé were to be believed, the relationship between the elected Sultan and his senior ministers, for long rather strained, had become almost intolerable. It was not therefore a complete surprise when the Prime Minister announced that a plebiscite was to be held in March to allow the Maldivians to decide whether their nation should remain as a sultanate or revert to a presidential republic. The previous flirtation with republicanism had lasted only from 1953 to 1954, its early demise brought about by the widespread belief among the Maldivians that the change from a sultanate to a republic had been largely responsible for the loss of imports and the onset of near-starvation in the archipelago. Now the mood had swung against the retention of the sultanate which had so overwhelmingly been voted back after swift disillusionment with the republican government of fifteen years ago.

The rumours proved to be true. The plebiscite was held on the 15th of March and resulted in a landslide victory for the republicans with thirty-five thousand votes cast in favour of a return to a republic and only eight thousand against. That left the way clear for Nasir, the leading contender for the post of President, to pursue his ambition to control the affairs of the nation from the highest office in the land. With such a dramatic change in the offing any atoll chief would understandably avoid making decisions which could be even remotely construed as political and if that were so throughout the archipelago it was obvious that at Addu Atoll the chief would be even more circumspect. Thus it came as no surprise that the chief's stock answer 'The RAF should take up the matter with the Maldivian Government' was used when the senior medical officer proposed that a health clinic should be established in each village, staffed by Maldivians who had been trained by the RAF in basic first aid.

The chief's response did not vary, even when it was suggested that, as part of the general Maldivianisation programme, some of the Adduans employed on Gan should be trained to undertake skilled, rather than semi-skilled, work. He was not interested in the fact that on both occasions the islanders stood to benefit if the proposals were accepted and the changes introduced. His focus was on self-preservation. He was similarly not prepared to bring to his government's attention the concerns of the traders at the atoll. Ever suspicious, they were convinced that the removal of excise duty in November 1967 had been a prelude to the curtailment of entrepreneurial trading through the introduction of obligatory licences for all external trade, both imports and exports.

Three of the traders had already fallen foul of their government and had been banished and those who retained their licences were well aware that they did so under sufferance. They would never be so foolish as to admit in public what they were prepared to say in private; they neither liked nor trusted Nasir. Certainly they were not likely to take issue with the then Prime Minister nor was the atoll chief, himself a trader as the government agent with the sole right to inspect and buy all RAF surplus items for shipment to Malé, likely to argue on their behalf. All they could do was to hope for the best and maximise their trading while they still had the opportunity to do so. The result was an ever-increasing demand for goods from the NAAFI, particularly for petrol, oil and lubricants, and an ever-increasing tendency to trade with visiting ships, an activity which the RAF was technically expected to discourage or curtail but was invariably powerless to do so without seriously damaging the working relationships with the Adduans.

In June, national and local events showed how wise the chief had been to avoid all political involvement. Affairs of state in Malé that month were running normally. Normally, that is, for Maldivian politics at that time. The discovery of an illegal press for producing counterfeit banknotes together with a cache of arms sufficient to support a coup against Ibrahim Nasir led to a series of arrests and the subsequent conviction of a group of dissidents which included the son and daughter-in-law of Nasir's predecessor.

The Adduan atoll chief, in Malé for the special assembly of the Majlis, rightly perceived that it was a bad time for anyone to be heard criticising the government, and a particularly inopportune moment for him to raise any issues related to the concerns of the traders and the islanders at Addu Atoll. Wisely, he kept quiet. Three hundred miles to the south, Abdullah Manikfu, deputising for the absent chief, was similarly inclined to keep his own counsel and was, if anything, even more reluctant than the chief to make any decision which might affect the working arrangements with the RAF. That situation, which was so often frustrating for the station com-mander, prevailed until well into August when the chief finally returned to Hitaddu after spending all of July taking part in the Majlis debates on the details of a constitution for the re-created Republic.

His return did not, unfortunately, mark a return to the friendly relationships of the past.

Throughout the operational life of RAF Gan there was never a period when the station commander could relax in the knowledge that events on the island would not become the subject of political point-scoring. Wing Commander Mullineaux was perhaps more fortunate than his predecessors in that respect because during the first half of 1968 there were very few occasions when national or local politics affected the day-to-day operation of the base. At the national level, the March plebiscite, the subsequent reversion to a republic and the election of a president kept the Maldivian ministers so occupied with domestic matters that they had neither the time nor the inclination to pick any squabbles with the British. At the local level all was generally quiet due in part to the atoll chief's reluctance to involve the central government ministers at that time and in part to the general awareness, among the servicemen and the expatriate civilians, of the Maldivians' sensitivities and of the atoll chief's readiness to politicise any local issue in order to maintain his reputation as a firm representative of central government.

Generally quiet, that is, until August when Moosa returned from Malé and lodged two formal complaints which could not be easily ignored because he might decide that his reputation could be enhanced if he were to bring the complaints to the attention of the Malé-based ministers.

The first incident which he complained about occurred when an Anglia TV film crew visited Gan in August. Their filming took several days and covered just about every aspect of life on the island, including the coral blasting. For some reason it had been decided at the Ministry of Defence that the Maldivians should not feature in that part of the film and instructions had been issued to that effect. Mohammed Fazel, the Pakistani foreman in charge of the blasting operation, followed the instructions and the Maldivian workers promptly complained to their representative who took up the matter with the atoll chief. He declared that Fazel had insulted the Maldivians and threatened that he would take up the matter with Malé and would withdraw Maldivian labour unless an apology was forthcoming together with the promise of additional filming to show the Maldivian workers. It was, like so many such incidents, a storm in a teacup. But he got his way. An apology was given and additional footage, which included the Maldivian workers, was shot.

As if to make sure that Mullineaux would remember the last few weeks of his tour as Gan's station commander, Moosa also complained, in September, that a Pakistani had assaulted a Maldivian. That was a complaint which was serious enough to warrant a police investigation. The chief, however, had ordered the Maldivians not to cooperate with the RAF police in any of their investigations and that led to a stalemate with the provost officer informing Moosa that without the help of the islanders his staff could make no progress. The chief, pursuing his own agenda, informed the Malé-based ministers that the RAF police were failing to investigate the matter. That led to the involvement of the Maldivian Government Representative in Colombo who passed on a complaint to the British High Commissioner, triggering off numerous signals between Colombo, Singapore and Gan.

At that time Moosa was quite obviously on the horns of a dilemma. He genuinely wanted to establish and maintain good working relations with the station commander but more than ever before it was essential, for his own political future, that he did not fall foul of Nasir who seemed almost certain to become the President of the Republic of the Maldives. Thus the atoll chief was apparently determined to use, as best he could, any incidents on Gan to establish a favourable reputation with Nasir whilst simultaneously trying to maintain a reasonably amicable, if somewhat businesslike, association with Mullineaux.

The result was a surprising combination of complaints and hospitality with the Maldivian Affairs officer being invited by the chief to tour Hitaddu and to join him for a meal in the atoll office in the same month that accusations were being made about the behaviour of Pakistanis towards the Maldivians. During the meal the chief explained that he would '...*always do his best to help the RAF but would always need approval from Malé for non-routine matters*', a comment which explained why he would not give permission for Maldivians to attend any education classes other than those which were intended to provide the Adduan employees with sufficient command of the English language to cope with the demands of the workplace. That restriction provided yet another example of the way in which good intentions, in this instance the inclusion of a Maldivian candidate amongst those who were sitting the O-level English language examination, had backfired. The Maldivian passed the examination, duly received his certificate and proudly displayed it to his relatives and friends. Word of his success reached Malé from where, *via* the Maldivian Government Representative in Ceylon and the British High Commissioner in Colombo, a formal complaint was lodged with the Foreign and Commonwealth Office in London. The upshot was that the atoll chief received instructions from his government and, almost without precedence, Gan's station commander received a letter from the Maldivian government stating that under no circumstances were Maldivians to receive education or training not directly related to their work. The atoll chief, instructed to ensure that the embargo was not broken, interpreted it literally, even to the extent of vetoing football coaching and training.

On the 27th of September the Maldivians voted in their presidential election. The ballot papers carried only one name, Ibrahim Nasir. Voters had to show their preference with a tick or a cross. Nasir was elected.

The new Republic of the Maldives was born on the 11th of November 1968 and was celebrated with a three-day public holiday. The transition from a sultanate to a republic marked a sea-change in the attitude of the Maldivian ministers towards the British government and, more importantly, towards the one-time rebels of Addu Atoll.

For Wing Commander Farmer, newly in post as Gan's station commander, political harmony would be more than welcome.

XV Political Harmony

The euphoria created by the imminent birth of the new Republic of the Maldives even flowed over into the negotiations, held in Malé on the 7th and 8th of November, on the pay and conditions for the eight hundred and eighty Maldivians employed on the RAF sites at Addu Atoll. The British representatives, the Far East Air Force Command Secretary, the Assistant Command Secretary, the Head of Chancery from the British High Commission in Colombo and the Maldivian Affairs officer from RAF Gan were pleasantly surprised when the five Maldivian ministers created an unexpectedly friendly atmosphere in which they sought to reach a fair agreement on the pay and conditions which had remained virtually unchanged since 1958. The British negotiators, obviously keen to take advantage of the prevailing spirit of goodwill, pressed for closer direct dealing with the atoll chief and were delighted, but slightly sceptical, when given assurances that closer liaison between the atoll chief, the officials in Malé and RAF Gan's station commander would be encouraged.

Throughout the negotiations the Maldivians proved to be hospitable, courteous hosts who were obviously enthusiastic about their re-formed Republic. The British were not, however, carried away by this new-found spirit of cooperation because experience had taught them that, for the Maldivians, blowing hot and blowing cold was something of an art form. They were well aware that their hosts were seeking to increase, by at least fifty per cent, the wages paid to the Adduans and that under those circumstances it was obvious that they would do nothing to sour the atmosphere, at least until they had got what they wanted. The British, whilst fully recognising an obligation to increase the Adduans' rates of pay, finally offered a range of increases which almost certainly failed to match the local inflation rate over the decade since last the islanders' pay had been reviewed.

Admittedly, some of the improved conditions of employment added a charge to the British exchequer but they did not generally increase the income of the individual employees. The new rates of pay finally offered by the British negotiators were based upon a six-day, forty-eight-hour working week, excluding meal breaks. Pay rates ranged over six pay bands corresponding to the six trade groups used for the Maldivian workforce. At the bottom of the new pay scales, in Band 1, were the room-boys and messengers whose daily rates of pay were increased to seven shillings and twopence (36p), with pay bands progressing through nine shillings and sixpence (47p) for labourers and cleaners, ten shillings and threepence (52p) for semi-skilled workers, thirteen shillings and elevenpence (70p) for skilled workers, fifteen shillings (75p) for clerks and interpreters up to the highest rate of seventeen shillings and fourpence (87p) for overseers, all of whom were in pay band 6.

Special allowances complemented the new pay scales, taking into account a variety of factors such as length of service, supervisory responsibilities, rowing time, time spent working at heights of fifty feet or more and overtime hours. Length of service allowances were paid to anyone continuously employed for at least two years since August 1968, adding sixpence (2½p) to the daily wages of those in trade groups 4 to 6 and just half that for those in the lower trade groups. For all employees, continuous employment for at least four years doubled the allowances paid. Supervisory allowances were paid only to leading hands and varied from sixpence (2½p) a day for trade group 1 employees up to three times that for those in trade group 5.

The workers who were living on Hitaddu, Huladu or Midu were obliged to row to and from Gan each day and were paid a rowing allowance of one shilling and fourpence (7p), regardless of trade group, for every working day. Very few Maldivians worked on the masts and aerials but those who did were paid an allowance for the time actually spent working at heights of fifty feet or more, receiving ninepence (4p) an hour when working at heights exceeding one hundred and fifty feet, sevenpence (3p) an hour for heights of more than one hundred feet but not more than one hundred and fifty feet and fivepence (2p) an hour when working at heights of not less than fifty feet but not more than one hundred feet. Hourly overtime rates were set, ranging from one shilling and a penny (5½p) for the lowest trade group to two shillings and eightpence (13p) for those in trade group 6. Overtime rates for public holidays attracted an extra premium, ranging from one shilling and fourpence (7p) an hour for trade group 1 workers to three shillings and threepence (16p) an hour for the top trade group employees.

Although these rates seem ridiculously low by today's standards they have to be put in the context of the Maldivian lifestyle, the rates paid by employers in Malé, where the cost of living was much higher than at Addu Atoll, and the general income levels at that time. Additionally, pay and allowances were only part of the story; improved conditions of employment were to be introduced which would provide benefits even though they would not provide higher wages.

The original conditions of employment contained only three significant safeguards; no Maldivian under the age of fifteen could be employed, nobody under the age of eighteen would be employed if an older worker were available and each worker was entitled to periodic health checks and free health care. But the Maldivian workers had no entitlement to holiday pay, sick pay or compensation for injuries sustained at the workplace.

Under the revised conditions of service every full-time employee would be entitled to be paid for the eleven days which were taken as public holidays each year or, if obliged to work on those days, would be entitled to receive overtime pay or paid time off in lieu. Workers with at least twelve months continuous service would be entitled to twelve days paid holiday each year in addition to the public holidays. Finally, entitlements to sick pay and to compensation for industrial injury or death were to be introduced as soon as the details were finalised in London. No deadline was set for the London-based staff, they were merely requested to finalise the details '...*as soon as possible*'. There was a hollow ring to that phrase for the British government's attitude towards the Adduans had been overtly exploitative ever since the old wartime base had been re-commissioned.

Since 1957 Britain had employed several hundred Maldivians, relying on them to provide a cheap and flexible workforce which could be increased or reduced without compensation almost on a week-by-week basis. Their availability had contributed greatly to the creation and subsequent operation of a strategic military airfield but the British government had shown little interest in their rates of pay and had never seen fit to grant them the fundamental conditions of employment which were to be introduced under the revised agreement. There was, understandably, some scepticism on the part of the Maldivians who found it hard to believe that '...*as soon as*

possible' would be interpreted as anything other than '... *when we feel like it*'.

The proposed changes were not all favourable for the Adduans. In particular, they were reluctant to accept both the introduction of a regulation requiring every Maldivian employee to carry a pass and the inclusion of a clause which gave the RAF police the right to search any Maldivian leaving Gan. But the Maldivian negotiators accepted them as a price they would have to pay as a *quid pro quo* for the benefits which they had negotiated. Within days the broad details of the new agreement had become common knowledge amongst the Adduans and it was inevitable that the Pakistanis, whose rates of pay had always been higher than those of the Maldivians, soon had word of the Adduans' imminent pay rises. The pay differentials were mainly justified by elementary job evaluation but were increased partly by comparison with rates of pay in Karachi and partly by the addition of an allowance to compensate for the lengthy period of employment as an unaccompanied expatriate.

Predictably, the Pakistanis saw no reason to accept an erosion of the differentials between their rates of pay and those of the Maldivians but they chose not to submit a general pay claim because they were well aware that any such claim would be rejected out of hand. They chose instead to develop a series of arguments for the rates of pay for various occupations to be increased for very good, but noticeably different, reasons. They started with the Pakistani firemen who had been recruited as trainees. Knowing that the establishment review had graded the jobs as firemen/drivers they successfully argued that those employees should be paid at a higher rate on the basis of a comparison with the rates of pay for firemen/drivers in Karachi. Success paved the way for the next argument and, although they could not always win, they continued to argue a series of cases until virtually every job undertaken by Pakistanis had been re-evaluated. At that point, with a significant number of successes to show for their efforts, the Pakistanis felt that honour was satisfied and accepted that they could do no more.

With the smooth transition from a sultanate to a republic the Maldivians seemed to be enjoying a general feeling of well-being. But it was nothing like as strong as that experienced by Mohammed Saeed, the ill-fated interpreter who, after being frequently shuttled to and from Malé and called to account for numerous offences, had eventually been banished for five years. For him, and for others in similar circumstances, the 11th of

November brought freedom under a political amnesty announced in celebration of the return to a republic. As a result, he re-appeared, much to everyone's surprise, alongside the atoll chief during an informal visit to the station commander in December. Not only that, the chief, who had generally been thought of as the main instigator of Saeed's frequent recalls to Malé, suggested that the one-time interpreter should return to his old job. That was a politically sensitive suggestion, which the station commander referred to the Far East Air Force Command Secretary and to the British High Commissioner in Colombo, leaving Saeed once more in limbo.

So a year which had been politically successful, both at national and at local level, drew to a close and, reinforcing the new spirit of cooperation, the atoll chief invited the station commander and a small group of RAF officers to tour Hitaddu as his guests on the 22nd of December to mark the end of Ramadan. Refreshments in the chief's house were followed by a tour of the village on foot and by car, culminating in a meal with the chief and members of the atoll committee.

The new spirit of friendship and co-operation flowed steadily through 1969, manifesting itself in a variety of ways. Virtually every month Farmer was invited to accompany a small group of servicemen and expatriate civilians on an escorted tour of Hitaddu. Relations became so cordial that at one stage Moosa even suggested a direct phone link between himself and the station commander, a suggestion which Farmer diplomatically declined. Nevertheless, there was still no agreement on the establishment of any first aid clinics in the villages even though villagers trained in basic first aid techniques would have staffed them. Nor was the RAF's hygiene squad allowed to visit any of the villages even though the senior medical officer was invited onto any of the islands at the first signs of any unusual or serious illness. Friendly cooperation, it seemed, was still constrained by the fear of criticism from Malé.

In March the station commander and the senior medical officer received invitations to make a goodwill visit to the Maldivian capital and on the 4th of April they started the thirty-one-and-a-half hour journey in one of the marine craft unit's launches. In Malé they enjoyed first class hospitality, were interviewed for the local newspaper and the local radio station and were generally treated as welcome guests. Farmer, aware that there was an acute shortage of books in local schools everywhere in the Maldives, became instantly popular with the local headmaster and his staff when he donated to their school some four hundred books which he had brought from Gan, all surplus to the requirements of the RAF but all of considerable value to the local schoolchildren. Many of the people they met, including the Prime Minister and the Public Prosecutor, spoke to them about Gan and asked them to pass on messages to relatives at Addu Atoll. On the 5th, the day before their departure, the company met Zaki for a one-and-a-half hour discussion and found it very difficult to believe that there had ever been any animosity between the Maldivians and the British. Farmer met the atoll chief soon after returning to Addu Atoll and, on telling him of the highly successful visit to Malé, learnt that the Maldivian government, which had previously condemned incipient Westernisation, had decreed that all atoll officials on a salary of one hundred rupees or more per month were to wear European-style clothes when on official business, a requirement which explained why Moosa Ali Didi had been to the NAAFI tailor's shop to be measured for a suit.

Best of all, co-operation brought an end to the escalation of trivial incidents into diplomatic complaints. Problems which would previously have found their way *via* Malé onto the British High Commissioner's desk in Colombo were dealt with locally and when the Air Commander of the Far East Air Force and the High Commissioner from Colombo visited Gan in April and invited the chief to meet them for a general discussion he not only agreed to meet them on Gan, he invited them back for an informal visit to Hitaddu as his guest. His invitation, readily accepted, provided a very useful opportunity for Moosa informally to discuss his difficulties and to gain some understanding of the situation as perceived by the British government and the RAF.

Cooperation and flexibility became so commonplace that special arrangements were made to accommodate the July independence day celebrations by the Maldivians. In addition to the usual public holiday many of the Adduans employed on Gan wished to take their paid leave entitlement at that time to visit Malé for the festivities. When they also asked for permission to take an additional month's unpaid leave to make the journey worthwhile their request was granted on condition that each absentee sent a relative or friend to substitute for him at work, an unusual concession but one which benefited both parties. The whole affair provided a noteworthy example of the way in which the entire political atmosphere had changed;

very few Adduans would have ventured anywhere near the capital in the mid-1960s.

By August the Maldivian government was showing an unprecedented willingness to allow personnel from Gan to visit other islands in the atoll, acceding to Moosa Ali Didi's suggestion that such visits would '...cement goodwill.' A precedent was set on the 16th of August when Farmer, accompanied by five other officers, travelled to Hitaddu on board a landing craft and was met at the jetty by Moosa, Mohammed Saeed and Abdullah Rashid, the atoll committee's secretary. The six officers and three Maldivians then made their way to Hulumidu on board a local trader's motor launch, powered by an ingeniously converted cement-mixer engine. There they visited the village school and, followed by thirty or forty schoolchildren, toured the village on bicycles, being welcomed into many of the villagers' homes and invited to photograph the villagers and their environment. By the end of August other parties of fifteen had accepted invitations and been given similar tours of Maradu and Fedu. Subsequently Moosa proposed that the RAF's Maldivian Affairs officer could arrange for groups of Gan's Pakistanis to make escorted tours of Hitaddu to develop cultural relationships with their Muslim brothers as prophesied in their religion.

As visits to Gan by the chief became easier to arrange, and consequently more frequent, he expressed a willingness to meet the most important of the many VIP's who were briefly the guests of the station commander. Some, such as the High Commissioner and the Air Commander were of significance to him because of their direct involvement in policy and with his own government. Others were significant to him because of their status. In particular he was always pleased to be invited to meet British royalty or those closely related to them and in August he readily accepted the invitation to meet Princess Alexandra and her husband during their brief stay at the atoll whilst en route to the Far East.

Easier associations were bound to bring some difficulties but both the chief and the RAF authorities dealt very firmly with anyone who overstepped the mark. The chief began to deal more severely with any Maldivian found to have consumed alcohol for, although there had always been a few offenders, the easier relations gave the Maldivians more opportunities to buy alcoholic drinks and there were always some Pakistanis prepared to sell to anyone. Maldivian employees convicted of consuming alcohol were automatically put under house arrest and, at the chief's request, were dismissed from employment on Gan. By the latter part of the year thirteen Maldivians had been convicted and exiled to an island in Malé Atoll and when some thirty other Adduans had been implicated the Maldivian government became sufficiently concerned to order an investigation into affairs at Addu Atoll. By then the RAF police had already mounted their own investigation and eventually the Pakistani suppliers were identified, their employment contracts were terminated and they were flown back to Karachi.

It was easy enough for the executives on Gan to sustain good relations with the Adduans because there were always opportunities to confer benefits on the islanders.

In addition to the well-established provision of health care, the search and rescue services and the use of materials, plant and expertise there were the recently re-introduced English language classes for Maldivians and the supply of commodities for the nominated traders. It was, however, becoming increasingly difficult to cope with some of the Maldivians' demands. By July, medical consultations were up to four thousand and the number of would-be English language students was some five times the number that could be accommodated without adversely affecting the RAF education officers' official duties.

As far as the bulk of the employees was concerned their 'chitty economy' was capable of providing nearly all they wanted from the RAF, but in 1969 they had the added benefits of increased rates of pay and improved conditions which, in spite of the none-too-generous review of over a decade's pay stagnation, had been generally well received. But the Maldivian traders were making ever-increasing demands for petrol, oil and lubricants with many traders travelling from Malé even though they knew that they were not allowed to trade directly with the NAAFI and would have to rely upon the provision of supplies from one of the atoll's authorised traders. In the last quarter of 1969 more than fifty thousand gallons of petrol, diesel and lubricating oil were sold to the Maldivians with one Malé-based trader known to have taken eleven thousand gallons on one trip.

The good relations with the atoll officials were obviously fostered by the favours so readily granted by successive station commanders, but, willing though they were, the British could not help the Maldivians out of every difficult situation in which they found themselves. That much became very obvious on the 18th of August when a Maldivian Vedi, a one-hundred-and-twenty-foot trading vessel, went aground on the outer reef of Hulumidu. The fully-laden ship, with thirty-two passengers on board and carrying a cargo of rice, sugar and flour, had taken a month to sail the three hundred miles from Malé only to be blown onto the reef whilst standing off Hulumidu waiting for daylight. Fortunately there were only minor injuries to the passengers. But the cargo, so precious to the Maldivians, was ruined and the ship was in danger of breaking up.

The RAF's Zodiac dinghy was able to rescue the injured and the three children who were on board; the remaining passengers were taken off by dhoni before the RAF's reef rescue vehicle, the Stalwart, arrived at the scene. The loss of the ship, however, was potentially disastrous for the owners and, ever obliging, the RAF's marine craft airmen offered to pull it off the reef. It resisted all their efforts. For five or six days they tried, on numerous occasions, to tow the Vedi to safety but it just could not be pulled clear. There it remained until September when HMS Rothesay arrived at the atoll. Her captain, hearing of the Maldivians' plight, immediately offered to tow the stricken vessel into the lagoon, never imagining that his ship would be unable to do that. But the Maldivian ship, stuck so fast that on one occasion the sixty-ton hauling rope broke without the Vedi moving, refused to budge. That left the islanders with little choice: abandon the ship or salvage what they could. They cut it up *in situ*, helped by the marine craft airmen who attached buoyancy bags to the sections which they then towed to Hitaddu where the Maldivians rebuilt the ill-fated vessel.

Moosa was much luckier when he asked for the RAF to help him obtain engine spares for his unserviceable launch. Britain's Permanent Secretary to the Ministry of Public Buildings and Works, Sir Michael Cary, happened to be visiting Gan when the chief made the request and he promised to do what he could to help. Discovering, on his return to England, that the S6 marine engine had long since been out of production, he contacted the chairman of Perkins, the manufacturers, and asked for help. The chairman rounded up all the available spares for the chief to buy, leaving the Permanent Secretary to get them to Gan which he did by asking the Air Member for Supply and Organisation, Air Chief Marshal Sir Thomas Prickett, to ensure that they reached the atoll. Moosa was delighted, but almost certainly had no idea of the way in which people in high office were doing favours to sustain the political goodwill at Addu Atoll.

In October, Wing Commander Farmer's tour ended and he handed over command to Wing Commander Spragg who had arrived at Gan on the 5th of October, five days before Farmer departed. Spragg was fortunate; local relationships at that time were as good as they had ever been and there was no reason to believe that that was likely to change.

A week later Gan's recently-arrived station commander found himself, in the company of the Air Commander and the Command Secretary, *en route* to Malé to meet the British High Commissioner and three of his senior staff, all taking up the Maldivian President's suggestion, made during Farmer's goodwill visit to Malé in April, that he was prepared to receive senior RAF officers and British diplomatic staff provided adequate notice was given.

The visiting party was taken from Hulule to the President's house on Malé island, enjoying the hospitality of the Prime Minister and the President during their brief stay. Zaki, the prime minister, was unusually forthcoming during the visit, disclosing that he wanted no dealings with the Russians nor with the Arabs even though he was under some pressure to support the Muslim brothers in the Middle East. He also expressed the opinion that the Adduans should not be paid as much as the Pakistanis employed on Gan and declared his support for the teaching of English to the Maldivians at Addu Atoll even though the previous government had been against that. He created the impression that he preferred the Adduans to be seen as cheaper labour than the Pakistanis so that when their English and their trade skills had improved they would be available for a full Maldivianisation programme.

All this cooperation and goodwill had one slight disadvantage as far as the Maldivian Affairs officer on Gan was concerned; the staff at the British High Commission and at the Far East Air Force Headquarters became complacent about the Adduan situation. At the atoll it was always easy to see that, even after the recent agreement, the Maldivians' pay and conditions were still poor. But after an eight-day round trip to Colombo and Singapore to discuss the matter the Maldivian Affairs officer had to report that neither the High Commission staff nor the Command secretariat were interested in improving the lot of the Maldivians whilst everything was running smoothly at the atoll.

1969 seemed almost too good to be true as far as local politics at Addu Atoll were concerned and at national level the improvement in the Maldivians' attitude towards the British use of the Gan and Hitaddu sites was quite remarkable. The only looming disagreement related to the Maldivian governments' declaration that, in accordance with the claim which they had first made in 1967, their territorial limits extended from 7° 10 ¼' North to 0° 45 ¼' South and from 72° 29 ¼' East to 73° 49' East. Britain had never previously taken issue with them over the claim but to delay doing so beyond 1969 could have prejudiced objections that the claim was contrary to international law. Accordingly, Britain informed the Maldivian government of her non-recognition of the claim, counterclaiming that the stated territorial limits amounted to annexation of the high seas. That dispute between Britain and the recently reconstituted Republic had no repercussions at Addu Atoll. Understandably, the islanders were completely indifferent as to the whereabouts of their invisible territorial limits in the Indian Ocean.

The easy relationships, developed through 1969, flowed smoothly into 1970. At the atoll, cooperation from the Maldivians was as high as at any time since 1957 even though the reducing works services programme meant that Pakistanis were not being offered re-engagement on completion of their contracts and eighty Maldivians had to be made redundant. The atoll chief accepted that the fifteen per cent cut in the work force was inevitable, viewing the situation with regret but without any strong reaction aimed at delaying or changing the decision. As far as the Adduan communities were concerned it was unfortunate that most of the dismissed Maldivians came from Hitaddu and Hulumidu but, given that most of the works services employees came from those islands, there was no easy way to spread such a significant number of dismissals across the different communities. It was also ironic that the redundancies came at a time when eighty Maldivians were attending English language classes as part of the steady progress towards the Maldivianisation of the jobs undertaken by the Pakistanis and the Ceylonese.

Conducted tours of the villages by parties of Europeans, usually including the station commander and the Maldivian Affairs officer, became frequent events with the visitors enjoying the hospitality of the Maldivians and the opportunity to see something of the islanders' lifestyle. For the Pakistanis, organised visits to the villages were commonplace in 1970, particularly during festivals associated with their religion. If anything, relations in that year became so good that some controls on reciprocal hospitality had to be introduced, especially after the chief and the atoll committee visited the Pakistani mess as lunchtime guests without the station commander being aware of their presence on Gan. Such occasions were not banned, merely made subject to Spragg's approval with casual invitations seen as undesirable.

One suggestion from Moosa was, however, turned down although it is difficult to see why. Several islands in the atoll had been connected by causeways during the Second World War but after 1946 they had been allowed to fall into disrepair. In 1970 the islanders, working with two ex-Costain tipper lorries, a dumper truck, rafts and dhonis had begun to rebuild the Hitaddu-Maradu-Fedu links. The RAF took aerial photographs of the work for the chief to send to Malé and arranged a flight for him in one of the Shackletons so that he could see from the air how the work was progressing. Pleased with the progress and the RAF's gesture he suggested that it would be a good idea for the works services department to rebuild the Gan-Fedu bridge, the wooden decking of which had long since disappeared, leaving only a row of stone piers to show that the two islands had once been joined by a road bridge built to cope with the heavy transport vehicles used throughout the atoll during the war.

The reconstruction and subsequent maintenance of a Gan-Fedu footbridge would have required only a minor investment of resources because the old piers had survived and were apparently sound. The benefits were easy to see. A bridge connecting Gan and Fedu would allow the dhoni line at Gan to be closed, the dhonis could be parked at Fedu, the Maldivians could walk to and from Gan through a check point on the bridge and the Maldivian women who visited the station medical centre from Fedu, Maradu and Hitaddu could go home when their business on Gan was finished, thus dispensing with the need for the accommodation provided in the Maldivian hotel. Finally, if Maldivians could travel from Hitaddu to Fedu on foot or bicycle and then walk across to Gan the RAF could save a large part of the annual sixteen thousand pounds spent on the hire of dhonis. In spite of the benefits, and the minimal investment required, the RAF was not enamoured of the idea and the chief stopped pursuing it.

The old problem of illicit trading by the Maldivians refused to go away and although the RAF maintained quite adequate control over illicit trading between the Maldivians and the expatriates it was virtually impossible to do anything other than make a token attempt to stop them trading with the crews of visiting ships. It was not really an RAF problem unless the goods sold to the Maldivians had been destined for the NAAFI, the works services department or the RAF and even then the RAF police were handicapped by the need to stop and search a fleet of dhonis if they were to put an end to the practices. The chief, however, on yet another unexpected gesture of co-operation, gave the RAF authority to do just that, to check for stolen goods, promising that the miscreants would be dealt with on Hitaddu. In a further clamp down on thefts, which had increased slightly with the easing of restrictions on association, the atoll committee mounted several investigations which led to the recovery and return of stolen property, much of it taken from the Pakistani camp. The culprits were, as usual, dismissed from their jobs on Gan and exiled for at least a year which was the minimum term decreed by the chief for any Maldivian convicted of the theft of property from the leased territories.

That other time-worn proposal, the establishment of a basic health care clinic on every inhabited island, was still not favoured by the chief although he was, by 1970, quite happy for the senior medical officer and the hygienists to visit the villages. That system meant that the medical staff were quickly able to deal with the occasional cases of typhoid among the islanders, and thus reduce the likelihood of an epidemic but it did not reduce to any great extent the number of Maldivians visiting the station's medical centre that year and by the end of June 1970 over five thousand islanders had used the services provided on Gan. Among that number was the atoll chief who, almost blind in his left eye, was flown to Changi in July for an ophthalmic appointment and treatment which improved his sight. Subsequently, he was embarrassed to be told that his government had arranged for him to be examined by an eye specialist in Colombo and although he was aware of the medical ethics of the situation he dared not express to his government any preference for treatment by the British. His Colombo appointment led to an operation which kept him away from the atoll for several weeks and which, whilst not restoring normal vision to his left eye, eventually led to considerable improvement. During his absence the acting chief was reasonably friendly but tended to be remote and to avoid making decisions when dealing with the RAF.

Since the latter part of 1969 football matches between Maldivian teams and RAF section teams had become quite common again after a period when relations had not been good enough for such fixtures to be arranged. Remarkably, after all the acrimony and mistrust of the previous years,

Hitaddu, the centre of the ill-fated secessionist movement, was chosen as the venue for the 1970 Maldivian annual inter-island football tournament. Rarely held outside Malé, the tournament was an event of sufficient importance for several government ministers to attend and, in anticipation of the widespread publicity which would be given to all the match results, a whole series of practice matches was held against RAF section teams in preparation for the August tournament. Unfortunately affairs of state prevented the ministers from travelling to Addu Atoll in August and the tournament was postponed. It had still not been held when Wing Commander Spragg completed his tour at Addu Atoll and handed over command to Wing Commander Gee who had arrived on the 2nd of October, eight days before Spragg left.

Gee, like his predecessors, had been briefed on the political aspects of his new appointment but within a matter of weeks he was given a classic example of the way in which the primary concern of many local Maldivian officials was political caution, even at the risk of human life. At that time the atoll chief was in Colombo and the acting chief, who was not unfriendly, tended to be cautious and to avoid any significant involvement with the British, even though relationships between the British and Maldivian governments were better at that time than they had been since 1957. His caution was never more clearly demonstrated than when a Maldivian sailing boat was in danger of foundering and lives were at stake. In the atoll office on Hitaddu an SOS was picked up at noon from a boat which, with twenty-one people on board, was in serious trouble some twenty miles off Gan.

Lashed by storm-force winds and pounded by heavy seas the boat was in imminent danger of going down. The acting chief's reaction was to contact Malé for permission to ask the RAF to mount a search and rescue operation. The result was a delay of some two-and-a-quarter hours and by the time Gan's Shackleton was airborne there was precious little daylight time left. The search continued until dark without success. A similar search the following day was also unsuccessful. Nothing more was heard of the boat and the best that could be hoped for was that it had carried the crew to another island. As it was not an Adduan boat its fate and that of its crew was only of passing concern to the Adduans; they regarded such risks as part of day-to-day life for Maldivians who went to sea.

It was difficult for Gan's expatriate Europeans to understand how the national inter-island football tournament could be postponed until such time as the government ministers could attend the opening ceremony but that is exactly what happened. As affairs of state continued to prevent the ministers from travelling to Addu Atoll the entire tournament was postponed month after month, finally taking place in December when the Maldivian Attorney General, the Minister for Trade and Development and the Under Secretary of State for Home Affairs arrived at the atoll.

The Maldivian minister opened the tournament with a short speech and Wing Commander Gee was invited to reply before performing the kick-off ceremony for the first match on the 7th of December. The speeches, which were recorded for later transmission over Radio Malé, were broadcast live on Radio Gan as were commentaries from every match throughout the tournament with that from the final being recorded and subsequently broadcast on Radio Malé.

Groups of ten expatriates were invited to attend each match and to tour the village, the hospitality being reciprocated by inviting the Maldivian VIPs to tour Gan and take tea in the officers' mess on the 9th of December. The tournament final, on the 18th of the month, was attended by Ibrahim Rasheed, the Maldivian minister for health and was watched by a selected group of thirty personnel from Gan together with spectators from every island in the atoll. It was all part of the changed political scene in which relationships seemed, after years of mistrust and acrimony, almost too good to be true, with Maldivian ministers feeling able to visit Addu Atoll in safety.

The ministers, convinced that the British military would remain at Addu Atoll for at least the next sixteen years, were blissfully unaware that in Britain, government ministers were asking questions of the Ministry of Defence about the future use of Gan. By 1970 the decision to reduce Britain's military commitments in the Far East had already been made and the intention to withdraw British forces from Singapore in 1971 and 1972 brought into question the long-term need for the mid-ocean staging post. The 1969 Ministry of Defence assessment of the suitability of the facilities available at Addu Atoll for the post-1971 needs drew the broad conclusions that Gan could continue to satisfy the Air Support Command requirements provided the engineering facilities were improved and additional service-men were established at the base to provide adequate security for Strike Command aircraft. It was also thought, in 1969, that the airfield operating hours could be reduced after 1971 but that assessment was changed when the use of Gan was reconsidered in the context of changes at Masirah and

Tengah. The intention was that RAF Gan would remain as a Far East Air Force station until the 1st of April 1971 when it would be transferred to Air Support Command to serve as a staging post between Cyprus and Hong Kong, providing airfield facilities for twenty-four hours a day at a time when Masirah did not and when the facilities at Tengah would be under the control of Singapore Air Defence Command, not the RAF.

As with 1970, so with 1971; a politically quiet year at both national and local levels. At Addu Atoll the order of the day seemed to be reasonably friendly co-operation with only two significant disagreements in the year. The first arose out of the need to reduce the number of Maldivians and Pakistanis employed by the works services department, the second out of the results of the local Maldivian elections.

The reduction of the works services labour force was intended to be a gradual rundown over a period of about six months. In general, Pakistanis whose contracts came to an end in 1971 were not being offered fresh contracts which meant that only twenty or so would have to be made compulsorily redundant before they had served their full time on Gan. The Maldivians, however, were not on fixed term contracts and it was expected that some reduction in the numbers employed could be achieved through natural wastage. Even so, over one hundred of them would have to be made redundant during the year. From April through October, natural wastage was expected to account for the loss of forty-one Maldivian employees with the addition of fifteen compulsory redundancies each month giving an expected workforce reduction of one hundred and forty-six by the 1st of November.

The bone of contention amongst the Pakistanis was that some of those who completed their contracts were not re-engaged even though there was still a demand for their work to be done. Under the Maldivianisation programme their jobs were allocated to Adduans who might otherwise have been made redundant. Understandably, the Pakistanis believed that the work should be reallocated to reduce the number of Pakistani redundancies, not to reduce the number of Maldivian redundancies. Invited to select redundancy candidates from among their number, the Pakistanis would have nothing to do with the idea, leaving the selection to the works services engineers.

For the Adduans there was a crumb of comfort. The effect of the redundancy plan on their community was to be temporarily offset by the need to transport a thousand tons of aggregate from Gan to the Hitaddu transmitter site, a job which would require labourers employed solely for the duration of the task. In addition, dhonis and crews would also be hired provided the dhonis were strong enough to carry the aggregate. The offer of employment was welcomed by the islanders but the atoll chief still felt obliged to obtain permission from Malé before agreeing to provide the fifty-six men and six dhonis which were needed for the job.

With dhonis available for hire at fifty pence a day and Maldivian labourers willing to work for less than five pounds a week, it was not surprising that there were numerous other occasions when the islanders were offered casual employment. There were never any objections from the Maldivian government but the chief did not feel confident enough to allow the islanders to accept any work until government approval had been received, occasionally creating frustrating delays for the works services engineers.

The overall situation was depressing for the Maldivian employees and in previous years would no doubt have provoked the atoll chief into ordering them to take some action to disrupt the work of the RAF. But attitudes had softened by 1971 and although Moosa expressed his concern he behaved rather philosophically, accepting the obvious fact that the workload had reduced and that job losses were inevitable.

His attitude was particularly remarkable in view of the fact that in February the islanders were due to vote in the biennial elections for the seven-man atoll committee with the candidate who polled the most votes becoming the atoll chief, subject to approval from central government. There were thirty-six candidates and approximately five thousand voters: all the Adduan men and women aged over twenty-one. The ballot boxes were sent to the capital on the 25th of February and the ballot resulted in a win for Ahmed Salih Ali Didi, a thirty-eight-year-old Hitadduan who had served on the committee for four years. Moosa Ali Didi who had been the atoll chief for several years came second. On learning of a government ruling that no government official would be permitted to serve as a committee member, three of the island headmen who were elected to the committee decided to resign; for them, government official status as headmen was preferable to the status enjoyed by committee members.

In March, Ahmed Didi was called to Malé to be interviewed before being confirmed as the Adduan atoll chief. Whilst he was away, the RAF virtually suspended all dealings with his deputy to avoid showing any preference for him over the recently-elected chief. It was May before Ahmed returned from Malé, his appointment as atoll chief confirmed and his briefing complete. His succession was marked, as far as the RAF was concerned, with a change in the relationship which had been established with his predecessor.

Ahmed started his period in office by being rather remote and cool towards any advances made by the Maldivian Affairs officer. The inference was that his briefing in Malé had made him very wary of having any dealings with the British which might reflect badly on him in the eyes of his Prime Minister. The hope was that this change would be temporary and that, once he had been in office a few months he would be confident enough in his dealings to adopt the same co-operative approach as Moosa.

At least Ahmed had confirmation from his government that previously unacceptable associations with the RAF were now approved; in April it had been agreed that the hygiene teams could visit all the islands at Addu Atoll provided three days notice was given to the atoll committee and each visit was made in the presence of the village headman. It was thus easy enough, within weeks of Ahmed Didi's return, to obtain his approval for the senior medical officer and his staff to conduct a survey of Hulumidu. Very little medical expertise was needed to identify the major sources of the diseases which so often afflicted the islanders; human faeces lay exposed on the island beaches together with rotting fish heads and fly-infested entrails. As far as the chief was concerned, that was the way the islanders lived and he was not prepared to act upon the obvious recommendation that they should be given basic education in hygiene even though he was keen that other education and training, intended to support the Maldivianisation programme, should continue.

One early indication of Ahmed Didi's approach was his insistence, immediately on his return from Malé in May, that his representative at all investigations and hearing of charges involving any Maldivian employee would be a member of the atoll committee. Initially accepted with some trepidation by the RAF, the arrangement actually worked very well with the various committee members who acted as the chief's representatives being as fair-minded as possible, presumably because Ahmed had made it clear to them that if they failed to be seen as open-minded in their consideration of the matters under investigation he, the initiator of the system, would lose face with the RAF.

July brought the breakthrough which indicated that Ahmed was feeling secure enough in his new position to take the initiative of inviting seventy Gan personnel to visit Hitaddu to watch the inter-island dhoni race and to tour the village. They formed the largest single contingent of Gan personnel ever to set foot outside the leased territories and enjoyed a highly successful, incident free, tour. It was an eye-opener for the visitors, most of whom had had no idea of the islanders' living conditions and could only wonder at the tenacity of the villagers whose domestic lives were in such stark contrast to their working lives on Gan. The chief then took the unprecedented step of asking his government for permission to invite the RAF's medical staff to conduct a mass vaccination programme in the villages and the works services engineers to clear coral growths from the dhoni routes off the main islands. Even more surprising was the fact that his requests were granted without argument. The result was that the medical officers arranged for smallpox vaccination teams to visit all the villages in September and the engineers made life less hazardous for the dhoni owners by blasting away the numerous coral heads which had developed in the channels off Maradu, Hitaddu and Hulumidu.

Political harmony in the Maldives meant that, as far as the British government was concerned, the only political cloud on the Indian Ocean horizon came from America, not from Malé. During the 1960s the Americans had become increasingly anxious to use the facilities on Gan; like the British, they needed an Indian Ocean base. It was an internationally sensitive matter and eventually their requests to use the RAF's staging-post facilities became so frequent and so strong that the British government decided to offer the island of Diego Garcia to the Americans so that they could develop their own base. To do that, Britain 'purchased' the Chagos Group of islands, renamed them the British Indian Ocean Territories, forcibly evacuated the islanders and, over the years, recouped from the American government far more than the entire cost of the operation. The advantages for the British were obvious; they would not have to be concerned about the possible use of Gan by American aircraft carrying nuclear weapons and, most importantly, RAF Gan and the United States Air Force base on Diego Garcia would provide diversion airfield facilities for each other. The last of the Ilois people were removed from Diego Garcia in 1970 and within months of their departure the American air base was under

construction, its progress monitored by Gan's Shackleton crews who would over-fly the Chagos Archipelago during their Indian Ocean patrols.

This shabby episode, a clear breach of the United Nations Charter, was made worse by the fact that many of the evacuees ended up living in poverty in Mauritius because inadequate arrangements were made for them to be decently resettled. Thirty years later the islanders had the belated satisfaction of obtaining a High Court ruling that their eviction had been unlawful and that they were entitled to return, adequately compensated, to their archipelago. In court, Lord Justice Laws slated the behaviour of the British officials who had brokered the secret deal with the Americans and effectively sent the islanders into exile and poverty.

In late August 1971, Wing Commander Gee completed his tour as Gan's station commander, by which time the Ministry of Defence staff had decided that, following the rundown of the Far East Air Force and the transfer of RAF Gan into Air Support Command, the mid-ocean staging post should be under the command of a Group Captain. Consequently Group Captain Sheppard arrived at Gan on the 26th of August, two days before Wing Commander Gee departed.

The timing of Sheppard's arrival meant that within days he was introduced to a Gan-style bank holiday festival with events enjoyed by the expatriates and the Adduans alike. It gave him an immediate impression of the off-duty relationship which the islanders had with the expatriates and at that time it was a fair impression for, at both local and national level, friendship was the order of the day.

The relaxed attitude displayed by the atoll chief in the early 1970s was undoubtedly a reflection of the attitudes adopted at national level where Nasir was apparently keen to let bygones be bygones, due in part to his understandable interest in the benefits which would continue to accrue for as long as the Maldivian and British governments remained on friendly terms. Aid from Britain had already amounted to five hundred thousand pounds over the previous five years and there was no reason for Nasir to imagine that it would end there. There was, in addition, the steady flow of revenue from Addu Atoll where the wage-earning islanders had become contributors to the national economy. Whatever Nasir's reasons were, they had led to a dramatic improvement in the relationships at Addu Atoll.

Exemplifying that and erasing any doubts which Sheppard may have had about the cooperative stance adopted by Ahmed Didi, the medical officers implemented the smallpox vaccination programme, as arranged, in September. With ninety per cent of the villagers vaccinated during the first round of visits and with arrangements made for the remainder to be seen the following month, it was an operation which could be justifiably regarded as a success. Within weeks the Maldivian government had also called upon the expertise of the Gan officers, asking the senior medical officer and the district works officer to visit Malé in October to advise on the repair and refurbishment of the hospital.

Their visit revealed that the hospital was actually in far better condition than they had expected and arrangements were made for works services engineers to visit Malé the following January to effect the necessary minor repairs.

Events in November showed that the Maldivian government, whilst quite prepared to accept offers of free medical treatment, was still not prepared, or not able, to pay for the Adduans to be protected against the potentially fatal outbreaks of typhoid which so often occurred at the atoll. When three villagers from Maradu contracted typhoid that month a request was received from Malé for a full immunisation programme for the villagers, a very different attitude from that previously shown. But, for the reasons given on page 324, the programme was not implemented, the number of typhoid cases increased, the planned Christmas party and firework display for the Maldivian children was cancelled and the toys were given to the chief for distribution.

1971 ended as quietly it had begun. Maldivian politics, both nationally and locally were running smoothly with the Adduans believing that Gan's future was assured, a belief bolstered by the creation of additional facilities on the base where a new squash court and a large extension to the education centre had recently been built. Older hands amongst the Gan personnel, already wondering whether the base would be needed after Britain's military withdrawal from Singapore, were taking such building as an indication that the station's days were numbered.

As far as Maldivian affairs were concerned 1972 was much like 1971. In January relations with the Maldivian government were further improved when some of the Gan-based works services engineers went to Malé and spent ten days repairing the hospital which they had inspected the previous October. Knowing that British aid and Department of the Environment goodwill had been accepted with appreciation by Nasir, the atoll chief

became even more amenable, readily responding to approaches made through Mohammed Saeed, the ill-fated Adduan who had been allowed to return to Addu Atoll as a result of the political amnesty declared at the end of 1968 and, once back in favour with the atoll chief, had been re-employed on Gan and promoted, becoming a Maldivian supervisor and senior interpreter.

Maldivianisation gathered pace during 1972, much to the satisfaction of the chief and the atoll committee who saw it as a way of mitigating the effects of the inevitable redundancies brought about by the reduced need for building and maintenance work. Over the course of the year the total number of Pakistani employees was brought down to one hundred and forty-seven whilst the number of Maldivian workers increased to eight hundred and forty-seven. Also satisfying from the Adduans' point of view was the fact that the Maldivianisation programme required a considerable amount of on-the-job training which benefited the local communities by improving the villagers' employment prospects and by increasing the range of craft skills within their society.

The Maldivian employees were also heartened to hear that they would be receiving a pay rise early in 1973, their second in sixteen years. In remarkably short time there were strong rumours that their wages would be increased by at least twenty per cent, substantially more than they had expected. If true, that could certainly be justified, partly because the previous increase, in 1968, had not really compensated for the rise in the cost of living since their wages had been set in 1957 and partly because the recent pay rise for the Pakistanis, made in order to counter their government's devaluation, had given rise to a reasonable expectation that the Maldivians would be fairly treated. Regardless of the rumours, the employees knew that the amount they would actually receive would be determined late in 1972 when a pay review team from London was scheduled to visit the atoll and investigate every aspect of the Maldivians' conditions of employment and cost of living.

Organised social contacts continued to increase with the Maldivian community on Hitaddu arranging monthly tours of their village for groups of about twenty Gan personnel, an arrangement which was by then working very smoothly and seemed to be enjoyed by the Maldivians as much as by the expatriates. The atoll chief even suggested, in March, that the Maldivian Affairs officer should make a car journey from Hitaddu to Fedu and from

Hankada to Maradu, demonstrating that the causeways were all in good condition.

Although the schedule of visits was interrupted through August and September after a case of typhoid had been reported among the villagers on Hitaddu, it was resumed in October when it was certain that the isolated case was not the precursor of a widespread outbreak. For his part, the chief readily accepted an invitation to tour Gan, to see for himself the working conditions for the Adduans, and to visit the powerhouse in which he had expressed a particular interest.

For some unexplained reason, the Maldivian government was apparently in favour of the visits which it had so strongly resisted in the past. Approval was even given for a team of five scientists from Imperial College London to set up camp on Wilingili for about six weeks to study the flora, fauna and geology of the island, an unusual concession which would have been difficult to obtain only a few years earlier. On a personal level the chief extended his hospitality to the station commander almost as a matter of course, inviting Group Captains Sheppard and Salmon to lunch at Hitaddu on the 25th of May, the day before Salmon took over from Sheppard.

The only international matter of any political significance to Gan during 1972 related to the use of the base by Australian and New Zealand aircraft and ships. It had always been assumed by Britain that such casual use was permitted under the terms of the lease but for some reason the Chief of the Defence Staff had queried the arrangement only to discover that, technically, the consent of the Maldivian government had to be obtained for each intended visit except for a ship or aircraft in distress. Common practice however was usually, but not invariably, to notify the Maldivian government of any non-RAF flights or of scheduled visits by non-British ships as a matter of courtesy, an arrangement which had been agreed between the Foreign and Commonwealth Office and the Maldivian Ambassador in April 1968. Such courtesy notification would apply to the use of Gan by Commonwealth ships and aircraft and appeared to be acceptable to the Maldivian government. The advice given to the Chief of the Defence Staff by the Foreign and Commonwealth Office was that, given good relations, the system seemed to work smoothly and it was therefore not really advisable to raise the issue with any thoughts of trying to regularise what was an irregular but widely accepted system.

On the 20th of November another pay review team arrived from London to investigate the pay and conditions of the Maldivian employees, spending a week checking the working arrangements and interviewing the Adduans, all of whom were delighted by the prospect of yet another pay rise. They were even more delighted when, early in January 1973, they received details of a pay award which was to be back-dated to the first of June 1972. Using the basic rates of pay on the 31st of May 1972 as a datum, the Maldivians were to receive an increase of thirty-two per cent for the period from the 1st of June 1972 to the 31st of December 1972 and a further increase on the 1st of January 1973 to bring basic pay rates thirty-six per cent higher than on the 31st of May 1972. Some allowances were also increased with the result that the award added an extra seventy-five thousand pounds to the annual wage bill for Maldivian labour. Even so, this, the first pay rise since 1968, still didn't fully compensate the islanders for increases in the cost of basic commodities purchased through the NAAFI where price rises since 1966 had been two hundred and twenty-seven per cent for rice, two hundred per cent for potatoes, two hundred and sixteen per cent for onions and one hundred and fifty-seven per cent for sugar. It was nevertheless welcomed by the atoll chief as a fair settlement, particularly as the Maldivianisation of jobs previously allocated to Pakistanis was continuing. If anything, that programme was seen by the chief as more important than the pay award because the population of the atoll had grown to over thirteen thousand and paid employment had become one of the foundation stones of the local economy.

1972 ended and 1973 arrived with the usual celebrations on Gan and a continuation of the amicable relations both at government level and at Addu Atoll; 1973 was to become noteworthy as a year of trouble-free relationships with the Adduans sustaining the smooth-running pattern of cooperation which had developed early in 1972.

The number of expatriates visiting the Maldivian villages during the year increased dramatically with some one hundred and fifty, many of them Pakistani Muslims, visiting the four inhabited islands of the atoll during the religious festival in January. In February the chief actively encouraged the RAF's hygiene teams to visit the island headmen to persuade them to initiate a refuse burning system and although the teams had little success their visits clearly showed that they had the chief's support and from then on their work became much easier. Co-operation at work had rarely been better, due in part to the obvious progress of the Maldivianisation programme which, by March, had been mainly responsible for reducing the number of Pakistani workers to one hundred and two and increasing the number of Maldivian employees to nine hundred and fifty.

By then the officer commanding RAF Gan was Group Captain Whitlock who had arrived on the 23rd of February, three days before Group Captain Salmon departed. Whitlock inherited the calm political atmosphere and the friendly local relationships which had been enjoyed for nine months by his predecessor and which were set, with one exception, to continue well beyond his nine-month tour.

The fact that British-Maldivian friendship in 1973 still extended to government level was demonstrated by Ahmed Hilmy Didi, the Maldivian minister of fisheries who, in an almost unprecedented gesture, wrote to the British High Commissioner in Colombo in December to comment on the good relations which existed at the atoll and to express his appreciation of the reception he had received and the hospitality which he had enjoyed on Gan when he had visited the atoll earlier that month.

1974 started with the promise of nothing unusual as far as the RAF was concerned, just a steady strengthening of the political arrangements which had worked so well for the last few years. The role of Gan in the British military network appeared, at least to the Maldivians, to be firmly established and the Maldivianisation programme, which would eventually lead to the removal of all Pakistanis from Gan, held the promise of a consequent increase in the general prosperity of the Adduans. Ahmed Didi, the atoll chief, having overcome any inhibitions about organised visits to the various villages, invited almost two hundred expatriates to visit the islands during the course of the Eid festival in January, the month when he also demonstrated that he had lost any earlier qualms about his dealings with the RAF by asking to purchase generator spares together with four unserviceable engines from the Department of the Environment and additional fuel for the traders. For good measure he asked for RAF technicians to effect the repairs to the atoll's radio telephone and, almost inevitably, for medical assistance to deal with an outbreak of measles among the villagers. That same month he extended the social contacts with the Adduans by agreeing to let a dozen officers camp overnight on Bushey where some of the Maldivian employees set up camp for them, acted as hosts and met all the expenses.

The informal weekend, unheard of in previous years, was spent swimming and shark fishing and even included a visit by a musical troupe from Hitaddu. It was the first of many such weekend camps on the uninhabited islands with the expatriates always invited as guests of the Maldivians who organised the camp. As the year progressed the host groups became more and more ambitious, steadily increasing the number of guests until, at the largest such gathering of the year, a group of forty-two officers, other ranks and civilians camped on Wilingili, the island leased by the Maldivian government to coconut farmers.

There was one unwelcome, but fortunately short-lived, trend at the beginning of 1974. A spate of minor thefts by Maldivians occurred in January, particularly of bicycles where the preferred technique for stealing them was to throw them into the lagoon just off the beach during the daytime, return at night by wading across the Gan-Fedu gap, retrieve the bicycles from the shallows and wade back to Fedu with them. From Fedu the bicycles could be ridden along the newly repaired inter-island causeways as far as Hitaddu.

Generally however the incidence of crime was reducing, due in no small measure to the presence of police dog patrols which made the Maldivians very wary indeed. Those who were not apprehended during their clandestine forays rarely remained undetected for long; thefts were generally followed by arrests and, as was the case after four Maldivians had been sent to Malé for trial on charges of stealing bicycles, the conviction of the thieves was invariably followed by a drop in the incidence of offences. The way in which Ahmed Didi dealt with any islander accused of theft showed that he had no sympathy whatsoever for those who thought they could get away with it and although the January offences were regrettable they were dismissed as an aberration on the part of a small number of Adduans.

Inevitably, illegal trading by the Adduans continued. Clamping down on the practice was not as easy as coping with petty crime but neither was it an RAF responsibility unless the expatriates were involved. Small-scale trading with Gan personnel was ignored. The islanders would offer to sell souvenirs such as models of the dhonis and buggaloes, inscribed sword-sticks and daggers, painted coconuts and carved shells. In exchange, they sought to buy items not readily available through the authorised traders, either clothing or utilitarian items such as waterproof glue, which meant that any expatriate going on leave or temporary duty was likely to be given a shopping list by his room boy or by the Maldivians in his workplace. Often the list would include articles which were very difficult to obtain in England such as a twenty-eight-inch black brassiere, suitable for a normal sized Maldivian woman whose colour preference for all clothes followed the trend for dark colours which was common throughout the atoll.

Trading between the Adduans and the crew of any visiting ship could not, however, be ignored because it was blatantly undermining the business of the authorised Maldivian traders. Even so, it remained a Maldivian problem; the RAF really only became involved when a visiting ship's captain could be persuaded to curtail the illegal trading, easy enough with the Royal Navy but not so easy with some of the visiting merchant ships. The chief was invariably co-operative but he had to balance his own popularity with the maintenance of good relations with the RAF and that could result in the kind of embarrassment caused in February when the RAF police went aboard the SS Mahout which was at anchor in the lagoon.

On board they found several Maldivians, none an authorised trader, purchasing goods from the crew. The Maldivians were evicted from the ship but when the police found sacks of flour in one of the dhonis they promptly confiscated them, declaring that all the goods on board the Mahout belonged to the NAAFI or the Department of the Environment. Ahmed Didi, however, declared that on this occasion the military police had no right to confiscate the flour. The police responded by stating that they had no intention of trying to stop the Adduans trading with a visiting merchant-man but every intention of stopping them if they were trading in RAF goods. The ensuing argument over the ownership of the flour went on until the RAF was obliged to return it to the Maldivians *via* Ahmed Didi rather than undermine the goodwill which had been built up since he had been elected.

Four years of harmony had resulted in a good lifestyle as far as the Maldivians were concerned. Health care was undoubtedly the biggest bonus with the annual consultations running at some ten thousand, of which over six and a half thousand were non-entitled Adduans. But they were also enjoying more and more of the benefits of a Western lifestyle, purchasing a whole range of utilitarian and luxury items, from motor launches to electrical equipment and the generators which were needed to provide the necessary power. Even when home was a very basic kadjan hut such luxuries were likely to be installed because they had become status symbols.

Many of the villagers owned mopeds, some of the more wealthy Adduans had bought ex-RAF cars and a few entrepreneurs, forecasting that before long many of the villagers would want to replace their kadjan huts by more substantial dwellings, had purchased the ex-Costain vehicles and plant.

Mechanisation was inevitably accompanied by a demand for petrol, diesel and oil and as early as 1972 the chief, claiming that the Adduans owned one hundred and thirteen vehicles, outboard motors and generators, had been granted an increase in the monthly allocation of four and a half thousand gallons of fuel supplied to the Maldivian traders by the RAF. By 1974 he was predicting that the demand would continue to grow.

Ahmed Didi was keen to see the good life extended and after he and Mohammed Saeed were given privilege flights to Singapore for a large scale shopping expedition he suggested that the authorised traders should be allowed to travel to and from Singapore as fare-paying passengers with the RAF. The request was turned down by the Ministry of Defence staff because it was obviously one which could not be granted without establishing a system which would undoubtedly have quickly become an embarrassment. But the reason given for the refusal was odd. The Ministry staff declared that they could not be seen to be competing for customers with civil airlines, giving the impression that the decision makers in London had little idea of the location of Gan or the fact that the nearest commercial airfield used by the international airlines was in Sri Lanka, some seven hundred and fifty miles across the ocean and a three week journey by a series of island-hopping trading boats.

From Malé, the government ministers were no longer instructing the atoll chief to refuse day-to-day offers of help from the RAF or the works services engineers and, willing to allow such help to be given to other atolls in the southern reaches of the archipelago, they even gave permission for an RAF launch to sail into Fua Mulaku waters to position reef marker buoys; a boon for the islanders and a useful navigation exercise for the marine craft crews. The ministers were also discussing possible commercial developments in the Maldives and, in particular, were exploring Nasir's idea for the development of tourism in the archipelago. Since his election to the presidency, he had been keen to pursue this idea, arguing that the two significant attractions which the Maldives offered, over and above their natural beauty and the attractive climate, were remoteness and autocratic government controls, a combination which could provide privileged tourism for the wealthy. The ministers, equally keen on the idea, issued instructions that every atoll chief was to allocate one island for tourism and build, or allocate, two four-bed bungalows for use by visitors. Ahmed Didi was far from happy with those instructions but he had no say in the matter

When Ali Maniku, the Maldivian government minister for tourism, visited Addu Atoll in February he was accompanied by three anthropology students, two Danish and one Finnish, who were on a world tour and were undertaking some research whilst travelling through the Maldives. They were certainly not run-of-the-mill holidaymakers but Ali Maniku regarded them as the atoll's first tourists and they were, if his government were to be believed, the forerunners of a steady flow of visitors who would pay handsomely for the privilege of holidaying in the archipelago. Although Maniku did not discuss his government's plans with the station commander it later became fairly obvious that his visit was partly planned to give him a chance to assess the daily usage of the airfield on Gan because his government obviously had hopes that holidaymakers would be able to fly to Gan rather than travel by sea.

Therein lay the snag as far as the British were concerned.

In May 1974, three months after Maniku had reported on his visits to those atolls which were expected to establish some local amenities for tourists, Ahmed Zaki, the Maldivian prime minister, visited London to discuss with the Foreign and Commonwealth Secretary the use of Gan airfield by civilian aircraft. He was hoping to get agreement on two separate plans.

Firstly he requested the use of Gan by the Maldivians' fledgling airline in order to provide a fortnightly or monthly communications shuttle between Malé and Addu Atoll. The Air Maldive aircraft would either be a Convair 440 or a charter aircraft owned by the Sri Lankan Air Force, themselves occasional visitors to Gan. The Air Maldive flights would, he hoped, start within four or five months when the airline had been established on Hulule.

His second request was for the use of Gan by international civil airlines bringing tourists to Addu Atoll for transfer either by boat or by light aircraft to Malé Atoll, a shuttle system which would only require the use of Gan until Hulule had been developed as an international airport.

The request to use Gan for Air Maldive communication flights was really undemanding and was politically difficult if not impossible to refuse.

There were no air staff objections and no security objections to those flights and Zaki was informed accordingly. The second request raised all kinds of potential problems from security to accommodation and aircraft servicing. Given that Admiralty charts of the atoll were freely available, the security aspects may have been exaggerated, but the fact remained that civil airliners would bring to Gan anyone who paid the fare and that would provide opportunities for aerial photography and airfield observation when the passengers left the aircraft. Accommodation on Gan was so limited that if crews or passengers had to stay on the island overnight it would be extremely difficult to provide bed space for them and almost impossible to maintain adequate security across the base. The idea of regarding them as a Maldivian problem and shipping them to Hitaddu was superficially attractive but would inevitably lead to political repercussions as soon as the passengers formally complained. Finally there was the difficulty posed by the need to provide basic aircraft servicing facilities. The RAF was in no position to provide such services because appropriately certificated engineers, equipment and spares for a range of civilian aircraft just did not exist on Gan and the Ministry of Defence could hardly consider establishing a suitable aircraft servicing facility in order to support the Maldivians' tourist industry. All those considerations were relevant to Gan's normal operational state but the situation would be compounded during any military exercise. At such times the arrival of tourists on civil airlines would be totally unacceptable.

By chance, Zaki's visit to London occurred only a matter of weeks after the British government had asked the Ministry of Defence to conduct a defence review setting out the policy options within set financial constraints. That allowed the Foreign and Commonwealth Secretary to inform Zaki that no decision could be made in response to his second request until Britain's future use of Gan was clarified within that defence review. Zaki thus became aware very early on that the review was taking place and was obviously astute enough to realise that with Britain's large scale withdrawal from the Far East there had to be some doubt as to whether the British would abandon Gan before the expiry of the lease. Although Callaghan could not pre-empt the findings of the defence review such a withdrawal was, he knew, a distinct possibility. Hinting at the provision, within limits, of aid if the British were to withdraw prematurely from Addu Atoll he suggested that the Maldivians would need to take care before considering the advances of other nations to fill any vacuum created when Britain did withdraw from the Maldives, regardless of when that was. Zaki, whilst hoping that Britain would stay, agreed that such care would be needed. He also referred to the 1975 government elections in the Maldives saying that he hoped to remain in office; the unspoken implication being that he hoped to gain some British support for the Maldives which he could publicly attribute to his visit to London.

By June the Defence Review Steering Committee had concluded that there was no military justification for the retention of overseas commitments at the expense of Britain's contribution to the North Atlantic Treaty Organisation. Britain could therefore withdraw from Gan in 1976 subsequent to the rundown of her Far Eastern military presence. In September, after the broader implications of such a withdrawal had been examined and the question of whether the base should be retained to provide a reinforcement capability had been considered, the decision was made that retention could not be justified and a 1976 closure was agreed. The government accepted the recommendation and informed the Chief of the Air Staff that withdrawal from Gan was to be completed during March 1976.

The military decision was simple; the political considerations were anything but. In November Callaghan outlined the complexities in a loose minute to the Ministry of Overseas Development and the Vice-Chief of the Air Staff saying:

'As a result of the defence review we have decided on a complete withdrawal from Gan by March 1976. . . . we have a responsibility to help the Maldives as far as we could to tide over the effects of our departure . . . it is important to ensure that the airport facilities at Gan should be available to use if we needed them in the future and that the Maldivians will not permit others whom we might not wish to see installed there settled in after our departure. . . . (a) severe effect on Maldivian economy. Five hundred thousand pounds (10 to 15 per cent of Gross National Product) transformed the Maldivian society by creating a money economy with a loss of traditional skills and with wages and hospital services helping to generate a large increase in population . . . we should be prepared to offer something more than current aid to retain Maldivian goodwill and our self respect. I would suggest an investment of some two or three million pounds over three to five years via the World Bank or the Asian Development Bank.

There are implications in all this for our military forces. Hulule airport will not be ready before 1978 and the Diego Garcia runway is not likely to be ready before 1976 so no alternative mid-ocean staging post will be available if Gan closes early in 1976. In theory the lease agreement for Gan runs to 1986 even if we withdraw: in practice it is not on to keep it on care and maintenance in order to exclude others and serve us in an emergency.

The Maldivians want an international air strip in the north of the archipelago, at Hulule island in Malé Atoll, and a southern airstrip for internal flights. Our best thrust is political not military. Let the current Air Maldive flights build up. If tourist flights arrive, the RAF should co-operate with the Maldivians as much as possible. What is needed now is careful negotiations with the Maldivian Government in order to achieve satisfactory withdrawal by April 1976, to ensure that access is denied to other military powers, to agree on aid disbursement and retain the good will of the Maldivians.'

The stage was set for a difficult year in which the British and Maldivian governments would have to hammer out an agreement which would compensate the Maldivians for Britain's premature withdrawal from the atoll. There was every reason to believe that, for the remaining months in the operational life of RAF Gan, acrimony between the two governments would spill over into the Adduan communities, souring relations between the Adduans and their British employers.

Remarkably, that was not to be so.

The decision to withdraw from Gan in 1976 was not generally know around the Ministry of Defence until late in 1974 and whilst the politicians were finalising their plans to abandon the base the Ministry of Defence staff were still planning the installation, by July 1975, of four radio transmitters to improve the radio facilities at the base. The transmitters were intended to replace obsolete equipment and, after the withdrawal from the Gulf and the Singapore rundown, to provide a maritime rear link and tactical communications cell. It was not that the Ministry of Defence departments were unaware that Gan's future was unclear it was just that, as a Directorate of Signals (Air) letter indicated ' . . . future unclear, go ahead pending clarification or a natural break'.

Zaki's second visit to London in 1974 lasted from the 27th of October to the 5th of November by which time Callaghan was aware that Gan was to be abandoned but was not apparently prepared to inform the Maldivian Prime Minister of the fact, probably because the decision would quickly be communicated *via* the Maldivians to everyone at Addu Atoll which was no way for them to find out.

By the time Zaki made that second visit to London the seeds had been sown for the development of a tourist industry in the Maldives, with holiday accommodation already built on several islands. In September the Maldivian airline had acquired three Convairs and in October the Prime Minister had been on board the Air Maldive inaugural flight to Gan. Zaki was thus understandably keen to discuss with Callaghan the growth of the tourist industry and the accompanying use of Gan's airfield by civil airlines. It seems that he had to be content with Callaghan's ready acceptance of frequent Air Maldive communications flights into Gan and his delay in responding to the proposal for civil airline flights to the island '...*pending the result of the defence review*'.

When Zaki and the British Defence Adviser from Colombo arrived at Gan on board a Maldive Air Convair later in November the minister gave no indication that he was aware of the imminent closure of the RAF base. Thirty-six other Maldivian passengers were on board that flight, all of them businessmen or politicians, all involved in some way with the intended development of Maldivian tourism, all used to a reasonable standard of living and all needing to be accommodated overnight. The station commander was sympathetic but this was obviously the first of many such visits and, quite apart from any security considerations, he was unwilling to establish a precedent by trying to accommodate such a large group in the Blue Lagoon transit hotel. The Maldivian hotel was far too basic for them and as there was a limited number of good quality houses on Hitaddu some of them stayed overnight as guests of the more wealthy families in various villages across the atoll. On this occasion assistance from the RAF was therefore restricted to the provision of a launch to ferry the visitors from island to island. It was a wise decision because the number of Air Maldives flights into Gan did increase and the Maldivian government accepted the Foreign and Commonwealth Office ruling that visiting groups of Maldivian businessmen and politicians could be offered the use of the RAF's transit accommodation only under tightly controlled conditions which set out such use as a privilege not a right thereby giving the station commander guidelines and control over a situation which could have got out of hand.

It was ironic that the Maldivians, unaware of the British decision to withdraw from Addu Atoll, were working on the development of a tourist industry to add to their national economy; the unfortunate truth was that, after April 1976, the Maldivians would be losing far more than they could hope to gain from tourism.

Section 5 – Expatriate Life at Addu Atoll

Fig 16.1. First sight of Addu Atoll islands and the barrier reef.

XVI   The Pioneers: 1957 – 1960

The unaccompanied tourists

The men of the Ship's Flag detachment pioneered the work on Gan but the servicemen and the civilians who arrived at the atoll at any time prior to the completion of the island-long runway and its ancillary buildings could justifiably regard themselves as pioneers for they had the unenviable task of converting the swampy, densely-wooded island into a fully operational staging post for the RAF's transport and combat aircraft. That latter group of pioneers began to arrive during June 1957 by which time Squadron Leader Schofield had settled in as the first officer commanding Royal Air Force Gan.

At the end of August 1957 the main airfield construction contract had been awarded to Richard Costain Ltd and by mid-September the airmen on Gan had been joined by the first of the civilian expatriates; a NAAFI manager, some of the senior Air Ministry Works Directorate staff and several of Costain's site engineers and plant operators. From then on, the number of newcomers increased week after week and that led to the development, during the latter months of 1957, of three domestic sites. The servicemen's camp was on the northern shore of the island, slightly east of the re-commissioned runway line with a community of European civilians alongside. Pakistani and Ceylonese civilians were also arriving, recruited and brought to Gan to work for Costain, the NAAFI and the Air Ministry because they offered cheap labour with skills and physical abilities which the Adduans could not match. With their arrival another domestic site was created or, more precisely, two sites within a newly established Asian village in the south-west sector of the island. The multi-cultural society had come to Gan.

Across the expatriate communities each individual's status was reflected in his conditions of employment, which varied significantly in the three major elements: rates of pay, the expected length of service at the atoll and the entitlement, if any, to annual leave away from the Maldives. Virtually all the expatriate civilians, European and Asian, were employed on contracts which set out their conditions of employment. They were, with the exception of a few senior executives, volunteers attracted either by the opportunity of earning a considerable sum of money or, as was the case for most of the Pakistanis, by the opportunity to qualify for a British passport after five years Crown Service. In contrast, few of the servicemen were volunteers, they did not benefit from any significant addition to their rates of pay nor did service on Gan necessarily enhance their career prospects. They, however, were not expecting to spend much more than six months at the atoll. The men of the Ship's Flag detachment had known that they would leave as soon as the old wartime runway had been re-commissioned and the normal tour length for airmen who arrived during the latter half of 1957 was six months.

That was a reasonably short period as far as the airmen were concerned but such a rapid turnover of personnel was obviously inefficient and as the base was rendered more hospitable the Air Ministry staff decided that any serviceman posted to Gan after 1957 would spend twelve months at the atoll and would not be entitled to take any mid-tour leave. The result was that for the first few months of 1958 there was a two-tier society amongst the servicemen with the newcomers facing what they saw as a double tour in comparison with those who had arrived in 1957. There were the inevitable jibes and niggles but there was never any real resentment over the issue.

Whilst the Air Ministry staff had been reviewing the tour length for the airmen posted to Gan, the Far East Air Force Command staff in Singapore had been considering the status of the station commander relative to the works department's district officer who, in the Air Ministry hierarchy, was accorded the status of a Wing Commander and was thus senior in rank, but not in position, to Squadron Leader Schofield. That didn't worry Schofield but it bothered the Command staff and by the end of the year RAF Gan's establishment had been upgraded and Schofield promoted to the rank of Wing Commander with his tour of duty extended from six months to twelve in line with the increased tour length of the airmen who were due to arrive at Gan in the new year.

Regardless of the many differences, the servicemen and the expatriate civilians did have one thing in common; they were not permitted to bring their families to the atoll. The Pakistani who hoped to be there for at least five years, the serviceman who had been posted to Gan for a matter of months and the European civilian who would be at the atoll for the duration of his contract, each was subject to the same embargo. Each was there without his family and each became a member of the heterogeneous group generally referred to as the unaccompanied tourists.

The new arrivals

Even those passengers who were fortunate enough to arrive at Gan during good weather would often not catch sight of the atoll until their aircraft was within five miles of it for at any greater distance the wooded spits of land were not easily discernible. Only the white breakers on the barrier reefs surrounding the atoll betrayed the presence of that small ring of islands in the middle of the Indian Ocean (Fig 16.1) and on the descent to Gan most passengers found it hard to believe that such a speck of land was large enough to accommodate an RAF airfield with a resident community of several hundred expatriates.

New arrivals, whether greeted by blazing sunshine or torrential rain, would generally walk down the aircraft steps, look around at what was to be their equatorial home for at least the next six months and think of a dozen questions. The weather, the accommodation, the food, the off-duty diversions, the NAAFI and the nature of the job; all, to a greater or lesser extent, occupied the minds of the newcomers who, rain or shine, would quickly have their attention diverted by the tropical environment and by the sight of some of the island's wildlife. Small lizards abounded and numerous geckos were to be found in and around the huts, tolerated or even encouraged to take up residence because they were the most effective fly-killers around. But it was the sight of the fruit bats which invariably took the newcomers aback. With a wing span and body size which led many transients to refer to them as flying foxes the bats tended to migrate between Fedu and Gan each day, the flight arriving on Gan late in the afternoon, hanging in the trees overnight and setting off for Fedu in the morning. They looked fearsome but were harmless enough if left alone.

Most newcomers expected to encounter voracious insects on the island, in particular they expected to become blood donors for the local mosquito population. Their fears were largely unfounded. In and around the domestic sites the 'swinging smokies' had virtually eradicated the mosquito population along with most other blood-sucking insects; those prospered only where the vegetation had been allowed to flourish untrimmed. Unfortunately, the cockroaches seemed to be impervious to the liberally dispensed insecticide and continued to multiply.

As every expatriate discovered, Gan was home to only a modest variety of wildlife. There were surprisingly few resident birds on Gan. Herons, white terns and turnstones could be seen at any time of the year, whimbrels would arrive late in the year and depart before May and occasional flocks of golden plovers would visit the island, tending to congregate on the golf course alongside the runway and always being encouraged to leave the airfield almost as soon as they arrived. The only other wildlife which was constantly on view on the island, apart from a small number of feral cats, was to be found on the beaches which were home for legions of crabs, mostly small scurrying creatures just anxious to be left alone and certainly keen to avoid the attention of any passing whimbrel. Often heard but less frequently seen were the rats. They foraged at night, their population large enough to survive the few losses inflicted by the feral cats and the rat traps deployed near each of the messes.

The weather

Within three months of the establishment of RAF Gan in 1957 the station's meteorological office was operational, providing forecasts for the military and data for the Meteorological Office Headquarters in Bracknell and thus, indirectly, for the World Meteorological Organisation. Initially only daytime readings were recorded but after mid-July 1959 hourly observations were made twenty-four times a day every day of the year, a process which continued throughout the operational life of the base. Primarily established to provide data and forecasts for the military, the meteorological officers, well aware that Gan's residents were interested in such a central aspect of life at the atoll, invariably publicised details of unusual or record-breaking observations. More frequently, they forwarded their observations to the station diarists who could generally be relied upon to record the information when it referred to some unusual weather pattern or event but, understandably, did not maintain a month-by-month record of the merely mundane.

What the majority of the pioneers wanted was something to write home about. For them, the meteorological officers provided an authoritative source of information on the local temperatures, the rainfall and the wind speeds; details of the hottest, coldest, driest, wettest day, week or month was always thought to be of interest to those living in cooler climes. After living on Gan for a few months most of the expatriates realised that, contrary to their first impressions, the maximum daytime temperatures were fairly constant at around eighty-six degrees Fahrenheit with minimum night-time temperatures, similarly constant, some ten degrees lower. They also discovered that there was no clearly defined wet season or dry season at the atoll; February and March tended to be the driest months and October the wettest, with wide variations from year to year.

The rainfall, commonly heavy enough to reduce visibility to less than half a mile and often torrential with visibility down to less than four hundred yards, was depressingly frequent as far as the pioneers were concerned because heavy rain created unpleasant working conditions, curtailed their off-duty activities and flooded their domestic accommodation. The sea breezes which generally made life pleasant were welcome but new arrivals quickly discovered that not-so-welcome gusts of over thirty-three knots, invariably accompanied by rain, sweep across the islands in that region around thirty times a year whilst winds of over twenty-five knots blow across the atoll at least three times as often as that.

That general picture was all so well and good but what the diarists and the letter-writers wanted, and what they got, were noteworthy events. In that sense, the rainfall often obliged by being remarkably frequent or remarkably heavy, satisfying diarists and correspondents alike whilst making life generally unpleasant for everyone and almost unbearable for those who were living under canvas or in kadjan huts. They soon became quite adept at mopping up during a normal month but their patience was sorely tested on several occasions in 1958 and 1959; the rain which fell on eighteen days in June 1958 was followed by a fall of thirteen inches in September, by nineteen wet days in October and a further fall of almost fifteen inches in December. That short-lived record was broken the following month when Gan's residents had to shelter from a fall of just over fifteen and a half inches, an exceptional start to a normal year in which the second highest rainfall figure in a month was just under ten and a half inches.

Surprisingly, the ferocious but fairly short-lived thunderstorms which occasionally hit the atoll did not necessarily occur during a month of continual heavy rain, as was evidenced in March 1960 which was not a particularly wet month even though it started with the dramatic storm which led to the ditching, described on page 290, of Hastings TG 579.

Just like the Maldivians who complained, whenever the daytime temperature dropped much below eighty degrees, that their rheumatism was painful during such cold weather, the expatriates quickly became acclimatised and on those rare occasions when the afternoon temperature dipped into the low seventies many of them would shiver whilst a bar of chocolate left out of the refrigerator would become ever softer.

The isolation

A sense of isolation struck every newcomer within days of arriving at the atoll.

It was difficult to ignore Gan's geographical remoteness because a constant reminder was prominently displayed for all to see: a multi-fingered sign post informed everyone that the island was five thousand seven hundred and fifty miles from London, four thousand two hundred and two from Cape Town, one thousand nine hundred and ninety-four from Delhi and two thousand one hundred and thirty from Singapore.

But the sense of isolation came not so much from the location, it came from the lack of external communications systems which made it impossible for an unaccompanied tourist to converse with anyone beyond the confines of the base or to listen to anything other than a tape recording or a record. The lack of a telephone link with other countries was not unexpected but almost certainly every European expatriate had assumed, quite wrongly, that a normal domestic radio set would be capable of receiving some English language broadcasts, probably those transmitted by the BBC World Service. What they found was that, prior to the 1960 birth of Radio Gan, described in chapter XXI, contact with the outside world was limited to a daily teleprinter summary of the main news items, the mail which was brought to Gan whenever an aircraft arrived from Ceylon and the newspapers and magazines which belatedly found their way to the atoll *via* Katunayake.

The domestic accommodation

The encampment created by the men of the Ship's Flag detachment, with tented sleeping accommodation and kadjan messes, was the first of the three early sites occupied by the expatriate communities. With the arrival of the

European civilians employed by Richard Costain Ltd, the Air Ministry's Works Directorate and the NAAFI, that first site was extended eastwards and when the Asian civilians from Pakistan and Ceylon came to Gan an Asian village was created in the south-west corner of the island.

Various standards of living accommodation were provided for the different communities. Whilst the European civilians enjoyed the comparative luxury of living in prefabricated wooden huts which had been shipped to Gan along with the airfield construction materials, the servicemen, in accordance with the Air Ministry policy which decreed that the airmen at Addu Atoll would have to live under canvas until the operational works had been completed, were accommodated in six-man tents which, in Gan's hot and humid atmosphere, provided even more uncomfortable living conditions than the kadjan huts which were occupied by the expatriate Asians.

Such differences were accepted with little comment during the last quarter of 1957 and the early days of 1958, when the steady increase in the resident population on Gan and in the number of Maldivians employed on the site during the daytime meant that there were urgent and essential works to be undertaken, not least the construction of a sewage plant to replace the rudimentary sanitation system in use at that time. But after a minor outbreak of dysentery the Air Ministry staff modified the policy on domestic accommodation, allocated additional funds for essential works and provided an allowance for the construction of a recreation room and sleeping quarters for some of the station's sixteen non-commissioned officers and eighty airmen. By the end of May 1958 the servicemen had not only been provided with additional washrooms and showers, they had occupied three newly-built kadjan huts.

Although the servicemen's tour length had been doubled it still carried no entitlement to mid-tour leave and by the time Wing Commander Kent was in post, the unofficial system introduced by Schofield had not survived. Even the competitive sportsmen who, earlier in the year, could reasonably expect to fly to Ceylon once during a tour at Addu Atoll, lost that opportunity when it was decided that RAF Gan would not be represented in any Ceylon-based competitions until such time as it was considered that the sportsmen could be collectively spared from their primary duties.

Thus, in June 1958, the servicemen, aware that the Air Ministry staff were disinclined to grant them any entitlement to mid-tour leave or to give

approval for the construction of their permanent domestic accommodation before the airfield complex had been completed, were facing an unbroken twelve-month tour on Gan and were living either under canvas or, for a fortunate few, in kadjan huts alongside civilian construction workers who had been provided with prefabricated accommodation.

There was nothing Kent could do about the length of the tour and little that could be done about the provision of mid-tour breaks in Ceylon but it was certainly possible to improve the domestic accommodation even more than was envisaged by the Air Ministry staff who had already allocated some funds for that purpose. So, in spite of the Air Ministry's policy on priorities and the use of the civilian workforce, the station commander prevailed upon Costain's construction engineers to use some of their Maldivian labourers to provide more kadjan huts for the airmen and to make an early start on the construction of prefabricated barrack blocks. The result was that, by August, the only airmen living in tents were the twenty-five RAF policemen who had decided to remain under canvas until the prefabricated accommodation became available.

The domestic accommodation was of no consequence to visitors who remained for only a few hours, but those who stayed overnight were invariably taken aback by the poor facilities even though they were always afforded the comparative luxury of a works department room whilst Kent's officers were living under canvas a few yards away. If the living conditions surprised the visitors during good weather, those who saw the results of the rainfall on the 9th of September must have been aghast. Heavy rain is quite common at Addu Atoll but the storm that day was truly exceptional with eight inches of rain falling in ten hours. The island was almost instantly converted into a quagmire that took days to dry out, affecting working conditions and leisure activities alike. Most of the airmen's kadjan huts were as much as six inches deep in water and it was almost a week before the accommodation was back to normal; for the men who had chosen to remain under canvas it was even longer than that before they had dried and cleaned their tents and their possessions. Costain's engineers were as obliging as they could be even though the September storm and a further six inches of rain in October left them juggling their priorities in an attempt to keep their construction programme on schedule. They redirected labour to work on the domestic accommodation and on the 13th of November, four days after more torrential rain had led to the cancellation of the Remembrance Day parade, the first of the airmen's prefabricated barrack blocks was handed over and occupied.

As the new year was welcomed in none of the expatriates could have imagined that within a few hours the Adduans would be rioting on Gan as a prelude to their unilateral declaration of independence. It transpired that their rebellion and the creation of a so-called republic, the United Suvadive Islands, described in chapter XIII, would be very much to the advantage of Costain's engineers, would sour the relationship between the British and Maldivian governments and, whilst complicating life for successive station commanders, would only occasionally have any direct impact upon the lives of the servicemen on Gan. There was, however, one immediate change which affected the servicemen: the construction of the additional prefabricated barrack blocks was postponed for a month because Costain's labour force was directed to concentrate on demolition work and site clearance.

With the full cooperation of the Adduans under Afif Didi's leadership the construction programme gathered pace and by April 1959, when Wing Commander Kent handed over to Wing Commander Thomas, there were still several kadjan buildings on the site but some of the prefabricated ancillary buildings had been completed, additional domestic accommodation was under construction and additional buildings were being erected month after month to provide workplace, domestic and recreational accommodation. It took almost three years to complete the scheduled works but the general impression of a hutted encampment on a building site changed quite rapidly so that by the time Thomas handed over to his successor, Wing Commander Constable-Maxwell, Gan was beginning to resemble a conventional RAF camp, albeit in an exotic environment.

The servicemen's domestic accommodation, still far from ideal, was steadily improved during 1960 but in the Asian camp, where the hastily-erected prefabricated huts had deteriorated, resentment over the living conditions had grown to such an extent that the Pakistanis went on strike, declaring that they would not return to work until something had been done to improve their housing. The station's RAF Regiment officer visited the camp and was forced to beat a hasty retreat in the face of a very real threat of attack. On reporting to the station commander he advised Constable-Maxwell to keep away from the site but his advice was ignored because the station commander had developed a close association with the Pakistanis' religious leaders and was confident that, with him, they would discuss their complaints without resorting to violence or abuse. He drove out to the camp and within minutes of his arrival he was surrounded by about a hundred of the three hundred and fifty Asians who were living there. He asked to see the cause of their complaints and was given a conducted tour, accompanied by some two hundred workers.

Two things struck him most about their accommodation: the appalling condition of the buildings and the presence of a photograph of the Queen or the late King in virtually every hut. A cursory inspection of the buildings was all that he needed. The prefabricated roofs and walls were leaking so badly that the huts had deteriorated almost to the point at which they were uninhabitable. Constable-Maxwell immediately agreed that the accommodation was unacceptable and promised that he would initiate all the necessary repairs. His relationship with the religious leaders was invaluable because they trusted him enough to call off the strike whilst he took up the matter with the Air Officer Commanding the Far East Air Force. The station commander stayed in the village long enough to have lunch and on returning to his office sent an immediate signal to the Air Officer stating the problem, supporting the Asians' claims and requesting urgent action. Within twenty-four hours a staff officer arrived at Gan, inspected the Asian's accommodation, agreed with their complaints and immediately sanctioned all the necessary repairs.

The continual arrival of inspecting officers from the Far East Air Force Headquarters made it easy to forget that, as on this occasion, they could, and frequently did, provide help when help was needed. It was an incident which provided a timely reminder that when the solution to a local problem was *ultra vires* for the station commander, it could still be implemented by a visiting staff officer.

Settling in

Newcomers never took long to settle in to the working arrangements referred to in chapter XIX, to sample the off-duty activities described in chapter XXI and to establish their individual communities, supplementing their imported cultures with local practices and rituals.

With no telephone links to the outside world and no radios to listen to they naturally tended to focus their everyday topics of conversation on personal matters and local events. Inevitably, a village-gossip culture developed across the island, with local incidents spawning temporary 'in' jokes with some eventually elevated to the status of Gan folklore.

At the heart of the socialising within the island's communities, these numerous incidents were significant to the expatriate population even if they were trivial in comparison with the political developments affecting, and already threatening, the redevelopment of the atoll base. As one of Costain's engineers succinctly put it:

> 'Cut off from the outer world as we are, shattering international events seem of little significance. This reduces subjects of conversation to tax and sex, since both are of outstanding importance to all of us.'

He could have added food and drink to his topics because they were the subjects of the complaints most commonly voiced by servicemen across the world and, in that respect, Gan was no different from anywhere else. The rations for the expatriates were usually flown thrice weekly from Ceylon and as far as the servicemen were concerned they left much to be desired for they included an element of so-called 'war stock rations', preserved food which had a shelf life and was issued for consumption before the expiry date so that it could be replaced by more recently preserved stock.

The supply of fresh fruit and vegetables was limited and, even more irritating for people living on an Indian Ocean island, so too was the supply of fresh fish. The NAAFI manager, as frustrated as the other expatriates, was very well aware of the shortcomings of the system, but had little control over bulk purchasing, which was undertaken in Ceylon. He did, however, make arrangements to charter a supply vessel, the *Starline Trader*, which, after visiting the atoll on the 14th of February 1958, was despatched to Ceylon for refitting as a four-hundred-ton refrigerated cargo ship. Refitted, the ship entered service in March and subsequently made monthly deliveries of refrigerated food to Gan. As the quality of the food improved, the expatriates had one less gripe although none would admit to being completely satisfied because the NAAFI was, and always would be, a favourite target for complaints, justified or not.

Drink, a common enough topic of conversation, provided another ready-made focus for those who needed something to moan about. Firstly, those who favoured draught beer complained that they were not catered for because none was imported; their complaints of deprivation understandably being regarded as an example of the serviceman's uncanny ability to find something to complain about. Secondly, and far more justified, was the complaint about the drinking water which had a peculiar, unpleasant taste which just could not be eradicated even by the water purification plant. Palatable only when consumed cold from the refrigerator or when its taste was masked by the addition of flavouring, it was used in the production of 'Ganade' and tonic water in the NAAFI's bottling plant, adding a distinctive and unwelcome flavour to the entire product range from the plant.

The complaints about the products from the bottling factory were justified but hardly the fault of the NAAFI because the Gan water which had to be used in the manufacture of all the drinks was guaranteed to taint every one of them, rendering some quite unpalatable. But the cost of importing branded soft drinks was high and Gan's population included several hundred low-paid Moslems who could ill afford to pay more for their non-alcoholic refreshment.

Moaning was pointless; draught beer remained unobtainable and the water remained unpalatable up to the day the base was abandoned.

Policing the community

Over the first three months of 1958 the expatriate population grew to more than four hundred as Ceylonese and Pakistanis were recruited and brought to Gan to work for the NAAFI, the Air Ministry and Costain. The Adduans resented this latest influx, partly because of their latent dislike of other Asians and partly because the employment of Pakistani construction workers would inevitably cast the Maldivians as little more than general labourers for the foreseeable future. Given that resentment, it was not really desirable to employ a large number of expatriate Asians on Gan but it would have needed a Maldivian government embargo to stop the influx; the feelings of the Adduans counted for little until simmering resentment led to confrontation.

With over three hundred Maldivian labourers employed on Gan during the daytime it was only to be expected that the cultural differences between the servicemen, the European civilians, the Pakistanis, the Ceylonese and the Maldivians would create some friction. Perhaps the surprise was not that there were the occasional confrontations but that there were so few of them; the communities were generally as law-abiding as any station commander could have hoped for. There were, of course, misdemeanours and there was, inevitably, some pilfering as the stream of supplies and equipment flowed onto the base. There was also the likelihood that, unless there was a general increase in security on the base, pilfering could get out of hand because the items which were so casually discarded by the servicemen and the European expatriates were, to the islanders, so desirable. The pre-Christmas theft from the NAAFI had clearly shown that, for some of the Maldivians, the temptation to take what they thought they could get away with was overwhelming and that created the potential problem that the interrogation of any Adduan by the RAF police was likely to become a political issue involving the atoll chief.

The need for extra security to protect the military supplies was obvious; what was unexpected, even after the January fracas referred to on page 123, was the need to increase the police presence on the island to protect the Asian expatriates. But the murder of Mr Symon, described on page 125, convinced the RAF police that the situation could easily spiral out of control and it was that which persuaded Costain's directors that whilst the feud continued it was inadvisable to employ Ceylonese construction workers on Gan. Within a few weeks they had all been paid off, repatriated and replaced by Pakistanis.

The difficulty of policing the site and the different communities was readily accepted by the Far East Air Force staff and sixteen days after the death of Mr Symon the arrival of a Warrant Officer, a Sergeant and fifteen Corporals brought the RAF police presence at the atoll up to twenty-five, a number which would gradually be increased over the coming years by the addition of Pakistanis recruited into the force, reflecting the increase in the number of expatriate Asians employed on Gan (Fig 16.2). For some unstated reason it was not, however, considered appropriate to recruit any Maldivians into the police force even though the number of Adduan employees was also increasing.

There was probably no need to employ as many RAF policemen on the island even in later years when the Vulcans Victors and Valiants were staging through the base because at such times the resident servicemen could mount special security patrols. But the high profile police presence was deemed appropriate in 1958 and it undoubtedly helped to persuade the Maldivians that troublemakers would soon be brought to book.

Identity and allegiance

By 1960 the pioneering expatriates had collectively adopted that most common symbol of male group membership, a conventionally striped Gan pioneer tie in the colours of the Maldivian national flag (Fig 17.5), openly identifying themselves as Gannites. They had also established rituals and symbols of sub-group identity among the Gannites and the hermits of Hitaddu, that select band who lived and worked in the Hitaddu enclave. Across the island the ubiquitous bicycles with their handlebar-mounted boxes reminiscent of the old fashioned butcher-boys' bicycles bore a variety of legends to identify the workplace sub-groups with the padre's chariot labelled 'Maker's Rep'. Decorated tee shirts for off-duty wear started to appear with section mascot motifs such as the roadrunner adopted by the staging aircraft servicing flight and the incredible hulk, usually shown swinging a roadrunner by the neck, which was adopted by the general engineering flight. Thus the airmen carried sectional allegiance into their off-duty hours, flaunting their motifs during the frequent, and often trivial, inter-section competitions which could never be held without the sectional chants such as that of the signals specialists who would loudly proclaim their departmental allegiance with shouts of 'siggies, siggies, siggies'. Such was life on Gan.

The Gan argot had also grown, with local terms being added to those imported from RAF stations around the world. New arrivals, or moonies as they were known until they developed a suntan, quickly adopted the jargon which was largely meaningless to outsiders: the sun worshippers invariably took up their positions with cries of 'bronzee, bronzee, bronzee', everyone, on hearing the shouted message 'the stickies are in', knew that the mail had arrived; 'getting over the hump' was nothing to do with being grumpy, that was 'getting a monk on', the hump was the mid-tour watershed which left just six months to go before the ultimate party or, as it was always referred to, the 'big gozome', when a tight-fisted individual or 'posbee', a modified acronym for the Post Office Savings Bank, would try to avoid paying for any alcohol.

The Navy, Army and Air Force Institutes

The NAAFI has been the butt of service humour almost since the day the organisation was created; even the acronym has been adopted to provide the derogatory description of a layabout as having No Aims, Ambitions or Flipping Interest. The servicemen on Gan were no different from their counterparts anywhere in the world; they needed a focus for their daily complaints and the NAAFI provided it. But theirs was very much a partial view of an organisation which had very wide commitments on the island and which fulfilled its remit without the executives ever pretending that the service was as good as they would have liked it to be. When the airmen complained they were generally complaining about the limited stock in the NAAFI shop or about the products of the bottling plant which produced the 'own brand' soft drinks and tonic water. Both complaints were justified up to a point and it was undoubtedly frustrating to find, on settling into Gan's all-male community, that the shop offered a selection of birthday cards 'For My Darling Husband' and that swimming trunks and sunhats were either out of stock or were available only in the smallest of small sizes. It was just as well that Alfred, the shop manager, was an amiable long-serving, and long-suffering, Asian character for he had the unenviable job of dealing with customers' complaints and explaining why requested items were not available. His deep rich voice could so often be heard across the shop sadly proclaiming '*Sorry sir, we are not having*' that the expression became a universal catchphrase on Gan, encapsulating, as it did, every deprivation experienced by the unaccompanied tourists.

What the complainants failed to take into account when generalising about the NAAFI was that the organisation was quite successfully, but by no means perfectly, catering for the diverse culinary tastes and religious tenets of Gan's multi-cultural society; running the bottling plant, the bakery, the tailor's shop, the boot and shoe repair services and the barber's shop; offering a mail order service, providing club facilities and sponsoring the Women's Royal Voluntary Service representative. Undoubtedly there were organisations which would have been only too happy to take over one or two elements of the NAAFI's operation on Gan but few if any would have been prepared to take over the organisation's entire remit; it was all too easy to overlook the broad picture and complain without giving credit where credit was due.

The visitors and transients

On the morning of the 1st of February 1957 the twelve men of the Ship's Flag detachment disembarked from HMS Modeste and established their camp on Gan. That same day Flight Lieutenant McNeil, the detachment commander, found himself hosting the first visitors to the camp, a team of signals specialists who flew in from Ceylon on board an RAF Sunderland, inspected the Hitaddu aerial site, discussed the survey which was to be undertaken later that month and then flew back to Ceylon, apparently satisfied with what they had seen and discussed.

So began the continual stream of visitors and transients which was to last throughout the operational life of the staging post.

During the early weeks of the re-commissioning project Flight Lieutenant McNeil was fortunate enough to have relatively few visitors apart from the cargo ships' crews but, inevitably, the numbers grew and by June he was only too happy to hand over his general hosting responsibilities to Squadron Leader Schofield, Gan's newly-arrived station commander. By September, when the old wartime runway had been re-commissioned, even more visitors began to arrive; some military, some civilian, some welcome for the support they gave, others not so welcome because of the interruptions they caused.

Schofield soon discovered that hosting the senior officers and the other VIPs who came to Gan was a time-consuming activity; in the course of four weeks he was to play host to Air Marshal the Earl of Bandon and other high-ranking officers; the Maldivian Prime Minister, Mr Ibrahim Ali Didi; the Maldivian Government Representative in Ceylon; the representative of the United Kingdom's High Commissioner in Ceylon and the project manager from Costain Limited.

As far as Schofield was concerned his hosting duties may have been time-consuming but they were rarely unwelcome. The visitors mostly tended to stay only for the few hours needed to satisfy their professional interests in the construction programme and almost without exception the senior officers commiserated with the servicemen working on Gan, appreciated the local problems and were as helpful as possible. It was obvious that such visits would become a regular feature of station life and although that seemed to be an onerous task it was one which Schofield and his successors were often able to turn to their advantage, developing contacts who were senior enough to pull a few strings for the benefit of the men at Addu Atoll.

Like those signals specialists who visited Gan on the day that McNeil and his men arrived, the visitors came with intent; some to conduct inspections, some to provide specialist skills on temporary-duty detachments and others to boost the morale of the expatriates. Their numbers increased over the years but they were, after the beginning of 1960, nothing like as numerous as the transients who, *en route* to their intended destinations, were obliged to while away some time at the staging post merely waiting for their aircraft to be refuelled. But for the RAF's insistence that passengers must disembark during refuelling, the majority of the transients could just as easily have spent their time on board the aircraft rather than in the transit lounge. There were, of course, some of the most senior VIPs who chose, on many occasions, to combine the intent of the visitor with the time-killing of the transient, using the refuelling stop to good effect whilst staging through Gan.

Prior to 1960, visitors who came by sea far outnumbered those arriving by air for there was a steady stream of supply ships bringing the materials, equipment and heavy plant for Richard Costain Ltd. Their captains were interested only in offloading their cargos and departing as soon as possible; they had no wish to remain at anchor in the lagoon long enough for the crew to go ashore, they were not party to the events on Gan and were generally only of passing interest to the station commander. He obviously had a general interest in the what they were bringing to the atoll and he invariably received a courtesy call from each ship's captain but he had no hosting commitments. It was the officer commanding the RAF marine craft section who generally made first contact with such visitors because he was responsible for piloting ships into and out of the lagoon. His making first contact with the visiting ship's captain and establishing a professional working relationship not only added variety to his job, it quite frequently led to an invitation for him and a group of his fellow officers to enjoy a few hours hospitality on board ship.

Although the merchant ships were generally of little interest to most of the servicemen, the ships of the Royal Navy were, after the visit by Admiral Biggs, the commander-in-chief, East Indies, always welcomed. The Admiral arrived at the atoll on board his flagship, HMS Ceylon, on the 18th of July 1957, intending to familiarise himself with the new military base in his bailiwick and to use the lagoon anchorage to refuel the Ceylon from the fleet auxiliary tanker the Wave King which arrived a mere half an hour before the flagship. The lagoon provided a good location for the rendezvous; so good, in fact, that fleet refuelling at Addu Atoll was to become a well-established arrangement for Royal Navy ships over the years with the Wave King's sister ships, the Wave Victor and the Wave Ruler, each spending several years at anchor in the lagoon.

The Admiral's visit, like subsequent visits by Royal Navy ships, developed into a social occasion as well as a working visit. He and the ship's crew took the opportunity to go ashore where seamen competed against airmen in a variety of impromptu sports fixtures before helping to consume some of the ample supplies of alcohol which had been delivered to the atoll by the Maskeliya. In an exchange of hospitality, all the servicemen were invited aboard the Ceylon where they were hosted by the crew and given a guided tour of the flagship, an experience which persuaded most of them that life in the RAF, even on Gan, was better by far than life on board ship. As far as the naval ratings were concerned, the reverse was true. They believed that the airmen deserved all the sympathy they got for having to serve on a 'stationary aircraft carrier' in the back of beyond and when news of the visit and the circumstances of the servicemen on Gan spread through the Royal Navy's grapevine such events, appreciated by the airmen and sailors alike, became part of the pattern of life at Addu Atoll for the next nineteen years.

In September most of the cargo ships which visited the atoll were, as usual, of little significance as far as the station commander was concerned but there was one which particularly interested him and the Maldivians, albeit for different reasons. For him, the cargo of one hundred thousand gallons of aviation fuel in forty-gallon drums was a welcome and timely addition to the airfield's fuel stocks but to the local Maldivian labour force it represented hours of hard labour helping to bring the drums ashore. To the Maldivian Government Representative who was with Schofield to watch the arrival of the ship, the fuel was of no significance. But the ship was. It was the SS Addyyatal Rahman, Britain's ill-fated gift to the Maldivian government. The four-hundred-ton motor schooner purchased from Sweden as the MS Freja and renamed at the request of the Maldivians had left Tilbury on the 17th of July bound for Gan, Colombo and Malé. In poor condition when she left Tilbury, the ship was in an even worse state when she arrived at Addu Atoll because she had suffered an engine room fire whilst crossing the Indian Ocean; an unwelcome experience at any time but a particularly dramatic event on a ship carrying some four hundred tons of high octane aviation fuel.

With the fire successfully brought under control, the Addyyatal Rahman had been able to continue her journey under reduced power but had arrived at Addu Atoll well behind schedule. Further repairs to the engine room were effected whilst the ship was at anchor in the lagoon and, with the engines seemingly having suffered no serious damage and the cargo discharged, the ship set sail for Colombo. *En route* those apparently serviceable engines broke down and she suffered the ignominy of being towed to her destination by a Russian ship which had answered her distress calls. Repaired in Ceylon, the Addyyatal Rahman eventually reached Malé and was handed over to the Maldivian government whose ministers were less than impressed by the sight of a small, rusty old vessel in obviously poor condition when they had been led to expect a gift which would more fairly reflect the goodwill and supposedly mutual co-operation between the two nations.

It was unfortunate that the rather shabby little Addyyatal Rahman arrived only a matter of days before Ibrahim Ali Didi, the Maldivian prime minister and Mr Zaki, the Maldivian government representative in Ceylon, were due to visit Gan to discuss the demolition of the Gan village and the resettlement of the villagers. Unfortunate, because their first sight of the ship must have influenced their attitude towards the British who seemed eager to take advantage of the strategic location of the Maldives but far from keen to reciprocate the Maldivian government's goodwill and generosity. They visited Gan in October, as did Mr East from the United Kingdom's High Commission in Colombo, but it was no surprise that their visit, like so many of the subsequent overtly political occasions, was of little value as far as the station commander was concerned because it yielded no local benefits for the site engineers who, hoping for a decision which would enable them to raze the Gan village, ended up with yet more prevarication.

Within three weeks Zaki, accompanied by Farouk Ismail, was back at the atoll, once again considering the evacuation arrangements for the Gan villagers. Hosted by the station commander, the visitors conducted their discussions in private and left without setting a timetable for the evacuation or agreeing on appropriate levels of compensation for the evacuees. It was, from Schofield's point of view, another rather pointless visit for it resolved none of the problems which were bedevilling the evacuation and which were to lead to the difficulties described in the early part of chapter XI. Ahmed Zaki and Farouk Ismail returned from Colombo to Hitaddu in November, continued their discussion with the islanders and left after once again keeping their own counsel. Whatever was being discussed or decided, it was obvious that they had no intention of sharing their knowledge with Schofield.

The man who was ultimately to become the driving force behind the construction programme, the Air Officer Commanding-in-Chief of the Far East Air Force, Air Marshal the Earl of Bandon, arrived in October, accompanied by two other Air Officers. Official visits by very senior officers were a normal part of service life but they were not usually events which were looked forward to by anyone and certainly not by the airmen on Gan for whom October was already developing into a particularly bad month. On this occasion, however, they were in for a pleasant surprise because the Earl of Bandon's visit turned out to be the great morale booster of the year. He spent hours touring the island talking and listening to as many men as possible. It was not every day that a Commander-in-Chief showed such a close personal interest in the living and working conditions of the junior members of his service and after that first visit the Earl's local reputation was such that he was assured of a genuine welcome whenever he cared to return to Gan which, as the political drama unfolded, was to be more often than he, or anyone else, could have imagined.

Two days before Christmas the sight of the civilian yacht 'Xarifa' sailing into the lagoon aroused the interest of the expatriates who, whilst used to the stream of cargo vessels and to the occasional Royal Navy or Royal Fleet Auxiliary ships, were understandably curious about the rather impressive yacht which had turned up just one day before the station stand-down and the start of the Christmas celebrations. Their curiosity was partially satisfied when they learned that Dr Hans Hass was on board the yacht with the team of scientists which was accompanying him on an expedition through the Maldives and the Laccadives.

The yacht's arrival, not planned with Christmas in mind but occurring quite fortuitously in time for the celebrations, meant that the Xarifa's crew was welcomed into the expatriates' communities to take part in the first Christmas festivities on Gan since the Commonwealth forces had left the atoll at the end of the Second World War. Maritime visitors were generally welcomed because they brought fresh, albeit brief, social contacts into the communities on the island; only the men obliged to work as temporary stevedores would have mixed feelings about some of the arrivals. But on this occasion even they could offer an unqualified welcome because the 'Xarifa' was on a scientific research expedition and was thus bringing social contact without a demand for labour. For six weeks the Xarifa remained at anchor in the lagoon whilst Hans Hass and his scientists explored the lagoon's coral shelves, becoming familiar figures on Gan, enjoying the hospitality that was offered them and returning that hospitality by inviting people aboard the Xarifa, by taking several servicemen scuba diving down to the lagoon reefs and by giving a series of talks in the various messes.

For Hass the presence of the Royal Air Force on Gan presented the possibility of a welcome bonus, an opportunity to view some of the Maldivian atolls from the air. Initially disappointed that a request for such a flight could not be officially entertained, he was delighted when, within a few days of his broaching the subject, the Air Headquarters' staff in Ceylon gave their approval for him to accompany the station commander on a two-hour reconnaissance flight over the atolls to the north of Gan, an arrangement described with appreciation by Hass in 'Expedition into the Unknown', the published account of the Xarifa's voyage.

With Christmas over and normal working arrangements resumed after a two-day stand-down to mark the arrival of the New Year, Schofield found himself meeting and hosting a variety of visitors, including a nine-man Maldivian Commission sent to the atoll in January with a remit to investigate the reports of the premature evacuation of Gan villagers described in chapter XI. Arriving on board an RAF Sunderland in the company of Mr East, who almost immediately returned to Colombo, they spent some considerable time with the station commander, quite reasonably discussing the evacuation arrangements and the recently declared strike by the Maldivian employees but offering no solutions to any of Schofield's problems; once again the visit seemed to have been, in the short term, a rather pointless exercise.

The other visitors that January included several very senior officers, a Flight Lieutenant criminal investigation officer sent to Gan to investigate the theft of cigarettes from the NAAFI and two, an RAF padre and a dental officer, who were to become such familiar figures on the island that they came to be regarded more as honorary residents than visitors. The padre was one of the many who would visit the island over the years because although a Church of England padre was later resident on Gan, the arrangement was that padres of other denominations would visit the base for several days each month, generally on detachment from Singapore. A similar arrangement brought an RAF dental officer to Gan each month during the years when no dentist was resident on the island.

February 1958, the month when scheduled Valetta flights were introduced, was one of the busiest months for Schofield with visitors arriving by air and by sea. Some, such as the Chaplain to the RAF, who arrived with his ecclesiastical entourage, and the Deputy Under Secretary of State for Air, were easy guests, others managed to complicate life for Gan's station commander. The Maldivian ministers created the biggest upset when they flew from Ceylon to Gan with a remit to investigate the Adduan claims for a pay rise and compensation for their destroyed crops. Their brief visit, described in chapter XI, became memorable because they had to be rescued from a crowd of angry villagers and, routed and considerably shaken, left Gan on the first available aircraft headed for Ceylon.

The other visitors who made that February a memorable month for Schofield exemplified the peculiarities of command at the atoll. The expatriates had all been made well aware of the political sensitivities of the Maldivians and were generally careful to avoid giving offence but as the number of visitors to Gan increased it seemed that almost any visitor, even a padre, was likely to offend someone. The intermittent visits by the padres from Ceylon seemed to be innocuous enough until one of them came close to creating a political furore by seeking to convert the Moslem islanders to Christianity, a remarkably naïve action given that the Maldivian government did not even allow non-Moslems to settle permanently anywhere in the archipelago. Fortunately the station commander became aware of the padre's missionary zeal in time to stop him distributing bibles amongst the islanders and arranging to preach the gospel to any who cared to listen.

Cultural and political sensitivity were not, of course, the sole prerogative of the Maldivians, as the station commander discovered when three Indian Navy ships sailed into the lagoon that month. The Maldivian government and the United Kingdom's High Commissioner in Ceylon had agreed, earlier in the year, that the Indian naval cruiser 'Delhi' and the escort frigates Thai and Kistna could visit the atoll during their Indian Ocean exercises. There was no significance about the arrangement, it was regarded by all concerned as no more than a courtesy visit which would provide an opportunity for an exchange of hospitalities ashore and afloat. That view, however, was not shared by Gan's Pakistani expatriates. They informed Schofield that there was a deep-seated hostility between the two nationalities and that it would be unwise to allow the Indian seamen ashore. At that time there were several hundred Pakistanis on Gan and it was fairly obvious from their thinly-veiled threat that they were likely to instigate trouble. The result was that no Indian crewmen were allowed ashore, the planned exchange of hospitalities was abandoned and only Schofield was entertained on board the flagship.

Criminal investigation officers were rarely called upon to bring their expertise to Gan but early in 1958 there were two such occasions, the first in January, the second in March. The pre-Christmas theft of cigarettes from the NAAFI brought the January visitor to the base but his investigation paled into insignificance in March when the murder of Mr Heengama Wattalidiniya Symon, referred to in chapter XI, led to the arrival of a criminal investigation team which undertook extensive but fruitless inquiries.

After those earlier episodes the subsequent visitors seemed unremarkable. In May there was one visit, by a staff officer from Singapore, which was memorable because it was reminiscent of, but fortunately not nearly as bad as, one of the wartime fiascos. As described on page 315, he arrived at Gan to undertake a pestological survey but almost immediately reported sick and returned to Singapore after only three days on the island. In June the pioneers hosted the first entertainers to visit the base; four airmen from Kuala Lumpur whose skiffle group performances in June are referred to on page 328.

By mid-1958, with the Valetta shuttle service between Gan and Ceylon adding three scheduled flights a week to the *ad hoc* arrivals, there was an almost month-by-month increase in the number of visiting officers so that Wing Commander Kent, within days of his arrival to take over from Wing Commander Schofield, was meeting and greeting visitors on three or four days every week.

Throughout the latter half of that year Air Marshal the Earl of Bandon almost certainly came to Gan more frequently than any other VIP for he had a very personal interest in the construction programme and was quick to resolve, whenever he could, any problems which were thought likely to delay the commissioning date for the new runway. He was invariably a welcome visitor as were some, but not all, of his staff officers, most of them coming to Gan out of a combination of professional commitment and an interest engendered by their enthusiastic commander's declared expectation that they should familiarise themselves with the construction programme.

The problem, as Kent soon discovered, was that most of the more senior among them expected him to be attentive throughout their stay which was not an unreasonable expectation for those who were only on the island for a few hours but irksome when the visitors stayed overnight, leaving him with little time to attend to his everyday commitments. But there was little he could do about it. That year the Earl of Bandon, having visited the island in May with Sir Robert Scott, commissioner general for South-East Asia, returned in August, October and November. Little did anyone imagine that when next he would visit Gan, in January 1960, he would be visiting a rebel community and a self-styled independent republic.

December 1958 started normally enough with the Europeans at the atoll finding it difficult to realise, as the dry sunny days became more frequent, that Christmas was only a few weeks away. The first of the visitors referred to in the station diary that month was Mr Lindsay, Costain's overseas manager, who was becoming increasingly concerned about the politically-motivated delays facing his construction engineers. He remained at the atoll long enough to gain as detailed an understanding of the situation as possible before returning to England to discuss the matter with the Air Ministry staff. Like the Earl of Bandon, he could never have imagined that the Adduans were about to pre-empt those discussions by declaring their independence and allowing Costain's engineers to do whatever was necessary to bring the construction programme back on schedule.

Within days of Lindsay's departure, and quite coincidentally, an Air Ministry team arrived, sent to the atoll as a result of the political manoeuvring which had developed around the plans to evacuate the Gan villagers. The members of the team used Gan as their base from which to visit Huvadu atoll and inspect a more northerly island of Gan which had been suggested as a possible resettlement site for the evacuated Adduans. Taken to Huvadu in an RAF launch, they informally surveyed the northerly island, returned to base and then flew back to England, blissfully unaware that events later that month would make their visit, and their report, irrelevant.

The days preceding the very welcome Christmas stand-down were largely uneventful although the servicemen did receive a practical reminder that, even on their tropical island building site, service practice still prevailed: on the 17th of the month Air Vice Marshal Grundy visited the island and took the salute at Gan's first annual parade for the Air Officer Commanding the Far East Air Force. Held on the airfield's hardstanding, the parade was a rather modest affair but the accompanying inspection was probably the most comprehensive ever on Gan with Grundy arriving on the

22nd of the month, taking the salute at the parade on the 24th and departing on the 25th; a schedule intended to give him and his entourage time to inspect the Gan and Hitaddu sites and to gain a better understanding of expatriate life at the atoll.

With the 1958 Christmas festivities behind them, the expatriates settled back into their normal working arrangements, little realising that the forthcoming visit by Ahmed Zaki, the Maldivian government representative in Ceylon, would lead to a rebellion by the Adduans. His was the visit which precipitated the riots described in chapter XI, led to the Adduans' subsequent declaration of independence and brought the Earl of Bandon hotfoot to Gan where he agreed with the station commander that Abdullah Afif Didi was to be recognised as the *de facto* leader of the breakaway republic: a decision which led to the years of political acrimony described in chapter XIII.

In those early days of the rebellion cargo ships continued to arrive in the lagoon as frequently as ever but there are no diary references to individual visitors to the station other than the Earl of Bandon and his usual entourage. Then, early in August, some four months after Wing Commander Thomas had taken over from Wing Commander Kent, there was a sudden spate of newsworthy arrivals. The first group of visitors arrived during the night of the 5th and were only of indirect interest to the station commander for they were the Huvaduan infiltrators whose capture is described on page 142. They may have been of little interest to Thomas but when news of their capture was relayed to the Far East Air Force Headquarters it triggered off a reaction which brought troops to Gan under the guise of an air mobility exercise.

Coincidentally, the British government, viewing the political situation with increasing concern, had by then decided that a Royal Navy ship should be stationed in the lagoon to deter the Maldivian government from sending its militiamen to the atoll and that led to the arrival, referred to on page 143, of HMS Cavalier the day before two Hastings and a Beverley flew in from Singapore, bringing a hundred men of the First Battalion, The Cheshire Regiment, complete with enough tentage for them to live under canvas on the airfield. Seven days later forty RAF Regiment airmen arrived and when the remainder of the two RAF Regiment flights arrived the following day the Cheshires left for Singapore, having spent just one week encamped on the airfield.

From then on, RAF Regiment personnel were shuttled between Singapore and Gan whenever trouble loomed at the atoll and that, over the next few years, occurred so frequently that there seemed to be a Regiment presence on the island more often than not. For the foreseeable future the presence of a Royal Navy gunboat at anchor in the lagoon was an even more permanent reminder that the Adduans believed themselves to be under siege, a belief accepted, to a lesser extent, by the British government. The rota system effectively made each guardship a short-stay visitor, generally remaining on station in the lagoon for a month before being relieved.

The crew of the Cavalier soon established what was to be a common pattern, becoming part of the local community, readily competing against the RAF and the Army in sports competitions, often inviting station personnel to go to sea when the ship was briefly patrolling beyond the atoll's outer reef and readily accepting any offers of air experience flights on board the search and rescue aircraft.

They also became known for their practical jokes, two of which were well remembered by Wing Commander Thomas many years later. On one occasion he happily granted their request to come ashore for an evening's fishing, a request which turned out to be a cover story for a very different kind of expedition. The morning after the naval party had been ashore the station commander discovered that he had lost the pennant from his car, that a White Ensign had been nailed to the station's flagpole, that each of the four faces of the water-tower had the message 'under Royal Navy protection' painted on it and, for the benefit of incoming aircraft, the same message had been painted across the runway.

The other well-remembered occasion occurred when HMS Caprice was due to relieve the Cavalier and it did at least show that the Cavalier's crew were even-handed in their choice of targets. Caprice's captain sought, and was given, advice from the Cavalier's crew on the sort of reception he could expect when first paying his compliments to Gan's station commander whom he was due to meet the following morning on Gan's main jetty. Wing Commander Thomas, accompanied by Arthington-Davy, drove down to the jetty in a Land Rover, the only suitable vehicle available in the days before a staff car was sent to Gan. Thomas was wearing normal working dress of khaki shirt and shorts and Arthington-Davy was wearing nothing more than khaki shorts and flip-flops; his normal casual attire,

Both were rather surprised when the captain of the Caprice was rowed ashore by an immaculately dressed crew of seamen whose oar drill was as impressive as the tropical whites, medals and sword carried by the captain. It transpired that the crew of the Cavalier had informed him that Gan's station commander was a punctilious individual who insisted on the highest standards and on correct protocol. It took some time before the visiting captain was persuaded that he had been met by Gan's commanding officer and not by one of the station's drivers.

By the end of August 1959 when the Cavalier left Addu Atoll for Singapore, the ship's crew had, like the seamen from HMS Ceylon some two years earlier, been accepted as competitors in a variety of sports on the island and it was correctly assumed that the visiting crews of the succession of guard-ships would continue to compete against Gan's expatriates.

At the beginning of October a medical team, led by Squadron Leader Rawll on detachment from Singapore, was undertaking an atoll-wide filariasis survey but, like Smith's pestological survey in May 1958, it was ill-fated because it had to be postponed after two and a half weeks when Rawll abandoned the work to help the clinicians to deal with the outbreak of food poisoning and dysentery, referred to on page 317, which afflicted over a hundred of the men on Gan. With virtually all of the Maldivian employees under orders not to report for work, additional servicemen were brought in from Singapore and accommodated under canvas on the airfield. With the extra work created by the epidemic, the consequent influx of servicemen and the ten inches of rain which flooded the island it was a month when the station commander had enough to do without spending time hosting VIPs who were staging through Gan but, even though the transients interrupted his day, it was a duty which could not be avoided. Unlike the official visits made by the Far East Air Force Command staff, hosting transients was a diversion with little immediate benefit except when it occurred at a time of local suffering and that October was a classic example of just such a time; it was a month when every unaccompanied tourist took the opportunity to welcome the transients and to persuade them that what they were seeing was nothing out of the ordinary on Gan.

November brought even more aircraft movements and even more VIPs, including the Earl of Bandon and a retinue of Air Officers. Theirs was a brief visit but it was long enough for the airmen to don their so-called 'panic kit' uniforms which they kept for the most important visitors and for the occasional parades. The Earl and his retinue were but one group out of the thirty-five VIP visitors that month, including the Permanent Under Secretary of State for Air and his entourage, all very anxious to familiarise themselves with the political aspects of the continuing rebellion.

They were not the only people intrigued by the situation at Addu Atoll; in England, there were many journalists who wanted to know more about Britain's involvement with Afif Didi and the United Suvadive Islands but most of them accepted that they would get nothing more than the press releases because Gan was Air Ministry controlled territory and was so remote as to make it almost inaccessible.

Admittedly, Mr Van Lief, a freelance photographer, had been given Air Ministry permission to visit the base in November 1957, and had arrived there, quite coincidentally, on the day Farouk Ismail and Ahmed Zaki returned to the atoll from Colombo. He had therefore had an opportunity to record both the environmental and the political impact of the British military presence in the archipelago but after the airfield had been classified as fully operational and had also become the focus of continual political argument, the Air Ministry had excluded photographers and reporters from the site.

There was, however, one enterprising individual, Bertram Jones, who created a furore by making his own way to Addu Atoll, arriving unannounced and triggering off the chain of events described on page 143. His visit paved the way for other reporters, giving Afif Didi an easy international outlet through which to publicise the Adduans' grievances and adding to the station commander's concerns over unwelcome publicity.

1959 was rounded off with the Christmas celebrations which fell almost automatically into the patterns established in 1957 and 1958 but it was a year when the competitions were much more keenly contested than usual for the participants included the visiting servicemen from the Army's Signals Installation Troop, and the seamen from the frigate St Mounts Bay and the destroyer Carysfort, both of which were anchored in the lagoon throughout the Christmas period.

By January 1960 there was talk of a new agreement between Britain and the Maldives which meant that Thomas found himself hosting an even greater stream of very senior visitors that month, when the Earl of Bandon brought his entourage to the station, and again in February when the Commander-in-Chief and his staff arranged to meet Mr Alport and Sir

Alexander Morley, the United Kingdom's high commissioner, for preliminary discussions at Addu Atoll before travelling on to Malé on board HMS Gambia.

Those visitors, all with serious intent, were highly respected but nothing like as congenial as the captain of HMS Cavalier which, rostered to relieve Carysfort on the 12th of January, sailed into the lagoon with an RAF ensign flying from the jackstaff, a memento of the incidents which occurred during the ship's previous tour of duty as the atoll guardship.

Early March brought a rare visitor into the lagoon, the aircraft carrier HMS Centaur, diverted in response to an Air Ministry request to deliver aviation fuel to Gan before the island's tanker farm ran dry. For the resident servicemen the visit provided a break in the daily routine with the opportunity to compete against the Centaur's crew in a hastily arranged football match and, for some, the opportunity to visit the ship and glimpse the living and working environment on board. Once again, those who toured the ship were unanimous in declaring that they would far rather serve for a year on Gan than sail the seas with the Royal Navy. For almost another sixteen years a variety of Royal Navy ships was welcomed by the expatriates but aircraft carriers were rare visitors to the atoll; the frigates and destroyers far more frequently represented the Royal Navy. By mid-1961 even they were outnumbered by the Royal Fleet Auxiliary ships which would visit the Wave Victor. They rarely remained in the lagoon long enough for the crew to spend time ashore but whenever a ship was at anchor for several hours the crew was generally granted enough shore-time to respond to a challenge to raise a sports team to compete against the Gannites. The Royal Fleet Auxiliary ships had fewer crewmen than the ships of the Royal Navy but their crews became well known for their on-board hospitality and were every bit as welcome as the crews of the frigates and destroyers.

At the beginning of April 1960 Wing Commander Constable-Maxwell took over from Wing Commander Thomas and he soon discovered that what he had been told about the number of visitors to the base was no exaggeration. In April alone, the list of visitors included the newly appointed Assistant Chaplain-in-Chief; the Air Ministry's Establishment Review Committee; thirty-two inspecting officers from Command Headquarters and a retired Group Captain who, as secretary of the Central Asian Society, had been given permission to film at the atoll.

In May the only significant visitors were the Air Officer Commanding and his entourage, conducting a three-day inspection of the station. For the station commander, that month provided something of a respite from the continual stream of visitors but for the airmen, the parade, which customarily provided a climax to the annual inspection, was unusually demanding. In their experience parades on Gan were generally modest affairs but those airmen who marched onto Gan's hardstanding on the 24th of May had already endured seven practice parades to ensure that the occasion lived up to the station commander's expectations. Almost certainly no other visiting officer ever reviewed a more impressive parade on Gan even in May 1962 when the Chief of the Air Staff, Marshal of the Royal Air Force Sir Thomas Pike, became the most senior officer ever to take the salute on the base.

Air Marshal the Earl of Bandon, accompanied by his wife and his retinue, paid a farewell visit to Gan on 8th June 1960 before relinquishing command as the Commander-in-Chief of the Far East Air Force. The occasion was, like all his visits, relatively informal and it was a sad day when the station bad farewell to the man who had been the driving force behind the construction programme from the time when the idea of a mid-ocean staging post had first been mooted. He had taken the initiative at a time when politicians were dithering, had used his influence to sort out as many problems as he could and had done his best to ensure that the project could be completed on time. His numerous visits to the island had always been welcomed for he had shown a genuine interest in the wellbeing of everyone working on the site. His soubriquet reflected the expatriates' opinion of him for as soon as he had agreed to recognise Afif Didi as the *de facto* leader of a breakaway republic they had dubbed him The Earl of Gandon.

There were one or two occasions in 1960 when RAF Regiment airmen were flown to the island as trouble loomed but their visits were far less frequent than in previous years and the demonstrations mounted by the Maldivians during 1960 were never on a scale which required Army personnel to be sent to the atoll as had been necessary in 1959 when the Cheshires had been called upon to provide a show of force on Gan. But some of the regiment's officers revisited the base in July 1960 and, at a reception in the transit hotel, they recalled the 1959 affair before formally presenting the station commander with a Cheshire Regiment shield in appreciation of the hospitality and cooperation which the men of that regiment had enjoyed during their short stay on the island the previous year.

For the second half of 1960 the station diaries refer to the introduction of the regular passenger flights, which brought so many transients to the island, and to the increasing number of combat aircraft staging through Gan. The diarists, however, provide very little information about the transients or about the visitors until December when there is a reference to Air Vice Marshal Grundy and the formal opening, on the 13th, of the station laundry by Mrs Grundy who had accompanied her husband to the atoll. That, for the servicemen was a far more important ceremony than the dedication service, conducted that evening by the Bishop of Maidstone, for the recently constructed Church of Saint Christopher.

Christmas celebrations

Unique among the diversions and festivities in the Gan calendar, the Christmas celebrations, which, in 1957, would be the first on the island since the departure of the Commonwealth forces at the end of the Second World War, provided a ready topic of conversation for the expatriates early in December. It would also be the first official bank holiday stand-down since McNeil's unit had arrived at the atoll for although the men of the Ship's Flag detachment had enjoyed several such respites during their seven or eight months on Gan there is no reference in the unit diary to bank holidays as such. They had, however, been invited to share the Maldivian celebrations on Hitaddu to mark the end of the Eid festival early in May when they had competed against a Maldivian football team, taken part in a dhoni race and established a basic pattern for every bank holiday sports day on Gan for as long as the station remained operational.

For the servicemen and the civilians alike, the 1957 Christmas festivities provided a welcome break at the end of an exhausting year. Religious services, Christmas fare, the very considerable consumption of alcohol, the dhoni race, the sports competitions and the chance to relax and swim in the lagoon provided the diversions necessary to sustain the morale of men whose thoughts of family Christmases could so easily have lapsed into morbid yearning for home. For the station commander there was one minor worry; with over four hundred men enjoying a two-day stand-down and an alcoholic celebration of Christmas there was a distinct possibility that the celebrations could get out of hand. He need not have worried. Even though the men did their best to outdo each other in every aspect of the celebrations and in every competition, including that for alcohol consumption, the two-day festivities remained remarkably trouble free.

A few of the European expatriates who experienced those 1957 celebrations may still have been on the island twelve months later but even if that were not so embroidered accounts of the festivities had been handed down and had established an early benchmark for the more recent arrivals. The result was that, as in the previous year, the 1958 celebrations combined the traditional and the exotic, starting early on Christmas Eve when the servicemen distributed toys, sweets and oranges to the Gan village children whose tranquil way of life had been so disrupted by the construction work. On Christmas Day, with the temperature in the eighties, a considerable consumption of alcohol accompanied by a turkey-and-plum-pudding dinner was followed by a variety of sporting, and often unsporting, competitions. But the surprise of the day was sprung in the evening when the station commander assembled the airmen and, after thanking them for all their hard work during the year, played a collection of Christmas messages tape-recorded by their families in Britain. The initial ribaldry quickly died down and gave way to an emotional atmosphere; it was, for everyone, a reminder that, although their tropical island was visited every week by merchant ships and by aircraft, their only contact with home was through the mail service which, reasonable though it was, could only ever be a poor substitute for the voices of those they had temporarily left behind.

Newcomers who arrived shortly after the celebration of that second Christmas were inevitably regaled with embroidered tales of marathon festivities and enviable stamina. The implication was clear; a pattern had been established and targets set, providing challenges which could not be ignored by successive generations of Gannites.

By Christmas 1959 Gan's airfield had been fully operational for several months, passenger aircraft were regularly staging through, combat aircraft were frequent visitors, the pioneering days were drawing to a close and the pioneers would be replaced by colonists.

Fig 16.2. The Pakistani police on Gan.

XVII   The Colonists: 1960 – 1976

The settled society

By 1960 Gan was fully established as the RAF's Indian Ocean staging post and the different communities on the island were allied in a society which accommodated their imported cultures. Where previously there had been pioneers there were colonists, occupying the island to the exclusion of the indigenous people but dependent upon them for the provision of a low-paid daytime labour force.

The new arrivals

Sometime in the early 1960s, when Gan's amenities were well established and the base no longer had the appearance of a construction site, a small booklet, 'Going to Gan', was produced at the base and published by the Ministry of Defence. Subsequently a copy of this modest little guide to life at the atoll accompanied the posting notice which was sent to every serviceman who was due to become one of Gan's colonists. Nevertheless, newcomers, who by then were arriving in some style on board a Britannia, a Comet or, by mid-1967, a VC10, invariably reacted in much the same way as the pioneers of the late 1950s; they stepped out of the aircraft, briefly looked around and immediately began to wonder what life on Gan would be like in the coming months. As the years passed, each new generation of unaccompanied tourists benefited from the improvements made by their predecessors and each new generation discovered that, on Gan, some things changed but little. The sense of isolation, the domestic accommodation, the work, the off-duty diversions and the introspective communities on the island were much the same in the 1970s as they were in the mid-1960s.

The weather

The colonists, like their predecessors, soon adjusted to the local weather patterns and they too, soon became interested in any noteworthy events. The meteorological office staff, knowing that by the mid-1960s Gan's expatriate residents had become avid collectors of records for every aspect of life on the island, invariably circulated details of interesting or record-breaking observations continuing to provide, as they had done for several years, authoritative answers to the friendly bar-room disagreements over the hottest, coldest, driest, wettest day, week or month experienced by the disputants. On occasions the enthusiasm with which the meteorological staff announced some unusual event was lost on most of Gan's residents because the scientific significance of the observation would only register with the amateur meteorologists among them. Thus, few people were any the wiser when, in February 1963, they were told that there had been several 'Green Flash' and 'Sun Pillar' sightings; without further explanation they simply accepted the comments as references to unusual optical illusions.

Like the pioneers, the colonists' main interest was in the temperatures, the rainfall and the wind speeds. The operations record books show that in every year the unaccompanied tourists could write home with news that several months had brought over ten inches of rain to the island whilst figures in excess of fifteen inches were not uncommon. None, however, could claim to have suffered more than those who had to shelter from the record eight inches which fell in ten hours on the 9th of September 1958 or the nineteen inches which fell in November 1963. Even the driest months tended to bring at least two inches of rain but when almost eighteen and a quarter inches in December 1961 was followed by over twelve inches in January, Gan's worst year began. The island's wettest 'dry season' contributed to a total of almost sixty-six and three quarter inches of rain by the end of August and to 1962's grand total of one hundred and five inches, well above the average annual figure of around ninety inches. Under those conditions the new arrivals soon adopted the common local practice of cycling to work wearing nothing but flip-flops and underpants under their voluminous cycling capes which provided more than enough cover for them and the plastic bags in which they carried their workplace uniforms.

1962 was a year to write home about, not just because of that remarkably high rainfall but because it was also a year of unusually high temperatures and unusually strong winds. The station diaries contain frequent references to wind speeds in excess of forty knots and in May the reference to fifteen inches of rain that month is accompanied by reports of frequent gale force winds with one unusually dramatic thunderstorm and a waterspout which, during the evening of the 15th, tore across the island at sixty-eight knots, causing considerable structural damage. In between times the diarists noted that the daytime temperatures, which were very rarely below eighty-two Fahrenheit or above eighty-eight, reached ninety on the 21st of March and again on the 14th of June, just one degree below the record set on the 8th of April 1964.

The expatriate Europeans did not take long to adjust to Gan's remarkably constant temperatures; many of them would react by donning their jackets on those rare occasions when the daytime temperature dropped into the low seventies and when a record low of sixty-nine point four Fahrenheit was recorded at two o'clock in the afternoon on the 23rd of July 1970, donning their jackets still left them shivering.

Heavy rain for an hour or two was fairly easy to live with except for those who had to continue working whilst being soaked. But continual rain, even when it was not that heavy, inevitably lowered morale because it curtailed so many of the off-duty activities enjoyed by the expatriates and raised the humidity in the domestic accommodation to an unpleasant level. Regardless of the amount which fell, May 1973 must have been a most depressing month with rain recorded on twenty-eight days out of the thirty-one. Conversely, in 1967 no rain fell for twenty-three days; from the 20th of February to the 14th of March not so much as a light shower interrupted life on the island. It remains as the longest recorded dry spell throughout the operational life of the base.

Dry spells generally, but not invariably, meant that ten or twelve hours sunshine would be recorded each day; more than enough for those residents whose ambition was to achieve a dark oak suntan. Two hundred hours sunshine in a month was thus not uncommon during the dry season, figures in excess of two hundred and fifty were rare and the figure of three hundred and nine and a half hours recorded in March 1965 set a record which had not been broken up to the time the base was abandoned in 1976.

The continuing isolation

The sense of isolation experienced by the pioneers was inherited by the colonists and remained with them even when scheduled passenger flights were staging through Gan every day of the week. Radio Gan provided a very welcome, albeit passive, link with England but for every unaccompanied tourist the post office still provided the only link with home. It was a rare expatriate who did not eagerly anticipate the arrival of the mail and when the Britannias began to deliver letters and parcels almost every day of the week, the morale of the European expatriates soared. Not only did the aircraft provide a frequent delivery service, they provided a direct postal service to England with mail handed in at Gan's post office being processed by the Army staff, put on board the staging Britannia and offloaded at RAF Lyneham, generally that same day. The expatriates soon adapted to the speed of the service, even occasionally sending perishables by post.

That trend started with the despatch of fresh coconuts, chosen because they came already gift-wrapped by nature and could survive all but the longest delay in the post. All that the sender had to do was to pluck the nut from the tree, carve the recipient's name and address into the green outer shell and take the addressed nut to the post office where, after it had been weighed and had the appropriate postage stamps stuck to the outer shell, it would be dropped into the mailbag with all the others. Numerous local postmen in Britain must have been initially rather taken aback on first seeing an addressed nut but they undoubtedly became used to the sight, merely regretting that the coconuts were so heavy (Fig 17.1).

In the early days, when there were few palm trees on Gan the Maldivians would always provide coconuts from the other islands but as Gan's trees matured they provided a free supply of nuts and as the flowering shrubs matured they provided flower buds which were favoured by the servicemen who found that a single frangipani bud, sealed in with a letter, would still be fresh when it arrived in England and would bloom within hours of being placed in water. 'Flowers by post' had come to Gan, courtesy of the works department gardeners rather than the NAAFI which provided a similar commercial service (Figs 17.2 & 17.3).

The postal service was not always as reliable as the unaccompanied tourists would have liked but there were only two occasions when that important link with home was severely disrupted; one in 1963 and one in 1971.

At the beginning of 1963, while Gan's European expatriates were living and working on their tropical island in the Maldives, their friends and relatives in Britain were experiencing a near-arctic winter and that, far from raising morale amongst those who had escaped to the sunshine, had exactly the opposite effect for the simple reason that the mail could not be delivered. According to RAF Lyneham's station diaries, heavy snows, high winds and freezing fog created near impossible operating conditions throughout January with little improvement during February. As news of Britain's severe winter was reinforced with the cancellation of scheduled Britannia flights through Gan many of the expatriates became worried about their families back home but had no way of contacting them and therefore no way of knowing how well, or how badly, they were coping. Understandably, the men's morale sank.

That uncharacteristic disruption of the postal service demonstrated just how important the mail deliveries were to the Gan communities, an obvious truth which was again clearly demonstrated almost exactly eight years later.

On the 20th of January 1971, the first day of a prolonged strike by the postal workers in England, the General Post Office service between Gan and the United Kingdom was suspended. The official mail was still being carried by the military but there was no service for private correspondence which meant that, with no telephone links from Gan to the outside world, those who arrived at the base whilst the strike was on could not even let their families in Britain know that they had arrived safe and well. As the postal strike continued, morale plummeted and after two weeks the Ministry of Defence introduced a system whereby their establishments in Britain offered a *poste restante* service for private mail from overseas and a delivery service whereby private mail handed in to any Ministry establishment in Britain could be sent overseas with the official mail.

The scheme was far from ideal because it could only serve those who were able to deliver and collect correspondence from the designated centres but it was the best that could be done and it did partially alleviate the problem. On Gan, many of the servicemen and expatriate civilians had left their families living within easy reach of a centre but the unaccompanied tourists had no way of informing their relatives that a *poste restante* system had been introduced; for them the frustration was enormous. For a few, word of mouth through the transit passengers and the aircrew solved the problem but there was no doubt that until the 8th of March, when the strike ended, morale amongst the unaccompanied tourists on Gan was as low as it had been for many years; fourteen years after the base had been created, the sense of isolation amongst the unaccompanied tourists was as strong as it had ever been.

The domestic accommodation

Following the Adduans' unilateral declaration of independence, prefabricated buildings were being constructed on Gan month after month to provide all the workplace, domestic and recreational accommodation needed. By the end of 1962 the last of the domestic accommodation for the European expatriates had been constructed with single room accommodation provided for each of the officers, senior non-commissioned officers and their civilian counterparts. From then on the domestic accommodation remained unchanged except for essential repair, routine maintenance and the need, in 1964 and 1965, to rebuild most of the prefabricated accommodation in the Asian village where the repairs undertaken in 1960 had proved to be inadequate.

Admittedly, the accommodation for the junior airmen, with four men to a room, remained much as it had been since early in 1960 with many of the occupants attempting to obtain some privacy by erecting temporary partitions around the bed-spaces, creating somewhat claustrophobic quarters commonly referred to as council flats. 'Adequate but certainly not generous' was a fair description of their accommodation. Understandably, most airmen preferred to spend their off-duty time outdoors or in the 180 club rather than in their billets.

Across the camp, the domestic accommodation was reasonable enough during good weather but it left a lot to be desired during prolonged periods of heavy rain when the attendant high levels of humidity would encourage mould to grow on everyone's clothing, even when it was hanging in one of the so-called 'heated wardrobes' which were in common use; wardrobes which each housed one electric light bulb. The only air-conditioned rooms were in the transit block, where slip crews were accommodated, and in the VIP suite in the station commander's bungalow. Elsewhere, ceiling fans were provided and the rooms had fine mesh window shutters rather than glazed fittings. Air-conditioning was not provided in the domestic accommodation partly because that would have led to an excessive demand for electrical power and partly because it was thought that any newly-arrived expatriate was likely to become acclimatised more quickly without it, an opinion supported by anecdotal evidence from those who worked in buildings where permanent air-conditioning was needed to maintain an appropriate environment for the temperature-sensitive equipment.

The open-mesh window shutters provided ventilation when there was a reasonable breeze but they did little to exclude the noise of a working airfield nor could they exclude the shouting and cheering from the nearby sports fields or the sounds of neighbours listening to their records or to Radio Gan. Peace and quiet was elusive on Gan but there was one popular air-conditioned centre where off-duty personnel could quietly relax with a magazine or newspaper in the afternoons or the evenings: the station library, air-conditioned to prolong the life expectancy of the books and coincidentally providing a cool refuge for readers.

The occupants of bedrooms fitted with mesh windows soon discovered another disadvantage; smoke filtered easily through the mesh. For most of the day that didn't matter, but at six o'clock every morning the 'swinging smokies' would start their rounds, trailing a cloud of insecticide-laden diesel smoke to contaminate the insects' breeding sites throughout the domestic area. This pungent cloud would filter through the mesh windows and pervade the atmosphere inside the domestic accommodation, fumigating the rooms and anybody unwise enough to be inside them at that time (Fig 17.4).

The solitary woman

One of the drawbacks to living in the village-gossip society on Gan was the lack of confidants; comments unwisely made to the wrong person had a nasty habit of becoming common knowledge. For a significant number of the non-Moslem expatriates, and particularly for those who attended confirmation classes, the Church of England Padre on Gan was generally accorded the role of resident confidant and adviser, becoming party to the worries which inevitably beset some of the men during their time on the island. He was also an important member of the community as far as the station commander was concerned, partly because of his standing as a respected neutral counsellor and partly because of his ability to inform the station commander, without breaking any confidences, of nascent problems in the communities. It was a role which he, and his successors, could perform far more easily than could the Singapore-based Roman Catholic and Church of Scotland padres who visited Gan for a week every month.

Obviously there were many airmen who were not inclined to share their personal concerns with a padre and there was, after the first week in October 1960, an alternative ear because the station gained a resident confidante,

Miss Gwen Caton. She was the first in a succession of Women's Voluntary Service, later the Women's Royal Voluntary Service, representatives who spent upwards of a year on the island, sponsored by the NAAFI and employed, for most of their time, in the airmen's 180 club where, apart from organising a variety of club activities and looking after the club's equipment, the library and the supply of magazines and newspapers, they were always willing to listen to anyone who needed a friendly neutral to talk to. Prior to Gwen Caton's arrival the description of Gan's expatriate community as 'all-male' had been legitimate because, although there were often women who were briefly at Gan, none was an established resident. But from October 1960 onwards such a description was incorrect; the resident expatriate workforce comprised some one thousand males and one woman.

Undoubtedly, the maternal presence of Gwen Caton and her successors tempered the atmosphere in the club for in Gan's male community, clubroom activities would tend to become rather vigorous and the jests obscene but in those days the airmen tended to moderate their language and their behaviour whenever the lady was present. Although the representatives would almost certainly not have described themselves as such, they were very much 'agony aunt' figures, perceived as good listeners, guardians of anything said in confidence and sympathetic advisers who were particularly valued when help was needed with the composition of those awkward personal letters which so many airmen needed to write at some time during a twelve-month unaccompanied tour. As far as the station commander was concerned, Gan's solitary woman was, like the padre, in a privileged position and he appreciated that she could, on occasions, give him some indication of the airmen's disaffections without in any way revealing any individual confidences. In that sense each trod a careful line but it says much for all of them that they were, without exception, well regarded by the airmen.

Gwen Caton completed her year on the island in October 1961 by which time she had come to be regarded as a trusted confidante by many of the airmen, as a valued and influential counsellor by the station commander and as a successful clubroom supervisor by the NAAFI manager, whose organisation was sponsoring her. With her presence on the island fully justified, her post was retained for the foreseeable future with her successor, Miss Hutcheson, similarly sponsored by the NAAFI, as were those who followed, including 'Roddy' Carpenter; Ann McGregor; Heather Ratcliffe;

Joy Sibbald, who returned for a second tour after a three year interval; Joan Parsons, who featured in the Anglia TV film 'The Lonely Men of Coral Command'; 'Roz' Howard and others whose records have been lost or buried deep in some archives. Each had volunteered to become Gan's solitary female resident for a year and each came to be highly regarded for the work she did and the influence she had. Collectively, these volunteers made a significant contribution to the morale of the expatriate airmen but theirs was a contribution which went largely unrecognised except by their sponsor and by successive station commanders.

Identity and allegiance

Few of the servicemen on Gan had volunteered for an unaccompanied tour on the island but within a few weeks of arriving, most were happy to identify themselves as 'Gannites', a breed apart from the rest of the RAF. That sense of identity manifested itself in many ways, not least in the wearing of a Gan pioneer tie even though the design meant little to a stranger. To overcome what they regarded as an inappropriate design some of the colonists designed an alternative tie for the unaccompanied tourists, using a 'club badge' pattern which incorporated a no-entry sign below the Roman numerals XII, amended to IX in 1971 when the tour length for newly-arriving servicemen was only nine months. (Fig 17.5)

Behind each serviceman's self-recognition as a Gannite there were other allegiances which surfaced most frequently and most obviously whenever there was a competitive event. Whether that allegiance was to a specialisation or a section depended on the nature of the competition but it was a feature of life on Gan which never changed; if anything, such allegiances grew stronger over the years.

Conversation pieces

Quite apart from the subjects of conversation referred to by the Costain's engineer, the expatriates were always quick to elevate local, frequently trivial, incidents in their isolated world into items of interest. Workplace incidents; interesting transients and visitors; unusual weather; inter-section sports fixtures; new facilities; eccentric behaviour and, occasionally, new arrivals all became topics of conversation. The first five featured quite often in the early diaries but as Gan's residents became somewhat blasé about visitors such as the Chief of the Defence Staff and the Admiral of the Fleet, the diaries reflected that, giving little more than passing references to the senior officers who spent a few hours on the base.

Somewhat surprisingly, the Adduan rebellion, which was referred to at some length in th station diaries was a significant topic of general conversation only when it led to demonstrations, riots and the withdrawal of labour; at other times it was largely ignored by most of the expatriates.

After February 1960, Radio Gan became an established feature of life at the atoll, adding to the topics of conversation on the island and satisfying most of the listeners most of the time. The programmes, obviously planned with the expatriate communities in mind, were listened to by many of the Adduans in their villages and were received by ships in the area, giving the radio announcer the opportunity to issue the usual sporting challenges to any crews heading for Addu Atoll. Whenever a visiting crew had the time to take up the challenge to compete against the Gannites in a variety of sports the welcome variation on the familiar local fixture list generally provided a topic of conversation for a few days, especially if the competitions were followed by an hour or two of naval hospitality on board ship.

But in 1961 there were two ships which were of particular interest even though neither carried a crew which could respond to the Gannites' sporting challenges.

The first was the Wave Victor which dropped anchor in the lagoon on the 30th of March, subsequently to become a feature of the atoll skyline for many years and to be instrumental in attracting other ships to the atoll. She was an eight-thousand-four-hundred-ton Royal Fleet Auxiliary tanker and was to be kept permanently on station in the lagoon, providing a refuelling facility for Royal Navy ships. On the 13th of April the captain secured the Wave Victor to a marine craft buoy some three miles from the Gan jetty, opposite Maradu island. At that point he considered the ship to be an RAF responsibility and he left the RAF's marine craft unit to provide Maldivian watchmen to guard the ship until such time as the Singapore-based Command staff resolved the question of responsibility for the vessel and for the extra crewmembers required. For several weeks the marine craft airmen maintained a watch over the ship, but eventually a Royal Fleet Auxiliary Captain was posted to the atoll to take command of the Wave Victor, becoming one more unaccompanied tourist, living ashore but spending his days on board ship. Maldivian crewmen were employed to man the ship day and night, receiving and subsequently redistributing fuel oil during the daytime and providing a night watch to guard the fuel stocks which, as far as the islanders were concerned, were valuable, attractive and easily disposed of.

The second ship to attract the attention of the Gan residents and to become, briefly, an interesting topic of conversation amongst the expatriates and the Maldivians alike was the Italian motor vessel Ornella Prima which ran onto the reef south of Gan just after one thirty a.m. on the 15th of September. Stuck so fast that a visiting Royal Navy ship, HMS Lincoln, was unable to free her, the motor vessel remained aground until the arrival of two tugs, Help and Schwitzer. Surprisingly, after undergoing some relatively minor repairwork the stricken ship was seaworthy enough to be towed to Colombo, salvaged by the two tugs.

In January 1963 Gan's village-gossip society found another outlet for its conversation pieces; the Gan Island Post, described in chapter XXI. It was a cyclostyled weekly news-sheet filled with local news, sports results, gossip and 'in' jokes and, like Radio Gan, was destined to become a feature of life on Gan until the base was abandoned in 1976. Throughout those thirteen years the Gan Island Post largely reflected the expatriates' cultures in which local trivia provided the most common topics of conversation day after day, week after week, month after month, year after year.

War in Pakistan

For Gan's unaccompanied tourists, family separation could be worrying at times but the worries were mostly related to domestic matters, not to the safety of the family which had been left behind. But in September 1965 many of the Pakistanis on Gan had far more to worry about than their family's domestic affairs; they received news that war had broken out between Pakistan and India. Almost immediately some of those who were employed by the works services department tried to persuade all their fellow Pakistanis to return home either to fight against India or to protect their families, many of whom lived in areas which were said to have become battle zones. A mixture of anger and worry, fuelled by the local Mullah's declaration that the war was a Jihad and that it was the religious duty of every Pakistani to go home to fight, soon had most of the Pakistanis asking to be repatriated. Suddenly the station commander, Wing Commander Scannell, was faced with the possible loss of the entire Pakistani workforce.

The district works services officer's attitude towards the request was based solely on the employees' contracts of employment; anyone who chose to leave before the end of his contract would have to pay his own fare home and would be offered no re-engagement. The Pakistanis, however, asked the RAF to fly them to a Muslim country, possibly to Teheran, from where they could make their own way home.

Within hours of receiving the requests for repatriation Scannell had asked the Command staff to provide up-to-date information on the war and to implement Operation Econium to cover the loss of the Pakistani workforce which, whilst predominantly employed on works services, also provided workers for a variety of jobs throughout the base. Within forty-eight hours Econium personnel from Singapore were arriving on Gan. That created a chain reaction, with the Singapore-based staff signalling the Ministry of Defence in London with a request for servicemen to be sent from England to Gan to allow the Singapore-based Econium personnel to return to normal duties. Whilst the Ministry of Defence staff, who had already agreed to fly the Pakistanis to Karachi at Ministry expense, were processing the request from Singapore the Pakistanis on Gan were beginning to assess the financial implications of returning home. Suddenly, repatriation did not seem to be such a good idea and, casting around for some justification for their rapid change of mind, they began to blame local activists for calling the war a Jihad. Some went as far as to send anonymous letters to the station commander naming those said to be agitators. There was obviously a shift in opinion which could be exploited for the benefit of the RAF and Scannell decided that some bluff would be in order. On the 13th of September he sent a signal to the Command staff saying:

'...will address all this afternoon saying I have received notice from Pakistani Government instructing them to stay and will post notice to this effect and ask those who wish to disobey government instructions, to break their contracts and return, to notify me and the District Works Services Officer in writing. . .'.

That was a neat enough idea but politically it was hazardous. If details of the ploy were to become known to the Pakistani government, as they so easily could via the monthly repatriation flights to Karachi, Scannell would find himself at the centre of a diplomatic row. Not surprisingly, the Command staff vetoed his idea, informed him that no Pakistani who wished to return home to fight was to be threatened with breach of contract, and instructed him to hold a secret ballot amongst the entire Pakistani workforce. Scannell was quite happy to go along with the idea but couldn't resist the opportunity of informing the Singapore-based staff, on the day that he received his instructions, of the latest report from the Pakistani camp. Unconfirmed, but almost certainly true, the report was of a Radio Karachi broadcast advising all Pakistani nationals working abroad to heed their government's advice to stay abroad and earn foreign currency for their nation.

Just to add to the general debate, the Vice-Chief of the Air Staff pointed out that if the Ministry of Defence were to repatriate the Pakistanis at British expense India would probably misconstrue the action, interpreting it as one of support for Pakistan in a war against India. He was understandably anxious to avoid such repatriation if at all possible and it was fortunate that a situation which seemed to be developing ever more complications was virtually resolved by the Pakistanis themselves. In the ballot which was held on the 14th of September over one hundred of them voted and not one expressed a wish to be repatriated. Ten RAF-employed Pakistanis and fifty-four of those employed by the works services department did not vote. As soon as the immediate threat of a dramatic loss of Pakistani labour had been withdrawn, most of the Econium personnel were allowed to return to normal duties in Singapore and the Ministry of Defence staff were able to cancel the plans to send RAF personnel from England.

On Gan, the station commander was still faced with the fact that a hardcore of malcontent Pakistanis was putting pressure on their compatriots with the result that some were requesting special leave. Scannell needed to stop that trend for although such an arrangement was contractually permissible it was impractical to grant such a concession to a large number of workers at the same time. Ideally he wanted to get rid of the agitators and the newly-elected Pakistani committee which had attracted more than its fair share of such people. Once again events worked to his advantage. Before the departure of the regular repatriation flight to Karachi at the end of September, India and Pakistan had agreed on a cease-fire and most of the moderate Pakistanis had lost any interest in special repatriation, preferring not to incur the considerable financial loss which that would bring. Only two of them requested, and were granted, compassionate leave, fourteen were due for repatriation anyway and a further twelve resigned. By chance, the main agitators were amongst those who were due to leave and the

recently-formed Pakistani committee had lost the cause which justified its campaigning style. The result, much to Scannell's relief, was a Pakistani workforce which once again focussed on local matters of little or no political significance. By mid-October the only noticeable reminders of the episode were a few vacancies in the Pakistani workforce, resulting from a cessation of recruitment in Karachi during the brief war with India, and a slight change of attitude on the part of some Pakistanis towards those of their compatriots who had agitated for repatriation.

The whole affair was typical of the way in which events on Gan reflected international activity and then sent ripples around the world. In the course of a fortnight, confrontation between India and Pakistan had created a potential manning problem on Gan which had resulted in personnel being moved at only a few hours notice from Singapore whilst others were on standby for rapid redeployment from England. A flurry of signals had travelled the globe and careful consideration given on how best to avoid a diplomatic incident. But it all ended in an anti-climax because the external events ceased to be significant. So it invariably was on Gan but at the time the concern was real enough and no station commander could afford to ignore the wider implications of virtually any event on the island; the day he did so would be the day when the worst-case scenario became reality.

From Command to Command to Command

On the 1st of April 1971, as the RAF rundown in Singapore began, Gan became an Air Support Command station. On the same date Gan's communications centre and the electrical engineering flight from the engineering squadron were combined to form N° 6 signals unit, becoming part of N° 90 Signals Group which had its Headquarters at RAF Medmenham.

Almost five months later Gan's station commander, Wing Commander Gee, completed his tour and handed over to Group Captain Sheppard who was appointed in accordance with the decision that, following the RAF withdrawal from Singapore, Gan should in future be under the command of a Group Captain.

Gan was an Air Support Command station for only seventeen months because on the 1st of September 1972 Air Support Command was assimilated into Strike Command and Gan became part of N° 46 Group. The chain of command then flowed from Strike Command Headquarters at

High Wycombe through the Group Headquarters at Upavon and thence down to Gan. The change had little impact on the day-to-day running of the staging post because the Strike Command policies and regulations which affected Gan were little different from those which had applied when the station was in Air Support Command. Additionally, most of the Headquarters staff at Upavon remained in post, becoming Group Headquarters staff instead of Command Headquarters staff. At Addu Atoll it was very much a case of business as usual, at least until the 1st of April 1973 when RAF Gan became part of the Near East Air Force with a chain of command which flowed directly to Gan from the Headquarters in Cyprus.

Devaluation

Many a Gan-based Pakistani had left home to work for the Ministry of Defence on the understanding that after five years Crown Service on the island he could become the proud holder of a British passport. It was a benefit worth having and to qualify for that most of the Pakistani expatriates were prepared to suffer separation from their families, modest wages and indifferent accommodation. But in 1971 the changes described on page 356 all but destroyed their dreams, leaving them to make what they could of a poor deal. Some, whose contracts expired that year chose to leave Gan for good; most, however, were left with little choice but to work on. They, whilst still coming to terms with the changes in the British legislation, then suffered another blow; a reduction in their standard of living brought about by a combination of their government's devaluation of the Pakistani rupee and the arrangements for setting their wage rates.

In 1971 the rupee had stood at 11.43 to the pound Sterling. An initial devaluation from 11.43 to 12.4 had effectively reduced the salaries of the Pakistani employees on Gan but had been accepted, admittedly with some discontent, as a loss which could be tolerated. The problem, as far as the Pakistanis were concerned, was that their salaries were set in rupees but they were paid in pounds. The monthly salary for a fireman, for example, was three hundred rupees which, before the devaluation, would convert to £26.25. After devaluation he would be paid only £24.20 a month. He was also prevented, by his contract, from drawing more than one third of his monthly pay on Gan, the balance either being transmitted to relatives at home or collected for use in Pakistan when he went home on leave. Trouble came in May 1972 when the Pakistani government again devalued

the rupee, this time from an exchange rate of 12.40 to 28.66. Overnight the Gan-based Pakistani fireman's salary went down from an already reduced level of £24.20 per month to £10.47 per month of which he could draw only £3.49 for use on Gan. It was just not possible to live on such a sum and the whole Pakistani community was incensed.

As tempers flared it became almost impossible for the Maldivian Affairs officer, whose remit also covered Pakistani and Sri Lankan affairs, to discuss the matter with the Pakistani representatives. But he did what he could, contacting the Air Support Command staff who referred him to the Ministry of Defence staff who referred him to the Foreign and Commonwealth Office on the basis that Gan was not the only place affected and it was not therefore a Ministry of Defence matter. In June, Air Support Command staff did come to Gan where they met the Pakistani welfare committee and were left in no doubt about the strength of feeling amongst the Pakistanis, many of whom were openly recommending disruptive industrial action unless the Ministry of Defence took some action to alleviate the problem. Regardless of the apparent lack of concern from London, the Command staff saw the situation as potentially damaging and by mid-June had persuaded the Ministry to provide pay rises for the Gan-based Pakistanis. The new rates did not fully compensate for the devaluation of the rupee but did considerably reduce the size of the earlier loss, giving a range of salaries from 273 rupees a month (£9.53) for a labourer through 780 rupees (£27.22) for the highest paid clerical grade to a top monthly salary of 906 rupees (£31.61) for the Asian camp supervisor. For their part, the Pakistanis remained angry but accepted that Britain could not be expected to protect them totally against their own government's financial decisions and that, having been given a pay rise which reduced the effects of devaluation by about fifty per cent, they had actually been treated very reasonably. They remained angry but their anger was directed towards their own government and at no time did they vent their feelings by reiterating their threats of disruptive industrial action.

The local overseas allowance

In comparison with the Pakistanis' loss of income caused by the devaluation of the Pakistani rupee, the threat to the servicemen's local overseas allowance was trivial. An overseas allowance was intended to enable anyone serving abroad to maintain a standard of living overseas which was approximately the same as that which would have been enjoyed at home. At Addu Atoll the allowance was low, some two shillings (10p) a day for a Squadron Leader and correspondingly less for more junior ranks. In mid-1972 a case was submitted to the Ministry of Defence for the local overseas allowance to be increased which meant that a team from London was obliged to visit Gan to investigate the claim. The result was not what anyone had expected; the allowance was to be frozen for the next twelve months and it was then to be discontinued. The only consolation was that those who were already serving at Addu Atoll did not lose their allowance. Neverthe-less, the team's decision provided the airmen with yet another niggle to mull over during the gradual decline, described on page 339, of the mid-tour leave arrangements.

Separated and evicted

For some of the servicemen, the impact of the postal strike at the beginning of 1971 added insult to injury because they had been virtually obliged to move their families out of service married quarters and into private accommodation on being posted to Gan. It was not that they wanted to move their families for the duration of what was at most a twelve month tour and was, for those who arrived in 1971, a nine month tour; in fact they would rather not have done so for it was an unwelcome short-term disruption. But at that time the family of any serviceman on an unaccompa-nied tour was not entitled to remain in the married quarter which had been allocated to him whilst he was on the strength of the home base. Whilst he was abroad his wife and children were classified as non-entitled occupants and could be moved out of their home at any time. The best they could hope for was that they would be offered a surplus married quarter elsewhere in the country, be that in Cornwall, Yorkshire or wherever there was unoccupied Ministry of Defence accommodation. There were servicemen on Gan whose families had been obliged to move and it was distressing for them because the family move and any associated domestic difficulties had to be resolved by writing to each other, a difficult process at the best of times and a near-impossibility during the postal strike.

The staff at the Ministry of Defence had never voiced any serious con-cerns for the evicted families of men on unaccompanied tours and seemed unlikely to amend the regulations until they were challenged, which is exactly what happened in 1971 when Gan's station warrant officer, previously employed in the recruiting office in Birmingham and on his last eighteen months of service in the RAF, was informed that his wife would have to move out of her home. He refused to give up his married quarter and that led to a series of interviews with the station commander whose sympathies were, understandably, with the Warrant Officer. There was little the Ministry staff could do about the situation without attracting adverse national publicity and eventually they let the matter drop and looked more closely at the effects of the policy and the difficulty of implementing the regulations in the face of a determined challenge. Later that year the policy was changed and by 1972 families living in married quarters were given security of tenure for the duration of a serviceman's unaccompanied tour.

The visitors and transients

From 1957 until the tail-end of 1975 a steady stream of visitors and transients descended upon Gan; the visitors arriving with a sense of purpose and a remit, the transients whiling away their time on the island whilst their aircraft was refuelled *en route* to their intended destination.

Transients were obviously few and far between in the early days but when the RAF introduced scheduled refuelling stops on Gan for the passenger aircraft on the trans-oceanic route the Britannias, Comets and, later, the VC10s brought several thousand passengers to the island every month. All were obliged to disembark and wait in the transit lounge whilst their aircraft was refuelled and they were permitted to return to their seats somewhat refreshed and ready for the next leg of the journey. This standard RAF refuelling procedure meant that, each month, several thousand passengers, many of them VIPs, had to be briefly hosted in accordance with their designated Air Ministry status which established the protocols to be observed.

Military visitors were obviously hosted according to rank with no-one below the rank of Group Captain, or its equivalent, categorised as a VIP. Public service civilians were similarly classed and there was, for example, no disputing the legitimacy of the status accorded to passengers such as government ministers and the senior civil servants. The result was that by mid-1960 it was a rare scheduled flight which did not have VIPs on board, all to be hosted, whilst on Gan, by a duty protocol officer. Inevitably, there were some passengers who were regarded as VIPs by the Air Ministry but were not seen in that light by the rostered protocol officers on Gan and with the hosting duties so often occurring well outside normal working hours, the seemingly overrated status of such passengers was all too frequently a source of irritation for the staff who had to observe the correct protocols regardless of personal perceptions. Occasionally, they could understand that inflated status was used as a control mechanism to inhibit the movements of particular passengers who, like all VIPs, would be the first to disembark, would be met at the aircraft steps by the duty protocol officer, taken by staff car to the VIPs' coffee lounge and hosted until it was time to be escorted back to the aircraft.

Not surprisingly, the use of VIP status to ensure such close control was most frequently applied to journalists who were invariably accorded privileged status after one or two had been left to spend their time with other passengers in the transit lounges along the route and, after talking to a few servicemen, had subsequently written distorted accounts of service life overseas. Close-hosting was a simple technique which was not much liked by transient journalists who, initially pleased to be regarded as VIPs, were far from pleased when they discovered the isolation controls which went with it, at least on Gan. The controls were quite effective but not foolproof for they could only be easily applied to individuals or small groups; an obvious fact proved by the duty protocol officer in November 1963 when thirty press correspondents staged through Gan on their way to Perth where they were to report on the exercise 'New Pastures'. They were only on Gan whilst their aircraft was being refuelled but a few of them still managed to gather enough information about life on the island to write several misleading articles for the British press.

By the end of 1960 Gan had also been designated as a scheduled refuelling stop for royal flights across the Indian Ocean and from then on the station diaries contain occasional references to the Duke of Edinburgh, the Prince of Wales, Princess Margaret, Lord Snowdon, the Duke and Duchess of Kent and Princess Alexandra, all of whom became transients on Gan during their various journeys to and from the Far East. It seems that most members of the royal family were easy guests who, whilst clearly able to please themselves what they did whilst on the base, generally chose to be driven on a brief tour of the island, to relax in the grounds of the officers' mess, or to swim off the adjoining beach. But there were occasions when royal transients opted for an informal tour of a few workplaces or messes, meeting some of the servicemen and civilian expatriates and talking to some of the Maldivian employees and their island officials. Such tours were necessarily brief but they were usually scheduled several weeks before the event and thus generally came to be regarded as informal royal visits with a set itinerary.

One of the first transient members of the royal family to spend more time on the island than was needed for the aircraft to be refuelled was Princess Alexandra who, with her entourage, staged through Gan *en route* from Rangoon to Aden on the 5th of December 1961. Hers was an informal visit with an all-ranks reception late that afternoon in the 180 club where she met Miss Hutcheson, the Women's Voluntary Service representative who had taken over from Miss Caton just two days previously. The royal party subsequently spent the evening socialising in the officers' mess, stayed overnight, met some of the Pakistani and Ceylonese employees the following morning, took a cruise in the marine craft unit's pinnace and found time to swim in the lagoon before departing just before mid-day. After that visit Gan seemed to hold a certain fascination for the princess; she subsequently staged through the base on several occasions, each time arranging her schedule to ensure that she had ample free time to relax on the island.

So it was that, by 1961, Gan's expatriates had settled into the demanding, but largely predictable, routines for hosting an annual flow of some forty thousand transients and visitors; a figure which would inevitably increase quite significantly. Over the years, a total of some three quarters of a million transients staged through the base, their brief presence such a normal aspect of life on the island that the station diarists tended to refer only to those who became involved in the life of the station or to the most senior of those hosted by the station commander under the protocol which dictated that he should host any VIP who was more senior than an RAF Group Captain. That was a time-consuming commitment but successive commanding officers generally agreed that the more senior transients tended to be easy conversationalists who were interested to hear about life on Gan and who could, on occasions, become useful contacts in high office.

Among those who were visitors rather than transients were the several hundred staff officers who came to Gan every year, many of them to conduct the annual inspections and audits which were such a routine aspect of life in the RAF that the inspection teams merited little more than a passing reference in the station diary. That taciturn style extended to all but the highly unusual, the inconvenient and the political; even the visits by the Chief of the Defence Staff and the Admiral of the Fleet tend to be noted rather than commented upon in any detail.

Few visiting officers came alone and during its relatively short life, RAF Gan was probably visited by more teams of investigators than any other RAF station in the world. Most came as a matter of routine, undertaking straightforward inspections and audits which required the collective expertise of a group of specialists; none with greater expertise or military seniority than those who formed the combined telecommunications and signals inspection teams which usually comprised an Air Vice-Marshal, an Air Commodore, a Group Captain, four Wing Commanders and an entourage of specialists. The routine and the mundane apart, Ministry of Defence teams and Command staff teams came, as did selected individuals, to study and report on almost every aspect of life at the atoll whilst civilians, singly or in teams, came with similar remits focussed on anything from the scientific to the political. In many instances the local circumstances which led to the arrival of such visitors, their investigations and the subsequent events flow through the Gan story but many visitors were noteworthy in their own right, not because local circumstances had led to their arrival as participants in the Gan saga. Some, such as the entertainers, came to Gan by invitation and were received as welcome guests; others, not specifically invited, were not always as welcome.

It is hardly surprising that every one of Gan's station commanders was left with an abiding memory of a stream of visitors which included royalty; prime ministers and other senior politicians; Maldivian ministers; senior military officers and senior civil servants, all coming to Gan for a purpose and all so senior that it fell to the station commander to host them. Even though numerous visitors, including the many Ministry of Defence and Command teams which spent time on the base, were left in the hands of section commanders the station commander's role as host remained the most demanding on the base.

The first four months of 1962 brought to the island the senior political figures and the mass demonstrations referred to on page 156 but there was certainly no lack of seniority amongst the later visitors that year for the list included the Chief of the Air Staff, Marshal of the Royal Air Force Sir Thomas Pike; the Right Honourable Julian Amery, secretary of state for Air; the Commissioner General for South East Asia; the Commanders-in-Chief for Transport Command and the Far East Air Force; Air Marshal Frazer, the inspector general; the Civil Lord of the Admiralty accompanied by four Members of Parliament; the Earl of Cosford and Air Vice-Marshal Sir Walter Pretty who revisited the island with his combined telecommunications and signals inspection team in November. Relatively speaking, the Wing Commanders, Squadron Leaders and Ministry of Defence civilians who came to Gan to conduct inspections and audits during that period were of minor significance.

As far as visitors and transients were concerned, 1963 was much the same as 1962 with Gan's station commander hosting the usual variety of very senior VIPs and meeting other visitors, among them Hammond Innes who spent twelve days on the island in late January and early February, gathering local information for his next book, 'The Strode Venturer', and bringing to the expatriates a brief insight into the world of the successful thriller writer.

Very few of the thousands of passengers who staged through Gan every year expected to spend more than an hour or so on the ground; those who did were invariably very senior transients whose flight schedules had been arranged to give them a prolonged stay on the island. Some, however, found themselves unexpectedly spending far longer than an hour or two on the base. They were the passengers whose aircraft had developed technical problems, been classified as unserviceable and was grounded until the staging aircraft servicing flight technicians had completed whatever repairs were required. Apart from near-tragedies such as that which befell those on board Hastings TG 579 when it ditched short of the runway in the accident described on page 290 the worst situation, as far as the Gan-based servicemen were concerned, arose when passengers were stranded overnight pending the arrival of a replacement aircraft. Under such circumstances 'Operation Fastbed', described on page 304 had to be implemented.

After the Wave Victor had been designated as an Indian Ocean refuelling centre Royal Navy and Royal Fleet Auxiliary ships became frequent visitors, their presence accepted as just another routine aspect of life at the atoll. But when the Royal Fleet Auxiliary Fort Langley sailed into the lagoon on the 17th of September 1963 she brought an unusual problem for the station commander; her captain requested permission to bury a Chinese steward, Chan Wan Pang, who had died whilst at sea. The problem for the captain was that the religious beliefs of the dead man and his compatriots made burial at sea unacceptable; the problem for the station commander was that the construction and operation of the base had led to a dramatic increase in the extraction of water from the island's subterranean supply and, because the water table was only two or three feet below the surface, there was a general embargo on interment on the island for fear of contaminating the water supply. Eventually the district works services officer agreed that the small disused Second World War graveyard on the south-eastern coastal strip would provide a suitable burial place and Chang Wan Pang was interred there during a ceremony attended by thirty of the Fort Langley's crew and three RAF officers.

In January 1964 Wing Commander Hill handed over command to Wing Commander Moss and he, like his predecessors and his successors, soon found that he had to adapt to a demanding schedule of disrupted days and nights. Some thirty years later he could still recall that virtually every day he was expected to host a few senior VIP transients who were briefly disembarked from the Transport Command Comets which staged through Gan, one arriving some two hours after midnight and another some eight hours later. Like the rostered duty protocol officer, he was thus obliged to leave his bed in time to arrive at the hardstanding before the VIPs disembarked and to host his temporary guests for an hour before returning to his bed, rarely much before four o'clock in the morning. Unlike the rostered officers, however, he was on call for every such flight throughout his tour.

Moss could also recall that, quite apart from the transients, virtually every senior staff officer in the Far East Air Force Headquarters tried to justify at least one annual visit to Gan. There seemed to be an endless list of air-rank officers waiting to visit their favourite watering-hole and it became obvious that the situation was getting out of hand when the Commander-in-Chief, after spending two days at the atoll with a sizeable entourage, expressed a wish to return for a fishing holiday. Fortunately, his plan was vetoed, effectively putting a stop to any future suggestions that Gan could be treated as a holiday resort for senior officers.

Every year some visitors and transients came by sea and, apart from the period when a Royal Navy guardship was on station in the lagoon, the officer commanding Gan's marine craft unit would make first contact with any non-Maldivian vessel which arrived at the atoll. That, together with the fact that he provided a piloting service for visiting ships, was responsible for the provision of the ferry service between Gan and Hitaddu and for the cargo handling on the marine craft unit's jetty meant that the RAF and the Royal Navy tended to regard the lagoon as Gan's military harbour although it was actually sovereign waters and could, with the permission of the Maldivian government, be entered by any vessel. In theory, there was nothing to stop Russia, China or any other nation from obtaining permission and sailing its ships into the lagoon; only the protection agreement and the continuing diplomatic relations with Britain prevented that from happening.

There was, however, no reason to exclude vessels which were unconnected with the cold war and every year a few private yachts would find their way to the atoll, some diverted out of curiosity after picking up the signals from Gan's beacon, others intentionally headed there after the lagoon had been chosen as a mid-ocean safe haven. Quite frequently the visiting crew would be taken aback to discover, on entering the lagoon, that they were in the company of a Royal Navy destroyer or frigate and a Royal Fleet Auxiliary refuelling tanker permanently at anchor alongside a military base.

Generally, those visiting captains and crews wanted nothing more than a respite from the Indian Ocean and after forty-eight hours at anchor in the lagoon they were usually refreshed and ready to put to sea again. Such casual visitors were rarely invited ashore by the Maldivians nor were they welcomed by the RAF but they were never refused help if it was needed and they were always invited to re-provision if necessary. That, however, was the limit of the RAF's contact with any crews who did not have Air Ministry clearance to land on either of the leased territories.

On those rare occasions when an ocean-going vessel did arrive in distress the RAF's marine craft technicians were invariably able to render assistance and over the years they proved that they could deal effectively with most of the technical problems which they encountered. Few ships, however, created as complex a situation for the station commander as that which arose on the 26th of April 1964 when an American yacht, the SS Te Vega, flying a flag of distress, sailed into the lagoon. Sponsored by Stanford University and employed on the International Indian Ocean Expedition, the ship had apparently been caught in a monsoon and suffered an explosion in the engine room when water poured into a hatch which had been left open. The explosion had resulted in an electrical failure and had left the engineer with a lacerated skull and second degree burns for which he received treatment in the RAF's medical centre where the facilities were better than those on board the ship. As soon as he had been treated he was, at his request, given permission to send a signal from Gan to the ship's owners. His message reflected his anger; he informed the owners that he intended to abandon ship and he demanded that a board of inquiry be convened to determine the cause of the accident which he claimed to be the result of negligence. Moss sent a copy of the signal to the Te Vega's captain but it was ignored, as was the protocol which required the captain of any visiting non-Maldivian ship to pay a courtesy visit to Gan's station commander who was also the officer commanding the harbour, a rarely used title but one which clearly established his status. When the Te Vega's captain failed to come ashore, Moss went out to the ship to explain that the crew, which included some thirty scientists, would be allowed ashore subject to certain restrictions which applied to all visitors to the RAF base. Some duly came ashore later that day and spent a rather boisterous evening in the sergeants' mess.

The following day, when the ship's captain ignored a message asking him to come ashore to see the station commander, Moss went aboard the Te Vega where he found the captain to be curt and decidedly inhospitable. Left standing in the rain outside the cabin, Moss was told that no assistance was needed even though several servicemen from the RAF marine craft unit were already helping with the repair work. The captain was quite offhand but he did inform Moss that the crew would not be allowed ashore again. Moss left. He had no idea what subsequently happened on board ship but within hours he received a signal from the captain stating that there appeared to be a mutiny brewing on board and that military assistance might be needed.

Moss read his copy of Admiralty Orders but was left pondering the complexity of a situation in which a mutiny might occur on board an American ship, employed on an international expedition, at anchor in Maldivian waters alongside a British military base. He sent an explanatory signal to the Command staff but by the time they had contacted the staff at the American embassy the possibility of a mutiny had faded and no action was needed. Moss, however, received a personal signal from the American Secretary of State deploring the problems which had arisen, expressing appreciation for the assistance given and promising reimbursement, without questions, of any costs incurred. Repairs to the ship were effected by the end of the month but it then remained in the lagoon until early in May awaiting

a replacement for the engineer who had left Gan earlier on a casualty evacuation flight.

Mid-1964 was a time when confluent events brought so many visitors to Gan that the facilities on the base were almost over-run. The airfield was cluttered with the V bombers heading east; the station's accommodation was filled to capacity with servicemen on temporary detachment or travelling with the V-force; the VIP transients and visitors, including the team sent to investigate the pay and conditions of the Maldivians, were as numerous as ever and the Adduan villagers were at loggerheads with their officials and with each other. When fighting did break out in the Adduan villages it did not spread onto Gan but the temporary loss of Maldivian labour meant that Operation Econium had to be implemented and that led to the arrival of personnel from Singapore and an increase in the demand for accommodation on the already congested base.

It was an odd time for the Command staff to decide that there was no longer any need for an RAF Regiment detachment on Gan but that they did, announcing that at the end of June the incumbent flight would be withdrawn and not replaced. Five weeks later the station commander was obliged to call for their return because trouble had flared up again in Hitaddu village. Compounding the situation, a large number of the Adduans failed to report for work that week and, with the Econium personnel on twenty-four hours standby in Singapore it became necessary to prepare additional accommodation on Gan ready for yet another influx of servicemen. For almost a month the expatriates coped without them but during the second week in September the reinforcements had to be brought in together with a flight of RAF Regiment airmen from Lyneham, detached to Gan because the Singapore-based Regiment airmen had already been despatched to other trouble spots in the Far East.

In something akin to a parallel universe, numerous scientists were at that time continuing to undertake their research in the Indian Ocean with one such group, from the University of Cambridge, arriving at the atoll on the 1st of July and embarking on a three-month study of the local marine ecology. The scientists had very little to do with the expatriates; they tended to keep themselves very much to themselves although they did discuss their work quite readily with Ley Kenyon, a visiting lecturer and scuba diving instructor who, during the last week of July, was making one of his occasional visits to the atoll, giving an entertaining series of lectures and accompanying some of Gan's scuba divers during their explorations of the reefs and the wreck of the British Loyalty.

The Adduans' unpredictability continued to complicate matters for Wing Commander Moss until well into the new year but by April 1965 an air of near-normality had descended on the Adduan communities and the Ministry of Defence decided that, after five tour extensions as Gan's station commander, Moss could be repatriated.

For the next three years his successors benefited from the gradual improvement in the relations between the British and Maldivian governments, the signing of a new agreement and a marked difference in the behaviour of the Adduans, all of which meant that RAF Regiment airmen and Econium reinforcements were infrequent visitors after 1965. Other visitors, however, continued to arrive week after week and the stream of transients staging through the base continued to include VIPs on virtually every flight; by 1966 life on Gan was back to normal and would remain so until the Adduans once again chose to disrupt it.

For Wing Commander Mullineaux, Gan's station commander for the last quarter of 1967 and for most of 1968, 'normal' brought two Lords, seven Members of Parliament, two Admirals, one Air Officer, the atoll chief, a Merchant Navy Captain and a journalist from a national newspaper, all to be hosted by the station commander during his first six days in post. It was an interesting, if somewhat demanding introduction to his hosting responsibilities.

There were, of course, some light-hearted moments to offset the almost daily demands which continued throughout his year on Gan, few more amusing than that which occurred on the 3rd of October 1968. That evening he was due to host the Chief of the General Staff who, accompanied by his lady and an entourage of eight VIPs was due to arrive on board a late evening Comet. The aircraft landed on schedule at a quarter to ten and was met by the station commander along with the escorting officers and the RAF police, all of them standing to attention at the foot of the aircraft steps ready to welcome the VIPs before escorting them to the staff car and the passenger coach.

The General was the first to emerge from the aircraft. He was in his swimming costume and was wrapped in a towel. The remaining members of the party then emerged, all of them in swimming costumes, some with towels, some without. After getting over his initial surprise, Mullineaux

extended the normal courtesies before rapidly changing the planned itinerary and arranging for the entire party to be taken to his bungalow instead of to the transit lounge. From there they were able to enjoy swimming in the lagoon by moonlight augmented by the bungalow's security lights. It was, perhaps, a fitting finale to Mullineaux's hosting commitments for later that month he completed his year as Gan's station commander and handed over to Wing Commander Farmer.

Farmer was fortunate. He took over from Mullineaux only a matter of days before the Maldivians' euphoric transition, in November, from a sultanate to a republic and the subsequent political harmony ensured that at Addu Atoll there would be no more demonstrations and confrontations because the islanders would no longer have a good reason to disrupt the operations on Gan. It meant that no guardship would have to return to the atoll, no RAF Regiment airmen would have to be despatched to the island and no Econium personnel would have to be ferried to and from the base to undertake the work abandoned by islanders who were on strike in protest against the British government's duplicity in handing them over to their central government. Without those temporary residents on the island, other visitors could more easily be accommodated and Operation Fastbed could be easily implemented whenever necessary.

As for Farmer, so it was for Wing Commander Spragg, his successor and for Wing Commander Gee who took over command from Spragg in October 1970.

By the 1st of April 1971, when Gan became an Air Support Command station, it was as if there had never been a rebellion, never been any acrimony between the British and Maldivian governments and never been any riots by the Adduans.

Three days after Gan's assimilation into Air Support Command, the Duke of Edinburgh staged through Gan *en route* to the Far East, his flight times arranged to give him two or three hours in which to pay informal visits to the officers' mess, the sergeants' mess, the 180 club and the corporals' club. In essence, his itinerary was to be similar to, but much shorter than, that arranged for Princess Alexandra in December 1961. But it had been decided that when Prince Philip staged through Gan on the 4th of April the occasion was to be treated as a royal visit rather than a mere refuelling stop and it was preceded by a staff visit to vet the schedule for the day and to discuss the details with Wing Commander Gee, the then station commander. The staff on that preliminary visit seemed to cover every detail, even down to the Duke's likely preference for gin and tonic, a suggestion which raised the amusing possibility that Prince Philip could be introduced to the rather obnoxious tonic water produced in the NAAFI's bottling plant. That product, made with Gan water, was no more palatable than the water itself and was a drink to offer to a guest only to make a point. But the NAAFI was the monopoly supplier and Schweppes tonic could not be imported to Gan, at least, not under normal circumstances. For the Duke of Edinburgh, however, an exception was made and several cases of tonic water, far more than necessary, were imported by an obliging VC 10 captain.

The fact that the visit was intended to be quite informal meant that very little planning had to be done. There was no guard of honour or station parade to be organised, just a small group of senior officers to be introduced to Prince Philip on the airfield hardstanding before he was taken by staff car to the officers' mess. Just hours before the arrival of the Duke's flight, with everything apparently well organised, Gee learnt that one important, and very basic, point had not even been mentioned during the preliminary staff visit. It was the Sergeant who was to be Prince Philip's chauffeur during the visit who realised that the flagstaff on the station commander's car would almost certainly not accommodate the royal standard.

When a rapid perusal of the RAF manuals provided no details of shaft sizes, the Sergeant made his way to the general engineering workshop where a Pakistani fitter manufactured a new flagstaff to the Sergeant's estimated specification of what was required, hoping that it would suffice. When the Duke's Aide-de-Camp came down the aircraft steps and handed the royal standard to the driver there was very little time to mount it on the car because the Duke was heading for the vehicle after being greeted by the station commander and briefly introduced to the four senior officers on the hardstanding. Gee, seeing that the Sergeant was having problems with the recently manufactured fitting, delayed the introductions as long as possible, finally escorting Prince Philip to the car when it seemed that the problem had been solved. The car set off for the officers' mess, moving slowly enough for the Duke to wave to the Maldivians who were lining the route. All seemed well and Gee began to relax, unaware that the unfortunate driver, in his effort to mount the standard, had made a most fundamental mistake. The standard was flying but it was upside down.

The station commander may not have noticed that but Prince Philip certainly had for, whilst continuing to wave to the crowd, he half turned towards Gee and out of the side of his mouth said *'That's the first time I've seen the lions pawing the bloody sky'*. That comment was typical of the Duke's informal style during his brief visit which, together with the fact that he made the effort to meet as many servicemen as possible whilst staging through, was appreciated by everyone. In each of the messes he met groups of men in their everyday uniforms, chatted informally to them, drank a beer with them and then moved on. His easy style was exemplified again when, on leaving the officers' mess, he expressed his appreciation of the work of all the unaccompanied tourists and ended his remarks with a smile and the comment *'… and you don't need to tell me what you will all be giving up for Lent'*. In each of the messes that evening Prince Philip's visit was remembered with appreciation as a fortunate few enjoyed his legacy, the taste of genuine tonic water, untouched because he had preferred to drink beer.

That same month the journalist John Blashill spent several days on Gan, subsequently writing an article which was published, under the title 'The Island of Not Having', in Time magazine on the 17th of May. It was an article which evoked a great deal of ill-feeling towards Blashill from the servicemen who had accepted him into their community and were angry that the published report said much about their sexual frustrations and their alcohol consumption but nothing of any significance about their work. It was just what the wiser, uncommunicative members of the expatriate community had expected. Others, who had been foolish enough to talk openly to him in the misguided belief that the published report would give a balanced account of expatriate life on the island, had learned a lesson; as far as they were concerned journalists were no longer welcome and were certainly not to be trusted.

Wing Commander Gee's successor, Group Captain Sheppard, had quickly discovered that the withdrawal from the Far East and Gan's assimilation into Air Support Command had had little effect on the number of visitors to the island. A steady stream of staff officers had descended upon the island during his first few weeks in post, many of them to conduct inspections, virtually all of them from Air Support Command Headquarters and the majority of them highly supportive.

That November a Harlech Television team visited the island to gather material for a documentary programme, Air Vice Marshal Durkin once again brought his inspection team to the atoll and Princess Anne staged through Gan *en route* to Akrotiri, her schedule giving her just one and a half hours on the island. It was but a brief interlude in her journey from Hong Kong but it was one for which some preparations had to be made, including the widening of the path from the officers' mess to the station commander's bungalow to ensure that the Princess and her escort did not have to walk in single file.

Sheppard's hosting commitments during December were little different from any other month with one significant exception; on the 9th of December Angus Mackintosh, the British high commissioner and ambassador to the Maldives, came to discuss with the Assistant Private Secretary to Her Majesty the Queen and his group of seven advisers the arrangements for the 15th of March 1972 when the Queen and Prince Philip would be visiting Gan. Apart from that, December was a normal month for the station commander. But it was certainly far from normal for those whose job it was to provide an efficient service for the island's transients. The two weeks leading up to Christmas were, as expected, exceptionally busy with the exodus from the Far East combining with the mass evacuation of Nº 40 marine commando unit. The exodus alone led to a significant increase in the number of passengers staging through Gan, every one of them anxious to arrive in England before Christmas and none of them wishing to be delayed *en route*. The mass evacuation of the commandos simply added to that month's workload with over six hundred troops disembarked from HMS Albion and flown back to England over a three-day period, the last of them leaving on the 19th, just three days before Gan's airfield was closed for the Christmas stand-down.

With Christmas and the New Year stand-down behind them, Gan's expatriates once again found themselves briefly hosting an unexceptional stream of visitors and transients each day. But when the royal yacht, Britannia, sailed into the lagoon on the 15th of March, it marked the beginning of the most significant visit in the history of RAF Gan for it was one of those rare occasions when Her Majesty was visiting the servicemen and civilians who were manning one the RAF's isolated outposts. To Gan's unaccompanied tourists and to the Maldivians in general the royal visit was an event to remember but for one small group of villagers it was far more than a royal visit, it was a never-to-be-forgotten reunion because on that day

seven islanders, the survivors out of thirteen people on board a missing dhoni, were brought safely back home.

Their boat had been adrift in the Indian Ocean since the 20th of January and as the days had run into weeks, hope had faded for all those on board. What no-one could have expected was that some of them would eventually be rescued and brought home by the Queen's escort ship. The first that the villagers of Addu Atoll knew of that development was on the 6th of March when they heard of a radio message from HMS Hydra, a Royal Navy survey ship some three hundred and sixty miles east of Gan, pinpointing the location of the drifting dhoni and arranging a rendezvous with the royal escort frigate HMS Arethusa. On the 11th of March the rescued Maldivians were transferred to the frigate, subsequently to be brought home. For them and their families the royal visit was forever to be remembered for the rescue more than for any of the other events of the day.

On the 15th the royal yacht anchored in the lagoon and just before twelve thirty the royal barge brought the Queen, Prince Philip and Earl Mountbatten to the marine jetty. The visit was not intended to be a formal affair and the Air Support Command staff had confirmed that the itinerary and hosting was to be largely determined by the station commander in consultation with the planning team which had visited the base the previous December. No official visit by the Queen could ever be informal but that day came as close to informality as was possible, an opinion which would no doubt have been shared by Corporal Panter, the Queen's driver that day, temporarily absent from his regular workplace in the marine craft unit where he could normally be seen driving a crane.

In the officers' mess, Ahmed Salih Ali Didi, the atoll chief, and Mohammed Saeed, his interpreter, were introduced to the Queen and Prince Philip, the chief dining as one of the honoured guests. The royal tour of the station included the messes and clubs which the Duke had visited the previous April, the civilian messes, the Asian village and several workplaces including the transit lounge where the tour ended with Prince Philip planting two trees outside the Blue Lagoon. During the tour the Queen formally opened Radio Gan's new studio, broadcasting a speech in which she said:

> 'This is a beautiful place and it is easy to see how visitors can become entranced by the colours and charm of the islands and the lagoon. But it is a long way from home and I realise that for many of you who are posted

here for a complete tour of duty the beauty is no compensation for the separation from your families and the absence of the diversions of a township. Here you have to make your own entertainment and for this Radio Gan is, of course, of great importance. Gan may be a long way from home but I need hardly remind you that the job you are doing here is of real value and that this is recognised'.

It was a brief speech but it was very well received for it succinctly expressed the feelings of virtually every expatriate at the atoll.

After taking tea in the station commander's bungalow, the royal party left Gan, later meeting Group Captain Sheppard and the twenty officers who had been invited to dine on board Britannia where Her Majesty bestowed a knighthood on Angus Mackintosh, the British high commissioner and ambassador to the Maldives. With the formalities concluded, the guests departed and at midnight the royal yacht sailed out of the lagoon, headed for the Seychelles.

Like every RAF station, Gan had benefited from an open purse approach to any work which was labelled 'royal visit preparation'. Around the world, such works remain as testimonies to that approach and although there was no grand building project on Gan the numerous small reminders of the visit included a glass-bottomed boat ostensibly built to enable the royal party to view the coral and the exotic marine life which abounded in the lagoon but coincidently providing a replacement for Gan's rather inferior model which had long since been condemned.

In comparison with the arrival of the royal yacht the three royal flights which staged through Gan in October aroused little interest. The first, with Princess Margaret and Lord Snowdon on board, was headed for Singapore *en route* to Australia; the second and third, carrying Princess Alexandra and Angus Ogilvie, were headed for Hong Kong on the 20th of that month and returning a week later. Whereas Princess Margaret and Lord Snowdon spent a mere hour on the base *en route* to the Far East, Princess Alexandra and Angus Ogilvie spent forty-eight hours on the island *en route* to Hong Kong, enjoying coral-gazing from the recently acquired glass-bottomed boat and taking the opportunity to relax on the island. For the station commander, hosting the couple during their stay involved the diplomatic curtailment of Princess Alexandra's tendency to get on a bike and set off around the island on her own; not a dangerous activity but one which was not to be encouraged. Fortunately, Sheppard's successor, Group Captain Salmon, was fit

enough to jump on his own bike and ride alongside her, combining the duties of a host with those of a minder.

It is difficult to see how the princess and her husband could justify such an extended stay for they were essentially treating Gan as a short-break holiday resort and that was not a popular thing to do on an island with a resident expatriate community of several hundred unaccompanied men. But there was one expatriate, possibly the only one, who benefited from the princess's extended stay; the solitary woman, the Women's Royal Voluntary Service representative. For her, there was an unexpected treat, an appointment with a Bond Street hair stylist, courtesy of the princess who was accompanied by her personal hairdresser.

Quite apart from the members of the royal family, the steady stream of transients and the usual visitors to the base, there were several visitors who attracted the attention of the unaccompanied tourists during the latter half of 1972, starting with the latest in a long line of researchers who had visited the archipelago over the decades: five scientists from Imperial College, London. They set up camp on Wilingili in August to begin their six-week study of the geology and the flora and fauna of the islands, extending the work of the Cambridge team which had spent three months at the atoll in 1964. They were the first of several scientists to visit the islands during September, October and November that year, a time when more scientific research was undertaken at the atoll than in any other comparable period throughout the operational life of the base.

As they were about to return to London, Ley Kenyon arrived on one of his occasional visits, spending ten days on Gan, once again giving a series of entertaining and informative evening lectures and leading a series of daytime scuba dives in the lagoon.

On the 29th of September, three days after Kenyon's departure, the first eight of the twenty-four Skua rockets referred to on page 295 were successfully launched, the remaining sixteen being fired during the first week of October. Finally, the study programme for the year was rounded off in November when a team from the Imperial College of Science undertook the research described on page 295 and the marine craft unit's airmen participated in the scientific survey referred to on page 307.

1973 started with an influx of troops on a combined mobility exercise. Brought to Gan by the Royal Navy, some two thousand troops camped on the airfield, their tents pitched down each side of the runway for over two weeks, the occupants coming to be regarded as temporary residents rather than visitors. They were lucky; January that year was an unusually dry month. Had they arrived four weeks earlier they would have experienced Gan at its worst for the airfield had been flooded twice in December, a month when almost eighteen and a half inches of rain fell on the island.

Apart from the five weeks when Gan's runway was partially closed for the repairs referred to on page 295, the first quarter of 1973 was little different from any other period as far as visitors and transients were concerned. The stream of transients continued unabated and the station commander and the duty protocol officers hosted the usual variety of VIPs including Prince Philip, who staged through on his way to England from Australia during the last week of March, a matter of days after the completion of the repairs to Gan's runway.

On the 1st of April 1973 the station became part of the Near East Air Force, the new chain of command flowing to Gan directly from the Command Headquarters in Cyprus. The transition from Strike Command, the third transfer of Command in two years, was accompanied by the anticipated arrival of the Air Officer Administration and a group of twelve staff officers, visiting the island for a week to familiarise themselves with their newly-acquired station.

Normality returned to Gan with a vengeance that month. The list of visitors included numerous staff officers from the Cyprus Headquarters and the Commander-in-Chief making his first official two-day visit to inspect the recent extension to his bailiwick. It was also the month when air mobility exercises were resumed with Nimrods, Phantoms and Victors staging through the base at a time when a contingent of Ghurkhas was obliged to remain on the island for two days because their aircraft was unserviceable.

The April flurry of staff visits from Cyprus was followed by a relatively quiet period when visiting ships and transient VIPs were no more numerous than usual. But in June there was one visitor who attracted the attention of the station diarist and the Radio Gan controller, a retired Army officer who spent three days on Gan at the beginning of the month. He was Major Wilfrid Manners MBE (Ret'd) who had been a member of the original survey party despatched to the atoll in 1940 and had been among the wartime pioneers who had developed the secret base, Port T. He had subsequently served at the atoll through most of the wartime years and had been invited to return in 1973 as a VIP guest of the Ministry of Defence.

Understandably, he found it hard to believe that what he remembered as a swampy, disease-ridden tented encampment manned by soldiers who spent several years at the atoll during the war, had been converted into something more akin to a holiday camp to which the servicemen were posted for only nine months. He was made very welcome for the duration of his stay, was interviewed on Radio Gan, was asked on countless occasions to describe his wartime experiences at the atoll and was duly issued with a new airfield driving permit to replace his Addu Atoll military driving licence which had expired at the end of the war (Fig 17. 6).

Of all the visitors who came to Gan the journalists were the ones who continued to be generally regarded as dissemblers, an opinion which was passed on from one generation of unaccompanied tourists to another and had been strengthened by the publication of John Blashill's 1971 magazine article. The majority of the servicemen on Gan were well aware of the risk of talking to a journalist who had travelled halfway round the world in search of a newsworthy story but inevitably some were naïve enough to share their private lives and thoughts with visiting writers only to find that their hospitality was abused without a second thought. A few reporters were prepared to present a balanced account of expatriate life at the RAF's mid-ocean staging post but far too many were only interested in writing a one-sided account of life at the atoll, emphasising minor aspects which could be described in sufficiently sensational terms to titillate the readers even if that came at the expense of their hosts' privacy. From Gan, it was virtually impossible to distinguish between those who would produce a balanced account of life on the base and those who would set out to produce an exposé but Group Captain Whitlock's request for the Near East Air Force staff to vet all the journalists who wished to visit Gan fell on deaf ears; they were as unresponsive as the Far East Air Force, Air Support Command and Strike Command staffs had been. Nothing changed.

Through the latter half of 1973 there were no extraordinary visitors or transients; Ministry of Defence teams, Combined Services Entertainers, VIPs, inspecting officers, Royal Navy and Royal Fleet Auxiliary ships, oil tankers, merchantmen and the occasional private yacht all came and went; some welcome, some not so welcome and only a few, such as the Duke of Edinburgh who staged through Gan *en route* to England in November, attracting much attention.

So it was for much of 1974, a year when the fuel shortage in Britain led to a significant reduction in the number of aircraft staging through Gan and in the number of Royal Navy and Royal Fleet Auxiliary ships putting into the lagoon, all subjected to the fuel conservation measures. The RAF's schedules for passenger flights to and from the Far East were not seriously affected during those early months of 1974 and although there was no significant reduction in the number of transient VIPs at that time there were slightly fewer visits by the more junior staff officers who seemed to be curtailing their travels even though visits by Air Officers, senior civil servants and senior members of the British government were no fewer during that period than at any other time.

The usual lengthy list of visitors from England that year included few out-of-the-ordinary arrivals apart from the British Museum curators, who briefly visited the atoll in April, and the artist Penelope Douglas who spent four days on the island producing preliminary sketches for an official painting of an RAF Britannia.

Only one transient, however, merited anything other than a passing reference in the station diary: the Prince of Wales who staged through Gan five times that year. Probably more familiar with the island than any other member of the royal family, he invariably chose to while away his time water skiing in the lagoon or swimming off the beach alongside the officers' mess.

It was the visitors from Malé who were of most interest in 1974 because they were openly declaring their intention to usher in a new era for the Maldives and for Addu Atoll in particular. Ever since Nasir had been persuaded that tourism could become as profitable an industry as fishing, his ministers had been working on the development of facilities in the archipelago and in October the Air Maldive inaugural flight brought twenty-eight Maldivian officials to Gan, all anxious to develop tourism facilities at Addu Atoll. Their enthusiasm meant that the airline's Convairs became frequent visitors, bringing numerous government officials and businessmen to the atoll, all used to a reasonable standard of living, all needing to be accommodated overnight and all hoping to stay on Gan. An awkward political situation was developing for Group Captain Moffat, the then station commander, but the Foreign and Commonwealth Office ruling referred to on page 241 was, somewhat unusually, made before the situation got out of hand and that saved Moffat from any embarrassment.

By the time Group Captain Edwards, who was to become the last of Gan's station commanders, arrived at the atoll the staging post's premature closure had been announced and he was thus bound to find himself hosting a variety of senior officers, British officials and Maldivian ministers who would be involved in the rundown, the withdrawal and the examination of the assets to be inherited by the Maldivian government.

The first really significant visitor with any information about the closure was Sir Andrew Humphrey, the chief of the air staff, who visited Gan in February 1975 to explain the implications of the recent defence review and to confirm that the staging post would be closed down at the end of March 1976. The effects of that decision on the Maldivians, the expatriate Asians, the Ministry of Defence civilians and the servicemen are described in chapters XXII and XXIII and although those were devastating for the Maldivians and severe for the expatriate Asians, day-to-day life on Gan was remarkably unaffected during 1975.

Throughout the first six months of 1975 all the usual activities continued, diverting the attention of the Pakistanis and the Adduans away from the painful fact that the staging post would be abandoned within twelve months. Even the mid-year groups of visitors contributed to the diversion; a five-day visit by a Combined Services Entertainment troupe in May, a June visit by a group of ten cadets from RAF Henlow and the arrival, a week later, of the BBC's Force's Chance team all helped to engender an air of near-normality in the workplaces.

But confirmation of the date of Britain's withdrawal inevitably led to a gradual change in the nature of the visits with routine inspections declining and investigative visits by teams of inspectors increasing. From Malé there came government ministers, teams of civil servants and senior representatives of organisations attracted by the investment opportunities internationally publicised by the Maldivian government. From Britain, Ministry of Defence representatives were sent to Gan, some to finalise the redundancy terms for the expatriate Asians and the Maldivians, some to work out the final pay award for the Adduans, some to offer advice to the European expatriates and the servicemen and some to provide technical advice on the removal of sophisticated military equipment such as that associated with Skynet.

By December, Gan's last full month as a staging post, there was little justification for staff officers to visit the base unless they were directly involved in the closure programme and, shortly before Christmas, the farewell visits made by the Commanders-in-Chief of Strike Command and the Near East Air Force signalled the end of the continual stream of visitors which had descended upon Gan ever since the days of the Ship's Flag detachment in 1957.

With the departure, on the 1st of January 1976, of the last of the regularly scheduled VC 10s to stage through the base the daily flow of transients ceased and from then on the only visitors to Gan were those associated with the closure and the hand-over.

Fig 17.1. Karen Doling receiving her 'coconut by post'

Fig 17.2. Frangipani on Gan, the favourite for 'flowers by post'

Fig17.4. One of the 'swinging smokies' on Gan 1971

Fig 17.3. A works services department gardener in the grounds of the officers' mess, Gan 1971

College of Arms
July, 1965

Clarenceux King of Arms
and Inspector of Royal
Air Force Badges

Fig 17.5. The Gan badge flanked by a 'Gan pioneer' tie and an 'unaccompanied tourist' tie.

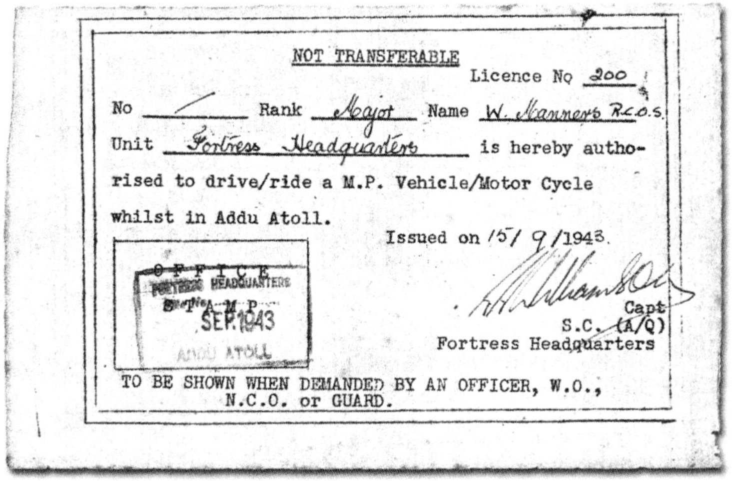

NOT TRANSFERABLE

Licence No 200

No ____ Rank Major Name W. Manners R.C.O.S.

Unit Fortress Headquarters is hereby authorised to drive/ride a M.P. Vehicle/Motor Cycle whilst in Addu Atoll.

Issued on 15/ 9 /1943.

OFFICE FORTRESS HEADQUARTERS SEP 1943 ADDU ATOLL

Capt S.C. (A/Q)
Fortress Headquarters

TO BE SHOWN WHEN DEMANDED BY AN OFFICER, W.O., N.C.O. or GUARD.

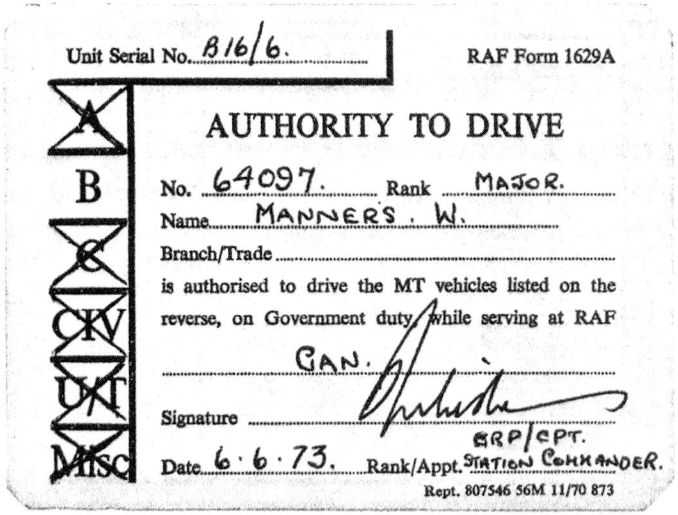

Unit Serial No. B16/6. RAF Form 1629A

A B C CIV UKT Misc

AUTHORITY TO DRIVE

No. 64097. Rank MAJOR.
Name MANNERS. W.
Branch/Trade
is authorised to drive the MT vehicles listed on the reverse, on Government duty, while serving at RAF GAN.
Signature
Date 6.6.73. Rank/Appt. GRP/CPT. STATION COMMANDER.

Rept. 807546 56M 11/70 873

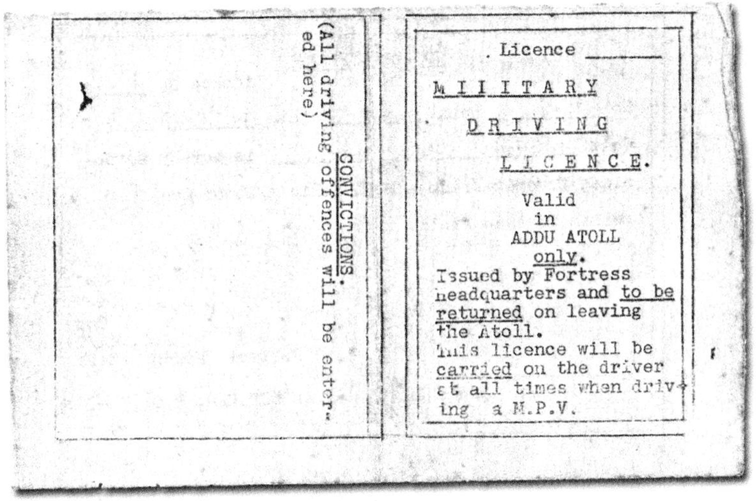

CONVICTIONS.
(All driving offences will be entered here)

Licence ____

MILITARY DRIVING LICENCE.

Valid in ADDU ATOLL only.

Issued by Fortress headquarters and to be returned on leaving the Atoll.
This licence will be carried on the driver at all times when driving a M.P.V.

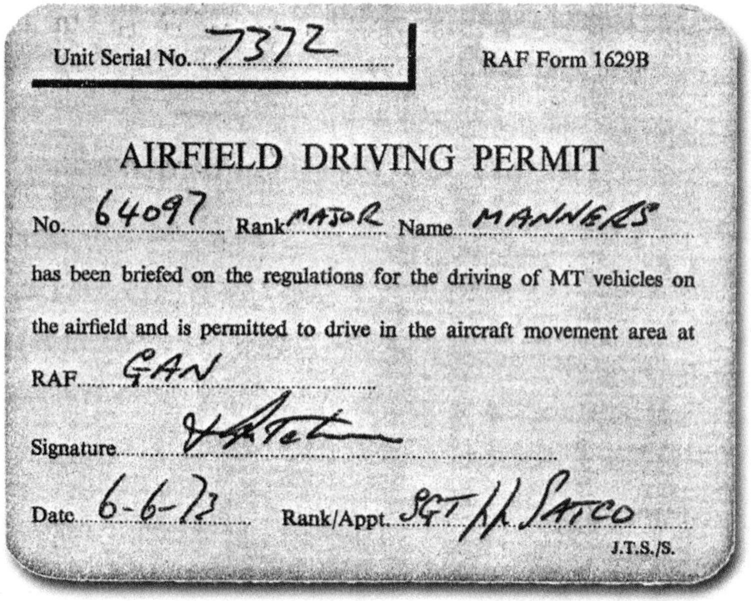

Unit Serial No. 7372 RAF Form 1629B

AIRFIELD DRIVING PERMIT

No. 64097 Rank MAJOR Name MANNERS
has been briefed on the regulations for the driving of MT vehicles on the airfield and is permitted to drive in the aircraft movement area at RAF GAN
Signature
Date 6-6-73 Rank/Appt. SGT/h.h. SATCO

J.T.S./S.

Fig 17.6. Driving licences issued to Major W Manners in 1943 and 1973.

XVIII   Airfield Operations

After the departure of the Commonwealth forces at the end of the Second World War the old wartime runway was left, like the rest of the island, to revert to scrub. Within a year it was completely overgrown. A decade later, when the men of the Ship's Flag detachment arrived at Addu Atoll, it was difficult to realise that the island runway had ever existed and even more difficult to visualise the airfield which had surrounded it. For seven months, whilst the Ship's Flag team worked to re-commission the old coral-surfaced runway the Sunderlands of Nᵒs 205 & 209 Squadrons provided an air link with Ceylon and Singapore, landing and taking off from the lagoon parallel to, but well clear of, the Hitaddu shoreline.

For the airmen who were responsible for refuelling the Sunderlands the island runway could not become fully operational quickly enough for that would signal the end of the flying-boat shuttle service and the manual refuelling operation. Week after week they greeted the arrival of the aircraft with mixed feelings; the mail and the newspapers were eagerly awaited but the work was unwelcome for it was both physically demanding and potentially dangerous. Whenever a Sunderland needed refuelling the airmen, assisted by Maldivian labourers from the fuel depot, undertook the back-breaking chore of manhandling forty-gallon drums of fuel from the shore depot onto a bomb tender or launch, taking them out to the flying-boat, using handpumps to transfer the fuel from the drums into the Sunderland's tanks, returning the empty drums to the store for refilling, manhandling more full drums into the launch and repeating the sequence of events until the aircraft had been refuelled.

Given the fuel capacity of a Sunderland, it was understandable that those who had to undertake the refuelling operation would view the arrival of a flying-boat with very mixed feelings, particularly in foul weather. In calm water the operation was straightforward enough and as the airmen watched the refuelled aircraft taking off they would often catch sight of the local dolphins, which frequently followed any flying-boat, performing aerobatics as they criss-crossed the wake before eventually being left behind as the aircraft approached its lift-off speed. But if the waters of the lagoon became choppy, as they frequently did, the refuelling operation could become a hazardous affair. Knocks and scrapes then became commonplace whilst significant injuries were not at all rare. Under such conditions there was also the possibility that the refuelling launch could be thrown against one of the aircraft's floats, puncturing it and leaving the flying-boat crew to adopt a take-off procedure which seemed rather bizarre but was apparently not an uncommon practice in such circumstances. The captain, in order to confirm that the punctured float was not hanging loose, would send his crew out onto the opposite wing with several filled sandbags to provide enough counterbalance weight to lift the suspect float clear of the water. When he was satisfied that the damaged float was still secure he would recall some of the crew, leaving the others out on the wing together with the sandbags. Using the asymmetrical loading to keep the punctured float clear of the water, the captain would then taxi towards the takeoff run and before the flying-boat lifted off, the remaining crew members would be invited to dump their sandbags and climb back into the aircraft.

Throughout August 1957 the airmen working on the old wartime runway had been employed on night shifts, laying and rolling the top surface when the temperature was normally below seventy-five degrees Fahrenheit. Their work was completed on the 29th of the month and, twenty minutes before noon on the following day, a Bristol Freighter of Nᵒ 41 Squadron, Royal New Zealand Air Force, arrived, stayed for two hours and then took off for Negombo. The newly-laid runway survived its first test and for the remaining months of 1957 it was used on an *ad hoc* basis, mainly by Bristol Freighters and Valettas, whilst the Sunderlands continued to provide the twice-weekly supply flights to the atoll from Ceylon. Within weeks *ad hoc* flights were commonplace and, with the main construction programme about to start, a steady stream of VIPs began to visit the island, establishing a pattern which was to continue for the next nineteen years.

October 1957, with a persistent combination of high winds and heavy rain making flying extremely hazardous, was not a good month to visit Gan: those VIPs who did arrive received a glimpse of the vagaries of life on the island and almost without exception they commiserated with the servicemen. None was more sympathetic or more impressed than those on board the aircraft which arrived during a sudden squall. They sat transfixed while their aircraft was buffeted as it flew into tropical rain which rattled so loudly against the fuselage that it almost drowned out the sound of the engines. The water streaming across the windows left only the lightning flashes visible and the passengers were well aware that the pilot had to be flying with almost zero visibility. Anxiously they counted the number of approaches which he made and aborted, opening the throttles and climbing into yet another circuit. On his fourth approach fortune favoured him; a sudden brief lull in the storm revealed the runway, showing it to be partially under water. As he landed his aircraft the pilot fought to prevent it from slewing off the runway, successfully bringing it to rest with its wheels only feet from the edge. The passengers, relieved that they were finally down safely, could only wonder at the fortitude expected of the servicemen who were required to spend a year working and living under canvas in such a climate. Understandably, the resident servicemen assured the passengers that what they had experienced was quite typical weather in that neck of the woods.

There were no problems with the re-commissioned runway whilst the Valettas and the Bristol Freighters continued to use it on an *ad hoc* basis but as the frequency of the flights increased, the surface began to disintegrate, necessitating the continual diversion of labour to effect the essential repairs that were needed to keep the airfield open. By January 1958, when a thrice-weekly Valetta shuttle service was added to the *ad hoc* arrivals, labour was almost permanently employed on repair work and as soon as that shuttle service was introduced the runway showed ominous signs of serious wear and tear. The repair programme was intensified and on St Valentine's day, after the runway surface suffered no ill-effects from the arrival and departure of aircraft XB 263, a Transport Command Beverley carrying a full complement of passengers and freight, the airfield was classified as '...*operational during daylight hours*.'

The respite from repair work was brief. Four weeks later, when the Director of Works Services for the Far East Air Force visited Gan, repairing the runway had once again become a regular activity and on his recommendation arrangements were made to remove the crushed coral surface layer and re-bed it to provide a much more substantial landing strip. It was an unwelcome, time-consuming task which put the runway out of action for a fortnight, necessitating the temporary reintroduction of the twice-weekly Sunderland flights from Ceylon but finally producing a runway surface good enough to last until the island-long concrete runway could be brought into service. Once again, Gan's airfield was classified as '...*operational during daylight hours*'.

'Operational' it may have been but that broad classification had to be qualified because the airfield facilities early in 1958 were still rudimentary. There was no air traffic control tower, just a small hut for the wireless operators who provided the crucial link with every Valetta flying from Trincomalee. Crucial, because a fully laden Valetta had a range of about four hundred miles and was thus not able to carry enough fuel for a round trip from Ceylon. There was no diversion airfield within range and the pilots were all well aware that at that time there were no search and rescue aircraft permanently operating out of Addu Atoll. It meant that if they were forced to ditch in the Indian Ocean a long-range rescue operation would have to be mounted from Ceylon; only if the aircraft ditched near Gan could the crew and passengers hope to be picked up by the air sea rescue launch operated by Gan's marine craft section.

Under those circumstances no pilot would fly beyond the point of no return without first receiving radio confirmation that the Gan airfield was operational and clear for landing. Even that precaution did not guarantee a trouble-free touch-down because the weather just south of the equator could deteriorate remarkably quickly and would occasionally force a pilot, who had been expecting a clear run, to search for the runway, or even for the atoll, in a tropical squall such as that encountered by the VIP flight the previous October.

In those early days there were no electronic landing aids on Gan. Pilots had to rely upon their eyesight and if visibility was poor they had to home in on flares fired from the touchdown point. Even when the runway was clearly visible it was unwise for any pilot to fly straight in for a landing; there were certain, somewhat unusual, precautions to take which a pilot would ignore at his peril.

As the aircraft approached the island the ground-based wireless operator would be asked to confirm that the ground staff had driven along the airstrip, checked for any significant surface defects and removed the debris which was commonly left behind by the Maldivians or dropped by the expatriate Asians working on Gan.

Each of the Valetta pilots also fell into the habit of making a low-level pass along the runway before lifting the aircraft into a circuit and final approach. In part that was done to check the wind effect, to confirm that the runway was clear, that a firetender was strategically positioned and that airmen were stationed at the road and runway junctions to control access to the landing strip. But there was another, probably more important, reason for the low-level sweep; it was made to deter the Maldivians from strolling across the runway. There was little that could be done to break them of the habit of taking the shortest route wherever they were going, regardless of whether that route took them across the airfield. They seemed to be quite unable to appreciate the risks they were taking and with few flights into Gan they had virtually no experience of aircraft movements across their island. Thus the low-level pass came to be used as a warning for the Maldivian pedestrians, making them aware that an aircraft was about to land and making them temporarily more cautious.

The introduction of the three scheduled Valetta flights to supplement the *ad hoc* arrivals every week provided a frequent fast passenger connection to Ceylon and led to a steady increase in the volume of airfreight being flown to the atoll. The consignments may have been small compared with those brought by sea but they were far from insignificant; when the three-hundredth Valetta flight from Katunayake landed at Gan on the 28th of October 1958 the twenty-two flights into the island that month had delivered a total of over sixty-five thousand pounds of air freight and, more importantly, had provided, on several occasions, an urgent-response service whereby a special request to Colombo had resulted in a delivery to Gan the following day. Obviously, there was a limit to the frequency with which such requests could be made but there was no doubt that in the latter months of 1958 the goodwill with which the Ceylon-based staff responded to any such requests significantly reduced, although it could never obviate, the problems brought about by the somewhat erratic scheduling of the sea-borne deliveries.

That three hundredth Valetta flight from Katunayake was not the only Valetta which merited a mention in that month's operations record book; there was an even more significant arrival on the 8th of the month. On that day, with a Valetta *en route* to Gan, an exceptionally strong wind blew up at ninety degrees to runway N° 33, the old wartime runway, creating hazardous landing conditions best avoided if at all possible. By then, work on runway

N° 28, the concrete runway being laid by Costain, had progressed to the point at which four thousand feet of lean-mix concreting had been completed and it was agreed that the inbound aircraft could land on that paved eastern end of the runway by skimming low over Costain's workers who were still operating their concreting trains towards the western end. The landing and subsequent takeoff were uneventful but that Valetta, the first aircraft to use the island's concrete runway, heralded a new era even though the runway, which would eventually split the island from end to end, was nowhere near complete.

Before Gan's station commander, Wing Commander Kent, left the atoll in April he had the satisfaction of seeing the island-long runway brought into use by an RAF Hastings which arrived on a trial run on the 18th of March 1959. The next day a Hastings freighter delivered a consignment of diesel for the marine craft section and from then on the staging post was ready to accept the scheduled trans-oceanic passenger flights made by the Changi-based Hastings of N° 48 Squadron which had relinquished its Valettas on being re-equipped with Hastings in 1957. At that point there was no longer any need for the regular Valetta flights between Ceylon and Addu Atoll and after the last such schedule on the 8th of April flights between Ceylon and Gan were once again arranged on an *ad hoc* basis.

Kent did not see the jet age brought to Addu Atoll because when he left Gan the runway loading tests had not been completed. It was the end of April before the final test confirmed that the big jets could safely use the mid-ocean staging post and on the 1st of May a Canberra, crewed by Air Ministry staff officers, became the first jet aircraft to land at Gan. The Adduans, initially taken aback by that foretaste of the sounds which the big jets were to bring to the atoll during the 1960s, soon became quite blasé about the sight and sound of the V bombers and the passenger jets which shuttled between Britain and the Far East.

Almost as soon as the runway was in regular use, incidents involving staging aircraft were being logged in the station's accident register. The first impression, on glancing through that register, is that for an airfield with so few aircraft movements each month, five hundred and twenty-nine recorded occurrences in twenty years is an unexpectedly high figure. A closer inspection, however, reveals that most of them were relatively minor mechanical or electrical problems; operational hazards to be regarded as facts of life, albeit unwelcome ones as far as the aircrews were concerned.

Relatively few of the recorded occurrences led to board of inquiry investigations and reports although some were so serious that it is a wonder that in the nineteen-year life of the station nobody was killed in an aircraft accident.

The first such near-tragedy occurred on the 4th of July 1959, a mere four months after the inaugural Hastings flight into Gan. Happily, the accident led to nothing worse than an incident that became part of Gan folklore with the Royal Navy enjoying the joke at the expense of the RAF. It started as a potential disaster when, on the 3rd of the month, a Hastings aircraft, TG 580, broke an undercarriage leg on landing and ended up on its belly some fifty yards from the runway. Fortunately, none of the crew or passengers was injured but the aircraft suffered category five damage and that left the station commander with the problem of finding the manpower and expertise to remove the wreck in the shortest possible time, a problem which was solved with the help of a visiting Royal Navy crew. Hearing of the difficulty, they volunteered to remove the damaged aircraft without explaining, until after the event, that they would do so by the simple expedient of blowing it up, leaving nothing but a hole in the ground surrounded by a vast quantity of fine debris which, they explained, could easily be removed by unskilled Maldivian labour. From then on, offers of help from the Royal Navy were understandably treated with suspicion and met with careful questioning.

After that, the first Hasting's engine change at the end of the month, executed with help from one of Costain's crane operators, was of little or no significance except to the aircrew, the station's aircraft servicing flight and the station commander. That engine change was the first real test of the station's ability to cope with the type of situation likely to arise at any time once the scheduled flights between Britain and the Far East began staging through Gan several times a week. Dealing successfully with the problem was good for morale, proving, as it did, that the aircraft servicing flight could already provide both the spares and the expertise expected of it.

In mid-1959 the aircraft servicing and air movements sections were still manned to an out-of-date establishment based upon sixteen aircraft movements a month, inadequate even under normal circumstances because the aircraft schedules had increased as soon as the new runway had become operational. The Far East Air Force Command staff largely ignored the situation until August when the routine schedules were overshadowed by *ad hoc* aircraft movements brought about by the reaction of the Singapore-based staff to the Adduans' fears of an attack.

During the first week of the month a Twin Pioneer and a Dakota were detached to Gan to take up reconnaissance duties alongside two Shackletons which had been sent from Ballykelly on detachment until the latter part of the month when they were scheduled to return to Northern Ireland, their role at Addu Atoll to be taken over by a solitary Shackleton from Singapore, notionally on a short detachment to Katunayake, but actually under the operational control of the officer commanding RAF Gan. The 10th of August saw the first Britannia to stage through the base, two days after a pair of Hastings and a Beverley brought a company of the Cheshire Regiment to Gan for security duties. On the 15th, two Comets brought a contingent of RAF Regiment airmen to the island, the first aircraft, XK 695, bursting three tyres on landing. Within twenty-four hours the Cheshires had handed over their security duties to the Regiment airmen and had left Gan on board the Comets.

For the next fortnight the servicemen at Addu Atoll were working in a constant state of readiness with daily reconnaissance flights checking all the shipping lanes in the region. The result was that by the end of the month a servicing flight established to deal with only sixteen aircraft movements a month had coped with one hundred and fifteen movements over a period of thirty-one days.

The general sense of urgency at that time inevitably led to unsatisfactory, but usually temporary, airfield practices exemplified by the way in which night-time flying had been introduced to accommodate the increase in the number of aircraft movements and the need for night-time vigilance. Airfield lighting had been installed as quickly as possible but night flying had been introduced before the controls for the lighting system had been installed in the air traffic control tower which meant that an electrician had to remain in the lighting control centre whenever night flying was in progress and that in turn necessitated the use of a two-stage communications link between him and the air traffic control officer who had to use his radio with a transmission link *via* a fire tender.

During the remaining months of 1959 the airfield became steadily busier, partly because Gan was by then established as the RAF's mid-ocean staging post and partly because political manoeuvring by the British and Maldivian governments was attracting so much attention that staff officers, politicians and civil servants were visiting the island in an attempt to gain some insight into the situation. In October, notwithstanding the foul weather and a food poisoning and dysentery epidemic, ninety-eight aircraft movements were logged and in November the number was up to one hundred and thirty-seven with even more VIPs visiting the island than usual.

If the tail end of that year was a busy period, January 1960 was the month when the Indian Ocean staging post really began to live up to its description. Two or three times a week the Comets and Britannias which plied between Britain and the Far East were refuelled, serviced, and sent on their way. The arrival of the first flight of Valiants in January heralded the beginning of a long association between Gan and the RAF's V-Force with the Valiants, Victors and Vulcans routinely avoiding Indian and Ceylonese air space by staging through the island base.

With this increase in through traffic came the increased risk of an aircraft accident which would require a search and rescue operation to be mounted and with that possibility in mind a rescue coordination centre was established and the Dakota and Shackleton which had, until the end of 1959, been deployed on search and rescue duties in the region, were replaced by two Shackletons from the Changi-based 205 Squadron, both on detachment to the island and flown by crews whose brief spell of duty on Gan was scheduled through a squadron roster.

The combination of *ad hoc* aircraft movements and scheduled passenger flights several times each week brought the aircraft movements for January up to one hundred and seventy-eight, some ten times the number on which the station's establishment levels were based whilst February, with two hundred and ninety-eight movements was even busier. Everyone who had a part to play in the provision of a safe and efficient refuelling and servicing facility was overworked but it was to be several months before a review recognised the imbalance and changed the establishment. Only after that were additional servicemen posted in to the sparsely-manned sections.

By the end of January 1960 the station boasted a newly-built transit mess, providing basic airport facilities and lounge amenities for transit passengers and for Gan personnel who were either arriving or departing. The facilities did include some air conditioned overnight accommodation, a rare luxury on the island, but that was reserved for use by aircrews whose remaining duty time was insufficient for the next leg of their journey and who would thus stay overnight as a slip crew, ready to take over from the crew of the next passenger aircraft staging *en route* to the Far East or to England. Gan was a military base but the first aircrew to enjoy the comparative luxury of this air-conditioned accommodation were civilians flying for Eagle Airways, the company which was contracted for trooping flights between England and the Far East.

With almost five hundred flight movements in the first eight weeks of the year, the demand for fuel began to outstrip the deliveries, virtually running the tanker farm dry and by the end of February stocks were critically low. But the Air Ministry staff, whose records indicated otherwise, were not persuaded that there was an imminent problem. Only when informed by Wing Commander Thomas, the station commander, that the next aircraft to arrive at Gan could not be refuelled until a fresh supply of aviation fuel had been delivered did they take the situation seriously. With no time to organise a delivery by tanker they were obliged to arrange for an emergency delivery to be made by HMS Centaur, an aircraft carrier which was in the Indian Ocean and which was diverted to Addu Atoll, arriving on the 7th of March and discharging one hundred tons of aviation fuel into Gan's bulk fuel installation. For Thomas, the diversion of HMS Centaur brought another bonus; it had been such a costly exercise that from then on the Air Ministry staff accepted without question any of his situation reports from Gan.

With the increasing number of aircraft movements it was only to be expected that there would be an increase in the number of aircraft incidents, particularly in the number of reported malfunctions. Sure enough, in 1960 there were twenty-six reported incidents involving a variety of aircraft types, starting with a 205 Squadron Shackleton, WG 525, on the 11th of January and ending with a Far East Communications Squadron Valetta on the 20th of December.

The other entries in the register provide seven references to Shackletons, four to Hastings, nine to Britannias, two to Valiants, one to a Comet and one to a Beverley. Britannias, the aircraft which were committed to the scheduled passenger services between Britain and the Far East, are over-represented on the 1960 accident report forms for Gan but most of the entries refer to 'occurrences' rather than accidents, an indication of the teething troubles experienced with some of the aircraft in those early days. Twenty-four of the twenty-six recorded incidents were regarded as normal operational hazards, one as a minor accident and one as a major accident.

That minor accident occurred on the 4th of February and is briefly described in the only 1960 accident register entry to refer to a Beverley. The aircraft, N° XM 112, landed safely which was remarkable in view of the fact that it had suffered some minor damage when the pilot used the undercarriage to remove the runway approach lights.

The major accident was a near-disaster. The earlier loss of Hastings N° TG580 so soon after the commissioning of the island-long runway had made everyone aware that on Gan's speck of an airfield tragedy was often little more than a lightning flash away. The spectre of a major accident involving a passenger-carrying aircraft was ever-present and on the 1st of March 1960 the air traffic controllers' worst fears were realised when the Changi-based Hastings N° TG 579 flew to Gan from Katunayake. The aircraft, with six crew members and fourteen passengers on board, arrived at the atoll during a night-time thunderstorm, forcing the pilot, whose visibility was impaired by the torrential rain, to overshoot on his first approach and bring the aircraft round for a second attempt. On the second approach the aircraft was about two miles out when a brilliant flash of lightning caused the pilot to look down into his cockpit to recover his night-vision. The second pilot then called out '...*approaching fifty feet*' and almost immediately the aircraft hit the sea short of the runway. It remained afloat long enough for all twenty people on board to take to the dinghies which, although it was dark and raining, were quickly located by a Shackleton which was airborne within twenty minutes of the ditching.

The Shackleton kept the area illuminated with flares and guided the search and rescue marine craft to the dinghies with the result that all the crew and passengers were picked up and checked into the station sick quarters within two and a half hours of the crash. The Hastings had been written off and the incident had been traumatic for all those involved but the search and rescue coordination centre had proved its worth, the rescue teams had demonstrated their ability and, fortuitously, no-one had been seriously injured.

The debriefing of all those involved in the rescue operation highlighted minor organisational aspects which needed to be improved but the incident left everyone better prepared for the accident which they hoped would never happen; the crash landing of a Britannia or Comet with a full complement of passengers on board.

With twenty-two entries in the register, 1961 was a slightly better year than 1960 and, far more importantly, there were no serious accidents. Two Beverleys featured in the register, the number of entries referring to Britannias went down from nine to three, there were three entries for Comets, eight for Hastings and three for Shackletons, all referring to everyday minor operating defects requiring the attention of the aircraft servicing technicians. The only V force aircraft referred to in the register that year was Victor XH 589 which returned to Gan shortly after takeoff because the pilot had been unable to retract the undercarriage. Potentially more serious was the incident on the 15th of April when Bristol Freighter NZ 5907, one of the two Freighters mentioned in the 1961 register, undershot the runway, and demolished five of the runway approach lights. Quite remarkably in view of the extensive damage to the aircraft's wheel strut fairings, the undercarriage was still sound enough to allow the pilot to make what he apparently regarded as a normal landing, albeit rather close to the end of the runway.

Over the next fourteen years the pages of Gan's register tell a familiar story with very few of the entries recording anything more serious than a special occurrence. There is, however, a familiarity about some of the entries. Bird strikes were not that unusual and although the gull struck by VC10 N° XR 809 was typical of a hazard which is common enough at many airfields, few RAF stations can have had reports of a heron strike, as happened to Hercules XV 196, or of fruit bat strikes, as reported by the pilots of Victor XH 618 and of Canberra XH 171, the former struck at two hundred feet whilst on circuit and the latter similarly struck whilst on final approach. Large though they are, the fruit bats did not present quite such a serious hazard as the heron but it was fortunate that in all three cases no serious damage was done, at least, not to the aircraft.

Tyres bursting on landing were quite rare but over the years there were bound to be several such incidents. They mainly occurred with the big jets, starting with the first Comet to land at Gan in 1959 and later with an Andover, a Victor, a VC 10 and, most notably, with a Valiant which ended up taxying onto the hardstanding with its wheels on fire. The most fortunate aspect was that on no occasion did burst tyres cause an aircraft to slew off the runway.

Runway approach lights were occasionally demolished, most notably by Comet XR 399 and Vulcan XA 910, because most pilots tended to land as close to the threshold as possible to avoid the risk of running out of concrete at the other end of the island. It was a practice which required fine judgment if an accident was to be avoided and in heavy rain it was decidedly hazardous, an obvious fact which was clearly demonstrated in October 1965 when the Eagle Airways' Britannia 'Endeavour' arrived at the atoll during a rainstorm, was put down prematurely, hit the coral beach just short of the runway, bounced into the air, landed back on the concrete, suffered a collapsed nosewheel and skidded down the runway before finally slewing onto the golf course and coming to rest (Fig 18.1). Incredibly, the passengers and crew suffered only minor injuries but the severely damaged aircraft was thought at first to be a write-off. Dragging it off the partially flooded golf course was a difficult operation but it was eventually brought back onto the runway, jacked up and moved across to the aircraft pan, allowing the debris-strewn runway to be cleared. Much to the surprise of the RAF technicians, the aircraft was not written off, it was repaired and eventually flown out of Gan.

Understandably, the aircraft type which features more often than any other in Gan's accident register is the Shackleton, the aircraft type on detachment to Gan for search and rescue duties from 1959 until January 1972. For twelve and a half years the Shackleton crews patrolled the region, responding to Mayday calls, to reports of lost or stricken vessels and to requests for humanitarian aid. Their declared role was to provide a search and rescue service but they were also employed on reconnaissance flights, checking on the activities of any Russian ships in the region whilst ostensibly scouring the ocean for vessels in distress, occasionally, and quite fortuitously, sighting unreported shipwreck survivors. The Gan-based search and rescue service was well known throughout the archipelago and to the crews of ships which plied the Indian Ocean, the aircrews' missions and success stories oft-repeated but rarely given the publicity which they deserved.

There were some false alarms, but most of the search and rescue missions were made in life or death situations in response to Mayday calls from stricken vessels either adrift in stormy seas or, like the Formosan fishing vessel, the SS Chin Glong Yin, in imminent danger of sinking.

It was mid-morning on the 22nd of March 1964 when a Mayday call was received from the Chin Glong Yin which was on fire approximately six hundred and fifty miles south-east of Gan. A Shackleton took off within the hour and located the burning ship three and a quarter hours later. The ship's crew, clinging to roughly-made rafts tied to the bow of the ship, was quick to clamber aboard the two dinghies which the Shackleton dropped along with the Lindholme rescue gear. With no other ships nearby the Shackleton continued to circle the area until informed by the operations centre on Gan that the SS Nuddea was proceeding to the scene and was expected to arrive in the early hours of the morning. The aircraft intercepted the Nuddea, and, using an Aldis lamp, the crew signalled a heading and distance for the stricken vessel before returning to the scene of the disaster and, whilst circling in darkness, dropping six marine marker flares. The Shackleton then flew back to Gan, landed just before midnight, refuelled and took off again almost two hours later to guide the Nuddea, by then only twenty miles away from the survivors, to the spot where the Chin Glong Yin had sunk but where the marine flares were still burning. The Nuddea was able to rescue all twenty-two crew members, later transferring them to another Formosan trawler. They were lucky. The presence of a Gan-based search and rescue aircraft which was able to spend more than twenty-two hours airborne in a twenty-four hour period almost certainly saved the lives of the men who seemed doomed to drift into the southern reaches of the Indian Ocean several hundred miles off the shipping lanes.

The humanitarian flights made by the Shackletons, referred to in chapter XIX, were rarely newsworthy because they invariably involved the air-dropped delivery of nothing more than medical supplies. Even when a supply of vaccine was delivered to Malé at a time when Afif Didi was still nominally the president of the United Suvadive Islands, the episode was not reported upon. Only the editor of the RAF News seemed to be interested in the aircrews' exploits, publishing a front-page report, on the 3rd of February 1962, of their flight over Diego Garcia to airdrop a supply of blood and a transfusion kit for a seriously ill woman.

By the end of 1962, Gan's monthly aircraft movements averaged well over two hundred and with the March peak of three hundred and seventy-five only seven higher than the November figure they gave some indication of the demands which would be placed on Gan's limited facilities in the years to come.

It was not the passenger aircraft which were likely to clutter the airfield and drain extraordinary quantities of fuel from the airfield's stocks, it was the combat aircraft on the frequently mounted air-mobility exercises which would do that. At best, Gan's airfield could accommodate eighteen large jets but manoeuvring that many around the solitary runway was a work of art. Refuelling was by bowsers but it was known that when paired exercises ran concurrently the demand for fuel could reach thirty-one thousand eight hundred gallons of Avtur and six thousand three hundred gallons of Avgas in any two-hour period, figures which were well below the station's fuel stocks but which would stretch the station's supply system almost to breaking point.

Predictably, the aircraft movements at the beginning of 1963 set new records even though the temporary closure of the runway at RAF Lyneham reduced the number of passenger flights staging through Gan. By the end of February eight hundred and ninety-eight movements had been logged with combat aircraft on exercises using the airfield virtually every day. The figures were lower in later months but they still consistently exceeded two hundred. There was even, for five days in June, four American aircraft from the United States' Weather Bureau operating from Gan, flying sorties out of the base and enabling the members of the United States' Indian Ocean Expedition to conduct a survey of the region.

The Americans conducted their survey from their B26, B57 and DC6 aircraft but other meteorological research was conducted from Gan's airfield in 1963 by the locally-based meteorological staff who released their Radio Sonde balloons from the airfield, tracking one of them to a height of one hundred and twenty-seven thousand feet in March.

The airfield traffic was not heavy during the latter months of 1963 but September brought one temporary addition to the airfield which was a novelty as far as the Adduans were concerned: a Sycamore helicopter. It was the month when a further detachment of RAF Regiment airmen had been sent to Gan to confront the belligerent islanders and the search and rescue helicopter, brought to the base on board a Beverley, was allocated for local reconnaissance flights at a time when the Adduans were demonstrably angry over the imminent demise of their so-called independent republic. The helicopter's value was as much in its symbolic presence as a spy in the sky as in its reconnaissance capabilities and it was retained on the island until well into 1965 before it was decided that there was no longer a need for any aerial reconnaissance over the atoll.

For the next two years the entries in the station diaries give little indication of the scale of the airfield operations; '...aircraft movements normal' is a common entry accompanying the figures for transient passengers and freight delivered and despatched. The exceptions, which are few and far between,

briefly refer to the airdropped delivery of arms to the Dunidu detachment on the 10th of April 1964, the supply and mail runs to Dunidu by the Valetta flights on the 10th and 13th of June, the large-scale air mobility exercises mounted by the Far East Air Force in August and November that year and the troop movements in September 1965. That trooping reference gives some indication of the scale of the operation by referring to the use of British Caledonian, British United and Eagle Airways, the civilian airlines contracted as carriers to supplement the limited capacity of the RAF's passenger fleet.

The station's diarists rarely bothered to mention minor flooding on the airfield because it occurred so often on Gan that it came to be taken for granted. Only the truly exceptional storms were logged and on each occasion, as the water drained away and the wind died down, the intensity of the squall could be gauged by the quantity of debris on the airfield and the nature of the items to be cleared from the runway, some potentially dangerous but none more amusing than the flying fish which were seen skipping from puddle to puddle in October 1965 after a particularly violent storm had swept across the island. The story, oft-repeated over the months, grew with the telling and always included a reference to the disbelieving Comet captain who was warned that on take-off he should beware of flying fish on the runway.

In contrast with the sparse comments in the station diaries during those two years, Gan's aircraft accident record book contains thirty-two entries for Britannias, seven for Comets and three for Hastings; all but one rated as special occurrences with no implications for passenger safety. The exception, the only major accident on Gan during that two-year period, occurred in October 1965 and involved the Eagle Airway's Britannia 'Endeavour' referred to above.

As with 1964 and 1965 so it was with 1966, 1967 and 1968. Far East Air Force exercises, photo-reconnaissance surveys and scheduled Transport Command flights were all much as expected. Among the few events which merited a diary entry was the arrival, in August 1966, of RAF VC10 XR 808 which took off for Lyneham from Fairford on the 21st of the month and then, *en route* to Hong Kong, staged through Muharraq and Gan. The proving flight, subsequently reported in the RAF News that October, was designed to provide training for the first VC10 aircrew and to show the aircraft to the maintenance and air movements staff at the staging posts along the route. The airmen on Gan, unable to ignore an opportunity to provide a welcome intended to reflect upon the navigator's sense of distance and direction, decked themselves out in a fanciful mixture of palm fronds and flowers, formed a gently swaying guard of honour on the hardstanding and displayed an artistically worked banner which read 'Welcome to The Cocos Islands', a greeting which had been given on several previous occasions, leaving some passengers convinced that they had actually staged through the Cocos (Fig 18.2).

Eight months after that inaugural flight the sight and sound of the Transport Command VC10s had become familiar features of life on Gan as the aircraft plied between England and the Far East.

Once again, the entries in Gan's aircraft accident record book show nothing other than 'special occurrences' for the passenger aircraft which staged through the base during 1966 and 1967. The demand for special occurrence rectification work was modest in 1966 with only three Britannias, one Comet, one VC10 and three Hastings logged in the record book compared with thirteen Britannias, two VC10s and two Hastings in 1967 and ten Britannias, nine VC10s and one Comet the following year.

The only major airfield incident during those three years involved the 899 Squadron (Royal Navy) Sea Vixen XN 691 which, piloted by an RAF Flying Officer, took off for Gan from the aircraft carrier HMS Eagle on the 27th of September 1967. On landing, the aircraft's starboard brakes failed and it ran off the end of the runway, coming to rest on the coral shelf in four feet of water. A team from HMS Eagle was sent to Gan to recover the damaged aircraft, a complex operation which was eventually completed with help from a group of airmen who claimed to have some experience of aircraft recovery from shallow water without disclosing that they were referring to flood water alongside the runway.

The location of Addu Atoll and the convenience of the airfield site attracted several meteorological research teams over the years, their work integrated into the normal airfield operations on the island. Among the first of the researchers was Dr Frith from the Ministry of Defence whose visit, in mid-September 1967, went virtually unnoticed except by the meteorological officers and the air traffic control staff.

After reconnoitring the area and discussing the arrangements for firing meteorological rockets into the upper atmosphere over the Indian Ocean, Frith was obviously satisfied that Gan provided a suitable location for his investigations because a year later he returned to the atoll with his research team and supervised the firing of ten rockets, each of which took some two and a half minutes to reach the desired height of sixty or seventy kilometres before ejecting a parachute and a cluster of measuring instruments. The whole assemblage then took about two and a half hours to float to earth. For the first one and a half hours after ejection continuous readings were obtained from the descending instruments, providing valuable data on the weather conditions in the upper atmosphere. Once again Gan featured in the RAF News with Dr Frith's research briefly described in the last issue in November 1968 under the headline 'Gan enters the space race'. Five months later seven more Skua rockets were fired from the airfield to complete the second phase of the programme.

The diary entries referring to airfield operations in 1968 tend to be restricted to statistics for freight and transient passengers although there is a brief reference to a January exercise involving N° 205 Squadron Shackletons working in conjunction with the Royal Navy, a later reference to a May exercise in which some four hundred troops from HMS Albion camped on the airfield and a September entry related to the Skua rocket firing programme.

Far more attracted the attention of the diarists in 1969, starting in January with a reference to Operation Piscator, an exercise designed to test the rapid deployment of Lightnings from RAF Leuchars to the Far East. On the 7th of the month the first pair of the ten deployed Lightnings arrived at Gan where Victor tankers and their ground servicing parties were waiting. For the next four days pairs of fighters and tankers from RAF Marham staged through the base and by the 11th of January the ten Lightnings and the sixteen tankers had all passed through without incident even though much of that month's sixteen and a half inches of rain had fallen during the first fortnight and had caused some flooding on the airfield.

Five weeks later three PR9 Canberras, with their six crews and a backup party of thirty-five airmen for ground servicing duties, arrived at Gan to conduct a photographic survey of the Maldive Islands. Between the 19th of February and the 5th of March they operated out of Gan, flying fifty-four sorties before completing the survey and returning to Malta.

On the 1st of April that year Air Support Command introduced new flight schedules, replacing the Britannias by C 130s from RAF Lyneham which would stage through Gan five days each week en route to and from

Singapore, leaving a solitary Britannia schedule each week for the carriage of dangerous and hazardous cargo, a description which covered the fuel needed on the island for that month's Skua rocket firing programme.

For the remaining months of 1969, for all of 1970 and for the first few months of 1971, airfield operations were as normal as they ever were on Gan with hundreds of transients each week, an Australian defence exercise for which Vulcans, Victors and Lightnings staged through in mid-69, several air mobility exercises and occasional flooding on the airfield.

Over the years many aircraft were obliged to land at Gan in torrential rain and it is therefore no surprise that in the station's register of aircraft accidents there are occasional references to Britannias aquaplaning or just skidding off a wet runway and coming to rest on the grass verge or on the neighbouring golf course. For the recovery-crew airmen, removing a Britannia from waterlogged grass was bad enough but on the night of the 16th of April 1971 they were faced with the problem of dragging Victor XL 193 back onto the runway in the most appalling conditions. The aircraft had taken off from Gan late at night in heavy rain but had developed hydraulic trouble, causing the pilot to return to the island after jettisoning fuel over the ocean. By then a thunderstorm had hit the atoll and the runway was partially under water. The pilot brought the aircraft in but it slid off the runway and came to rest on the waterlogged grass, creating an airfield hazard which had to be cleared as soon as possible. The recovery team had no choice but to work under floodlights in heavy rain which was being driven by a near gale-force wind. By the early hours of the morning they were exhausted but they had successfully completed one of the most demanding operations they ever encountered, dragging the aircraft back onto the runway and towing it onto the hardstanding.

In 1971, with Britain's military withdrawal from the Far East gathering momentum, it was inevitable that aircraft movements during the latter half of the year would be much higher than normal even without the occasional air mobility exercises and the survey of the Seychelles and the Amirante Islands to be undertaken by two photo-reconnaissance Victors of N° 543 Squadron which, with their ground servicing crews, were detached to Gan from the 3rd of May to the 1st of June. Airfield movements during July and August were heavy but not exceptionally so. September, however, was an unpleasant month for the airmen whose accommodation was close to the airfield; they not only had to cope with fifteen inches of rain, they had to endure sixteen days of aircraft noise as Operation Panther Trail was played out. That operation effected the withdrawal of N° 74 Squadron's Lightnings from the Far East and when they arrived at Gan in the company of the Victor tankers from RAF Marham they established a daily routine, flying thirty-five Victor sorties and twenty-seven Lightning sorties over a sixteen day period. Each day, tankers and fighters made test flights (Figs 18.3, 18.4 & 18.5) and each morning three Lightnings would take off for Akrotiri with the intention that one would return to Gan, leaving a pair to complete that leg of their trans-global journey.

It was only to be expected that December would be an exceptionally busy month for Gan with the exodus of servicemen and their dependents from the Far East, all understandably anxious to arrive in England before Christmas. What had not been expected was the combination, in the week before Christmas, of the exodus from Singapore and the evacuation of over six hundred troops, during the 17th, 18th and 19th of December, when N° 40 marine commando unit disembarked from HMS Albion and was flown back to England, accounting for the fact that that month's unusually high number of aircraft movements continued until two days before Christmas when the withdrawal was virtually completed and the staging post airfield was closed for the Christmas stand-down.

The departure, on the 17th of January 1972, of the last of the Shackletons to operate from Gan marked the end of an era for, unlike the Shackletons, the Nimrod and Hercules aircraft which took over the search and rescue role in the region did not provide a permanent presence on Gan; they were generally on detachment to the base only at times of intense airfield activity such as that which occurred during exercises. For one group of islanders it was fortunate that in February Exercise Pirate Trail brought Buccaneers, Victors, a Nimrod and a C130 to Gan because on the 20th of the month, in the early hours of the morning, a report was received from the atoll chief that two Adduan dhonis, with a total of twenty-six people on board, had been lost at sea late at night on the 19th.

A two-hour early-morning search by Gan's rescue and target towing launch failed to locate either of the lost boats. A second search was undertaken by the marine craft crew at ten o'clock and a visiting Hercules took off at half past ten to conduct an airborne search over a seventy-five mile radius. One of the dhonis was located at eleven o'clock but the other was not found even after further searches on the 21st by a visiting Canberra and on the 22nd by a Nimrod *en route* from RAF Tengah to Britain. As the days passed, hope faded for the islanders in the second dhoni but they were lucky; eventually they were brought back to Addu Atoll in the rescue operation described on page 277.

The withdrawal from Singapore meant that air mobility exercises became more frequent as rapid deployment to the Far East replaced the permanent presence of the past. The result was that Victor tankers were to be seen more often at Addu Atoll, providing air-to-air refuelling for the fighters deployed across the Indian Ocean and adding to the wear and tear on the runway which, some thirteen years after the inaugural Hastings flight, was beginning to look so much the worse for wear that the works services engineers decided that, sometime early in 1973, it would have to be partially closed for resurfacing.

For the airmen whose barrack blocks abutted the airfield that was a period to look forward to because in September 1972 they had suffered three weeks of disrupted nights when a 216 Squadron Comet, at the base on a crew training detachment, was regularly airborne on night-flying circuits. For each of the weary servicemen the opportunity to see their island base from the air during one of the many flights offered by the Comet's captain was inadequate compensation for three weeks of disturbed sleep but there was nothing they could do about that.

On the 29th of that month, the day before the Lyneham-based Comet left Gan, the meteorological office staff extended the work which had been started by Dr Frith's team in 1968 and 1969 by firing eight Skua rockets into the stratosphere with a further eight being fired on the 2nd of October and the final eight three days later, providing further information for the research into gravity waves. Shortly after the last of the rockets had been launched a research team from the Imperial College of Science arrived at Gan and, led by Dr Clarke, rounded off the year in November by launching two large Radio Sonde balloons from Gan's airfield, seeking to obtain information for their research into negatively charged atomic nuclei in the cosmic rays arriving at the upper atmosphere.

1973 started with the influx of some two thousand troops who camped on the airfield for over two weeks, outnumbering Gan's expatriates by some two to one. With their departure the island seemed to become a much quieter place but it was even quieter after the 15th of February because the runway was partially closed for repairs which started at seven o'clock in the

morning on the 16th, just one hour after the departure of the monthly Britannia flight to Karachi. For the next five weeks Gan became non-operational whilst six of the runway's concrete panels were replaced at a cost of some two thousand five hundred pounds. The repair project was organised so that at least one third of the runway was always available for use by the C130 Hercules which was on detachment from RAF Lyneham to Gan throughout that period and which, in short take-off and landing mode, could easily operate from the clear section, thus maintaining a search and rescue service in the region and a shuttle service between Gan, Tengah and Colombo, the temporary staging post for the Britannias flying to and from the Far East. The possibility that an international incident might cause the British government to initiate trans-oceanic flights which would need to stage through Gan was remote but it could not be ignored and the repair project was organised so that, quite apart from providing an adequate facility for the C130 Hercules, it could, if necessary, be rapidly brought back into use by filling in the excavated area to provide an 'emergencies only' airstrip.

Servicemen posted to Gan while the runway was being repaired were flown to Singapore on board a VC 10 and then flown to Gan on board the Hercules which, for five weeks, provided a shuttle service between Singapore, Sri Lanka and Gan, carrying passengers and the mail, the crucial link between the Gannites and home.

Among the servicemen who arrived at Gan by that circuitous route was Group Captain Whitlock, the station commander designate who was due to take over from Group Captain Salmon during the third week in February. For him, that non-operational period was invaluable because it allowed him to concentrate on his new command without being engaged on hosting duties which were an inevitable part of the station commander's life in normal times. Ironically, it was a period when the services of the search and rescue crews were very much in demand, giving Whitlock an insight into the RAF's commitments in the region.

The runway repairs were completed by the 23rd of March and two days later a VC 10 staged through the base *en route* to the Far East. From then on Gan's airfield operations were back to normal for a year which was to be marked by an unusually large number of air mobility exercises across the Indian Ocean, occasionally testing the facilities on Gan almost to the point of collapse as they added to the scheduled aircraft movements each month. Phantoms, Victor tankers and Nimrods were close-parked around the airfield in April. Vulcans, troop-carrying Hercules and Britannias staged through *en route* to Australia in May, the month when photographic reconnaissance Canberras began operating out of Gan, undertaking an eight month survey of the Chagos Archipelago.

With the increase in the number of aircraft movements came an increase in the number of serious incidents, because many Maldivians showed a casual disregard for danger on the airfield, both to themselves and to incoming aircraft. Over the years numerous Maldivian drivers had been suspended for ignoring the airfield warning notices or for driving across the runway threshold when the crossing lights were on red and if it was difficult to instil a sense of responsibility into some of the drivers it was almost impossible to make some of the other Adduan workers aware of the risks associated with an active airfield.

Even worse, there were those who seemed unable to appreciate the significance and the importance of the airfield equipment; a fact which became painfully obvious during Group Captain Salmon's tour as Gan's station commander. He recalled, some sixteen years after he left the island, that petty pilfering by the Maldivians was rife throughout his time at the atoll even though the punishments which the atoll executives meted out to convicted offenders were severe. Mostly, the items stolen were not really valuable and their loss was inconvenient rather than serious but matters came to a head when some of the runway approach lights, heavy items securely bolted to the coral shelf, were stolen.

Whilst a search was conducted, no Maldivian was permitted to take home any item obtained on Gan, even if ownership could be proved by the production of a signed chit. Usually, when the 'no chitties' rule was invoked it quickly led to the identification of the islanders who had so inconvenienced their fellow workers but on this occasion no culprit was identified. But the loss of the approach lights was so serious that the atoll chief came to see the station commander, a gesture which would have been unheard of in previous years but one which showed the level of cooperation existing at that time. He had already made his displeasure known to the villagers and, unbeknown to Salmon, his personal involvement in the case had already led to the discovery of the lights. It soon became obvious that he intended to deal with the problem in his own way because all he would say to Salmon was *'Are you sure you have lost them?'* and *'Why not look again?'* Salmon took the hint, a second check was made and the lights were found lying on the coral shelf where they had apparently fallen over after the heavy-duty bolts had unscrewed themselves.

With honour satisfied and no obvious loss of face, the chitty system was reinstated, life went back to normal and the airfield operations were unaffected. Such was life on Gan.

When, on the 1st of April 1973, RAF Gan was assimilated into the Near East Air Force the transition, which settled Gan into its fourth RAF Command in two years, had little effect on Gan's expatriates or on the airfield operations; those continued to revolve around scheduled flights, an unusually high number of air mobility exercises and further atmospheric research during June with Dr Clarke, once again leading a research team from the Imperial College of Science, overseeing the launch of two large Radio Sonde balloons and gathering data which, even before detailed analysis back at the college, appeared to be all that could have been hoped for.

Throughout the remaining nine months of the year the frequency and duration of the exercises and the number of participating aircraft meant that for most of the time a C 130 Hercules was detached to Gan for search and rescue duties, occasionally called upon, occasionally conducting joint exercises with the marine craft crews and generally giving a sense of security to those who might need their help, not least the Maldivians. Even during the Christmas stand-down, when no scheduled passenger flights were routed through Gan, the airfield was operational for twenty-four hours to accommodate the Vulcans which staged through on the annual westabout exercise, adding to the traffic generated by the six air mobility exercises which had occurred in October and November.

1974 was appropriately ushered in and with the New Year celebrations behind them, the servicemen expected that life on the island would once again go back to what they regarded as normal. But the contrast between the airfield operations in 1973 and those at the beginning of 1974 could hardly have been greater. In Britain, the fuel shortage was affecting the military because the Ministry of Defence had decided to cancel many non-essential operations and had set targets for fuel conservation across the three services. With the cancellation or postponement of a number of exercises for combat aircraft and the loss of a few of the scheduled passenger flights there was a consequential reduction of some twenty per cent in the number of aircraft movements at Addu Atoll; the airfield was quieter at that time than at any other normal operating period for several years. The RAF's schedules for passenger flights to and from the Far East were not seriously affected but the fuel conservation measures, which included a late start to the air display season, were obviously effective with the Strike Command returns showing a saving of one and a half million gallons of Avtur that year.

Then, just as the fuel supplies were being increased, conflict in Cyprus led to the cancellation of several planned air mobility exercises to and from the Far East and the number of aircraft movements on Gan's airfield fell to sixty-three in July and seventy-seven in August, virtually all accounted for by the scheduled passenger flights. As the troubles in Cyprus continued, the airfield on Gan remained relatively quiet, presenting the emergency services with opportunities to conduct some realistic training with the fire section tackling hot fires (Fig 18.6) and the marine craft unit and medical staff running a reef rescue operation in which twenty-four volunteers played the part of aircraft casualties in the shallow waters off Chicken Island to the west of Fedu.

It was November before the number of aircraft movements increased to something approaching the normal level and by then there were signs that the Maldivian government was hoping that civilian airlines would be permitted to use Gan's airfield, bringing tourists to the southern islands. That idea had been briefly discussed in London when Ali Maniku met Callaghan and although nothing had been agreed, an Air Maldive inaugural flight brought twenty-eight Maldivian officials to Gan in October, all intent on bringing tourism to the southernmost reaches of the archipelago. It was the first of many visits by the airline's Convairs because after the December announcement of the British government's intention to abandon the base, the Maldivian government, ignoring the nineteen inches of rain which flooded the island that month, became even more interested in the development of tourism in the region.

Three air mobility exercises in January 1975 signalled a brief return to normality for the staging post's airfield in a year when the number of aircraft movements each month was certain to decline as a result of Britain's reducing military commitments in the Far East. There was a brief period of activity in June when the major exercises, 'Unfix' to Singapore and 'Snow/Reindeer' to Fiji, brought eighty aircraft to Gan but after that the monthly figures for aircraft movements declined rapidly with a combined total of fewer than one hundred and seventy for September and October.

November brought to the airfield one of the few Argosies still in service with the RAF, a radar calibration aircraft instantly recognisable by its livery and its proboscis. Ever since Gan's airfield had become fully operational the calibration Argosies of N° 115 Squadron had been regular visitors and in November 1975 one spent a month on detachment from RAF Cottesmore to Gan, calibrating the airfield's navigation aids for the last time before the station was handed over to the Maldivian government. The aircrew, familiar figures on the island during the month, were particularly popular with the airmen who were given what would almost certainly be their last opportunity to take air experience flights over the area, to see and photograph the atoll and their island base.

An incident-free December included the customary stand-down over Christmas followed by a brief return to normality with the last of the regularly scheduled VC 10s staging through the base on the 1st of January 1976, marking the end of Gan's operational life as a mid-ocean staging post. With the departure of that VC10, Gan's role changed to that of a temporary diversion airfield open for only eight hours a day for the minor operations described in chapter XXIII.

There are obviously no extant records identifying every type of aircraft which landed at Gan but the station's aircraft accident register, containing brief details of five hundred and twenty-nine incidents logged by twenty different aircraft types during the seventeen years in which the main runway was operational, gives some indication of the variety of problems which Gan's aircraft servicing engineers had to be prepared to tackle.

Of those twenty aircraft types, the Andover the Buccaneer and the Sea Vixen are the only ones with solitary entries in the register; the Bristol Freighter and the Argosy each feature twice; the Lightning and the Phantom each have three entries; the Nimrod and the Valiant have four; the Beverley is the only type to have five entries; the Valetta has eight; the Vulcan, seven; the Canberra, twenty and the Victor, twenty-six. Understandably, the majority of the entries in the register refer to the Gan-based Shackletons and the freight and passenger carrying aircraft. Seventy-one entries refer to incidents involving a Shackleton; the Belfasts and the Comets each have twenty-six entries; the Hastings, twenty-seven; the Hercules, sixty-six; the VC 10s, ninety-seven and the Britannias, one hundred and twenty-nine.

That register is comprehensive but it does not necessarily provide details of every aircraft incident which had to be dealt with on Gan, nor are some of the incidents, remembered by servicemen who were on the island at the time, recorded. The record book does not, for example, include details of the 1963 episode, involving an eastbound Britannia, although Wing Commander Hill, Gan's station commander at the time, could clearly recall the circumstances some thirty years later. The Britannia was mid-way between the east coast of Africa and Gan when one engine developed a fault which left it permanently racing, leaving the pilot to coax the aircraft across the Indian Ocean to Addu Atoll. He brought it in safely but on later examination parts of the aircraft's runaway engine were found to be near-molten, leaving the servicing engineers to wonder how the pilot had ever managed to bring it safely to Gan.

The story of the airfield operation at Gan is essentially a story of success in spite of the oft-times treacherous nature of the airfield when subjected to the vagaries of the local weather. Thousands of aircraft movements took place at Gan with very few major incidents and although there was the near disaster with Hastings TG 579, no passengers or crew suffered serious injury during the operational lifetime of the base.

Fig 18.1. Eagle Airways Britannia 'Endeavour' on Gan's golf course.

Fig 18.3. The arrival of a Victor tanker on operation 'Panther Trail'.

Fig 18.2. A tropical island greeting.

Fig 18.4. One of the 'Panther Trail' Lightnings coming in to Gan.

Fig 18.5. Test flight for a 'Panther Trail' Lightning and Victor.

Fig 18.6. Valetta shell used by Gan's fire-fighters.

XIX   All in a Day's Work…

The daily round, the uncommon tasks

When Costain's engineers arrived at the atoll they, like the servicemen posted to RAF Gan, were somewhat surprised by the daily schedule because most of them had expected to work what were generally referred to as tropical hours, starting very early in the morning and finishing before two p.m. What they found was that, for the most part, servicemen and civilians alike worked a nominal eight-hour day six days a week, starting at half past seven each morning, taking a two-hour break in the middle of the day and finishing at half past five, roughly half an hour before sunset. But anyone could be called upon to work as a stevedore when a supply ship arrived and that, after August 1957, happened with increasing frequency, often on a Sunday and occasionally long after normal working hours. For every visiting ship's captain, the turnaround time was all-important; each wanted an immediate response from the stevedores whatever the time of day or day of the week and each became frustrated when having to wait. But by October that year ships were delivering construction materials and equipment ever more frequently and it was not unusual for four or five to arrive within a few hours of each other and have to remain at anchor in the lagoon whilst their captains waited impatiently for their cargos to be offloaded. As a contributor to the Costain house journal commented,

> 'Owing to the isolation everything except bananas has to be imported from the UK or Colombo, mostly by Messrs Brocklebank of Liverpool. The stevedores are controlled by a new addition to the firm, Keith Watson, generally known as 'Captain' in polite circles. His efficiency and personality is evident because Brocklebank skippers now dare not complain unless there are at least three ships in the lagoon awaiting discharge.'

Undoubtedly, working life on Gan during those early months was far from comfortable but it bore no comparison with the daily grind in the early 1940s when Gan's first airstrip was built and as 1957 drew to a close it was obvious that with the men, materials and machinery at the disposal of the contractors the construction work of 1958 would be very different from that of 1942.

The 1957 Christmas and New Year celebrations ended a difficult year for the men who had been brought to live and work on that spit of a coral island just south of the equator. Few of them had anticipated what life would be like on Gan yet their morale had remained remarkably high because there were significant mitigating factors, not least of which was the fact that virtually everyone had remained in good health throughout those early months. Above all there was a sense of purpose: the creation of an RAF staging post in an unpleasant environment and in such a remote part of the world presented a challenge to be met. For the servicemen there were particular compensations. The tour length in the early days was generally six months and there was usually an opportunity to take a mid-tour break in Ceylon even though that was not an entitlement. There was minimal military formality and the everyday working dress, comprising shirt, shorts, long socks, anti-mosquito boots and green jungle hat, emphasised the functional more than the aesthetic for there were very few occasions when the men were required to be formally on parade. They were, however, expected to present a better image whenever a VIP was visiting the base and by 1958 that was becoming an all-too-common occurrence.

Wing Commander Kent, who had taken over from Wing Commander Schofield early in June 1958, soon found himself meeting and hosting visiting officers on three or four days every week. Most of them were surprised by the seemingly disorganised Maldivian labour force employed on the site and by the working hours which were still nominally eight hours a day, six days a week. For the servicemen, those hours were certainly not likely to be reduced while Air Marshal the Earl of Bandon was the Commander-in-Chief of the Far East Air Force for on first meeting Wing Commander Kent he had pointed out that the increasing number of personnel based on Gan was beginning to cause him some concern and he had emphasised that although he was anxious to keep the construction programme on schedule, the number of servicemen at the atoll was to be kept to a minimum even if that meant that their workloads were exceptionally heavy. Those nominal working hours were therefore retained but, as was usual on Gan, the urgency of some works over-rode the nominal arrangements. The airmen, used to the demands of service life, accepted that. They also accepted, admittedly without any great enthusiasm, the normal military routines which, in-between the storms which brought rain to the atoll on eighteen days during Kent's first month on Gan, included two parades, one to mark Prince Philip's birthday on the 10th and another, to mark the Queen's birthday, on the 12th. Such birthday parades were regular, and often quite impressive, events in the service calendar but on Gan they were very modest affairs practised by participants who were not very enthusiastic because the living conditions and the lack of proper laundry facilities made it very difficult for any airman to maintain a smart uniform for such occasions and, given the atrocious weather that month, most of them would have preferred to dispense with the formalities of birthday parades.

To compare military service with civilian employment is difficult but whenever airmen and civilians work alongside each other comparisons are inevitable and that was as true on Gan as it was anywhere else. The European civilians had the obvious advantages of premium rates of pay for working on Gan, of receiving extra pay for any overtime worked, of living in better accommodation and of enjoying an informal lifestyle. The airmen were obliged to take the longer view of life in the service, to regard a posting to Gan as an aberration and seek out what few compensations there were to balance against the unattractive aspects of life on the island in 1957 and 1958. But by the time Kent took over from Schofield the compensations were reducing. The airmen who had been posted to Gan for only six months had left, each of those remaining was on a one year tour and the changes taking place in 1958 meant that virtually every one of them would be confined to camp for twelve months.

Throughout the previous year it was quite common for small groups of servicemen to be invited to visit the village on Hitaddu but the dramatic increase in the number of expatriates brought to Gan during the first few months of 1958 had inevitably meant that towards the end of Schofield's tour the official policy, which classified such visits as exceptional, had been resurrected, dusted off and complied with. Subsequently the only servicemen permitted to tour Hitaddu did so at the specific invitation of the atoll chief and after June 1958 very few expatriates received such an invitation. Similarly, the unofficial arrangements for providing mid-tour leave were withdrawn when the increasing demand and the reducing number of spare seats on the aircraft seemed likely to create a small but very privileged group of servicemen who had enjoyed the luxury of a mid-tour break in Ceylon whilst their colleagues covered for them at work. Even the competitive sportsmen who, in late 1957 and early 1958, could expect to represent Gan in the Ceylon-based tournaments, lost that opportunity when RAF Gan was withdrawn from the inter-station competitions until such time as it was considered that the sportsmen could be collectively spared from their primary duties.

Somewhat surprisingly, the servicemen's lot was improved sooner than expected as a result of the Adduans' unilateral declaration of independence which swept aside all the embargos affecting the airfield construction programme. The double shift system introduced by Costain's site engineers brought the concrete runway into use by the Changi-based Hastings early in March 1959, additional buildings were being commissioned almost daily, leisure facilities were being improved as the operational works were completed and the increasing number of aircraft using the airfield was creating an atmosphere akin to a regular overseas base, albeit one with a fairly tolerant regime in recognition of the fact that the servicemen were expected to spend twelve months living on what was still largely a construction site.

The Adduan rebellion may have led to some short-term benefits for the servicemen and the construction engineers but there was a longer-term price to pay as was made clear in March 1959. What none of the servicemen on Gan had expected was a call to arms but that was what they got that month when the Adduans became convinced that they were about to be attacked by the Malé-based militia and, as described on page 139, called upon the RAF for help. The servicemen were all alerted, the available arms were issued and an expedition mounted. The islanders' fears were unfounded but the servicemen had suddenly realised that for as long as the Adduans persisted with their unilateral declaration of independence, life on Gan was likely to be very different from what they, and everyone else, had imagined.

Over the next few months several similar, but less dramatic, events occurred, each one adding to the servicemen's workload. By the end of August the airmen were working in a constant state of readiness, RAF Regiment personnel had been sent to Gan and the arrival of reconnaissance aircraft had significantly increased the number of airfield movements and the demands made upon the servicing technicians. By September, political manoeuvring by the British and Maldivian governments had persuaded an increasing number of politicians and civil servants to visit the base in an attempt to gain some insight into the situation and their arrival added to the servicemen's already demanding workload.

November brought even more aircraft movements and even more VIPs, including the Earl of Bandon and a retinue of Air Marshals. Theirs was a brief visit but it was long enough for the airmen to don their so-called 'panic kit' uniforms which they kept for the most important visitors and for the occasional parades. Worn infrequently, and then only briefly, those uniforms were as well maintained as possible under the circumstances, a fact which was accepted by the station commander who, whilst generally condoning a standard of working dress in keeping with the climate and the workplace conditions, expected the airmen to make an obvious effort on special occasions. For those servicemen who wondered why Gan should so often attract the attention of the Earl and his Air Officers, the Daily Express provided an answer by publishing an article, on the 25th of November 1959, about the rebel islanders of Addu Atoll. Written by the enterprising Bertram Jones, whose expedition to Addu Atoll is described on page 143, the article, which appeared under the headline 'MIDNIGHT – and I anchor unannounced in lagoon of the forbidden isles', gave readers a somewhat fanciful account of life at the atoll since the Adduans' unilateral declaration of independence but it did raise the general public's awareness of the Adduan affair.

January 1960 was the month when the staging post really began to live up to its title. Two or three times a week the airmen of Gan's staging aircraft servicing flight demonstrated their slick routines as the Comets and Britannias which plied between Britain and the Far East were refuelled and sent on their way. The welcome increase in the number of scheduled flights created a two- or three-day postal service between England and Gan, generally brought to the atoll newspapers which were only two days old, reassuringly provided emergency flight opportunities from the base and, perhaps above all else, created a sense of purpose for the expatriates who, living and working on Gan, had very little contact with the outside world. The price to be paid for those benefits was an increase in the workload for everyone who had a part to play in the provision of a safe and efficient refuelling and servicing facility.

In February, the Gan-based Shackleton patrolled the Indian Ocean whilst passenger aircraft and combat aircraft staged through the base almost every day, raising the number of aircraft movements to two hundred and ninety-eight that month, one hundred and twenty more than in January and some fifteen times the number on which the station's established manning levels were based. The workload had increased as dramatically as forecast but it was to be several months before a review recognised the imbalance and changed the establishment; only after that were more servicemen posted in to the overworked sections.

As the number of scheduled flights increased, more and more passengers, obliged to follow Ministry of Defence procedures, were having to be shepherded to and from the aircraft which they had to vacate whilst it was being refuelled. By February the station boasted a newly built transit hotel, 'The Blue Lagoon', providing some air conditioned overnight accommodation for 'slip' crews, arrival and departure check-in points for Gan personnel and basic airport facilities for transit passengers who, in the normal course of events would spend less than an hour on the island. The basic facilities were perfectly adequate for the transients' brief stopovers although there were initially few diversion activities for children, a deficiency which was remedied within a few months when money was raised to build, equip and floodlight a play area alongside the Blue Lagoon, enabling the transient children to work off their surplus energy outdoors, weather permitting, during the day or night.

The transients, transported by coach between the aircraft and the Blue Lagoon saw the atoll from the air as they approached the island base but saw very little of Gan once they were on the ground. What they did see, apart from the buildings which flanked the main road from the aircraft pan to the transit hotel, were significant numbers of airmen who had, until then, been subjected to minimal dress regulations and as the number of transients increased to several hundred each week the airmen were required to present a somewhat smarter image than that which had been acceptable during the earlier construction phase. The 'panic kit' approach for the more formal occasions was retained because there was still no station laundry but the airmen's workaday uniforms necessarily became more presentable and by mid-1960 the workplace atmosphere on Gan had evolved into something akin to a conventional overseas station in the tropics.

With Gan's transition from a nascent military base to a fully operational RAF staging post, much of the daily round settled into a pattern similar to that on any RAF station for there was obviously a hard core of common routine tasks to be undertaken. But on Gan the routine tasks often paled in comparison with the uncommon demands made upon the servicemen and as the base became ever busier the phrase 'all in a day's work' took on a meaning which was peculiar to Gan, embracing such diverse activities as the extraction of coral rock from the underwater quarry, the provision of medical services for the indigenous population, the removal of aircraft from the station's golf course and the organisation of search and rescue missions in the Indian Ocean.

Many demands were made outside normal working hours because Gan's residents, cloistered in their compact domestic sites, were readily available day or night and were often called out at odd hours. For the servicemen on the duty rosters there was nothing unusual about that but for the station commander the demands were to become more and more frequent as he was called upon to host an increasing number of very senior VIPs every month. By mid-1960, when the staging post was fully operational, the station commander's role as host to all visiting and transient VIPs of air rank or its equivalent had become an almost daily occurrence and was to remain so throughout the operational life of the base.

His was undoubtedly a heavy burden but any serviceman was likely to be called upon at any time of the day or night. Quite apart from the shift workers whose normal hours ran into the afternoons, evenings and nights there was the usual complement of personnel covering the duty rosters and others who were either officially on standby for emergency callouts or who, like the accountant officer, were considered by some to be available on a goodwill basis should a VIP or an aircrew imprest holder need access to the RAF's financial services. But, with the exception of the station commander, the servicemen who tended to work the longest hours were the medical officers whose commitments are described in chapter XX; for them, and for all the others who willingly gave of their free time, serving on Gan was a temporary way of life, not a job.

During Wing Commander Thomas's year as Gan's station commander the transition from a building site to a fully operational airfield was virtually completed, even to the extent of having an internal telephone network installed; a feature which was a mixed blessing as far as he was concerned for, as he recalled,

> 'When no phones existed and enquiries could only be made by walking or cycling from one section to another, everyone tended to get on with his job and make decisions for better or for worse. It was very noticeable that the advent of the telephone service was followed by a general tendency for people to make decisions only after making more checks or obtaining authority; the efficiency of the station went down.'

March 1960 was a month which became etched on the memory of every serviceman on the island for it brought home to them, and everyone else, the very real threat to any aircraft attempting to land at Gan whilst a tropical storm was raging around the atoll. Anyone who had not taken that threat seriously before the 1st of March was forcibly reminded, by the accident described on page 290, that disaster was often no more than a lightning flash away. The conditions which could so easily have caused the pilot to crash that Hastings onto the runway were quuite common in the region and as the Comets and the Britannias were brought into service the worst-case scenario was for a fully laden Britannia to crash, killing most, if not all, of those on board, putting the runway out of commission and leaving the station commander to cope without any outside assistance. It was a scenario which was never seriously addressed by the Far East Air Force staff whose approach was to leave the matter in the hands of the local executives. Successive station commanders were thus left to ensure that contingency plans were made and that station staff were as well prepared as possible to cope with a near-impossible situation. Apart from that they just had to hope that nothing more serious than routine aircraft engineering problems would arise. Those were, in fact, not that uncommon and the station's contingency plan, Operation Fastbed, for the accommodation of passengers who were stranded on Gan overnight, had to be quite frequently implemented.

The plan focussed firstly on the capacity of the Blue Lagoon and then on buildings such as the gymnasium and the education centre which could be utilised as dormitory accommodation for up to two hundred people, albeit with limited washing and toilet facilities. The only air conditioned bedrooms, primarily intended for use by the 'slip' crews, were in the transit hotel where there were four VIP rooms, twenty-four rooms for officers, and twenty-two multiple-occupancy rooms, each containing five or six beds. There was no shortage of camp beds for use in the various buildings and in total it was possible to provide emergency dormitory accommodation for over three hundred and fifty people. The plan was straightforward enough and was used on numerous occasions over the years with little more than some inconvenience for the passengers and the station staff who would be called upon to organise the dormitory accommodation, distribute and assemble camp beds, organise the catering and the other passenger services and eventually clear the temporary accommodation when the stranded transients had departed.

For many of the delayed passengers the inconvenience of an overnight stay was offset by the thought that they would be able, briefly, to enjoy the tropical island environment. Those who harboured such thoughts were soon disillusioned; Gan was a military base with security restrictions and closed, multicultural, communities. It was not acceptable to have stranded passengers loose around the island even if it could be guaranteed that they would all be back in the departure lounge in time to board their delayed flight.

For the station staff, control and diplomacy had to go hand-in-hand particularly when a passenger aircraft had been declared unserviceable in the morning or early afternoon because at those times most of the passengers would be wide awake, understandably keen to see something of the island and not particularly happy to find that they were not permitted to wander outside the grounds of the transit hotel. But practice makes perfect and after several such delays the staff became adept at tactfully controlling the movements of one hundred or more passengers pending the repair or replacement of their unserviceable aircraft.

Increasing the frustration of the stranded passengers who were cloistered in the Blue Lagoon, and looking out at the sun shining on the tropical landscape, was the disconcerting discovery that there were no telephone links from Gan to the outside world and it was therefore impossible to contact any of the friends or relatives who were waiting for them at their destinations. The military communications system meant that the stations along the route were aware of the situation but concerned relatives could only learn of the delay by contacting the air movements staff at the destination airfield. The absence of any telephone links with the outside world was a fact of life which Gan's unaccompanied tourists were only too happy to bring to the attention of the more senior passengers who were temporarily marooned on the expatriates' tropical island.

Control was sometimes not quite as simple when VIPs were briefly delayed. Most of them were understanding and readily accepted the offer of a guided tour of the island in the station's staff car but there were occasionally those who had ideas of their own and would want to enjoy the enforced break by going swimming, or even sailing, in the lagoon. Fortunately, as far as the duty protocol officers were concerned, the most senior of the VIPs were privileged to be hosted by the station commander and it was left for him to provide them with appropriate diversions.

For the transients who briefly saw the conventional RAF airfield with its associated buildings and the tropical foliage along the main route from the airfield to the transit hotel there was no indication of the effort which had to be made by every expatriate to counter the effects of Gan's isolation and create the impression of a station which was as easy to run as a mainland base in England. Behind the scenes there was a widespread tendency to achieve results even if the process was not quite legitimate; Gan was a place where rules could often be bent because local circumstances were exceptional and Gan was not just a long way away from authority, it was virtually incommunicado. For the station commander, this freedom to use his initiative was very welcome even if he was continually having to make decisions in circumstances which were peculiar to the locale, highly unusual in the context of an RAF station and occasionally intuitive because they had to be made without the benefit of outside opinion. Quite apart from the difficulties encountered during the rebellion and long after the local version of normality had returned to the island, successive station commanders had their initiative tested in situations which had never been envisaged by the authors of the Air Force manuals. There were the issues raised by the sudden deaths on Gan; by the political sensitivities of many Pakistanis, by the local reaction to external events such as the war between India and Pakistan and, bizarrely, by the events surrounding the arrival of the SS Te Vega, described on page 274.

Anti-riot training

Since the islanders' first large-scale demonstration, the Gan-based airmen had often been called upon to control crowds of Adduan demonstrators, occasionally having to stand fast against the Maldivians pending the arrival of RAF Regiment reinforcements who were sent from Singapore whenever a demonstration threatened to develop into a riot. It was a role which they accepted even though they had received no relevant formal training. At times, and the early part of 1964 was one such period, a Regiment flight was retained on Gan because of the likelihood that trouble would flare up at any moment. But by the middle of that year, the hopes of an amicably renegotiated revision of the 1960 agreement between the British and Maldivian governments had increased to such an extent that the Far East Air Force staff decided that there was no longer a need to maintain a rostered Regiment flight on Gan and at the end of June the airmen were recalled, no replacements were detached to the atoll and the rostered rotation arrangement was ended.

It was a premature move because trouble flared up almost immediately and the Regiment airmen were called back to Gan for station defence duties in August and September. When they were finally withdrawn during October an RAF Regiment officer and one senior non-commissioned officer, both on detachment from Singapore, remained on the island to establish a ground defence training programme for the four hundred and sixty-one atoll-based servicemen, helping them to acquire the skills needed to handle local emergencies pending the arrival of reinforcements from Singapore where one of the Regiment squadron's flights was always on call for duty at Addu Atoll. By November, Gan-based airmen were being weekly inculcated in the art of dealing with a large number of unarmed rioters but few of them could be given weapons training because the station's rifle range was not then constructed and, as the photograph in the RAF News in May 1966 shows, the airmen had to demonstrate their range skills by firing at floating oil drums whilst on board a marine craft launch on the seaward side of Gan.

For the airmen on the island, the expectation that they might well be required to confront large numbers of Maldivians, who had so frequently and so violently demonstrated their hostility to their government officials, added to their already unusual inventory of commitments. That addition, and the lack of a rifle range on Gan, was recognised by the Singapore-based Command staff who decided that the ground defence training programmes on Gan ought to be regarded as specialised programmes which concentrated on the local situation and they accordingly added weapons proficiency certification to the list of pre-embarkation requirements for any serviceman posted to Gan; from then on every airman was obliged to undertake firing range practice at his home station before starting his embarkation leave.

With the initial training programme completed, the Regiment officer and his senior non-commissioned officer returned to Singapore, each being replaced by the first incumbents in the newly established posts on Gan. Even after the construction of the rifle range shown on the south- eastern shore of the island on the map at Appendix D, the pre-embarkation certification was retained although, as demonstrations by the Adduans became a thing of the past, it gradually came to be disregarded, leaving Gan's resident RAF Regiment officer to add weapons practice to the local ground defence training programme.

Search and rescue

Gan's location and the siting of the Hitaddu complex meant that the lagoon was as much a part of the base as was the airfield. Each day, people and supplies had to be ferried between the islands (Fig 19.1) and each month ships had to be piloted into and out of the lagoon, cargos unloaded and oil discharged from tankers. The activities in the lagoon, which were all straightforward enough, justified the establishment of Gan's marine craft unit but the marine craft crews had, like the search and rescue Shackleton crews who patrolled the region, a wider remit; they were expected to go to the assistance of those in distress anywhere within range of their sea-going launch (Fig 19.2).

The search and rescue service had been established primarily for the benefit of the British military traffic across the Indian Ocean but only rarely were Gan's search and rescue teams called upon to assist those who were their primary concern; most of the calls for assistance came from Maldivian boats, from merchant ships or from private yachts. Invariably they came from people in dire straits, often they were from weary Maldivians who merely wanted to be towed home against the prevailing wind and, on rare occasions, they came from some concerned individual who, believing that others were in distress, unwittingly raised a false alarm.

Distress calls could never be ignored and although there were occasionally calls which were later discovered to be false alarms, Gan's rescue co-ordination centre was at the heart of many newsworthy operations over the years, few more dramatic than the rescue of the crew of the SS Chin Glong Yin, described on page 291. Every week the Gan-based Shackleton crews patrolled thousands of square miles of ocean, their reconnaissance reports being analysed by the Gan centre before the island's marine craft, which was most frequently called upon to go to the aid of Maldivians, was called out on a rescue or humanitarian mission, such as that described on page 324; not exactly all in a day's work, but another example of the uncommon tasks which fell to the servicemen on Gan.

Even when the runway repair work, described on page 295, prevented a Shackleton from operating out of Gan the search and rescue service was maintained by using a C 130 Hercules which could take off and land on a short stretch of the runway. Several calls for assistance were made from Hitaddu on behalf of Maldivian dhoni crews, some of whom were eventually found in dire straights whilst others were merely in need of a little help from a powered vessel. The marine craft unit even answered a call to go to the rescue of an Adduan motorboat which had broken down in the lagoon but was in danger of being swept into the Indian Ocean by the strong current running to the north of Gan. One call, however, was unusual because it came from the American air base at Diego Garcia with a request for a medical evacuation flight for a sick airman who could apparently not be treated at the base even though the facilities there were at least as good as, and probably better than, those on Gan. The C130 Hercules, with Gan's medical officer on board, duly collected the airman and flew him to Singapore where he was hospitalised.

Search and rescue missions came at a cost, as did humanitarian aid and whenever the RAF's services were called upon someone had to submit to the Ministry of Defence a financial return for the operation. As the example given at Fig 19.3 shows, the return for even a simple rescue operation would be quite detailed, giving the Ministry staff the information needed to prepare an invoice should that be considered appropriate which, for the poverty-stricken Maldivians, it rarely was.

Although search and rescue operations were rarely mounted to assist Britain's military or civilian personnel in the region, they did occur; the most dramatic being the rescue operation mounted by the marine craft airmen when Hastings TG 579 ditched short of the runway. The only occasion when an airborne search had to be mounted for Gan personnel occurred in September 1971 when it was reported that one of the sailing club dinghies was missing, raising the obvious possibility that any of the thousand or so expatriates could have boarded the dinghy and been swept out to sea. Whilst the airborne search continued, a head count of every serviceman and every civilian on the base was undertaken. After four hours Group Captain Sheppard, Gan's newly-arrived station commander, was satisfied that no-one was missing and, on the assumption that the dinghy had been empty when it had gone adrift, called off the airborne search.

Ocean research

For Gan's RAF marine craft unit, 'all in a day's work' did not just refer to a mixture of the mundane and the dramatic, it also covered occasional participation in oceanographic research in a region which was of considerable interest to institutes around the world. Thus, in November 1972, the airmen of N° 1125 marine craft unit took their pinnace out into the Indian Ocean where they could be seen over a period of several days, towing three small barrage balloons whilst allowing their boat to drift with the current. They were taking part in an investigation, conducted on behalf of the Wood's Hole Oceanographic Institute, into the ocean currents in the region and the barrage balloons were to enable the institute staff to track the boat's drift on radar.

Helping research scientists to increase the collated knowledge of the surrounding ocean was satisfying but even more satisfying was the discovery made towards the end of 1974 when the marine craft airmen made their biggest contribution to oceanographic research in the region. 'The sea mountain find by coral island sailors' was the headline in the RAF News on the 4th of January 1975 over a report of the Indian Ocean survey which they made on behalf of the Scripps Institute of Oceanography and which led to the discovery of a previously uncharted sea mountain. The surveys showed that the seabed around Gan appears to consist of flat valleys separated by large and precipitous mountains with the uncharted peak, subsequently named Pinnace's Peak after RAF pinnace N° 1382, rising some three thousand five hundred feet from the sea bed and extending for almost four miles.

That topographical discovery was news-worthy but it was actually incidental to the mid-1970s research in that region where the institute was one of three Western oceanographic or other establishments working with the World Meteorological Office on a vast project to attempt to explain the causes of the world's climatic cycles and to produce a method of forecasting them. The aim of the project was to conduct research into current flow at various depths and try to determine whether there was any correlation with surface movement, whether the flow changed with the change of the monsoon and whether the deep current changes affected the weather above. The topographical discovery was made because one of the survey tasks to be tackled by the Gan pinnace crew was to lower current recording meters onto the submerged mountain peaks and, at the end of each two-month recording period, to return to the same areas with a special echo sounder which could send a coded pulse to the meters to release them from the seabed and allow them to float back to the surface for recovery.

Currency decimalisation

On the 15th of February 1971 decimal currency replaced Britain's familiar pounds shillings and pence. The change brought very little extra work to accounts sections throughout the RAF, except on Gan where, as usual, the local situation complicated what should have been a very straightforward process. The Maldivians were initially very suspicious of the decimal currency, believing that any system which replaced twelve large old pence by five small new pence was designed to rob them of more than half of their hard-earned savings. But when they eventually accepted that they were not being swindled they presented the accounts staff with far more work than had been expected. Every villager who had ever been paid in Sterling had saved money and, because nobody would save pound notes in a climate where paper could go mouldy within weeks, every one of them had a large box filled with coins. The accounts staff were thus faced with the job of counting and exchanging several tons of pre-decimal coinage which then had to be shipped back to Britain. It was a task which had to be spread over several months but which brought a bonus for many of those officers who were waiting for indulgence flights to England for mid-tour leave; they became cash couriers, escorting a few hundredweights of coins and thus travelling on duty with no chance of being offloaded *en route*.

The continuing construction work

When, early in 1960, the last of Costain's engineers left the atoll, the Air Ministry Works Directorate took over the direct responsibility for all construction and maintenance work, employing some three hundred and fifty of the Pakistanis who had been working for Costain and retaining the unskilled and semi-skilled Maldivian employees to maintain the buildings and the infrastructure, lay the roads and landscape the island. For the next two years the works department employees were fully occupied erecting new buildings and generally improving the environment which, early in 1960, was still very much that of a building site. By 1962 the main building programme had been completed and although, as the plans at Appendix D show, buildings were still being erected until well into the 1970s they were, almost without exception, *ad hoc* structures built to improve the existing facilities.

Throughout the 1960s and the first half of the 1970s Gan's underwater quarrying continued with Maldivian labourers drilling deep into the coral shelf and RAF armourers laying and detonating the hundreds of pounds of explosives needed to split the coral into slabs which could be pulled out of the water by dragline cranes and transported to the crushing plant. Subsequently used as aggregate for road works and in the manufacture of building blocks, kerbstones and the ubiquitous slotted support blocks for the hundreds of bicycles in daily use on Gan, the quarry-workers' harvest was visibly utilised across the island.

Quite apart from the completion of the main building programme, Gan at the end of 1962 was no longer a barren building site because Maldivians had been employed to convert the bare, dusty, and occasionally waterlogged acres into a tropical garden. It was a huge undertaking, requiring specialist knowledge of plants which would not be eaten by the island's voracious insects, would thrive in shallow soil on a coral island with a water table no more than three feet below the surface, could withstand tropical rainstorms during the wet season, weeks of near-drought during the dry season, salt-laden winds, constant daytime temperatures in the mid- to upper-eighties and night-time temperatures consistently some ten degrees lower. Botanists from Ceylon and from Kew Gardens were invited to visit Gan and, following their advice, thousands of seeds and hundreds of small shrubs and trees were planted in a propagation area three hundred yards east of the Asian camp alongside the station's water catchment area.

As the seedlings took root they were attacked, the first crop by a plague of snails which ate every young plant in the area, and the second by swarms of flies which took a liking to the roots of the newly-germinated grass seed and which, like the snails, had to be eradicated before fresh plants could be grown. After one more serious setback, when a Maldivian employee killed several thousand young plants by mistakenly spraying them with a particularly potent herbicide, the propagation centre developed into a very efficient nursery, helping to maintain Gan's tropical garden image and eventually exporting surplus plants to other RAF stations such as Masirah.

By the late 1960s the cultivation of the trees and shrubs listed at Fig 19.4 had softened the landscape, converting large areas of the base into a tropical garden, rarely appreciated by the residents as much as it should have been but certainly impressive as far as visitors and transients were concerned. The gardens thus created and maintained by the works department staff thrived with just one exception: no fine-bladed grass survived on the island. The broad-leafed plant which everyone referred to as grass was perfectly acceptable for the so-called grassed areas around the site and on the football pitches; it was somewhat coarse for the cricket table and when it was planted on the golf course greens the indignant golfers immediately re-christened them the semi-roughs.

Construction work and routine maintenance was very much the public face of the works department, earning the organisation its 'bricks and sticks' soubriquet but the engineers on the base were responsible for all the utilities, from the sewage farm to the power house, and if those were not properly run and maintained RAF Gan would quickly become non-operational and the communications site on Hitaddu would cease to function. Inevitably, problems arose but the engineers became adept at dealing with them in spite of the fact that any materials and spare parts not held on the island had to be imported. What was probably the most frustrating of all the problems encountered over the years did not happen on Gan or Hitaddu; it happened in the lagoon where the main underwater power cable ran from Gan to the Hitaddu site. In January 1962 that had broken and the engineers, without the means of recovering the broken ends for re-jointing, had been obliged to rely on a standby generator to provide power for the Hitaddu site whilst they spent two weeks preparing and laying a new underwater cable; a difficult, expensive operation.

The following month, fortune favoured the engineers; HMS Owen, employed on a hydrographical survey in the area, arrived at the atoll and the captain was prevailed upon to employ his ship and his crew in the lagoon for four days, locating and raising the broken ends of the old cable which was subsequently re-jointed and re-laid, providing a very welcome second link from the main power station on Gan to the Hitaddu site.

After that the works department's operations continued with little more than the common or garden problems until 1973 when a major project had to be undertaken: the repair of Gan's badly-worn runway. The operation, costing some two thousand five hundred pounds, had to be organised in a way which ensured that the restricted airfield operations described in chapter XVIII could be maintained whilst six of the runway's concrete panels were broken up, removed and replaced by fresh concrete which had to be laid and left to cure before being subjected to loading tests. The operation started, as planned, on the 16th of February and was completed on time five weeks later. That was no more than expected; on Gan such projects were normally started and finished on schedule because the engineers were very much in control of their own affairs. For anyone familiar with the bureaucracy in England, the procedures for implementing a building project on Gan were refreshingly simple. When the extension to the education centre, for example, was approved by the Air Support Command staff in the latter half of 1971, the works engineer called into the centre on his way to lunch and made a note, literally on the back of a cigarette packet, of the location, style and size of the additional building required. He promised that the work would begin as soon as possible and two hours later a team of Maldivians had marked out the site and were digging the foundation trenches. Such was life on Gan.

The runway repair was one of those rare activities which focussed the attention of Gan's unaccompanied tourists onto the work which was going on around them every day of the week, every week of the year. Even so, it is almost certain that very few of Gan's residents would have been able to estimate the level of expenditure on new works and on maintenance during the first five financial years of the 1970s; figures given by Brynmor John in a written parliamentary answer in November 1975 as five hundred thousand pounds on new works and two million and eighty-seven thousand pounds on maintenance.

When, in December 1974, Roy Mason announced that the base was to be abandoned, the works engineers shelved all their plans for new works and concentrated on the completion of projects already started and the repair and maintenance of the existing facilities. By April 1975 they had received details of the works, referred to in chapter XXII, to be undertaken as part of Britain's contractual obligations to return some of the land on Gan to its earlier state on relinquishing the lease. Other works were undertaken, with

Ministry of Defence approval, for the general benefit of the community but the number of Maldivian and Pakistani employees was steadily reduced so that by 1976, of the few Pakistanis who remained on the payroll some were employed to train the Maldivians who would be responsible for the works programmes after the British withdrawal and others were retained solely to deal with the inevitable problems which would arise during the final stages of the rundown.

Maintaining operations

Considering the impact of Britain's 1974 defence review and the briefing given by the Chief of the Air Staff when he visited Gan in February 1975, events at Addu Atoll during March and April that year were remarkable for their normality. The Adduans seemed almost to have taken the devastating news in their stride, mounted no demonstrations and remained as amicable as they had been for years. Maldivian affairs aside, the only immediate sign that a new era was dawning was the arrival of Ministry of Defence staff and resettlement advisers, despatched to Gan during those two months to assess the impact of the decision to abandon the base, to offer advice to the servicemen and the Department of the Environment staff and to re-examine the redundancy arrangements for the Adduans and the Asian expatriates.

For most of 1975, working life on the island was much the same as usual for the majority of the servicemen and the civilian workforce, if not for the executives; for them, operations would no longer follow the usual pattern because outline plans were already being made for the gradual rundown of the base even though no detailed arrangements could be finalised until the politicians had decided what would be shipped out and what would be left behind.

What could be done, well before those decisions had been made, was to apply tight controls to the RAF's supply chain, ensuring that the only supplies to be ordered were either operationally essential or were items which would be consumed well before march 1976. That would ensure that by February, when the Maldivian team would begin to compile an inventory of assets to be handed over, the stocks of consumables, with the exception of medical supplies, would have been reduced to an operational minimum throughout the base. Achieving that was not as straightforward as it seemed because orders for essential materials and equipment still had to be placed during the last few months of 1975 and into the first few weeks of 1976. Given that airfreight deliveries to the atoll were always likely to be delayed for a week or two and that sea-borne freight would rarely if ever arrive until several weeks after it had been ordered, the last six months in the life of Gan were marked by a very careful assessment of needs, a virtual embargo on orders for sea-borne freight and a series of *cries de couer* over delivery dates.

The reducing population

Steadily reducing the number of civilian employees on the base during 1975 was simply a matter of making the Maldivian and expatriate Asians redundant, repatriating the Pakistani and Sri Lankan employees either at the end of their fixed-term contracts or earlier if necessary. Maintaining an appropriate number of servicemen at the atoll during the last few months was not quite so simple. Each of them had been posted to Gan for a nine-month tour and was due to be posted elsewhere at the end of that period with the arrival of his replacement maintaining the RAF's normal cycle of personnel movements.

Many of the servicemen were willing to spend more than the customary nine months at the atoll, volunteering to take two weeks leave at the end of that normal tour of duty before returning to the base to work through to the end of March but the RAF's personnel management staff, continually trying to take into account the broader picture and the disruptive effect of changing the normal pattern of personnel movements, preferred, for the last few months of 1975, to maintain an adequate manning level on the base by continuing to withdraw servicemen on completion of the regular nine-month tour, sending very few replacements to the atoll and leaving the remaining established posts vacant.

The result was that during the last quarter of the year the number of servicemen on Gan declined significantly with six of the thirty-six officers disestablished and the number of other ranks reduced from five hundred and thirty-three to three hundred and fifty-eight. Extended tours remained the exception rather than the rule until the early weeks of 1976 after which it was possible to sustain the steadily reducing military presence by extending the tour length for key personnel and for some other servicemen whilst only very rarely replacing anyone who left the base at the end of a nine-month tour.

Fig 19.1. Gan's landing craft ferry.

Fig 19.2. Gan's rescue and target towing launch.

Fig 19.3 (a). A search and rescue financial return.

GAN/9/9/Air   July 1964

The Under-Secretary of State
M.O.D. Air (Ops(SAR), F.6y F.3g.)
Whitehall
London S.W.1

Sir,

                Financial Return on Search and Rescue Operation
                    Conducted from Gan R.C.C. on the
                            3rd July, 1964

1.   I have the honour to submit this financial return in accordance with
paragraph 94 British Supplement to ATP 10A (Search and Rescue).

2.   On the 3rd July 1964 a signal was received from the M/V Garrybank
with a request for assistance to enter harbour on behalf of a Male
Government dhow "Rachmad Rahman" which had been becalmed for 22 days with
57 people on board and as a result of sending a distress message by light
to M/V Garrybank was towed by that vessel to within four miles of the
lagoon entrance to Haddumatti Atoll (approximately 150 miles north of Gan)
where the tow had to be dropped because of shoal waters and no large scale
charts being available.

3.   The S.A.R. Shackleton was scrambled and the Marine Craft Section
Rescue and Target Towing Launch slipped mooring and proceeded with all
despatch for the given position. It was intended that the Shackleton
captain would investigate and signal back to Gan when the R.T.T.L. would
be recalled if it was considered that assistance was not necessary.

4.   Upon arrival at the scene the dhow was observed to be under full sail
and making approximately three knots toward the lagoon entrance. The M/V
Garrybank drew the Shackletons attention to a rowing boat with eight
persons on board who appeared to have been cast off from the dhow and were
rapidly drifting in the heavy sea toward the western edge of the coral
reef upon which large rollers were breaking. The Shackleton captain
decided to make a Lindholme drop in the hope that the rowers would board
the light draft J Type dinghy and the seas carry them clear across the
reef to the shallows beyond.

5.   The drop was successful and two of the rowers boarded the dinghy but
were then seen to only remove the paddles before returning to their own
craft when the additional paddles were put to use in assisting their boat
out of danger. The Lindholme Gear disappeared across the reef and all
eight persons were seen to make land safely farther along the coast. When
it was observed that the dhow was in the lagoon and the rowers safely
landed both the Shackleton and the R.T.T.L. returned to Gan.

6.   (a) The aircraft employed was Shackleton Mk. 2. Airframe No. WL 745.
             (205.Squadron Detachment to Gan for S.A.R. Standby duty.)

        (b) The aircraft was not already airborne when ordered to under-
             take this operation. The flying times involved were as follows:-

                  Airborne 030735Z   Landed 031140Z

                        Total 04 hrs. 05 mins.

        (c) Flying was undertaken during a period of one half day.

                                                        /(d)....

- 2 -

(d) The following aircrew were employed and flew the sortie as a crew, their flying hours are, therefore, the same and as shown in sub-para.(b).

2 Flight Lieutenant G.D./Pilots
1 Flight Lieutenant G.D./Navigator
1 Flying Officer G.D./Navigator
1 Flight Lieutenant G.D./A.E.O.
1 Master Engineer
2 Flight Sergeant A.E. Ops.
2 Sergeant Signallers

(e) A list of equipment expended on the operation other than P.O.L. is attached as an appendix.

(f) The task involved the use of the following man hours/labour:-

(i) Servicing Personnel:

1 Corporal Engine Fitter — 3 hours
Aircraftmen A/F Mech. — 2 hours
1 Corporal Wireless Fitter — 5 hours

(ii) Safety Equipment Personnel:

1 Corporal S/E Worker — 6 hours
1 Aircraftman S/E Worker — 6 hours

(iii) Armament Personnel:

1 Corporal Armourer — 6 hours
1 Junior Technician — 6 hours

(iv) Signals Personnel:

1 Aircraftman Wireless Op. — 7 hours

(v) Marine Craft Section Personnel:

1 Flight Lieutenant M.C. Capt. — 7 hours
1 Chief Technician Fitter/Marine — 7 hours
2 Sergeant Coxswains — 14 hours
4 A/C's. Motor Boat Crew — 28 hours
2 A/C's Wireless Operators — 14 hours
1 A/C Sick Berth Attendant — 7 hours

(vi) The following Motor Transport was used during the task:-

Crew Coach — 2 miles
Land Rover — 2 miles

(g) There are no local charges which could not be assessed by the Ministry of Defence (Air).

(h) It is recommended that the Commonwealth Relations Office be requested to inform you of the political situation before any decision is made regarding the raising of charges.

(j) The operation was considered to be of limited training value to all sections concerned.

I have the honour to be,
Sir,
Your obedient Servant,

(N.F. TOMLINSON)
Flight Lieutenant

Copy to:-

Headquarters Far East Air Force

APPENDIX 'A' TO
GAN/9/9/AIR
DATED   JULY, 64

Items used on Sea Rescue Operation Friday,
3rd July, 1964

Sect.	Ref.	Description	Denom.	Qty.
5A	4216	Lights McMurdo	EA	3
5J	3411	Batteries, Sea Activated	"	4
6D	633	Heads, Operating, Type "F"	"	1
"	634	Housing Soluble Plug	"	1
"	9430546	Cylinder, CO2 Mk. 3	"	1
9A	02440	Kits, First Aid, Large	"	2
15C	382	Slings	"	1
"	383	Sling Removers	"	2
"	384	Containers, Inner	"	1
"	385	Containers, Outer	"	1
"	391	Bags, Water Proof	"	4
"	392	Containers, Equipment	"	4
21D	153	Cards, Playing	Sets	2
22C	860	Suits Water Proof	Ea	2
"	1,186	Whistles Aircrew	"	1
27C	1,880	Bellows Breast	"	1
"	2,035	Covers Weather Desalters	"	1
"	2,161	Desalter Apparatus	"	17
"	2187	Dinghies Type J.L. 4	"	1
"	2339	Balers	"	2
"	2364	Heliographs	"	3
"	2390	Stills Solar	"	4
27P	8	Water Canned	"	
"	25	Rations Emergency	"	
"	27	Rations Universal	"	3
"	29	Milk Condensed	"	
5J	3476	Batteries Sarah	"	1
"	3475	Transister P/U	"	1

Fig 19.3 (b) & (c). Search & rescue financial return

Trees

Latin name	Common name
Andira surinamensis.	Cabbage bark tree
Bauhinia purpurea	Camel's foot
Cassia var	Cassia
Casuarina equisetifolia	Cassia
Cocus nucifera	Coconut
Delonix regia	Flamboyante
Acacia aurieulifermis	Acacia
Meringa cleaferia	Drum stick tree
Parmentiera cerifera	Candle tree
Peltophorum pterocarpum	Copper pod
Plumeria acuminata	Frangipani
Spathodea	African tulip tree
Terminalia catappa	Indian almond
Thevetia var	Thevetia
Pisang Rajah	Banana

Shrubs

Latin name	Common name
Acalypha wilkesiana	Acalypha
Caesalpina pulchirrima	Caesalpina
Codiaeum	Crotons var
Gardenia var	Gardenia
Hibiscus R S	Hibiscus
Ixora var	Ixora
Jatropha var	Jatropha
Lagerstroemia indiea	Queen flower
Tecoma stans	Tecoma
Thumbergia erecta	Thumbergia

Fig 19.4. The trees and shrubs on Gan in 1971.

The wartime sickness records gave a clear indication of the health hazards likely to be encountered by the men of the Ship's Flag detachment who were sent to Addu Atoll in 1957 to re-commission the runway. By then Gan, having largely reverted to scrubland and marsh, provided ideal breeding conditions for the disease-carrying insects and the bacteria which had wrought such havoc amongst the troops who were based at Port T during the Second World War. Fortunately, the lessons from the wartime experiences had been well learnt and the health care regimes implemented in 1957 were so successful that the RAF medical officer was never under any real pressure even though his tented medical centre was rudimentary by normal RAF standards.

With the arrival of Squadron Leader Schofield and the establishment of RAF Gan the servicemen who were being posted to the island for a six-month tour were being subjected to pre-tour vaccinations, medical examinations and dental treatment, the latter an essential because there was no resident RAF dentist on Gan nor were there any plans to base one there. The expatriate Asians were required to submit to a similar, but less demanding, medical regime before being accepted as contract workers and brought to Gan and most of the European civilians employed at Addu Atoll had followed the advice to have a medical examination, to undergo dental treatment and to be vaccinated before embarkation even though they were under no obligation to do so. The result was that the expatriate communities on Gan were in good health when they arrived and had been well protected against the most likely diseases to be encountered at the atoll.

For the Maldivians, however, health problems were an ever-present fact of life with influenza, malaria, elephantiasis, dysentery, typhoid, scrub typhus and dengue fever all-too-common in the southern reaches of the archipelago. Malaria and scrub typhus had been endemic at the atoll before the Second World War and elephantiasis had, like typhoid and Asian flu, not been all that uncommon. But during the war the incidence of most of those diseases had reduced quite significantly as a result of the treatments and preventative measures introduced for the troops who established their bases on virtually every island in the atoll until 1945. By the end of 1946,

some time after the last of the Commonwealth forces had been withdrawn, the islanders had begun to revert to their normal way of life and by the mid-1950s they were once again suffering from a variety of diseases, most of them insect-borne. Within their homes the Maldivians were generally neat and tidy but their villages had no sanitation systems and it was common practice to defecate on the ground, particularly on or near the beaches. Fly-borne disease was thus a normal aspect of life at the atoll and was at its worst during the main fishing season when the discarded remains of the fishermen's catches would be left to rot in the sun. The swampy areas of land, the discarded rotting coconut husks and the open wells which existed in every village all added to the health hazards because they all provided breeding grounds for malaria-carrying mosquitoes. Finally there was a sizeable, and seemingly ineradicable, population of rats living in and around every village, increasing the health risk by adding the possibility of Weil's disease to the already formidable list of maladies commonly found throughout the atoll.

The men of the Ship's Flag detachment and their successors ensured that on Gan the newly-created camp areas and their surrounds were kept as clean as possible. Every day the contents of the latrines were transferred into large drums which were then transported by lorry and emptied into the open sea on the edge of the southern reef. Good housekeeping, sensible dress and hygiene regulations were complemented by the employment of a group of Maldivians whose job was to create clouds of insecticide-laden smoke throughout the camp; smoke which would carry and deposit the insecticide onto the breeding sites for the insects which swarmed across the island. Every day the Maldivians, known to everyone as the 'swinging smokies', would trail their clouds of smoke into the bushes, the buildings, the tents, the hundreds of water-collecting nooks and crannies and across the swampy areas of ground. The smokies were never expected to eliminate the mosquito population on Gan, never mind the atoll, for that was obviously impossible; their objective was to reduce the risk of disease by waging war on the insect population and in that the measures were highly successful.

During the last few months of 1957, the arrival of more servicemen and the civilians from Britain, Ceylon and Pakistan increased the workload of the RAF medical officer and his staff who, working from the tented medical centre, had a general remit to provide health care for everyone who had been brought to the island to work on the airfield construction programme. They also had to provide basic health care for the increasing number of Maldivian employees and their families and were authorised to treat any other Maldivians when time and resources permitted. Such 'goodwill' care, provided entirely at the discretion of the medical officer, had to be carefully controlled because, given the slightest encouragement, the Adduans would have been queuing outside the medical tent from dawn to dusk. October, however, brought a situation which could not be ignored by the medical staff; a severe outbreak of Asian flu, known since ancient times as the scourge of the Maldives, hit the islanders.

Believed to have been brought to the atoll from Ceylon by the crew of a trading ship, the virus spread from village to village at an alarming rate. By the middle of the month four hundred and fifty Adduans had fallen ill and the medical staff were working unstintingly to control the epidemic, partly on humanitarian grounds and partly to help prevent the disease from spreading into the Gan communities. For the islanders, usually seeking non-urgent treatment for malaria or venereal disease, the rapid provision of widespread medical aid during the epidemic provided a dramatic example of one of the major benefits of living alongside a British military base. The results of the treatment astounded them. Many Adduans could recall epidemics of this particularly virulent form of influenza and they had clear memories of the death toll in every epidemic which they could recall. But on this occasion there were no fatalities.

The medical officer, having suddenly acquired demigod status, took full advantage of the situation by issuing instructions that every Maldivian family was to observe fundamental, but previously ignored, hygiene practices. Although he could not conduct domestic inspections in the villages he was satisfied that, for at least as long as the memories of the epidemic remained, his instructions would be followed by most villagers, partly out of respect and partly out of fear that future medical treatment would be withheld from anyone reported to have ignored them.

For the next six months all seemed to be well. The Maldivian labourers continued to receive whatever medical treatment was necessary, no epidemics hit the islanders' communities and, with the relocation of the medical centre into prefabricated accommodation, the medical staff were better equipped to provide the health care required. That was just as well because more and more expatriates were living on Gan and working alongside the steadily increasing number of Maldivian employees who daily commuted to Gan from the neighbouring islands. Under those circumstances it was only to be expected that the next epidemic at the atoll would spread from the Maldivian villages into the expatriates' communities, and that it did. In the first week of May 1958 there were reports of an outbreak of dysentery on Maradu and in a matter of days there were reports of cases in virtually every village.

Over six hundred Maldivians were said to have been struck down, twenty-two fatally. By the middle of the month a number of servicemen were suffering from diarrhoea and seven cases of dysentery had been confirmed, all quickly dealt with by the medical staff who soon had the Gan outbreak under control. Coming, as it did, after six months in which there had been no significant health problems that epidemic provided a timely warning that the RAF base could easily be closed down by any one of a dozen diseases which commonly struck the atoll communities. The scare had three immediate consequences. It made everyone on the base more hygiene conscious, it increased the urgency of some of the building work and it led the Principal Medical Officer for the Far East Air Force to initiate a pestological survey of Gan.

The building work was all straightforward and by the end of May the kitchen had been rendered fly-proof, an annex had been added to the sick quarters and improvements had been made to the ablutions and latrines. But the intended pestological survey did not go well. On the 24th of the month, as the finishing touches were being put to the newly-extended sick-quarters, Flying Officer Smith arrived from Singapore to undertake the type of survey which had last been attempted by Surgeon Lieutenant Ross in November 1942. On that occasion the survey had been abandoned after Ross contracted bush typhus, developed the type of psychological disturbances which so often accompany the disease and fell foul of the fortress commander before being hospitalised. Nearly sixteen years later there was an air of *déjà vu* as Smith arrived, almost immediately reported sick and returned to Singapore after only three days on the island. The survey, so quickly abandoned, was not resurrected.

In the latter half of 1958 there were good reasons for the medical staff to feel optimistic about the general health of the expatriates for there had only been that one minor health scare to deal with during the first six months of the year. By the end of November they also had the satisfaction of working in the newly-built hutted accommodation which incorporated x-ray facilities and a basic operating theatre, completing the complex which had been started in May with the addition of the annex. Word of the improved medical facilities quickly spread and within a few weeks it was not unusual for there to be an early-morning queue of twenty or thirty Maldivians, none of them employees, all waiting outside the sick-quarters and all hoping to receive 'goodwill' treatment from the medical officers who, understandably, found it very difficult to turn their backs on anyone who was sick or injured. By the end of the year, the word had spread beyond Addu Atoll and a few badly afflicted Maldivians began to arrive from Fua Mulaku and Huvadu atoll.

The improvements to the facilities on the base were reassuring enough for the expatriates but they also had the consolation of knowing that, with the runway operational, anyone in need of hospital treatment could very rapidly be evacuated to Ceylon, a procedure which had already been used to good effect in July when a Pakistani worker had suffered a fractured skull during a fight in the Asian village where, on the 26th of the month, a Moslem holiday was being celebrated rather too vigorously by some of Costain's employees. The knowledge that the casualty evacuation procedure had been established and successfully utilised was reassuring both for the expatriates and for Gan's two medical officers, one a general practitioner and the other a surgeon, who were only too well aware of the limitations of the local service they could provide.

They, like the Ceylon-based dental officer who visited the island each month, were established to treat only the servicemen, the expatriate civilians, the Maldivians employed on the construction programme and the Adduan employees' families. But they had never stuck rigidly to that remit, partly because it was against their nature and partly because they were presented with a rare opportunity to practise amongst people who had been virtually isolated from Western medicine since the end of the Second World War. Although they had to limit the number of non-entitled Maldivians whom they could treat they had, even when working in the tented sick-quarters, justifiably built up a reputation for their sympathetic approach towards the islanders who affectionately dubbed them Medi Didi and Cutti Didi.

With the approval of Gan's station commander, Wing Commander Kent, the medical officers continued to treat as many of the non-entitled Maldivians as they could, subject to the overriding criterion that the provision of such treatment did not distract them from their primary duties. Kent's attitude to this was not shared by the Singapore-based Command staff nor by the Air Ministry staff who, convinced that such a gesture would quickly lead to an open-ended commitment, preferred to have the medical officers working strictly to the book. It took a great deal of argument and advocacy before Kent, convinced that the goodwill created by the limited provision of health care for the islanders would more than repay the cost, managed to persuade the Command staff to agree with him, winning, in the process, the concession that basic medical supplies would be provided for such care.

With the 1959 departure of most of Costain's engineers and many of their Pakistani employees the primary demands on the RAF's medical staff reduced which meant that they were able, quite legitimately, to spend more time attending to the increasing number of Maldivians who were finding their way to the medical centre. It had been obvious for some time that the doctors' largesse was attracting so many islanders that they would threaten to overwhelm the facility and by September 1959 they were close to doing just that. Would-be patients and their relatives would arrive each morning and, with infinite patience, would wait outside the medical centre for hours, hoping to be seen by a doctor but quite prepared to return the following day if necessary. Initially they would gather in a straggling semblance of a queue but as their numbers grew the queue became a crowd, hampering the medical staff and others who were going about their normal business in that area.

For the doctors this daily gathering provided clear evidence, if any were needed, that on every inhabited island at the atoll there were people suffering from medical problems which could be at least alleviated and possibly cured if the military's medical expertise were to be employed to that end. But, professionally frustrating though it might be, they had to control a situation which was in danger of getting out of hand. Solving the overcrowding problem was easy enough but they would only overcome their professional frustrations if they could simultaneously help to improve the provision of health care across the atoll. Afif Didi was the man who could help or hinder any such developments and he was very much in favour of any which would benefit the Adduans, particularly if he were to be largely in control of the arrangements; control and patronage would help him to retain his presidency.

Informed of the difficulties facing the medical staff, Afif readily agreed to the introduction of controls based upon the medical staff's assessment of the number of islanders for whom goodwill health care could be provided and he promised that any Maldivian not employed by the British would only be allowed to visit the RAF medical centre if in possession of a chit issued through the atoll secretariat. The controls were introduced within a matter of days and although the Adduans were not very happy with the quota system they were mollified when informed that Afif had also asked the medical staff to conduct a survey across the atoll, visiting every village and determining the health care needs of every community. The survey, he explained, was the first step in his long-term plan to provide every island with a healthcare clinic staffed by Adduans who had been trained by, and who worked under the control of, the RAF.

Coincidently, but seemingly as if to prove that what Afif promised, Afif delivered, a specialist team, led by a medical officer from Singapore, arrived at Gan to conduct an atoll-wide filariasis survey, starting in the village on Fedu early in October 1959.

With Gan's airfield fully operational and the construction programme on schedule, morale amongst the expatriates was running high. Then food poisoning and dysentery hit the camp. The first cases were reported on the 22nd of October and within days over one hundred personnel had been struck down. The Maldivian employees were, with very few exceptions, told not to report for work on Gan, effectively isolating the island from the rest of the atoll. Emergency wards were created by requisitioning all the accommodation near the medical centre, extra medical staff were brought in from Singapore and Ceylon, the filariasis team abandoned its survey to work in the wards and the catering staff who had been afflicted were replaced by cooks and kitchen staff flown in from Singapore. Then, at the height of the epidemic, the station's piped water supply failed. For three days everyone was dependent upon the limited supplies available from the bowsers which were driven around the camp by the RAF Regiment airmen who, although on detachment to Gan for station security duties, drove the bowsers and

worked shifts in the sick quarters, the messes and wherever else they were needed, whenever they were needed.

The passengers who staged through Gan during the epidemics were still obliged to follow the RAF's standard procedure and disembark whilst the aircraft was refuelled but, tightly controlled, they were shepherded from the aircraft steps into a coach, driven to one of the recently constructed buildings which was serving as a temporary transit lounge and kept there until it was time for them to be shepherded back onto the coach and driven to the aircraft. Aware of the epidemic on the island, they were only too happy to conform with the tight security which surrounded them throughout their brief stay. The expatriates, knowing that the Parliamentary Under-Secretary of State for Air was among the passengers staging through Gan that month, enjoyed the quiet satisfaction of believing that he, along with all the other transient VIPs, must have gone away with the impression that Gan was one of the more undesirable postings in the world.

By November the epidemics were well under control and life on Gan was very much back to normal after yet another example of the way in which such incidents could complicate the operation of the staging post and have repercussions in Singapore. Controlling such minor epidemics on Gan was not difficult because the medical staff were quick to implement established procedures throughout the expatriate population and amongst the Maldivian employees but the medical officers were well aware that typhoid and lesser diseases would never be eradicated from the atoll without the total support of the islanders and the Maldivian government and that, unfortunately, was never given. There developed instead a standard pattern of behaviour; outbreaks occurred, the Adduans asked for help, the medical staff responded, an epidemic was either prevented or controlled and everyone then waited for the next outbreak.

The filariasis survey team, its research so dramatically interrupted, resumed work in November, taking blood samples from the villagers on every island, undertaking the analyses and providing treatment. The three hundred and fifty Asian workers based on Gan were also tested and treated but only four were found to be positive, three of those with filarial disease and one with filarial infection; a negligible count compared with the five hundred and ninety-two positive results obtained from the survey of the Maldivians. The team continued to treat the expatriate Asians and the Maldivians until its departure on the 13th of July by which time four hundred and fifty-three of the islanders who had received treatment had been re-tested with negative results, leaving only one hundred and thirty-nine to receive further treatment in Gan's medical centre.

Through the early 1960s the medical facilities on Gan were continually improved with the new medical complex eventually comprising consulting rooms, outpatient facilities, wards, an operating theatre and dental facilities. It was also a period of continuing demand from the Maldivians but not from the servicemen and the civilian expatriates for they were still generally very healthy, largely as a result of the pre-embarkation examinations and vaccinations which they had been given.

Civilians and servicemen alike had been told that there was no resident dentist on Gan and, with treatment only available during the monthly visits made by an RAF dental officer from Singapore, they had been warned to make sure that any necessary treatment was completed before embarkation. That advice never varied but it was not always correct because in March 1962 an RAF dental officer was posted to Gan for a normal tour of duty. He arrived with a remit to treat the expatriates, the Maldivians who were on the British payroll and, in an emergency, any transit passenger. Rarely did he provide treatment for anyone else although he was occasionally told by the Command staff to offer his services to local Maldivian dignitaries.

After a year it was decided that the demand for dental treatment was not enough to justify the provision of a full-time dental service at the base and after March 1963 the service was generally provided by one of the Singapore-based dental officers on detachment to Gan for one week each month. Only after the withdrawal from Singapore was a dental officer's post established on Gan and even then it was only intermittently staffed with interim cover provided by officers briefly detached from Hong Kong.

As news of the improved medical facilities on Gan spread across the region and as the reputation of the staff grew, requests for help in emergencies came from as far afield as Mauritius and from ships traversing the Indian Ocean. The requests were made in the knowledge that the Gan-based Shackleton could deliver medical supplies whenever and wherever they were needed and the station's marine craft launch could transport medical staff and equipment to rendezvous with ships some two or three hundred miles away from Addu Atoll. The result was that the medical officers and their staff, already practising in what was arguably the most professionally interesting station medical centre in the RAF, were occasionally faced with urgent and unusual requests for help.

The provision, by parachute-drop from a Shackleton, of much needed medical supplies was generally straightforward enough as was proved in June 1961 when a supply of antibiotics, needed to combat an outbreak of enteric fever, was dropped at Rodriguez, some three hundred and fifty miles west of Mauritius where the aircraft refuelled before returning to Gan.

Many such humanitarian flights were carried out over the years including one, in August 1961, to Malé Atoll where a typhoid outbreak was threatening to develop into an epidemic. On being informed that there was apparently a shortage of vaccine in the capital, the United Kingdom's High Commissioner in Colombo arranged for a supply to be dropped at Hulule by the Gan-based Shackleton. The drop was trouble free, the vaccine was collected and the Maldivian Prime Minister wrote a letter of appreciation to the High Commissioner, an unheard-of gesture in view of the sour inter-governmental relations at that time.

Such operations came to be regarded as rather routine events which was certainly not a description which could be applied to the response, in January 1962, to an emergency signal from Mauritius requesting help for a woman on Diego Garcia. Her plight was desperate; unless she could be given a blood transfusion she was almost certain to die. Within hours of the request reaching Gan a Shackleton had dropped a transfusion kit and a supply of rhesus negative blood, given by four donor servicemen, their crucial contributions to the mercy-mission providing a human-interest story for the RAF News. Those four servicemen were not the only newsworthy blood donors from Gan; some four and a half years later the RAF News dubbed the station's two medical officers 'the Good Samaritans of Gan', reporting how they had undoubtedly saved the life of a Maldivian woman who had been brought from Fedu to Gan in the middle of the night. She had given birth some four hours previously, was in great pain, weak from loss of blood and in need of an operation which could not be performed until she had been given a blood transfusion. After the operation she needed a second transfusion before leaving the theatre and a third transfusion after being transferred to the ward. But at that stage the only donors immediately available were the two doctors who consequently bled each other to provide the two pints which the woman needed. Two days later she was allowed to return home, undoubtedly owing her life to the two officers.

The good health of the servicemen and the civilians who had been brought to the atoll meant that they made only limited demands on the medical service, primarily seeking treatment for workplace or sportsfield accidents and for minor illnesses. In the early 1960s the medical officers were spending most of their time providing health care for Maldivians, establishing environmental health controls and reacting to occasional epidemics. Their workload was heavy but manageable throughout Afif Didi's reign as the so-called president of the United Suvadive Islands because he ensured that the quota system, introduced to control the number of Maldivians arriving at the medical centre each day, was properly applied. But when he left the atoll and settled in the Seychelles the controls were relaxed and eventually the system fell into disuse. Inevitably an increasing number of Maldivians then sought medical treatment, controls and quotas had to be reintroduced with the help of the then atoll chief and the cycle started all over again with declining controls followed by increasing demand and reintroduced quotas *ad infinitum* over the years.

What did happen during the 1960s was an increase in the number of admissions and operations. Even though the vast majority of the Maldivians who received treatment at the medical centre did so as outpatients, a significant number was admitted and each of those, in accordance with the Maldivian culture, was likely to be accompanied by a healthy relative who would settle into the medical centre until the in-patient was discharged. As a result the occupants of the so-called Maldivian wards, one for women and one for men, comprised the sick or injured in the beds and healthy wives, husbands or parents who would sleep on the floor in the spaces below the bedsprings.

By 1964, the year following Afif Didi's departure, the quota controls had all but been abandoned by the atoll chief and, as the number of Maldivian patients grew, the goodwill of the medical staff was stretched almost to breaking point. At the end of a year when no more than a thousand Adduans had been employed on Gan the statistics (Fig 20.1) clearly showed the extent of the problem but it was several months before the atoll chief could be persuaded to reintroduce quota controls.

The one aspect of the medical officers' role which could never be forgotten, even though everyone hoped that it would never have to be put into practice, was the treatment of aircraft crash survivors, the certification of the dead and the subsequent care and disposal of the bodies. Contingency plans for dealing with such a situation had been drawn up after the Hastings crash in March 1960 and occasional practices had been held but the medical staff were only too well aware that, even with the improved facilities, the station was ill-equipped to cope with the number of injured or dead should there be a major accident involving a fully-laden passenger aircraft. It would not be too difficult to set up temporary wards, akin to those in a field hospital, to supplement the medical centre facilities and, provided there was no wreckage blocking Gan's runway, emergency support staff and equipment could be flown in from Singapore in a matter of hours. But without such assistance, those attending to the injured would face severe problems whilst those attempting to care for a large number of dead would find their job almost impossible because of the lack of facilities and resources on the island.

Repatriation of more than three bodies would be impossible until suitable coffins could be manufactured or flown in to Gan to supplement the three which were normally held in the medical centre. Multiple interments on the island were not possible even though many of the Indian Army soldiers who had died at Addu Atoll during the Second World War had been buried on Gan and the disused Maldivian graveyard on the island provided evidence of numerous earlier burials. But the small cemetery near Gan's south-eastern shore was rarely used for fear of contaminating the island's water supply and in the tropical climate bodies not buried at sea or flown home in a suitably sealed coffin would obviously have to be refrigerated. Complicating the situation was the fact that the station's mortuary was not large enough to hold more than six bodies and any stored elsewhere could not easily be kept cold enough even by packing them in ice in one of the few rather modestly air-conditioned buildings.

The whole situation was unsatisfactory but it was not seriously addressed by the Far East Air Force Command staff whose approach was to leave the matter in the hands of the station commander. Given that there had already been several aircraft accidents at Gan that left successive station commanders with the worrying possibility that a fully laden passenger aircraft might crash and block the runway, leaving the ill-equipped station staff to deal with the tragedy as best they could.

Inevitably, there were deaths amongst the expatriates but the tragedies, fortunately rare, came singly. When they did occur, the station staff had to determine the cause of death so that a death certificate could be issued, contact the next of kin to ascertain their wishes for the funeral and, often the most problematical, arrange repatriation or an appropriate local funeral. In spite of the general policy that there were to be no more burials on the island the small cemetery near the south-eastern shoreline was used for four interments; in 1958 for Costain's murdered employee, in 1963 for the burial of a deceased Chinese steward from the Royal Fleet Auxiliary ship Fort Langley, and for two Pakistanis who had died of natural causes, one in 1964 and one late on Christmas day in 1973.

Among the station diary entries for November 1974 there is a reference to the death of a works department employee, who, whilst working on a barge on the marine craft unit slipway, fell backwards and fractured his skull. He later died in the station's medical centre and his body was repatriated to England. It seems, from the station records that he was the only expatriate European civilian to die on Gan. In comparison, five servicemen died at the atoll during Gan's nineteen-year lifetime; a Flight Sergeant who died in 1966 from the injuries he received after falling from a moving bus, a Flying Officer who was electrocuted in 1970, a Chief Technician who committed suicide in 1971, a visiting Sergeant who had a heart attack whilst out walking on the reef in 1973 and a catering squadron Sergeant who died after a heart attack in 1975. In accordance with the wishes of the deceased's next of kin, all were repatriated except the Flight Sergeant who was buried at sea in what was probably the only peacetime occasion when such a ceremony had been conducted at an RAF station.

Every death was a tragedy but one which was more poignant than any other was that of a serviceman's young wife who was being medically evacuated from Singapore to England in 1971 but died on board the aircraft as it was on the final approach to Gan. The aircraft was on a normal refuelling stop and was expected to be on the ground for no more than an hour, giving the station commander very little time to unravel the complex regulations relating to the death and the repatriation of the deceased. The preferred solution was to leave the young woman on board the aircraft which was headed for England but with no suitable refrigeration facility on board that was not an option for such a long flight unless a sealed coffin was available and there was no time to prepare one of those. Gan's emergency telephone link enabled Wing Commander Gee to seek the opinion of that Friday night's duty officer at Air Support Command Headquarters whose advice was in line with the provisional plan, already formed by the station

commander, which was to transfer the young woman's body into Gan's mortuary and accommodate the bereaved husband on the base until a death certificate had been issued and the deceased could be repatriated in a sealed coffin. In the event, the husband elected to continue on the flight to England, there to await the repatriation of his wife's body.

Whenever an expatriate died on Gan the senior medical officer was required to issue a death certificate. Without that, a burial ceremony could not be performed nor could a body be despatched from the atoll. If there was no doubt about the cause of death, there was no problem issuing such a certificate and the remaining difficulties were organisational, not legal or medical. But if the cause of death was not obvious a post mortem was required and that created complications. The likely dilemmas were brought to the attention of the Command staff on numerous occasions but a succession of staff officers at the Far East Air Force, at Air Support Command, at Strike Command and at the Near East Air Force Headquarters did not wish to address the issue. When Group Captain Whitlock, Gan's station commander for most of 1973, raised the matter with the Cyprus-based staff he was informed that nobody had died at Gan for at least ten years, which was patently untrue.

He must have had a premonition when he raised the issue because partway through his tour a visiting non-commissioned officer collapsed whilst out walking on the reef and was declared dead on arrival at the station's medical centre. It was an occasion when there was some doubt about the cause of death and that meant that a post mortem had to be performed. As the senior medical officer explained to Whitlock, he was not qualified to conduct a post-mortem which, in any case, was not his job. Compounding the situation was the fact that the incident occurred at a weekend which meant that enquiries to the Near East Air Force Headquarters had to be dealt with by the duty staff who were understandably reluctant to make decisions on a matter which was obviously outside their experience and was likely to involve them in some subsequent inquiry into the legality of any actions taken. A flurry of signals between Gan and the Headquarters eventually resulted in a decision from Cyprus to the effect that '... *if the senior medical officer believes that the cause of death was a heart attack, issue a death certificate on that basis*'. He did that and, in accordance with the wishes of the next of kin, the deceased was repatriated.

Deaths among the expatriates were so rare that most of the medical officers who served on Gan never encountered the problems associated with such tragedies; for them, the daily round was filled with consultations, some surgical operations, public health matters, the occasional epidemic and, for the senior medical officer, a seemingly interminable battle against the political machinations of the atoll chief. It was incredibly frustrating for the medical staff to spend their time treating so many Maldivians whose illnesses could have been avoided if the atoll chief had been prepared to follow the example set by Afif Didi and allowed the RAF-employed hygiene teams to work on all the inhabited islands of the atoll. But successive chiefs, ever conscious of the political ramifications of agreeing to such an arrangement, would not allow any non-Maldivians to work in the villages, even though their work would so obviously benefit all the Adduan communities.

The result was predictable.

In May 1965 an outbreak of malaria and infective hepatitis on the islands was so serious that it seemed to be only a matter of time before some islanders died. The senior medical officer, anxious to prevent an epidemic which could threaten the operation of the RAF base, offered to employ the Maldivian villagers on hygiene duties at a fair rate of pay but when the Maldivian Minister of Health learnt that the proposal would involve the presence of European supervisors in the Adduan villages he vetoed the plan. By good fortune the epidemic caused fewer deaths among the villagers than had been feared and frequent health checks of the Maldivians employed on the military sites helped to prevent the diseases from spreading into the expatriate community. Then, in October, typhoid broke out among the Adduans, effectively forcing the Maldivian Minister of Health to permit the RAF's medical staff to visit the various villages in the atoll.

On the 18th of that month the senior medical officer confirmed four cases of typhoid among the Maldivians on Hitaddu. The Maldivian Minister of Health, appraised by the atoll chief of the seriousness of the situation, had little choice but to give permission for an RAF medical team to visit any of the villages to treat the sick and to supervise the environmental spraying programme. The team worked in the villages through November 1965, brought the outbreak under control and reinforced the message that, if given permission to work within the local communities, the hygiene teams could virtually guarantee to prevent such epidemics. The message was ignored.

Local and national politics continued to bedevil the provision of preventative health care for the Adduans throughout the following year with one issue, the use of sterilisation powder in the village wells, becoming the focus for the political manoeuvring described in chapter XIV and the frustrations referred to on page 213.

As Maldivians continued to arrive at the medical centre day after day the only good news for the medical staff was that the re-introduced quota system, controlled by the atoll committee, was generally working well, allowing the medical officers to provide treatment for around a thousand Maldivians each month; a figure which was manageable provided there were no unexpected demands on their services from their primary patient groups.

As always, many of the Maldivians' health problems stemmed from the unhygienic environments in their villages but in spite of all the senior medical officer's efforts to persuade the islanders to adopt simple hygienic practices in their villages they largely ignored him except when they were facing the immediate threat of an epidemic, as they were in February 1966 and again in September 1967. The typhoid outbreak in 1966, referred to on page 212 was bedevilled by political manoeuvring but when the villagers on Hitaddu faced another epidemic in September 1967 the Maldivian politicians were only involved to the extent that they gave the atoll chief permission to work as closely as necessary with the medical staff who quickly confirmed that three villagers had typhoid.

The by-now-familiar procedures, based upon the World Health Organisation's reports from previous years, were immediately implemented. Isolation wards were prepared in the medical centre and in the Asian village for any expatriates who might be affected. All Hitadduans were sent home with instructions to report to Gan's medical centre the following day. The health records of all food handlers were checked and the staff re-immunised as necessary. In all areas in which food was handled, police guards were set up at the entrances and exits and ordered to ensure that everyone who went into those areas observed the hygiene regulations. Failure to do so had always been a disciplinary offence but with the threat of a typhoid epidemic on Gan such failure would be treated for more seriously; for a Maldivian employee it merited instant dismissal.

This latest outbreak came shortly after the renovation of the so-called Maldivian hotel, a building which had been occasionally used as an isolation ward during previous epidemics but which had been closed immediately after the 1965 typhoid outbreak and subsequently condemned by the works engineers, on the grounds that it needed rewiring, and by the senior medical officer who described it as a health hazard. In May 1967 the decrepit kadjan roof had been replaced by corrugated metal, the building rewired, refurbished and brought back into daily use only to be almost immediately requisitioned to provide isolation ward facilities for those Maldivians found, or even suspected, to be suffering from typhoid.

Throughout the operation the atoll chief had been kept informed of everything the medical officers were doing and he, in his sudden new-found spirit of co-operation on health matters, helped to trace all those Adduans who had recently been in contact with the isolated patients. With his help, a selective immunisation programme was implemented, adding to the general feeling that this latest outbreak was over and done with.

That feeling didn't last long because within a month there was another typhoid scare among the Maldivians with five suspected cases and one confirmed case from Fedu. The immunisation programme, however, had proved its worth because only five cases were confirmed and only two deaths recorded; one being that of a two-year-old Maldivian girl who had died in the Maldivian hotel. By December, when no further cases had been confirmed, the outbreak was deemed to be over, the Maldivian hotel reverted to its normal function and a typhoid epidemic on Gan had been averted.

The medical staff's sustained contribution to the improved health care of the Adduans together with the successful containment and treatment of the 1965 and 1967 outbreaks of typhoid at the atoll was officially recognised when Gan was awarded the Wilkinson Sword for Peace for 1967. In the Cutlers' Hall in London on the 25th of June 1968 the chairman of Wilkinson Sword Ltd presided over the ceremony at which Dennis Healey presented the sword to Wing Commander Mullineaux who was accompanied by Wing Commander Hourston, Gan's senior medical officer in 1967. The citation accompanying the award paid tribute to the efforts of all the servicemen on Gan during the typhoid outbreaks, adding:

'The brunt of the work involved in combating the outbreak fell upon the laboratory staff who at one time performed four thousand eight hundred and fifty tests in a month; on three state registered nurses who had responsibility for the day-to-day care of cases and suspects, inoculations

and normal duties which continued unabated; and the hygiene section, which was required to double its vigilance and efforts in all aspects of hygiene. All ranks and individuals performed their tasks without fuss or complaint.'

In making the presentation, Healey was able to comment on the fact that he had recently been Wing Commander Mullineaux' guest on Gan, a reference to his overnight stay on the island when, with a large entourage which included the Chief of the Defence Staff, he had staged through the base en route to the five-power conference in Kuala Lumpur, arriving at Gan on the 8th, stopping overnight and leaving on the 9th. The timing of that visit had been fortuitous for Healey, because it gave him the opportunity to learn something of the local health-care problems and the services provided by the RAF's medical staff.

If variety is the spice of life, the medical staff on Gan could have had few complaints in 1968 for, apart from the wide-ranging ailments brought to their attention by the Maldivians, they often found themselves dealing with extraordinary problems, either on the base, as was the case when they diagnosed an advanced case of tuberculosis of the spine in a young Maldivian boy, or at sea as happened in July when they responded to an urgent request to attend to a seriously injured Pakistani seaman on board the SS Mahronda.

The case of the seven-year-old Maldivian boy was a success story which deservedly featured in the RAF News the following month. When the senior medical officer made the diagnosis he knew that without proper treatment the boy faced a short life as a hunchback. The necessary drugs were available but prolonged immobilisation was an essential part of the treatment and that presented a challenge for the staff because no suitable equipment was available. Whilst the medical officers designed and constructed a plaster jacket which could keep the boy's spine permanently extended one of their state registered nurses designed a frame to support the patient in a way which would allow him to be nursed and turned without any spinal movement. The frame was subsequently manufactured in the station's general engineering workshop where the design was modified slightly after suggestions by the carpenter and the fitters, the co-operative venture providing yet another example of the way in which the Gan expatriates would work with each other to prove that on Gan, 'anything is possible'.

The adventure at sea occurred in July when the captain of the S S Mahronda, at that time almost three hundred miles to the south-west of Addu Atoll, called for help. The airmen from Gan's marine craft unit immediately prepared the search and rescue launch for sea and within an hour they were ferrying Gan's surgeon and two medical orderlies out to the ship which, by then, was headed for Addu Atoll. A rendezvous took place some two hundred miles from Gan and after the injured seaman had been examined by Gan's surgeon he was, with some difficulty, transferred from the ship into the launch which was riding the choppy waters. The patient was brought back to Gan where the surgeon, convinced that the injuries could best be treated in a major hospital, arranged for the seaman to be flown to Britain on board a casualty evacuation flight.

The 11th of November 1968, the date on which the Maldivians abandoned their monarchy and reverted to a republic, marked the beginning of a welcome change in the attitude of the Maldivian government towards the provision of health care for the Adduans. A spirit of friendship and cooperation developed and although the politics of health care did not disappear overnight, relationships continued to improve year after year, enabling Gan's medical staff to help the Adduans, and indirectly to reduce the risk of an epidemic on the base, more during the 1970s than at any time since the departure of Afif Didi.

Providing help, however, did not guarantee any great measure of success because the Adduans' lifestyle and the island environment tended to legislate against any dramatic improvements in the general health of the indigenous population. Compounding the situation was the fact that the population of the atoll was increasing more rapidly than at any time in living memory; the Foreign and Commonwealth Office annual review of the Maldives gave the 1971 population of Addu Atoll as thirteen thousand one hundred and forty-nine with five thousand nine hundred and twenty-two islanders living on Hitaddu, two thousand nine hundred and thirty on Midu, two thousand one hundred and twenty-nine on Maradu and two thousand one hundred and sixty-eight on Fedu.

With the customary lack of sanitation on the islands and the Maldivians' general disregard for basic hygiene, disease was inevitable and was certain to spread more rapidly as the population increased. But the islanders seemed to be content to rely upon the RAF's medical staff to deal with any epidemic as it occurred; for them, the answer to their prayers was treatment, not prevention. For the medical staff there was the constant worrying thought that epidemics far worse than the 1959 outbreak of dysentery or the 1967 typhoid outbreak could so easily spread to Gan, infect transit passengers and be carried into some distant communities. Although that possibility was ever-present, their worries faded as the months went by because the atoll chief became amenable to the presence of Gan's hygiene teams in the Adduan villages and openly appreciative of the service given to the islanders, even to the extent of thanking the senior medical officer for the treatment of two islanders in particular; one a tragic case, the other a success story.

The tragedy involved a young Maldivian man who had been so severely burnt that the medical officers could only wonder how he had survived. He was brought to the medical centre where he was isolated in a sterile environment and nursed through the shock until he was considered strong enough to cope with the first of many skin grafts. As the weeks ran into months and the operations continued the medical staff had high hopes that he would make a full recovery but he suddenly seemed to lose heart and although his skin grafts remained clear of infection he became deeply depressed and died.

The success story started with a bitter disappointment for a young Maldivian boy, aged about twelve, who had extraneous bone growth around and below both knees on the inside of his legs, splaying his lower limbs and preventing him from walking normally. Like any Maldivian with severe medical problems, he faced a bleak future at the atoll unless the RAF medical services could come to his rescue. He was examined in the medical centre where, like many other islanders, he was told that his problems were so severe that he required major surgery beyond the skills of the incumbent surgeon on Gan. Nevertheless, details of his condition were, as was usual in such cases, carefully recorded on the off chance that surgery might be possible sometime in the future. Later that year an unexpected opportunity arose; an orthopaedic surgeon who was temporarily employed in Gan's medical centre was able to operate on the youngster who was walking about in a matter of weeks and running around within three months.

The atoll chief's new-found spirit of cooperation had always been susceptible to the general political climate in Malé and to his interpretation of local events and perceived slights but in September 1971, a mere four months after the newly re-elected chief returned from his post-election briefing in Malé, that susceptibility seemed to have become a thing of the past. Lifting the last embargo, he welcomed smallpox vaccination teams into all the villages. With ninety per cent of the villagers vaccinated during the first visits and arrangements made for the remainder to be seen the following month, the medical staff were confident that, whatever else was on the horizon, a smallpox epidemic was most unlikely.

The easier relationships could hardly have come at a better time; in November 1971 three typhoid cases had been diagnosed on Maradu and the chief asked for help to prevent yet another epidemic. Quite remarkably, his request was followed by another from Malé asking for a full immunisation programme for the Adduan villagers. Gan's medical staff would have been only too happy to do all that was asked of them but they could not mount such a programme without approval from the Air Support Command staff and when that approval was sought it was given subject to the Maldivian government paying thirteen hundred pounds to cover the cost of the vaccines. The Maldivian government declined to pay that and an appeal from the British High Commissioner in Colombo to the Overseas Development Officer to fund most, if not all, of the programme was to no avail. The only Maldivians given immunisation were those employed on Gan. By December there were six confirmed cases of typhoid on the atoll, and for the first time, the planned Christmas party and fireworks display for the Adduan children was cancelled, the toys being given to the atoll chief for distribution.

There was, however, one development which the chief would never accept. In spite of all the arguments in favour of the establishment of a Maldivian-run clinic on each of the inhabited islands at the atoll and in spite of the obvious benefits which would come from having such clinics staffed by selected villagers who had been trained by the RAF, he was not prepared to seek his government's approval for such a scheme and he would never dare to agree to the suggestion on his own initiative.

For the final five years of the station's operational life the expatriate community continued to make few demands upon the medical officers whilst for the Adduans it was the period when they benefited most from the presence of the RAF's medical services because the Maldivian government condoned, if not actually encouraged, the cautious cooperation practised by the atoll chief. The senior medical officer and the hygienists were invited to make regular visits to the atoll villages and were welcomed whenever they did so. The villagers gradually began to adopt a more responsible attitude towards the health hazards in their communities and although occasional outbreaks of typhoid did occur, they were quickly controlled as a result of the hygienists' frequent visits. Maldivians continued to visit the station's medical centre for consultations, surgical operations, maternity deliveries, laboratory tests and outpatient treatments given by the RAF staff and the Maldivians under the supervision of Don Tutu, the senior Maldivian dresser.

Although the number of civilians who attended Gan's medical centre during 1974 was not as high as in 1964, the figures given by Brynmor John in a written parliamentary answer on the 1st of December 1975 clearly show the scale of the service provided on Gan. The Ministry of Defence civilians, a group which included the expatriate Pakistanis, accounted for only two hundred and fifty-nine consultations and four hundred and eleven treatments, including eighteen as in-patients. The Maldivians, however, accounted for fourteen thousand seven hundred and fifty-five consultations, and eighteen thousand two hundred and eighty-five treatments including one thousand one hundred and forty as in-patients.

When, at the end of 1974, it was announced that the military base on Gan was to be abandoned the Adduans clung to the hope that the military withdrawal would not occur for several years. But with the 1975 confirmation that the British would depart by the end of March 1976 their hopes were dashed and they then became anxious to make the most of what little time there was left before the RAF's medical services were withdrawn. Predictably, more Maldivians availed themselves of the medical centre's facilities during that last calendar year on Gan than at any time since 1957.

As always, some of the so-called routine consultations and treatments were often anything but routine and the medical staff never ceased to be surprised by some of the problems which the Maldivians brought to the centre. The demands upon their expertise did not, of course, end there for they continued to be available for search and rescue mercy missions in the region, justifiably featuring in the RAF News again in March 1975 as a result of their response to an SOS from the Motor Vessel Bycle, a freighter which, *en route* from Bremerhavan to Taiwan, had on board a seriously ill seaman who was in need of urgent medical treatment.

The collection of the seaman and his eventual transfer to Gan's medical centre became a military operation involving an RAF Argosy which had located the freighter and was in radio contact with Gan's rescue coordination centre, helping to guide the station's search and rescue launch to a rendezvous with the ship. The launch intercepted the Bycle some one hundred miles from Gan and although the heavy seas prevented the transfer of the seriously ill man from the freighter to the launch, Gan's medical officer and one of the station's state registered nurses managed to board the ship and attend to the seaman. The freighter was then headed for Addu Atoll and as soon as it heaved to in the calm waters of the lagoon the sick man was transferred to the marine craft unit pinnace and thence by ambulance to the medical centre where he received emergency treatment which enabled him to make a full recovery.

By the end of 1975 the Adduans and the RAF's medical staff were becoming concerned about the post-withdrawal provision of medical services at the atoll. Quite apart from the fact that the islanders had become used to the standard of medical care provided on Gan there were some one hundred and twenty of them who were dependent upon regular medication, some of them suffering from diabetes, some with heart disease and a few with epilepsy; they were all living month-to-month on life-saving drugs supplied by the RAF. Yet, at the end of the year, no doctor had been recruited to provide health care at the atoll after the RAF withdrawal and the staff at the Ministry for Overseas Development seemed to be dragging their heels, much to the concern of the Ministry of Defence staff who were determined not to have any involvement with the Adduans after the military withdrawal.

The Adduans' fears were not to be allayed until the last week in January 1976 when Group Captain Edwards was informed that the Ministry for Overseas Development would recruit the necessary medical staff and arrange for them to be in post before the end of March.

The Ministry staff had cut things rather fine but, as promised, they did recruit a surgeon and a state registered nurse, arranging for them to run the medical services at the atoll on a one-year contract. Dr Roger Wolstenholme and Peta his wife, who was a state registered nurse, arrived on the 20th of March, much to the relief of the Adduans who felt that they had been granted a last minute reprieve.

Given that the doctor and his wife would be the only medically qualified practitioners in the southern reaches of the archipelago, would be running the only Western-style medical centre in that part of the world and would be expected to provide healthcare for any Maldivian who needed it, their arrival was much closer to the final withdrawal date than was desirable. As they were adjusting to life at the atoll, taking over the medical centre, reading case notes, examining patients and trying to familiarise themselves with their multi-island bailiwick the RAF staff were packing their bags.

On the 29th of March the last contingent of servicemen boarded the landing ship logistics Sir Percival, leaving the two practitioners with a fully-equipped medical centre, thirteen thousand local patients and a bailiwick which extended across the southern islands of the archipelago. They were left with no illusions about the potential demand for their services; even a brief study of the medical centre's records for the past year showed that they were unlikely to have much time to relax on their tropical island over the next twelve months. From April 1975 until the end of January 1976, nine thousand six hundred and six islanders had visited the medical centre and by the end of February the figure was up to nine thousand eight hundred and fifty-four, of which only one thousand six hundred and three had actually been entitled to use the services provided by the RAF.

personnel	RAF and entitled non-Maldivians	Maldivians
consultations	3217	14337
outpatient treatments	4561	21900
admissions	369	681
x-rays	286	2966
surgery	60	511
laboratory examinations		8897

Fig 20.1 RAF Gan medical centre statistics for 1964.

Diversions and Excursions

The Gan calendar

Gan was undoubtedly a place where time would drag for any individual who did not take the opportunity to enjoy any of the unique experiences available at the atoll. But there were airmen who regarded a tour on Gan as a custodial sentence and chose inactivity as a way of passing their time, marking off their days on a wall calendar. The 'countdown convicts', as they became known, featured in a variety of jokes and lifestyle stories, some of which were printed, duplicated and circulated, including the countdown diary comprising three hundred and sixty-five cryptic comments, with one extra for those unlucky enough to spend a leap year on the island (Fig 21.1).

For those whose sole focus was the countdown to the day they could bid farewell to Gan, regular flight schedules and the bank holiday festivals served to measure the passage of time in a far more obvious way than did the passing of the seasons because on Gan the terms 'winter' and 'summer' are meaningless. The daytime and night-time temperatures vary but little throughout the year and there is no significant change in the daylight hours from one month to another; only the students of the rainfall figures, of the slight variation in the location of the setting sun and in the appearance of the seed pods on the deciduous trees which carry green leaves throughout the year were able to use natural phenomena as a guide to the seasons.

Tropical island attractions.

For the first of the servicemen to be posted to Gan, the short six-month tour and the prospect of a mid-tour break in Ceylon meant that the lack of off-duty diversions was of no great significance; most of them were content to relax on their tropical island during their limited free time, to get away from their work, their tents, their huts or their colleagues, and to savour the novelty of the environment, either by beachcombing, by strolling in those parts of the island which were not out of bounds, by fishing or by swimming in the lagoon where the water remained comfortably warm throughout the year. Few of them had ever seen a tropical island, let alone lived on one, and over the course of the year most of them enjoyed many hours swimming and admiring the exotic marine life which lived in and around the magnificent coral reefs. While television audiences in Britain were being introduced to the underwater world of Hans and Lotte Hass in their series 'Diving to Adventure', the newcomers to Addu Atoll were experiencing at first hand the pleasures and the minor risks of snorkelling and scuba diving along Gan's northern shore.

The risks were real enough but most of them could easily be avoided or reduced. The most obvious one, that of severe sunburn, was largely ignored until a few expatriates needed medical treatment after being unwise enough to relax in the lagoon shallows during their two-hour mid-day break and discovering that the mid-day sun was indeed something to be avoided by anyone who was not fully acclimatised. Less obvious was the danger posed by the coral but those who rubbed against it whilst swimming or were foolish enough to go barefoot into the shallows, where razor-sharp coral proliferated, quickly learnt that calcareous splinters could be painful, that the wounds would take a long time to heal in a climate which caused most people to perspire throughout the day and that the scrape would, in many cases, turn septic.

Even without the coral there was good reason for not paddling barefoot in the shallows: the warm waters of the Indian Ocean play host to a remarkable variety of venomous fish, some of which were certain to be found in the lagoon. There was thus the slight risk of painful, serious, or even fatal, poisoning as a result of being stung or impaled by the spines which feature so prominently in the defensive armoury of several species of tropical fish and which are as effective as hypodermic syringes when delivering a poisonous injection.

Conversely, the threat posed by the barracudas and the few sharks which frequented the lagoon was not as great as many imagined and could be virtually eliminated by the simple expedient of never swimming or diving alone or by continually keeping a wary eye open for such unwelcome company. Even then there was one far-from-obvious risk regardless of the time of day. A powerful current traversed the lagoon, flowing between the islands of Gan and Fedu, running almost parallel to the north shore of Gan and out into the Indian Ocean through the Gan gap. A swimmer could only avoid being sucked out of the lagoon if, when first caught at the edge of the current, he struck out for the shore, did not panic and was happy to land a few hundred yards east of the Gan-Fedu gap. Even the strongest swimmer could not make headway against the central current which often ran fast enough to carry a twelve-man dhoni off course in spite of the oarsmen's frantic rowing.

Swimming apart, the lagoon provided an opportunity for any fisherman to practise his skills in a spectacular location, enjoying his sport and supplementing the military rations which made up the servicemen's diet in 1957. The old stone piers in the Gan-Fedu gap, the sole remnants of the wartime bridge, provided ideal seating for rod-and-line fishing (Fig 21.2), an activity which many of the airmen found uninteresting, believing that it lacked the excitement which could be found among the coral outcrops which they had explored whilst snorkelling. Progressing to scuba diving, they added the excitement of spear fishing to their expeditions without fully appreciating the associated risks. Handled correctly, their spear-guns were no more dangerous than firearms but the death throes of a speared fish were quite likely to attract predators, particularly the sharks which, never very far away, were occasionally lured into the lagoon by the big-game fishermen who developed their own technique for hooking and landing them. They would bait a large hook which they had attached, by cable, to one or two sealed, floating, and loosely captive forty-gallon oil drums. Once hooked, a shark would either escape by biting through the cable or would struggle to the point of exhaustion when it could be easily landed, killed and added to the dinner menu.

Eventually the practice was banned, as was spear fishing, and the Maldivians and the crews of visiting ships were requested not to dispose of offal by throwing it into the lagoon. As a result, sharks became less frequent visitors with many servicemen spending a year at the atoll without ever setting eyes on one. Less exciting, but far more desirable, was the occasional capture of a large Indian Ocean turtle. Those docile creatures tended to be infrequent visitors to the lagoon and were highly prized both by the servicemen and by the Maldivians for they were not only good to eat, they provided a large, valuable turtle shell from which the local craftsmen could produce a variety of hand-carved curios, many of which could be sold to the expatriates on Gan who would pay far higher prices than would the middlemen from Malé. As the number of expatriates grew that local market began, illicitly, to trickle Sterling currency into the Maldivian community, a trend which was destined to grow as the islanders applied their craftsmanship and their ingenuity to the production of a range of curios designed to attract the interest of newcomers to their atoll.

The cinemas

The exotic location, the beaches and the lagoon inevitably palled when they were the only diversions and it was obvious that the morale of those airmen posted to Gan for twelve months was bound to suffer unless active leisure facilities became available; they could hardly spend a year just relaxing throughout their off-duty time on the island. There was a limited range of outdoor activities but there were few, if any, wet-weather leisure facilities on Gan in 1957 which meant that continual rain for a few days was enough to lower the expatriates' morale as they sheltered in their tents and huts. Even during fine weather the outdoor facilities could not be fully utilised because sunset, at around six p.m. every day of the year, signalled the beginning of the long evening when the only outdoor facilities were the open-air cinemas in the European and Asian camps where, weather permitting, two current-release films were shown each week.

Gan's Astra cinema was opened in the late 1950s but in the European camp outdoor cinema screens were retained in the grounds of the senior messes where the mess members would gather twice a week to watch the same current-release films which had been hired from the Services' Kinema Corporation and had already been shown in the Astra. The films were the same but the atmosphere was different. In the cinema the environment could temporarily persuade the customers that they were in a camp cinema back home until, that is, the sound track was rendered inaudible by the torrential rain on the corrugated iron roof. The audience in the Astra also had a tendency to be quite participative whereas the mess audiences were inclined to sit back in their easy chairs and enjoy a beer or two whilst watching the film.

Regardless of which film was being shown, mess members tended to gravitate towards their open-air cinema simply because it was one of the few after-dinner activities which provided a relaxing diversion at the end of a tiring day. Unlike the cinema-goers who were cocooned in the Astra, those who watched the films on the open-air screens in the mess grounds invariable saw them against a backdrop of silhouetted palm trees and a moon bright enough to cast dark shadows; it was just not possible, under those conditions, for the members of the audience to imagine that they were back home.

The first sports facilities

Even during the early labour-filled days of 1957 there were some men who had the energy and the enthusiasm, regardless of the tropical climate, to take part in the various impromptu ball games which would occur whenever a few like-minded men found themselves at a loose end. On Gan, the quality of the so-called pitches or courts for those impromptu games left much to be desired because they had to be created either on a dusty coral surface or on a patch of ground-hugging weeds. Even the Adduans, who would occasionally field a football team to play the expatriates, played their matches on the local coral-surfaced pitches.

By November 1957, when the population of servicemen and expatriate civilians had grown to over four hundred, Gan's station commander was becoming increasingly concerned about the limited leisure-time facilities. They would suffice whilst the men were preoccupied with the creation and operation of a military base but they would obviously be inadequate once the newcomers had settled in. Everyone was aware that the operational works programme took priority over all else and that the provision of under-cover leisure facilities would have to wait until the essential ancillary buildings for the airfield had been erected but it was obvious that unless some such facilities were to be included on the list of works to be started within the next two months, morale would suffer and the overall efficiency of the construction workers would decline.

By the end of the year Wing Commander Schofield had reached an agreement with the district works officer over the use of labour to improve the off-duty amenities and during the first few weeks of 1958, some ground was being cleared ready for the first of the sports pitches to be laid. The work was started during Schofield's tour but it was left to his successor to bring the plans to fruition.

The visiting entertainers

As if to prove that some under-cover leisure facilities were sorely needed on Gan, rain fell on eighteen days during June 1958, the month when Wing Commander Schofield handed over to Wing Commander Kent. Given such atrocious weather it was obviously a month when off-duty diversions were particularly welcome as was made clear to the four airmen from Kuala Lumpur who became the first entertainers to visit RAF Gan, their skiffle group performances in the airmen's canteen and in Costain's bar being rewarded with enthusiastic applause far in excess of their expectations or their due.

Their visit ought to have put Gan on the map for other entertainers but it is quite remarkable that a station which was a scheduled refuelling stop on the RAF's route between Britain and the Far East, which had over a thousand resident expatriates but had no live radio, television or telephone links with the outside world was largely ignored over the years. From June 1958 until the latter part of 1962 the only performances referred to in the station diaries are those of the RAF's Far East Air Force band which arrived on the island and gave a series of very popular concerts during the last week of March 1959. For the next three and a half years the station diaries contain no references to entertainers; after that, visits by the Singapore-based band are mentioned five times with one unusually prolonged visit of seven days in November 1962. Not until January 1964, when the BBC's Treble Chance quiz team came to the island, do the diaries refer to any visits by civilian entertainers. Over the following twelve years there were nine Combined Services Entertainment shows at the base, the first in March 1966 and the last in May 1975.

The entertainers may have been few and far between but there was no denying their standing for among those whom the expatriates welcomed over the years were Acker Bilk and his jazz band, Eve Boswell and Ken Dodd. Every one of their performances was well received but it was understandable that Gan's unaccompanied tourists were mostly interested in the attractive female members of any show which meant that Ken Dodd had to work much harder for his applause than did the Karlin Sisters and their like. In-between the Combined Services shows the BBC's Forces Chance quiz teams made two visits to Gan, the first in April 1969 to record two programmes for the series and the second in May 1972 when the team ran and recorded three quiz competitions in the Astra.

Between 1958 and 1975 there were long periods when no entertainers visited Gan but those expatriates living on the island through the last quarter of 1968 and the first half of 1969 were unusually well catered for; they received two visits from the RAF's Far East Air Force band; two from Combined Services entertainers, the Carl Denver Show and the Raindrops; a BBC quiz team and Acker Bilk's jazz band. As usual, each of the Combined Services troupes put on two shows in the Astra cinema and one on Hitaddu whilst the RAF's Singapore-based band, which was at Gan from the 24th to the 30th of May, went out of their way to give as many performances as they could, appearing in the Astra cinema, in the various messes, the Imperial Club, the corporals' and airmen's clubs, the Royal Air Forces' Association clubroom and the Hermitage on Hitaddu. Acker Bilk and his jazz band, at Gan on the 31st of May and the 1st of June, somehow managed to cram in as many performances as did the RAF band and, for good measure, featured on Radio Gan to conclude the most exhaustive and exhausting series of concerts ever given at the base.

League football

Even though bad weather and political manoeuvring delayed the construction programme in mid-1958 work continued on some of the general amenities and by September the sports pitches were in use whenever the weather permitted. It was just unfortunate that, like so many of the island's recently-created facilities, they were all too often unusable during the latter months of that year because frequent rainstorms left them badly flooded.

When the Adduans made their unilateral declaration of independence at the beginning of 1959 the increased tempo of the construction work inevitably meant that very little labour could be employed on general amenity projects but in spite of that the expatriates still found time to bring some organisation to their previously casual leisure pursuits, starting, among other things, an eight-team soccer league with the teams, perhaps appropriately, named after proprietary brands of beer. The league thrived to such an extent that in August Wing Commander Thomas, who had taken over from Wing Commander Kent in April, gave permission for an RAF Gan team to travel to Singapore and compete in the Far East Air Force championships. By then it was over a year since the previous representative team from Gan had been allowed to leave the atoll to compete in an outside tournament but that 1959 morale-boosting excursion was merely the forerunner of a host of similar trips; from 1960 onwards representative teams from Gan travelled to Singapore every year to compete in tournaments for virtually every sport.

Escapism

For those who preferred escapism to the confrontations on the football field there was the welcome arrival, at the end of 1958, of the station's first batch of sailing dinghies which, after the creation of Gan's sailing club, provided everyone with the opportunity to spend hours off the island, sailing in the lagoon. As always at the atoll, the sense of freedom was illusory but welcome nonetheless.

Sailing, however, was not an escapist activity which appealed to everyone; there were many who preferred to remain on dry land, strolling or casually cycling around the island to get away from the slightly claustrophobic atmosphere of the domestic site. For them, the condition of the unsurfaced roads was not that important although they obviously appreciated the improvements brought about as a result of the extensive repairs continually undertaken by the works department staff. No longer the axle-breakers of the previous year, the roads were still essentially compacted coral tracks and although the casual walkers and cyclists accepted them for what they were, they were still not highly thought of by those enthusiastic walkers, runners and cyclists who continually attempted to set new records for their round-the-island journeys.

Sub-aqua

Of all the off-duty diversions the most exotic was undoubtedly the exploration of the underwater world of the lagoon. The majority of the expatriates were content to don snorkelling gear to view the stunning coral formations and the tropical fish which inhabited the warm shallow waters off Gan's northern beaches whilst for those who could not swim, the glass panel which Gan's marine craft technicians had fitted into the bottom of a small boat provided tantalising glimpses of the exotica, encouraging some of them to become modest swimmers. That glass panelled boat did not last long and with its demise the non-swimmers were left with a simple choice; learn to swim or miss some of the most memorable sights at the atoll. It was not until the royal visit in 1972 that a replacement boat was built, ostensibly to enable the royal party to view the coral and the marine life which abounded in the lagoon but surreptitiously to use the royal visit funding to provide another general amenity item for the benefit of Gan's residents.

For the experienced scuba divers, riding in a glass-bottomed boat or snorkelling in the shallows was obviously of little interest; they formed Gan's sub-aqua club, organised regular deep-water dives to explore the lagoon and occasionally checked moorings and anchoring for the marine craft unit. The members even made a valuable discovery in 1961 when diving in the lagoon with visiting members of RAF Changi's sub-aqua club; they located a seven-and-a-half-mile length of submarine cable, obviously a Second World War relic, with a scrap value of some one hundred and thirty-two thousand pounds. During the early 1960s the club members made several dives to explore the wreck of the British Loyalty and an even deeper dive down to one hundred and ninety feet in 1964, the year when their most ambitious undertaking was the construction of a diving cage to enable them to study the behaviour of the sharks which were known to visit the lagoon.

The eight-feet-high, six-feet-square cage was lowered on test on the 7th of December before being suspended eighty feet below the surface in the Man Kanda channel during the afternoon of the 9th and again at seven p.m. that same day. Even though there was not a particularly bright moon that night there was enough light for the divers to see each other's hand signals at a depth of eighty feet. Not one shark was sighted during the three dives. The episode was described in the Gan Island Post as a successful experiment but Wing Commander Moss, Gan's station commander at that time, recalls that the young officer who had been instrumental in the construction of the cage, and had been one of those who had made the descent, was sufficiently worried about the safety aspects of the project to have the cage dismantled and the study abandoned.

Radio Gan

As far as off-duty diversions were concerned, life improved for everyone on the island on the 13th of February 1960 when Radio Gan's first transmission provided the expatriates on Gan with their own radio station, relaying BBC programmes as well as broadcasting local interest news, interviews and record request hours. As Michael Butler describes in his book 'Return to Gan', Radio Gan was created by a group of enthusiasts who begged and borrowed equipment to set up a medium wave radio station in a spare room at the end of the communications centre.

For those expatriates with a penchant for inactivity it was a development to savour because it meant that they could lay back and listen to the radio, a pastime previously denied them because in the southernmost reaches of the archipelago a normal domestic receiver was not powerful enough to pick up any English language broadcasts. The station, listened to throughout the atoll, was not just an instant success; it was destined to become a Gan institution. By the 1970s Radio Gan was on the air for an hour and a half early in the morning and from early afternoon until midnight with the programme schedules published in the weekly Radio Gan Times which would frequently carry a cover picture obviously designed to attract the attention of Gan's young unaccompanied tourists (Figs 21.3 & 21.4).

Record request programmes were always popular, particularly those which included requests and messages from home for Gan's expatriates. Gan rarely featured on the BBC's 'Two Way Family Favourites' but on Christmas Day 1971 the BBC broadcast a special programme which included recorded messages from service personnel based at some of the remotest stations in the world, including Gan. The programme was so popular that Jack Dabbs, the producer, repeated the format in subsequent years, his visit to Gan in 1972 featuring in the Christmas issue of the RAF News which carried an account of his travels and published a photograph of him under the palm trees, recording messages and requests from five of the station's unaccompanied tourists.

The improving amenities

The amenities on the island still left a lot to be desired during 1960; even those who were determined to make the most of their time at the atoll could find plenty to complain about. But in 1960 the main building programme was nowhere near completion and the operational imperative determined the priorities. It was also easy, at that time, to forget that the atoll was notionally the capital of a breakaway republic formed after the rebellion just over a year earlier and Gan was, as a result, the focus of considerable activity which had little to do with improving the lot of the expatriates.

Nevertheless, most of the promised improvements had been made by the end of the year. The new NAAFI club facilities and the recreation room had been well received even though they were considered somewhat limited for the numbers who wished to use them. Three or four films were shown each week in the recently built Astra cinema, a conventionally furbished cinema which had quickly become very popular even though the soundtrack could hardly be heard when heavy rain rattled on the building's corrugated iron roof. The outdoor sports facilities had been increased and a floodlit tennis court had been provided. A newly built education centre had been opened and an education officer established on Gan to take over the general education scheme services which had previously been provided under a parenting arrangement from Ceylon. He provided the permanent on-site education facilities which were common to all home stations and included a station library service which was obviously superior to the mess libraries which had been built up over the previous two years.

Clubland

By mid-1961 there was no shortage of outdoor sports pitches but the indoor leisure facilities were still limited. The sportsmen had the gymnasium but until the latter part of the year there were few indoor venues apart from the respective messes, the station cinema and the clubroom attached to St Christopher's Church. The situation changed in the latter part of the year because many of the European civilians were leaving and as their accommodation was handed over to the RAF it was converted into a recreation centre. Located towards the eastern end of the island, the centre was officially opened on the 2nd of September and as more accommodation was vacated, the complex grew, eventually housing a games room, a bar, a restaurant, various hobby clubs, a bowling alley and meeting places for the Gan branches of the Royal Antediluvian Order of Buffaloes and the Royal Air Forces' Association.

Clubland had arrived.

Gan, arguably the smallest fully operational RAF station in the world, almost certainly boasted more clubs and bars by the mid-1960s than any other station anywhere. The booklet 'Going to Gan', which was given to every serviceman before embarkation, referred to the general sports facilities which were normally to be found on any RAF station and then added brief references to the golf course; the Go Kart club; the floodlit tennis, the football and basketball facilities; the sailing club; the sub-aqua club and the other lagoon activities, which by then included water skiing. Among the clubs and societies referred to in the booklet were the local branches of the Royal Air Forces' Association and the Royal Antediluvian Order of Buffaloes; the music circle; the photographic club; the drama society; the amateur radio club; the hobbies club and the small arms club which had been provided with an indoor firing range. But that was not the end of it; the key to the buildings shown on the maps at Appendix D, identifies several buildings which were later constructed to provide additional clubrooms and others which were re-allocated as demand arose.

Most of the clubs were either local versions of those to be found on any RAF station or were reflections of the Gan environment and although many of them remained active for years some were merely eccentric local creations, as ephemeral as the members who were pursuing their own particular interests during their twelve months on the island. There had, for example, never been a railway on Gan even during the Second World War but there was, in 1965, a Gan railway society which had been formed with the declared aim of meeting each Wednesday at eight p.m. in the church clubroom for a 'natter and a noggin'. There was even, briefly, a Caledonian society with no obvious objectives except the one which related to the consumption of Scotch whisky.

There remained, however, the basic problem that there was really no alternative society on the island; every resident was an unaccompanied tourist living and working in a small enclave from which there was no escape month after month. Those who saw each other at work every day saw each other at leisure every day, day after day, week after week, month after month. The nearest thing to an alternative society was actually provided in Gan's Asian village where the Sri Lankans had named their mess The Imperial Club and had extended an open invitation to all other Gannites to use the club as though it were their 'local'. It was a remarkably generous gesture by a popular section of Gan's community and was accepted, at one time or another, by most of the island's residents. Once The Imperial Club had been well established the Sri Lankans offered another facility which was very much appreciated; a small restaurant, 'The Barn', which could be booked for an all-ranks dinner party. The Sri Lankans who were employed by the NAAFI would make all the arrangements, obtaining, preparing and serving the food which the diners had ordered some days earlier. Curry was the chefs' speciality and there can have been very few Gannites who completed a tour on the base without enjoying an 'Imps Curry' in The Barn.

With the exception of the church clubroom and the indoor firing range, club premises were invariably equipped with a bar. The result was that the number of established bars on the island was rarely fewer than fifteen. Every one was well controlled for the simple reason that it could be closed down if excessive drinking created problems. 'Excessive' was, of course, open to interpretation and there was one bar in which heavy consumption was the norm: The Marine Bar, managed by and for the men of the staging aircraft servicing flight but open to anyone. Located just off the beach to the rear of station headquarters, the bar had a justifiable reputation as a downmarket public bar where rank did not count, where the more accomplished drinkers could gather and where the evenings were raucous.

Apart from the general clientele and the male members of the slip crews spending the night on Gan, the bar seemed to attract a number of Eagle Airways stewardesses and Women's Royal Air Force air quartermasters; transient females who were well aware that no woman was allowed into this male-orientated establishment unless she donated an item of underwear to add to the collection which was pinned onto the wall behind the bar. Judging by the number of items hanging on the wall, such a donation was apparently considered by many a price worth paying.

The remarkable thing about the Marine Bar was that it maintained the same downmarket style year after year and never ran foul of authority because the raucous, boisterous customers never became violent; there seemed to be a general awareness amongst the patrons when their behaviour was dangerously close to the level which would lead to the loss of their bar licence.

On-board hospitality

Although fewer cargo ships came to the atoll each month after 1961 the arrival of the Wave Victor and the designation of Addu Atoll as a fleet refuelling base led to a significant increase in the number of Royal Fleet Auxiliary and Royal Navy ships which briefly visited the lagoon. Refuelling was usually a smooth and rather brief operation which left the visiting crew no time to go ashore but on occasions a ship would spend several hours in the lagoon and when that happened the crew was generally granted shore-time and would invariably respond to a challenge to raise a variety of sports teams to compete against the Gannites. It was also common practice for some of the landlubber expatriates to be invited aboard to tour the ship and to enjoy an hour or two of naval hospitality, an invitation which was always appreciated and accepted because a few hours spent socialising on board ship provided a welcome reversal of the normal hosting roles, an opportu-

nity to talk to men who were not Gan residents, a brief period in a different environment and contact with an alternative society.

Those other frequent visitors, the oil company tankers, were too sparsely crewed to raise competitive sports teams but were always welcomed for their onboard hospitality, which was legendary amongst the Gan expatriates.

Moonie-baiting and trophy hunting

There were always those who, tired of the day-to-day recreational facilities, could dream up other diversions. Among the simplest was moonie-baiting, an age-old game intended to provide amusement for the old hands at the expense of any newcomer. The most popular, and the most durable, on Gan was the invitation to the Saturday evening collar-and-tie party in the nurses' mess on Bushey island, that tiny coral islet between Hitaddu and Mahira. The nurses' mess was, of course, a total fiction but the innocent victim was unaware of that and, having been persuaded that his unaccompanied tour had suddenly taken a turn for the better, he would be told that the marine craft launch would leave the jetty promptly at eight p.m. and would return to Gan at midnight, leaving behind anyone who had been lucky enough to be invited to stay the night with the nurses on Bushey. Suitably dressed, the newcomer would arrive at the jetty only to be told that the launch always left at seven p.m. and that he was quite mistaken to think that he had been given a later departure time. From then on the art was to sustain the newcomer's belief that he had missed out on a great night, to console him over numerous pints in the mess and to promise him that his newfound friends would do all that they could to get him another invitation. With luck the fiction could be extended to the workplace for a day or two by which time some other moonie would be lined up, giving the previous victim an opportunity to do to someone else what had been done to him.

Far more challenging were the trophy hunts perpetrated by small groups of raiders, usually members of the same section at work or of the same club. They would target a trophy, such as Gan's multi-finger signpost, and mount a night-time raid to remove it, subsequently to display it outside their workplace or their clubhouse. Inevitably, some other group would respond to the challenge, remove the trophy, display it and start another cycle. In trophy hunting there were just two generally accepted rules; successful raiders were allowed at least a fortnight to gloat and display their trophy before anyone attempted to remove it and no trophy was to be set in concrete although it could be bolted down. Some of the raids were remarkably well organised, leaving the victims wondering how, for example, that much-coveted signpost could be lifted out and transported to the Hitaddu enclave without any of the temporary owners noticing what was going on.

Even more remarkable was the initiative displayed by the trophy hunters who successfully made off with a pair of Second World War gun barrels. Early in December 1971, the barrels had been recovered from the sea in a combined operation mounted by airmen from the marine craft unit, the hermits of Hitaddu, the works department staff and the crane operators from the mechanical transport section. Following the recovery one of the barrels was displayed outside the marine craft unit billet, one was left in the works department yard and the third was left near the marine craft unit jetty pending its transfer to a display site outside the Hermitage Club on Hitaddu. An enterprising group of airmen promptly borrowed and hid the hermits' barrel before it could be taken to Hitaddu, and several members of the local branch of the Royal Air Forces' Association raided the works department yard, removed the stored barrel and left it outside station headquarters as a Christmas present for Group Captain Sheppard.

It is difficult to believe that a group of people could abscond with an eight-ton gun barrel without being apprehended but trophy hunting on the island was something of a fine art and was based on the premise that on Gan, anything was possible.

Gossip In Print (GIP)

On the 10th of January 1963, when the mail service was being disrupted as a result of the snowbound airfield at RAF Lyneham, the first edition of Gan's local news–sheet, The Gan Island Post (GIP), was published and included, under the heading 'Arctic London', the considered opinion of the principal scientific officer in the local meteorological office that the world was getting colder after warming up for nearly fifty years.

That first edition, very much an experimental issue, included a personality profile section introducing to the readers the characters in their midst and, by doing so, helping to improve the cross-cultural associations which were so important for the smooth operation of the base. From the editor's point of view that section was one of several which could continue *ad infinitum*; there was certainly no shortage of personalities to feature in the articles because the numerous characters already on the island were continually being joined by a steady flow of newcomers.

The cyclostyled news-sheet, immediately dubbed the GIP, was the innovation of the year. Appreciated by virtually everyone, it undoubtedly came second only to Radio Gan in terms of widespread appeal for it carried a mixture of news, sports results, gossip, cartoons and 'in' jokes which extended to the 'coming shortly' film reviews which included, for every film, the reviewer's P and B score, understood by everyone on the island to indicate the extent to which 'pubes and boobs' appeared on the screen. Scheduled for distribution every Friday, the GIP quickly became such a common feature of life on the island that whenever publication was delayed the editor's office would receive numerous telephone calls from would-be readers, all wanting to know how much longer they would have to wait for their news-sheets.

Within a year the general style and content of the Gan Island Post was familiar to everyone but as the jokes and cartoons progressed from the innocuous to the risqué to the crude there were occasional complaints that copies containing material considered unsuitable for family reading had been found on board the passenger aircraft which had staged through Gan. Such complaints were briefly heeded by successive station commanders but were not taken too seriously; the news-sheet was essentially good for morale and any censorship was a local matter not to be determined by the reaction of outsiders who happened to come across copies which were not to their liking.

Not everyone agreed with that opinion; for some, there was a period when GIP stood for 'Garbage In Print' but as editors came and went the tone of the news-sheet varied even though the content remained familiar, indulging the unaccompanied tourists with the usual mixture of local news, sports reports, informative articles, cartoons, jokes, competitions and gossip. The ever-popular references to recently set records and the servicemen's obvious preoccupation with local achievements led to the occasional publication, as a supplement to the news-sheet, of updated versions of the Gan book of records, providing a few interesting details about the island, an insight into the bizarre world of some claimants and a few tongue-in-cheek claims which were just plausible enough to leave the reader wondering whether they were true or false. The Gan Island Post had its fair share of critics, some of whom were quite disdainful but theirs were obviously minority opinions for the news-sheet remained hugely popular from the day it was born until the final issue in 1976 (Figs 21.5, 21.6 & 21.7).

The film stars of Gan

The men who were responsible for refuelling and servicing the VC 10s which staged through Gan proudly claimed that no-one could complete the operation as smoothly and as rapidly as they. Their experience, the frequency of the flights staging through the base and Gan's generally fine weather attracted the attention of the Ministry of Defence staff responsible for the production of training films and in June1968 a film crew arrived and spent a week on the island, shooting scenes for use in a work study film on the turnaround procedures for a VC10. The men who featured in that film were the first of the film stars of Gan but, unlike those who were chosen to feature in an Anglia Television production, they were not destined to be seen by a million viewers.

Unbeknown to the Ministry of Defence film crew the Anglia Television executives were already thinking of making a documentary film about the RAF's mid-ocean staging post. The Ministry of Defence staff, regarding the idea as a useful addition to the annual recruiting campaign, had readily agreed to the company's proposal and had arranged for the producer and a film crew to make a preliminary visit to the base at the end of June 1968, a few days after the departure of the Ministry's own film crew. The Anglia Television team spent four days at the atoll reconnoitring locations, liked what they saw and persuaded the producer that life on the RAF's coral island staging post would be an ideal subject for a thirty-minute documentary, provisionally titled 'The Lonely Men of Coral Command'.

The full film crew duly arrived on the 5th of August and spent eight days filming almost every aspect of life on the military sites. In accordance with the rather insensitive instructions issued by the Ministry of Defence staff the Anglia team excluded from the film the Maldivians who normally assisted with the coral blasting operations in Gan's underwater quarry, their exclusion causing the minor upset which led to the atoll chief's protest, referred to on page 223, and the additional filming needed to pacify the Maldivians.

The end result of eight days filming was as balanced a picture of life on Gan as could be expected in a thirty-minute documentary. The environment, the work, the operational efficiency of the airmen, the sense of isolation, the frustrations and the tolerant society were fairly illustrated and commented upon. Inevitably, some of the local rituals attracted the attention of the film crew but, unlike most of the journalists who came to Gan, they were not seeking to create an exposé, they were more interested in the quaint than in the sensational. Thus they ignored some rituals but included a short sequence on men who were all dressed up with nowhere to go, a fair comment on the officers who, dressed in accordance with their mess regulations, could be seen every evening enjoying their sundowners whilst watching the sunset from the comfort of a deck chair in the grounds of the officers' mess. The participants could see that this would seem quaint to a stranger but what they did not say was that even they thought it odd that for their formal dining-in nights the collar-and-tie regulations were abandoned and the diners were required to wear short-sleeved, open-neck shirts with epaulettes attached.

For the Gannites, however, the opportunity to make a few tongue-in-cheek comments about life on the island was too good to miss and they regaled the producer with examples of strange behaviour brought on as a result of spending month after month on Gan. Whether those tales were believed or whether they were just thought to be entertaining is debatable but, much to the amusement of the unaccompanied tourists who saw the Anglia film on Christmas day that year, the narrative included references to men who had been known to break down and weep out of sheer geographical frustration; men who, missing their children, would peer over the railings of the transit hotel kiddies corner at other men's children playing in the sun and men who, missing their wives and sweethearts, would turn up at the flight pan any hour of the day or night, the hum of a jet engine their music to watch the girls go by.

But the comment which provoked the loudest outburst of laughter was that which referred to men who, suddenly feeling that they were about to snap because they couldn't take it any longer, would head off to the provost flight where, on asking to be detained for the night, they would be sympathetically accommodated.

The 'Lonely Men of Coral Command' who subsequently saw the documentary were left to wonder what could have been made of the true life tales of men who, on arrival, took one look at the base and promptly tried to sneak onto the next homeward-bound aircraft; of the airman whose mental state led him to set fire to the communications centre and of the airman who, several months into his unaccompanied tour, managed to contract a sexually transmitted disease after making the acquaintance of a remarkably friendly woman on board a passenger aircraft during its one hour refuelling stop on the base.

The stand-down festivities

English bank holidays were celebrated on Gan with a station stand-down and a festival of sport to ensure that everyone was provided with a healthy outlet for any surplus energy and given as little time as possible to either brood or to over-indulge in one or more of the station's bars.

In essence, the arrangements at Easter and in August were practice sessions for the December marathons even though, by the 1970s, the bank holiday revelries, combining events which were peculiar to the local environment with some which were loosely based on those in the popular British TV series 'It's a Knockout', had developed a reputation of their own as great festivities and significant fund-raising occasions for favoured charities (Figs 21.8, 21.9, 21.12, 21.13, 21.14, 21.15 and 21.16).

The Christmas celebrations

The pattern for Christmas celebrations on Gan had been established by the pioneers and a decade later it was virtually unchanged with the 1968 diary referring to a programme which seemed, that year, to develop into an even longer marathon than usual. The 1968 events started with the Christmas dinner and draw in the Hitaddu enclave on the Sunday evening followed, three days later, by the festivities on Gan which flowed through Christmas Day, Boxing Day and into Friday. It was a year when the familiar events were supplemented by a gala night in the gymnasium; a personality-dunking event to conclude the water polo tournament; the Imperial Club open house sessions and the Posbee film shows which included the Anglia Television film 'The lonely Men of Coral Command', a film which greatly amused those members of the audience who had been on the island during the filming in August and had regaled the film crew with stories of life on Gan.

For nineteen years European tradition combined with Gan diversions to make every Christmas on Gan an event to be remembered. The carol service, the turkey lunch and the consumption of an over-generous amount of alcohol blended, but did not always combine well, with two solid days of physical competitions, the variety of which grew year by year until it was virtually impossible to think of any activity which had been overlooked. The mundane became permanent fixtures in the Christmas calendar, as did the dhoni races, but some events had to be abandoned after a year or two, either because the risk of serious injury was too high or because of the damage to property; or both. Thus the bicycle races around the island (Fig 21.11) were retained but bicycle polo, in which the contestants wielded croquet mallets, was banned after far too many incidents in which mallet shafts were thrust into the wheels of overtaking cycles.

The dhoni race was arguably the most spectacular of the events, attracting section teams from across the base and from the Maldivian villages although it was difficult to understand why islanders who were obliged to spend several hours rowing to and from work every day would wish to take part in a dhoni race on a holiday afternoon. Such races had become an accepted part of every sports day since 1957 and as the number of competing teams increased, a festive streak was grafted onto the event with teams donning fancy dress, often hampering their rowing ability but adding humour to an otherwise highly competitive event. The surprise, for most of the expatriates, was the frequency with which the slightly-built Maldivians were the winners, proving that with such ungainly craft technique was every bit as important as brute strength. The crew of any naval vessel at anchor in the lagoon on the day of the dhoni race would always be invited to compete in the event and, fondly imagining that they could beat any opposition, the sailors invariably set off at a cracking pace only to end up trailing behind the lightweight Adduans and having to suffer the inevitable jibes from their watching colleagues.

Fancy dress inevitably played a part in other events and somewhere along the line it was combined with the idea of a billet bar competition which, like so many other elements of the Christmas celebrations on Gan, gained in popularity as the years went by. It was a simple competition. In every billet the occupants created a theme bar, the station commander judged the results (21.10) and the winner was presented with the billet bar plaque and an impressive quantity of alcohol. Over the years the quality of the workmanship which went into the entries improved to such an extent that some were under construction as early as October, turning the creation of the bars into something of a marathon for the airmen.

As the popularity of the competition increased, the judging developed into something of an endurance test for the station commander for it generally came immediately after he had made his Christmas rounds of the clubs and the messes, accepting the hospitality proffered by the members and subsequently being expected to imbibe at each of the billet bars where the airmen would have been only too happy to have provided him with just that one drink too many.

Every Christmas the Gannites would attempt to set new records, their every achievement from dhoni racing to alcohol consumption being compared with those of their predecessors. Inevitably, alcohol consumption during the stand-down became a yardstick used by many of the expatriates to judge the intensity of the celebrations and when a new NAAFI club was opened on Christmas Eve 1959 the occasion was celebrated by the sale of sixty-three thousand bottles of beer over the two-day holiday, a record which stood for six years before the contents of sixty-eight thousand five hundred and thirteen bottles were consumed during the forty-eight hour stand-down, setting a new record which was seemingly never broken.

Competitions and consumption were not, however, the only marathons for there was another, very different, side to the Christmas celebrations on Gan: charity fundraising which underpinned a whole variety of activities including, after 1960, variety shows in the cinema and marathon record request programmes broadcast over Radio Gan. The fundraising, which started well before Christmas, always had two beneficiaries: Adduan children and a British charity of the year. For the Moslem children, the Christian celebrations meant presents and a pre-Christmas party for some five hundred youngsters. For the nominated charity, invariably the Wireless for the Blind, the fundraising meant a donation of several hundred pounds. Every Christmas the fundraisers would set a target of four hundred and fifty pounds, a significant amount of money in the 1960s and early 1970s, and every year they surpassed it. In 1967, when the nominated charity was the Guide Dogs for the Blind Association, the Radio Gan appeals ran through Christmas and into the New Year, contributing to the grand total of nine hundred pounds, enough to pay for the training of three guide dogs which were duly named Addu, Shearn and Stager.

After the introduction of the nine month tours in 1971 there were many servicemen who completed a tour on Gan without experiencing the Christmas marathon which had become so much a part of life at the atoll.

Nevertheless, the pattern of events remained virtually unchanged because the Christmas experience was described to all newcomers, with some embellishments, by those who had survived it. In addition, those word-of-mouth accounts were tempered by the memories of civilian expatriates, many of whom spent more than a year on the island and were able to recall most, if not all, of the previous years' events.

The 1972 Christmas celebrations were, in most respects, just like those of earlier years with the usual festivities, competitions and alcohol immunity trials. There was, however, a variation in the entertainment with the production and presentation, by the airmen, of an old-time music hall show in the cinema, the participants unaware that they were reflecting, in far better circumstances, the music hall performances of the amateur thespians who had been among the earliest arrivals at the atoll during the Second World War. But there was something else to remember about that Christmas. For the first time there was a satellite telephone link from every mess to the Ministry of Defence switchboard and thence into the public network, enabling everyone to make a brief phone call to family or friends in Britain. The link was not retained; after Christmas the only telephone connection to Britain was the emergency line provided for the station commander.

Rarely if ever were the Christmas celebrations curtailed although in the 1960s the children's party fell victim to the political manoeuvring and in 1971 their party had to be cancelled because there was a minor outbreak of typhoid in one of the villages.

In 1975, just three months before the RAF base was abandoned, the festivities were tackled as enthusiastically as ever, possibly even more so than usual in an attempt to achieve temporary notoriety and to leave a lingering impression with the Maldivians for whom this would be the last such occasion.

Leave

Although the servicemen's tour length had been doubled towards the end of 1957 they still had no entitlement to mid-tour leave. Wing Commander Schofield, concerned about the impact of that on the men's morale, had agreed, as early as 1957, that, dependent upon the availability of spare seats on the Sunderlands, Bristol Freighters or Valettas, any airman not in a specialist digital post could take up to two weeks leave in Ceylon. It was an unofficial system but virtually every serviceman was able to enjoy a short break away from the island at some time during his tour and although Schofield saw no reason why the arrangement should not continue it had to be curtailed for operational reasons through the latter half of 1958 and it was not generally reintroduced until well into 1959. Not until the early 1960s were the servicemen permitted to take mid-tour leave in Singapore or in England.

During the early part of 1960 the increase in the number of scheduled flights staging through the base provided further opportunities, for a select few, to fly to Singapore to represent RAF Gan in the Far East Air Force sports tournaments. Those with little sporting prowess were less fortunate; they still faced the prospect of serving at the atoll for twelve months without a break because local leave was banned and they had no entitlement to leave the atoll for mid-tour leave elsewhere. Given that seats were so often available on staging aircraft, that seemed unreasonable to the airmen and it was quite obvious to Wing Commander Thomas, Gan's station commander at that time, that they would gradually become resentful unless something was done about the situation. He could not create an entitlement to mid-tour leave but he could, and did, introduce a local arrangement whereby any atoll-based serviceman could apply for one period of privilege leave and the accompanying indulgence flights at any time during the last six months of his twelve-month tour on Gan.

Granting the leave was easy because, except for the few servicemen in digital posts, any airman's colleagues would stand in for him at work whilst he was away. But the flight arrangements posed a problem. On RAF passenger aircraft any seats not allocated to personnel travelling on duty would be made available for so-called indulgence passengers, or indulgees, who would pay a nominal fee for the off-duty flight. An indulgee had to accept the risk of being offloaded anywhere, any time, if the seat were re-allocated to a duty passenger. Indulgees could thus be left stranded at any staging post *en route* and left to their own devices.

The direct flights between Gan and Singapore carried no such risk but the regulations carried a sting in the tail. For service personnel there was a regulation requiring indulgees to show that they could return to duty on time even if they were unable to do so on a service aircraft and with no scheduled civilian flights to the atoll the servicemen at that isolated outpost were thus not legitimately permitted to take an indulgence flight to anywhere. Gan however, was a Far East Air Force base and, in a generous interpretation of the regulations, Gan's airmen were informed that provided they returned to RAF Changi on the due date they would be regarded as having returned to duty.

That liberal interpretation of the regulations was subsequently retained for the benefit of those who, under the later arrangements, were granted indulgence flights to England, a much riskier journey for indulgees because the aircraft were scheduled to stage through one the RAF's Near East Air Force stations where the passenger list was quite likely to be revised and indulgence passengers offloaded. Quite apart from the possibility that Gan personnel could be stranded *en route* to or from England, there was a further consideration; in 1960 there were not enough vacant seats on the west-bound flights to accommodate all those who would like to spend their leave in Britain and that led to the introduction of the arbitrary rule which permitted bachelors to spend their leave in the Far East and allowed only married men to be offered the choice of applying for mid-tour leave in either England, with the attendant risk of being off-loaded *en route*, or in Singapore. The system, far from perfect, was accepted by everyone and worked well in the early days of the scheduled flights. It was not long, however, before the number of empty seats began to dwindle and the number of applicants began to rise and that led to the introduction of a lucky draw each month for the few available seats, a system which was seen as the fairest way of allocating what had become a prized privilege. It was a system which was only briefly necessary although whenever the number of applicants exceeded the number of available seats the lucky draw system was reintroduced.

Over the next decade servicemen posted to Gan were given various versions of the mid-tour leave arrangements. By 1964 the information booklet 'Going to Gan' was declaring that '*Personnel posted to Gan start a new leave year from the date of their posting and one period of fourteen days leave may be taken after six months*'. The servicemen actually on the island were well aware that they might not be permitted to take any leave and that, even if they were given permission to do so, they might not be offered an indulgence flight. Nevertheless, very few airmen were obliged to spend a full tour on Gan without being given the opportunity to take fourteen days leave with an indulgence flight either to England or to Singapore.

That was the situation in 1971 when the tour length for the newly-arrived servicemen on Gan had been reduced from twelve months to nine and each of them had been told, on receipt of his posting notice, that he would have no leave entitlement during such a short tour. In part that was justified in view of the intended withdrawal from Singapore during 1971 and the consequential reduction in the number of spare seats on the passenger aircraft staging through Gan.

Nine months was certainly a significantly shorter tour but the servicemen on Gan would still have to spend that time in close confines, sharing that spit of a coral island with the same people day after day, with no alternative society and nowhere else to go. Wing Commander Gee, Gan's station commander at that time remained sympathetic towards the unaccompanied tourists and continued to allow them to take fourteen days leave in the Far East or in Britain whenever seats were available on the VC10s which staged through the base virtually every day. Predictably, as the withdrawal from Singapore gathered pace the requests for indulgence flights to England exceeded the number of seats available and for westbound flights a lucky draw system was introduced.

By September, after Gee had handed over to Group Captain Sheppard, the unofficial provision of mid-tour leave and indulgence flights for Gan-based personnel was under review by the senior Command staff but there had been no open declaration that the unofficial breaks were to be discontinued. As there were only about six hundred servicemen at the base there were generally about a dozen men taking indulgence flights out of Gan each week and a similar number returning; rarely since the introduction of Transport Command's scheduled flights through the staging post had there been insufficient spare seats on the aircraft to satisfy this rather limited demand.

As far as morale was concerned, it would be difficult to imagine anything more demoralising than the cancellation of this unofficial perk whilst VC 10s with empty seats were staging through the base almost every day of the week. The fact that on most of the aircraft there were indulgence passengers flying to and from stations where the servicemen were accompanied by their families was likely to generate even more resentment if the Gan-based airmen were to be denied the opportunity of a mid-tour break from their tropical exile. It was not as if they could take local leave at the atoll for that was specifically prohibited; without the indulgence flights the servicemen would be confined to camp for nine months with only the bank holiday stand-downs to interrupt their nine months of working 5½ days every week. For all of those reasons, Sheppard ignored the technicality of the regulations and continued to grant mid-tour leave and indulgence flights whenever possible, arguing that every station commander's remit required him to ensure that all personnel took their annual leave unless prevented from doing so by operational necessity and although Gan had no establishment allowance to cover for absences on leave there was no such operational impediment for anyone except a very few men in digital, and critical, posts.

But waiting in the wings was RAF Masirah.

The servicemen at Masirah were, like those at Gan, on an unaccompanied tour but their environment was nowhere near as pleasant as that at Addu Atoll. It was their misfortune that Masirah did not have scheduled passenger flights in anything like the numbers which staged through Gan so they were very rarely offered indulgence flights, legitimate or not. Successive station commanders at Masirah were almost certainly aware that the rules were being flouted for the benefit of the men at Addu Atoll but there was no reason for them to blow the whistle on someone else's good fortune. Until, that is, their airmen made an issue of it, which is precisely what happened halfway through Sheppard's tour. His tolerant regime came under the spotlight when an airman from Gan took an indulgence flight to England on board a C 130 Hercules and was obliged to stop overnight at Masirah. He was unwise enough to let it be known that it was quite normal for Gan's servicemen to be granted indulgence flights so that each could enjoy one brief mid-tour leave either in Britain or in the Far East even though the tour length had been reduced to nine months. When word of that arrangement got around, it caused some resentment amongst the Masirah airmen and eventually their station commander was persuaded to contact the Air Support Command staff and question the inequity.

Sheppard became aware of this rather too late to try to nip it in the bud; the matter had reached the ears of Air Vice-Marshal Clementi, the air officer administration at Air Support Command. He informed Sheppard that the practice was to cease and from then on every serviceman posted to Gan was informed, on arriving, that he would be unlikely to leave the atoll during his nine month tour. Those who had already been informally assured that they would be able to take a brief mid-tour leave in Britain or in the Far East were told that every effort would be made to honour that arrangement even though the Air Officer's instructions and the reducing number of passenger flights through Gan would make it extremely difficult to do so. From then on every device which could be used to honour the informal assurance was used; reasons were found for servicemen to travel as duty passengers in order to attend sports events, conferences and courses on anything from hockey refereeing to moral leadership. The result was that the number of indulgence passengers fell dramatically even though there was no significant change in the number of servicemen who were enjoying a mid-tour break away from the atoll. For the remainder of his tour as Gan's station commander, Sheppard tried to persuade Clementi to rescind his instruction but he had no success even when the matter was discussed during the Air Officer's inspection of Gan in May 1972.

Two weeks after that inspection Sheppard completed his tour and handed over to Group Captain Salmon who was thus left to deal with the situation knowing that he stood next to no chance of persuading Clementi to change his mind. Sure enough, it fell to Salmon to wield the axe.

It was impossible to carry out the Air Vice-Marshal's instructions without affecting the servicemen's morale because many of them were bound to feel disgruntled. But it was possible, if Clementi's instructions were to be loosely interpreted, to develop a compromise which would ensure that very few servicemen would have to spend an entire nine months on the island. What was offered by Salmon, and readily accepted as the best that could be hoped for, was a steady decline in the number of indulgence flights to Britain with the monthly lucky draw resurrected until the westbound indulgence flights were finally discontinued. Concurrently, a short, illegitimate, mid-tour break would continue to be granted with indulgence flights to and from the Far East for as long as seats were available on the scheduled flights. With scheduled flights from Britain to the Far East staging through Gan each day at noon and with return flights arriving at the staging post each evening, it seemed likely that the mid-tour break in the Far East would remain available for everyone for the foreseeable future, as indeed it did.

Fig 21.1. Extracts from one man's countdown diary.

365	Arrived today, bloody hell it's hot.
363	What a place to work.
362	Can't find anyone I know.
360	Found two old mates propping up bar.
359	Had a lot to drink.
358	God, what a hangover.
340	Can't understand the Gan language yet.
339	What's a GIZZIT or a MONK?
310	Can't believe how long I still have to do.
300	Went to library – still no porn.
280	Roomboy keeps wanting GIZZITS.
279	Going to learn to speak Maldivian.

278	No I'm not.
250	Bought case of beer, put it under bed.
249	Beer's gone, monk having.
200	Five days and no stickies.
190	Maybe wife has run off with milkman.
189	Six stickies together today, bloody postal service.
185	Going very white again, bar tan having.
170	Rained all day today.
169	Rained all day today.
168	Rained all day today.
167	Must be a plot so you can't see the sun moving.

110	Ten more days and I'll be down to the hundred.
109	Started crying when I realised how much longer to go.
108	I wanna go home.
107	Tried to stow away on VC10. Got caught when skirt slipped. Big monk having
105	I wonder if the sun ever moves?
104	Beginning to like the taste of Charlies.
103	Went to gozome party. Got drunk.
102	Nobody tries to ride a bike up a palm tree.
100	Saw sun move – backwards.
99	Bought radio from NAAFI.
98	Sold radio, bought beer.
97	No stickies today, monk having.
96	Got parcel, sold contents for beer.
90	Got bicycle.

89	Fell off. Sold bike, bought beer.
86	Missed leave draw - again. I'll never live to get off this bleeding island.
85	Had request played on radio – happy having. Request for wrong person – monk having.
80	Got get well card from AA.
79	Guinness book of records want my name.
78	Got asked to extend tour – now in guardroom. What's the penalty for striking an officer?
75	Pleaded insanity. Plea rejected, padre got me off.
74	Joined church, wine having.
73	Got drunk, padre monk having.
72	Guardroom tour .
68	Freedom having.
67	Night walk, got lost. Met police dog.
66	Reported sick with dog bite. Covered mouth with toothpaste, doctor got monk on.
65	The sun has definitely stopped.
64	This calendar is lasting a bloody long time.
55	Building aeroplane, must escape.

54	Sold aeroplane, bought beer.
50	Get repat jabs up to date.
49	Got lecture on how to behave in UK.
48	Practise wearing shoes.
47	Bought Gozome presents.
46	Sold presents, bought beer.
44	Checked POSB book. Mein Gott.
43	Sneered at moony today - nobody has that long to do.
40	Getting excited at sight of aeroplanes.
39	Practise doing up shoe laces and flies.
38	Long day, bloody sun stopped moving again.
37	Practise saying please and thankyou.
34	Mates all leaving, monk having
33	Hope I go a few days early.
32	Wonder if I'll be frightened crossing the roads?
31	Shaving every day now, need to practise.
30	Bought new razor.
29	Sold new razor, bought beer.
28	Repair flip flops, not buying new at this stage.
27	Got flight date.

26	Gave present to movements officer.
25	Gave bigger present to movements clerk.
24	Wrote home, sent repatriation warning. (see Appendix E)
20	Practise running up aircraft steps.
19	Fell off steps, monk having.
18	Final lecture on how to behave in UK.
17	Panic tanning every day now.
16	Sunburnt, monk having.
15	Practise packing.
14	Send crate of charlies to movements staff.
13	Gozome party.
12	Ouch.
11	Sell flip flops, buy beer.
7	Stare hard at VC 10, practise behaving casually. Failed.
6	Out of weeks – tear down calendar, ceremonial burning.
5	Write last letter.
4	Have last haircut, keep boss happy.
3	Sold all porno posters collected during last year.
2	Clear today, collect repat warning document.
1	Board aircraft, kiss pilot.

Fig 21.2. Evening-time fishing in the Gan-Fedu gap.

Fig 21.3. A Gan 'Radio Times' cover. Source: G Brown

7.00	News & Press Review + Met Forecast	BBC
7.15	The Later On Early Show	Duty Controller
10.15	Morning Service	Padre
10.30	Letters From Home	Bernie Thompson
Noon	Sunday Sounds	Gerry Bee
1.00pm	The Jaunt	Mick Johnson
2.00	Don't Stand In The Eggshell Mum	Merv Perry + Mick
3.00	Top Twenty	Rog Haynes
4.00	Pet Clark Story	Transcript
5.00	Round The Horn	Transcript
5.30	Evening Star	Records
6.00	News	BBC
6.15	Band Beat	Transcript
6.30	Navy Lark	Transcript
7.00	What's New	Chris Thrower
7.30	My Way Again	Dave Bill
8.30	Dr Finlay's Case Book	Transcript
9.00	News	BBC
9.15	World Of Music	Rog Phillips
10.15	Soul Spectrum	Tape
11.00	News & Met Forecast	BBC
11.15	In The Still Of The Night	
11.45	Epilogue	Tape
12.00	Close Down	—

VHF

6.00	News	BBC
6.15	An Emotional Experience	Tape
7.00	I.S.I.R.T.A.	Transcript
7.30	Let's Dance	Tape
8.30	Sounds Progressive	Rog Haynes
9.30	Ronnie Aldrich	Transcript
10.00	Anyone's Guess	Duty Controller
11.00	News	BBC
11.15	Evening Melodies	Tape
12.00	Close Down	—

Fig 21.4. Typical Radio Gan programme schedules. Source: G Brown

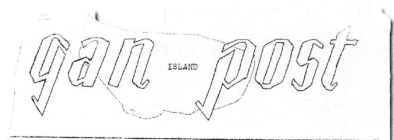

ISLAND

10 JANUARY, 1963   EDITION NO. 1.

EDITORIAL

This first edition of the "Gan Island Post" is intended to be experimental in both format and content. The intentions behind the publication of this newsheet, which will be produced at first on a limited basis, are to provide personnel with news and views of island life and activities, to provide a survey of events of interest at home, and to be a means by which personnel can express their views and opinions. The first issues will be restricted to a six page broadsheet but should demand warrant it will increase both in size and circulation.

GAN TOP SIX

	Title	Artists
1.	You Know What I Mean	Vernon Girls
2.	Some People	Valerie Mounta
3.	Return to Sender	Elvis Presley
4.	Lovesick Blues	Frank Ifield
5.	P.S. I Love You	The Beatles
6.	What Now My Love	Shirley Bassey

CINEMA

Friday 11th January, 1963

"MAN IN THE GREY FLANNEL SUIT"

Gregory Peck   19.30 hrs.

Saturday 12th January, 1963

"THE HOODLUM PRIEST"

Don Murray   18.30 hrs.
Cindi Wood   20.30 hrs.

U.K. TOP TEN

	Title	Artists
1.	Return to Sender	Elvis Presley
2.	The Next Time/ Bachelor Boy	Cliff Richard
3.	Sun Arise	Rolfe Harris
4.	Lovesick Blues/ You Taught Me How To Yodel	Frank Ifield
5.	Bobby's Girl	Susan Maughan
6.	Dance On	The Shadows
7.	Guitar Man	Duane Eddy
8.	Rocking Around The Xmas Tree	Brenda Lee
9.	Let's Dance	Chris Montey
10.	Desafinado	Stan Getz and Ch. Byrd.

AIRMEN'S CLUB GOSSIP

"Write an article" said the Editor. "You know the kind of thing - amusing stories you heard in the Airmen's Club.   About 500 words and could I have it by Monday?"

Let's face it, nothing funny has happened down in this end of the Island since the night the roof blew off the Asian latrine.

Take this morning for instance in the Airmen's Club; on all sides can be seen the soles of flip-flops poised among the coffee cups on the tables, each pair of soles attached, at varying distances, to an airman diligently reading "The Farmers' and Stockbreeders' Journal" (July, 1960), "Homes and Gardens" (December, 1959) or the "Bird Fanciers' Gazette" of last March. With the possible exception of the last - and a sad disappointment that turned out to be - this is no indication of the personal tastes of the readers but a sure sign that we've really dredged the bottom of the magazines and that if the mail doesn't arrive soon we'll all be swapping knitting patterns. The tattered old tom-cat yawns, stretches himself and tries a few tentative scales and departs in mid-howl with his no-tail well tucked in. One flip-flop is retrieved.

A file of anxious moonies shuffle nervously across the verandah on their way to the Guardroom. They are lavishly clad in Boer-war type K.D. and the "Bird Fancier" is lowered to allow its reader to comment compassionately on their probable feelings. His asterisks are neatly capped by the agricultural student with a witty speculation in dots and dashes and mild laughter flutters the dog-eared pages of the magazines. A sleepy game of gin-rummy springs to picturesque life with the discovery that the pack has only 50 cards in it; a gust of wind slams the doors and windows and a bowl of plastic roses topples slowly off the ledge and bounces soggily on the floor. Nobody moves. On inaccessible parts of the ceiling little tatters of Christmas decorations flutter in the wind like forlorn hopes on a Tibetan prayer-wheel and I need only say "Om mane padme hum" three or four times to bring me up to my "approximately 500 words".....
                                                                          E.H.

Fig 21.5. Extracts from the first issue of the Gan Island Post.

3

PERSONALITY PROFILE   No. 1   Sergeant Hurst   Post Office

Service in the R.A.F.V.R., Merchant Navy, Rifle Brigade, Parachute Regiment and Royal Engineers, plus a spell as a Civil Servant, - and we thought that all he did was to sell stamps and weigh coconuts.

Sergeant Charles Hurst was born in Rothes, Morayshire and his first job was as a tally clerk in the Forestry Commission; this job he stayed in until the age of 17½ when he joined the R.A.F.V.R. as a W. op./Air Gunner. Alas! much to his disappointment there was a surplus of aircrew at that time (December, 1943) and so it was that A.C.2 Hurst, without much ado, became Rifleman Hurst of the Rifle Brigade. He soon found the pace (180 to the minute) far too hot for him and transferred to the Queen's Own Cameron Highlanders seeing, with them, action in the last few months of the North Western Europe campaign, including the Rhine crossing.

Another transfer in 1948, this time to the Parachute Regiment as a volunteer! After this tour of 4 years back to the Camerons and eventually demobilisation.

The Merchant Navy next took his fancy and in keeping with his love of travel he visited New Zealand, Australia and the Far East three times. Then Mr. Hurst took a rest, he became a civilian, working as a Civil Servant at a Government Experimental Establishment, but the army called again and "Postie" took up his present occupation in the Royal Engineers (Postal Service).

Sergeant Hurst is very interested in motor racing, and indeed once owned an Austin Healey Sprite (until he spritely heeled it into a wall, leaving himself with £10 of scrap metal and a fractured skull.)

Of course "Postie" won't be at Gan for ever (he hopes) and says that although he's enjoyed his stay with the R.A.F. he's longing for his ain (Pongo) folk!   D.A.

Fig 21.6. The personality profile article from the first issue of the Gan Island Post.

Fig 21.7. The front cover of the two hundredth edition of the Gan Island Post.

Fig 21.8. The RAF Regiment team bringing Boadicea to open the Easter festivities in 1964.

Fig 21.10. Wing Commander Moss, Gan's station commander, judging the 'Verge Inn', one of the Christmas 1964 billet bar competition entries.

Fig 21.9. Boadicea's team recuperating, Easter 1964.

Fig 21.11. The start of the *tour de Gan* cycle race, Christmas 1964.

Fig 21.12. Crews arriving for the dhoni race, Easter 1971.

Fig 21.13. One of the dhoni figureheads, August bank holiday 1971.

Fig 21.15. Around the landing craft, the halfway point in the dhoni race, August bank holiday 1971.

Fig 21.14. The line-up for the dhoni race, August bank holiday 1971.

Fig 21.16. Winners of the 1971 August bank holiday float competition; Nº 11 radio fitting party.

Section 6 – Finale

XXII   Towards the Withdrawal

Although the decision to abandon the RAF's Indian Ocean base had been made in June it did not become public knowledge until the 3rd of December 1974 when Roy Mason, the British secretary of state for defence, outlined the shape and nature of the defence review in a statement to the House of Commons. Referring to '...*the decisions taken by the Labour Government in 1968 about the reduction of the British presence east of Suez*' he later included the comments that '...*we would withdraw our forces from Gan and Mauritius*' and '*Given the effects of these decisions in the Indian Ocean area and the Soviet naval presence there, we have decided to agree to proposals from the United States Government for a relatively modest expansion of the facilities on the island of Diego Garcia ...*'

At the end of that week the front page of the RAF News carried Mason's statement, comments from the Chief of the Air Staff, a message to the Ministry of Defence civilian staffs from the Permanent Under Secretary of State and a cryptic headline: '*Gan to go*'.

On 11th December Group Captain Edwards, Gan's station commander designate, arrived at Gan five days before Group Captain Moffat departed, leaving Edwards to begin his tour knowing that his Indian Ocean staging post was due to be abandoned in the not-too-distant future. By then the servicemen and the civilian expatriates on Gan had all heard of Mason's announcement and although word must have spread to the Adduans it seemed to have had little immediate impact. For them, Britain's decision to abandon the atoll base had sounded the death knell for their recently acquired lifestyle and yet they continued through 1974 and into 1975 seemingly unconcerned about the threat hanging over them.

The only grievance which they expressed related to their rates of pay. Since the 1973 award the annual wage bill for the Maldivian workforce had risen to approximately three hundred and sixty thousand pounds but the islanders' cost of living had continued to rise, as had their aspirations. Evidence of their changing, more expensive, lifestyles was everywhere and there was a growing demand for more extensive, and more affordable, education for all Adduan children.

Although basic primary education was available at Addu Atoll, secondary education could, at that time, only be obtained in Malé. There, the tuition was free but parents had to pay for their children to travel to the capital and had to meet all accommodation costs and general living expenses as well as the cost of educational materials. On Hitaddu an English school had been established to provide secondary education in some core subjects but it was an expensive facility which received no funds from the central government.

Financial problems were becoming all too common in the Adduan communities and were by no means affecting only the parents who were anxious to obtain secondary education for their children. Many islanders, tempted by the goods available, had been given credit by the traders and were beginning to have problems meeting their repayments. By the end of 1974 virtually every Adduan employee believed that he was underpaid whilst the dhoni owners, convinced that they were particularly poorly rewarded, were claiming that they could not manage financially just by using their dhonis as ferries, they needed full time employment on Gan as well. The arrangement was that the islanders started work on Gan at six a.m., which, for those who had to row across the lagoon, meant setting out at about three a.m. The commuters rowed themselves and, unlike the arrangement in earlier years, did not have to pay for the privilege. The dhoni owner was paid by the RAF for each day that his dhoni was checked in at Gan, the short dhonis at a rate of forty-five pence a day and the long dhonis at sixty-seven and a half pence a day. Once the commuters had landed, the dhoni had to stay at Gan for the rest of the day because the owner had no crew to row it back or to take it out fishing. The owners of the motor launches were better off. They charged each passenger two pence for the journey from Fedu to Gan or five pence from Hulumidu to Gan but they were able to take the launch away for use elsewhere during the day.

The widespread dissatisfaction with the low wages led the Maldivians, who were convinced that their government had no intention of seeking a pay rise on their behalf, to mount a deputation to see the district works officer, the major employer. That annoyed the atoll chief who claimed that such behaviour undermined his authority as well as that of the atoll committee. More to the point, he was worried that his government might believe that he had initiated the deputation and might sack him. That certainly would not have been to the RAF's advantage, given the good relationship with the present chief and the likelihood that any successor would, under such circumstances, adopt the very cautious, remote style which had been the hallmark of the relationship during the 1960s.

The event was therefore described, for the benefit of the atoll chief and the committee, as a deputation whose request had been pre-empted by the district officer's earlier decision to recommend that the pay scales for all Adduans employed in the works department should be reviewed. Thus in June the Near East Air Force Command staff suggested that a team from Cyprus should visit Addu Atoll and interview Maldivians in the villages to establish the local cost of living and to set fair levels of pay. One hundred islanders volunteered to be interviewed in the presence of an inter-preter/observer from the atoll committee with the result that the review was perhaps the most thorough study of Maldivian pay and cost of living since RAF Gan had been established.

Thorough investigation, however, takes time and the increase in pay did not occur until mid-1975 with the Maldivians waiting patiently on the assumption that the review would result in a fair award which they would eventually receive. Meanwhile they had to cope with a dramatic increase of one hundred and eighty per cent in the cost of fuel which meant that many of them were obliged to return to their old ways of living without generators, rowing and sailing instead of using outboard motors and walking instead of paying to ride on motor vehicles.

It was in February 1975 that the Adduans' dreams of a prosperous future were finally shattered. That was the month when Air Chief Marshal Sir Andrew Humphrey, the chief of the air staff, visited the station to brief the officers on the provisions of the defence review and to provide details of the timetable for the military withdrawal from the atoll. In doing so he confirmed that the base would be closed early in 1976; news which came as no great surprise to his audience who had been aware that Gan was likely to be abandoned within eighteen months of the December announcement of the closure.

For one executive, Sir Andrew's announcement soon had an impact; the station commander was asked to extend his tour by three and a half months to oversee the rundown and final departure from the atoll. He had no strong objections to that, in fact he saw it as a sensible suggestion, but it is unlikely that he would have been able to refuse without some very strong justification. He was thus left to maintain the operational efficiency of the base throughout 1975 and into 1976, with every expatriate and every Adduan painfully aware of the personal implications of the imminent closure.

As far as the Maldivian ministers were concerned it was likely that Zaki, in spite of the noncommittal style he had adopted during his November visit, would have had a shrewd idea that the British could be intending to vacate the atoll well before the lease expired; he may even have been discretely prepared to consider the possibility of early closure. Given that he, with another contingent of Maldivian businessmen and politicians, had visited the atoll in January, the Adduans may also have got wind of such a possibility, leaving them half-expecting bad news but hoping that it would either never come or would be long-delayed. If that were so, the briefing killed off their hopes, leaving them with no option but to come to terms with the fact that in little more than a year's time the British would have abandoned the base and left them to eke out a living as best they could.

Most of them had been hoping that the leasehold agreement, far from being ended prematurely, would be extended, ensuring that the RAF base would remain operational for generations to come. More to the point, they knew that the present agreement did not expire until 1986 and the news that the withdrawal would occur almost ten years sooner than was required took them aback. It was bad enough to be told that Britain would abandon the base prematurely but to be told that the withdrawal would be completed within little more than a year left most of them feeling angry and betrayed. Surprisingly, given the volatile nature of the islanders and their tendency to react dramatically to news or events that threatened their livelihoods in any way, they did not become disruptive or demonstrative, possibly because they were well aware that the decision which had cast a cloud over their lives had been made five thousand miles away and that local action would not change it.

They apparently decided that all they could do was to make the best of the time that remained and hope that when their government took issue with the British government the Malé-based ministers would argue their case strongly enough to delay the withdrawal until the end of the original agreement or, at the very least, to extract generous compensation for the islanders who would suffer the effects of the withdrawal.

What they wanted immediately was as much information as possible from the Chief of the Air Staff and they expected Ahmed Salih Ali Didi, their atoll chief, to gather it. He was just as anxious as they to hear of the future plans for Gan and sufficiently confident of his relationship with Malé and with the RAF to miss the main Friday prayer meeting in order to visit Gan and discuss the matter with Sir Andrew. He learnt little that the Adduans did not already know but at least he could rightly claim that he had the authoritative version of the current plan, albeit one that did not yet cover the details of greatest interest to the villagers.

It was quite remarkable that although the islanders had just been told that they were facing a very bleak future virtually all of them remained as compliant and cooperative as they had been at any time since 1957. If anything, the atoll chief became more friendly, readily accepting an invitation for himself and several headmen to be dinner guests in the officers' mess later that month and continuing to allow occasional organised visits by Gan personnel to the village communities on Hitaddu. It was on such an occasion, in March, that one not-so-obvious effect of the RAF's withdrawal was brought home to the visitors. A group of sixteen servicemen, including the station commander, was shown around the English school which had been established in 1974. Whilst at lunch with their hosts in the school hall they learnt that although the school had benefited greatly from the gifts of books from the RAF it was a costly facility and it was facing almost certain closure through lack of funds. The atoll committee, extant at that time and its members unaware that their days in office were numbered, had asked the Maldivian government for funds but had received nothing. There seemed to be little doubt that when the British left and the atoll economy declined to little more than subsistence level, education beyond the most basic standard would become an unaffordable luxury.

News of the imminent British withdrawal led to an unwelcome, but not unexpected, increase in the incidence of theft by the Adduans, reversing the trend which had shown a general decline during the 1970s. Most worrying was the increasing number of illegal landings on Gan, usually very late at night or in the early hours of the morning and patently linked to thefts from the island. The reason for the increase was obvious. Knowing that the British would be leaving the island early in 1976, some villagers were anxious to steal what they could while there was still anything left to take. They seemed not to care that the penalties for anyone convicted of organised theft were far more severe than those for petty pilfering; the perpetrators were obviously of the opinion that the rewards were attractive enough to make the risk worthwhile.

Unfortunately some also believed in violence as a legitimate means of evading capture if detected and the situation came to a head on the 21st of March when about eleven Maldivians from Fedu were seen landing on Gan's northern beach and when pursued by a Maldivian watchman they set upon him and made good their escape. They were inevitably apprehended in their home village, tried and banished from the atoll. The affair marked a turning point as far as illegal landings were concerned because the convictions and banishments demonstrated that the rewards were probably not worth the risk after all and that, combined with the widely publicised increase in the number of shoreline security patrols on Gan, was enough to deter all but the most determined thieves. From then on there were few such incursions. Pilfering, however, was to become ever more rife as the year wore on.

The weeks passed, and still the Maldivians' reactions to the British plan to abandon the base remained muted. At the local level, the Adduans, effectively trapped in a remote, poverty-stricken atoll, had a certain fatalism about their future, born out of years of living in a culture where day-to-day survival, disease and death featured more prominently than any five-year plan for prosperity. For them, the re-appearance of the British military in 1957 had been a stroke of good fortune and had materially enriched their lives beyond their dreams. Over the years very few of them had given any thought to the possibility that the British would leave the atoll and most of those that did briefly consider it did not care to dwell on the implications. A few visionaries, in the mould of Afif Didi, dreamed of the commercial possibilities for the airfield and its amenities but they were only too well aware that the remoteness of their atoll would make it unattractive for significant commercial exploitation. Basically, the islanders' philosophy was to enjoy the good times while they lasted and to hope that they would continue.

As far as the Maldivian government was concerned, Britain's premature withdrawal from Gan could be viewed with mixed feelings. Nationally, Britain's military use of Addu Atoll had been of limited financial benefit. The income from the lease was probably little more than the government could have received in aid over the same period and the revenue generated at the atoll had not greatly increased the central government's income, partly due to the reaction of the Adduans towards any form of direct taxation. Politically, the British presence had been an irritant for much of the time and a great embarrassment during the Afif Didi era when the British had effectively undermined Maldivian sovereignty. There had been some benefits but it could certainly be argued that, at least during the 1960s, they had inadequately compensated for the problems which the military base had brought to the archipelago. Once those problems had been overcome and political stability restored, Britain's military presence at Addu Atoll had become both useful and financially attractive. Now, just as the Maldivian government was beginning to enjoy those benefits and was expecting to continue doing so for at least ten more years, the military withdrawal would bring them to an end.

But the withdrawal did offer one big attraction. The Maldivians stood to inherit a fully operational airfield together with all the accommodation and amenities needed for a holiday resort or some other commercial venture. With that in mind, the President, well aware that the British decision to abandon the atoll could be neither reversed nor postponed, became determined to argue forcefully for the entire airfield to be handed over to his government as a fully operational international airport.

The British government may have been expecting acrimony and confrontation but matters rarely developed as expected in the Republic and it transpired that 1975, the last full calendar year in the operational life of RAF Gan, was marked more by the turmoil in Maldivian politics than by argument over Britain's decision to abandon her atoll base.

The turmoil began with the Maldivian elections in February. A new atoll committee was elected on the 14th of the month, eight days before a general election was held to appoint a successor to Mr Zaki, the prime minister. He was re-elected but his pleasure was short-lived because on the 6th March he was sacked by Nasir who blamed him for all the problems besetting the Maldivian economy and the lives of the islanders. The President then took over control as an emergency, effectively reverting to his earlier style as an elected dictator. News of Zaki's sacking and Nasir's control reached Addu Atoll on the 10th of March and, with no detailed explanation of why Zaki should have been banished from Malé and the post of Prime Minister abolished, the islanders began to fear that these latest moves signalled a return to the confrontations of the past. Their fears were fuelled when they heard that a special conference was being held in Malé to amend the Maldivian constitution.

It transpired that the amendments actually had very little impact on the daily lives of most Maldivians. Throughout the archipelago few islanders would have been in a position to take advantage of the relaxation of the rules on foreign travel and the declaration that there was no requirement for everybody to be able to read and write Arabic or Divehi, to study Islam or recite the Koran was of little significance for adult Maldivians although it was likely to affect the nature of primary education throughout the Republic. For a few ambitious politicians there was the minor disappointment that nobody below the age of thirty could become a government minister, whilst for those who lived in Malé and aspired to high office there was the more immediate disappointment that membership of the Majlis was reduced from fifty-four to forty-eight with all six of the lost seats being taken from the Malé allocation which was reduced to two.

Those changes, however, were the forerunners of others which all reflected Nasir's ambitious plans for the Maldives. Two were significant as far as other nations were concerned; the first declaring that the Republic's territorial boundaries extended twelve miles beyond the outer reef of every island, the second permitting the employment of foreigners throughout the archipelago and giving them the privilege of leasing land for periods in excess of five years without reference to the Majlis.

What made the Adduans nervous were the changes to the structure of the government. Nasir had strengthened his control by appointing four Vice-Presidents, each dependent on the President's patronage rather than an elected majority. With those appointments, the cabinet then consisted of the President, four Vice-Presidents, the Attorney General, four Ministers and the Speaker of The Majlis. It was obvious that, with the reconstituted cabinet, Nasir could introduce almost any changes he wanted.

The Adduans' fears were soon heightened. Ahmed Salih Ali Didi, their atoll chief, was called to Malé on the 6th of April and dismissed from office on the 17th. Moosa Ali Didi, who deputised for Salih whenever the chief was away, was formally promoted and became the atoll chief in May. That move upset many of Salih's supporters, some of whom vented their anger by setting fire to Moosa's trading boat at Hitaddu. Most thought it wiser to keep their own counsel but their resentment was clear to everyone and it was equally obvious that a combination of fear and resentment could easily lead to the kind of violent political demonstrations which had previously been all too common at the atoll.

The Adduans were not the only angry islanders; serious trouble was brewing in Malé, stemming from the offshore presence of eight Japanese fishing boats which were trawling the areas normally fished by the Maldivians. By feeding their catches to a mother ship the trawlers were able to operate almost continuously, leaving little for the local fishermen and creating a shortage of fish in the market places of the northern atolls. In June five or six hundred demonstrators took to the streets of the capital and became so rowdy that the militiamen were called out. Machine guns were set up near the Hukuru Miskit and, as matters got out of hand, shots were fired. By the time order was restored to the streets four demonstrators had been killed and many others seriously injured. The Minister of Agriculture, blamed for publicising the reason for the fish shortage and thus indirectly sparking off the demonstrations, was sacked and banished. A curfew was imposed in Malé and the President was forced to embark on a damage limitation exercise because the affair could not be kept secret even though the Radio Malé staff were warned not to discuss the matter and all the Malé islanders were told not to talk about the incident outside their own communities.

That same month the Adduans learnt that Nasir had initiated the abolition of all atoll committees. On the 9th of June a radio broadcast informed the nation that the Majlis had passed a law disbanding all atoll committees with immediate effect and that each atoll chief was required to recruit clerks to replace the committee members. The effect was simple. The clerks would have no say in local policies and would be dependent upon the chief for their job security. With no elected local government officers the affairs of the atoll would be in his hands. He in turn would be dependent upon central government, which effectively meant upon the President, for his security of tenure in office. A direct chain would thus be established from the President down to one-man local government.

The Adduan committee was disbanded on the 10th and the chief began to recruit the necessary clerical staff, leaving the villagers to wonder whether this was the beginning of another period of confrontation between them and their central government.

Given that stream of events in Maldivian politics during the first six months of the year it was hardly surprising that neither Nasir nor his ministers had the time to argue with the British about the premature withdrawal from Gan.

By June 1975 the Adduans were in no doubt whatsoever that the British forces would be leaving Gan early in 1976 even though they knew that on the 15th of March their government had started negotiations with Britain in an attempt to stave off the seemingly inevitable. The only development which helped the islanders to look forward to something more than a return to a subsistence-level lifestyle was the appearance, in May, of advertisements setting out the investment opportunities in the archipelago. Placed in several international publications by the Maldivian Minister for External Affairs, they extolled the virtues of the Republic of the Maldives and the benefits of investing there. Potential investors were invited to consider a variety of opportunities including manufacturing; tourism; fishing; international banking and the creation of an oil refinery with bunkering for shipping. The attractions referred to were one hundred per cent tax free and duty free concessions; free and unrestricted repatriation of profits; free currency movement; no exchange restrictions; one hundred per cent secrecy in banking with laws to protect depositors from outside interference; free entry to skilled personnel connected with any of the enterprises; unrestricted residency permits and, rather optimistically in view of the recent history of Maldivian politics and the soured relationships with the southern islanders, one hundred per cent political stability with total protection of all investments.

The advertisements brought a glimmer of hope for the longer term but the Adduans were still having to face up to the realisation that they were now under near-direct rule from Malé and that the only outside employer at the atoll would be leaving in less than a year.

They, of course, were not the only ones faced with redundancy as a result of Britain's defence review; throughout the Far East, locally employed civilians were losing their jobs as the British military rundown gained momentum. The difference was that for the Adduans the closure of the RAF base would almost inevitably force their entire community to return to subsistence-level living and the islanders, understandably, had no interest in the fate of workers elsewhere.

On Gan the Pakistanis were also facing more than the loss of their jobs. Most of them were losing the opportunity to qualify for British citizenship which could have been granted to any Pakistani who completed five years

Crown Service at the atoll. The opportunity to acquire a British passport and the right to reside in the United Kingdom was an attractive privilege which was extolled by the Karachi employment agents who recruited the Gan workforce on behalf of the British government. With such a prize in mind, many of the Pakistanis had given up good jobs in Pakistan and had been prepared to spend the necessary qualifying years living and working on Gan. The first blow to their ambitions had come in 1971 when the qualifying length of Crown Service had been dramatically increased at a time when Maldivianisation was resulting in the repatriation of many Gan-based Pakistanis who had expected to be offered re-engagement at the end of their short-term contracts. For them the opportunity to qualify for British citizenship had gone. Now, all but a few of those remaining at the atoll in 1975 would be prevented, by Britain's premature withdrawal, from completing the necessary period of employment. They made a collective plea for special treatment under the legislation which allowed the British immigration authorities to exercise some discretion but their pleas fell on deaf ears: no concessions were granted.

The Sri Lankans employed by the NAAFI were not much better off. Some would be able to work for the NAAFI elsewhere in the world but with the reduction in the number of British bases overseas there would be fewer such opportunities.

The Ministry of Defence civilians who expected to return to Britain when they left the atoll were not under any immediate threat of compulsory redundancy as a result of the withdrawal from Gan. They were, nevertheless, facing an uncertain future with Mason's statement referring to a manpower reduction ' …over the period up to 1978-79…' of '…about thirty thousand directly employed civilians, about half of whom would be civilians locally entered abroad.'

Finally, there was the totally unexpected announcement that the overall reduction in Britain's armed forces over the coming four or five years would be achieved in part by natural wastage and in part by redundancies, some voluntary, some compulsory. It would have been easy enough to reduce the number of servicemen simply by failing to offer re-engagement to many of those who were approaching the end of their contracted period of service but that approach would not have resulted in the departure of an appropriate mixture of ages and ranks and the redundancy programme was therefore designed with the primary aim of retaining a balance of skills, ranks and ages

amongst those who remained in the service. The details of the selection process and the redundancy terms were far from clear and on the 15th of April an RAF resettlement advice team visited Gan to offer clarification and advice to anyone who was either intending to volunteer for redundancy or was likely to be among those forced to leave the service.

The fact that Britain's defence review had so affected the lives of the expatriate civilians and the servicemen at the atoll was no consolation for the Adduans but the realisation that the wholesale redundancies included some servicemen helped them to understand that the British government intended to reduce its defence commitments with little regard for the people affected. That insight was almost certainly behind their reluctant acceptance that nothing could be done to dissuade the British from abandoning the base in 1976 and with that acceptance came a willingness to continue working normally until such time as the withdrawal was completed. In spite of the impact which the premature closure of the base would have on the local communities that attitude was common at every level with Moosa Ali Didi, the newly-appointed atoll chief, setting an example by being as amenable in 1975 as he had ever been. Happy to sustain, and even extend, the social contacts which had been enjoyed since 1971, he continued to permit expatriate visits to the villages, even relaxing the notice requirements to allow visits by slip crews who were only on Gan for less then twenty-four hours.

By mid-1975 visits to the village communities by groups of servicemen and civilians had become a feature of life for the Adduans. Selected groups, such as the BBC's Forces' Chance team which toured Hitaddu on the 8th of June and the RAF Henlow cadets who were given permission to tour Fedu, Hitaddu and Maradu during their forty-eight-hour visit to Gan that same month, would be met and accompanied by the atoll chief. Other influential Adduans tended to follow his example with the result that the villagers must have been photographed more often during the remaining months of 1975 than at any time in the history of the base. Quite remarkably, the chief even allowed some private visits during July when Gan personnel were able to visit the local communities as guests of their Maldivian employees.

The Maldivian ministers never formally commented on these local arrangements but they were not averse to relaxing the hospitality rules, especially when there was a quid pro quo, as was evidenced in April when they sought the help of the RAF's marine craft unit to lay a mooring buoy at

Fua Mulaku. Once the buoy was in position, the station commander and the Maldivian Affairs officer were given a conducted tour of the island and invited to send a group of twenty-five servicemen and civilians to Fua Mulaku on the 10th of May to camp overnight before returning to Gan on the 11th. The ministers even arranged for the visitors to be taken to and from the island on board a trading vessel, owned by the Hulumidu headman, and to be left free to wander during their stay.

There was one significant disappointment in 1975; whilst so many Adduans were inviting expatriates into their villages and their homes others were intent on stealing whatever they thought they could get away with, causing Edwards to record, in September, that '...*thieving continues apace and nothing is sacred*', a sentiment confirmed when thieves removed some of the runway approach lights. With the intervention of the atoll chief those were quickly recovered, as were the components from a works department dumper truck which was left overnight on Hitaddu when some work was being undertaken on the island as a favour for the chief.

Whilst life was continuing almost as normal at Addu Atoll the British High Commissioner and Ambassador to The Republic of the Maldives was meeting the Maldivian ministers in Malé to discuss the closure of the RAF's staging post and to negotiate the terms under which Britain would prematurely terminate the leasehold agreement for the atoll sites. The first round of talks started on the 15th of March and ran for three days with Sattar, the finance minister; Hilmy Didi, the fisheries minister and Shihab, the attorney general, consistently voicing their fears for the Adduans' future. Indeed, their over-riding concern throughout the subsequent negotiations appeared to be the effect of the withdrawal on the lives of the Adduans whom they described as a generation of islanders who, after being seduced by the British into losing their primitive life skills, were being abandoned ten years prematurely with only twelve months warning. They made the point that, with ten years of the original agreement still to run, nobody had started planning for the post-withdrawal period and now there was insufficient time to do so.

The Maldivian negotiators insisted that they were not objecting to the military withdrawal *per se*, they were objecting to the speed with which it was to be implemented and the apparent intention of the British to leave the airfield site unoccupied. They argued that under the 1965 agreement the British presence at the atoll was assured until the end of 1986, at least in spirit if not in words, and that under the spirit of the agreement Britain should either retain the RAF base on Gan or should continue paying the Adduans at Ministry of Defence rates until December 1986 whilst running Gan as a civil airport. They declared that if Britain were to fail to honour that spirit the Maldivian government would consider the agreement to be terminated when the leased territories were abandoned and under those circumstances would be free to do what it liked with the facilities at the atoll, even to the extent of inviting another foreign power to fill the vacuum created by the British withdrawal.

Their concern for the Adduans rang hollow in view of the ill-feeling which had existed between those southern islanders and their government from the late 1950s into the 1970s. To the British High Commissioner it seemed far more likely that the Maldivian ministers believed that the best way to approach the negotiations was to display a sense of moral outrage on behalf of the Adduans.

At the end of the three-day debate, Mr Smedley, the British ambassador, reported to London, clarifying the situation and setting out what he believed to be his best approach for future negotiations. He pointed out that, in essence, the Maldivians saw the 1965 agreement as their strongest bargaining point, thinking that they could get the best result by emphasizing the spirit of the agreement and their freedom, if Britain were to go against that spirit, to offer a ready-made military base to some other foreign power. Although well aware that Britain feared the arrival of the Russians or the Chinese into the Indian Ocean Smedley believed that Nasir had no real wish to enter into an agreement with any other power and suggested that Britain should not be panicked into any ill-considered arrangement. Commenting that the Maldivians could well make overtures to other nations before the withdrawal, he described those as negotiating tactics; he still considered that there was no real risk of another power moving in. Concluding that it would be pointless to debate the status of the 1965 agreement, he proposed that the best approach would be to get on with the negotiations over the details of redundancy compensation, disposal of assets and post-withdrawal aid.

Conceding that the Americans' interest in the Indian Ocean could cause them to be concerned over the future of Gan, he suggested that other suitors could be deterred and American fears calmed if Britain were to declare that the 1965 agreement remained valid even after the military withdrawal.

Arguing that there was nothing in the agreement allowing unilateral cancellation, he also made the point that the Maldivians could not assume that Britain would just stand idly by and allow them to cancel the agreement and offer the facilities to anyone else.

Smedley's analysis and his suggested negotiating stance were accepted by the British Prime Minister and the Ambassador was left to focus on those aspects which he saw as central to the British case. He thus continued to negotiate without making an issue of the possible unilateral cancellation of the lease by the Maldivians, simply preferring to make them aware of Britain's feelings about the presence of another power at Addu Atoll and hoping that the promised aid would be enough to persuade the President that his nation's best interests lay with Britain rather than with Russia or China, the two nations which already had occasional contact with the Maldivians.

Whilst the terms and conditions of Britain's withdrawal were being debated in Malé, the Ministry of Defence staff were working on an unusual combination of financial awards: the details of the Maldivians' final pay rise and their redundancy payments. The two-stage pay rise was generous, as it could afford to be in view of its short life expectancy. The first stage was to take effect on the 1st of July 1974 and last until the 30th of June 1975. That doubled the pay rates prevailing in June 1974. The second stage took effect from the 1st of July 1975 and provided a further pay rise equal to forty-five per cent of the June 1974 pay rates. Thus, by the 1st of July 1975 the rates of pay for the Maldivians were almost two and a half times what they had been twelve months earlier.

Given that a determination to pay not one penny more than was absolutely necessary had characterised the Defence staffs' attitude to all previous investigations into the rates of pay for the Maldivians, this unexpectedly generous settlement could only be seen as a sop to the islanders, a short-lived sweetener to help counteract their grievances. The proposed redundancy payments, however, were far from generous and, set at one week's pay for each year of service, applied to Maldivians, Pakistanis and Sri Lankans alike. The result was that most of the Maldivians would benefit more from the backdated pay rises than from the redundancy payments.

As expected, the Adduans welcomed the generous pay rises, but they, and the Pakistanis, quickly described the redundancy terms as unfairly biased in favour of the Sri Lankans who, on being made redundant, would receive larger cash settlements than either of the other two nationalities. The reason lay in the fact that the contracts which the Sri Lankans had with the NAAFI entitled each of them to be paid a terminal gratuity equal to three weeks pay for each year of service and that gratuity, when added to the proposed redundancy payments, would mean that each of the Sri Lankans would leave Gan with four weeks pay for every year of service. Although it was easy to argue that, like the Maldivians and Pakistanis, they would only be getting an extra week's pay over and above their contractual entitlement to a terminal gratuity, there was a perceived injustice. The Maldivians, ever ill-disposed towards their Malé-based ministers, were convinced that their own government had accepted such paltry redundancy payments out of indifference towards their plight. They became sullen but did not vent their obvious anger through non-cooperation. The Ministry of Defence staff, faced with the reaction of the Maldivians and the arguments propounded by the Pakistanis, recognised that there was an apparent injustice and, feeling that at that stage of the game there was little point in arguing over what was a relatively trivial amount of money, increased the redundancy payments for the Maldivians and the Pakistanis so that their total remuneration would be in line with that paid to the Sri Lankans.

That satisfied the Maldivians and although the increase was welcomed by the Pakistanis they were quick to point out that the redundancy payments were insignificant in comparison with the loss of their qualification for British passports.

The Maldivian ministers, aware that the base would be handed over to them at the end of March 1976, asked the British Ambassador for an assurance that the buildings and facilities which would be left on the site would be in sound condition. Smedley not only gave such an assurance, he added a commitment to undertake additional works for the benefit of the islanders. The result was that after the 1st of April 1975 the works department staff, although primarily employed on the repair and maintenance of the facilities which the Maldivian government would inherit, also undertook a variety of other tasks. Some of those, such as the preparation of the Hitaddu site for yam cultivation and the restoration of the Gan aerial farm to a coconut and banana plantation, were ordered by the Ministry of Defence as work which had to be done under the terms of the original leasehold agreement. Others were requested by the atoll chief and undertaken, with approval from London, as goodwill work. By mid-1975, the chief, only too well aware that time was running out as far as construction work favours were concerned, produced an exhaustive list of demolition and construction work which would benefit the islanders by improving the atoll environment whilst providing employment for Adduans who would otherwise be made redundant. Thus for the latter part of 1975 and for a few weeks in 1976 Adduans employed by the works department were busy clearing the heavy undergrowth along Gan's southern shoreline; removing coral outcrops which threatened the Maldivians' boats; repairing village roads; installing pipe-work to drain the Hulumidu swamp; demolishing the redundant wartime slipway at Maradu and repairing the storm-damaged causeways between the islands of Huludu and Midu, Fedu and Maradu, Maradu and Hankada and Hitaddu.

The only two significant requests which had to be refused were the repair of the Gan-Fedu bridge and the deepening of the channel into Fua Mulaku. It was December before the chief resurrected the idea of a Gan-Fedu bridge, asking for that to be reconstructed without apparently realising that the works staff could never have obtained the materials and completed the work in time to leave the atoll by the end of March. The other request was seemingly more reasonable but had to be refused because by the end of 1975 the RAF's marine craft personnel were fully occupied on the preparations for the withdrawal and without their craft the works staff had no way of transporting their equipment to Fua Mulaku.

It was not just the chief who was anxious to make the most of the last few months of the British presence at the atoll. The villagers were just as keen as he was, although they had slightly different priorities. Their requests for goods and materials increased month by month as they desperately tried to stockpile the type of commodities which would be very difficult to obtain once the RAF base had been abandoned. They also began to appear in ever increasing numbers at the medical centre with the result that the medical staff were eventually spending eighty per cent of their time on consultations for Maldivians. By November they had seen over nine thousand islanders, seven and three quarter thousand of whom were not, strictly speaking, entitled to consult the medical staff on Gan. As always, the staff were more than willing to help anyone in need but enough was enough and the senior medical officer felt obliged to contact the atoll chief and insist that he restrict the number of islanders travelling to Gan for routine medical examinations and treatment, promising that if that were done the level of midwifery care and surgery would be sustained for as long as the medical facilities and staff were available.

The chief, as appreciative as ever of the goodwill services provided at the medical centre, readily accepted that the situation had got out of hand and duly introduced the necessary controls. He rationed health care across the islands but ensured that no woman was denied access to midwifery care, a service to which the islanders had become emotionally attached because it had, over the years, led to such a dramatic improvement in the survival rate of newborn children that in every village there were grateful families only too happy to testify to the quality of the services which the RAF provided.

The majority of the Maldivian employees were, like the expatriate Asians, on the Department of the Environment payroll and as the demand for works services declined many of them were made redundant as were the many Pakistani and Sri Lankan employees who were repatriated, either at the end of their fixed-term contracts or earlier if necessary.

The military operations on Gan were also gradually reducing but maintaining an appropriate number of airmen at the atoll during the latter part of 1975 was not quite so simple. Each of them had been posted to Gan for a nine-month tour and was due to be posted elsewhere at the end of that period with the arrival of his replacement maintaining the RAF's normal cycle of personnel movements. Many of the servicemen were willing to spend more than the customary nine months at the atoll, volunteering to take two weeks leave at the end of that normal tour of duty before returning to the base to work through to the end of March 1976. But the RAF's personnel management staff, continually trying to take into account the broader picture and the disruptive effect of changing the normal pattern of personnel movements, preferred, even during the last few months of 1975, to maintain an adequate manning level on the base by continuing to withdraw servicemen on completion of the regular nine-month tour, sending very few replacements to the atoll and leaving the remaining established posts vacant.

The result was that during the last quarter of the year the number of servicemen on Gan declined significantly with six of the thirty-six officers disestablished and the number of other ranks reduced from five hundred and thirty-three to three hundred and fifty-eight. Extended tours remained the exception rather than the rule until the early weeks of 1976 after which it was possible to sustain the steadily reducing military presence by extending the tour length for key personnel and for some other servicemen whilst only very rarely replacing anyone who left the base on completion of a nine-month tour.

For the first eight months of 1975, working life on the island was much the same as usual for the majority if not for the executives who were beginning to work on the gradual rundown of the base even though no detailed arrangements could be finalised until the politicians had decided what would be shipped out and what would be left behind. Until those decisions had been made the executives could do little more than publish a set of milestone plans for the various units and sections, all of which would continue to function until the end of the year with some remaining operational until the dying moments of the mid-ocean base.

By the end of August 1975 it was becoming obvious that if the Gan and Hitaddu sites were to be cleared ready for the departure at the end of March there was precious little time left for the British and Maldivian governments to reach an agreement on the disposal of the assets. What could be done, well before that had been decided, was to apply tight controls to the RAF's supply chain, ensuring that the only supplies to be ordered were either operationally essential or were items which would be consumed well before the 31st of March. That would ensure that, come the handover, the stocks of consumables, with the exception of medical supplies, would have been reduced to an operational minimum throughout the base.

Achieving that was not as straightforward as it seemed because orders for essential materials and equipment still had to be placed during the last few months of 1975 and into the first few weeks of 1976. Given that airfreight deliveries to the atoll were always likely to be delayed for a week or two and that sea-borne freight would rarely if ever arrive until several weeks after it had been ordered, the last six months in the life of RAF Gan were marked by a very careful assessment of needs, a virtual embargo on orders for sea-borne freight and a series of *cries de couer* over delivery dates.

Acutely aware that time was running out, a Ministry of Defence team accompanied by the Defence Adviser from Colombo and the Maldivian Affairs officer from Gan flew to Malé early in September, submitted to the Maldivian ministers a provisional list of the assets expected to become surplus to British requirements when the leased territories were vacated, and sought to reach an agreement on the revised wage rates and the amended terminal payments for the Maldivians employed at Addu Atoll.

Ali Maniku, the vice-president and minister for commercial affairs, explained that his government wished to take over the entire base as a going concern with an operational airfield and working public utilities. He therefore wished to send to Gan, prior to the RAF's withdrawal, a team of trained engineers to take over the essential services before they were shut down and decommissioned. Other assets could initially be taken over on a care and maintenance basis with plans to bring them back into use and operate the airfield as an international airport as soon as possible. That rather grand scheme conflicted with Britain's general policy on withdrawal from overseas bases which decreed that those fixtures, fittings and equipment which were required to maintain the operational status of the base could be left *in situ* only if there was no immediate operational requirement for them to be transferred to some other site. Non-surplus items could be purchased provided the Ministry of Defence did not require them elsewhere, but items which had been purchased from non-public funds had to be removed unless the original benefactors or the funding organisations, such as the Nuffield Trust, agreed to alternative arrangements. The British government could, of course, leave everything behind as a gift but that would be for the politicians to decide, not the Ministry of Defence staff.

The situation at Addu Atoll was, however, demanding of special consideration on two counts: the military interest in the abandoned base shown by other powers and the interest already shown by the media in the way Britain had behaved towards the Maldivian government through the early 1960s and towards the Ilois people, who had been evicted from their homes to allow the United States Air Force to build an airfield on Diego Garcia. For the British, an amicable and successful handover would help to defuse possible media and parliamentary criticism and would probably help to exclude other foreign powers from the archipelago but if the withdrawal from Addu Atoll looked as if it might result in economic and social disaster for the Adduans, the British government could be internationally embarrassed.

With those thoughts in mind a meeting was arranged to take place on Gan from the 17th to the 19th of November between Ministry of Defence representatives and a Maldivian government team led by Ali Maniku. By then the British approach to the disposal of the assets had been broadly clarified but there were still some matters to be resolved. In essence the plan was to abandon the land and to give to the Maldivians some fixed assets and some movable assets, asking for payment for the remainder. The non-public assets, mostly belonging to the NAAFI, would be available for the Maldivians to purchase if they so wished. By October, Maniku had been provided with a list of the assets to be left at the atoll under the above arrangements and in November he, accompanied by two engineers and Mrs Ismale, the matron from the Malé hospital, flew to Gan from Hulule. They said very little to the local population and, inevitably, that helped to fuel the many rumours related to the Adduans' future.

The British representatives clearly began by doubting whether the Maldivians were capable of converting an abandoned RAF airfield into an international airport but as the meetings developed into detailed negotiations over the disposal of assets Ali Maniku's grasp of the problems, his energy and his determination for Gan to succeed persuaded them that he was the one person who might be able to mastermind such an enterprise. Apart from his position as Vice-President and Minister for Commercial Affairs he was a leading entrepreneur in the region with wide interests, including joint ownership of Air Maldives; Nasir obviously had great faith in his ability for he had made him responsible for reclaiming the leased lands at the atoll and for planning the future commercial exploitation of Gan. As far as Maniku was concerned, he was anxious to obtain the best deal that he could because that would further enhance his standing with Nasir and if his plans for tourism came to fruition they would create valuable job opportunities and increasing demand for Air Maldives flights.

Much as Ali Maniku would have preferred to keep all the movable assets, he had a limited budget and could only afford to purchase the available non-public assets, leaving Britain to remove those which had been purchased out of public funds. He did, however, explain that he was particularly anxious to retain all the communications equipment necessary to maintain the worldwide links which he believed to be essential for the long-term development of the Republic and, although no promises were made, he was asked to provide a written statement of his requirements for comparison with the existing equipment.

Ali Maniku's other major ambition was to inherit the RAF's medical centre as a fully equipped, fully stocked, operational centre providing an uninterrupted service which would immediately satisfy the needs of the Adduans and the requirements of an international airport whilst being gradually developed to provide health care services for at least the southern half of the archipelago. His laudable, if somewhat grand, plan far exceeded the British government's more modest intention which was, at that time, to leave the medical centre reasonably well equipped and adequately stocked to satisfy the immediate needs of the Adduans pending the adoption of the facility as a government-run centre.

The British negotiators were well aware that the Adduans, and many other islanders in the southern reaches of the archipelago, had become partially dependent on the RAF's medical staff, and had decided on a generous approach because it was obvious that, for the Adduans, the loss of the RAF's medical services would be one of the most distressing aspects of the withdrawal. Quite apart from the fact that thousands of the islanders sought medical advice and treatment year after year, some one hundred and twenty of them were living month-to-month on life-saving drugs supplied by the RAF. There was every reason to believe that after the departure of the RAF's medical staff typhoid and other diseases would occur more frequently and the death toll would probably rise. Finally, there were the potential short-term problems associated with the improved lifestyle of the Maldivians, brought about by the British presence. The arrival of the NAAFI store had enabled them to change their diet and had undoubtedly helped to improve the islanders' general health but it was also thought to have contributed to the general increase in the size of the children born to Maldivian women, a change which had necessitated occasional Caesarean births as well as creating a need for the modern midwifery services available at the medical centre. There was a worrying possibility that when such facilities were no longer available there would be an increase in deaths in childbirth. If Britain were to strip the medical centre when abandoning the base the plight of the Adduans would become an immediate focus for media criticism and the British ministers were anxious to avoid that.

There was really no problem acceding to Maniku's requests for he was effectively asking for little more than the British government had initially been prepared to donate rather than face the criticism which would accompany a decision to remove all that the Maldivians could not afford to purchase. It was the subsequent operation of the airfield with its sophisticated communications systems, the power station and the fuel supply depot which gave the greatest cause for concern. In particular, the tanker farm and the power station, on which every facility depended, could be destroyed by mismanagement of the fuel storage and supply systems and the works engineers openly expressed their opinion that Maldivians were not yet capable of running those potentially lethal utilities. Ali Maniku, accepting that such was the case, explained that he intended to recruit specialists for the operation of the utilities, the communications systems and the medical centre. He added that he had already contacted the World Health Organisation to ask for help and if medical specialists could not be recruited to work on Gan, the medical centre would be operated by the existing RAF-trained Maldivian staff.

The upshot was that the meetings ended amicably on the 19th of November with agreement on the disposal of the assets and on an arrangement whereby a Maldivian team would spend February and March on Gan compiling a total inventory of all the assets which were to be handed over to the Maldivians. For his part, Ali Maniku readily agreed to abide by the British stipulation that the assets which his government would inherit were not to be given, loaned or sold to any third party.

With the meetings over, the Maldivian negotiators flew back to Hulule. Within days of their return to Malé, Nasir made a formal request, through the British High Commissioner, for Britain to provide specialists who could be employed at the atoll for twelve months after the military withdrawal, taking over the communications systems, the utilities and the medical centre, operating those facilities and training Maldivians in as many skills as possible. The President's view was that, by mid-1977, his government would be able to manage Gan's international airport with minimal help from foreign contractors.

For William Rodgers, Britain's minister of state for defence, Nasir's request rang a few alarm bells. Throughout 1975 he had been corresponding with Ted Rowlands, the parliamentary under-secretary of state for the foreign and commonwealth office, and with Reginald Prentice, the minister of state for overseas development, making it clear that he had no intention of becoming embroiled in any post-withdrawal support for the Maldivians. He saw that as the concern of the ministers for overseas development and the Foreign and Commonwealth Office. Emphasising that handing over the assets was an RAF responsibility and that the wider questions of aid and resource development were of no concern to the Ministry of Defence, he made it quite clear that the message to Nasir must be '...*nothing will delay our departure beyond 1 April 1976*'. He also pointed out that if the British government wished to help the Maldivians to use the donated assets to convert Gan's airfield into an international airport, some non-surplus items with an estimated value of one hundred and fifty thousand pounds would have to be handed over in addition to the assets already identified and offered to Ali Maniku. In particular, he pointed out that the airfield would be of very little value without those associated communications and navigation aids which were not among the assets due to be given to the Maldivians.

His assessment left the British ministers with a dilemma which would have to be resolved before February when the Maldivian team would start to compile an inventory of the British assets at Addu Atoll.

The Adduan employees, seemingly resigned to their indeterminate future and without any faith in their government's interest in them, continued to be remarkably cooperative throughout 1975, apparently consoling themselves with the short-term benefits in November, when they received their increased rates of pay and their arrears, and in December, when each of those who would be entitled to a redundancy payment in 1976 received half of that payment in advance.

For the Adduans, the enhanced redundancy rates, which were linked to the combined gratuity and compensation awards for the Sri Lankans, and the increased wages were the only bright spots on the horizon. In theory it was possible for a Maldivian who had been employed in a highly rated job since 1957 to collect a terminal payment of almost two thousand pounds, a small fortune in Adduan society. The reality was that very few qualified for more than half that and the majority would each receive considerably less than two hundred pounds.

When Brynmor John, Britain's parliamentary under-secretary of state for defence for the Royal Air Force was asked to give an estimate of the redundancy payments to be made to the locally employed civilians as a result of the RAF's withdrawal from Gan he stated , in a written answer to the House, that the total cost of the redundancy payments ' ...*for the Ministry of Defence, Department of the Environment and NAAFI employees... [was] ...about one hundred and thirty-four thousand pounds in total and one hundred and forty-five pounds per employee.*'

Given that the Pakistanis and the Sri Lankans were generally longer serving and higher paid than the Maldivians, the average figure seems to suggest that the majority of the Maldivians received redundancy payments of less than one hundred and fifty pounds each.

The problem for the Adduans was how best to utilise the money. So many were being made redundant that they couldn't all become traders nor could all those with skills learnt on Gan become tradesmen; there just wasn't enough demand for so many artisans. For most of them the money would serve to buy items to make life easier for a while, to pay for the purchase of a fishing boat or to pay for their children's education, albeit for an indeterminate future.

The only glimmer of hope for the islanders was their government's plan to convert the military base into an international airport and bring tourism and trade to the atoll. It was a proposal which the islanders wanted to believe but which they regarded with considerable scepticism, convinced that nothing would come of those grand ideas. Nevertheless, they could not afford to ignore the possibility that even some modest developments could lead to employment opportunities for those who could offer appropriate skills and could speak, read and write English. The result was that training and education for Maldivians became a regular feature of life on Gan during the last few months of 1975 and into the early weeks of 1976. For the Adduans who enrolled on the programmes it was an act born out of hope rather than faith because even though most of them believed that their government was unlikely to carry out its grand scheme they were prepared to spend their time learning anything which just might improve their prospects.

XXIII   The Final Weeks

The final agreement

It was early in January 1976 when Ali Maniku made what was to be his last visit to London before he sent a team of Maldivian inspectors and recorders to Gan with instructions to compile a total inventory of the assets which were to be inherited by his government. He came hoping to add to the already lengthy inventory of items which were due to be handed over in accordance with the November agreement but he was not really expecting to be given all that he was asking for and, with little to offer during any negotiations, he was convinced that he would have to make his case, once more, by arguing that Britain had a moral obligation to treat the Maldivians far more generously than was required under a strict interpretation of the British government's long-standing policies on military withdrawals from overseas bases. What he did not expect was that there would be no need for him to argue his case: the British ministers had already discussed the disposal of the surplus movable public assets which he had said he could not buy and they had decided to donate everything which could be said to be reasonably necessary for the continued operation of the Gan airfield as a civilian airport after the 31st of March 1976. They specifically excluded from their offer the Skynet communications equipment which was designed for military use and had no civil application but, with that exception, whatever was there would be left. In addition, the major works would all be backed up by the donation of spares and general stores to support a civil operation.

Given the reservations about the Maldivians' ability to run a facility as complex as that on Gan, the British offer was extremely generous and there were, inevitably, misgivings that much of the equipment would not be utilised but would be left to deteriorate. There was, however, one certainty: Britain could not be accused of making any failure inevitable by depriving the Maldivians of essential equipment.

When Maniku realised the full extent of the British offer he was taken aback. The fuel storage depot would be left with enough fuel to run the airfield for at least a month and any empty storage tanks would be made safe before the handover by filling them with water to purge them of explosive vapours. The powerhouse would be handed over in full working order and although two generators would be removed for use elsewhere those which remained had the capacity to meet the requirements set out by the Maldivians during the November meeting on Gan. Standby generators, powerful enough to meet the needs of an airport in the event of a main power failure, would be left behind. The airfield was offered complete with all landing lights in working order and navigation aids comprising the instrument landing system, the approach radar, the precision approach radar, the tactical aid to navigation, the non-directional beacon and the airfield equipment for ground-to-air communications. The control tower, complete with mini-communications systems, would be handed over in the condition seen during the November inspection, the meteorological station would be left with equipment ranging from barometers to cloud searchlights and with balloons and a hydrogen supply to satisfy the requirements of an international airfield. A miscellany of equipment, ranging from aircraft steps to three operational sets of air conditioning equipment for use on parked aircraft, completed the airfield package. Also offered was Gan's complete cold storage facility which, with a capacity of fifteen thousand cubic feet, was large enough to satisfy the demands of an embryonic international airport.

The communications equipment to be left behind was all that the Maldivians could desire. The Hitaddu transmitter station, with aerial alignments which covered the United Kingdom, Cyprus, Mauritius and Singapore incorporated Marconi equipment with power ratings from three and a half kilowatts to thirty kilowatts. On Gan the co-located system control section and receiving station included receiving antennae with provision for alignment with the United Kingdom, Cyprus, Singapore and Mauritius. The automatic telephone switchboard was to be left *in situ*, as was the entire Radio Gan complex.

To indemnify Britain against any subsequent claims, Ali Maniku was advised that everything would be left '...*as seen by the Maldivians who were to start taking over the assets with effect from mid-January 1976*'. Similarly justified clauses were included in the agreement, recommending that the Maldivian minister should make arrangements for a professional safety survey to be undertaken on every mast, should raise a maintenance contract for the test equipment which his government was to inherit and should, on his return to Malé, immediately organise familiarisation training for the Maldivians who would be employed to operate the donated equipment after the end of March. Delighted with the outcome of his visit to London, Maniku readily accepted all the recommendations and informed the British ministers that he had made arrangements for a survey team to assemble on Gan on the 15th of January and to begin compiling the inventory of assets which would be handed over as they fell out of use.

At that point Ali Maniku was left with nothing else to ask for, the meeting was brought to a close and he left, almost certainly unable to believe that, without having to argue his case, he had been handed more than he had ever expected; the movable public assets which his government was about to inherit were worth at least a million pounds and the fixed assets were valued at almost ten times that.

The assets on land were all relevant to the Maldivians' plans for the creation of a civil airport but were of little immediate value to their economy. The donated assets from N° 1125 marine craft unit, however, were of immediate use for they included the twenty-five-foot cutter used to service the Wave Ruler; launch N° 1667; four dumb barges; pinnace N° 1382 which was fit only for scrap; three general purpose landing craft, one of which had no power unit; two marine tenders, one of which was beyond repair; one sampan and some nine hundred and fifty tons of naval buoys, representing the balance of the unit's holdings after a mere thirty tons of buoys had been recovered for use elsewhere.

Maniku's visit provoked the head of DS8 at the Ministry of Defence to write, in January, to the Permanent Secretary to the Parliamentary Under-Secretary of State for Defence for the Royal Air Force, expressing opinions which quite clearly showed that he had few, if any, qualms about the premature abandonment of the Adduans. Commenting on the unwelcome possibility of employing RAF personnel to run the medical centre and the communications systems at the atoll after the 31st of March 1976 he pointed out that the Maldivian minister had not specifically referred to the use of RAF specialists, would probably prefer to employ civilians and had said that he could find medical staff and doctors from India. Arguing that the employment of any British servicemen would have to be undertaken by personnel on three-month detachments because of the remoteness of the atoll he pointed out that such an arrangement would, in any case, merely delay the inevitable whilst providing a medical service which would be too sophisticated for the Adduans' culture. Suggesting that it might well be better to stop providing such medical care sooner rather than later, he added his voice to those already in favour of total withdrawal, strongly recommending that no RAF personnel should remain at the atoll after the 31st of March 1976.

By the 15th of January, when the Maldivian survey team was expected to assemble on Gan to start compiling the inventories, RAF Gan would have been out of daily use as a staging post for a fortnight. Consequently, much of the equipment which had been designed specifically for military rather than civil use would have been transferred to bases elsewhere in the world, as would some of the general equipment which was no longer required on Gan but which was needed on other sites. The inventory would reflect that and would also show that by February the stocks of consumables, with the exception of medical supplies, would have been reduced to an operational minimum throughout the base, a process which had been going on for several months.

The transfer of assets

After the usual Christmas break Gan once more became a fully operational staging post, albeit for less than a week. On the 1st of January, when the last of the regularly scheduled VC 10s to stage through Gan took off for Brize Norton (Fig 23.1) it signalled, for the expatriates, the beginning of twelve weeks of sorting, packing and stacking.

At that point, an air of finality seemed to develop among the Maldivians. It was as though that last schedule marked the end of their long association with the British military and their inexorable decline into a subsistence-level economy, the like of which had never been experienced by an entire generation of Adduans. In every village there were young adults who could not remember what life had been like before the arrival of the RAF and for them the idea of regression into a subsistence lifestyle seemed particularly threatening. For those who were parents, it was not just their own future which looked bleak, it was their children's future as well and for their sakes Adduan parents across the atoll were desperately hoping that life on the islands would improve in the longer term. For many of them it meant that they would have to decide whether to spend the redundancy payments on modest but immediate benefits for the family or on the provision of education for their children who were facing an indeterminate future.

Not surprisingly, the station diary for January includes comments such as 'The locals' hearts are not in their work ...they need supervising or they work very slowly' and '...petty crime continues, now with impudence as illustrated by the theft of the runway approach lights.' But after the 15th of the month theft and general pilfering became a matter of interest to the Maldivians who were compiling the inventory of assets to be handed over. To them, theft from Gan was in essence theft of property soon to belong to the Maldivian government. Thus it was that towards the end of January fifteen Maldivians were recruited, trained and employed by the RAF as security guards on Gan, working for the RAF police until the end of the Adduans' last complete day shift on the 28th of March when they formed an independent Maldivian security corps responsible for all security and police matters related to Maldivians on the leased territories on Gan and Hitaddu. Their employment solved the problem. After January, significant thefts became quite rare and, although it was almost impossible to assess the level of petty pilfering, there was a general impression that it had been dramatically reduced.

The compilation of the inventory was far less troublesome than had been envisaged, largely because the British government's approach, intended to ensure that the Maldivians inherited a going concern, was to give them anything not previously earmarked for removal and use elsewhere. There were some local sales of small items to servicemen but none to the Adduans except those who were also nominated as traders and even they were permitted to buy only the assets that the Maldivian auditors were prepared to release.

By the end of January everyone had begun to appreciate the effectiveness of the controls which had been imposed on the supply chain to the base; they had significantly reduced the volume of stores and equipment to be packed ready for removal and had ensured that the few items in the pipeline at the end of January would arrive well before the end of March.

Questions in Parliament

In Britain the withdrawal and the attendant benefit to the Maldivians of inheriting most of the assets had attracted the attention of several members of parliament, one of whom, Geoffrey Finsberg, questioned the govern-ment's generosity in giving away movable assets and suggested that perhaps the Maldivians should be asked to pay for some of them. In reply, Brynmor John set out the case against such a proposal saying:

> 'The fixed assets and the land on which they stand revert free of charge to the Maldivian Government under the terms of the agreement. Those assets amount to £9.8 million. The donated movable assets, with a value of £1.044 million were items which were either of no further use to Britain or would cost more to bring home to the UK than to replace. The agreement permitted the sale of such items only to nominated traders and this effectively removed any local market for them. The list of movable assets was very wide ranging. None was to be replaced.
>
> The only alternative was to destroy all of them which would have gone against all that Britain was trying to achieve. As it was, they will be of value to the Maldivians, helping towards the creation of an international airport with benefits for the Maldivians which their government could not have created from its own resources. A limited range of non-surplus Department of Environment (Property Services Agency) and defence equipment to a value of two hundred and seventy-five thousand pounds was to be given to the Maldivians because it makes an essential contribution to the airfield. The cost would be covered by the Spring Estimates. In essence the donated assets are of great use to the Maldivian Government but of almost no value to Britain who has acted to help preserve the Maldivian economy and good relations.'

Finsberg didn't let the matter rest. He came back to Brynmor John about the cold store in Gan and the fact that there was a need for such a store in Cyprus. Not only that, he suggested that Brynmor John had been in breach of parliamentary procedure by agreeing, without first informing the House, to donate assets on the assumption that the cost would be covered by supplementary estimates. John's final answer made it clear that the only assets which could be handed over were those covered by the Treasury minute which lay before Parliament for the obligatory fourteen days. The non-surplus items, to be covered by supplementary votes to Defence and the Department of the Environment, could not and would not be handed over until the supplementary votes were approved. A Ministry of Defence supplementary vote would be required to provide the cold store needed in Cyprus because the fifteen thousand cubic feet cold store on Gan could not be regarded as a surplus item, it was being given to the Maldivian government only because it was not feasible to operate a civil airport on Gan without cold store facilities.

Last minute recruitment

Ali Maniku, whilst obviously interested in the inventory of assets to be handed over, had an additional concern; the post-withdrawal provision of medical staff and a communications specialist . There were similar concerns in London where the Under-Secretary of State for Defence for the Royal Air Force feared that, unless appropriate staff could be recruited and in post at Addu Atoll before the 1st of April, the Ministry of Defence would be called upon to save face for the British government by providing post-withdrawal medical services at the atoll, operating the islands' communications systems and training Maldivians until they were competent enough to take over all the site facilities.

It was not too difficult to recruit a communications specialist but recruiting a doctor and a nurse was not so easy and it was the last week in January before Group Captain Edwards was informed that the Ministry for Overseas Development would definitely recruit the necessary medical staff and arrange for them to be in post before the end of March. That news came as a welcome relief for the atoll chief, Moosa Ali Didi, who learnt from the station commander on the 30th of January that *The United Kingdom's Overseas Development Ministry will recruit medical officers to take over the regional medical centre'*. The Ministry staff had cut things rather fine but, as promised, they did recruit a surgeon, Dr Roger Wolstenholme, and his wife, Peta, a state registered nurse, arranging for them to run the medical services at the atoll on a one-year contract.

Exploiting the inheritance

Whilst Ali Maniku's team of inspectors was compiling the inventory of assets and the British were recruiting the medical and communications specialists, the Maldivian ministers were still considering how best to exploit the airfield facilities at Addu Atoll, making overtures to several potential leaseholders and resisting approaches from others. The Russians and the Chinese were both interested in using the island as a military base but neither was welcome as far as the Maldivian government was concerned; companies were sought after, not nations and certainly not communist states. In essence, the Maldivians had decided that, if they could not keep the British military at the atoll, they did not want servicemen from any other nation to be based there.

The facilities which the British had created offered one obvious and immediate possibility; they could be converted into a holiday resort. With that in mind, Ali Maniku, occasionally accompanied by the British Defence Adviser from Colombo, became a frequent visitor to Gan during the first three months of 1976, meeting representatives from any organisations which showed an interest in the island's facilities, taking the opportunity to examine the non-public assets which his government was to inherit, checking on the progress of his audit team and inspecting the infrastructure which was to be handed over at the end of March.

At the beginning of the year he had commissioned International Aeradio Ltd (United Kingdom) to compile a report on the conversion of Gan from a military to a civil airport and, within days of receiving that report, he had flown to Gan to meet two groups of representatives, the first from British Airways, the second from a German tour operator. At that stage, he was becoming rather anxious because the Malé-based staff in the Department of External Affairs had received virtually no response from their government's advertising campaign of May 1975. Almost certainly that was because potential investors had been put off by memories of the southern insurrection which made the offer of one hundred per cent political stability ring rather hollow. Tourism, it seemed, was to be the sole option for the regeneration of Gan's facilities.

On the 19th of February, while Ali Maniku was meeting those representatives on Gan, the Russians applied for their Academy of Science ship the Vityaz to conduct marine biology surveys in the southern regions of the archipelago and, more specifically, in the vicinity of Addu Atoll. Aware that, if the Maldivians acceded to the request, the Russian crew would, after the 1st of April, be able to land at the atoll and inspect the Gan and Hitaddu sites, the British government sent word to the Maldivian President that the Vityaz would be an unwelcome visitor in that region, that the Russians should most certainly not be permitted to land at either Hitaddu or Gan and that, in this context, Britain regarded the 1965 agreement as binding even after abandoning the sites.

That message left Nasir with little choice. Were he to allow the Vityaz into the southern waters there was a possibility that Britain would remove every significant piece of equipment from the atoll sites, leaving little or nothing for the Russians to inspect. The President chose not to take that risk. He excluded the Russian ship from the southern region even though it was no stranger to Malé, having been previously employed as a survey ship in the more northerly waters.

The closure invitation

Even though politicians, civil servants and military chiefs had been working since December 1974 on the rundown and withdrawal from Addu Atoll it was not until the 9th of March that the Air Officer Commanding-in-Chief of the Near East Air Force received a letter from Air Commodore Hamilton, the director of organisation and administrative plans at the Ministry of Defence to provide the formal authorisation for the closure of RAF Gan. The letter was actually couched as an invitation, reading:

CLOSURE OF RAF GAN

I am directed to state that executive authority is given for the closure of RAF Gan by 31 Mar 76, the exact timing to be at the discretion of the Air Officer Commanding-in-Chief, Near East Air Force. You are invited to implement this decision and to notify Ministry of Defence ...on completion....

The last of the assets

The bulk of those assets which were to be removed from the island were destined to be taken on board the Royal Fleet Auxiliary landing ship logistics Sir Percival but during the first three months of 1976 the Hercules aircraft, which were frequent visitors to the base, removed a diverse collection of military equipment and a significant volume of general freight, including a number of unique items such as the station's Wilkinson Sword and Frank Wootton's painting of Gan.

On the 16th of March the Sir Percival arrived at the atoll and as the loading began the Adduans realised that within a matter of days their twenty-year association with the RAF was about to end. The following day, the medical centre became the first of the major facilities to be formally handed over to the Maldivian government and from then on ownership of the assets at the base was transferred almost day by day. Whilst that process was continuing the officer commanding N° 1125 marine craft unit was organising the transfer of several hundred tons of miscellaneous stores and equipment onto the Sir Percival.

On the 19th Gan's residents bad farewell to the Royal Fleet Auxiliary refuelling hulk, the Wave Ruler, towed away for scrap after being at anchor in the lagoon since October 1970 when she replaced the Wave Victor.

The transfer of the assets built up to a major handover of the communications equipment, the airfield, the meteorological office, the utilities and over six hundred thousand gallons of fuel on the 27th, by which time the station commander was seriously beginning to doubt whether the Sir Percival had the capacity to take all that was to be removed. He was under instructions not to leave behind anything which had not been gifted to the Maldivian government and as the departure deadline approached he watched the loading operation with increasing concern. On the 28th of March he breathed a sigh of relief as the last pallet was hoisted aboard ship and he realised that, with virtually no spare capacity on board, the entire loading operation had been successfully managed, leaving only the marine craft unit, the vehicles and the remaining facilities to be handed over to Ali Maniku on the 29th.

The last Pakistanis and Sri Lankans

Throughout 1975 the number of expatriate Asian employees at the atoll had been continually reduced and by the beginning of March the remaining thirty-three Pakistanis and twenty-seven Sri Lankans were packing their belongings and getting ready to leave. The Sri Lankans left for Colombo on the 21st of the month, the day before the Pakistanis were flown to Karachi. On each of the two flights the passengers' baggage weighed more than the passengers because every one of them had been on a six-month spending spree at the NAAFI, purchasing anything, from a watch to a refrigerator, which was either unobtainable or extremely expensive in Sri Lanka or Pakistan . Waiving the normal baggage weight restrictions, the RAF carried some seven hundred pounds of luggage for each passenger, a final goodwill gesture for the Asian employees who had supported the RAF at the atoll and had, in many cases, had their dream of British citizenship through Crown Service shattered by Act of Parliament and the premature closure of the RAF's mid-ocean staging post.

The last Maldivian employees

With the cessation of the daily passenger flights staging through Gan and the removal of much of the military equipment, the redundancy rate among the Maldivians gathered pace; of the seven hundred and ninety-nine employed at the beginning of January, three hundred and forty-nine had been made redundant by the end of February.

Four hundred and fifty Maldivians remained on the payroll until the 31st of March but many of them did not bother to report for work after the 25th for the simple reason that on that day they were all finally paid off. Those who chose to honour the agreement to work until the end of the month remained dependent upon the dhoni services across the lagoon and those, fortunately, continued to operate for two reasons. Firstly, the passengers, who were rowing themselves to and from Gan were, by their rowing, enabling the owners to collect bulky items such as empty oil drums or wardrobes from the scrap yard, a legitimate, well-established practice controlled by the RAF (Fig 23.2). Secondly, and more importantly, none of the dhoni owners wished to forfeit the last-minute payment of fees from the RAF because those would include a considerable lump sum award to cover an increase, back-dated to July 1974, in the daily hire rates.

The last servicemen and European civilians

With Christmas behind them and the departure of the west-bound VC10 on the 31st of December Gan's dwindling population of European civilians together with the remaining servicemen, thirty RAF officers and three hundred and fifty-eight other ranks, welcomed in the New Year. Within hours, those who were to remain on the island were bidding farewell to the last scheduled VC 10 as it took off for England, carrying the last of the personnel from Nº 6 signals unit which had, since April 1975, gradually shed most of its full complement of two hundred servicemen. With their departure the communications networks were left in the hands of Gan's signals personnel and a detachment of Nº 38 Group Tactical Communications Wing specialists.

For the next twelve weeks Gan's twenty-seven officers and two hundred and ninety-two other ranks, supported by a declining number of expatriate civilians and Maldivian employees, were to spend their time preparing for the departure, running a shadow of a staging post whilst sorting, stacking and packing the remaining assets.

Throughout that period there was a rapid reduction in the number of servicemen at the atoll as men were repatriated on completion of a normal nine-month tour. Rarely was anyone replaced during those first few weeks of 1976 and, other than the key personnel who were needed in post until the final hours, very few of those who volunteered to remain beyond the end of a normal tour were asked to do so.

The last hundred Gannites departed on board the Sir Percival on the 29th of March after the final ceremony had marked the end of the British military presence in the Maldives.

The final ceremony

The British Ambassador to the Maldives, Mr D P Aiers, accompanied by Lieutenant Colonel R G Woodhouse, the defence attaché, came to Gan from Colombo for the final ceremony on the 29th of March, the day when the RAF ensign was lowered for the last time (Fig 23.3) and when Group Captain Edwards, the last of Gan's station commanders, formally handed back the leasehold lands to Ali Maniku with a farewell message from the British Prime Minister to the President of the Republic of the Maldives saying:

> 'On the occasion of the departure of the Royal Air Force from Gan, I send you, on behalf of Her Majesty's Government, our thanks for the generous cooperation which we have received throughout our stay, and our best wishes for the future prosperity of the Maldivian people'

So ended the RAF's nineteen-year association with the atoll and its inhabitants.

Ali Maniku could have been forgiven had he shown a wry smile at the wording of that final message for he could well remember the acrimony during the days of the Adduans' rebellion and as for future prosperity, Britain's unexpectedly early withdrawal from the atoll had left the Adduans and his government with a severe short-term problem, no matter what the distant future might bring.

The departure

As the Sir Percival sailed out of the lagoon the last contingent of Gannites looked back at the islands with mixed emotions; some had volunteered to serve on that spit of a coral island, some had been unwilling conscripts, very few were sorry to be leaving but almost certainly none would wish that he had never experienced life on Gan.

The new expatriates

The departure of the last of the Gannites left three expatriates at the atoll. Mr Little, an ex-RAF Chief Technician recruited to operate and maintain the communications systems for the next six months, Dr Wolstenholme and his wife Peta, a state registered nurse.

All three had arrived much closer to the RAF's withdrawal date than was desirable with Mr Little being welcomed on the 21st, just twenty-four hours after Dr Wolstenholme and his wife had been greeted by Gan's senior medical officer and briefly introduced both to the departing staff and to the Maldivians who would continue to work in the medical centre after the departure of the military.

For the newly arrived expatriates, the 30th of March marked the beginning of life as the only westerners in an isolated Maldivian society. From then on they would not be able to call upon the resources of the British military, there would be no RAF aircraft linking the atoll to the Far East or Cyprus, no works department staff, no NAAFI facilities and no regular supply ships bringing Western commodities to Gan.

It was to be an interesting experience.

Fig 23.1. Farewell to the last of the regularly scheduled VC 10s.

Fig 23.2. Furniture collection by dhoni.

Fig 23.3. The RAF ensign being lowered for the last time at Gan.

The Gan Shoreline.

Appendices

Appendix A: Gan's Commanding Officers

THE DETACHMENT COMMANDER

Flt Lt G M McNeil BSc was the officer commanding the Ship's Flag detachment from the third week in January 1957, when the twelve-man unit was formed in Ceylon, until he left Gan in September. The first officer commanding Royal Air Force Gan was Squadron Leader R A Schofield whose tour as Gan's station commander began whilst McNeil and his men were still working on the island.

THE STATION COMMANDERS

Jun '57 - Jun '58	Squadron Leader/Wing Commander R A Schofield
Jun '58 - Apr '59	Wing Commander W Kent AFC
Apr '59 – Apr '60	Wing Commander I Thomas DFC
Apr '60 – Oct '60	Wing Commander M H Constable-Maxwell DSO DFC MA
Oct '60 – Oct '61	Wing Commander E W Cropper
Oct '61 – Dec '62	Wing Commander P C Ellis DFC
Dec '62 – Jan '64	Wing Commander P G Hill
Jan '64 – Apr '65	Wing Commander G Moss OBE AFC
Apr '65 – Apr '66	Wing Commander M Scannell OBE DFC AFC
Apr '66 – Apr '67	Wing Commander H K Rees
Apr '67 – Sep '67	Wing Commander R B Fleming DFC AFC
Sep '67 – Oct '68	Wing Commander R H Mullineaux
Oct '68 – Oct '69	Wing Commander H T C Farmer
Oct '69 – Oct '70	Wing Commander B J Spragg
Oct '70 – Aug '71	Wing Commander B Gee BSc
Aug '71 – May '72	Group Captain H L Sheppard
May '72 – Feb '73	Group Captain R S Salmon
Feb '73 – Nov '73	Group Captain A J Whitlock OBE
Nov '73 – Dec '74	Group Captain D F Moffat OBE
Dec '74 – Mar '76	Group Captain W Edwards AFC

Appendix B: 1942 Map of Gan

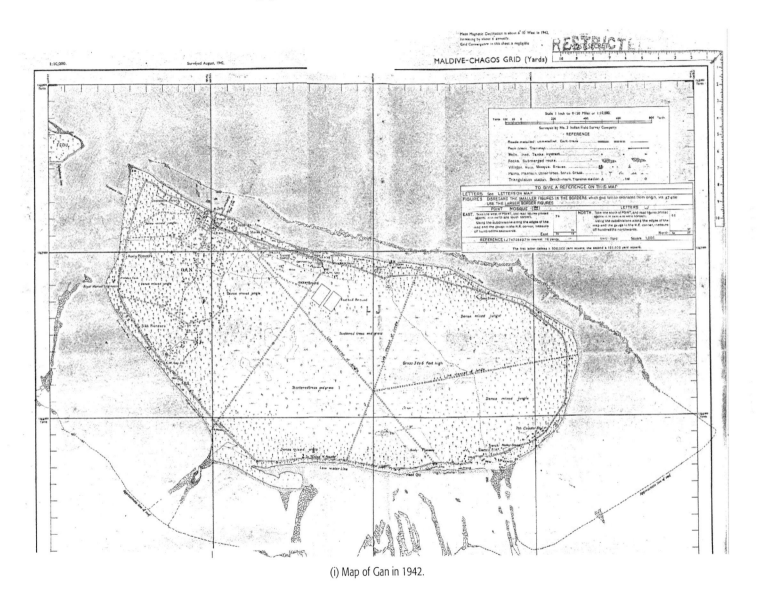

(i) Map of Gan in 1942.

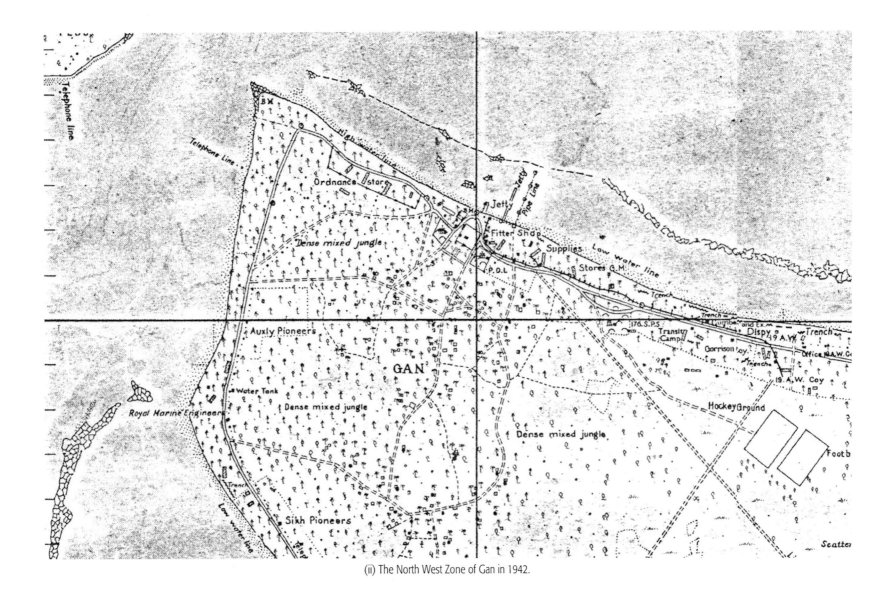

(ii) The North West Zone of Gan in 1942.

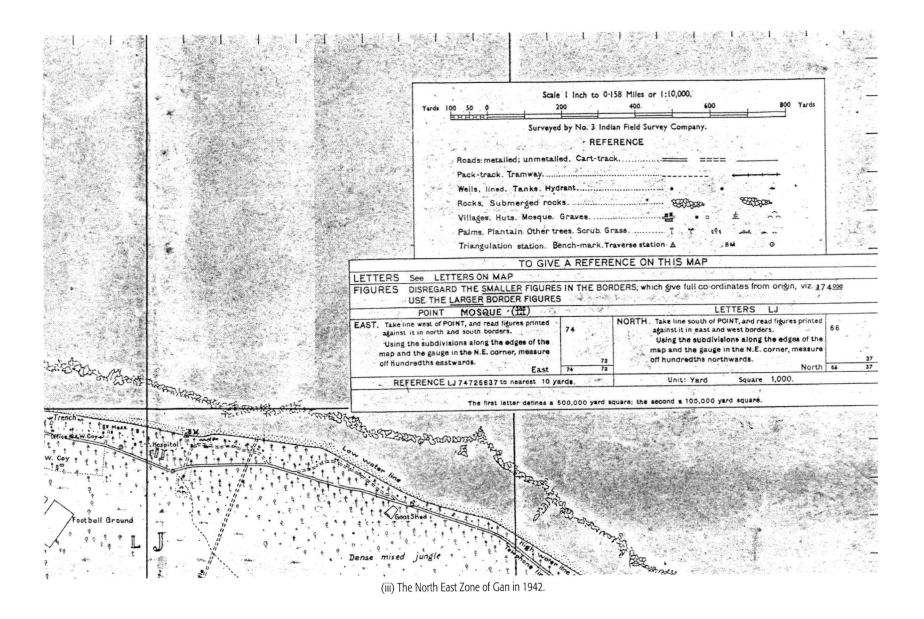

Scale 1 Inch to 0·158 Miles or 1:10,000.

Yards 100 50 0   200   400   600   800   Yards

Surveyed by No. 3 Indian Field Survey Company.

REFERENCE

Roads: metalled; unmetalled. Cart-track..........

Pack-track. Tramway..........

Wells. lined. Tanks. Hydrant..........

Rocks. Submerged rocks..........

Villages. Huts. Mosque. Graves..........

Palms. Plantain. Other trees. Scrub. Grass..........

Triangulation station. Bench-mark. Traverse station △   BM   ⊙

TO GIVE A REFERENCE ON THIS MAP

LETTERS   See   LETTERS ON MAP

FIGURES   DISREGARD THE SMALLER FIGURES IN THE BORDERS, which give full co-ordinates from origin, viz. 374.000
USE THE LARGER BORDER FIGURES

POINT MOSQUE (iii)		LETTERS LJ	
EAST. Take line west of POINT, and read figures printed against it in north and south borders. Using the subdivisions along the edges of the map and the gauge in the N.E. corner, measure off hundredths eastwards.	74	NORTH. Take line south of POINT, and read figures printed against it in east and west borders. Using the subdivisions along the edges of the map and the gauge in the N.E. corner, measure off hundredths northwards.	66
East 74 72	72	North 66 37	37
REFERENCE LJ 74726637 to nearest 10 yards.		Unit: Yard Square 1,000.	

The first letter defines a 500,000 yard square; the second a 100,000 yard square.

Trench
Mess.
Office   R.A.W. Coy
Hospital
W. Coy

Low water line

Football Ground

L   J

Goat Shed

Dense mixed jungle

High water line

Telephone line

(iii) The North East Zone of Gan in 1942.

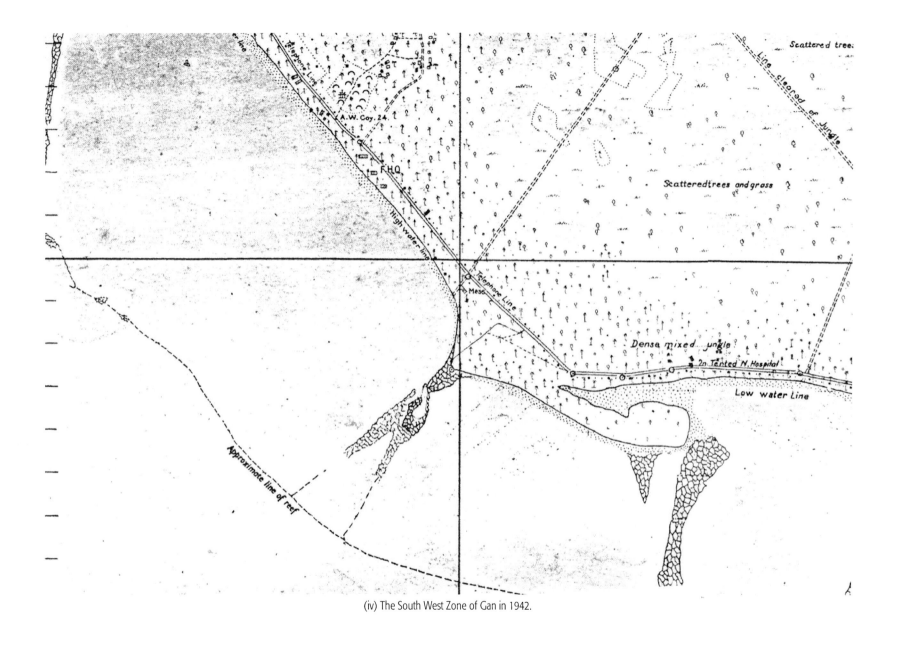

(iv) The South West Zone of Gan in 1942.

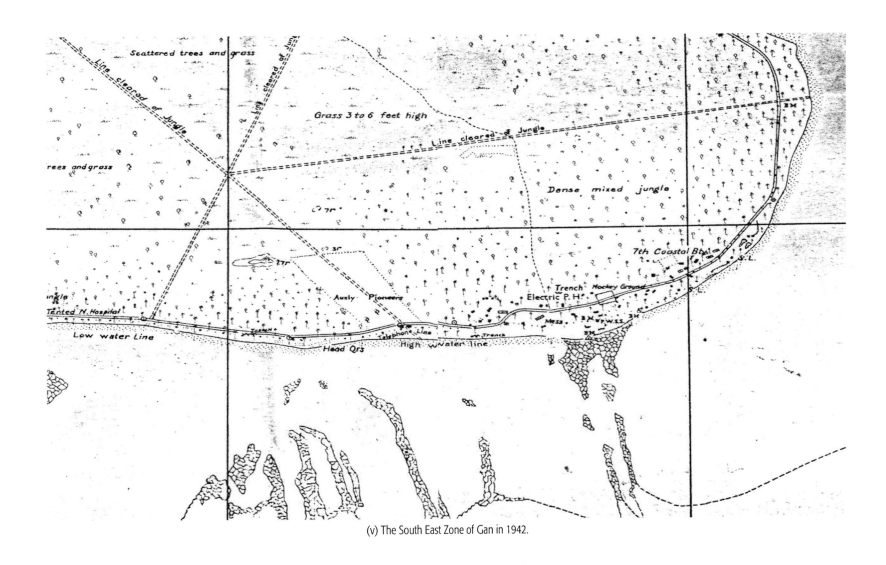

Scattered trees and grass

Line cleared of Jungle

Line cleared of Jungle

Grass 3 to 6 feet high

Line cleared of Jungle

rees and grass

Dense mixed jungle

7r

3r

27r

7th Coastal Bty.

S.L.

S.L.

ngle

Trench

Hockey Ground

Auxly Pioneers

Electric P. H.

Tented N. Hospital

Trench

Mess

S.M.

W.S.S.

3M

Low water Line

Trench

3M

Head Qrs

Telephone Line

Trench

High Water line

3M

(v) The South East Zone of Gan in 1942.

Appendix C: Aerial Photo of Gan in 1967

RAF Gan from the air in 1967 (source: K. Rees).

Appendix D: RAF Gan Buildings and Other Significant Structures Standing in January 1976

Number	Feature
1	Station commander's bungalow
2-5	Senior officers' quarters
6-9	Junior officers' quarters
10	Officers' tennis court
11	Aircrew quarters
12-21	Senior non-commissioned officers' quarters
22	Senior non-commissioned officers' tennis court
23	Guardroom
24	Airmen's tennis courts
25	Church
26-38	Airmen's quarters
39	Transit block
40	Airmen's quarters
41	Squash court
42	Aircrew quarters
43/44	Non-commissioned officers' quarters
45	Mortuary
46	Medicine store
47	Dhoni-line police post
48	Gymnasium
49	Maldivian rest room ('Maldivian hotel')
50	Mosque
51	Navy Army and Air Force Institutes' shop (European)
52-54	Female transients' quarters
55	Airmen's quarters
56	Aircrew quarters
57	VIP quarters
58	Marine engine repair shed
59	Marine servicing and boatwright shop
60	Boatwright shop, offices and stores
61	Marine craft unit office
62	Petrol, oil and lubricants store
63	Rigging shop and paint store
64	Crew room
65	Pyrotechnics store
66	Rigging store
67	Cable store
68	Chemicals store
69	Supply squadron
70	Technical supply flight
71	Nº 605 signals troop store
72	Nº 605 signals troop vehicle shed and cable store
73	Hobbies centre
74/75	Education centre
76/77	Transmitters
78	Airfield transmitter generator shed
79	Fire section store and RAF Regiment accommodation
80	Nº 6 signals unit cleaning shed and workshop
81	Nº 6 signals unit message centres workshop
82	Ground radio and Nº 6 signals unit engineering coordinating centre
83	Fire section garage
84	Satellite receiving station (meteorological)
85	Meteorological section enclosure
86	Air traffic control pyrotechnic store
87	Communications centre, telephone exchange, meteorological office and operations centre
88	Staging aircraft servicing flight control centre
89	Meteorological balloon filling shed
90	Radio Gan studio
91	Archery club/station warrant officer's store
92	Post Office, Navy Army and Air Force Institutes' office and civilian administration office
93	War memorial
94	Angling club store/boat shed
95	Yacht club
96	Sailing club and bar
97	Bakery
98	Navy Army and Air Force Institutes' cold store
99	Navy Army and Air Force Institutes' bulk store
100	Navy Army and Air Force Institutes' dry goods store
101	Maldivian trading post (Navy Army and Air Force Institutes)
102	Navy Army and Air Force Institutes' mineral water bulk store
103	Navy Army and Air Force Institutes' cold store
104	Barrack store
105	Gan island dairy
106	Navy Army and Air Force Institutes' cold store for potatoes and flour
107	RAF laundry and Department of the Environment workshop
108	Department of the Environment blacksmith and welding shop
109	Agricultural plant store and office
110	Department of the Environment offices
111	Department of the Environment workshops
112	Department of the Environment paint shop
113	Department of the Environment main store
114	Department of the Environment general store and cycle shop
115-122	Department of the Environment stores
123	Supply squadron bulk store
124	Department of the Environment oil store
125	Department of the Environment cement store
126	Mosque
127	Department of the Environment agricultural office
128	Cement mixer plant shed
129	Mechanical transport servicing section
130	Mechanical transport control section
131	Coach shed
132	Tanker refuelling bays
133-136	Civil Service accommodation
137	Department of the Environment accommodation
138	Civil Service mess office
139	Civil Service recreation block
140	Compressor house
141-146	Floodlight tower
147	Civil Service mess and kitchen
148/49	Civil Service officers' quarters
150	Sea and air movements office
151	Crash equipment bay
152	Mosque
153	Battery charging block
154	Pyrotechnic store
155	Avionic and safety equipment servicing centre
156	Oil, paint and dope store
157	Ground equipment servicing bay
158	Ground equipment servicing office
159	Carpenters' shop
160	Ground electrics workshop, mechanical engineering office
161	Engineering gas store
162	Engineering squadron headquarters and library
163	Engine bay and armoury
164	Photographic section rest room
165	Staging aircraft servicing flight equipment shed
166	Ground support equipment shelter
167	Staging aircraft servicing flight ground handling equipment section
168	Compressor house
169	Staging aircraft servicing flight control centre
170	Camera and radio club workshop

171	Mosque	197	Tactical aid (navigation) building
172	Power house store	198	Aerial tower
173	Power house	199	Cathode ray direction finder
174	Diesel transfer pump house	200	Oil and paint store
175	Diesel fuel storage tanks	201	Rifle range store
176	Trailer shed	202	Police dog training centre
177	Petroleum storage depot	203	Incinerator
178	Fuel oil catchment pit	204	Police dog kennels
179	Petroleum storage depot pump house	205	Hydrogen generation plant
180	Petrol oil and lubricants shelter	206	Radio Sonde balloon filling shed
181	Fuel pump house	207	Radio Sonde
182	Petroleum storage depot samples store	208	Radio Sonde transmitter store
183	Avpin storage	209	Anemometer tower
184	Petroleum storage depot offices and crewroom	210	Oil and paint store
185	Trailer shed	211	Gas producing plant
186	Petroleum storage depot office and Department of the Environment store	212	Caustic pit
187	Royal Antediluvian Order of Buffaloes' lodge accommodation	213	Oil store and acid store
188	Indoor rifle range	214	Gas plant office and store
189	Skittle alley	215-217	Compressed gas stores
190	Royal Air Forces Association's club accommodation	218	Batching plant equipment store
191	Police flight accommodation annex	219	Cement blockyard office
192	Air traffic control storage	220	Blockyard office
193	RAF police quarters	221	Blockyard shed
194	Instrument landing system (Glidepath)	222	Coral crushing plant
195/196	Arrester gear barrier plinth	223	Blockyard office and restroom
		224	Police dog kennels
		225	Dangerous goods store
		226	Explosives store
		227	Pyrotechnic store

228	Aerial mast	266	Shower block
229	Nº 6 signals unit systems control centre and receiving station	267	Pakistani club
		268	Pakistani sick quarters
230	Classified waste destructor	269	Navy Army and Air Force Institutes' European staff bungalow switch room
231	Approach radar aerial tower	270	Pakistani Nº 1 mess and staff quarters
232	Approach radar building	271-273	Pakistani staff quarters
233	Special stores	274	Pakistani senior staff quarters
234	Precision approach radar	275	Pakistani camp office and superintendent's residence
235	Coral blast area rest room		
236	Water pump house	276	Storm warning radar transmitter
237	Golf course implements store	277	Storm warning radar tower
238	Pakistani camp open air cinema	278	Instrument landing system (localiser)
239	Nº 2 and Nº 3 Pakistani messes	279/280	Arrester gear barrier plinth
240	Charcoal store	281	Anemometer tower
241	Pakistani tailor's shop	282	Angling club shop
242	Skittle alley, barber's shop and Navy Army and Air Force Institutes' ironing room		
243	Shower block		
244	Sri Lankan club (Imperial Club)		
245	Sri Lankan mess		
246-248	Sri Lankan quarters		
249	Pakistani mosque and mullah's residence		
250	Asian Navy Army and Air Force Institutes' shop		
251-257	Pakistani labourers' quarters		
258	Latrine block		
259	Hygiene section		
260-265	Pakistani labourers' quarters		

The unlisted features comprise a miscellany of small structures such as sheds, latrines, transformer distribution centres and static water tanks. Details of those can be found on the key to the Department of the Environment/Property Services Agency Grid Layout Plan F/034k as updated on the 29th of January 1976, a drawing which also provides details of the water lines, foul drainage lines, field pipes and storm drains which existed on the island at that time.

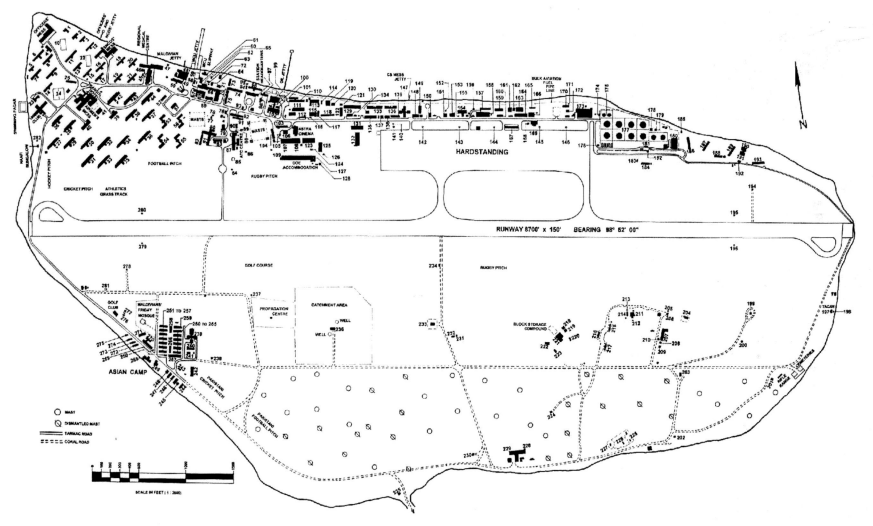

Entire island of Gan. (Based on DOE/PSA Layout Plan F034k dated 29.1.76.)

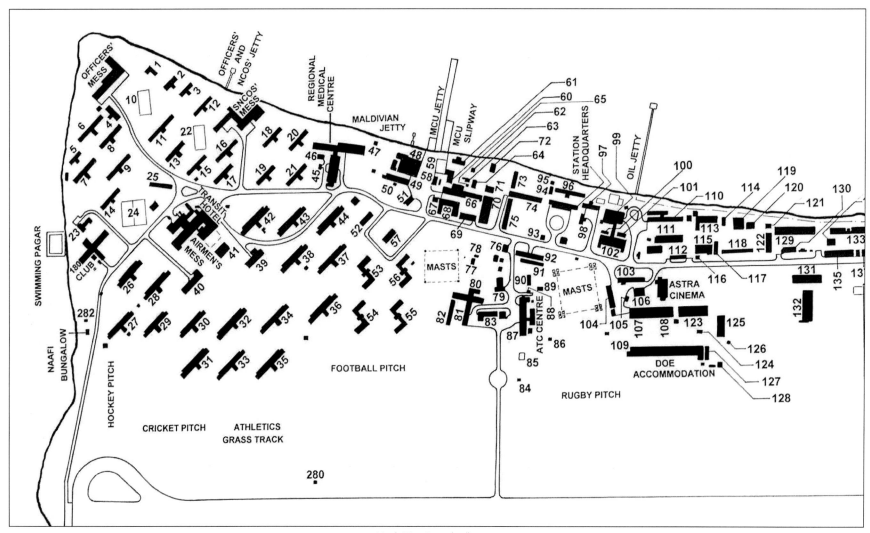

North West Zone detail.

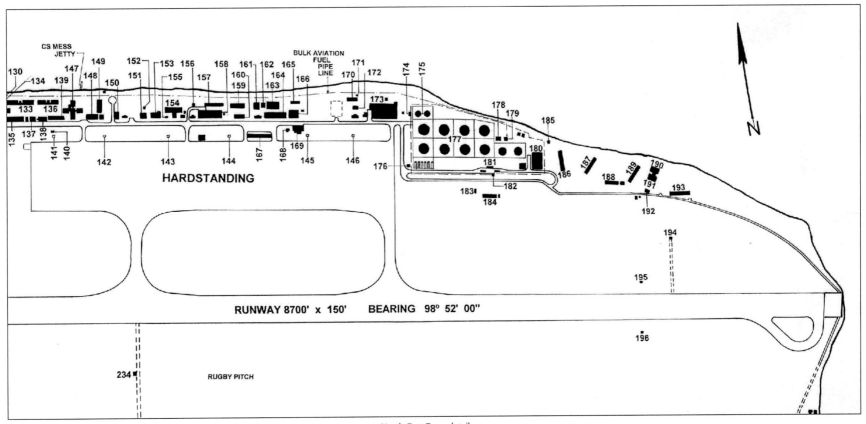

CS MESS
JETTY

130
134
139
147
148
149
150
151
152
153
155
156
157
158
160
159
161
162
163
164
165
166

BULK AVIATION
FUEL
PIPE
LINE

170
171
172
174
175

173

133
136
135
137
138
141
140

154

142
143
144
167
168
169
145
146
176

HARDSTANDING

178
179
177
185

180
181
182
186
187
188
189
190
191
193
183
184
192

194

195

RUNWAY 8700' x 150'   BEARING 98° 52' 00"

196

234
RUGBY PITCH

N

North East Zone detail.

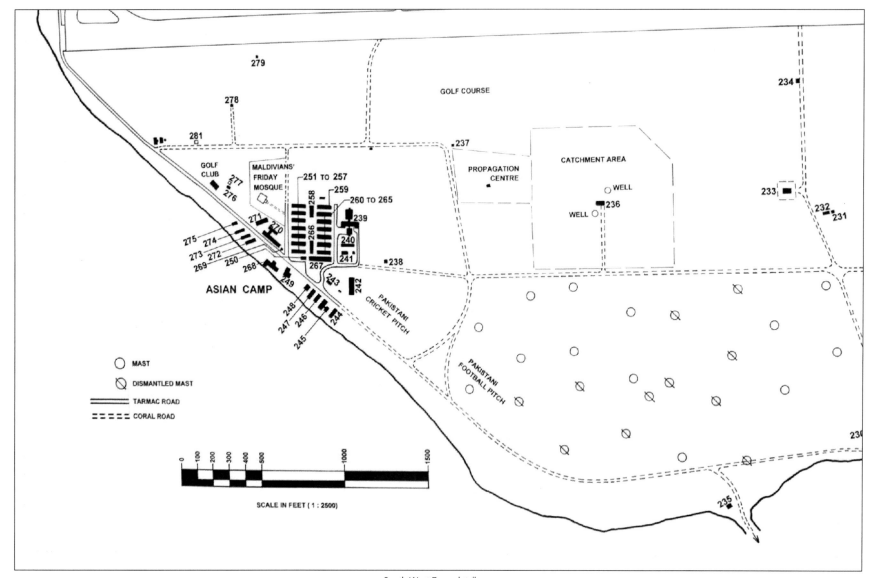

279

GOLF COURSE

234 ■

278

281

.237

CATCHMENT AREA

233 ■

GOLF
CLUB

MALDIVIANS'
FRIDAY
MOSQUE

PROPAGATION
CENTRE

232
231

277
276

251 TO 257

○ WELL

258

259

260 TO 265

236

WELL ○

271
270

239

275 274

266

240

273 272

241

269 250 268

267

238

ASIAN CAMP

249

243 242

PAKISTANI
CRICKET PITCH

248

244

247 246

245

PAKISTANI
FOOTBALL PITCH

230

○ MAST

○⃥ DISMANTLED MAST

▬▬▬ TARMAC ROAD

▭ ▭ ▭ ▭ CORAL ROAD

0 100 200 300 400 500 1000 1500

SCALE IN FEET (1 : 2500)

235

South West Zone detail

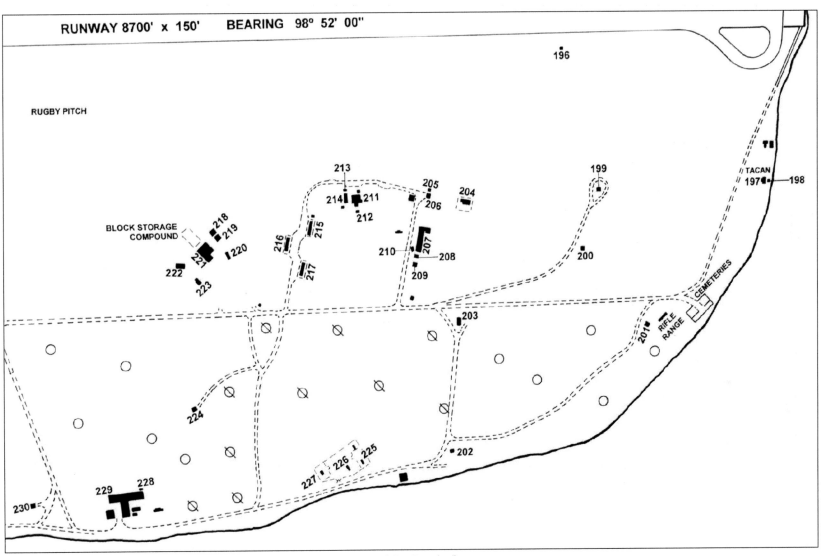

South East Zone detail.

Appendix E: Text of Document Issued to Each Airman Four Weeks Prior to Repatriation

The following is a warning, issued to all relatives, friends and neighbours of

No......... Rank............ Name............

In a short while the above-mentioned airman will be returning to your midst, dehydrated and demoralised, to take his place once again in normal civilised society.

In preparation for his arrival it is recommended that these steps and precautions be taken:

> ➢ *get those civvies out of mothballs*

> ➢ *lay on large quantities of beer*

> ➢ *lock your daughters in their rooms*

With these essential preliminaries completed, you will have taken the first steps towards assisting him in his struggle to become once again a human being enjoying peace, freedom, justice and the somewhat delayed resumption of the pursuit of happiness.

During the protracted period of recuperation which is to follow, you must continually give much consideration to the environment which has been his lot for the past nine months.

For instance, it may have been noticed that his manners and habits lean towards the Asiatic. Do not be alarmed by this, it will pass with the passage of time.

In order to foster the illusion that he is once again a member of the family, show no surprise should he prefer to sit on his haunches rather than on a chair, insist on removing his shoes before entering the house, call for a Tiger (this, we hasten to add, is not one of his pets but a potent beer found in the Far East) or exhibit a fiendish delight in calling everyone including complete strangers "moonies".

No form of horror should be expressed if, on entering his bedroom, you find him sleeping in the nude or removing his mattress from the bed to a place on the floor. Likewise, do not show alarm if, early in the morning, you see him clutching a razor, soap and toothbrush and clad only in the towel, running distractedly around the garden in a frantic search for the showers.

Similarly, should you find him in a trance-like state, standing rigidly to attention on the front lawn, lead him gently back into the house, murmuring comforting words such as "It's all right dear, Daddy doesn't want a parade this morning."

At times like this, be especially careful not to make flattering remarks about the Royal Air Force or ask why the boy down the road has a higher rank than he. Failure to observe this important rule can cause a relapse, thus undoing any good that may have been achieved hitherto.

Flip-flops and towel will have been his preference for normal dress since leaving the United Kingdom, so reintroduce him gently to socks, shoes, shirts, trousers, ties and jackets and this in conjunction with the somewhat more severe climatic conditions should be instrumental in bringing about his speedy conversion to the requirements of modern civilised society.

Eating habits

Our next problem is the mealtime, or feeding time, as it has been in the past. Here again is a problem that only time and patience can conquer. Keep cool, therefore, when he pours gravy on his desert or has mashed potatoes with his peaches. Humour him when he states that he would prefer fried rice or even ususfu-young-ha to boiled beef and carrots. At mealtimes he will approach the kitchen with hallowed reverence, intrigued by the delicious smells issuing forth. From long habit he will devour his food at a breakneck speed in order to eat it before the cockroaches get at it.

As far as food goes, you can feed him on practically anything, since his stomach and palate will be very hard after surviving Gan's cuisine for nine months.

Beware of taking him to tea with strangers, as he will astonish and embarrassed you by carefully examining his slices of bread, sometimes holding them up to the light for closer inspection. In this case, never make the terrible mistake of asking him what he expects to find in the bread, lest he should shock your host by first describing a species of beetle, finishing by giving his own pet name for it.

Having broken him in at the dining table, you should gently unfurl his fingers from such things as fistfuls of cabbage or potato, then demonstrate how, with great dexterity, food may be conveyed to the mouth by means of a fork.

Inform him also that the knife need no longer be held dagger fashion, as all foods on the plate from now on will be already dead.

Persevere in these things and his final complete readjustment to eating correctly will be your reward.

Outdoor activities

Do not allow him to go shopping alone, for sometimes, as the local store-keepers, unaccustomed to being beaten down to half their normal retail price, may misinterpret his haggling gestures as a prelude to physical violence. Should this occur, lead him gently away, at the same time explaining to the storekeeper that the reference to him as a "dirty, robbing, black-enamelled bastard" was not intended as a reflection on his own personal character. As a safeguard therefore, it is suggested that all friends and relatives of the returning airman play shop with him until he learns to purchase goods in the western manner once more.

His behaviour at the cinema will at first be rather alarming, as he will cheer the villain, boo the hero and continually shout very pointed advice to the projectionist throughout the performance.

Be especially careful when he seeks the company of the opposite sex, particularly when the same is young and attractive, as having watched beautiful actresses being wooed on the screen of his station cinema over the past nine months, he now imagines himself to be a master of the art, and will be over-enthusiastic. Whilst his intentions will be perfectly sincere, they will also be definitely dishonourable. Therefore do not allow yourself to be lulled into the false sense of security, thinking that his prolonged absence from women has dulled his senses to such an extent that he won't know one when he sees one. On the contrary... we lose a lot of daughters that way.

Despite these seemingly endless barriers to a happy reunion and a return to the peaceful coexistence which you all knew before, let it be known that beneath his rugged exterior there beats a heart of gold.

Finally, treasure his heart of gold, for it will be the only thing of value that he will have left. Treat him with kindness, patience, great tolerance and an occasional quart of good ale and you will have the joy of seeing emerge, from this shell of a man, the man you once knew and loved.

We wish you the best of luck in your arduous task.

Signed ....
Rehabilitation Officer
Royal Air Force Gan, BFPO 180

List of Source Documents

1940 – 1946

Published texts:

- Francois Pyrard de Laval, Voyage to the East Indies, the Maldive, the Moluccas and Brazil (1614), translated by Albert Gray and Harry Charles Purvis Bell, (Hakluyt Society 1887-1890)

- Ibn Batuta, Abu Abdullah. The Maldives and Ceylon, translated by Albert Gray, { Journal of the Royal Asiatic Society (Ceylon Branch) 1882 }.

- Thomas William Hockly, The Two Thousand Isles. (Witherby, London 1935).

- Harry Charles Purvis Bell, The Maldive Islands: Monograph on the History, Archaeology and Epigraphy. (Ceylon Government Press 1940).

- Stephen Wentworth Roskill, The War at Sea (HMSO London 1954-1961)

- Clarence Maloney, People of the Maldive Islands, (Orient Longman 1980)

- Thor Heyerdahl, The Maldive Mystery, (London. Allen and Unwin 1986)

- Ben Warlow, Shore Establishments of the Royal Navy, (Maritime Books. 2000)

Official papers:

- Ceylon Sessional Papers 1881.

- Meteorological Office data, RAF Gan, Addu Atoll.

- Report of an analysis of water from the Maldive Islands by T F Garvan MD, Public Analyst Ceylon, (Ceylon Government Publication 1879)

- Indian Ocean, Maldive Islands, Addu Atoll Surveyed 1923, (. Admiralty, London)

- HM Governor of Ceylon's despatch to the Secretary of State for the Colonies dated 20th March 1944

- HM Governor of Ceylon's despatch to the Secretary of State for the Colonies dated 20th March 1944

- War Losses of the Second World War, Vol I, (Lloyds of London 1989)

- ADM 1 Series documents held at the Public Record Office:
  - Addu Atoll, Indian Ocean: … medical reports (1941-45)
  - Eastern Fleet: arrangements for maintenance and buildup of supply depots in Indian and Australian waters (1941-42)
  - Addu Atoll naval base; policy, development, reduction and closure (1942-45)

- ADM 116 Series documents held at the Public record Office:
  - Addu Atoll, Indian Ocean. Signals and Messages (1941- 1945)

- ADM 199 Series documents held at the Public record Office:
  - Eastern Fleet: War Diary and East Indies War Despatches (1939-43)

- Ceylon Command War Diaries 18 June 42 - 31 Aug 43

- ADM 202 Series documents held at the Public record Office:
  - Reconnaissance reports - Port T, Addu Atoll, Maldive Archipelago --- Sep - Oct 1941
  - Diary of Force Piledriver
  - Diary of Force Shortcut
  - Port T orders 5.28
  - Port T orders 17.82
  - WO 172 Series documents held at the Public record Office:
  - War Diary of OC Engineering Troops Addu Atoll, Port T.
  - The Addu Atoll War Diaries, Jan - Dec 1943
  - The 1943 War Diaries of Addu Atoll
  - The 1944 War Diaries of Addu Atoll.

- Files studied at the RAF Air Historical Branch:
  - Air 20/5327 AHB II J57/2/6 Trade Protection in the Indian Ocean 1941 File 151/2/Air AHB II J 51/40/6/356 (B) Indian Ocean Bases- Defence.
  - File 141/6/Air GR, AHB II J 51/40/6/331(G.). GR Bases - Progress Reports 1943

1946 – 1976

Chapters VIII through XXIII overlap chronologically. Most of the following sources have provided information relevant to more than one chapter.

Official papers

- RAF Forms 540 Operations Record Books, Ship's Flag Detachment and RAF Gan.
- DO 35 Series documents held at the Public Records Office:
  - o War Graves: Maldive Islands.
  - o Air Forces: General. Proposed air route across the Indian Ocean and proposed survey of Addu Atoll in
  - o the Maldives.
  - o Economic assistance for the Maldives.
  - o Maldive islands: The Colombo Plan.
- ADM 53 Series documents held at the Public Records Office
- DO 196 Series documents held at the Public Record Office.
- Air 28 Series documents held at the Public Record Office.
- Folders from the RAF Air Historical Branch archive collection:
  - o South Indian Ocean Air Routes (Maldives/ Gan). (AIR MIN: V/CAS folder).
  - o Far East Air Route (Maldives/Gan). (AIR MIN: CAS folder).
  - o Seychelles and Maldive Islands survey – 'Ship's Bunk' (inc Gan). (AIR MIN: D. D. Ops. (M) folder)
  - o Maldivian Affairs - Summaries and Briefs (RAF Gan: Org)
  - o Liaison with the Maldivians – Policy (RAF Gan: Org)
  - o Liaison with the Maldivians – Correspondence (RAF Gan: Org)
  - o Maldivian Labour – Pay and Service Negotiations (RAF Gan: Org)
  - o Adduan Trading – Policy (RAF Gan: Org)
  - o Export of Parts for Atoll Chief
  - o Gan – Policy (FEAF Air Plans)
  - o Defence Review 74/Closure of Gan (RAF Gan: Org)
  - o Gan Withdrawal (RAF Gan: Ops)
  - o Gan Overseas Reinforcements (RAF Withdrawal) (AMSO)
  - o Report on The Maldives by J M Healey
  - o Operation NAWAB – Reinforcement of RAF Gan
  - o Operation Saintly – Replacement of Local Labour in Gan.
  - o Gift of Assets to the Maldivian Government.
  - o Aircraft Accident Register: RAF Gan.
- RAF Aircraft Accident Record Cards (Forms 1180) held at the RAF Museum, Hendon
- Hansard, 1959, 1974, 1975, 1976.
- DOE/PSA RAF Gan Grid Layout Plan F/034k dated 29-1-76.

Published texts:

- Hans Hass, Expedition into The Unknown, (Hutchinson and Co Ltd 1965)
- Tony Fairbairn, Action Stations Overseas (PSL 1991)
- Michael Butler, Return to Gan, (Woodfield Publishing 2000)

Newspapers and journals:

- Contemporary national newspapers.
- Gan Island Post
- The Globe and Laurel
- The Royal Air Force News.
- Soldier; the British Army magazine.